MW01532406

Field Manual
No. 3-21.20 (7-20)

Headquarters
Department of the Army
Washington, DC, 13 December 2006

The Infantry Battalion
Contents

Page

*This publication supersedes FM 7-20, 6 April 1992.

Figures

Contents

Tables

Preface

This manual defines the role, operational requirements, mission tasks, battlefield functions, and command and control relationships of Infantry battalions organic to the Infantry Brigade Combat Team (IBCT). Users of this manual must understand the elements of doctrinal literature and their relationship to each other. The commonly used terms, tactics, techniques, and procedures are both interrelated and mutually supportive. However, each term has its own usage, level of detail, and place in the hierarchy of doctrinal publications. FMs provide doctrine, tactics, and some techniques, while mission training plans (MTP) provide techniques and procedures. Procedures can also be found in publications such as unit standing operating procedures (SOP) and Soldiers' manuals as well as others. Tactics, techniques, and procedures, in that order, become more prescriptive and require less judgment as these elements are applied.

This manual is provided for use by Infantry battalion commanders and staffs, company commanders, and special platoon leaders. The term Infantry unit, as used in this context throughout this manual, refers to all Infantry and Ranger units unless otherwise specified. Air assault and airborne mission trained units are organized as Infantry units and are not differentiated in this manual. This manual is also provided for use by instructors of US Army Infantry battalion operations. It provides the doctrine for Infantry battalions to use in combat training and combat. It establishes a common base of tactical knowledge from which specific solutions to battalion-level tactical problems can be developed. It is designed to increase the effectiveness of battalion-level operations by providing doctrinal principles and selected battlefield-proven tactics, techniques, and procedures.

While this manual is primarily written for US Army Infantry units, it is also a source of information for other branches of the US Army and US military, and for multinational forces while working in a joint environment. It applies to the Active Army, the Army National Guard (ARNG), the National Guard of the United States (ARNGUS), and the US Army Reserve (USAR), unless otherwise stated.

The *Summary of Change* lists major changes from the previous edition by chapter and appendix. Changes include lessons learned.

The proponent for this publication is the US Army Training and Doctrine Command. The preparing agency is the US Army Infantry School. You may send comments and recommendations by any means, US mail, e-mail, fax, or telephone, as long as you use or follow the format of DA Form 2028, *Recommended Changes to Publications and Blank Forms*. You may also phone for more information.

E-mail.......... arthur.durante@us.army.mil
Phone .... COM 706-545-7114 or DSN 835-7114
Fax .... COM 706-545-7500 or DSN 835-7500
US Mail.......Commandant, USAIS
ATTN: ATSH-ATD
6751 Constitution Loop
Fort Benning, GA 31905-5593

Unless this publication states otherwise, masculine nouns and pronouns may refer to either men or women.

Also, to improve clarity, some graphics show Soldiers' uniforms without the camouflage pattern.

Summary of Changes

Chapter 1	UPDATED .... Infantry battalion organization ADDED...................... Discussion of modularity issues ADDED...................... Organization of IBCT ADDED...................... Discussion of COE
Chapters 1, 4, 10	ADDED...................... Discussion of weapons company
Chapters 1, 10	ADDED...................... Forward support company
Chapter 3	ADDED...................... ISR ADDED...................... Integration of UAS into collection and surveillance plan
Chapter 4	ADDED...................... Discussion of sniper squad employment
Chapter 5	NA
Chapter 6	ADDED...................... Stability operations
Chapter 7	UPDATED .... Civil support operations
Chapter 8	ADDED...................... Tactical enabling operations
Chapter 9	ADDED...................... Command post operations
Chapter 10	CHANGED.................. BOS to WFFs CHANGED.................. CSS to sustainment ADDED...................... IBCT operations
Chapter 11	ADDED...................... Urban operations
Appendix A	ADDED...................... Risk management and fratricide avoidance
Appendix B	ADDED...................... Movements and assembly areas
Appendix C	ADDED...................... Air assault operations
Appendix D	UPDATED .... Operations with Heavy and Stryker
Appendix E	UPDATED .... Aviation support to ground operations
Appendix F	UPDATED .... Sniper operations ADDED...................... Squad designated marksman.
Appendix G	ADDED...................... SOF, joint, interagency, and multinational operations
Appendix H	ADDED...................... Continuous operations
Appendix I	ADDED...................... Operations in CBRN
Appendix J	ADDED...................... Media considerations
Appendix K	ADDED...................... UAS and A2C2
Appendix L	ADDED...................... Lethal/nonlethal capabilities
Appendix M	ADDED...................... Forward operating bases
Appendix N (TBP)	TO BE PUBLISHED ... Counterinsurgency operations

Chapter 1
Introduction

The Infantry battalion is the first level of command that includes an assigned staff supporting a commander. The battalion can deploy rapidly, execute early-entry operations, and execute missions throughout the full spectrum of operations. It can conduct effective combat or other operations immediately upon arrival to assist in the prevention, containment, stabilization, or resolution of a conflict.

Section I. MISSION, CAPABILITIES, AND LIMITATIONS

The Infantry battalion can execute military operations in varying terrain and under any visibility conditions throughout the full spectrum of operations. Infantry battalions use, and even seek out limited visibility conditions in tactical and training situations to continually enhance their capabilities. Darkness, fog, heavy rain, and falling snow offer the battalion opportunities to maximize its technical abilities and tactical skills. Infantry battalions are also well suited for restrictive terrain such as mountains, jungles, and urban areas. They are best when used in a combined arms formation, especially when armor, artillery, engineers, aviation, and other joint assets are integrated into the operation. Task organizing combined arms with access to joint capabilities tailors the organization to the mission. This flexibility allows the commander to apply combat power at a designated time and place. An Infantry battalion can be completely wheel mobile using trucks from the forward support company (FSC) and more trucks from the brigade support battalion (BSB). However, the Infantry brigade combat team (IBCT) can only provide this mobility to one Infantry battalion at a time.

MISSION

1-1.   The primary mission of the Infantry battalion is to close with the enemy by means of fire and maneuver. Its purpose is to destroy or capture him, to repel his assaults by fire, close combat, and counterattack, or all of these. Infantry battalions can deploy rapidly and can be sustained by an austere support structure. They conduct operations against conventional and unconventional enemy forces in all types of terrain and climate conditions. The battalion's composition and training uniquely equip it to conduct its mission. In addition to its primary war-fighting mission, the Infantry battalion might be tasked to perform other types of operations, including stability operations and civil support operations, semi-independently or as an integral part of a larger force. The Infantry battalion can routinely be task organized as part of an IBCT, Heavy brigade combat team (HBCT), Stryker brigade combat team (SBCT), or possibly to a supporting brigade.

CAPABILITIES

1-2.   The inherent capability of the Infantry battalion is linked to that of the BCT to which it is assigned or task organized. The BCT is the primary fighting headquarters of the US Army tactical fight. The Infantry battalion's relatively small, light organization allows it to move rapidly and strategically. As a result, the Infantry battalion functioning as part of the IBCT often arrives in a theater of operations before the HBCTs and SBCTs. BCTs have assigned robust intelligence collection, fires management, and command and control systems. These systems allow the Infantry battalion to maneuver to points of advantage before making physical contact with the enemy. In doing so, the battalion is less likely to conduct movement to contact tactical offensive operations; it is more likely to conduct maneuver to a known point and to execute deliberate tactical offensive operations. It can accomplish this by using its assigned Army Battle Command System (ABCS) to—

- Quickly access the BCT and higher intelligence databases.
- Maintain a clear picture of friendly force locations.
- Communicate over distance via satellite and digital means.
- Quickly communicate orders without the need for face-to-face coordination.

1-3.   All Infantry battalions share the same table of organization and equipment (TOE) and can conduct air assault operations. However, some Infantry battalions receive regular, intense, and specialized training in air assault and airborne operations.

LIMITATIONS

1-4.   Once the Infantry battalion is deployed to an area of operations, lack of rapid mobility is a limitation. While insertion means vary, all Infantry battalions are comprised mostly of foot-mobile Soldiers, and thus require organic or supporting unit vehicles for enhanced ground movement of troops or supplies. In addition to limited mobility, the Infantry battalion lacks the firepower and protection of an SBCT Infantry battalion or HBCT combined arms battalion. While moving, Infantry battalions are especially vulnerable to enemy indirect fires and chemical, biological, radiological and nuclear (CBRN) attacks. Also, the Infantry battalion can only conduct independent operations for short periods. Sustainment must be carefully planned. It must focus on quantities of supplies immediately available to the unit, forecasted requirements, and a distribution plan that is synchronized with the maneuver plan.

Section II. ORGANIZATION AND FUNCTION

The Infantry battalion is designed for employment in full spectrum operations, specifically, offense, defense, stability operations, and civil support operations. The combination of rifle companies, weapons company, and specialty assets such as the scouts, mortars, and snipers, allows the commander to internally task-organize capabilities as needed.

COMMAND AND CONTROL STRUCTURE

1-5.   In addition, the command and control structure can readily accept external task-organized elements, to include combat arms, combat support, and sustainment. Close attention must be paid to the command and support relationship of task-organized elements to ensure adequate command, control, and logistical support.

FUNCTION

1-6.   The Infantry battalion normally functions as part of an IBCT. Figure 1-1 and Figure 1-2 (page 1-4) show, and the following paragraphs discuss the organization of the two basic Infantry battalions: Infantry and Ranger. Appendix D discusses the integration of Infantry, Heavy, and Stryker forces; and Appendix G discusses integration with SOF, joint, interagency, and multinational operations. Each battalion has three rifle companies, a weapons company, and a headquarters and headquarters company (HHC). The battalion also has a habitually associated FSC task-organized for sustainment from the BSB. The HHC has two elements: the headquarters section and the headquarters (HQ) company:

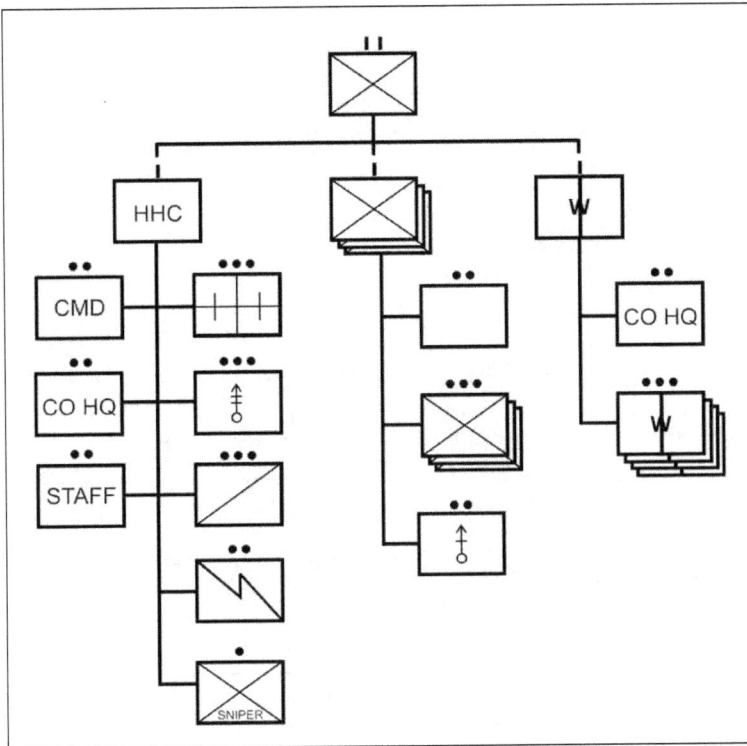

Figure 1-1. Infantry battalion.

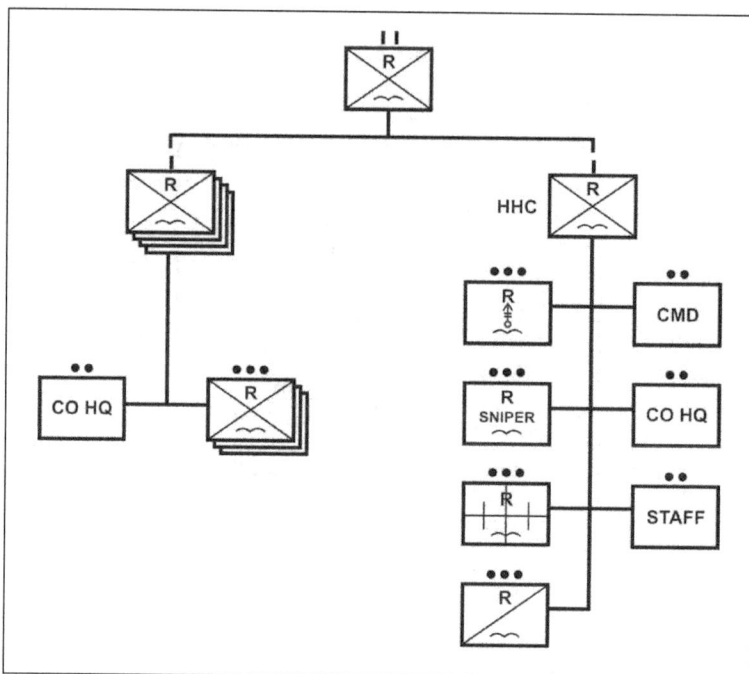

Figure 1-2. Ranger battalion.

HEADQUARTERS SECTION

1-7.   The headquarters section includes the battalion command section and the coordinating, special, and personal staff members. (See FM 6-0 for more on staff responsibilities and characteristics.)

Battalion Command Section

1-8.   The battalion command section consists of the battalion commander, the battalion executive officer (XO), the battalion command sergeant major (CSM), and supporting enlisted Soldiers such as vehicle drivers. The commander locates where he can observe and influence the critical points and actions on the battlefield and communicate orders and guidance. The battalion command section has several wheeled vehicles to assist with the command, control, coordination, and transportation of command section personnel, but during execution of their duties, they are often on foot.

Battalion Executive Officer

1-9.   The battalion XO exercises the duties and responsibilities of second in command, chief of staff, and logistics coordinator. His primary duties include—

- Exercising command in the absence or incapacitation of the commander.
- Integrating and synchronizing staff activities to optimize control of battalion operations.

- Directly supervising the battalion main command post.
- Overseeing the synchronization of information management within the battalion.
- Closely monitoring administrative and logistics issues within the battalion.
- Executing any other duties prescribed by the commander.
- Supervising military decision-making process (MDMP) and orders production.
- Managing commander's critical information requirements (CCIR).

Battalion Command Sergeant Major

1-10.   The CSM is the senior noncommissioned officer (NCO) within the Infantry battalion and advises the commander concerning the enlisted ranks. He is the battalion's senior enlisted trainer and works closely with company commanders when coaching and training company first sergeants and platoon sergeants. He acts as the commander's representative in supervising aspects vital to battalion operations, as determined by the commander and by himself.

Battalion Coordinating, Personal, and Special Staffs

1-11.   The battalion coordinating staff consists of the sustainment section (S-1 and S-4), the intelligence section (S-2), the operations section (S-3), the communications officer (S-6), the liaison officer (LNO) and, if authorized, the civil-military operations officer (S-9). The personal staff includes the chaplain and the CSM. Special staff officers include other personnel with specific technical and functional area expertise such as the fire support officer (FSO), the chemical officer (CHEMO), the FSC commander, and the battalion surgeon. All staff elements assist the commander with planning, organizing, employing, and sustaining the battalion. See Chapter 10 for a detailed discussion of the duties and responsibilities of the fire support element (FSE) and the FSO. See Appendix I for a detailed discussion of the duties and responsibilities of the CHEMO.

Sustainment Section

1-12.   The sustainment section consists of the human resources (S-1) and logistics sections (S-4).

Human Resources Section

1-13.   The human resources or S-1 section, led by the battalion adjutant, is responsible for maintaining unit strength and conducting personnel actions. The S-1 identifies and reports critical human resources shortages to the commander and higher headquarters. The S-1 section ensures assigned personnel transition smoothly into and out of the battalion. It handles routine day-to-day tasks such as preparing battalion status and strength reports, monitoring and preparing personnel awards and orders, scheduling, and other administrative support as required. During tactical operations, the S-1 section operates with the S-4 section to provide support to the battalion, including unit strength reporting to higher headquarters and coordination of unit replacements as directed by the battalion commander. Elements of the S-1 locate with the FSC to receive and sort mail, to monitor and track battalion personnel changes, such as receiving incoming replacements or outgoing Soldiers, and tracking casualty and KIA flow as they return to or through the BSA. Casualty tracking continues through Level III care. The S-1 is also the staff point of contact (POC) for activities such as inspector general, public affairs, and judge advocate general issues. The S-1 coordinates the medical platoon leader's actions when he is in his role as special staff.

Logistics Section

1-14.   The logistics or S-4 section, led by the battalion logistics officer or S-4, is responsible for providing logistical planning and support to the battalion and operates the battalion's combat trains command post (CTCP). The S-4 functions as the commander's primary logistics planner, with assistance from the FSC commander, and provides timely and accurate logistical information required to support and sustain the individual maneuver companies and specialty platoons with all classes of supply. The S-4 section staffs the CTCP in conjunction with elements of the S-1 section and FSC personnel. The CTCP provides human resource and logistics reporting (on hand status and forecasted requirement) to the FSC and the brigade support battalion (BSB) command post (CP). It also coordinates logistics resupply and unit replacements as required. The CTCP functions as the alternate battalion tactical operations center (TOC) and monitors the current fight. As such, the S-4 and the logistics section anticipate the logistical requirements of the battalion and ensure the XO is knowledgeable of the unit's status.

Intelligence Section

1-15.   Intelligence is one of the commander's most important decision-making tools. The S-2 section is responsible for providing timely and accurate intelligence analyses and products in support of the commander, staff, and subordinate units. The S-2 supervises and coordinates collection, processing, production, and dissemination of intelligence, and integrates this into the S-3's operational planning for tasking. The section makes analytical predictions on when and where enemy, noncombatant, and weather effects will occur. It also provides analysis on the effects of the battlefield environment on friendly and enemy courses of action and capabilities. The S-2 is responsible for evaluating the enemy in terms of doctrine and or pattern analysis, order of battle, high-value and high-pay-off targets, capabilities, and vulnerabilities. In conjunction with the XO and S-3, the S-2 coordinates the battalion staff's recommended priority intelligence requirements (PIR) for inclusion in the commander's critical information requirements (CCIR). The S-2 section integrates staff input to intelligence preparation of the battlefield (IPB) products for staff planning, decision-making, targeting, and combat assessment. The S-2 also plans and manages intelligence, surveillance, and reconnaissance (ISR) operations in coordination with the S-3 and FSO. The S-2 or his intelligence representative also participates in the targeting meetings to provide the most current threat information to assist with updating the target priority and methods of delivery

Operations Section

1-16.   The S-3 section is the commander's primary staff for planning, coordinating, prioritizing, and integrating all battalion operations. The S-3 section runs the battalion main CP, under XO supervision. The S-3 is generally the senior staff member of the tactical CP, commonly called the TAC, if the commander employs one. The operations section's main duties are to plan, prepare and produce the battalion operations orders, control current operations, and coordinate critical support operations, as required, with the other staff sections. In addition, the operations section develops and synchronizes the intelligence, surveillance, and reconnaissance (ISR) collection plan. They also manage the battle rhythm of the TOC, to include orders production; battle tracking, operations updates and briefings, rehearsals, receipt of reposts, and reports to higher headquarters. Chapter 9 provides additional information on the operations section and command post operations.

Communications Section

1-17.   The communications section, led by the S-6 communications officer, is responsible for all communications for the battalion. Together, they ensure proper setup and operation of all communications equipment in the TOC, TAC, CTCP, and the field trains CP. The communications section also ensures all retransmission (retrans) operations for the battalion are set up and operational. The section monitors maintenance on communications equipment and performs 10-and 20-level maintenance when necessary.

Liaison Section

1-18.   The liaison section is comprised of one LNO and an enlisted assistant. The joint and multinational nature of operations requires that the Infantry battalion have the capability to conduct liaison operations. The liaison team facilitates and coordinates the operations of the battalion with other units or agencies as directed by the battalion commander. During combat operations, the LNO keeps other units informed of the status, disposition, and location of the battalion, and assists in deconflicting boundaries and fires with adjacent units. The LNO section is normally augmented with interpreter support when conducting multinational operations. During the conduct of stability operations and civil support operations, the LNO can also act as a coordinator with the civil-military operations center (CMOC), governmental and nongovernmental organizations, as required.

Chaplain

1-19.   The unit ministry team (UMT) is composed of a chaplain and one enlisted chaplain's assistant. The unit ministry team facilitates and coordinates religious support across the battalion's area of operations (AO). The chaplain is also a special staff member who serves as a confidential advisor to the commander on the spiritual fitness and ethical and moral health of the command. The unit ministry team advises the commander on humanitarian aspects and the impact of command policies on indigenous religions. He provides and coordinates privileged and sensitive personal counseling and pastoral care to the unit's command, Soldiers, authorized civilians, and families. The unit ministry team locates where it can best coordinate, communicate, and facilitate religious support. The S-1 section in the CTCP is normally the coordinating staff that monitors UMT activities and location.

HEADQUARTERS COMPANY

1-20.   The headquarters company consists of the HHC headquarters and the battalion's scout, mortar, and medical platoons, and the communications and sniper section. The HQ Company provides intelligence, fire support, protection, and very limited sustainment to the battalion through its specialty platoons and HQs section. The attached FSC provides most sustainment to the battalion.

Company Headquarters Section

1-21.   The company headquarters section provides the immediate leadership, supply, and human resources support to all HHC personnel, including the battalion's command group, coordinating, special, and personal staff, and specialty platoons and squads. It includes the HHC commander, first sergeant (1SG), executive officer, and supporting supply and chemical sections. In a tactical environment, the HHC HQ section provides flexibility to the battalion commander. The HHC commander, 1SG, and XO do not have a set location from where they conduct their duties and as such, can be placed where they can most effectively help the battalion to execute the mission.

1-22.   For example, the HHC commander might locate in the TOC to oversee mortar, scout, and sniper operations, as well as to maintain CP security. The 1SG locates in the field trains as the noncommissioned officer in charge (NCOIC) and assists in logistics package (LOGPAC) operations. The XO locates with the FSC commander to provide tactical requirements advice and assistance. The HHC HQs section might be used as a combat headquarters, for example, to lead a battalion reserve with task-organized elements from different companies. The HHC HQ section also provides support to the battalion's TOC with regard to coordination of security and displacement operations. It has several wheeled vehicles to help support HHC elements, including two small decontamination apparatuses for limited but immediate tactical decontamination.

Medical Platoon

1-23.   The medical platoon provides force health protection (FHP) for the battalion using its organic medical capabilities. The medical platoon is dependent on the health service support (HSS) system for direct support (DS) and augmentation/reinforcement, when required. The medical platoon is organized with a headquarters section, a treatment squad, four ambulance squads, and a combat medic section. The medical platoon is responsible for providing Level I medical care. This care includes emergency medical treatment for wounds, injuries, or illness, advanced trauma management, and sick call services. It also includes casualty collection and medical evacuation from the supported unit to the battalion aid station (BAS) or forward aid station (FAS). The medical platoon habitually establishes the BAS where it can best support the battalion and has the capability to split into a BAS and a FAS for wider area coverage. It normally operates under the direction of the CTCP.

Headquarters Section

1-24.   The headquarters section provides command, control, communications, and resupply for the medical platoon. The platoon headquarters consists of the field surgeon/medical platoon leader, the field medical assistant, and the platoon sergeant. It normally collocates with the treatment squad to form the BAS. The battalion surgeon, assisted by the field medical assistant and the platoon sergeant, is responsible for the FHP plan for the Infantry battalion. The field medical assistant is the operations/readiness officer. He plans, coordinates, and executes the FHP plan. See FM 4-02.4 and FM 8-55 for more information on planning, preparation, and execution of HSS activities for FHP.

Treatment Squad

1-25.   The treatment squad consists of two treatment teams; Alpha and Bravo. These teams operate the BAS and provide Level I medical care and treatment. This includes sick call, emergency medical treatment (EMT), and advanced trauma management (ATM). The treatment teams can operate for limited times in split-based operations in DS of battalion units. Typical operations for the treatment squads are as follows:

- The battalion surgeon/platoon leader is located with Team Alpha, which is staffed by a health care sergeant (SGT) and two health care specialists.
- Team Bravo is staffed with a physician's assistant (PA), a health care SGT, and two health care specialists. They are trained to provide EMT and assist with ATM procedures.
- The treatment teams can operate for a limited amount of time in split-based operations in DS of battalion units for wider area coverage. Split based operations normally do not exceed 24 hours, otherwise efficiency and capability of the teams is reduced.
- Each team employs treatment vehicles with two medical equipment sets (MES's); one trauma field MES, and one sick call field MES.
- During periods where the Infantry battalion is not deployed, the battalion surgeon is normally attached to the local medical care facility using the Professional Officer Filler Information System (PROFIS; AR 601-142). As a result, the platoon's field medical assistant/operations/readiness officer often serves as the medical platoon leader.

Ambulance Squads

1-26.   Medical platoon ambulances provide medical evacuation and en route care from the Soldier's point of injury or a casualty collection point (CCP) to the BAS. The ambulance team in support of the maneuver company works in coordination with the trauma specialists supporting the platoons. In mass casualty situations, non medical vehicles may be used to assist in casualty evacuation as directed by the supported commander. Plans for the use of non medical vehicles to perform casualty evacuation should be included in the Infantry battalion's tactical standing operating procedures (TSOP) or operations order (OPORD).

Combat Medic Section

1-27.   Trauma specialists are allocated based on one trauma specialist per each rifle platoon in the battalion's rifle companies. The platoon trauma specialist normally locates near the platoon sergeant. The rifle company trauma specialist normally collocates with the 1SG. When the rifle company is engaged, he remains with the 1SG and provides medical advice as necessary. As the tactical situation allows, he manages the company CCP, provides treatment, and prepares patients for medical evacuation (MEDEVAC). For definitive information on medical platoon operations, see FM 4-02.4 and FM 8-55.

Scout Platoon

1-28.   The battalion scout platoon serves as the forward "eyes and ears" for the battalion commander. The primary mission of the scout platoon is to conduct reconnaissance and security to answer CCIR, normally defined within the battalion's ISR plan. The platoon can conduct route, zone, and area reconnaissance missions. The platoon can also conduct limited screening operations and can participate as part of a larger force in guard missions. The platoon has one officer and 21 enlisted personnel. The platoon leader is assisted by his platoon sergeant (PSG), who assists and advises the platoon leader and leads the platoon in his absence.

1-29.   The scout platoon is organized into a platoon headquarters and three squads of six men each. Each squad leader is responsible for controlling his squad's movement and intelligence collection requirements. He reports critical intelligence information obtained by his squad to the scout platoon leader or battalion TOC.

1-30.   In either offensive or defensive operations, the commander may deploy his scout platoon to conduct screening operations of the battalion's front, flank, or rear. The scout platoon may also occupy outposts from which it can relay critical information to the TOC concerning enemy composition, disposition, and activities.

Mortar Platoon

1-31.   The primary role of the battalion mortar platoon is to provide immediate, responsive indirect fires in support of the maneuver companies or battalion. The battalion mortar platoon consists of a mortar platoon headquarters, a mortar section with fire direction center (FDC), and four mortar squads. The platoon's FDC controls and directs the mortar platoon's fires. Infantry battalion mortar squads are equipped with 120-mm and 81-mm mortars, but are only authorized enough personnel to operate one of the two systems at any one time (arms room concept). For a more in-depth look at mortars and their characteristics, see Chapter 10.

1-32.   The mortar platoon provides the commander with the ability to shape the Infantry's close fight with indirect fires that—

- Provide close supporting fires for assaulting Infantry forces in any terrain.
- Destroy, neutralize, suppress, or disrupt enemy forces and force armored vehicles to button up.
- Fix enemy forces or reduce the enemy's mobility and canalize his assault forces into engagement areas.
- Deny the enemy the advantage of defile terrain and force him into areas covered by direct fire weapons.
- Optimize indirect fires in urban terrain.
- Significantly improve the Infantry's lethality and survivability against a close dismounted assault.
- Provide obscuration for friendly movement.

1-33.   Each mortar system can provide three primary types of mortar fires—

- High explosive (HE) rounds are used to suppress or destroy enemy dismounted Infantry, mortars, and other supporting weapons and to interdict the movement of men, vehicles, and supplies in the enemy's forward area. Bursting white phosphorus (WP) rounds are often mixed with HE rounds to enhance their suppressive and destructive effects.
- Obscuration rounds are used to conceal friendly forces as they maneuver or assault, and to blind enemy supporting weapons. Obscurants can also be used to isolate a portion of the enemy force while it is destroyed piecemeal. Some mortar rounds use bursting WP to achieve this obscuration. Bursting WP may be used to mark targets for engagement by other weapons, usually aircraft, and for signaling.
- Illumination rounds, to include infrared illumination, are used to reveal the location of enemy forces hidden by darkness. They allow the commander to confirm or deny the presence of the enemy without revealing the location of friendly direct fire weapons. Illumination fires are often coordinated with HE fires both to expose the enemy and to kill or suppress him.

Sniper Section

1-34.   The primary mission of the sniper section in combat is to support combat operations by delivering precise long-range fire on selected targets.

Mission of Snipers

1-35.   Snipers create casualties among enemy troops, slow enemy movement, frighten enemy Soldiers, lower morale, and add confusion to their operations. They can engage and destroy high payoff targets. The secondary mission of the sniper section is collecting and reporting battlefield information. The sniper section is employed in all types of operations. This includes offensive, defensive, stability operations and civil support operations in which precision fire is delivered at long ranges. It also includes combat patrols, ambushes, counter sniper operations, forward observation elements, military operations in urbanized terrain, and retrograde operations in which snipers are part of forces left in contact or as stay-behind forces.

Composition of Sniper Section

1-36.   The Sniper section has 10 enlisted personnel, 3 long range sniper rifle systems, and 3 standard sniper rifle systems. The section leader is the primary advisor to the battalion commander on sniper employment. If the commander does not directly control sniper employment, he should designate a sniper employment officer (SEO) to command and control the sniper section. The HHC commander or XO could be used in this role.

Sniper Teams

1-37.   There are three sniper teams in the sniper section organized with a sniper, observer, and security. As a result, the sniper section can effectively employ three sniper teams at any one time, although the commander could employ up to five ad hoc sniper teams for limited duration missions by employing two man teams. Sniper teams can be task organized to any unit in the battalion or employed directly under battalion control. Snipers are most effective when leaders in the supported unit understand capabilities, limitations, and tactical employment of sniper teams. See FM 3-22.10 and Appendix F for more information on planning, preparing, and executing sniper team employment.

Common and Other Potentially Task Organized Elements Providing Special Staff

1-38.   The following are common and other potentially task organized elements that provide special staff:

United States Air Force Tactical Air Control Party

1-39.   The augmenting USAF TACP consists of the air liaison officer (ALO) and two enlisted terminal attack controllers (ETACs). The TACP assists the commander with the planning, integration, and execution of fixed wing close air support (CAS) operations. It is the commander's primary link to Air Force CAS assets that are made available to support the battalion's mission.

Psychological Operations

1-40.   Psychological operations (PSYOP) units (Appendix G) are often attached or in direct support to units, particularly in stability operations. An important potential byproduct of PSYOP can be additional intelligence of the AO.

Civil Affairs

1-41.   Civil Affairs (CA, Appendix G) will often be attached or in direct support of units, particularly in stability operations and civil support operations. CA can be vital to gaining the support of the local population and can provide important information about the AO and key local leaders. However, CA cannot overtly collect intelligence. CA is also a related activity of IO that should be considered in any IO campaign.

Engineers

1-42.   Typically combat engineers; the senior engineer advises the commander on how best to employ his assets in mobility, counter mobility, and survivability roles. During stability operations and civil support operations the engineer will be required to provide technical advice in a wide range of engineering related areas, to include construction and general engineering subjects

Air Defense

1-43.   Short range air defense (SHORAD) units are unlikely to be attached or placed in DS or general support (GS) of Infantry battalions. Regardless of the availability or relationship, air defense units may require specific terrain within the battalion AO to accomplish their mission.

FORWARD SUPPORT COMPANY

1-44.   The FSC is a multifunctional sustainment unit organized to provide habitual and direct support to the Infantry battalion. The FSC is habitually DS to the Infantry battalion and a close SOP supported relationship exists between the units. Both the BSB and Infantry battalion commanders ensure the FSC is tightly integrated into the Infantry battalion's operations in garrison, training and in combat. In the Modular Force, the FSC is responsible for conducting the majority of the sustainment operations that were previously conducted by the Infantry battalion HHC. These responsibilities include—

- Unit level vehicle and equipment maintenance and recovery.
- Resupply operations for all classes of supply (except medical) and water.
- Transportation for all classes of supply and personnel.
- Supplemental transportation of personnel with no organic wheel movement capability.
- LOGPAC operations.

INFANTRY COMPANY

1-45.   The Infantry Company consists of a headquarters section, three Infantry platoons, and a 60-mm mortar section. The Infantry Company is strategically mobile. Each Infantry platoon has three Infantry squads and a weapons squad. Each weapons squad has two Javelin (close combat missile) command launch units and two medium machine guns.

WEAPONS COMPANY

1-46.   The mission of the weapons company is to provide mobile heavy weapons and long range close combat missile fires to the Infantry battalion. The weapons company consists of a headquarters section and four assault platoons. Each assault platoon has two tube-launched, optically tracked, wire-guided (TOW) close combat missile systems fired from the improved target acquisition system (ITAS). In addition, each platoon is equipped with a .50 cal heavy barrel machine gun and a Mark 19 automatic grenade launcher.

BATTLEFIELD ORGANIZATION

1-47.   Commanders visualize their battlespace and determine how to arrange their forces. Spatially, commanders may find it useful to organize this area into deep, close, and rear areas. However, this framework is more appropriate for a linear battlefield than a non linear battlefield such as when conducting stability operations and civil support operations. Battlefield organization is the arrangement of subordinate forces according to purpose, time, and space to accomplish a mission.

1-48.   The purpose-based framework centers on decisive, shaping, and sustaining operations. Purpose unifies all elements of the battlefield organization by providing the common focus for all actions. Forces act in time and space to accomplish a purpose. The nested effects caused by accomplishing these purposes drive the framework. Main efforts are identified within the decisive, shaping, and sustaining operations for the activity that the commander determines constitutes the most important task at the time.

1-49.   As a full-spectrum combat force, the Infantry battalion organization design includes capabilities tailored specifically to the unique requirements of the battalion's mission set. The battalion organization allows the commander to scale his force to accept additional Infantry organizations and units or elements that are not organic to the battalion structure such as heavy, Stryker, engineers, or civil affairs. This organizational flexibility allows the battalion to function in its primary role as a major participant in combat operations as part of a BCT or to serve as the base modular combat force in stability operations. When the battalion has a temporary grouping of units under one commander designed to accomplish a particular mission, it becomes a task force.

Section III. WARFIGHTING FUNCTIONS

A warfighting function (WFF) is a group of tasks and systems (people, organizations, information, and processes) united by a common purpose that commanders use to accomplish missions and training objectives. Integration and synchronization of the WFF occurs horizontally and vertically throughout the battalion. Commanders visualize, describe, direct, and lead operations in terms of the WFFs. Decisive, shaping, and sustaining operations combine all the WFFs to generate combat power. No WFF is exclusively decisive, shaping, or sustaining. The six WFF plus leadership combine to become the seven elements of combat power. Figure 1-3 shows the warfighting functions.

• **Fire Support**
• **Movement and Maneuver**
• **Protection**
• **Command and Control**
• **Intelligence**
• **Sustainment**

Figure 1-3. Warfighting functions.

FIRE SUPPORT

1-50.   The fire support WFF is the related tasks and systems that provide collective and coordinated use of Army indirect fires, joint fires, and offensive information operations. It includes tasks associated with integrating and synchronizing the effects of these types of fires with the other WFFs to accomplish operational and tactical objectives. Lethal and nonlethal fires, including offensive information operations, are integrated into the concept of operations during planning and targeting based on the targeting guidance. The three components of the fire support WFF are—

- Fire support command and control.
- Target acquisition systems and assets.
- Fire support assets and resources.

1-51.   The fire support WFF encompasses the collective and coordinated use of all fire support assets needed to conduct indirect fires in support of the scheme of maneuver. The fire support system acquires and tracks targets; delivers timely and accurate fires; provides proactive counterstrikes; and plans, coordinates, and orchestrates Army and Joint fires. The battalion FSO receives guidance from the commander regarding the task, purpose, method, and effects desired. He then plans, coordinates, and achieves the desired effects using organic and non-organic means. Each FSE has subordinate fire support teams that support the weapons company and each rifle company. Each fire support team assists the maneuver company commander with establishing targeting information and assessment of effects and acts as the liaison for all fire support assets. The TACP, consisting of an air liaison officer and enlisted tactical air controllers, integrates into the battalion headquarters alongside the FSE, providing the ability to request, coordinate, and control close air support. Some operations may include the United States Marine Corps (USMC) or air and naval gunfire liaison company (ANGLICO) assets task-organized to the battalion, typically to assist in controlling supporting naval gunfire.

MOVEMENT AND MANEUVER

1-52.   The movement and maneuver WFF is the related tasks and systems that move forces to achieve a position of advantage in relation to the enemy. It includes those tasks associated with employing forces in combination with direct fire or fire potential (maneuver), force projection (movement), mobility, and counter mobility. Movement and maneuver are the means by which commanders mass the effects of combat power to achieve surprise, shock, momentum, and dominance.

1-53.   The rifle companies and the weapons company of the Infantry battalion, maneuver to achieve a position of advantage with respect to the enemy. The rifle companies are most effective in close combat but also employ organic close combat missile and shoulder fired munitions/close combat missile weapons for use against armored vehicles, buildings, bunkers, and fortifications. The weapons company provides mobile heavy weapons fire, to include long-range close combat missile (antiarmor) fires, and the ability to destroy buildings, bunkers, and fortifications. All other battalion assets support the maneuver elements. The battalion achieves decisive action by means of combined arms effects at the company and platoon level to achieve the desired purpose. Maneuver is usually supported by the integration of fire support; however, protection and sustainment must be integrated throughout. Army aviation and fixed wing support are also assets that may conduct operations in support of the battalion. Attack helicopters can conduct enemy and terrain oriented combat missions using movement and maneuver. Aviation assets can also provide timely reconnaissance and surveillance information to ground maneuver commanders and conduct air movement and sustainment operations in support of Infantry forces.

1-54.   Mobility operations preserve the freedom of maneuver of friendly forces. These missions include breaching obstacles, controlling battlefield circulation, improving or building roads, providing bridge and raft support, and identifying routes around contaminated areas. Counter mobility operations attack and deny mobility to enemy forces using obstacles and smoke generation.

1-55.   Infantry units conduct mobility, counter mobility, and survivability missions with or without engineer support. Combat or construction engineers may augment the battalion; provide expertise, equipment, and limited manpower. The senior engineer unit leader advises the commander on employment and placement of engineer assets and obstacles. He also provides technical construction advice in stability operations and civil support operations. The Infantry battalion may conduct missions that include the construction of obstacles, emplacement and clearing of minefields, demolitions, road improvement, and bridging.

1-56.   Infantry battalions may be augmented with military police (MP) support from the BCT. If the MP platoon is not attached, the Infantry battalion will still often find portions of the BCT MP platoon operating within its AO. The BCT MP platoon provides twelve 3-Soldier teams that habitually operate in pairs (two weapons platforms) to perform mobile and/or dismounted operations. The six pairs of MP teams rotate to cover 24 hour operations. Working with civil affairs planners and the S-3, MPs can also monitor refugee routes and control points.

1-57.   The teams or mobile patrols provide a combination of the following capabilities as prioritized by the commander:

- Maneuver and mobility support (MMS) for vehicle traffic, circulation control points, checkpoints, roadblocks, holding areas, and mobile patrols.

- Area security/force protection mobile patrols for reconnaissance, detection, and response to threat incidents.
- Operation of the detainee initial collection point.
- Incident response to maintain law and order and to collect and report on information to support police intelligence operations.
- Security for small critical sites, facilities, or storage areas.

PROTECTION

1-58.   The protection WFF is the related tasks and systems that preserve the force so the commander can apply maximum combat power. Preserving the force includes protecting personnel (combatant and noncombatant), physical assets, and information of the United States and multinational partners. It includes the following task areas at the Infantry battalion level:

- Safety.
- Fratricide avoidance.
- Survivability.
- Air defense.
- CBRN.
- Defensive information operations.
- Force health protection.

1-59.   Survivability operations protect friendly forces from the effects of enemy weapon systems and from the environment. Survivability measures include: hardening of facilities, fortification of battle positions, deception, dispersion, and CBRN defense measures.

1-60.   Infantry units are trained to operate in a CBRN environment to survive and accomplish their missions. They increase their survivability through adherence to the CBRN defense fundamentals including contamination avoidance, CBRN protection, and CBRN decontamination. Decontamination assets within the battalion are limited; however, they can provide for initial measures to control the spread and lessen the risk of contamination. The BCT has an assigned chemical reconnaissance platoon that may operate in support of the battalion. Smoke generating units may be task organized to an Infantry battalion. They are used to obscure and deceive.

1-61.   The battalion and BCT have no organic air defense artillery (ADA) assets. ADA support comes from an ADA battalion at echelons above the BCT. Infantry battalions employ the passive measure of remaining undetected as their primary form of defense against air attacks. Other measures include: the use of camouflage and moving in limited visibility. In the event of an air attack, the battalion should employ combined arms for air defense (CAFAD) and the air defense procedures described in Chapter 10.

COMMAND AND CONTROL

1-62.   The command and control (C2) WFF is the related tasks and systems that support commanders in exercising authority and direction. C2 has two components: the commander and the C2 system. The C2 system supports the commander's ability to make informed decisions, delegate authority, and synchronize the WFFs. Through C2, commanders initiate and integrate all systems and WFFs toward mission accomplishment.

1-63.   As with all C2, the Infantry battalion's C2 system is the arrangement of personnel, information management, procedures, equipment, and facilities essential for the commander to conduct operations. Personnel constitute the battalion commander, his subordinate commanders, and staff. Information management is the provision of relevant information to the right person at the right time in a usable form to facilitate situational understanding and decision making. Procedures are standard and consist of detailed courses of action that describe how to perform a task. Equipment and facilities provide sustainment and a work environment for the other elements of a C2 system.

1-64.   By virtue of rank and assignment, the commander exercises command and control over his battalion. He executes battlefield missions through his leadership coupled with his tactical knowledge, visualization of the battlefield, situational understanding, and with the assistance of his subordinate commanders and staff. The battalion commander positions himself on the battlefield where he can most influence and direct combat actions. He must be able to see and feel the battle in order to command actions. His presence on the battlefield must be apparent to his subordinates. The subordinate commanders must understand and execute missions in accordance with his intent. The battalion commander leads by example and maintains control over his unit while still allowing subordinate commanders to exercise initiative to the extent possible. His staff assists him in the control of the battalion through the CPs, orders production, manning and maintaining the communications system, and enforcing established procedures.

1-65.   Information management uses procedures and information systems to collect, process, store, display, and disseminate information. Information management consists of relevant information and information systems (INFOSYS). Information systems are the equipment and facilities that collect, process, store, display, and disseminate information. These include computers; hardware and software, and communications, as well as policies and procedures for their use.

1-66.   Procedures allow common repeated tasks to be standardized and executed quickly and efficiently. Procedures govern actions within a C2 system to make it more effective and efficient. Adhering to procedures minimizes misunderstanding and hesitance, as commanders make frequent rapid decisions to meet operational requirements.

1-67.   Equipment and facilities in the Infantry battalion consists of the main CP, also referred to as the TOC, TAC, the CTCP, and the field trains CP. For more information on CP operations, see Chapter 9.

INTELLIGENCE

1-68.   The intelligence WFF is the related tasks and systems that facilitate understanding of the enemy, terrain, weather, and civilian considerations. It includes tasks associated with ISR. It is a flexible, adjustable architecture of procedures, personnel, organizations, and equipment. These provide relevant information and products relating to the threat, civil populace, and environment to commanders. The intelligence WFF focuses on four primary tasks:

- Support to situational understanding.
- Support to strategic responsiveness.
- Conduct ISR.
- Provide intelligence support to targeting.

1-69.   The Infantry battalion has limited organic means outside of the S-2 section to dedicate to information collecting and reporting. The battalion relies mainly on the scout platoon, sniper teams, Infantry patrols, and organic short range unmanned aircraft systems (UAS) to gather information. One other important, internal source of information is the Soldier. Every Soldier in the battalion is a sensor and is expected to observe and report relevant information in a timely manner. Most staff officers have access to sources of intelligence. These sources can include their Soldiers on the ground such as CA, Air Defense, and Engineers, or their counterparts at the next higher HQs or supporting brigade. They can also use the "reverse WFF" method and give the S-2 logical assessments about how the adversary would employ any of his assets that fall in the staff officer's functional area of expertise. Other intelligence information must be received from the BCT and higher echelons. This information helps the commander develop a situational understanding (SU) of the battlefield by applying his judgment to the COP, and it should answer his PIR. Situational understanding and information superiority enable the force to avoid surprise, develop rapid decisions, conduct movement and maneuver with synchronized fires and effects, and achieve decisive outcomes.

SUSTAINMENT

1-70.   The sustainment WFF is the related tasks and systems that provide support and services to ensure freedom of action, extend operational reach, and prolong endurance. It includes those tasks associated with—

- Maintenance.
- Transportation.
- Supply.
- Field services.
- Explosive ordnance disposal.
- Human resources support.
- Financial management.
- Health service support.
- Religious support.
- Related general engineering.

1-71.   Considering the nature of the Infantry battalion's mission, the sustainment structure is adequate to provide for logistical needs, with the habitual DS relationship of the FSC. The battalion headquarters and headquarters company includes the staff needed to plan sustainment and plan and conduct HSS operations. Constrained vehicle assets allow the unit to operate in terrain that is more restrictive and increase strategic and operational maneuverability. However, the FSC has sufficient sustainment assets to provide for the conduct of continuous sustainment operations. The battalion executive officer orchestrates sustainment activities in conjunction with the S-1, S-4, and FSC Commander. Together they plan and employ sustainment assets to facilitate operations and ensure success of the battalion's mission. Chapter 11 provides a detailed outline of the sustainment WFF.

Section IV. CONTEMPORARY OPERATIONAL ENVIRONMENT

Potential enemy states and non-state actors in various regions of the world generally see the United States as the world's dominant power, with large technological, economic, and material advantages and an overwhelming military capability. Given this strategic assessment, potential US enemies seek to avoid US military strengths while exploiting perceived US weaknesses. In this way, our enemies hope to achieve their own regional or international goals without US intervention or, failing this, without the US military defeat of those objectives. If it comes to a fight with US forces, our enemies are unlikely to fight the same way they would fight their regional peers or lesser forces in their region.

ASYMMETRY

1-72.   Asymmetry is an ideological, cultural, technological, or military imbalance that exists when there is a disparity in comparative strengths and weaknesses and in how a force generates combat power and applies or focuses the effects of combat power. In the context of the COE, asymmetry, or an asymmetric threat, means an adaptive enemy approach to avoid or counter US strengths without opposing them directly, while seeking to identify, target, and exploit US weaknesses to achieve goals or objectives. For example, an enemy without long-range artillery or missiles may use improvised explosive devises to target Infantry and military vehicles to achieve the same destructive effect.

THREATS

1-73.   In today's world, commanders must be prepared to go into any region or operational environment and perform the full range of missions while dealing with a wide range of threats. Some threats come in the form of nation-states; this may be a country or a coalition of countries. Threats can also come from entities that are not states, including insurgents, terrorists, drug-traffickers, and other criminal organizations. These non-state actors may use force of arms to further their own interests and threaten the interests of the US or other nation-states. Non-state threats may exist in isolation or in combination with other non-state or nation-state threats.

> "The unresting progress of mankind causes continual change in the weapons; and with that must come a continual change in the manner of fighting."
>
> Alfred Mahan

SCOPE

1-74.   The COE is more than one specific threat or force. It is the complete *environment* in which US forces operate worldwide. It includes the physical environment and all other factors, such as political, military, economic, ethnic, religious, and tribal factors, that can affect US operations. These factors also affect where our enemies will operate against us. Operating in the COE requires a change from viewing the enemy only through the traditional line and block, time-phase, Soviet motorized rifle regiment paradigm, to considering the *entire* operational environment to understand the adaptive and opportunistic enemies that US forces will continue to combat worldwide. As part of his planning and execution of operations, the commander must remain acutely aware of and carefully consider the differences in the relationship between strategic, operational, and tactical goals, plans, and actions. He considers those of both US and enemy forces relative to each situation in order to appreciate the nature of the conflict at his level, and in his AO/AI).

VARIABLES

1-75.   During operations in the COE, commanders will encounter a variety of conflicts in a number of different operational environments. *Eleven critical variables define the nature of the operational environments where those conflicts or other US military activities can occur.* They are called *variables* because the exact nature of the conditions, circumstances, and influences that make up the operational environment varies by situation, region, and political considerations.

1-76.   Whether or not these operational variables might significantly affect the strategic, operational, or tactical environment, they must at least be considered during any analysis of the mission or changing situation.

VARIABLE 1--PHYSICAL ENVIRONMENT

1-77.   The physical environment has always been a key factor in military operations. History has demonstrated that those forces able to obtain an advantage by using various aspects of the physical environment have a much higher probability of defeating their opponents, regardless of size and capability overmatch. Potential opponents clearly understand that less complex and open environments favor the US with its standoff technology, precision guided munitions (PGM) and sophisticated ISR capability. For this reason, they will seek to use complex terrain and urban environments in confrontations with US Forces.

VARIABLE 2--NATURE AND STABILITY OF STATE

1-78.   Understanding the nature of the state involved in the conflict and its degree of stability is critical in calculating the center of gravity, nature of the military campaign, and true end state. A state that must commit significant resources to maintain internal control represents less of a threat in conventional combat and more of a threat in stability operations. The question then becomes: Is the real strength of the state; the military, the police, or the population?

VARIABLE 3--SOCIOLOGICAL DEMOGRAPHICS

1-79.   The demographics and sociological aspects of the population provide significant complexity to military operations. States will fail due to cultural, ethnic, resource, or opportunity issues. Stopping those conflicts would involve training a broader set of leader and unit competencies. In addition, states fragmented by these types of issues and who have sophisticated military capability normally behave more aggressively and violently within their regions.

VARIABLE 4--REGIONAL AND GLOBAL RELATIONSHIPS

1-80.   Regional and global relationships of potential opponents serve to define the scale of military operations. They also give indication of escalation or limiting factors. In an unaligned world, these relationships are much more fluid and unpredictable. Alliances within a region may add significantly to the military capability of an opponent or globally broaden the AO. This could occur in the middle of deployment or after the force has been introduced into the area of responsibility (AOR).

VARIABLE 5--MILITARY CAPABILITIES

1-81.   Existing military capabilities are the most critical variable for military operations. Once easy to define, this variable is rapidly becoming the most complex of all. Hybridization, rapid technological advancement, and capabilities developed from asymmetrical concepts generate constant change.

VARIABLE 6--INFORMATION

1-82.   Sophisticated and unsophisticated opponents alike understand the value of information operations. Some argue that it will be the decisive factor in future conflicts. Most potential opponents feel this is the most productive avenue to take to offset US conventional battlefield capabilities.

VARIABLE 7--TECHNOLOGY

1-83.   Advanced technology serves to level the playing field either symmetrically or by development of asymmetrical capabilities. The presence of sophisticated technology indicates where opponents expect to achieve the greatest advantage or perceive the greatest threat. The nature of the environment can change dramatically with the introduction of a new or advanced system.

VARIABLE 8--EXTERNAL ORGANIZATIONS

1-84.   Increased globalization of individual economies and the development of world wide information systems are generating enhanced worldwide awareness. This has resulted in the increase of United Nations, regional, nongovernmental, and private organizations. In addition, these organizations are growing in influence and power as well as in willingness to become involved in crises. In the past, many of these organizations have become actively involved in crisis areas and are having a growing impact on operations.

VARIABLE 9--NATIONAL WILL

1-85.   Clearly, US national will is viewed by most countries as its strategic center of gravity. The degree to which a state can attack its opponent's national will and still preserve its own, represents to a large degree, its ability to achieve favorable conflict resolution. In today's world of transparent military operations, this attack and defense of national will has tactical as well as strategic implications.

VARIABLE 10--TIME

1-86.   Time is always a critical factor. It drives the operation. In most cases, opponents view time as being to their advantage in that the longer the amount of time between crisis and response, the greater the opportunity for games of brinkmanship and adjusting the nature of conflict. Time is an operational factor and a tool to manipulate tactical and strategic advantages.

VARIABLE 11--ECONOMICS

1-87.   Economic position represents a nation's ability to rapidly purchase military capabilities or to conduct sustained operations. It also gives indication of external relationships that could result in political or military assistance. Criminal elements will want to profit from the US deployment by pilfering, by manipulating contracts, and by preying on local and national employees in the service of the US.

This page intentionally left blank.

Chapter 2
Battle Command

Battle command is the exercise of command in operations against a hostile, thinking enemy. It is the application of the leadership element *combat power* to operations. Principally, battle command is an art that employs skills developed by professional study, constant practice, and considered judgment.

Assisted by staff, the commander visualizes the operation, describes it (states his intent and provides guidance); and directs the actions of subordinates within his intent. He directs operations in terms of the WFFs. He directly influences operations by his personal presence, supported by his command and control system.

Command of the battalion remains a personal function. The functions of command and control are planning, preparing for, and executing the other warfighting functions; to synchronize activities among them; and to assess the situation continually.

Section I. ART OF COMMAND

Command is the authority that a commander in military service lawfully exercises over subordinates by virtue of rank and assignment. Leaders possessing command authority strive to use it with firmness, care, and skill. Command is more of an art than a science; although it exhibits characteristics of both. The "art of command" requires expert performance of a specific skill, using intuitive faculties that the leader cannot gain solely by study or education. Command also requires a conscious and skillful exercise of authority to fulfill command responsibilities using decision making and leadership.

ROLE OF COMMANDER

2-1.   The Infantry battalion commander's knowledge, experience, and personality determine how he interacts with his unit. He drives the process through mission command. He establishes a command climate for his unit, prepares his unit for operations, commands his unit during operations, and assesses his subordinates. The commander refines the battalion's command and control system, and he runs it based on his personality. He establishes a system to meet the unique demands that he places on his unit, balancing the abilities and personalities of his subordinates, and the capabilities of the equipment in the Infantry battalion. Once the commander decides what he wants to do, he relays his intent to his subordinates.

COMMANDER'S INTENT

2-2.   The commander's intent is a clear, concise statement of what the force must do and the conditions the force must meet to succeed with respect to the enemy, terrain, and the desired end state. The commander makes his own independent and sometimes intuitive assessment of how he intends to win. The final expression of intent comes from the commander personally. The commander formulates and communicates his intent to ensure unity of effort during operations, allowing subordinates to exercise disciplined initiative. Intent, combined with mission, directs subordinates toward mission accomplishment

---

in the absence of orders. When significant opportunities appear, subordinates use the commander's intent to orient their efforts and display initiative.

SUBORDINATE INITIATIVE

2-3.   Initiative is the assumption of responsibility to decide and initiate independent actions when the commander's concept or order is no longer applicable or when an unanticipated opportunity presents itself that leads to the accomplishment of the commander's intent. Subordinates decide how to achieve their assigned missions within the delegated freedom of action and the exercise of disciplined initiative during execution; they have an absolute responsibility, however, to fulfill the commander's intent.

COMPONENTS

2-4.   The components of the commander's intent include: end state, key tasks, and expanded intent (if desired).

End state

2-5.   At the operational and tactical levels, an end state consists of those conditions that, when achieved, accomplish the mission. The commander normally articulates an operation's end state by describing the relationship between friendly forces and the enemy, terrain, and the population.

Key Tasks

2-6.   Key tasks are those tasks that the force must perform as a whole, or are the conditions the force must meet to achieve the end state, and the stated purpose of the operation. Key tasks are not tied to a specific course of action (COA); but rather, they identify what the force must do to achieve the end state. Acceptable COAs accomplish all key tasks. In changed circumstances, when significant opportunities present themselves or the concept of operations no longer fits the situation, subordinates use key tasks to keep their efforts focused on achieving the commander's intent. Examples of key tasks include; terrain that must be controlled, the operation's tempo and duration, and the operation's effect on the enemy. Key tasks are not specified tasks for any subordinate unit; however, they may be sources of implied tasks.

Expanded Purpose

2-7.   If the commander's intent addresses purpose, it does not restate the "why" of the mission statement; but rather, it addresses the broader operational context of the mission.

LOCATION OF COMMANDER

2-8.   In the past, the commander has been torn between the conflicting requirement to visualize the battlefield and the requirement for his presence in the main or tactical command post (TACCP) to participate in the MDMP. This dilemma slowed the planning and execution of operations while frustrating the commanders' efforts to "get out of the command post."

2-9.   Infantry battalions must have the ability to visualize the battlespace in all dimensions and to share a common operational picture (COP). In addition, battalion commanders retain the ability to recognize and protect their own and other friendly forces. The commander cannot, however, fully visualize the battlefield while directing and synchronizing the efforts of his battalion from the command post. He must move from the CP to assess the situation face-to-face with subordinate commanders and their Soldiers. The C2 infrastructure within the Infantry battalion permits a commander to position himself where he can best command without depriving himself of the ability to respond to opportunities and changing circumstances.

2-10.   The commander can be any place on the battlefield where he can best affect current operations but not disrupt the planning and preparation for future operations. He will need information updates and continuous assessments to make command decisions. He may need to make brief trips to the CP to approve and personally deliver plans and orders from battalion to company level. However, the commander is not tethered to the CP if he needs to review developed COAs, WARNOs, OPORDs, and FRAGOs or provide guidance for planning. If the commander chooses, he can receive, review, edit, and disseminate orders and issue guidance from his ABCS suite.

SCIENCE OF CONTROL

2-11.   The commander is the key to command and control in the battalion. Foremost among his roles is his ability to combine the art of command and the science of control. He must use a method of visualizing the battlespace, describing his visualization to subordinates, directing action to achieve results, and leading the unit to mission accomplishment, with continuous assessment throughout the mission.

VISUALIZE

2-12.   The commander's visualization is the core mental process that supports his decision making and by which he combines the art of command and the science of control. It is the process of achieving a clear understanding of the battalion's current state with relation to the enemy and the environment, developing a desired end state that represents mission accomplishment, and determining the sequence of activities that moves the battalion from its current state to the end state. The commander begins to visualize the desired end state when he receives a mission or perceives a change in the mission. He applies his current situational understanding to the received or perceived mission. As he analyzes or receives staff analysis of the mission, he develops a mental image of the friendly forces in relation to the enemy, the environment, and possible future operations at the conclusion of the operation. The commander's visualization is his assessment tool throughout the operation. He should focus on the following factors.

Understand Current State of Friendly and Enemy Forces

2-13.   The commander derives situational understanding from applying his judgment, experience, expertise, and intuition to all of the information gathered on the current situation. Situational understanding includes physical factors, human factors, and the relationships between friendly and enemy forces and the environment that represent potential opportunities or threats for the battalion.

Common Operating Picture

2-14.   The COP is an operational picture tailored to the commander's requirements based on common data and information shared by more than one command. The COP includes friendly, enemy, and environmental elements and helps the commander to make timely, accurate decisions. The COP is displayed at a scale and level of detail that meets the information needs of the commander. Depending on how long it takes friendly and enemy situational information to reach a particular unit, the COP will represent varying degrees of accuracy of the actual picture at any given point. As technology continues to push toward state-of-the-art digital communications to enhance near-real-time situational understanding, the accuracy of the COP between the various units on the battlefield will be increased. C2 systems fuse information from a variety of sources. Rapid distribution of information is enhanced as information systems (INFOSYS) continue to be updated with digital devices on the battlefield.

Situational Understanding

2-15.   SU is the product of applying analysis and judgment to the COP to determine the relationships among factors of METT-TC (mission, enemy, terrain, troops, time available, and civil considerations). It enhances decision making by identifying opportunities, threats to the force or mission accomplishment, and information gaps. However, SU is imperfect, particularly with respect to the enemy situation.

Foresee a Feasible Outcome

2-16.   The commander must identify a feasible outcome to the operation that results in mission success and leaves the battalion postured for the next operation.

Visualize Dynamics Between Opposing Forces

2-17.   The commander must identify the dynamics of opposing forces throughout the sequence of actions. This includes evaluating possible enemy reactions and friendly counteractions. This evaluation may lead to the identification of possible critical decision points throughout the operation.

DESCRIBE

2-18.   The commander describes his visualization by participating in the MDMP during planning and preparation for an operation and during execution. Specifically, his commander's intent, planning guidance, anticipated decision points, and commander's critical information requirements all serve to guide and focus the C2 system to support his decision making and to communicate his decision for execution. He must apply his judgment, experience, expertise, and intuition before making a decision and describing that decision to subordinates. During preparation, the commander uses the rehearsal to describe further his intent and concept to his subordinates, to identify and discuss options at decision points, to synchronize activities within the battalion and among subordinate units, and to add to his own visualization. During execution, the commander continues to visualize the implication of events, and he describes his conclusions to his staff and subordinates through updated CCIR and guidance and to his higher HQ's through a situation report.

DIRECT

2-19.   The commander directs when he has made a decision and communicates that decision to his subordinates through an order.

Plan

2-20.   Orders should enable subordinates to understand their situation, their commander's mission and intent, and their own mission. Clear direction is essential to mission success; however, commanders must strike a balance between *necessary but minimum direction* and *overly detailed direction*. The commander, or his staff, assigns graphical, written, or procedural control measures (permissive or restrictive) to prevent units from impeding one another and to impose necessary coordination. The commander should impose only the minimum control measures necessary to provide essential coordination and deconfliction among units.

Prepare

2-21.   The commander must update and validate his visualization during preparations as the results of reconnaissance and surveillance operations become available. The earlier the commander identifies the need for modifications, the easier it is for him to incorporate and synchronize them into his plan. He describes the implications of his updated visualization and directs actions to effect his changes to the plan throughout the orders process.

Execute

2-22.   Execution includes a continuous process of assessing the current state of the operation and making adjustments to exploit opportunities and to account for unforeseen enemy actions. Combining the art of command and the science of control is most evident during execution. The commander exercises judgment and initiative continuously, assessing the situation and making decisions often with incomplete, conflicting, and vague information. Waiting for perfect information is rarely an option. During execution, the commander uses his visualization, along with continuous updated information, to ensure that his subordinate units execute appropriate measures for the actual situation. A major part of the "art of command" is to know when the plan must change and what criteria indicate a need for changes and then to determine what changes will maximize unit effectiveness. The commander directs these actions primarily through a FRAGO.

Section II. COMMAND AND CONTROL

Command and control has two components: the commander and the C2 system. The commander uses the C2 system to exercise C2 over forces to accomplish a mission.

SYSTEM

2-23.   The C2 system is the arrangement of personnel, information management, procedures, and equipment and facilities essential to the commander to plan, prepare for, execute, and assess operations.

INFRASTRUCTURE

2-24.   The C2 infrastructure is a system of intelligence, surveillance, and reconnaissance collection and processing procedures, information management, organizational structures, personnel, equipment, facilities, communications, and computers essential to conduct operations. It is designed to exercise C2 over forces to accomplish the mission. It supports a commander's exercise of C2 across the range of military operations through regulation of forces and functions IAW the commander's intent. The C2 infrastructure provides the commander and staff with the ability to plan, prepare, and execute using resilient voice and data communications networks to enable effective C2 on the battlefield. This capability includes the conduct of operations from alert through redeployment. It also includes conduct of counterintelligence operations to deny the adversary's ability to do the same. The battalion integrates the C2 infrastructure through maneuver, fires and effects, logistics, force protection, information operations, and intelligence.

EXERCISE

2-25.   The battalion commander must place the C2 system into action to exercise C2. Exercising C2 is dynamic throughout the operations process. Although planning, preparing, executing, and assessing occur continuously in operations, they need not occur sequentially. The battalion must prepare to perform all four actions simultaneously, and the commander is at the center of the process (Figure 2-1). The operations process is execution-focused rather than planning-focused.

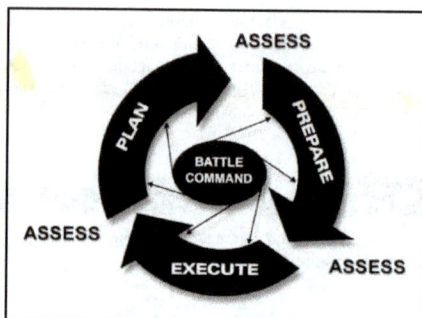

Figure 2-1. Operations process.

DISTRIBUTION AT BATTALION LEVEL

2-26.   The battalion's staff sections are normally distributed among three C2 organizations: the command group, main command post, and combat trains command post. The battalion commander organizes his staff within each command post to perform essential staff functions to aid him with planning and in controlling operations. These C2 organizations are normally positioned within the battalion's AO to maintain flexibility, redundancy, survivability, and mobility. See Chapter 9 for more information.

COMMAND GROUP

2-27.   The command group usually consists of the commander, the fire support officer and or air liaison officer, and other key staff officers as directed by the commander. Its purpose is the direct C2 of the battalion. The command group is not a permanent organization; rather, it is formed anytime the battalion commander goes forward to control an operation. The command group is equipped to operate wherever the battalion commander feels it is necessary to influence operations with rapid decisions and orders. The commander determines the actual placement of personnel within the command group.

2-28.   The commander fights the battle from the command group and positions himself in the best location, normally near the main effort, to influence the battle without losing situational understanding. From this forward location, he is better able to observe critical events, maintain communications, and sense the battle. Whenever possible the commander uses the C2 system to free himself from the main CP so he can physically visualize his subordinates and the terrain he is to fight on without affecting his decision-making ability.

2-29.   In determining his location on the battlefield, the commander considers—

- Where on the battlefield he must position himself so that he can exert the greatest influence.
- Time and location of critical events and decision points that have the greatest impact on mission accomplishment. Ideally, the commander selects a location where he can observe the conditions that aid in making a critical decision.
- Security for the command group, including the commander's personal protection.

MAIN COMMAND POST

2-30.   The main CP is the battalion commander's principal C2 facility. The main CP operates from a stationary position and moves as required to maintain control of the operation. In linear operations environments, it locates behind the Infantry companies' CPs and, if possible, out of enemy medium-artillery range. In nonlinear and or noncontiguous operations, it locates where it can best support battalion operations and is least vulnerable to potential hostile actions. The battalion XO is responsible for supervising all staff activities and functions within the main CP. The main CP serves the following functions:

- Synchronizes combat, combat support, and sustainment activities in support of the overall operation.
- Provides a focal point for the development of intelligence.
- Supports information understanding for the battalion commander and subordinates by monitoring, analyzing, and disseminating information.
- Monitors and anticipates the commander's decision points.
- Plans future operations.
- Coordinates with higher headquarters and adjacent units.
- Keeps higher headquarters informed.
- Serves as net control station for the operations and intelligence radio net and backup net control station for the command radio net.
- Provides a stable, secure planning facility.
- Produces and disseminates the commander's orders.
- Plans and controls reconnaissance and surveillance operations.

COMBAT TRAINS COMMAND POST

2-31.   The CTCP controls and coordinates the administrative and logistical support for the battalion. It consists of the battalion S-1 and S-4, and it usually collocates with the BAS. The battalion S-1 and S-4 work closely with the forward support company (FSC) commander and the BSB support operations officer to coordinate sustainment for the battalion. The CTCP serves the following functions:

- Tracks the current battle and is prepared to assume the functions of the main command post.
- Provides sustainment representation to the main CP for planning and integration.
- Forecasts and coordinates future requirements.
- Monitors main supply routes (MSRs) and controls sustainment traffic within the battalion's AO.
- Coordinates the evacuation of casualties, equipment, and enemy prisoners of war (EPWs).

INFANTRY BATTALION FIELD TRAINS COMMAND POST

2-32.   The attached FSC commander controls the field trains and all units that reside in it. The battalion's field trains will usually reside in the brigade support area (BSA); however, the field trains may locate within the Infantry battalions AO. The field trains usually include the personnel administration center (PAC), elements of the S-4 section, elements of the company supply sections, elements of the FSC, and any other support elements that are not forward in the combat trains. Infantry companies normally locate their supply sections with elements of the HHC headquarters section in the field trains. The HHC 1SG is typically the senior battalion representative in the field trains. The battalion S-4 coordinates all unit supply requests, and ensures the logistics needs of the battalion are coordinated with the FSC commander. This includes coordination of LOGPACs moving forward into the battalion AO, and satisfactory completion of all maintenance requests.

COMMAND AND SUPPORT RELATIONSHIPS

2-33.   A subordinate unit falls under the direct command of a specific commander if that subordinate unit is organic, assigned, attached, or under operational control to that specific commanders unit

---

COMMAND

2-34.   Command responsibility and authority are established routinely through these following standard relationships:

Organic

2-35.   This unit forms an essential part of an Army organization and is listed in its TOE or table of distribution and allowances (TDA).

Assigned

2-36.   This unit is placed in an organization on a permanent basis and is controlled and administered by the organization to which it is assigned.

Attached

2-37.   In this relationship, a unit is assigned temporarily to a command other than its parent unit. The attached unit is under the command of the unit's commander to which it is attached.

- The commanding officer exercises the same degree of C2 as with his organic units.
- C2 is subject to limitations specified by the commander directing the attachment. This relationship includes the responsibility for logistics, training, operations, and uniform code of military justice; however, the parent unit retains responsibility for transfer and promotion.
- Having a unit attached imposes an administrative and logistical burden on the unit to which the attachment is made.

Operational Control

2-38.   This relationship places a unit under the control of a commander for specific operations. The relationship is limited by function, time, or location. OPCON does not imply responsibility for administration, logistics, discipline, internal organization, or training. The commander's relationship with OPCON units is otherwise the same as with organic or attached subordinate units.

Tactical Control

2-39.   TACON is the authority normally limited to the detailed and specified local direction of movement and maneuver of forces to accomplish a task. This is a command relationship where a combatant commander delegates limited authority to direct the tactical use of combat forces. TACON is often the command relationship established between forces of different nations in a multinational force.

SUPPORT

2-40.   Support is the action of an element or unit that aids, protects, complements, or sustains another unit IAW an order requiring such support. A supporting unit assists another unit but is not under the command of that unit. The commander's relationship with supporting units is as follows:

- He ensures that the supporting unit establishes liaison and communications with his unit.
- He keeps the supporting unit informed of the situation and the support needed.
- The leader of the supporting unit advises him on its employment considerations.
- A supporting unit honors his request for support as an order. In case of a conflict, the supporting unit leader refers the matter to his parent unit commander. However, the request or order in question is honored, until the conflict is resolved.

Direct Support

2-41.   A unit in DS supports another specific unit, but remains under the command of its parent unit commander. The supporting unit answers directly to the supported unit's requests. The company commander may not reallocate, reassign, or task-organize the DS force supporting him.

General Support

2-42.   Units in GS to the battalion are under control of their parent unit commander. They support the battalion as a whole, not any specific company. Company commanders may request support from the GS unit through the battalion.

Reinforcing Mission

2-43.   Reinforcing is a tactical artillery mission in which an artillery unit augments the fire of another artillery unit. Coordination for support is normally provided through the DS artillery unit.

General Support-Reinforcing Mission

2-44.   General Support-Reinforcing (GS-R) is a tactical artillery mission where an artillery unit has the mission of supporting the force as a whole and of providing reinforcing fires for another artillery unit. Coordination for support is the responsibility of the DS artillery unit.

Section III. PLANNING PROCEDURES

Planning for operations leads the commander to make decisions during execution. At its core, decision making is knowing *if* to decide, then *when* and *what* to decide. It includes understanding the consequences of decisions. The MDMP is an established and proven analytical process. This tool helps the commander and staff develop estimates and a plan. The recognition of the criticality of WFFs, and the digitization of the Army, have not changed the steps of the MDMP; they have enhanced them. The analytical aspect of the MDMP is continuous, occurring before, during, and after operations with constant feedback and updates of information. In the end, the MDMP is the commander's planning tool to be implemented as he deems appropriate.

PARALLEL, COLLABORATIVE, AND DISTRIBUTED PLANNING

2-45.   Parallel planning allows each echelon to make maximum use of time available. Collaborative planning is the real-time interaction of commanders and staffs at two or more echelons. Distributed planning allows the commander and staff members to execute planning from different locations.

PARALLEL PLANNING

2-46.   Parallel planning occurs when two echelons conduct their planning almost simultaneously. It requires significant interaction between echelons. Parallel planning can happen only when higher headquarters produce timely warning orders and share information with subordinate headquarters as it becomes available.

COLLABORATIVE PLANNING

2-47.   Collaborative planning is the real-time interaction among commanders and staffs at two or more echelons developing plans for a single operation. It must be used judiciously.

2-48.   Collaborative planning is most appropriate when time is scarce and a limited number of options are being considered. It is particularly useful when the commander and his staff can benefit from the input of subordinate commanders and staffs.

2-49.   Collaborative planning is not appropriate when the staff is working a large number of courses of action or branches and sequels, many of which will be discarded. In this case, involving subordinates wastes precious time working options that are later discarded. Collaborative planning is also often not appropriate during ongoing operations in which extended planning sessions take commanders and staffs away from conducting current operations.

2-50.   As a rule of thumb, if the commander is directly involved in time-sensitive planning, some level of collaborative planning is probably needed. The commander, not the staff, must make the decision to conduct collaborative planning. Only the commander can commit subordinate commanders to using their time for collaborative planning.

DISTRIBUTED PLANNING

2-51.   Digital communications and INFOSYS enable members of the same staff to execute the MDMP without being collocated. Distributed planning saves time and increases the accuracy of available information in that it allows for the rapid transmission of voice and data information, which can be used by staffs over a wide geographical area.

MILITARY DECISION-MAKING PROCESS

2-52.   The MDMP is a process used by a commander and his staff to develop and thoroughly examine numerous friendly and enemy courses of action. Based on the commander's estimate, the MDMP can be adjusted to meet the current situation. The commander and staff typically conduct this examination when developing the commander's estimate and operation plans (OPLANs), when planning for an entirely new mission, and during extended operations. This process can be performed slowly and deliberately or quickly with heavy commander involvement. It also helps the commander and his staff to examine a specific situation and, by applying thoroughness, clarity, sound judgment, logic, and professional knowledge, reach a logical decision. (See Section IV for a detailed explanation of the MDMP and the use of MDMP in a time-constrained environment.)

2-53.   The MDMP relies on doctrine (FM 5-0), especially the terms and symbols (graphics) consolidated in FM 1-02. Using approved terms and symbols facilitates the rapid and consistent assessment of the situation and the creation and implementation of plans and orders by minimizing confusion over the meanings of terms and symbols used in the process.

ROLES OF COMMANDER AND EXECUTIVE OFFICER

2-54.   The commander is in charge of the military decision-making process. From start to finish, the commander's personal role is central. His participation in the process provides focus and guidance to the staff; however, there are responsibilities and decisions that are the commander's alone. The amount of his direct involvement is driven by the time available, his personal preferences, and the experience and accessibility of the staff. The less time available, the less experienced the staff, and the less accessible the staff, the greater the commander's involvement in the MDMP. See paragraph 2-19 for a discussion of increased commander involvement in the decision-making process.

2-55.   The XO manages, coordinates, and disciplines the staff's work and provides quality control. He ensures the staff has the information, guidance from the commander, and facilities it needs. He determines timelines for the staff, establishes briefback times and locations, enforces the information management plan, and provides any unique instructions needed to guide the staff in completing the MDMP process.

2-56.   Warning orders are used to facilitate parallel planning. By issuing guidance and participating in formal and informal briefings, the commander and XO guide the staff through the decision-making process. In a collaborative environment, the commander can extend this participation directly to subordinate commanders and staffs. Such interaction helps the staff and subordinates to resolve questions and involves all staff and subordinates in the complete process.

ROLE OF RECONNAISSANCE AND SURVEILLANCE

2-57.   The battalion commander deploys the battalion scout platoon and other assets early in the planning process to facilitate early intelligence collection. However, the scout platoon is a primary source of the battalion's intelligence. It should only be deployed after he first considers, as a minimum, the reconnaissance and surveillance planning factors found during mission analysis.

2-58.   The commander and staff ensure reconnaissance and surveillance is continuous during planning, preparation, and execution of the mission. Data collected during reconnaissance and surveillance may result in initial plans or courses of action being modified or even discarded. Further, when the plan changes, the commander must modify his reconnaissance and surveillance objective to support the new plan.

2-59.   Reconnaissance assists significantly in developing courses of action. Conducted early in the planning process, it can help confirm or deny the commander's initial assessment (visualization). Information may also allow him to focus immediately on a specific course of action or to eliminate courses of action that the reconnaissance shows to be infeasible.

2-60.   When conducting a reconnaissance, the commander must determine if the benefits outweigh the risks. During defensive, stability operations, and civil support operations, the reconnaissance can often be conducted with little risk. During offensive operations, reconnaissance involves more risk.

2-61.   When the commander deploys reconnaissance assets, particularly human intelligence, minimum planning guidance is given to ensure the survival of the asset while still enabling mission accomplishment. This guidance includes—

- Mission statement to include eyes-on-target time and anticipated length of mission.
- Priority intelligence requirement.
- Enemy situation in the operational area.
- Commander's intent for intelligence (can be stated by the S-2 or S-3).
- Method of deployment and insertion with abort criteria. Coordination time and place are included, if applicable.
- Fire support plan to include assets available.
- Communication plan (primary and back-up).
- Casualty evacuation plan.
- Exfiltration plan.
- Resupply plan.

Section IV. MILITARY DECISION-MAKING PROCESS

The MDMP has seven steps. Each builds on the outputs from the previous steps. Each then produces its own output that drives subsequent steps (Figure 2-2). Errors committed early in the process, especially with a faulty mission analysis, affect later steps. Estimates go on continuously to provide important inputs to the MDMP. Each staff section produces estimates. Both these estimates and database updates support the planning process, as well as mission execution. This section summarizes the MDMP. (See FM 5-0 for a more detailed discussion of the MDMP.)

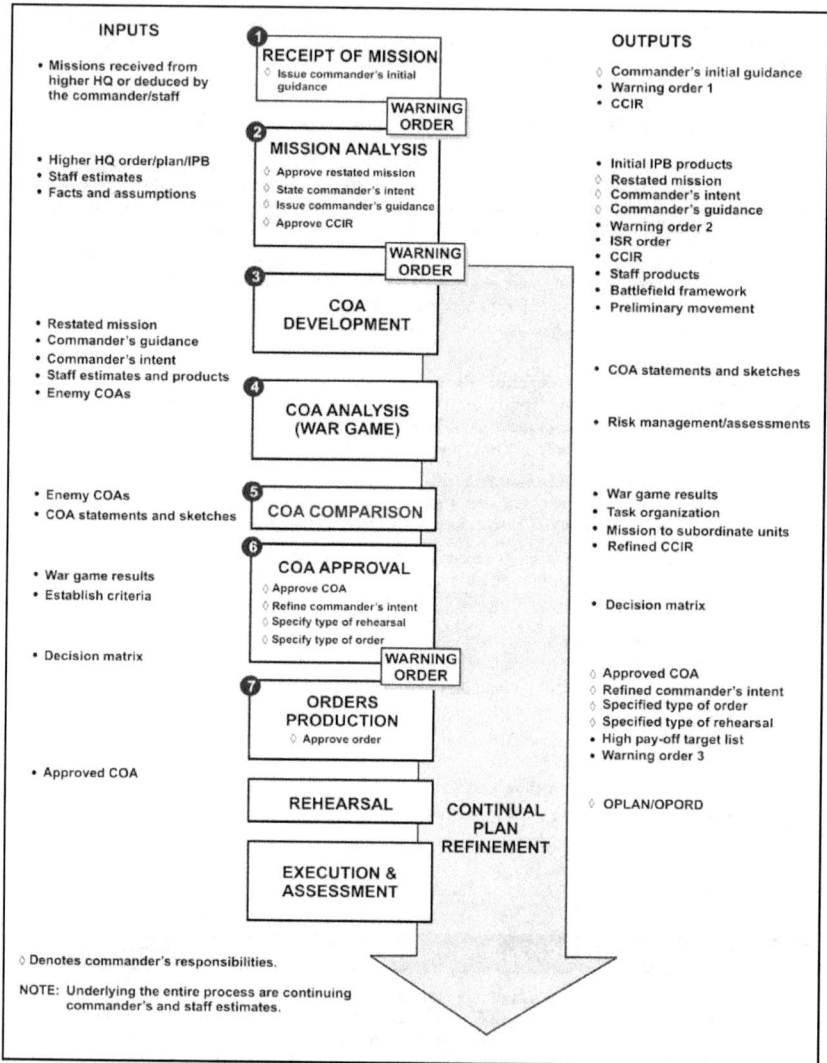

INPUTS

- Missions received from higher HQ or deduced by the commander/staff

- Higher HQ order/plan/IPB
- Staff estimates
- Facts and assumptions

- Restated mission
- Commander's guidance
- Commander's intent
- Staff estimates and products
- Enemy COAs

- Enemy COAs
- COA statements and sketches

- War game results
- Establish criteria

- Decision matrix

- Approved COA

1 RECEIPT OF MISSION
◊ Issue commander's initial guidance

WARNING ORDER

2 MISSION ANALYSIS
◊ Approve restated mission
◊ State commander's intent
◊ Issue commander's guidance
◊ Approve CCIR

WARNING ORDER

3 COA DEVELOPMENT

4 COA ANALYSIS (WAR GAME)

5 COA COMPARISON

6 COA APPROVAL
◊ Approve COA
◊ Refine commander's intent
◊ Specify type of rehearsal
◊ Specify type of order

WARNING ORDER

7 ORDERS PRODUCTION
◊ Approve order

REHEARSAL

EXECUTION & ASSESSMENT

CONTINUAL PLAN REFINEMENT

OUTPUTS

◊ Commander's initial guidance
- Warning order 1
- CCIR

- Initial IPB products
◊ Restated mission
◊ Commander's intent
◊ Commander's guidance
- Warning order 2
- ISR order
- CCIR
- Staff products
- Battlefield framework
- Preliminary movement

- COA statements and sketches

- Risk management/assessments

- War game results
- Task organization
- Mission to subordinate units
- Refined CCIR

- Decision matrix

◊ Approved COA
◊ Refined commander's intent
◊ Specified type of order
◊ Specified type of rehearsal
- High pay-off target list
- Warning order 3

◊ OPLAN/OPORD

◊ Denotes commander's responsibilities.

NOTE: Underlying the entire process are continuing commander's and staff estimates.

Figure 2-2. MDMP steps, staff inputs and outputs.

TIME CONSTRAINTS

2-62.   The MDMP is the foundation for planning in a time-constrained environment. The products of the MDMP are used in later planning sessions, when time is too short for a thorough reexamination, but when significant parts of existing information and analysis of METT-TC factors -have not changed substantially. Quickly developed plans are not likely to anticipate every possible branch or sequel, enemy action, unexpected opportunity, or change in mission directed from higher headquarters, but this can be mitigated by continuing staff planning after the order is given. Fleeting opportunities or unexpected enemy actions may require a quick decision to implement a new or modified plan. The commander decides how to abbreviate the MDMP; steps of the process should never be dropped; however, they may be done in a shortened timeframe. What works for a unit depends on its proficiency and the factors of METT-TC in a given situation. For more detailed information on the abbreviated decision making process, roles the commander and staff play in it, and time saving techniques, see FM 5-0.

TRAINING ON THE MDMP

2-63.   Before a unit can conduct decision-making in a time-constrained environment, it must train on, and master, all of the steps in the MDMP. A unit can only abbreviate the MDMP if it fully understands the role of each step of the process and the requirements to produce the necessary products. Training on these steps must be thorough and result in a series of staff battle drills tailored to the time available. Training on the MDMP must be stressful and replicate realistic conditions and timelines. There is only one process, and omitting steps of the MDMP to meet time constraints is not the solution. Anticipation, organization, and prior preparation are the keys to success in a time-constrained environment. Well-trained staffs will know where they can abbreviate actions and planning, focusing on only the most critical factors.

ABBREVIATION

2-64.   The unit abbreviates the MDMP when there is too little time for a thorough and comprehensive application of the process. The most significant factor to consider is time. It is the only nonrenewable, and often the most critical, resource.

TECHNIQUES

2-65.   There are four primary techniques for abbreviating the MDMP:

- Increase the battalion commander's involvement, allowing him to make timely decisions without waiting for detailed briefings after each step.
- Limit options. When the commander is more prescriptive it saves the staff time by allowing them to focus more closely.
- Maximize parallel planning. Although parallel planning should be normal during the MDMP, maximizing its use in a time-constrained environment is critical.
- Limit the number of courses of action. If the commander conducts a personal assessment and chooses a course of action, he can direct the staff to refine that one course of action only. This technique normally saves the most time. It is highly dependent on the commander having an accurate grasp of the relevant tactical situation facing the battalion.

2-66.   In a time-constrained environment, the importance of warning orders increases as available time decreases; a verbal warning order now, followed by a written order later (or posted to a database), are worth more than a written order one hour from now. The same warning orders used in the MDMP should be issued when abbreviating the process. In addition to warning orders, units must share all available information, (particularly intelligence preparation of the battlefield [IPB] products) with subordinates as soon as possible. The C2 INFOSYS greatly increase this sharing of information and the commander's visualization through collaboration with his subordinates.

2-67.   While the steps used in a time-constrained environment are the same, many of them may be done mentally by the battalion commander or with less staff involvement than during the MDMP. The products developed when the process is abbreviated may be the same as those developed for the MDMP; however, they may be much less detailed and some may be omitted altogether. Unit SOPs and mission requirements tailor this process to the commander's preference for orders in this environment.

2-68.   When developing the plan, the staff may initially use the MDMP and develop branches and sequels. During execution, they may abbreviate the process. A unit may use the complete process to develop the plan while a subordinate headquarters abbreviates the process.

ADVANTAGES

2-69.   The advantages of using the abbreviated MDMP include the following:

- It maximizes the use of available time, and may be the required solution due to mission requirements.
- It may allow subordinates more planning and preparation time.
- It focuses staff efforts on the commander's specific and directive guidance.
- It facilitates adaptation to a rapidly-changing situation.
- It compensates for an inexperienced staff.

DISADVANTAGES

2-70.   An abbreviated MDMP--

- Is much more directive; also, limits staff flexibility and initiative.
- Ignores some available options during the development of friendly courses of action.
- Can result in only an oral OPORD or FRAGO.
- Increases the risk of missing a key factor or failing to uncover a better option.
- Might decrease the coordination and synchronization of the plan.
- Requires more focus to rehearse, and could require more face --time between commanders.

Section V. PREPARATION FOR OPERATIONS

Preparing for operations includes activities conducted by the battalion before executing to improve its ability to conduct an operation. At a minimum, these activities include: plan refinement, rehearsals, reconnaissance and surveillance, coordination, inspections, and movement. Preparation occurs anytime the battalion is not executing. Ideally, preparation begins with the receipt of an order (as does planning) and ends as execution begins. Assessment during preparation monitors the progress of a unit's readiness to conduct the operation. The commander evaluates preparations against his criteria for success to determine variances and to forecast the significance of those variances for mission accomplishment.

RECONNAISSANCE AND SURVEILLANCE

2-71.   During preparation, the battalion commander receives answers to some of his CCIR and improves his intelligence about the enemy and terrain through the scout platoon and other ISR assets available to him. A reconnaissance and surveillance operation is planned and executed with the same level of importance as any operation. As the scout platoon and other assets gather information (answering the CCIR), the staff should modify the collection plan to account for new information requirements and to redirect efforts to collect additional information. The staff should focus collection efforts on the most important unknowns remaining, emphasizing the current CCIR. The battalion commander must balance his need for information--

- With the ability of the scout platoon and other assets to gather the information.
- On the risk to the scout platoon to collect it.
- On the ability of the battalion to sustain and provide indirect fire support to the scout platoon over time and distance
- On the requirement to have the scout platoon available at critical times and places to support the decisive action
- On the availability (time, type, and quantity) of other ISR assets.

SECURITY

2-72.   Security during preparation prevents surprise and reduces uncertainty through local security and operational security. Local security and operations security (OPSEC) prevent the enemy from discovering the battalion's plan and protect the force from unforeseen enemy actions. The goal in conducting security operations is to prevent the enemy from gathering its CCIR. Security is a dynamic effort that anticipates and prevents enemy intelligence-gathering efforts.

FORCE PROTECTION

2-73.   Force protection includes a combination of active and passive measures to deter, defeat, or mitigate enemy actions. It is not a discrete mission assigned to a single subordinate unit but a continuous effort executed by the battalion and all of its subordinate units regardless of their mission, location, or threat. The commander and staff develop and initiate actions during planning but conduct the actions during planning, preparation, and execution.

PLAN REVISION AND REFINEMENT

2-74.   The battalion commander adjusts plans based on new information. The enemy is also acting while the battalion is preparing for an upcoming operation. As assumptions prove true or false, as the scout platoon (or other ISR assets) confirms or denies enemy actions and dispositions, and as the status of subordinate units change, the battalion commander determines whether the new information invalidates or validates the plan, or requires him to adjust the plan.

COORDINATION AND LIAISON

2-75.   During preparation, the battalion conducts necessary coordination with higher, lower, adjacent, supporting, joint, interagency, multinational, or SOF units or organizations (Appendix G). This may include sending and receiving liaison teams. Coordination includes deconflicting operations (to include information operations), exchanging graphic control, fire support, and direct fire control measures. Coordination should also include establishing communication links to guarantee continuous contact and prevent fratricide during execution. This coordination is essential for synchronizing different unit and organization actions during execution.

COORDINATION

2-76.   Exchanging information is critical to successful coordination. Coordination may be both internal and external. Internal coordination occurs within the battalion staff. External coordination, often referred to as collaborative planning, involves subordinate and supporting units or staffs and higher headquarters. Coordination has four objectives:

- It ensures an understanding of the commander's intent and an understanding of subordinate and supporting unit roles.

- It ensures that all affected and interested personnel have been consulted or informed so they may respond as desired or adjust their plans and actions.
- It avoids conflict and duplication of effort among subordinate units, reducing the risk of fratricide and the expenditure of resources.
- It ensures that the commander and staff consider all relevant factors and effectively employ all available assets.

LIAISON

2-77.   Liaison provides a means of direct communications between headquarters. Liaison may begin with planning and continue throughout preparation and execution.

REHEARSALS

2-78.   The intent of a rehearsal is to practice actions to improve performance during execution. The extent of rehearsals depends on the time available. Rehearsals allow participants to become familiar with the plan and to translate the plan into a visual impression that orients them to the environment and other units when executing the plan. Rehearsals imprint a mental picture of the sequence of key actions within the upcoming operation. Rehearsals also provide a forum for coordination among subordinate and supporting leaders. Rehearsals emphasize times, locations, and solutions for coordinating actions to achieve synchronization at critical points during execution. Key to success is for the staff, normally the S-3, to advise participants about any needed focus areas to be discussed in advance.

Section VI. EXECUTION

Execution is putting a plan into action by applying combat power to accomplish the mission using SU to assess progress and make decisions. Inherent in the dynamic nature of execution is deciding to execute planned actions as well as deciding to adjust the plan based on changes in the situation. Combining the art of command and the science of control is most evident during execution. The commander exercises judgment and initiative continuously. He assesses the situation and makes decisions, often with incomplete, conflicting, and vague information. During execution, the commander uses his visualization, continuously updated with a current COP, to assess the progress of operations. The commander's current SU determines what CCIR needs to be updated against the COP.

COMMAND AND CONTROL

2-79.   During execution, the C2 system must continuously manage relevant information. It must compare the COP against the commander's intent, identify variances from the plan, and recommend ways for the commander to correct or exploit the variances. Finally, the C2 system must direct actions to counter unforeseen enemy or friendly actions and to exploit opportunities.

ASSESSMENT

2-80.   During execution, assessing the operation is an essential, continuing task. It is a deliberate comparison of forecast outcomes to actual events to judge operational success at any point during the operation. Commanders and staffs assess the probable outcome of the ongoing operation to determine whether changes in the current operation are necessary to achieve the mission, react to unexpected threats, or take advantage of opportunity. Commanders and staffs also assess the probable outcome of the current operation in terms of its impact on potential future operations in order to develop concepts for these operations early. Assessment supports the commander in making both execution and adjustment decisions.

2-81.   The most important question when assessing the conduct of an operation is whether the current plan is still valid. Assessment supports the commander in making both execution and adjustment decisions.

As the commander develops his assessment, he describes his conclusions to his staff and subordinates to guide them in supporting him. After he makes a decision, the staff readjusts the plan to include adjustments to the criteria of success required by his decisions and the focus returns to executing and assessing.

MONITORING OF OPERATION

2-82.   The commander and staff monitor the ongoing operation to determine if it is progressing satisfactorily according to the current plan (including any FRAGOs that may have modified it). The staff monitors the facts and assumptions that formed the basis of the plan. They must ensure that these remain valid, or they must identify the need for new facts and assumptions that could affect current and future operations. Monitoring uses relevant information (RI) to develop a clear understanding of the battalion's current state in relation to the enemy and the environment. The staff processes this RI and presents it to the commander as a clear operational picture.

EVALUATING OF CRITERIA FOR SUCCESS

2-83.   The commander and staff continue to evaluate the commander's criteria for success during execution. The staff must continually update staff estimates and sources of assessment to supplement and support the commander's visualization

DECISIONS

2-84.   The battalion commander should not hesitate to modify his plan if it is necessary to: minimize casualties, accomplish the mission, exploit an unanticipated opportunity, or achieve greater success. Adhering to a plan when the situation has changed can waste resources and opportunities. The flexibility to adapt to changing situations is the hallmark of a good commander. The battalion must train to take advantage of unforeseen developments. The commander makes two basic types of decisions during execution: execution decisions and adjustment decisions.

EXECUTION

2-85.   Execution decisions implement anticipated actions and are directed by the order. The most basic form of this type of decision is applying combat power or conducting activities as outlined within the plan or commander's intent. Executing branches and sequels are execution decisions.

Critical Routine Functions

2-86.   The battalion must accomplish routine tasks during execution. Although these tasks occur routinely, the commander must consciously consider them during execution. His failure to consider these routine tasks can waste resources, squander opportunities, or lead to mission failure.

Continuous Reconnaissance and Surveillance

2-87.   Reconnaissance and surveillance continuously feeds the commander's SU and affects his decision making. The battalion commander should never keep the scout platoon and other ISR assets in reserve. During execution, these assets should be focused on answering the CCIR, looking for opportunities for the battalion to exploit, or beginning to shape future operations.

Commander's Critical Information Requirements

2-88.   The commander and staff must continue to review the CCIR during execution. The staff continues to analyze IR against the mission and updated commander's intent to identify those indicators that may directly affect the commander's decision making. As CCIR are answered or the situation changes, the commander may be required to develop new CCIR or establish new priorities to answer the IR. The staff must disseminate these new CCIR or priorities to subordinate and supporting units. The staff must develop a new collection plan and allocate assets (scout platoon, other ISR assets, or company teams) to answer the new CCIR.

Tracking of Battle

2-89.   Battle tracking is monitoring designated elements of the COP that are tied to the commander's criteria for success or tied to a decision. Battle tracking requires special attention from all staff officers. The XO and S-3 must continue to monitor the progress of movement and recommend changes as required. The staff cannot simply update maps and charts. It must analyze the information and be prepared to provide its assessment to the commander. This provides the commander the information he needs to gain an understanding of the situation.

Refinement of Targeting Process

2-90.   The commander's decisions provide the basis for targeting decisions made in support of the continuing operation. The commander remains alert to situations when he must give or modify targeting guidance to the staff. His guidance synchronizes the targeting process to continue achieving effects on the enemy.

Management of Movement and Positioning of Fire Support, Protection, and Sustainment Units

2-91.   Massing the effects of combat power at a decisive point requires not only the maneuver of combat forces, but also the movement of fire support, protection, and sustainment forces. Using fire support, protection, and sustainment forces to shape or sustain must not interfere with the movement of combat forces to the decisive point. In the heat of executing a mission, it is easy to lose sight of the time required to reposition fire support, protection, and sustainment forces. The commander and staff must analyze triggers to move fire support, protection, and sustainment assets to ensure that the movement of combat units does not outpace the movement of fire support, protection, and sustainment units. The commander's visualization should include the time required to move all battalion assets to get to the right place at the right time.

Continuation of Terrain Management

2-92.   The battalion must carefully track the location and land use by all units within the area of operations. Deconflicting land use among units in the battalion's area of operations is difficult but necessary during execution. The staff must ensure that adequate space, including the use of routes, is available at the right time to support critical activities. The commander's visualization should determine what space is required for what force at what time to support the decisive action.

Planned Actions

2-93.   The commander or staff must recognize that a particular event or action directed by the OPORD has met preconditions (events or triggers) for execution and direct the execution of this planned action. Modifying planned actions to fit the current situation is still considered a planned action. Branches and sequels to an order (or plan) are planned actions.

Section VII. ADJUSTMENT DECISIONS

Adjustment decisions modify the plan to respond to unanticipated threats or opportunities. Typically, a commander's adjustment decision requires further synchronization across the WFFs. Adjustments take one of two forms; reallocation of resources or changing the concept. The commander describes his visualization of the adjustment through additional guidance. He must pay particular attention to the effects of adjustment decisions on targeting and give sufficient guidance to support the targeting process. The commander's most important adjustment decision is the commitment of the reserve. Employing the reserve successfully requires anticipation and visualization, and allows the commander to task-organize, position, and move the reserve force in a manner that minimizes any loss of momentum with its commitment.

METHODS

2-94.   When adjusting to a unique or complex situation, the MDMP is preferred if time is available. When there is not sufficient time for a staff MDMP such as during fast-paced combat operations, decision making may become more internalized for the commander. This decision making emphasizes the commander's knowledge, judgment, experience, education, intellect, boldness, perception, and character.

MDMP

2-95.   The first way a commander can adjust to the situation is to use an abbreviated MDMP, focusing the staff on one course of action. This method also uses intuitive decision making. It begins with the commander using his current SU to visualize and mentally formulate a single course of action that solves the unforeseen problem. He directs the staff to analyze and refine the COA. The commander resolves any inadequacies the staff detects through its analysis by revising or modifying the given course of action rather than developing a new one.

RECOGNITION DECISIONS

2-96.   The second way a commander can adjust to a situation is to use "recognition decisions." This type of decision making requires the greatest involvement of the commander and the least involvement from the staff. It relies on the commander's experience in the use of intuitive decision making to be successful. The commander visualizes the solution to a problem immediately, with little or no analysis of alternatives or outcomes. Recognition decisions do not necessarily follow the MDMP; however, the commander's decisions are well grounded in an understanding of the enemy and terrain, the updated commander's estimate and staff estimates, and the OPORD that began the operation. This approach focuses on situational understanding, assessing significant variances, and selecting or refining an acceptable decision mentally instead of comparing multiple options to select the optimal answer.

DIRECTION OF ACTION

2-97.   Any decision to change a plan requires a change in the application of combat power and a resynchronization to mass effects on the enemy. The battalion commander must direct action that applies combat power to effect execution or adjustment decisions. The FRAGO is the normal means to direct changes during execution.

SYNCHRONIZE OPERATIONS

2-98.   After the battalion commander makes a decision during execution, his staff must resynchronize the ongoing operation to maximize the application of combat power against the enemy. This resynchronization includes informing subordinates, integrating assets, incorporating the decision into the targeting process, and deconflicting subordinate actions. Resynchronization should be used only to the extent required to ensure mission accomplishment. Excessive synchronization may waste valuable resources and opportunities.

MAINTAIN CONTINUITY

2-99.   Continuity (making as few changes as necessary) allows for a greater chance of successful execution. Continuity does not inhibit flexibility; the battalion commander and his staff should only make the changes to current operations necessary to solve a problem. Maintaining the current plan as much as possible allows subordinates to focus on only a few discrete changes. The commander and staff should avoid changes that may preclude options for future operations.

TRANSITION

2-100. Today's battlefield requires that units conduct operations continuously. During continuous operations, units will constantly be in transition from one type of operation to another. Staff leaders should plan for transitions, units should train for them, and all leaders should anticipate them. For example, units may be in transition from operations such as from the offense to the defense, from the defense to the offense, or from combat to stability operations. In order for operations to continue smoothly, it is essential that units anticipate and are prepared for these transitions. The flow of battle should not be interrupted, and security must always be maintained. It is important to remember that a transition to another type of operation may begin before the current operation concludes.

Section VIII. BATTLE RHYTHM AND TARGETING

Targeting is the process of selecting targets and matching the response to them, taking account of operational requirements and capabilities. It is a process specifically designed to manage DECIDE, DETECT, DELIVER and ASSESS (D3A) functions. Targeting occurs within the MDMP when the battle staff is developing an operations order (OPORD) and occurs outside of the MDMP once the plan is completed (in this respect validating previous D3A decisions while planning for future D3A decisions). It's an integral part of every unit's battle rhythm, especially during stability operations.

INTRODUCTION

2-101. Infantry units must establish and maintain a specific battle rhythm to ensure continuity of operations during protracted combat. Each commander's personality and leadership style impacts on his unit's battle rhythm. The unit's battle rhythm may also be event driven. Regardless of the commander, however, the established battle rhythm must be nested with the higher headquarters' requirements.

CYCLE

2-102. The targeting cycle is normally a fixed cycle within a unit's battle rhythm, but the desired outcome may come in just a few hours or may take several months. Traditionally, smaller units have shorter targeting cycles.

APPLICATION

2-103. Units conduct targeting during all types of Army operations: offense, defense, stability, and civil support.

SYNCHRONIZATION

2-104.   Targeting synchronizes the battalion's lethal and nonlethal fires across the warfighting functions. It can also help synchronize nontraditional requirements such as sphere-of-influence visits, ribbon-cutting ceremonies, and other media events. It is not a planning meeting. It specifically focuses on desired outcomes and recommends the appropriate resources to achieve those outcomes. Rather than producing a separate directive to subordinate units, it incorporates decisions made during targeting into operations or fragmentary orders. Examples of achieving a desired outcome might be destroying an enemy target using lethal fires, or developing popular support to a local government by improving infrastructure.

DECIDE-DETECT-DELIVER-ASSESS **METHOD**

2-105.   Using the *Decide-Detect-Deliver-Assess* method, commanders assign responsibility of targets to subordinate units or staff sections. Subordinate units attack targets with lethal or nonlethal fires, and the battalion staff analyzes the outcomes of a specific attack and adjusts the method based on the results. To achieve the desired outcome, targets must be constantly reviewed within the battle rhythm and targeting cycle. The staff constantly provides the commander their assessment of a target, and the commander adjusts his guidance and priorities accordingly. The targeting cycle continues until the desired outcome is achieved.

GUIDANCE

2-106.   The commander is responsible for providing the targeting guidance with a clearly articulated desired end state. The targeting working group, normally led by the Battalion Executive Officer, develops courses of action during the targeting meeting. In a process similar to the traditional MDMP, courses of action are presented to the commander for decision. After the commander approves a course of action, each battalion staff officer develops appropriate requirements for subordinate units. The Battalion Operations Officer synchronizes the staff's efforts and includes the targeting tasks and purposes in the unit operations order or fragmentary order.

This page intentionally left blank.

Chapter 3
Intelligence, Surveillance, and Reconnaissance Operations

Intelligence, surveillance, and reconnaissance, a tactical enabling operation, is a broad category of activities designed to support the battalion's intelligence development, planning, and decision-making. The goal of ISR operations is to answer the battalion commander's critical information requirements and other information requirements to enable timely and effective decision-making. The Infantry battalion scout platoon is still the primary eyes and ears of the battalion commander and provides him with an organic reconnaissance capability.

Section I. OVERVIEW

The Army has conducted reconnaissance and surveillance tasks since its inception. The production of intelligence; the product gained by analyzing combat information for its relevance to the unit's mission, has always been critical to successfully accomplishing the mission. In today's Army, information is a critical element of combat power. The speed, reliability, and availability of combat information have changed considerably from the methods of the past. For example, the availability of unmanned aircraft systems (UAS) and the addition of snipers to the Infantry battalion organization have significantly increased the ability to collect combat intelligence. (See Appendix F for more information about sniper employment; see Appendix K for more information about UAS.) To use such intelligence effectively, one must act on it in a timely manner, and then hit the enemy from unexpected directions. Doing so disrupts the enemy's operations and allows friendly forces to disrupt, dislocate, or destroy enemy formations.

DEFINITIONS

3-1.   ISR is the term presently applied to a combined arms enabling operation that combines what was previously described as reconnaissance and surveillance, (a maneuver task) with the production and dissemination of intelligence (previously shown as a staff task). ISR is a continuous operation focused on the collection of relevant information that is analyzed to create intelligence that helps form the commander's visualization and supports the operational cycle. The following definitions of ISR are extracted from FM 3-0.

INTELLIGENCE

3-2.   Intelligence is (1) the product resulting from the collection, processing, integration, analysis, evaluation, and interpretation of available information concerning foreign countries or areas; (2) information and knowledge about an adversary obtained through observation, investigation, analysis, or understanding.

SURVEILLANCE

3-3.   Surveillance is the systematic observation of aerospace, surface or subsurface areas, places, persons, or things by visual, sound, electronic, photographic, or other means.

RECONNAISSANCE

3-4.   Reconnaissance is a mission undertaken to obtain by visual observation or other detection methods information about the activities and resources of an enemy or potential enemy, or to secure data concerning the meteorological, hydrographic, or geographic characteristics of a particular area.

FUNDAMENTALS

3-5.   Commanders integrate ISR missions into a single plan that capitalizes on the different capabilities of each element and other information-gathering assets. They synchronize reconnaissance and surveillance missions that employ maneuver units with both the ISR plan and scheme of maneuver. The battalion uses intelligence products developed at higher echelons to identify gaps in the intelligence process. The battalion conducts reconnaissance and surveillance operations to fill the battalion CCIR. Successful battalion reconnaissance and surveillance depend on the following battalion-level fundamentals.

CONDUCT RECONNAISSANCE CONTINUOUSLY AND EARLY

3-6.   Reconnaissance, surveillance, and security are continuous processes that should be conducted 24 hours a day. For security and surveillance missions, the scout platoon should be augmented with elements from maneuver companies, sniper teams, and other combat and combat support elements assigned or attached to the Infantry battalion.

FOCUS RECONNAISSANCE AND SURVEILLANCE ON CCIR AND DECISION POINTS

3-7.   The priority intelligence requirements (PIR) derived from the CCIR; identify the information about the enemy needed by the commander to support his battlefield visualization and to make critical decisions. PIR help the commander filter information available to him by defining what is important to mission accomplishment. The commander and the staff use PIR to focus collection efforts and avoid wasting reconnaissance resources. With the limited number of reconnaissance and surveillance assets available at the battalion level, it is vital that the reconnaissance and surveillance effort be focused. However, the increasing number of organic and attached reconnaissance and surveillance assets require greater planning and monitoring efforts by the battalion staff. In addition to the battalion's PIR, there will also be PIR from the BCT and higher that will influence the focus of battalion reconnaissance and surveillance efforts. Focusing the reconnaissance and surveillance effort ensures that the commander's PIR and IR are answered and assets are not wasted looking for the wrong information. The reconnaissance and surveillance plan should focus on the collection of information required to support the ground maneuver plan and provide observation of the decision points on the battlefield.

INITIATE APPROPRIATE RECONNAISSANCE AND SURVEILLANCE FORWARD

3-8.   Reconnaissance and surveillance assets are normally not held in reserve. Maximum reconnaissance force forward has always been stressed. In the contemporary operational environment (COE), the fluid, nonlinear and noncontiguous nature of operations requires that reconnaissance and surveillance be continuous throughout the AO. However, men and machines cannot indefinitely conduct 24-hour operations as required by the COE. The battalion staff must plan rest and maintenance of reconnaissance and surveillance assets while still ensuring CCIR are continuously answered and decision points are covered. In some situations, the critical reconnaissance objectives may not be forward of the maneuver forces.

INCLUDE STAFF IN RECONNAISSANCE AND SURVEILLANCE PLANNING

3-9.   The S-3 and S-2 rely upon the entire staff to assist in the planning and execution of the battalion ISR plan by providing—

- A combined arms focus to the ISR plan.
- Subject matter expertise in respective WFF.
- Augmentation to the scout platoon (snipers, engineers, artillery observers).
- Communications planning.
- Information requirement submissions.

MAXIMIZE RECONNAISSANCE AND SURVEILLANCE ASSETS

3-10.   The battalion must maximize the capabilities of its limited reconnaissance and surveillance assets. For the battalion to conduct its operations, collection requirements should specify exactly what needs to be collected and where and when it needs to be collected and reported. Close coordination and integration with the BCT staff is required to ensure that BCT and battalion assets are not being tasked to find the same information. The S-3 must ensure that artillery observers are integrated into the effort.

REPORT, PROCESS, AND DISSEMINATE INFORMATION RAPIDLY AND ACCURATELY

3-11.   Once information arrives at the S-2, it is processed and disseminated to users such as the battalion commander, key staff officers, and the FSE. Combat information goes directly (unprocessed) to the commander for his consideration. To conduct reconnaissance and surveillance continuously, the battalion supplements its organic reconnaissance and surveillance assets with intelligence from the BCT and additional maneuver, fires and effects, or force protection assets. These assets provide the battalion with a variety of options to draw upon, each with its own capabilities. Table 3-1, shows the ISR collection assets that generally support a BCT which the battalion S-2 can request.

Table 3-1. Intelligence, surveillance, and reconnaissance collection assets.

Asset	Planning Range	Function	Interoperability
IREMBASS	Detection range: Personnel: 3 to 50 m Wheeled: 15 to 250 m Tracked: 25 to 350 m	Detects moving targets: personnel, wheeled, and tracked vehicles Uses seismic, acoustic, magnetic, and infrared sensors	ASAS-RWS
Common Ground Station	300 km	Has a receiver/preprocessor; serves as primary gateway for brigade	GS/ASAS, ASAS-RWS, AQF/JSTARS, GRCS, A2C2s, UAS, GBS/BADD
Raven UAS	10 km	Performs reconnaissance, surveillance, and target acquisition	Stand alone
Ground Surveillance Radar	6 km personnel 10 km vehicle	Performs surveillance and target acquisition	Stand-alone
CI Teams and Interrogators	N/A	Questions sources to obtain information to satisfy intelligence requirements	G-2/S-2, ASAS-RWS
Long Range Surveillance Teams	150 km	Conducts surveillance, reconnaissance, target acquisition, and damage assessment	G-2/S-2, ASAS-RWS
Prophet	300 km	Controls and receives ESM data from Prophet land and air systems	ASAS-RWS, FBCB2
Sentinel	40 km	Provides search and track functions against fixed and rotary wing aircraft	FAADC31, Avenger
Q-36 RADAR	Artillery, mortars: 12 km Rockets: 24 km	Uses mortar- and artillery-locating radar, set for short-range, high-angle weapons	AFATDS/FBCB2
Q-37 RADAR	Artillery: 30 km Rocket: 50 km	Detects long-range, low-angle weapons fire	AFATDS/FBCB2

RESPONSIBILITIES

3-12.   The battalion commander is responsible for the planning and execution of the reconnaissance and surveillance operation. He is an integral member of the planning team and must provide the staff with clear and concise guidance. His involvement in the planning process is critical, and he must provide the staff with his CCIR early in the process. He must clearly articulate to the staff and XO their responsibilities in the planning, and execution process and what risk to reconnaissance and surveillance assets he is willing to accept. These responsibilities are discussed in the following paragraphs.

COMMANDER'S GUIDANCE

3-13.   The battalion commander must provide specific guidance to the reconnaissance force. The commander's guidance for reconnaissance includes focus, tempo, and engagement criteria. This guidance is an extension of the commander's intent, and is designed to focus the reconnaissance commander's efforts in relation to the battalion mission.

3-14.   Focus is the expression of what types of information the battalion commander is most concerned. The commander's focus for reconnaissance usually falls in three general areas: CCIR, targeting, and voids in information. The commander's focus allows reconnaissance to prioritize taskings and narrow the scope of operations. An operation may have a terrain focus where status of routes, bridges, and obstacles are more important than the enemy. Conversely, the operation may focus on the enemy, where locating his security zone, main body, and reserves are essential. Also, commanders may express the focus in terms of reconnaissance information pull and push.

Reconnaissance Pull

3-15.   Reconnaissance pull is used when the enemy situation is not well known and or the situation is rapidly changing. The commander uses ISR assets to confirm or deny initial PIR before the decision on a COA or maneuver option; thus "pulling" the battalion to the decisive point on the battlefield. Success of the reconnaissance pull requires an integrated reconnaissance plan that can be executed before the commander making a COA decision.

Reconnaissance Push

3-16.   Reconnaissance push is used once the commander is committed to a COA or maneuver option. The commander "pushes" his ISR assets forward, as necessary, to gain greater visibility on specific named areas of interest (NAIs) to confirm or deny the assumptions on which the COA is based. Information gathered during reconnaissance push is used to finalize the battalion's plan.

3-17.   The commander uses tempo by establishing the time requirements he envisions for the reconnaissance force and expresses them in a statement that describes the degree of completeness, covertness, and potential for engagement he is willing to accept. The following describes the rate battalion commanders use to control the momentum of reconnaissance operations.

Deliberate Operations

3-18.   Deliberate operations are slow, detailed, and broad-based. They require the accomplishment of numerous tasks. This is a description of the degree of completeness required by the commander. Significant time must be allocated to conduct a deliberate reconnaissance.

Rapid Operations

3-19.   Rapid operations are fast paced, focused on key pieces of information, and entail a small number of tasks. This is a description of the degree of completeness required by the battalion commander. It describes reconnaissance operations that must be performed in a time-constrained environment.

Stealthy Operations

3-20.   Stealthy operations are conducted to minimize chance contact and prevent the reconnaissance force from being detected. They are often conducted dismounted, and require increased allocation of time for success. This is a description of the level of covertness required by the commander.

Forceful Operations

3-21.   Forceful operations are conducted without significant concern about being observed. They are often conducted mounted or by combat units serving in a reconnaissance role. It is also appropriate in stability operations or civil support operations where the threat is not significant in relation to the requirement for information.

Aggressive Operations

3-22.   Operations have permissive engagement criteria and allow the reconnaissance commander to engage in combat to meet his IR. This is a description of the potential for engagement.

Discrete Operations

3-23.   Operations have restrictive engagement criteria and restrain the battalion reconnaissance forces from initiating combat to gain information. This is a description of the potential for engagement.

3-24.   The battalion commander establishes engagement criteria by explaining what enemy forces he expects reconnaissance forces to engage, and with what level of force. This decision assists the reconnaissance leadership in planning direct and indirect fires and establishing bypass criteria. It is particularly important when the reconnaissance force is augmented with combat systems to conduct reconnaissance in force or security operations. If engagements significantly degrade the ability of the force to gain the needed intelligence, the commander should consider allocating additional assets to the reconnaissance effort.

Executive Officer

3-25.   The XO is responsible for staff synchronization during reconnaissance and surveillance planning. He helps direct execution of the reconnaissance and surveillance effort along with the S-3, S-2, the battalion staff, and the HHC company commander (if designated to assist in these operations).

S-1

3-26.   The S-1 and his staff section provide projected personnel status of reconnaissance and surveillance assets at the time the reconnaissance and surveillance commences. The S-1 also coordinates and plans health service support for the reconnaissance and surveillance assets, to include casualty evacuation (CASEVAC) and MEDEVAC.

S-2

3-27.   The S-2 and his staff section recommend initial information and priority intelligence requirements. Also, the S-2 staff section—

- Collects IR from other staff and special staff sections.
- Conducts IPB with staff input and develops the modified combined obstacle overlay (MCOO), enemy situation templates, and event template.
- Conducts pattern analysis on enemy actions, locations, and tactics, techniques, and procedures (TTPs).
- Identifies intelligence gaps.
- Translates the commander's PIR into specific information requirements and specific orders and requests.
- Determines and designates named areas of interest (NAIs).
- Identifies sources and nonorganic assets that can be used to answer the battalion PIR.
- Prepares and submits requests for information (RFIs) to the BCT.
- Has overall responsibility for developing the reconnaissance and surveillance matrix.
- Develops portions of the reconnaissance and surveillance annex and order: Paragraph 1 (situation), Paragraph 2 (mission), and Paragraph 3c (assignment of specific collection tasks [specific orders and requests (SOR)] and when and where to look [NAIs] for each asset).

S-3

3-28.   The S-3 and his staff section are responsible for overall execution of the reconnaissance and surveillance plan. They also—

- Identify and task battalion assets.
- Coordinate times and locations of linkup and logistics support relationships for attached reconnaissance and surveillance assets.
- Deconflict terrain with BCT and adjacent units for reconnaissance and surveillance assets forward of the line of departure (LD) and or line of contact (LC).
- Coordinate Army airspace command and control (A2C2) for all assigned and attached aerial assets. This may include submission of flight routes, times, and altitudes to be included in the air tasking order (ATO).
- Work with the battalion S-2 to ensure that all information requirements are covered to include the secondary asset assigned if the primary can no longer conduct the mission.
- Develop the initial graphics overlay.
- Develop portions of the reconnaissance and surveillance annex and order: Paragraphs 3a and 3d (concept of operations and coordinating instructions).

FIRE SUPPORT OFFICER

3-29.   The FSO and his fire support element (FSE) develop a fire support plan to support reconnaissance and surveillance assets, ensure observers are integrated into the reconnaissance and surveillance plan to execute the battalion indirect fire plan, and facilitate fire effects coordination between battalion and the combat observation lasing teams (COLTs). They also ensure fire support coordination measures are in place to protect friendly troops during reconnaissance and surveillance operations and coordinate and integrate battalion mortar platoon and company mortar section support.

S-4

3-30.   The S-4 and his staff section develop the logistical support plan for the operation and develop paragraph 4 (in conjunction with the S-1) of the reconnaissance and surveillance annex and order (service support and resupply).

SCOUT PLATOON LEADER

3-31.   The platoon leader is responsible for the tactical employment, collective training, administration, human resource management, and logistics of the platoon. He must know his Soldiers and how to employ the platoon and its weapons. He is personally responsible for positioning and employing all assigned or attached weapons. The platoon leader—

- Leads the platoon in supporting the battalion missions. He bases his actions on the missions the battalion commander assigns to him and on the battalion commander's concepts.
- Informs his commander of his actions when operating without orders.
- Plans operations with the help of the platoon sergeant, squad leaders, and other key personnel.
- Stays abreast of the situation and goes where needed to supervise, issue FRAGOs, and accomplish the mission.
- Requests necessary support from the battalion for his platoon to perform its mission.
- Provides guidance to the platoon sergeant in planning and coordinating the platoon's sustainment effort.
- During planning, receives on-hand status reports from the platoon sergeant, section leaders, and team leaders.
- Reviews platoon requirements based on the tactical plan.
- During execution, supervises the platoon sergeant and squad leaders.
- Develops the fire support plan with the platoon sergeant, squad leaders, and team leaders.
- Coordinates the obstacle plan.

- Analyzes tactical situations, disseminates information, and employs the full capabilities of his platoon's equipment to accomplish the mission.
- Ensures that situation reports (SITREPs) are accurate and are forwarded to the commander and staff as applicable.
- Analyzes and then disseminates pertinent tactical friendly and enemy updates to his subordinates.
- During limited visibility, employs all available night-vision device (NVD) assets to designate targets for the direct and indirect fire weapons and for situation updates.

MEDICAL PLATOON LEADER

3-32.   The medical platoon leader directs force health protection (FHP) support for the battalion. He is responsible for ensuring that FHP is provided for the battalion's attached, OPCON, and organic reconnaissance and surveillance assets. The medical platoon leader coordinates with the battalion S-1 to provide medical support to the units executing ISR operations.

Section II. INTEGRATION

The BCT and battalion staffs must coordinate their ISR efforts to prevent duplication of effort. Without integration, the battalion scout platoon; the BCT reconnaissance squadron; and the battlefield surveillance brigade (BFSB) could easily be tasked to find the same information while leaving gaps in other parts of the collection plan. Reconnaissance elements from these units and the Infantry battalions might unknowingly compete for the same observation post (OP) positions. One reconnaissance section can conceivably call for fire on another. It is easy to task multiple UAS assets to observe the same location. Without proper A2C2 coordination, this can cause damage and destruction of manned aerial platforms.

RECONNAISSANCE SQUADRON AND R&S ASSETS

3-33.   The battalion scout platoon and reconnaissance squadron can work together to perform their reconnaissance missions in several ways.

OFFENSE

3-34.   During a BCT and or division movement to contact (MTC), the reconnaissance squadron reconnaissance platoons can hand over key observation post positions to the battalion scout platoon as it advances through the AO. The reconnaissance squadron elements can vector the battalion scout teams into position and keep them informed about terrain, enemy positions, and obstacles that have already been found. The battalion scout teams can provide over-watch for the reconnaissance squadron elements as they continue on to their next series of OPs or reconnaissance of the area.

DEFENSE

3-35.   In the defense, the primary mission of the scout platoon is to provide security and early warning for the battalion. Battalion reconnaissance may also be integrated or connected into the BCT's counterreconnaissance mission. Infantry battalion and reconnaissance squadron elements provide stealthy observation and early warning of the enemy's reconnaissance elements.

3-36.   The scout teams maintain a low signature by not engaging targets. Rifle platoons, assault platoons, and sniper teams in the counterreconnaissance team kill the enemy reconnaissance. The scout teams locate the enemy reconnaissance forces and then vector the counterreconnaissance elements to them.

3-37.   The reconnaissance squadron elements and battalion reconnaissance can be employed in depth to provide multiple screens for the counterreconnaissance force (Figure 3-1). Reconnaissance squadron scouts and counterreconnaissance teams occupy the most forward positions. Battalion reconnaissance elements screen behind the counterreconnaissance force. Each battalion employs a counterreconnaissance force to its front capable of fixing and destroying the enemy reconnaissance forces.

3-38.   For the battalion scout platoon and the reconnaissance squadron elements to work together, the battalion and IBCT staffs must coordinate the following:

- Communications.
- C2 architecture.
- Terrain management.
- NAI and target area of interest (TAI) coverage and intelligence gaps.
- Fire support control measures.
- Fratricide avoidance measures.

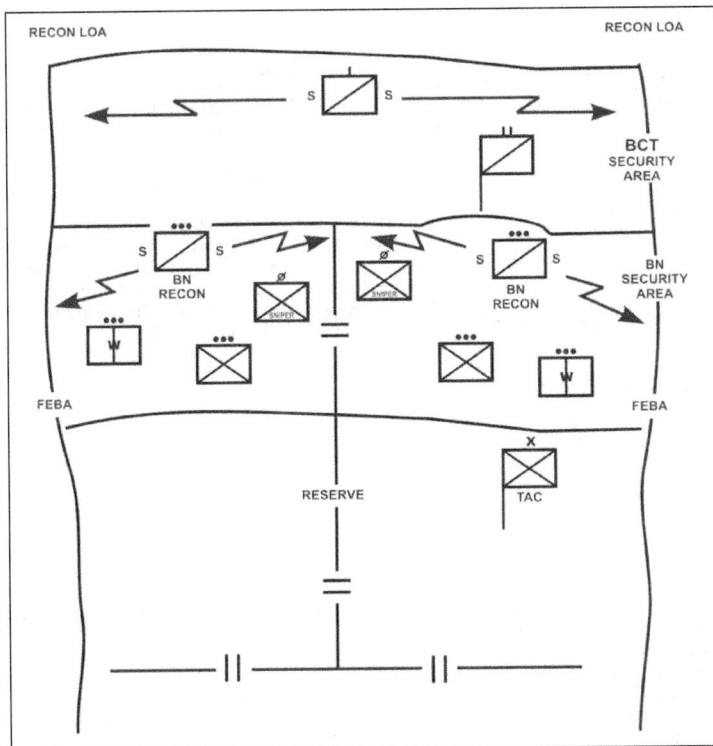

Figure 3-1. Counterreconnaissance organization reconnaissance squadron troop and battalion scout platoon.

CAPABILITIES

3-39.   The scout platoon is the battalion's primary means of conducting reconnaissance and surveillance. The battalion scout platoon may be augmented with additional assets such as the following.

SNIPERS

3-40.   Snipers are assigned to each Infantry battalion. Sniper missions include surveillance and reconnaissance. Snipers have excellent long-range observation and expert camouflage and stealth movement capability. They can attack and destroy targets in excess of 2,000 meters. When selecting surveillance and reconnaissance missions for snipers, consideration is given to the follow-on target. For example, a sniper team is assigned to conduct surveillance on an NAI during the counterreconnaissance phase and a TAI during the defense phase of the operation. The sniper team should be able to conduct both missions from the same general location to minimize movement requirements and possible compromise of their location.

ENGINEERS

3-41.   Engineers are attached to provide expertise on obstacle belts, minefields, and route and bridge classification. Sappers can provide preparation of obstacle breaches during limited visibility.

JAVELIN TEAMS

3-42.   Infantrymen from the line companies may form Javelin teams to augment the platoon for surveillance and target acquisition purposes during limited visibility operations. The nondisposable section of the Javelin is the command launch unit (CLU). The night sight and day sight of the Javelin are integrated into the CLU. Under most conditions, the thermal sight's range is more than 3,000 meters. The Javelin uses a passive infrared system for target acquisition and lock-on. This means that it emits no infrared or radar signature that enemy systems or smart munitions can detect.

CBRN RECONNAISSANCE

3-43.   The scout platoon may also be augmented with CBRN reconnaissance assets from the IBCT.

FIRE SUPPORT TEAM

3-44.   An FO team may be attached to the scout platoon to provide fire support.

COLT TEAMS

3-45.   Occasionally the scout platoon will be augmented with the COLT team assigned to the Infantry battalion HHC. The COLT team performs fire support and reconnaissance missions as directed, and is equipped with the lightweight laser designator rangefinder (LLDR) that lazes targets for munitions requiring reflected laser energy for final ballistic guidance. They are also equipped with the forward observer system computer for digital connectivity.

MULTISENSOR TEAM

3-46.   The multisensor team from the military intelligence (MI) company is another asset that may be task-organized to the battalion. The improved remotely monitored battlefield sensor system (IREMBASS) is an unattended ground sensor that will detect, classify, and determine direction of movement of intruding personnel and vehicles. The ground surveillance radar (GSR) is an attended ground sensor that will detect, classify, and determine the direction of movement of intruding personnel and vehicles. The Prophet is an attended emitter-locator sensor that can detect, intercept, determine direction of bearing, and possibly determine the location of intruding personnel communications emitters.

COMMUNICATIONS

3-47.   FM net structure and reporting procedures are unit- and SOP-dependent. The battalion scout platoon uses the battalion operations and intelligence (OI) net for reporting enemy information and asset locations. The scout platoon also has an internal platoon net for C2 within the platoon. When the scout platoon is acting as part of a counterreconnaissance force, it communicates on the counterreconnaissance unit command net. Reconnaissance teams from the battalion will need to communicate with elements of the counterreconnaissance force to pass information and deconflict OP positions. This may be done on the counterreconnaissance unit command net, platoon nets, or internal platoon nets.

EXECUTION

3-48.   Commanders depend on subordinate initiative to accomplish missions, even in the absence of orders. Information systems will fail, either of their own accord or because of enemy action. Commanders develop and communicate their vision to subordinates with enough clarity to allow them to act when this happens. Subordinates complement initiative with constant coordination and by keeping their higher commanders informed.

EMPLACEMENT AND ROUTES

3-49.   The battalion staff develops a general picture of where assets should locate on the battlefield. By understanding the SOR and NAIs to cover, the scout platoon leader or squad leaders determine the exact OP locations and routes for the reconnaissance teams. The battalion S-3 and S-2 must closely monitor OP locations to ensure that there is no conflict with the other elements or other BCT assets. The battalion S-3 must also conduct direct coordination with the reconnaissance squadron as necessary.

INSERTION AND EXTRACTION ROUTES

3-50.   While deconflicting terrain with the S-3, the S-2, and scout platoon leader identify the methods the platoon will use to infiltrate or bypass enemy forces to enhance its survivability and ensure mission success. Inserting assets requires the coordination of the entire staff and may require the battalion to conduct a forward passage of lines for the scout platoon. Critical coordination tasks and actions should be listed in the reconnaissance and surveillance tasking matrix.

PROCESSING AND DISSEMINATATION OF INFORMATION

3-51.   The battalion S-2 must be able to quickly review the incoming combat information, sort it according to criticality and the PIR and IR it answers, and transmit it to the user in the shortest amount of time. Command post personnel must be aware of the CCIR. The CCIR are essential elements of friendly information, friendly force information requirements (FFIR), and PIR. When CCIR are answered, the commander must be notified immediately because these answers often influence his decision-making process and battalion employment. While fused intelligence may be the best intelligence, partially analyzed intelligence or combat information may cue the commander to enemy intentions that were not previously addressed during the war gaming process.

PLAN MODIFICATION

3-52.   Whether modifying reporting requirements because of new reporting criteria; new or adjusted PIR; loss of a scout squad, sniper team, UAS, or other asset; or changes in the mission, the battalion S-3 must be ready to adjust the reconnaissance and surveillance plan to fit the commander's needs and continue the reconnaissance and surveillance mission. The following questions need to be considered during the modification of the reconnaissance and surveillance plan:

- What asset needs to be moved?
- Do any other assets who can cover the requirement use electronic or visual collection methods that are easier to retask?
- What are the new collection requirement and or focus?
- What is the risk in moving the scout squad, sniper team, or other manned asset? Is the risk worth the potential information that might be gained?
- Do the communications require modification?
- Does the fire support plan need to change?
- Does the sustainment support plan need to change?

3-53.   During the planning process, the staff should also consider how to compensate for the loss of a reconnaissance and surveillance asset during critical points in the mission. Staffs will need to consider which unit or asset will replace the lost surveillance and target acquisition asset and issue a "be prepared mission" to the unit or asset in the operations order.

Section III. SUPPORT

The IBCT and Infantry battalion staffs must plan, prepare, and synchronize fire support, health service support, and communication and logistical support for the ISR assets. Concurrent with other operational planning, the staff develops its plan during mission analysis and refines it in the war gaming portion of the MDMP. Fires and sustainment rehearsals should be an integral step in preparation for reconnaissance and surveillance operations. (See Chapter 10 for detailed discussions of the six warfighting functions.)

FIRE

3-54.   The S-3 ensures that indirect fires support the reconnaissance plan and that communication links are maintained with observers and the main CP at all times. The distance the scout platoon can operate away from the main body is normally limited to the range of supporting indirect fires. For some missions, however, the staff and commander need to assess the risk and value of operating the scout platoon beyond the range of supporting fires.

LOGISTICS

3-55.   Providing service support to reconnaissance and surveillance assets forward of the LD and or LC provides a significant logistics challenge because the support elements also risk exposure to enemy contact. It is dangerous to conduct logistics resupply operations across the forward line of own troops (FLOT) with thin-skinned cargo vehicles.

3-56.   A maintenance team or LOGPAC can be dedicated to the scout platoon. The team responds to the needs of the platoon and is brought forward by the headquarters 1SG, the HHC XO, or another responsible individual. The LOGPAC links up with the scout platoon's PSG at a specifically-designated release point as far forward as possible. The PSG is then responsible for the distribution of supplies to the scout teams.

3-57.   The actual time when the scout platoon needs to resupply often does not coincide with the standard LOGPAC times for the rest of the battalion. The HHC commander, battalion S-4, scout platoon leader, and platoon sergeant must anticipate events to coordinate the best time for resupply. When the battalion scout platoon is augmented with assets from the IBCT, the battalion will assume responsibility for logistics support.

3-58.   To minimize risks during logistics operations, the HHC commander and scout platoon leader may choose to adopt the following procedures:

- Develop Soldier load plans to carry Class I, water, and Class V.
- Coordinate for aerial resupply (METT-TC dependent).

3-59.   In some instances, the reconnaissance squadron may be able to assist the Infantry battalion deployed reconnaissance and surveillance elements. The HHC commander and battalion S-4 should consider this when developing the sustainment plan.

MEDICAL

3-60.   Treating and evacuating wounded Soldiers provides another challenge to reconnaissance and surveillance planning because the reconnaissance and surveillance asset has most likely been engaged by the enemy and possesses no dedicated medical support. Sending ground-based medical assets in a manner that enhances their survivability, such as attached to a combat patrol or moving undetected under the cover of darkness, often contradicts the necessity to treat wounded Soldiers quickly. During aerial evacuation of wounded in action (WIA), planners need to consider landing zone (LZ) security, weather, terrain, possible compromise of the reconnaissance and surveillance effort, possible loss of the aircraft, and the actual urgency of patient care. To help the survivability of Soldiers in the scout platoon, the battalion needs to train the scout platoon Soldiers in basic and advanced combat lifesaving techniques. Also, the scout team members should rely primarily on their teams and sections to transfer wounded to designated casualty collection points or pickup zones (PZs) for ambulance or aerial evacuation.

COMMUNICATIONS

3-61.   The S-3, S-2, and signal section develop the signal architecture to support the scout platoon and other reconnaissance and surveillance assets deployed throughout the area of operation. All reconnaissance and surveillance assets must have continuous, two-way, secure communications with the battalion main CP. This requirement and the size of the reconnaissance and surveillance area of operations may require the battalion to establish retrans sites forward in the battalion AO.

This page intentionally left blank.

Chapter 4
Offensive Operations

Offensive action is the decisive form of any engagement. The primary purpose of the offense is to defeat, destroy, or neutralize an enemy force. A commander may also take offensive actions to deceive or divert the enemy, deprive him of resources or decisive terrain, collect information, or fix an enemy in position. Even in the defense, offensive action is normally required to destroy an attacker and exploit success. The key to a successful offensive operation is to identify the enemy's decisive point; choose a form of maneuver that avoids the enemy's strength and one that masses overwhelming combat power. This will result in accomplishing the unit's purpose regarding terrain and the enemy. This chapter discusses the basics of the offense which apply to all offensive actions. It also discusses the concept of synchronized attacks that maximize the battalion's unique capabilities, and the planning and executing of offensive operations.

Section I. FUNDAMENTALS

The Infantry battalion gains and maintains the initiative and keeps constant pressure on the enemy throughout its AO. The Infantry battalion transitions from one offensive action to another without pausing. Planning and preparing for the next and for follow-on operations occur simultaneously with execution of the current action. Success in offensive operations depends on the proper application of the fundamental characteristics of the offense discussed in the following paragraphs. The Infantry battalion's ability to maneuver through restricted and severely restricted terrain and relatively low electronic and audible signatures are key attributes.

SURPRISE

4-1. A force achieves surprise by attacking the enemy at a time or place and in a manner for which the enemy is not physically or mentally ready. The Infantry battalion commander must have sufficient information for a clear understanding of his current state in relation to the enemy and environment; a sound understanding of what the end state is for the assigned mission, and a vision of how to move his force from the current situation to the end state. A battalion achieves surprise by--

- Gaining and maintaining information dominance by conducting thorough reconnaissance and surveillance and denying enemy reconnaissance efforts. The IBCT and higher echelon unit intelligence assets provide depth to the effort and are used by the Infantry battalion to assist in planning follow-on operations. Short range reconnaissance and surveillance assets of the reconnaissance squadron and organic collectors in the Infantry battalion allow them to see, decide, and act inside the enemy decision cycle.
- Striking the enemy from an unexpected direction at an unexpected time using intelligence, rapid movement, and the ability to cross any type of terrain.
- Quickly changing the tempo of the operation. The constant application of pressure on the enemy's decision making cycle prevents him from regaining the initiative.
- Maintaining the element of surprise and unpredictability is critical in offensive operations. Tactical actions should be sound but also always mixed and varied. Enemy forces have can and will conduct pattern analysis.

CONCENTRATION

4-2.   A force achieves concentration by massing the effects of combat power. Superior timing, precision maneuvers and fires (made possible by shared information dominance), and speed allow the Infantry battalion commander to mass the effects of his forces. He can do this when and where needed, and he can shift quickly from one objective or direction to another. Because he has the advantage in information he receives, he better understands the effects of his actions. For example, it is easier for him to see if he has succeeded, or if he needs to continue an attack. If so, he can then apply available combat power more efficiently and focus his main effort more effectively. Once the Infantry battalion succeeds through the concentration and control enabled by this understanding, it can quickly disperse, if needed, to avoid enemy counteractions. A battalion achieves concentration through the following:

- Designation of a decisive operation and allocation of resources to support it.
- Careful planning and coordination based on a thorough analysis of terrain and enemy, combined with accurate, timely reconnaissance and surveillance.
- Positions that allow it to mass effects.
- The ability to synchronize direct, indirect, and nonlethal assets.

TEMPO

4-3.   Tempo is the ability to adjust the rate of operations relative to battle circumstances and relative to the enemy's capability to sense and react. It is the controlled rate of military action. While a rapid tempo is often preferred, tempo should be adjusted to ensure synchronization. The goal is to maintain pressure on the enemy, whether it is done quickly or slowly. Controlling and altering tempo promotes surprise, keeps the enemy off balance, denies the enemy freedom of action, and contributes to the security of the battalion.

AUDACITY

4-4.   Audacity is a simple plan of action boldly executed. Audacity inspires Soldiers to overcome adversity and danger. Audacity is a key component of any successful offensive action and increases the chance for surprise. It depends on the commander's ability to see opportunities for action, to decide in time to seize opportunities, and to accept calculated risks. Leaders must assess risks, understand when and where to take risks, identify control measures, and execute boldly. The sharing of combat information electronically between leaders at all echelons reduces the risk but does not eliminate the many uncertainties associated with battle. Digitization improves the commander's ability to make quick situational assessments, to conduct on-the-spot risk assessments, and to make bold decisions based on near-real-time information.

CONTACT CONTINUUM

4-5.   Traditionally, the Infantry battalion made contact with the scout platoon and lead company to develop the situation while in contact with the enemy. The lead company then fixed the enemy, allowing the remainder of the battalion to maneuver against an assailable flank. This method was based on the Infantry battalion's ability to maneuver over all types of terrain with little signature. With additional combat power (the weapons company) and information systems (INFOSYS) in the battalion, a new method of making contact is required. This new contact continuum consists of understanding the situation and maneuvering to a position of advantage to make contact with the enemy on the Infantry battalion's terms (Figure 4-1). Within the new contact continuum, the Infantry battalion can mass overwhelming combat power at the decisive point to achieve its purpose more efficiently and effectively. The Infantry battalion commander must also consider that the BCT reconnaissance squadron may provide the first situational understanding (SU) of the enemy or may be in contact with the enemy, allowing the Infantry battalion to maneuver out of contact to a position to initiate first contact with the enemy on the best terms for the battalion.

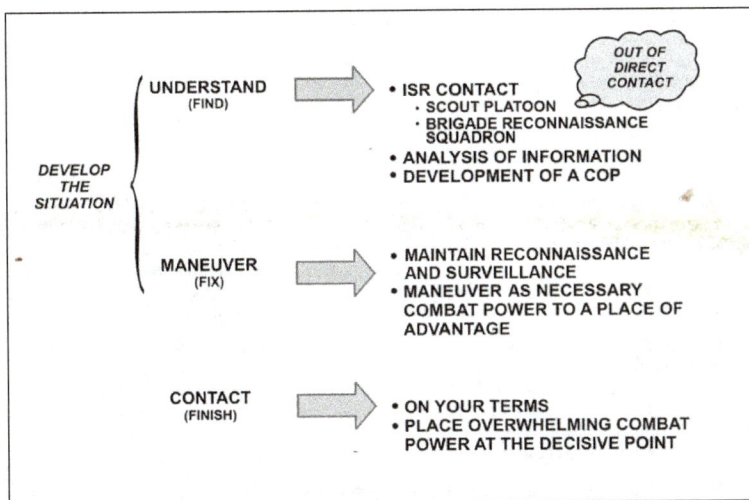

Figure 4-1. Contact continuum.

Section II. ORGANIZATION

Commanders organize forces according to purpose by determining whether each unit's operation will be decisive, shaping, or sustaining. The purpose-based framework centers on decisive, shaping, and sustaining operations. Purpose unifies all elements of the battlefield organization by providing the common focus for all actions. However, forces act in time and space to accomplish a purpose. These decisions form the basis of the concept of operations. Alternatively, commanders may choose to use the decisive point, or main effort methods to articulate their organization of forces if this better facilitates their ability to visualize, describe, and direct actions, especially since Infantry battalions operate at the tactical level of war. Commanders also synchronize operations in time and space. When circumstances require a spatial reference between friendly and enemy forces, commanders may describe them in terms of deep, close, and rear areas. These spatial categories are especially useful in combat operations that are generally contiguous, linear, and feature a clearly defined enemy force.

DECISIVE OPERATIONS

4-6. Decisive operations directly achieve the mission and intent of the higher headquarters. Decisive operations conclusively determine the outcome of battles and engagements. There is only one decisive operation for any major operation, battle, or engagement for any given echelon. The decisive operation may include multiple actions conducted simultaneously throughout the depth of the AO. Commander's weigh the decisive operation while economizing on the effort allocated to shaping operations.

4-7. In the offense and defense, decisive operations normally focus on movement and maneuver. Conversely, logistics may be decisive during the mobilization and deployment phases of an operation or in support operations, particularly if the mission is humanitarian in nature.

4-8. A reserve is a portion of a body of troops that is kept to the rear or withheld from action at the beginning of an engagement but remains available for a decisive movement. Until committed, reserves shape through their placement within the AO while planning for and preparing to conduct operations.

When committed, they usually either become the decisive operation or reinforce the decisive operation. Commanders can use reserves to influence circumstances or exploit opportunities. When commanders anticipate uncertainty, they hold a greater portion of the force in reserve to posture the force to seize and maintain the initiative as a situation develops. Reserves deploy and reposition as necessary to ensure their protection, availability, and prompt reaction.

SHAPING OPERATIONS

4-9.   Shaping operations create and preserve the conditions for the success of the decisive operation. Shaping operations include lethal and nonlethal activities conducted throughout the AO (Appendix L). They support the decisive operation by affecting the enemy's capabilities and forces, or by influencing the opposing commander's decisions. Shaping operations use the full range of military power to neutralize or reduce enemy capabilities. They may occur simultaneously with, before, or after initiation of the decisive operation. They may involve any combination of forces and occur throughout the depth of the AO.

4-10.   Some shaping operations, especially those that occur simultaneously with the decisive operation, are economy-of-force actions. If the force available does not permit simultaneous decisive and shaping operations, the commander sequences shaping operations around the decisive operation. A shaping operation may become the decisive operation if circumstances or opportunity demand. In which case, commanders weigh the new decisive operations at the expense of other shaping operations. The concept of the operation clearly defines how shaping operations support the decisive operation.

4-11.   Security is an important shaping operation. Security enables the decisive operation of the next higher headquarters. Security protects the force and provides time for friendly forces to react to enemy or hostile activities. It also blinds the enemy's tries to see friendly forces and protects friendly forces from enemy observation and fires.

SUSTAINING OPERATIONS

4-12.   The purpose of sustaining operations is the generation and maintenance of combat power. Sustaining operations are operations at any echelon that enable shaping and decisive operations by providing logistics, rear area and base security, movement control, terrain management, and infrastructure development.

4-13.   Sustainment encompasses activities at all levels of war that generate and sustain combat power. It provides the essential capabilities and performs the functions, activities, and tasks necessary to sustain all forces in theater.

4-14.   Rear area and base security include measures taken by a military unit, an activity, or an installation to defend and protect itself against all acts that could impair its effectiveness. It has four components: (1) intelligence, (2) base and base cluster self-defense, (3) response force operations, and (4) combined arms tactical combat force (TCF) operations (FM 100-7).

4-15.   Movement control includes the planning, routing, scheduling, controlling, and security of the movement of personnel and materiel into, within, and out of the AO. Maintaining movement control, keeping lines of communications (LOCs) open, managing reception and transshipment points, and obtaining host nation support are critical to movement control.

4-16.   Terrain management includes the process of allocating terrain, designating assembly areas, and specifying locations for units and activities. The process includes grouping units together to form bases and designated base clusters as necessary.

4-17.   Infrastructure development applies to all fixed and permanent installations, fabrications, or facilities that support and control military forces. Infrastructure development focuses on facility security modifications and includes area damage control (ADC) and repairs.

4-18.   Although they are neither decisive nor shaping, sustaining operations are inseparable from decisive and shaping operations. Failure to sustain operations normally results in mission failure. Sustaining operations occur throughout the AO, not just within the rear area. Sustaining operations determine how quickly forces reconstitute and how far forces can exploit success. At the tactical level, sustaining operations underwrite the tempo of the overall operation; they assure the ability to immediately take advantage of any available opportunity.

MAIN EFFORT

4-19. Within the battlefield organization of decisive, shaping, and sustaining operations, commanders designate and shift the main effort. The main effort is the activity, unit, or area the commander determines constitutes subordinate element conducting the most important task at that time. The main effort and the decisive operation are not always identical. The commander anticipates shifts of the main effort throughout an operation and includes them in the plan. However, when a main effort is designated, the commander weights it with resources and priorities. All other elements of the Infantry battalion support the main effort. In planning the scheme of maneuver, the main effort must have sufficient combat power and support to accomplish its mission. To weight the main effort, the commander may perform the following:

- Assign the main effort to the company with the greatest combat power.
- Allocate additional combat platoons in task organization to weight the main effort.
- Attach protection elements in direct support of the main effort.
- Position overwatch or support by fire elements to support the main effort.
- Assign priority of fires (artillery, mortars, PSYOP, and joint fires/close air support [CAS]) and priority of targets.
- Coordinate adjacent unit or attack helicopter support by fire.
- Assign priority of sustaining operations to sustain the main effort.
- Narrow the scope of main effort responsibility by geographical area or specified tasks.

4-20. Enemy actions, minor changes in the situation, or lack of success by other elements must not divert forces from the main effort. The commander commits the main effort at the decisive point where the unit's total combat power can be massed to achieve decisive results with respect to terrain, the enemy, and time to achieve the unit's purpose. Once committed, the unit may conduct the following:

- Secure key and or decisive terrain.
- Seize key and or decisive terrain.
- Destroy designated enemy forces.

4-21. The Infantry battalion commander may change the unit designated to conduct the main effort during the course of an operation. Rapidly shifting the main effort as changes in the situation occur is challenging. Time and distance factors determine which forces the combined arms battalion commander uses if he shifts the main effort. If the commander designates a new element as the main effort, he must then shift priorities of resources to support the new main effort.

RESERVE

4-22. The Infantry battalion designates a reserve when the BCT has no reserve, an inadequate reserve, or when faced with an uncertain situation that requires flexibility in the plan. The Infantry battalion reserve provides additional combat power during critical points in the fight, the ability to exploit the success of the main effort, and a hedge against uncertainty. The reserve should be based on the level of detail known about the enemy and should be sized to mitigate risk. The Infantry battalion's information dominance over the enemy allows the commander to capitalize on the capabilities of digitization to apportion his available troops to the tasks required to affect his concept of attack. The composition of the reserve should also be based on the firepower, mobility, and type of forces needed to meet its anticipated mission requirements based on the enemy. Solid intelligence can lead the commander to concentrate his committed units against specific enemy weak points and identify reserve requirements. The composition of the reserve should be discussed and agreed on by the BCT commander to reflect the organization of the IBCT as a two Infantry battalion organization. The BCT commander should provide specific guidance to the Infantry battalions regarding the composition of the reserve as well as the rules for the use of the reserve.

4-23. The Infantry battalion reserve can be as small as an infantry platoon or an assault weapons platoon. The commander and staff must look for opportunities to use other assets, such as fires and situational obstacles, to assist with the reserve mission. To generate larger ground maneuver reserves, the Infantry battalion commander must redirect committed elements after they have accomplished their initial tasks or when the enemy's defeat frees them for other tasks.

4-24. The speed and agility of the combat platoons allow them to be committed, withdrawn, redirected, and recommitted during the fight. The rotation of units into the reserve role requires the best possible information available. Moving a unit from one area (left to right or front to rear) requires everyone in the unit to know where they are, where the enemy is, and where other friendly units are located. Also, the movement of ground forces over the distances expected in the expanded battlespace requires time. The time and distance relationship for both mounted and dismounted actions, especially under limited visibility conditions and rough terrain, is a key factor in determining which units the commander can realistically consider as a possible reserve force.

4-25. The Infantry battalion reserve follows the main attack at a distance sufficient to keep it from interfering with the movement of the lead company and to maintain its freedom of maneuver. The reserve maintains the flexibility to shift its attack if the main effort changes.

4-26. The reserve commander must understand the commander's intent, especially the decision points and conditions for commitment of the reserve. The reserve commander must remain updated on the situation and possess the same common operational picture (COP) as the combined arms battalion commander.

FOLLOW AND SUPPORT

4-27. In exploitation and pursuit operations, the Infantry battalion is normally not employed by BCTs and higher echelon units in a follow and support role. Follow and support is a task in which a committed force follows and supports the unit conducting the main attack. A follow and support task is assigned to a unit to prevent the unit conducting the main attack (usually the Infantry battalion main effort) from having to commit its combat power away from its primary task. A follow and support force executes one or more of the following tasks:

- Destroy bypassed enemy forces.
- Block movement of enemy reinforcements.
- Secure routes or key terrain.
- Clear obstacles or reduce additional obstacle lanes.
- Guard or secure enemy prisoners, detainees, key areas, and installations.
- Recover friendly battle losses.
- Control refugees.
- Reinforce the main effort.

4-28. When operating as a follow and support force, the Infantry battalion's movement techniques are similar to those used in a movement to contact. The Infantry battalion coordinates plans with the unit it follows. Both units exchange situation reports frequently to coordinate operations.

FOLLOW AND ASSUME

4-29. Follow and assume is a task in which a committed force follows another force, normally the main effort, and is prepared to assume the mission of the other force if that force is fixed, halted, or unable to continue. The follow and assume force maintains contact with the trail elements of the other force and monitors all combat information and intelligence. It can maintain this contact through digital tools or by physical contact. The COP should provide the same picture of the battle to the follow-on force as is available to the lead force.

4-30. The follow and assume force is prepared to conduct a forward passage of lines but should try to pass around a flank of the lead force when assuming its mission. Also, the following force avoids becoming decisively engaged with enemy forces bypassed by the force it is following. The Infantry battalion S-2 must ensure that the following force is provided current information and disposition of the bypassed enemy forces as well as a current picture of the enemy forces the lead element faces and those it expects to face.

4-31. Crucial actions to support the commitment of the follow and assume force include the following:

- Maintain current information on the enemy and friendly situation.
- Shift observers and reconnaissance assets as required.
- Develop graphic control measures to ensure a rapid passage of lines or passing on a flank.
- Ensure terrain is allocated for rapid movement while maintaining force protection.
- Be prepared for the shift in priority of support. Reposition assets and retask organize as required.
- Activate emergency resupply operations as necessary.
- Establish direct-fire control measures and fire support coordination measures (FSCMs) such as restrictive fire lines (RFLs).

Section III. SEQUENCE

The commander and staff consider preparation and execution as they plan an offensive mission.

PREPARATION

4-32. The battalion conducts extensive reconnaissance and surveillance of the objective to support the commander's decisions on how to employ his combat power against the enemy. He normally does not make final decisions as to the exact conduct of the operation until reconnaissance and surveillance operations determine, to the greatest extent possible, the enemy situation. The commander and staff direct and supervise mission preparations to prepare the battalion for the battle. The battalion employs security forces to protect and conceal attack preparations from the enemy while exercising OPSEC. Preparation time is also used to conduct precombat checks and inspections, rehearsals at all levels, and sustainment activities.

EXECUTION

4-33. Execution generally consists of the following five sequential events:

- Movement to the line of departure.
- Approach to the objective.
- Actions on the objective.
- Consolidation and reorganization.
- Transition.

MOVEMENT TO LINE OF DEPARTURE

4-34. When attacking from positions not in contact, battalions often stage in assembly areas, road march to attack positions behind friendly units in contact with the enemy, conduct passage of lines, and begin the attack. When attacking from positions in direct contact, the line of departure is the same as the line of contact. In certain circumstances (noncontiguous operations), there may not be a line of departure.

APPROACH TO OBJECTIVE

4-35. The commander and staff plan the approach to the objective to ensure security, speed, and flexibility. They select routes, techniques, formations, and methods that best support actions on the objective. All leaders must recognize this portion of the battle as a fight, not a movement. The battalion may have to fight through enemy combat forces, obstacles, artillery strikes, security elements, possible spoiling attacks, and other combat multipliers to reach the objective. The commander employs techniques that avoid the enemy's strength when possible and conceal the battalion's true intentions. He tries to deceive the enemy as to the location of the decisive operation, uses surprise to take advantage of his initiative in determining the time and place of his attack, and uses indirect approaches when available to strike the enemy from a flank or the rear.

ACTIONS ON OBJECTIVE

4-36. The battalion's objective may be terrain- or force-oriented. Terrain-oriented objectives require the battalion to seize or secure a designated area. However, to gain a terrain-oriented objective often requires fighting through enemy forces. If the objective is an enemy force, an objective area may be assigned for orientation, but the battalion's effort is focused on the enemy's actual location. The enemy may be a stationary or moving force. Actions on the objective start when the battalion begins placing fires on the objective. This action usually occurs with preparatory fires while the battalion is still approaching the objective.

4-37. The battalion immediately reorients and continues the reconnaissance and surveillance effort beyond the objective to detect enemy repositioning, counterattack forces, and to look for exploitation opportunities.

CONSOLIDATION AND REORGANIZATION

4-38. The battalion reorganizes and consolidates as required by the situation and mission. The consolidation and reorganization plan needs to be as detailed as the assault plan.

Consolidation

4-39. Consolidation consists of actions taken to secure and strengthen the objective and defend against enemy counterattack. The unit providing the shaping effort during the assault may or may not join the assault force on the objective. Planning considerations should include unit locations, sectors of fire, forces oriented on enemy counterattack routes, and provisions to facilitate transition to follow-on operations.

Reorganization

4-40. Normally conducted concurrently with consolidation, reorganization occurs as necessary to prepare the unit for follow-on operations. Detailed planning provides the battalion with a plan for evacuating and recovering casualties, recovering damaged equipment, providing for prisoners of war, and integrating replacement personnel. As a part of reorganization, the battalion positions forces to prepare for enemy counterattacks, the commitment of enemy reserves, and friendly forces follow-on missions. This includes repositioning mortars to extend organic indirect fire coverage, establishing security forward of the objective, covering likely enemy avenues of approach to the objectives, and shifting indirect fire targets to beyond the objective.

Transition

4-41. The battalion executes follow-on missions as directed by the higher commander. The most likely mission is to continue the attack. Other missions may include supporting a passage of lines for a follow-on force, defending, or participating in an exploitation or pursuit. The battalion develops plans for follow-on missions based on the higher headquarters' plan, the higher commander's intent, and the anticipated situation.

Section IV. FORMS OF MANEUVER

The battalion uses the five basic forms of maneuver during an attack: envelopment, turning movement, infiltration, penetration, and frontal attack. When the battalion is executing a form of maneuver, the subordinate units may execute different forms of maneuver to assist the decisive .operation and the battalion in accomplishing their purpose and executing the battalion's concept of operation. Forms of maneuver are conducted in relation to or relative to an enemy force.

ENVELOPMENT

4-42. Envelopment seeks to apply strength against weakness. Envelopment avoids the enemy's front; where he is strongest, where his attention is focused, and where his fires are most easily concentrated. The battalion tries to fix the defender with shaping attacks which typically consist of one or more companies. The remaining companies of the battalion, the main attack, maneuver out of contact around the enemy's defenses to strike at assailable flanks, the rear, or both. The shaping attack must have sufficient combat power to keep the enemy engaged, while the enveloping force maneuvers to close with the enemy.

4-43. Envelopments may be conducted against a stationary or moving enemy force. Sometimes the enemy exposes his flank by his own forward movement, unaware of his opponent's location. In a fluid battle involving noncontiguous forces, the combination of air and indirect fires may isolate the enemy on unfavorable terrain and establish conditions for maneuver against an assailable flank or rear. The attacker needs to be agile enough to concentrate his forces and mass his combat power before the enemy can reorient his defense (Figure 4-2).

4-44. Variations of the envelopment include the double envelopment and encirclement. Battalions do not possess the resources to execute these variations independently, but rather, as a part of a BCT or higher operation.

Double Envelopment

4-45. The attacker seeks to pass at the same time around both flanks of the enemy. This type of envelopment requires two assailable flanks, precise coordination, sufficient combat power, detailed timing, and precise fire control measures. The potential for fratricide increases significantly with this form of envelopment.

Encirclement

4-46. Encirclement occurs when the battalion severs all LOCs, and prevents any reinforcement interdiction using inner and outer encircling arms. Battalion fires are synchronized to complete the destruction of the encircled force. Forces are positioned to block or interdict the enemy's try to break through and link up from the encirclement. Encirclements are likely to be an extension of an exploitation or pursuit. Battalions normally participate in encirclements as part of a larger force.

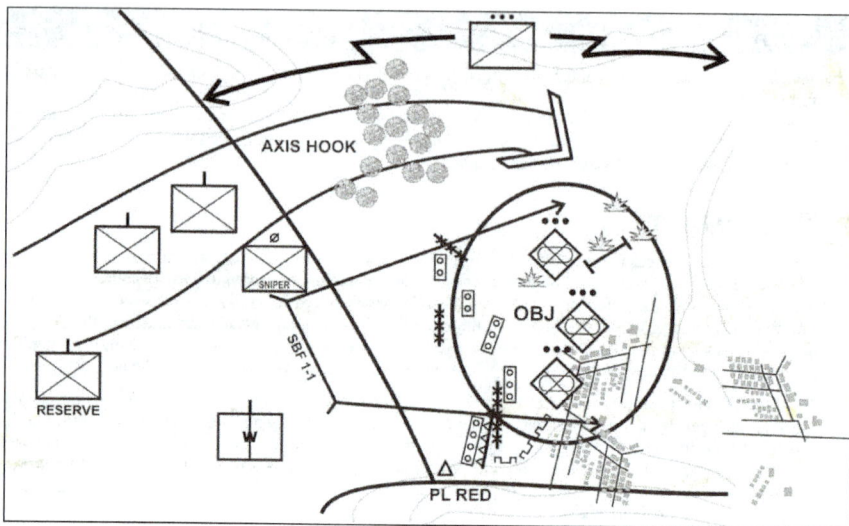

Figure 4-2. Envelopment.

PENETRATION

4-47. In a penetration, the attacker concentrates forces to strike at an enemy's weakest point and rupture the defense and break up its continuity to create assailable flanks. The attacker then uses the gap created to pass forces through to defeat the enemy through attacks into his flanks and rear. A successful penetration depends on the attacker's ability to suppress enemy weapons systems, to concentrate forces to overwhelm the defender at the point of attack, and to pass sufficient forces through the gap to defeat the enemy quickly. A penetration is normally tried when enemy flanks are unassailable or when conditions permit neither envelopment nor a turning movement such as an attack against the enemy's main defensive belt (Figure 4-3). Usually, when the penetration is successfully completed, the battalion will transition to another form of maneuver.

CONCENTRATION

4-48. The penetration of an enemy position requires a concentration of combat power to permit continued momentum of the attack. The attack should move rapidly to destroy the continuity of the defense since, if it is slowed or delayed, the enemy is afforded time to react. If the attacker does not make the penetration sharply and secure objectives promptly, the penetration is likely to resemble a frontal attack. This may result in high casualties and permit the enemy to fall back intact, thus avoiding destruction.

STEPS

4-49. A penetration is conducted in three steps.

Step 1: Penetration of Main Line of Resistance

4-50. A reinforced company can execute the initial penetration. The weapons company has the potential to play a significant role in this initial step.

Step 2: Widening of Gap to Secure Flanks

4-51. The battalion seizes enemy positions behind the obstacles and widens the shoulders of the penetration to allow assaulting forces room to attack deep objectives.

Step 3: Seizure of Objective and Subsequent Exploitation

4-52. Exploitation of the penetration is made as companies complete the destruction of the enemy and attack to secure deeper objectives. Objectives for the assaulting force are deep enough to allow an envelopment of the rest of the enemy position and should facilitate attack by fire against second echelon enemy positions and enemy counterattack routes.

PLANNING CONSIDERATIONS

4-53. To allow a penetration, the terrain must facilitate the maneuver of the penetrating force. The concentration of the battalion is planned to penetrate the defense where the continuity of the enemy's defense has been interrupted such as gaps in obstacles and minefields or areas not covered by fire. Multiple penetrations are normally only conducted at the operational level. When essential to the accomplishment of the mission, intermediate objectives should be planned for the attack.

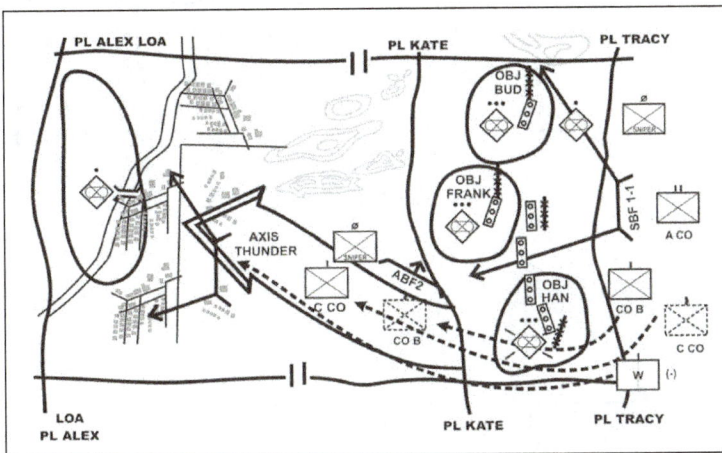

Figure 4-3. Penetration.

TURNING MOVEMENT

4-54. In a turning movement, the unit passes around and avoids the enemy's main force. It then secures an objective that causes the enemy to move out of its current position or divert forces to meet the threat (Figure 4-4). The objective of the turning movement is to make contact with the enemy, but at a location of the unit's advantage and out of the enemy's established kill zones. The battalion conducts a turning movement as part of a larger unit's operation. The battalion can also conduct a turning movement with subordinate companies.

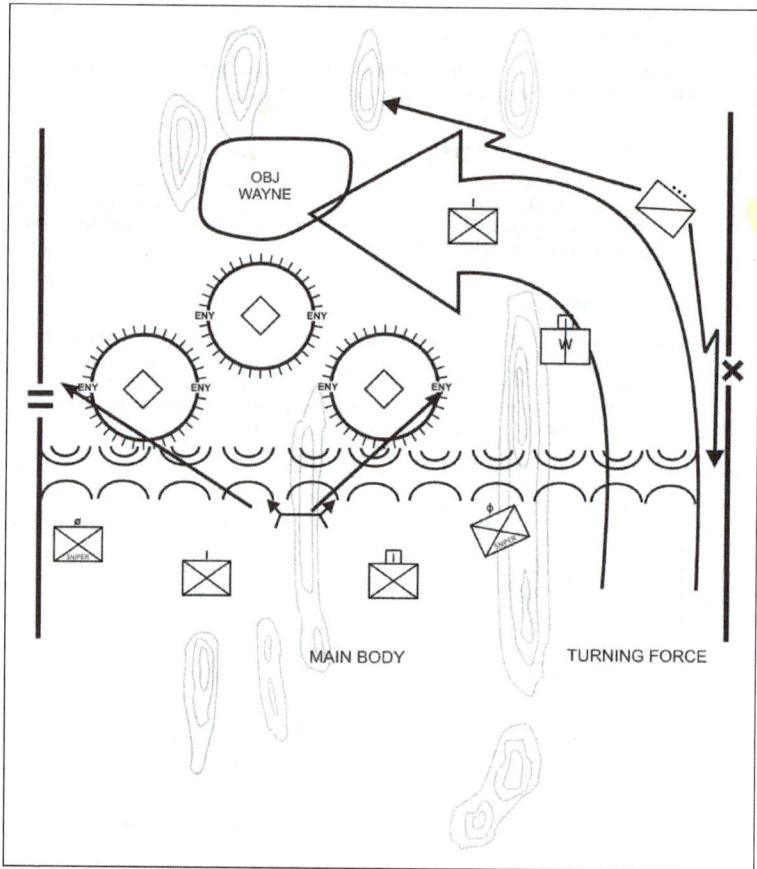

Figure 4-4. Turning movement.

INFILTRATION

4-55. Infiltration is a form of maneuver in which combat elements conduct undetected movement through or into an area occupied by enemy forces to occupy a position of advantage in the enemy's rear (Figure 4-5, page 4-14). The commander uses infiltration to—

- Attack lightly defended positions or stronger positions from the flank and rear.
- Secure key terrain in support of the decisive operation.

- Disrupt or harass enemy defensive preparations/operations.
- Relocate the battalion by moving to battle positions around an engagement area.
- Reposition to attack vital facilities or enemy forces from the flank or rear.

4-56. Detailed METT-TC analysis will dictate the location of infiltration routes, the number of infiltration lanes, the size of the infiltration lane(s), the anticipated speed of movement, and the time of departure. An infiltration should be planned during limited visibility through areas the enemy does not occupy or cover by surveillance and fire. Planning should incorporate infiltration lanes, rally points along the route or axis, and contact points. Companies and platoons usually conduct infiltrations, but it is possible to execute at a battalion or squad level also. Careful planning considerations for the integration of the weapons company throughout an infiltration must be exercised.

4-57. Although the weapons company may provide a larger and louder signature, the speed, mobility, shock, and firepower of the weapons company may provide an overwhelming advantage to either set conditions for or execute a decisive operation. The weapons company may have its own infiltration lane, follow another unit on a lane, or may be held as a reserve element. Another consideration for the infiltration means is the vertical infiltration. Due to limited resources, this means of infiltration may be limited to reconnaissance and/or weapons company assets. Single or multiple infiltration lanes can be planned.

SINGLE INFILTRATION LANE

4-58. Using a single infiltration lane—

- Facilitates navigation, control, and reassembly.
- Reduces susceptibility to detection.
- Reduces the area requiring detailed intelligence.
- Increases the time required to move the force through enemy positions.

MULTIPLE INFILTRATION LANES

4-59. Using multiple infiltration lanes—

- Reduces the possibility of compromise.
- Allows more rapid movement.
- Makes control more challenging.

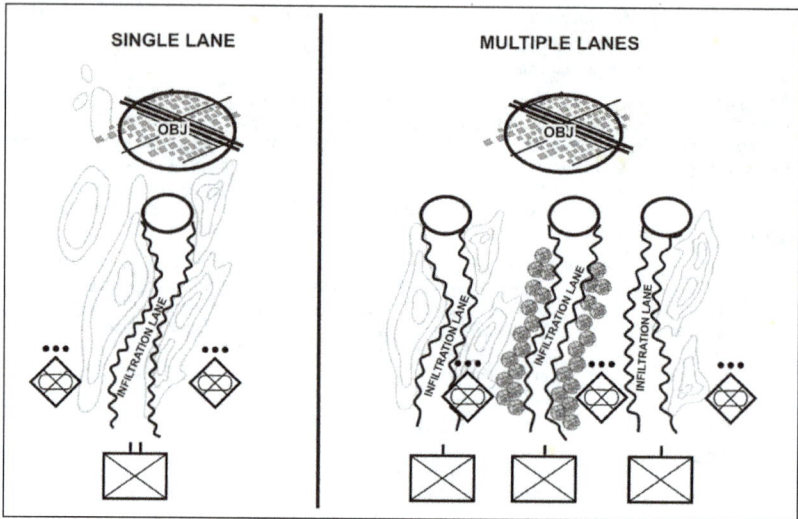

Figure 4-5. Infiltration.

FRONTAL ATTACK

4-60. The frontal attack is usually the least desirable form of maneuver because it exposes the majority of the offensive force to the concentrated fires of the defenders. The battalion normally conducts a frontal attack as part of a larger operation against a stationary or moving enemy force (Figure 4-6). Unless frontal attacks are executed with overwhelming and well synchronized speed and strength against a weaker enemy, they are seldom decisive. The battalion attacks the enemy across a wide front and along the most direct approaches. It uses a frontal attack to overrun and destroy a weakened enemy force or to fix an enemy force. Frontal attacks are used when commanders possess overwhelming combat power and the enemy is at a clear disadvantage or when fixing the enemy over a wide front is the desired effect and a decisive defeat in that area is not expected. The frontal attack may be appropriate in an attack or meeting engagement where speed and simplicity are paramount to maintaining battle tempo and, ultimately, the initiative; or in a shaping attack to fix an enemy force.

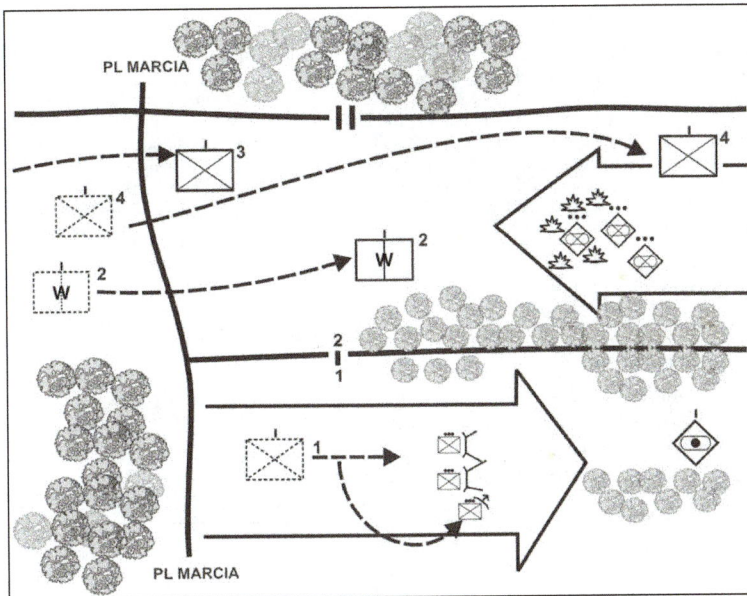

Figure 4-6. Frontal attack against a moving enemy.

MOVEMENT TECHNIQUES AND FORMATIONS

4-61. The selection of movement techniques and attack formations for the battalion depends on the factors of METT-TC and the probable line of contact.

MOVEMENT TECHNIQUES

4-62. The battalion uses traveling, traveling overwatch, and bounding overwatch movement techniques. It does not usually move as a unit using only one movement technique. The battalion commander will rarely dictate which technique his companies will use except in rare instances. When moving as a unit along a single avenue, the battalion commander designates the movement technique to be used by the lead unit(s) based on the likelihood of enemy contact. For example, the battalion may be moving to contact in column formation, while the lead company may be in a wedge formation using the traveling overwatch technique dictated by the battalion commander. Movement techniques are used when not in contact with the enemy; they end when the unit--

- Transitions to maneuver
- Comes into contact the enemy
- Begins actions on contact and overwatching force begins suppressive fires (maneuver).

4-63. The battalion should try to make enemy contact with the smallest possible friendly force. This technique allows the majority of the battalion freedom to maneuver against the enemy force.

FORMATIONS

4-64. The battalion may move in any one of these basic formations: column, wedge, vee, echelon, and line. The battalion may use more than one formation in a given movement, especially if the terrain changes during the movement. For example, the battalion commander may elect to use the column formation during a passage of lines and then change to another formation such as a wedge. Companies within a battalion formation may conduct movement using formations different from that of the battalion. Although the battalion may be moving in a wedge formation, one company may be in a wedge, another in an echelon right, and yet another in a column. Other factors, such as the distance of the move or the enemy dispositions, may also prompt the commander to use more than one formation. Distances between units depend on the factors of METT-TC.

Column Formation

4-65. The battalion moves in column formation when early contact is not expected and the objective is far away (Figure 4-7). The battalion's lead element normally uses traveling overwatch while the following units travel. The column formation—

- Speeds movement, eases control, and increases usefulness in close terrain.
- Allows quick transition to other formations.
- Requires flank security.
- Places most of the firepower on the flanks.

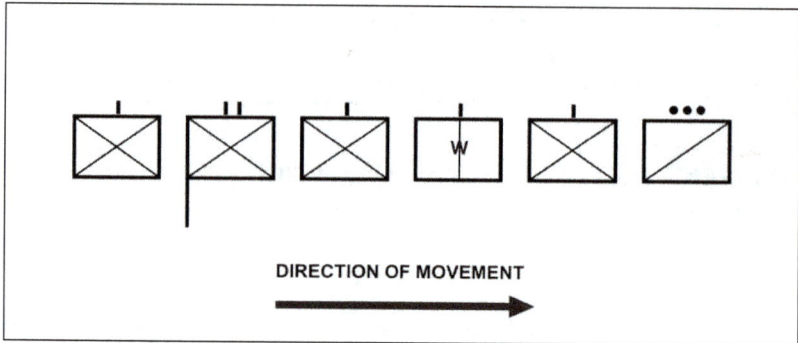

Figure 4-7. Battalion in column formation.

Wedge Formation

4-66. The wedge formation postures the battalion for enemy contact on its front and flanks (Figure 4-8). The force uses the wedge when enemy contact is possible or expected but the location and disposition of the enemy is vague. When not expecting enemy contact, it may use the wedge to cross open terrain rapidly. The wedge formation:

- Facilitates control and transition to the assault.
- Provides for maximum firepower forward and good firepower to the flanks.
- Requires sufficient space to disperse laterally and in depth.

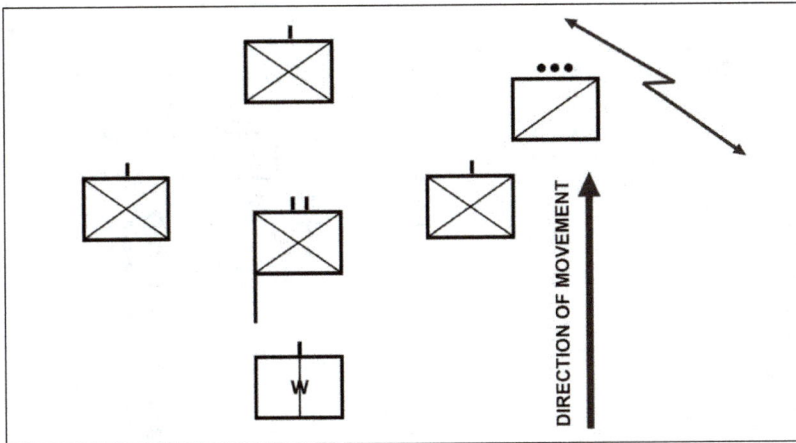

Figure 4-8. Battalion in wedge formation.

Vee Formation

4-67. The vee formation postures the battalion with two companies abreast and one trailing (Figure 4-9). This arrangement is most suitable to advance against an enemy known to be to the front of the battalion. The battalion may use the vee when enemy contact is expected and the location and disposition of the enemy is known. The following planning considerations apply:

- Formation is hard to orient and control is more difficult in close or wooded terrain.
- Formation provides for good firepower forward and to the flanks.

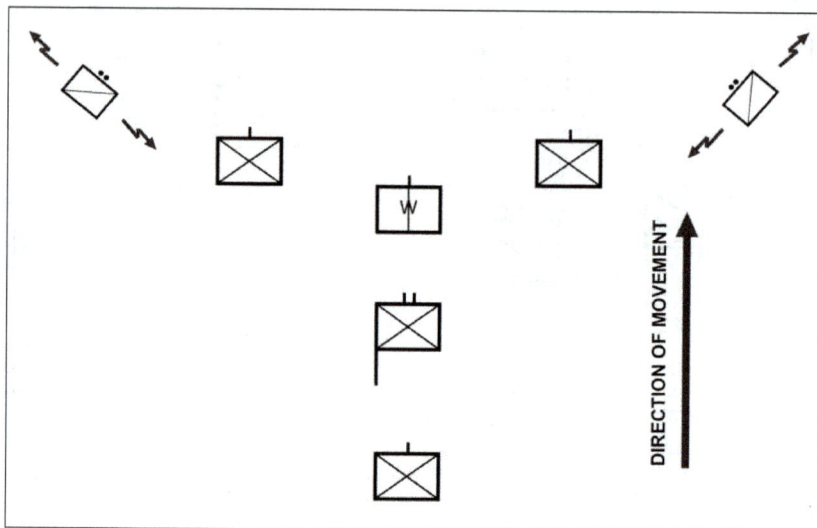

Figure 4-9. Battalion in vee formation.

Echelon Formation

4-68. The echelon formation arranges the battalion with the companies in column formation in the direction of the echelon (right or left) (Figure 4-10). The battalion commonly uses the echelon when providing security to a larger moving force. The echelon formation—

- Provides for firepower forward and in the direction of echelon.
- Facilitates control in open areas but makes it more difficult in heavily wooded areas.

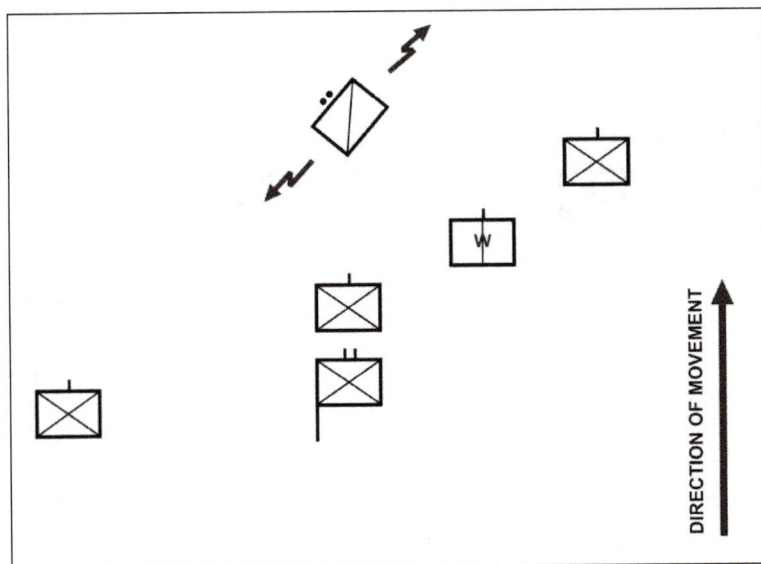

Figure 4-10. Battalion in echelon left formation.

Line Formation

4-69. The line formation postures the battalion with companies on line and abreast of one another (Figure 4-11). Because it does not dispose companies in depth, the line formation provides less flexibility of maneuver than other formations. The battalion uses the line when it requires continuous movement with maximum firepower to the front in an assault.

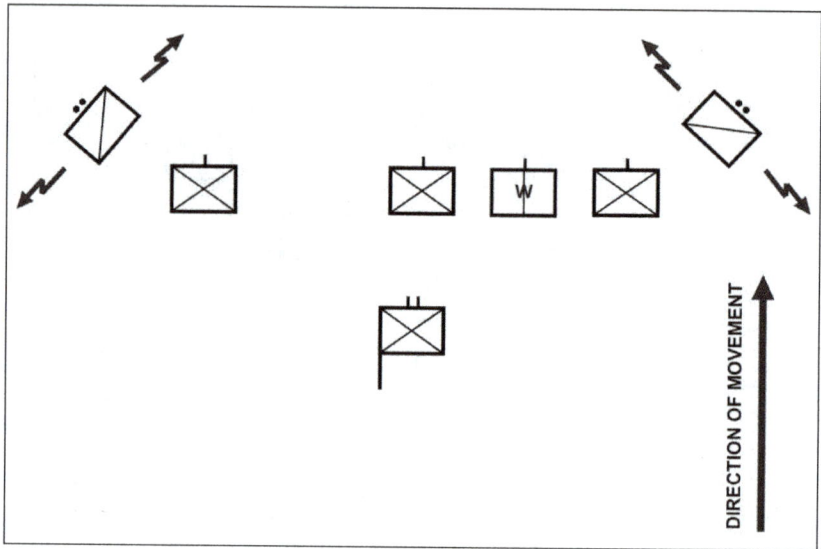

Figure 4-11. Battalion in line formation.

Section V. FORMS OF TACTICAL OFFENSE

At the battalion level, the offense takes the form of either a deliberate or a hasty operation such as a movement to contact, attack, exploitation, or pursuit across the full spectrum of conflict. The battalion may also be given the mission to conduct special purpose attacks such as a raid, demonstration, spoiling attack, or counterattack. Attacks, exploitations, and pursuits may be conducted sequentially or simultaneously throughout the AO.

HASTY OPERATIONS

4-70. The battalion conducts a hasty offensive operation after a successful defense or as part of a defense; due to a movement to contact, a meeting engagement, or a chance contact during a movement; or in a situation where the unit has an unexpected opportunity to attack vulnerable enemy forces. A hasty operation uses immediately available assets to perform activities with minimal preparation or task organizing, trading planning and preparation time for speed of execution. Hasty operations maximize the effects of speed, agility, and surprise, but sacrifice a certain degree of synchronization. Reconnaissance and surveillance assets are still deployed as soon as possible to gather the information needed by the commander to make decisions. As a result, the commander can convert a hasty operation into a deliberate operation without a substantial increase in planning time

DELIBERATE OPERATIONS

4-71. A deliberate offensive operation is one in which a commander's detailed intelligence allows him to develop and coordinate detailed plans and tailor his task organization. The result is a fully synchronized operation that employs all available assets against the enemy's defense and is characterized by detailed planning based on available information, thorough reconnaissance, preparation, and rehearsals.

MOVEMENT TO CONTACT

4-72. Advanced ISR technologies have provided Infantry battalions with an enhanced COP; however, these systems will never provide the commander with perfect intelligence which answers all of the unknowns about the enemy force. The battalion conducts movement to contact when the tactical situation is not clear or when the enemy has broken contact. Battalions conduct movement to contact independently or as part of a larger force. The purpose of a movement to contact is to gain or reestablish contact with the enemy. The battalion will normally be given a movement to contact mission as the lead element of an attack or as a counterattack element of a BCT or higher level unit. The battalion conducts movement to contact in a manner that allows it to maneuver to develop the situation fully, to maintain freedom of action, and if required, to defeat the enemy once contact is made. Reconnaissance, surveillance, and flexibility are essential in gaining and maintaining the initiative. The movement to contact terminates with the occupation of an assigned objective or when enemy resistance requires the battalion to deploy and conduct an attack to continue forward movement. A battalion given a movement to contact mission is assigned an axis of advance and an objective at a depth to ensure contact with the enemy.

ORGANIZATION

4-73. When executing a movement to contact, the battalion normally organizes into a security force comprised of a reconnaissance and surveillance force, an advance guard, the main body, and flank and rear guards (Figure 4-12).

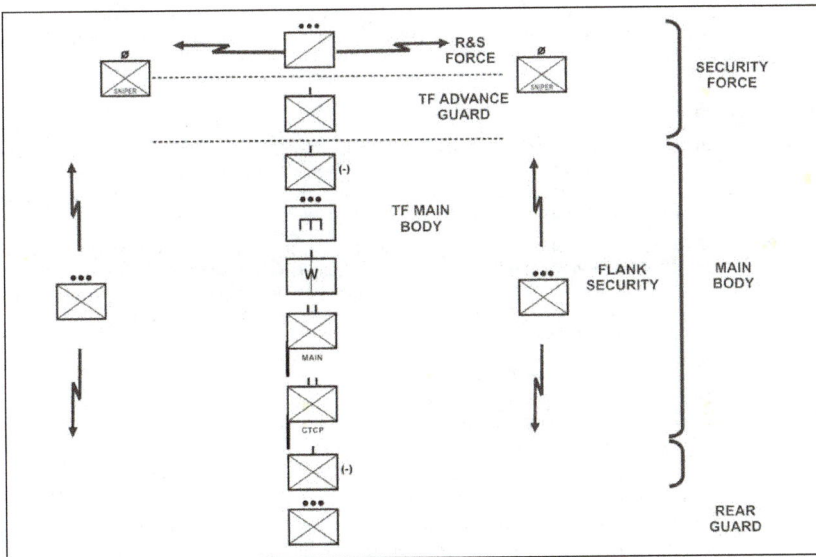

Figure 4-12. Battalion movement to contact.

Reconnaissance and Surveillance Forces

4-74. The reconnaissance and surveillance force for the battalion is normally the scout platoon augmented with snipers and UAS. Engineers and forward observers (FOs) are attached to the reconnaissance and surveillance force as necessary. Normally, the reconnaissance and surveillance force has initial priority of indirect fires. The mission of the reconnaissance and surveillance force is to determine the size, activity, location, and depth of the enemy force. Specifically, the reconnaissance and surveillance force must answer the PIR established by the commander. Other tasks, similar to an area reconnaissance, normally include—

- Reconnaissance of routes, bridges, and roads.
- Reconnaissance of obstacles and restrictive terrain.
- Surveillance of critical areas, danger areas, or key terrain.

4-75. The reconnaissance and surveillance force covers the frontage of the battalion axis of advance. It avoids decisive engagement, but once found it must keep the enemy under surveillance and report his activity.

4-76. The reconnaissance and surveillance force is far enough ahead of the advance guard to provide adequate warning, a detailed picture of the enemy force, and sufficient space for it to maneuver. The R&S force will normally remain within supporting range of the battalion's indirect fires unless task organized with internal indirect fire support. However, the reconnaissance and surveillance force must not be so far ahead that the advance guard cannot rapidly assist it in disengaging from the enemy, should that become necessary. The advance guard keys its movement on the movement of the reconnaissance and surveillance force.

4-77. The reconnaissance and surveillance force must be able to receive the latest information available from the BCT reconnaissance squadron as well as information available from adjacent units, other battlefield surveillance assets, and the S-2. With this information, the reconnaissance and surveillance force can confirm information provided by these assets to greatly reduce the risks and unknowns normally associated with a movement to contact mission. This information is also made available to the battalion subordinate elements.

Advance Guard

4-78. The advance guard for a battalion is usually a company team. Its composition depends on the factors of METT-TC. The engineers follow or are attached to the lead elements to ensure mobility and provide route/bridge classification expertise and may have attachments from the weapons company. The two lead companies are task-organized accordingly when a battalion moves in parallel columns.

4-79. The advance guard operates forward of the main body to provide security for the main body and ensure its uninterrupted advance. It protects the main body from surprise attacks and develops the situation to allow time and space for the deployment of the main body when it is committed to action. The advance guard accomplishes this by destroying or suppressing enemy reconnaissance and ambushes, delaying enemy forces, and marking bypasses for or reducing obstacles. The advance guard—

- Remains oriented on the main body.
- Reports enemy contact to the battalion commander.
- Collects and reports all information about the enemy.
- Selects tentative fighting positions for following battalion units.
- Tries to penetrate enemy security elements and reach or identify the enemy main force.
- Destroys or repels enemy reconnaissance forces.
- Prevents enemy ground forces from engaging the main body with direct fires.
- Locates, bypasses, or breaches obstacles along the main body's axis of advance.
- Executes tactical tasks such as fix, contain, or block, against enemy forces to develop the situation for the main body.
- May conduct a forward passage of lines (FPOL) with the main body.

4-80. Until the main body is committed, the advance guard is the battalion commander's initial main effort. Priority of fires shifts to the main body once committed.

4-81. In planning the movement to contact, each contingency operation should revolve around the actions of the advance guard. The lead elements must be well trained on battle drills, especially those involving obstacle reduction and actions on contact.

Main Body

4-82. The main body's rate of movement is dictated by the advance guard. It maintains current information of the advance guard's activities and enemy locations. The main body, remaining attuned to the advance guard's situation, provides responsive support when it is committed.

4-83. The main body contains most of the battalion's combat elements and is arrayed to achieve all-round security. The combat elements of the main body are prepared to deploy and attack, giving them the flexibility to maneuver to a decisive point on the battlefield to destroy the enemy.

4-84. The use of standard formations and battle drills allows the battalion commander, based on the information available to him, to shift combat power rapidly on the battlefield. Companies employ the appropriate formations and movement techniques within the battalion formation. Company commanders, based on their knowledge of the battalion's situation, anticipate the battalion commander's decisions for commitment of the main body and plan accordingly.

Flank and Rear Security

4-85. The flank and rear security mission may be given to one company as a shaping operation or may be given to platoon-size elements from the companies within the main body to conduct guard missions under organic company control. These elements remain at a distance from the main body to allow the battalion time and space to maneuver to either flank or the rear. Flank and rear security elements also operate far enough out to prevent the enemy from placing direct or observed indirect fires on the main body. Indirect fires are planned on major flank and or rear approaches to enhance security. Because of its enhanced observation capabilities, firepower, and mobility, the weapons company may be used to conduct the security mission.

SEARCH AND ATTACK TECHNIQUE

4-86. The search and attack technique is a decentralized movement to contact; requiring multiple, coordinated patrols (squad, platoon, or company-size) to—

- Destroy enemy forces.
- Protect the friendly force.
- Deny an area to the enemy.
- Collect Information.

4-87. The unit conducting a search and attack is organized into a finding force, a fixing force, and a finish force. The procedure for conducting this technique is to organize the battalion in purpose as well as space. It is most often used against an enemy operating in dispersed elements. When conducting a search and attack, units can expect to spend significant time reconnoitering in an area of operations. The battalion may conduct a search and attack as a coordinated battalion level operation or decentralized to independent company level operations.

4-88. A coordinated battalion level search and attack uses its reconnaissance and surveillance assets (scouts, snipers, and UAS) to assist in finding and potentially fixing a dispersed enemy. Once the enemy is found, the finding force must determine if they can achieve fire superiority to fix the threat or if the battalion must fix the enemy with its fixing force (usually consisting of a company size force). Once the threat is fixed, the fixing force must determine if it is able to conduct the attack the finish force would normally execute. If not, another company designated as the finish force will execute the assault. The battalion may direct each individual company to conduct find, fix, and finish procedures at their level; however, the battalion will provide the appropriate level of support in terms of assets, fires and effects, and sustainment to each of the companies. Companies may use UAS to assist in finding the enemy. Whether conducting a consolidated or decentralized operation, the battalion must designate a decisive operation and shaping efforts that enable it to maintain the amount of flexibility the situation dictates.

Purpose

4-89. Search and attack can be conducted for many reasons. The commander's concept focuses the battalion on one or more of the following:

Destruction of Enemy

4-90. The battalion must destroy enemy units operating in the area or render them combat ineffective.

Area Denial

4-91. The battalion must prevent the enemy from operating unhindered in any area, for example, in any area he is using for a base camp or for logistics support.

Force Protection

4-92. The battalion must prevent the enemy from disrupting and destroying friendly military or civilian operations, equipment, and property such as key facilities, headquarters, polling places, or dams.

Information Collection

4-93. The battalion must conduct IPB as soon as it enters an area and before it conducts any of the above activities. The battalion must also verify or answer certain unknowns about the terrain and the enemy.

Tasks

4-94. Search and attack operations can be conducted in a company- or battalion-size area of operations. Figure 4-13 shows an example of dispersing to search, and Figure 4-14, page 4-26, shows an example of a unit massing to attack. The unit can be tasked to—

- Locate enemy positions or routes normally traveled by the enemy.
- Destroy enemy forces within its capability or fix or block the enemy until reinforcements arrive.
- Maintain surveillance of a larger enemy force through stealth until reinforcements arrive.
- Set up ambushes.
- Search towns or villages (a host nation representative should accompany the search party).
- Secure military or civilian property or installations.
- Act as a reserve.
- Develop the situation in a given area.

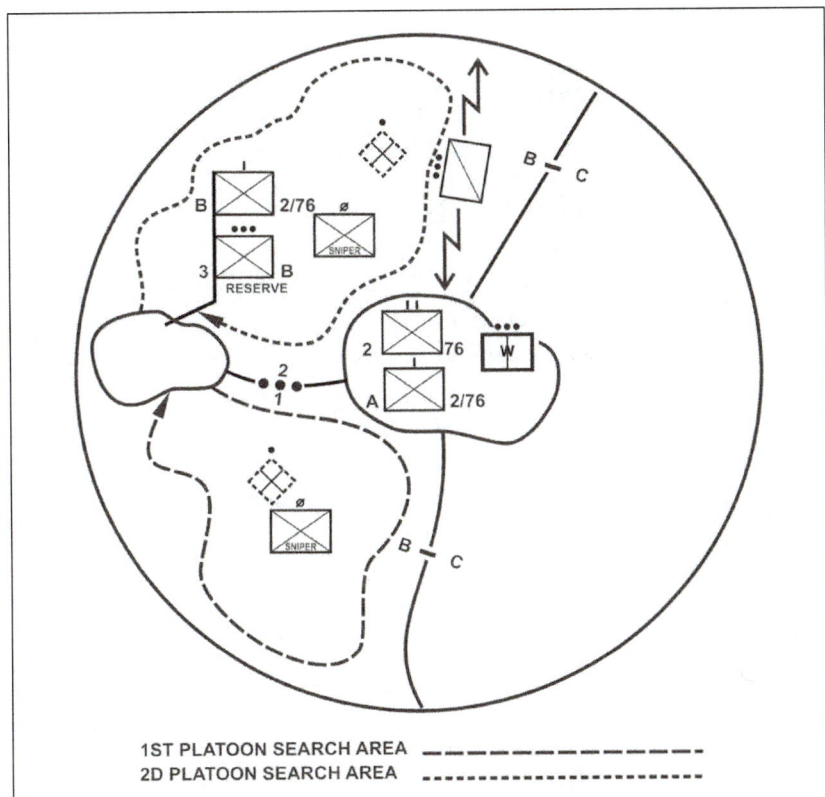

Figure 4-13. Example of unit dispersing to search.

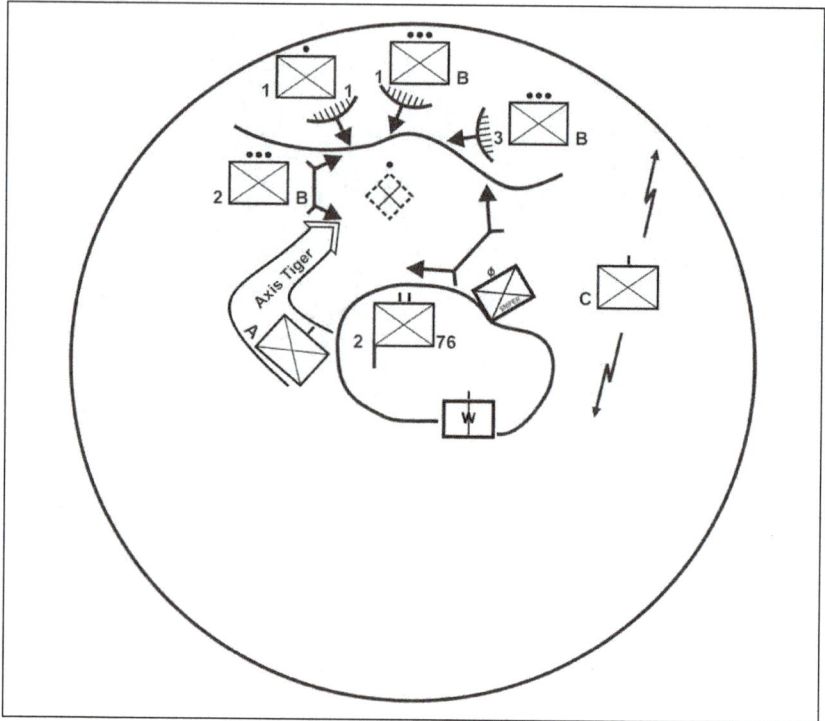

Figure 4-14. Example of unit massing to attack.

Concept Development

4-95. The concept for the search and attack is based on thorough IPB. The S-2 combines his own predictive and pattern analysis with information available from the brigade's and the battalion's reconnaissance and surveillance assets to determine likely enemy locations, capabilities, patterns, and actions. The friendly concept can then be developed to capitalize on the battalion's fires and maneuver. The commander must understand higher echelon unit's concept and provide a clear task and purpose for each of his subordinate elements. The commander must consider the following when developing his concept.

Find Enemy

4-96. Much time should be dedicated to determine the pattern of enemy operations. The commander and his decisions are most effective once the pattern has been identified; however, it may take more time than is available to accurately establish an enemy pattern.

4-97. The commander may consider using another technique to find the enemy. He can subdivide his area of operations into smaller ones and have the scout platoon reconnoiter forward of the remainder of the battalion (Figure 4-15). The scout platoon may be reinforced for this operation with snipers and UAS. In

Figure 4-15, the scout platoon conducts zone reconnaissance in AO Green, while the remainder of the battalion conducts search and attack operations in AO Blue. At a designated time, the commander directs the battalion to link up with the scout platoon at contact point 1 to exchange information. If necessary, the scout platoon guides the battalion to sites of suspected or confirmed enemy activity. The scout platoon can then move on to reconnoiter AO Red. This process is repeated for other AOs until the commander terminates it. The commander may decide to emplace sensors, when available, along the border from AO Red to AO Blue to identify enemy tries to evade the battalion. In Figure 4-15, an Infantry squad and a sniper team have been tasked to emplace and monitor the sensors.

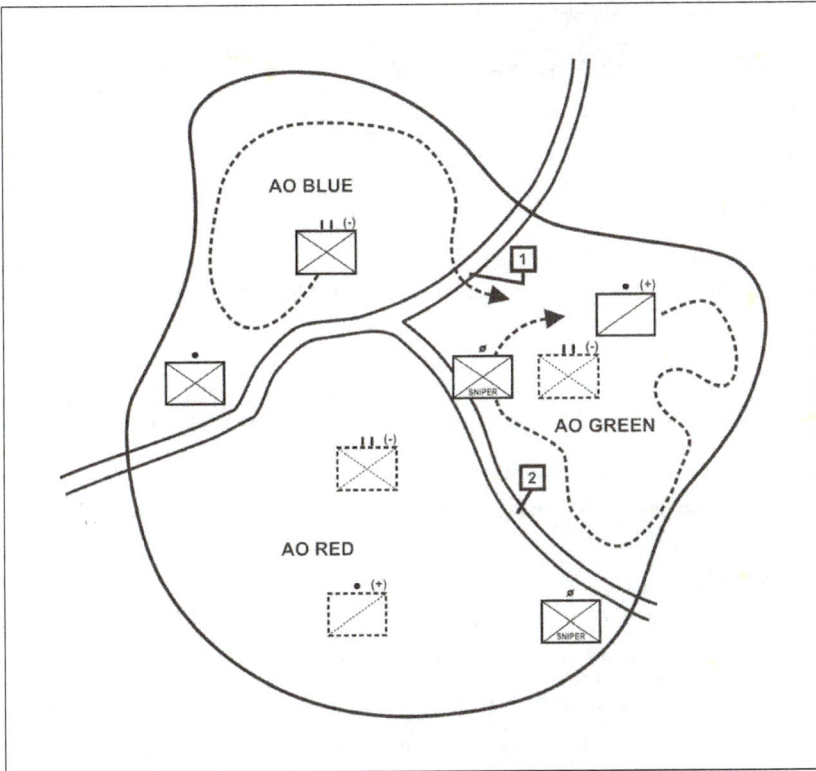

Figure 4-15. Example search and attack method with scout platoon forward.

4-98. The successive method of reconnaissance, discussed in paragraph 4-102, in which the scout platoon reaches the area of operations before the remainder of the battalion, allows the scout platoon more opportunities to gain information on enemy activity in the area. It also helps the battalion commander focus his search and attack operation when the battalion moves to the new area. Cache or airdrop most often provides logistical support for the reinforced scout platoon.

4-99. The battalion will rarely use the scout platoon designated as the finding force, as a potential fixing force. The scout platoon is organized to find information and the enemy, not to become decisively engaged with the threat.

Fix Enemy

4-100. The unit conducts one of the following actions after developing the situation, based on the commander's guidance and METT-TC factors.

Prepare to Block Enemy Escape and Reinforcement Routes

4-101. The unit maintains contact and positions its forces to isolate and prevent the enemy from moving to a position of advantage and prevent the interdiction of reinforcements. This facilitates the conduct of attack by the finishing force. Control measures and communications must be established between closing units to prevent fratricide. Unmanned aerial vehicles can assist in preventing fratricide by observing forward of the moving units and identifying friendly and enemy units as they approach. Overt UAS flights are also a nonlethal means to potentially fix enemy units.

Conduct an Attack

4-102. The fixing force can conduct the finishing attack when it is consistent with the commander's intent with respect to tempo, and if the available friendly forces can generate overwhelming relative combat power. Sniper fires can be used to disrupt the enemy and contain his movement as the main attack approaches.

Maintain Surveillance

4-103. The unit avoids detection so it can report enemy order of battle and activities. The unit must use stealth to be successful in this effort and must always retain the ability to fix the element.

Remain Undetected and Follow the Enemy

4-104. The unit does this to continue to gather information. It must be careful to avoid an enemy ambush and must always retain the ability to fix the element.

Finish Enemy

4-105. Battalions destroy enemy forces during a search and attack by doing the following:

- Rapidly concentrate combat power to conduct hasty or deliberate operations (attacks) or maneuver to block enemy escape routes while another unit conducts the attack.
- Conduct reconnaissance and surveillance activities and collect information to develop the situational template while remaining undetected.
- Employ indirect fire or CAS to destroy the enemy. The battalion may establish an area ambush and use these assets to drive the enemy into the ambush.

Follow Through after Finish Enemy

4-106. The battalion's operations do not end at the destruction of the enemy. The battalion must immediately conduct consolidation and reorganization and prepare for follow on offensive or defensive missions.

Execution

4-107. The commander must do the following to help ensure successful synchronized and decentralized operations:

4-108. Specify where each unit will operate, establish measures to consolidate units before attacks, and establish fire control measures for each unit. The commander seeks the most likely locations of enemy base camps, supplies, C2 sites, and mortars. He designates the company most likely to make contact as the decisive operation and prepares to shift the decisive operation, if necessary.

4-109. Concentrate battalion combat power. The commander does this so that once a patrol finds the enemy; the battalion can quickly fix and destroy him.

4-110. Each company operating in a dispersed company area of operations can be tasked to destroy the enemy within its capability. The battalion commander can direct each company to retain a reserve, or he can retain a battalion reserve. He tries to arrange for indirect fire weapons that can respond to all companies, as needed. He uses the reserve, priority of fire, and other available assets to weight the decisive operation.

4-111. The battalion commander considers means to fix or contain the enemy if the company cannot destroy him. The commander uses the battalion reserve, indirect fires, or CAS to do this.

4-112. The battalion commander provides control but allows for decentralized actions and small-unit initiative. Reconnaissance and surveillance assets are redirected and repositioned to support execution, but also to identify enemy counterattack forces entering the area of operations.

4-113. The battalion commander ensures that fire support and protection assets support the decisive operation while remaining responsive to the rest of the battalion. Mortars remain GS to the battalion. If the mortar platoon cannot support the entire dispersed battalion, the commander may consider splitting the platoon into sections.

4-114. The commander must consider the size of the area to conduct the search and attack. This should be dictated by the number of available forces and the time available. The staff must conduct analysis to establish the duration of the mission. They need to assess the battalion's ability to conduct continuous operations in order to develop and resource a plan to maintain the battalion's combat effectiveness.

Employment of Support Assets

4-115. Synchronization of fire support, protection, and sustainment assets is more difficult to achieve in search-and-attack operations than in most other types of operations. Distances between units, the terrain, and a vague enemy situation contribute to this difficulty. Movement and maneuver, fire support and protection assets are employed as follows:

Movement and Maneuver

4-116. The antiarmor element selects close combat missile (CCM) TOW missile positions where it can provide long range direct fire support. Based on his estimate, the commander can use the MK 19 or the .50-caliber machine gun in place of the CCM TOW. However, the weapons company can also provide mobility and additional firepower for the reserve. During limited visibility, the weapons company with its advanced optics can augment security forces at key locations, monitoring areas where the enemy is expected to travel at night.

4-117. Engineers provide expertise to help identify breach points in enemy defenses and assist with mobility. When the battalion has armored vehicles available, engineers can conduct route reconnaissance, determine bridge classifications, and find or make bypass routes where necessary. Engineers can clear landing zones for helicopter support.

4-118. Aviation units (assault and attack) can reconnoiter, guide ground forces to the enemy, provide lift and fire support assets for air movement, direct artillery fires, aid C2, and protect exposed flanks. Attack helicopters can reinforce when antiarmor firepower is needed to block the enemy (Appendix E).

4-119. Battalions must position TACPs well forward to increase the timeliness and accuracy of CAS. The battalion staff should not disregard the option to attach the TACP to company level. This may provide requests that are more responsive for CAS. To reduce the danger of fratricide, the battalion must develop means of friendly identification of both the aircraft and the Soldiers.

Fire Support

4-120. The FSO prepares fire plans for attacks and contingencies, recommends positioning of attached COLT team to support the decisive operation, and deconflicts airspace between the BCT assets and internal indirect fire and UAS assets. Mountainous terrain increases the need for combat aviation, close air, and mortar fire support (Appendix E).

4-121. The priority of battalion mortars during the search and attack is normally to the decisive operation. Mortars usually locate with another unit for security. The Companies employ organic mortars to support the attack, block ingress/egress routes, and prevent repositioning of enemy reserves.

Protection

4-122. The battalion may have Stingers or Avengers in a direct support role during a search and attack. In addition to providing security for the CP or moving with the main body, AD elements can also operate from key terrain overwatching a key route or air avenue of approach. If this is done, the battalion must consider providing the attachment with security.

Command and Control

4-123. The commander positions himself to receive information and transmit orders during the search and attack. He plans for shifting assets or committing the reserve. The command post must be positioned to best influence the battle and to allow the commander the best vantage point to see the battlefield. This may not necessarily be with the main effort.

INTEGRATION OF FIRE SUPPORT, PROTECTION, AND SUSTAINMENT ELEMENTS

4-124. The battalion commander determines how to integrate and maximize the employment of additional combat enablers.

Movement and Maneuver

4-125. Priority of engineer support is to mobility. Elements of the supporting engineer unit will likely join the reconnaissance and security force to reconnoiter obstacles and routes. Engineers travel with the advance guard to assist in mobility of the advance guard and main body. Situational obstacles are planned to support the security forces and the advance guard.

Fire Support

4-126. The lead elements will usually remain within supporting distance of the artillery to allow responsive fires. Priority targets are allocated to the reconnaissance and security force and the advance guard. Given the emphasis on proactive counterfires and the likelihood for operating in close terrain, the battalion must rely on its organic mortars.

4-127. The battalion mortars are normally placed under the operational control of the advance guard to reinforce the company's organic mortars and to provide responsive fires and smoke to support initial actions on contact.

4-128. Close air support, if available, interdicts enemy counterattack forces or destroys defensive positions (Appendix E).

Protection

4-129. Air defense artillery assets generally provide area coverage for the battalion and cover movement through restricted areas. However, some AD assets may provide direct support for the advance guard. Regardless of the command relationship, AD elements operate well forward on the battlefield.

Sustainment

4-130. The object of sustainment operations is to provide support as close to the point of need as possible. Decentralized support allows the FSC commander to weight the battle logistically or surge as required.

4-131. The XO and S-4 determine and anticipate mission requirements for more support of Class V. This support can be pushed forward from the brigade support battalion (BSB), configured, uploaded, and positioned at the combat trains. The FSC may push emergency resupply of Class V forward to logistics release points (LRPs) or to company locations as needed.

4-132. The battalion medical platoon habitually establishes the battalion aid station under the direction of the battalion TOC and CTCP and locates it where it can best support the battalion's operations. Company medical teams are generally attached to each company to provide medical coverage to each rifle platoon. The battalion medical platoon's evacuation squads are normally positioned forward with one squad per company to augment the company medical teams and assist with the evacuation of casualties. The maneuver company's 1SG has operational control of the squad(s).

4-133. In the offense, the factors of METT-TC determine whether casualties are evacuated by ambulance to a casualty collection point or back to the BAS. Medical evacuation personnel and a ground ambulance from the FSB/BSB medical company are normally pre-positioned with each BAS. The supporting medical company may also establish an ambulance exchange point (AXP) between the supported BAS and the medical company Level II medical treatment facility (MTF). The AXP enhances medical evacuation operations by shorting the amount of time supporting medical company ambulances are away from the supported BAS. The AXP operations also permit reevaluation of patients to determine if their condition and or priority for evacuation have changed.

PLANNING CONSIDERATIONS

4-134. Planning for movement to contact begins by developing the concept of the operation with the decisive point on the objective. The commander then plans backward to the line of departure while considering the conduct of the breach and the position of the isolation, support, assault, and breach assets.

Reconnaissance and Surveillance

4-135. The first consideration for a movement to contact is reconnaissance and surveillance planning. The battalion is one of several elements executing the reconnaissance and surveillance plan.

4-136. The first priority is to determine anticipated enemy locations, strengths, and actions. Potential enemy mission, intent, objectives, defensive locations, use of key terrain, avenues of approach and routes, engagement areas, and obstacles are among the items that must be identified early and incorporated into the reconnaissance and surveillance plan.

4-137. Various elements within the battalion conduct reconnaissance and surveillance operations.

Scout Platoon

4-138. The scout platoon has the Soldiers that are best trained to function as the "eyes and ears" for the battalion and is the element that can be committed the quickest. The battalion scout platoon's primary role is to monitor NAIs and TAIs. It is also used to confirm and identify enemy locations, orientations, compositions, and dispositions. Before, during, and after the movement to contact, it reports its observations and significant changes in enemy activity.

Ground Surveillance Radar

4-139. Ground surveillance radar (GSR) detects moving vehicles and personnel in open terrain at long ranges and provides information on the number, location, disposition, and types of targets. Normally, GSR covers open, high-speed approaches where early detection is critical. It also monitors defiles and detects enemy reconnaissance elements using oblique shots across the battalion's sector along open, flat areas. The integration of GSR allows the scout platoon to focus on complex, urban, close, and restricted terrain.

Remote Sensors

4-140. Remote sensors are assets that belong to units outside of the battalion, but they are frequently placed in DS of the battalion. These assets must be emplaced and monitored with the information going to the battalion S-2 who relays it to higher headquarters.

Snipers and Other Individual Weapon Platforms

4-141. The sniper squad is trained and equipped to man observation posts (OPs) in support of the reconnaissance and surveillance effort (Appendix F). Each weapon platform, especially during patrolling or manning observation points, is a source of information that needs to be integrated into the overall ISR effort. The weapons company also has vehicle mounted optics which can observe and positively identify enemy forces at extended ranges.

Unmanned Aircraft Systems

4-142. Numerous UAS are available to support the reconnaissance and surveillance plan. Small UAS provide the battalion organic and responsive capabilities which can reconnoiter and observe suspected enemy positions and activities. However, small UAS are limited by their short range which could compromise manned positions. Longer range tactical UAS at the BCT level can be tasked to contribute to the effort or observe areas not covered by other assets.

4-143. A strong reconnaissance and surveillance effort requires relevant and rapid information exchange between the battalion and the BCT. Intelligence, surveillance, and reconnaissance actions result in information dominance and, once established, can convert the movement to contact into an attack.

MOVEMENT AND MANEUVER

4-144. The battalion plan for a movement to contact should be flexible and promote subordinate initiative. Developing a simple scheme of maneuver, issuing a clear commander's intent, and developing plans to execute likely maneuver options that may occur during execution contribute to flexibility and subordinate initiative.

4-145. In developing his concept, the commander anticipates where he is likely to meet the enemy and then determines how he intends to develop the situation that leads to an attack under favorable conditions. The commander focuses on determining the battalion's organization and formation that best retains his freedom of action upon contact and supports his concept against known or anticipated enemy forces.

4-146. The commander and his staff develop plans for the maneuver options of attack, report and bypass, defense, and retrograde based on the higher commander's intent and the situation. They define the conditions in terms of the enemy and friendly strengths and dispositions that are likely to trigger the execution of each maneuver option. They identify likely locations of engagements based on known or suspected enemy locations. The commander states the bypass criteria for the advance guard. He must recognize the loss of tempo that is created by the lead element fighting every small enemy force it encounters. The advance guard may attack small enemy forces that it can quickly destroy without losing momentum. However, larger or more stubborn enemy forces are best bypassed and destroyed by the main body or a follow and support element.

4-147. The scheme of maneuver covers the battalion's actions from LD to occupation of the final objective or limit of advance (LOA). The scheme of maneuver specifically addresses—

- Actions at known or likely enemy locations.
- Methods for moving through and crossing danger areas.
- The battalion's formation, movement technique, and known locations where each will change.
- Actions and array of forces at the final objective or LOA to prepare for future operations.
- Decision points and criteria for execution of maneuver options that may develop during execution.

4-148. The following fundamentals guide the commander in developing the scheme of maneuver for a movement to contact:

- Focus all efforts on finding the enemy by developing a strong reconnaissance, surveillance, and target acquisition effort and through the employment of robust security forces.
- Make contact (if possible) with electronic means or observation by UAS first. If that is not possible, then make contact with the smallest force possible, consistent with protecting the force.
- Make initial contact with small, self-contained forces to avoid decisive engagement of the main body. This procedure allows the commander maximum flexibility to develop the situation.
- Task-organize the force and use movement formations and techniques that enable the battalion to deploy and attack rapidly in any direction.
- Maintain the ability to mass combat power rapidly in any direction.
- Keep forces within supporting distances to facilitate a flexible response.
- Maintain contact, once gained, regardless of the maneuver option adopted.
- Rely on SOPs and drills to develop the situation and maintain tempo. The massing of all available combat power against the enemy once contact is made is critical to achieving success.
- Develop a flexible scheme of maneuver since the location of the engagement with the enemy is not known. Flexibility is achieved by incorporating multiple DPs and triggers into the plan based upon where engagements are likely.

4-149. The following are key considerations for the scheme of engineer operations.

- Task-organize engineer forces and mobility assets well forward with the advanced guard to support potential breaching operations.
- Ensure the reconnaissance plan integrates the collection of obstacle and terrain information.
- Maintain the flexibility to mass engineers to breach complex obstacles.
- Plan obstacle belts, obstacle control measures, and situational obstacles to support flank security. Develop and adjust obstacle locations and triggers for execution based on the battalion's movement and the enemy situation.
- Develop plans for the handoff of marked obstacles, lanes, and bypasses.
- Consider the requirement for route maintenance, clearance, and repair.

FIRE SUPPORT

4-150. The following are key considerations for the fire support (FS) plan.

- Facilitate responsive and decentralized fires by establishing a clear understanding of the essential fire support tasks for each phase of the operation. This understanding is critical to the success of the FS plan. Once the battalion makes contact, it shifts control of all available fires to the observer who is in the best position to control fires against the enemy.
- Plan targets based on known or suspected enemy locations and danger areas and to support future operations. Refine targets based on the reconnaissance effort as the operation progresses.
- Maximize the use of priority targets along the axis of advance. Plan triggers to put these targets into effect and cancel them based on the movement of the battalion.
- Ensure immediately responsive fire support to the lead elements by assigning priority of fires to the advance guard.
- Position observers effectively and maximize the use of lead maneuver forces to call for fires since they often have the best view of the enemy. Observers must understand the essential fires and effects tasks for each phase of the operation.
- Synchronize the movement and positioning of artillery and mortars with the tempo of the battalion and the FS requirements.
- Decide if spilt based mortar platoon operations best support the battalion movement to contact.

PROTECTION

4-151. The following are key considerations for CBRN planning (Appendix F):

- Ensure the scout platoon is prepared for CBRN reconnaissance tasks.
- Immediately disseminate CBRN threats, once detected, throughout the BCT.
- Integrate and synchronize the use of smoke to support critical actions such as breaching or assaults. Ensure artillery and mortar smoke and any DS smoke support assets attached to the battalion complement each other.
- Develop decontamination plans based on the commander's priorities and vulnerability analysis.

SUSTAINMENT

4-152. The following are key considerations for the sustainment plan.

- Ensure the sustainment plan is responsive and flexible enough to support all battalion maneuver options.
- Support the battalion using the FCS for Class I, Class II, Class V, medical, and maintenance and repair parts support.
- Always maintain internal security whether conducting resupply operations or remaining static in the battalion rear area or the BSA.
- Use all available assets (FM, digital, visual) to develop and maintain an accurate enemy picture behind the lead maneuver elements.
- Plan and rehearse for enemy contact.
- Plan and coordinate the locations, displacements, and routes of sustainment assets to maintain responsive support.
- Plan and coordinate for aerial resupply.

Preparation

4-153. During preparation, the battalion commander and staff will receive the most current information from organic and higher echelon unit's scout and surveillance assets. They must ensure that FRAGOs are published and that plans are updated to reflect any changes. The battalion commander must ensure his subordinates understand his concept and intent and their individual missions as new information becomes available. He normally uses backbriefs and rehearsals to ensure his intent is understood and all actions are integrated and synchronized. Simple, flexible plans that rely on SOPs and are rehearsed repetitively against various enemy conditions are essential to success.

Inspections

4-154. The commander inspects subordinate unit preparations to ensure they are consistent with his intent and concept of operations. He emphasizes subordinate plans to move through danger areas, conduct actions on contact, and transition into a maneuver option. The commander ensures each subordinate force understands its assigned mission during the movement and the potential maneuver options that may develop during execution.

Rehearsals

4-155. The battalion's leadership rehearses the plan against a wide range of likely enemy COAs that would cause the battalion to execute various maneuver options at different times and locations. The goal is to rehearse the battalion's subordinate commanders on potential situations that may arise during execution and force them to make decisions under the anticipated conditions of the battle. This promotes flexibility and agility while reinforcing the commander's intent.

4-156. The commander seeks to rehearse the operation from initiation to occupation of the final objective or LOA. If done properly, the rehearsals will also include the decision points and actions taken upon each decision. Often, due to time constraints, the commander prioritizes the maneuver options and enemy COAs to be rehearsed based on the time available. The rehearsal focuses on locating the enemy, developing the situation, executing a maneuver option, exercising direct and indirect fire control measures, and exploiting success. The rehearsal must consider the potential of encountering stationary or moving enemy forces. Other actions to consider during rehearsals include—

- Actions to cross known danger areas.
- The advance guard making contact with a small enemy force.
- The advance guard making contact with a large force beyond its capabilities to defeat.
- The advance guard making contact with an obstacle the reconnaissance and surveillance force has not identified and reported.
- A flank security force making contact with a small force.
- A flank security force making contact with a large force beyond its capability to defeat.
- Actions to report and bypass an enemy force (based on the bypass criteria).
- Transition into a maneuver option.

Reconnaissance and Surveillance

4-157. The ISR effort is on-going during the preparation for the movement to contact. The primary focus of the reconnaissance and surveillance effort is to locate the enemy without being detected.

Locate Enemy

4-158. Locate the enemy early in order to--

- Confirm or deny the situational template
- Update the course of action
- Attack the enemy in depth
- Select favorable terrain and positions for the direct fire engagement
- Position observers, and
- Deploy before contact.

4-159.   When they detect enemy forces, reconnaissance and surveillance assets shift to determine the full extent of the enemy's strength and disposition. Reconnaissance assets gather vital information on the enemy force and try to determine the enemy force's vulnerabilities, such as an exposed flank, and the enemy's strengths. BCT elements, such as the reconnaissance squadron, will execute a reconnaissance hand over of located enemy positions in the battalion's area to the battalion scout platoon. If the scout platoon encounters obstacles, it determines size, location, and composition and seeks bypasses. If it finds a bypass, the reconnaissance elements mark and/or assist in guiding following units to the bypass. If it cannot find a bypass, the scout platoon advises the commander on locations for a breach and assists in guiding forces to the breach site. Snipers provide long range observation and precision fires to overwatch the potential breach site.

4-160.   The battalion advance guard maintains contact with the scout platoon to coordinate combat actions and exchange information. As the scout platoon locates enemy positions, it hands these locations off to the advance guard. In some cases, elements of the scout platoon maintain visual contact with the enemy and guide the advance guard maneuver forces. Regardless of the technique used, these actions should be rehearsed and closely coordinated during execution to prevent fratricide and confusion. The advance guard often uses UAS to locate and target enemy units overwatching the breach site.

Support Battalion's Movement

4-161.   Due to the need to maintain a rapid tempo, the scout platoon emphasizes terrain and obstacle reconnaissance primarily focused along the battalion's axis of advance. The scout platoon seeks to identify and confirm restricted terrain, trafficability of roads and routes, conditions of bridges, and locations of fording sites. The platoon also reconnoiters potentially dangerous areas such as obstacles, defiles, likely enemy positions, or possible ambush sites. If the scout platoon cannot clear these areas, the advance guard must assume a more deliberate movement technique.

Support Actions upon Contact

4-162.   Once a reconnaissance and surveillance element locates an enemy force, the battalion continuously observes it. Reconnaissance assets assist friendly forces by guiding them along the best routes to engage the enemy. As contact develops, reconnaissance assets report enemy actions and battle damage assessment.

EXECUTION

4-163.   The battalion moves rapidly to maintain the advantage of a rapid tempo. However, the commander must balance the need for speed with the requirement for security. He bases this decision on the effectiveness of the reconnaissance and surveillance effort, friendly mobility assets, effects of terrain, and the enemy's capabilities. The battalion must closely track the movement and location of subordinate companies and other battalion units. This ensures that security forces provide adequate security for the main body and that they remain within supporting range of the main body, mortars, and artillery. The movement of fire support, protection, and sustainment units is controlled by the Infantry battalion or their parent organizations (depending on command and support relationships), which adjust their movements to meet support requirements, avoid congestion of routes, and ensure responsiveness.

Actions at Obstacles

4-164.   Obstacles pose a significant threat to the battalion's momentum because the battalion's ability to breach obstacles is limited.

4-165.   Once a battalion element detects an obstacle, it immediately disseminates the location and description throughout the battalion. The battalion seeks a secure and favorable bypass. If a bypass is available, the unit in contact with the obstacle exploits, marks, and reports the bypass. Enemy forces normally overwatch obstacles. Units should approach all obstacles and restricted terrain with the same diligence with which they approach a known enemy position.

4-166. When the battalion must breach, it maneuvers to suppress and obscure any enemy forces overwatching the obstacle and then reduces the obstacle to support its movement. Engineer forces from the main body support the breach effort by creating lanes, improving the marking of lanes, and guiding the main body through the obstacle. Battalion snipers can provide long range observation and fires on enemy units overwatching the obstacle.

Destruction of Enemy Forces

4-167. The battalion destroys enemy forces with a combination of indirect fires and maneuver.

4-168. Depending on the commander's bypass criteria and the composition of the advance guard, the advance guard may fix company or smaller size enemy forces identified by the reconnaissance and surveillance force. Once committed as the fixing force, the advance guard fixes the enemy until the main body can destroy it.

4-169. The advance guard must provide the location of such a fixed enemy force to the battalion S-2, who then disseminates the information to all units in the battalion. Cross-talk between main body and fixing force commanders is critical to coordinate actions and avoid fratricide. The fixing force directs or guides the finishing force to the best location to attack the enemy. Once the battalion destroys the enemy, all forces continue the advance.

Report and Bypass

4-170. When conducting a movement to contact as part of a larger force, the higher commander establishes bypass criteria that allow the battalion to report and bypass enemy forces of a specific size.

4-171. When an enemy force meets the criteria, the battalion fixes the enemy force and leaves a small force to maintain contact while the remainder of the battalion continues the advance. Once bypassed, the destruction of the enemy force becomes the responsibility of the BCT.

4-172. Bypassed forces present a serious threat to forces that follow the maneuver elements, especially sustainment elements. As they move around these threats, it is imperative the bypassed enemy forces' locations and strengths are disseminated throughout the battalion to enable following units to properly orient their security forces.

Meeting Engagement

4-173. A meeting engagement is a combat action that occurs when the battalion, not completely deployed for battle, engages a sizable enemy force at an unexpected time and place. The enemy force may be moving or stationary. A meeting engagement is most probable during a movement to contact. The goal, once in contact, is to maneuver and overwhelm the enemy with combat power before he can react. This requires the commander to keep his force in a posture ready to act immediately to contact and develop the situation. Subordinate companies must act on contact, develop the situation, report, and gain a position of advantage over the enemy to give the battalion time and position to act effectively. The battalion's success depends on its subordinate units' ability to effectively develop the situation. The steps necessary to accomplish this follow:

- Usually, the reconnaissance and surveillance force makes initial contact. They must determine the size and activity of the enemy force and avoid being fixed or destroyed. If possible, the reconnaissance and surveillance force avoids detection.
- If the enemy is moving, the reconnaissance and surveillance force determines the direction of movement and the size and composition of the force. The reconnaissance and surveillance force's observers can disrupt lead enemy forces by placing indirect fires on them. Speed of decision and execution is critical when the enemy is moving.

- If the enemy is stationary, the reconnaissance and surveillance force determines whether the enemy is occupying prepared positions and is reinforced by obstacles and minefields. The reconnaissance and surveillance force tries to identify any crew served weapon or antitank weapon positions, the enemy's flanks, and gaps in his positions.
- The advance guard maneuvers to overpower and destroy platoon-size and smaller security forces. Larger forces normally require deployment of the main body. The advance guard protects the main body by fixing enemy forces larger than platoon size, which allows the battalion main body to retain its freedom to maneuver.
- In developing the situation, the advance guard commander maintains pressure on the enemy by fire and movement. He probes and conducts a vigorous reconnaissance of the enemy's flanks to determine the enemy's exact location, composition, and disposition. The advance guard transmits this information to the battalion commander.
- The battalion commander uses this information to develop a plan of action by selecting a maneuver option from the several actions-on-contact options developed during planning.

Maneuver Options

4-174. It is paramount that the battalion commander has timely intelligence so he can select the appropriate maneuver option. Normally, the commander makes the final decision for execution of a maneuver option based on the progress of the initial engagement of the advance guard. The movement to contact generally ends with the commitment of the main body. The following paragraphs provide a general description of the options that may develop after a movement to contact.

Bypass

4-175. If rapid forward movement is required, and if the BCT commander has authorized bypass of enemy forces, the battalion can bypass. If the size and mobility of the bypassed force represents a threat, the battalion must fix or contain the enemy force until released by the BCT.

Hasty Ambush

4-176. Ambush is effective against a moving or infiltrating force that is not aware of the presence of the battalion. Instead of immediately engaging the enemy, the advance guard (and possibly the entire battalion) moves into hasty firing positions oriented on an engagement area. The battalion commander continues to maneuver reconnaissance and surveillance assets to gather information on the enemy and prepare for the next engagement. When most of the enemy is in the engagement area, the battalion uses massed fires and maneuver to attack the enemy.

Attack

4-177. The battalion commander directs an attack when he--

- Has detailed knowledge of the enemy provided by his reconnaissance element,
- Has greater combat power than the enemy, or
- Determines that the battalion can reach a decisive outcome.

4-178. Then, he--

- Develops a scheme of maneuver and concept of fires for the attack
- Distributes orders to subordinate companies.
- Employs fires, CAS, and situational obstacles.
- Controls movement, deployment, and any changes in the task organization of the battalion's forces.

- After a successful attack, continues the movement to contact or executes other missions as directed by the BCT commander.

Defend

4-179. The battalion commander directs a defense when the battalion has insufficient combat power to attack, or when the enemy's strength forces the battalion to halt and prepare for a more deliberate attack (Figure 4-16). The battalion maneuvers to the best available defensible terrain. The commander may direct the advance guard or another security force to delay an enemy attack. The purpose of this is to provide time for the battalion to deploy.

4-180. The companies deploy, establish security, launch small UAS, array their forces, and develop fire plans. The company commander emphasizes flank protection and coordination with adjacent units. As the enemy attacks, the battalion commander repositions and maneuvers forces to defeat the enemy through massed fires, situational obstacles, and counterattacks. The battalion commander seeks to defeat an attacking enemy force and create the opportunity for offensive action. In some cases, the battalion may need to retain its position to allow the BCT commander time to commit additional forces.

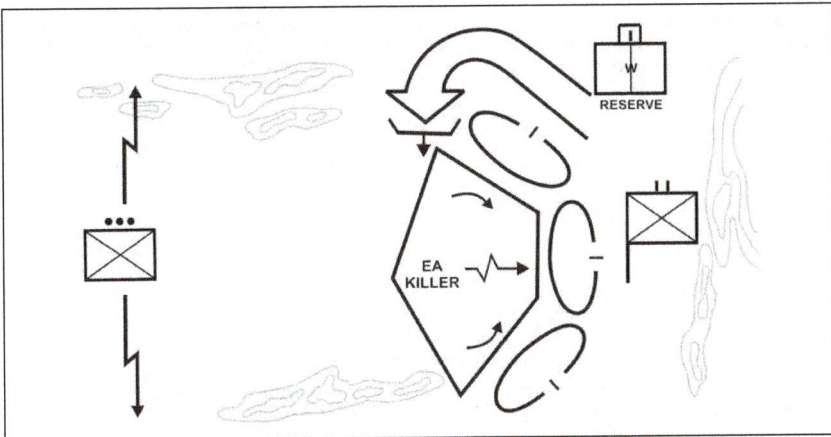

Figure 4-16. Concept of defense.

ATTACKS

4-181. Attacks range along a continuum defined at one end by fragmentary orders that direct rapid execution and at the other end by detailed plans and orders. Attacks rely more on an implicit understanding than on electronic communication with detailed orders and appropriate branches and sequels that make understanding explicit. At one extreme of the continuum, the battalion discovers the general enemy situation through a movement to contact and conducts an attack as a continuation of the meeting engagement to exploit a temporary advantage in relative combat power and to preempt enemy actions. At the other extreme of the continuum, the battalion moves into an attack from a reserve position or assembly area with detailed knowledge of the enemy, a task organization designed specifically for the attack, and a fully rehearsed plan. Most attacks fall somewhere between the two ends of the continuum.

CHARACTERISTICS

4-182. An attack at the battalion level is a type of offensive action characterized by close combat, direct fire, and movement and supported by indirect fires. When the battalion commander decides to attack, he masses the effects of overwhelming combat power against a portion (or portions) of the enemy force with a tempo and intensity that the enemy cannot match. The following paragraphs discuss the tactics for conducting—

- A force-oriented attack against a stationary enemy force.
- A force-oriented attack against a moving enemy force.
- A terrain-oriented attack.

4-183. A terrain-oriented objective requires the battalion to seize, secure, or retain a designated geographical area. A force-oriented objective requires the battalion to focus its efforts on a designated enemy force. The enemy force may be stationary or moving. All attacks depend on synchronization and integration of all WFF assets for success. They require planning, coordination, and time to prepare.

FORCE-ORIENTED ATTACK AGAINST A STATIONARY ENEMY FORCE

4-184. The battalion may attack a stationary enemy force as part of a counterattack, spoiling attack, or as an initial attack against an enemy defense. The battalion may also attack a stationary force as part of a BCT movement to contact or exploitation.

Planning Considerations

4-185. The focus of planning is to develop a fully synchronized plan that masses all available combat power against the enemy.

Scheme of Maneuver

4-186. The battalion directs its decisive operation against an objective, ideally an identified enemy weakness, which will cause the collapse of the enemy defense. The battalion seeks to attack the enemy's flanks, rear, or supporting formations causing disintegration or dislocation. By so doing, the enemy loses control of its systems and the enemy commander's options are reduced. Concurrently, the Infantry battalion retains the initiative and reduces its own vulnerabilities.

4-187. The commander seeks to identify: an unobserved or covered and concealed avenue of approach to the objective, a small unit lacking mutual support within the enemy defense, or a weak flank that he can exploit to gain a tactical advantage. When attacking a well-prepared enemy defense, the commander normally plans to isolate and then destroy small vulnerable portions of the enemy defense in sequence. The commander and staff develop the plan using a reverse planning process starting from actions on the objective and working back to the LD or assembly area. They incorporate plans for exploiting success and opportunities that may develop during execution. They emphasize synchronization of movement, precise direct and indirect fires, and support throughout the attack.

4-188. The commander and staff consider the enemy's strengths and obstacles to determine when and where the battalion may need breaching operations. The size of the enemy force overwatching the obstacle drives the type of breach the battalion conducts. The commander and staff consider the enemy's ability to mass combat power, reposition his forces, or commit his reserve. The battalion then develops a scheme of maneuver to mass sufficient combat power at an enemy weakness. The location selected for breaching and penetration depends largely on a weakness in the enemy's defense where its covering fires are limited.

4-189. The reverse planning process is an essential tool in building an effective plan to attack a defending enemy. By starting with actions on the objective and working back to the line of departure, the staff can allocate combat power, mobility assets, and indirect fires (suppression and obscuration).

Fire Support

4-190. The following are considerations for the FS plan:

- Position fire support assets to support the reconnaissance effort.
- Plan suppressive and obscuration fires at the point of penetration.
- Plan suppressive and obscuration fires in support of breaching operations.
- Plan fires in support of the approach to the objective. These fires engage enemy security forces, destroy bypassed enemy forces, and screen friendly movement.
- Synchronize fires on the objective to suppress, neutralize, or destroy critical enemy forces that can most affect the battalion's closure on the objective.
- Plan fires beyond the objective to support an attack or defense, or to isolate the objective to prevent the egress or ingress of threat forces.
- Use indirect fires and CAS to delay or neutralize repositioning enemy forces and reserves.
- Plan locations of critical friendly zones (CFZs) to protect critical actions such as support-by-fire positions, breaching efforts, and mortar assets.
- Use risk estimate distances (RED) to determine triggers to initiate, shift, and cease loading of rounds.
- Use echelon fires to maintain continuous suppression of enemy forces throughout the movement to and actions on the objective.

Movement and maneuver

4-191. Maintaining the mobility of the battalion in offensive operations is critical. The battalion engineer must plan and allocate mobility resources to the security forces (reconnaissance and surveillance and advance guard) and to the main body. The security force has just enough mobility resources to cover its own movement and to complete the reconnaissance mission. The advance guard needs enough resources to conduct breaching operations such as reducing obstacles and opening lanes for the main body to pass. If the obstacle is dense or covered by a relatively larger force, the main body deploys to conduct a breaching operation. Engineer task organization is based on supporting battalion in-stride breaching operations with minimal engineer assets under battalion control to transition to a battalion deliberate breach, if needed. The battalion uses situational obstacles to attack an enemy's vulnerability or a specific course of action and can use mobile obstacle detachments to help secure the battalion flanks. The following are considerations for the scheme of engineer operations:

- Always search for a bypass to an obstacle.
- Plan for adjustment of the breach location based on the latest obstacle intelligence.
- Ensure information on obstacles receives immediate battalion-wide dissemination, including fire support, protection, and sustainment platforms and units.
- Ensure adequate mobility support is task organized well forward during the approach to the objective to support breaching requirements.
- Retain ability to mass engineers to support breaching operations.
- Support assaulting forces with engineers to breach enemy protective obstacles.
- Ensure adequate guides, traffic control, and lane improvements to support movement of follow on forces and sustainment vehicle traffic.
- Use situational obstacles for flank security.

Protection

In offensive operations, air defense units move to the position from which they can best protect the battalion. The S-2 and AD officer must determine where likely enemy air avenues of approach are located, and plan positions accordingly. Priorities for protection may include companies, fire support, engineer elements, C2 nodes, and logistics assets. AD coverage is increased in areas and activities most vulnerable to air attack such as breaching operations or movements through restricted terrain. The following are considerations for CBRN support:

- The scout platoon should be prepared for CBRN reconnaissance tasks.
- Disseminate any detected CBRN threats throughout the battalion immediately.
- Integrate and synchronize the use of smoke to support critical actions such as breaching or assaults. Ensure artillery, mortar, and mechanical smoke are complementary.
- Develop decontamination plans based on the commander's priorities and vulnerability analysis.
- Disseminate planned and active decontamination sites.

Sustainment

4-192.   The following are considerations for the sustainment plan:

- Synchronize the movement and positioning of sustainment assets with the scheme of maneuver to ensure immediate support of anticipated requirements. This synchronized plan must cover movement from SP to the objective.
- Ensure adequate sustainment support to the reconnaissance and surveillance effort. The HHC commander must plan and integrate timely resupply and evacuation support of forward reconnaissance and surveillance assets into the reconnaissance and surveillance plan. He focuses on medical evacuation, especially air evacuation.
- Plan immediate support to high-risk operations such as breaching or assaults through the forward positioning of support assets.
- Plan for reorganization on or near the objective once the battalion secures the objective. Articulate clear priorities of support during reorganization.

Preparation

4-193.   The battalion uses available time before the attack to conduct extensive reconnaissance and surveillance, precombat checks and inspections, and rehearsals while concealing attack preparations from the enemy. The commander and staff refine the plan based on continuously updated intelligence. Subordinates conduct parallel planning as well as start their preparation for the attack immediately after the battalion issues a FRAGO. As more intelligence becomes available, the battalion commander revises orders and distributes them; thereby giving subordinates more time to prepare for the attack. Regardless of the time available, the commander must conduct detailed planning and supervision of subordinate preparations. The commander will also use this preparation time to conduct brief backs and back briefs with his subordinate commanders to ensure they understand their tasks, purposes, and are planning/executing within his intent. Usually during the battalion's preparation phase, the reconnaissance element is collecting information to confirm or deny the situational template. This allows the commander and staff time to incorporate any changes to the original course of action before executing.

Inspections

4-194.   The commander supervises subordinate troop leading procedures to ensure planning and preparations are on track and consistent with his intent. The commander may inspect subordinate unit order briefs and rehearsals. He focuses his inspections on the decisive operation and critical events such as assaults, breaching operations, and passage of lines. Since the commander cannot be everywhere at once, he maximizes the use of other key leaders and technology to assist him. The requirement that subordinate graphics and/or orders are provided back to the battalion staff allows the staff the opportunity to ensure they are consistent with the battalion plans.

Rehearsals

4-195. The battalion usually conducts rehearsals, but the type and technique may vary based on time available and the security that is required. During the combined-arms rehearsal, the battalion S-2 portrays a thinking, uncooperative enemy with emphasis on enemy repositioning, employment of fires, and commitment of reserves. The primary focus of the rehearsal is actions on the objective. Each subordinate commander addresses the conduct of his mission as the rehearsal progresses. The rehearsal places special emphasis on triggers and the coordinated maneuver of forces. All subordinate commanders must accurately portray how long it takes to complete assigned tasks and how much space is required by their force. Direct and indirect fire plans are covered in detail, to include the massing, distribution, shifting, and control of fires. The commander ensures subordinate plans are coordinated and consistent with his intent. The rehearsal also covers the following:

- Plans to execute follow on missions or exploit success.
- Likely times and locations where a reserve is needed and what are the commitment criteria.
- Execution of the FS plan, to include shifting of fires, employment of CAS, adjusting of FSCMs, and positioning of observers.
- Breaching operations.
- Passage of lines.
- Contingency plans for actions against enemy counterattacks, repositioning, commitment of reserves, or use of CBRN capabilities.
- Consolidation and reorganization.
- Execution of branches or sequels assigned by the brigade.
- Execution of the sustainment plan, to include unit maintenance collection point (UMCP), CASEVAC, movement and activities of combat trains, rear area movement and activities, and emergency resupply.

Reconnaissance and Surveillance

4-196. Effective and current intelligence is a prerequisite for a successful attack. Before conducting an attack, the commander needs to determine the enemy's strength and disposition. During hasty operations the entire intelligence collection, analysis, and dissemination process must rapidly respond to the commander's critical information requirements. The commander must receive an accurate picture of the enemy's defense so he can decide on a COA and act faster than the enemy can react.

4-197. When preparing for a deliberate operation, the commander and staff participate in development of the ISR plan. This well-resourced and coordinated ISR effort paints a detailed picture of the enemy situation before an attack. This reconnaissance effort must include redundant information gathering systems to ensure continuous flow of information to the battalion and correspondingly from the battalion to the companies. The battalion commander uses this intelligence to decide on a COA and make refinements to the plan. The ISR effort also provides him with continuous updates during the attack so he can adjust execution of the operation based on the enemy's reactions.

Enemy's Current Array of Forces

4-198. The intelligence available to the battalion comes from a continuous stream of information that begins with Joint Interagency Intergovernmental Multinational (JIIM), and SOF assets that funnel down to the BCT and then to the battalion (Appendix G).

4-199. The first priority is to confirm information available on the enemy's strength, composition, and disposition. The next priorities are the effects of weather and terrain, and how the enemy is likely to fight. The S-2 tries to identify what the enemy will do and what information the battalion needs to confirm the enemy's action. The battalion ISR effort focuses on identifying indicators required for confirming the enemy's actual COA. This information is vital in answering the commander's information and intelligence requirements and helps the staff in developing and refining plans. Ideally, the battalion does not make final decisions on how to execute the attack until it can identify the current array of enemy forces. Key areas to identify for a defending enemy force include—

- Composition, disposition, and strength of enemy forces along a flank or at an area selected for penetration.
- Composition, strength, and disposition of security and disruption forces.
- Location, orientation, type, depth, and composition of obstacles.
- Locations of secure bypasses around obstacles.
- Composition, strength, and disposition of defending combat formations within the enemy's main battle area (MBA).
- Composition, strength, and location of reserves.
- Location of routes the enemy may use to counterattack or reinforce his defense.
- Type of enemy fortifications and survivability effort.

4-200. Reconnaissance forces patrol to collect information. As time permits, reconnaissance and surveillance assets observe the enemy defense from advantageous positions (OPs) to locate gaps in the enemy's defense, identify weapons systems and fighting positions, view rehearsals and positioning, and determine the enemy's security activities and times of decreased readiness. The S-2 must discern any enemy deception efforts such as phony obstacles, dummy emplacements, and deception positions designed to confuse an attacker.

Enemy Engagement Areas

4-201. The battalion commander, supported by the S-2, seeks to define the limits of the enemy engagement areas. This includes where the enemy can mass fires, weapon ranges, direct fire integration with obstacles, ability to shift fires, and mutual support between positions. This analysis requires effective terrain analysis, confirmed locations of enemy weapons systems (by system type), and a good understanding of the enemy's weapons capabilities and tactics. Reconnaissance forces report locations, orientation, and composition of defending weapons systems and obstacles. The analysis of the enemy's direct fire plan assists the commander in determining where the probable line of contact is, when the battalion must transition to maneuver, how to echelon indirect fires, and how feasible his scheme of maneuver is. The use of long-range indirect fires allows the commander to shape what the enemy can do relative to engagement areas. Key to such actions is the emplacement of obstacles.

Enemy Vulnerabilities

4-202. The overall ISR effort also seeks to identify enemy vulnerabilities that may include—

- Gaps in the enemy's defense.
- Exposed or weak flanks.
- Enemy units that lack mutual support.
- Unobserved or weakly defended avenues of approach to the enemy's flank or rear.
- Covered and concealed routes that allow the battalion to close on the enemy.
- Weak obstacles or fortifications in an enemy defense, especially along a flank.

Support on Approach to Objective

4-203. Reconnaissance elements initially focus on the enemy's security and disruption forces forward of his main defense to locate enemy positions and obstacles along the battalion's planned routes of advance. Reconnaissance forces also locate gaps and routes that allow them to infiltrate into the enemy main defensive or rear area. The reconnaissance and surveillance effort seeks to locate enemy forces that may reposition and affect the battalion's approach to the enemy's main defense. Successful attacks depend on reconnaissance forces to call indirect fires on targets in the enemy's rear that isolate the enemy front line forces and prevent them from being reinforced. A rapid, secure advance to the enemy's main defense depends on the reconnaissance effort to locate enemy security forces and obstacles.

Execution

4-204.   The battalion commander positions reconnaissance and surveillance assets to maintain observation of enemy reactions to the battalion's maneuver on the objective. Reconnaissance assets focus on areas that the enemy will likely use to reposition forces, commit reserves, and counterattack. As the engagement on the objective develops, reconnaissance forces report enemy reactions, repositioning, reinforcements, and battle damage assessment (BDA). Again, reconnaissance elements target and engage with indirect fires enemy repositioning forces, reserves, counterattacking forces, and other high-payoff targets. Early identification of enemy reactions is essential for the battalion to maintain the tempo and initiative during the attack.

Approach to Objective

4-205.   During the approach, the battalion is prepared to—

- Bypass or breach obstacles.
- React to all seven forms of contact (visual, physical, indirect, obstacles, aircraft, CBRN, and electronic warfare).
- Transition to different formations and techniques based on the terrain and enemy situation.
- Employ forces to screen or guard flanks that may become exposed or threatened during the approach.
- Avoid terrain features that are likely enemy artillery reference points, locations for chemical strikes, or locations for situational obstacles.
- Destroy or force the withdrawal of opposing enemy security and disruption forces.
- Minimize the effects of enemy deception.

4-206.   When the situation permits, a defending enemy generally establishes a security area around his forces to provide early warning of an attack, deny friendly reconnaissance, and disrupt the friendly force's attack. The strength of the enemy's security area depends on the time available, forces available, and his doctrine or pattern of operations. The battalion must counter the effects of enemy security forces to ensure an unimpeded and concealed approach. This starts before the attack when reconnaissance forces seek to locate enemy security forces. Once located, the commander has the following options available—

- Destroy them immediately with indirect fires and CAS (preferred option).
- Destroy them with indirect fires and CAS during the approach to the objective.
- Conduct limited objective attacks before execution of the main attack.
- Employ a strong advance guard to destroy or force the withdrawal of enemy security forces during the approach to the objective.
- Attack with sniper fire to reduce their effectiveness.

4-207.   The battalion must maintain a steady, controlled movement. Speed and dispersion, facilitated by information dominance, are the norm with massing of weapons effects to destroy the enemy's defense. If the formation is too slow or becomes too concentrated, it is vulnerable to massed enemy fires.

Actions on Objective

4-208.   Before the attack is initiated, the objective is isolated to prevent the ingress or egress of threat forces. The battalion commander must set favorable conditions before committing his forces. He does this using artillery, fixed wing and rotary wing CAS, organic mortars, a shaping operation from another maneuver battalion, and the use of any JIIM or SOF assets. The battalion commander then maneuvers combat forces and employs direct and indirect fires, situational obstacles, and smoke to execute decisive maneuver against the enemy. The commander commits maneuver forces and fires to isolate and then rupture a small vulnerable portion of the enemy's defense to gain a flank or create a penetration.

Dislocation

4-209. Attacking from an unexpected direction and time can also limit or even change the enemy courses of action. This is called dislocation; its effect is fleeting and must be exploited rapidly before the enemy can recover. If the battalion is successful in locating and attacking a position that is unexpected, the enemy defense may become untenable. The battalion uses precision attacks that target key enemy systems such as C2, indirect fires or reserve forces. Effective destruction of these key systems reduces the enemy control and causes enemy organizational collapse.

4-210. Attacking from an unexpected direction and time can also limit or even change the enemy courses of action. This is called dislocation; its effect is fleeting and must be exploited rapidly before the enemy can recover. If necessary, the battalion achieves final destruction of the enemy force through the attack of assaulting forces.

Fires

4-211. The battalion employs fires to weaken the enemy's position and set the conditions for success before closure within direct fire range of the enemy.

4-212. Initially, preparatory fires focus on the destruction of key enemy forces that can most affect the scheme of maneuver. For example, during an attack to penetrate an enemy defense, the initial focus of preparatory fires is to destroy the enemy positions at the selected point of penetration. Preparatory fires may also—

- Suppress or neutralize enemy reserves.
- Emplace artillery delivered situational obstacles to block enemy reserve routes into the objective.
- Deceive the enemy as to the battalion's actual intentions.
- Destroy enemy security and disruption forces.
- Obscure friendly movements and deployment.
- Destroy or neutralize the enemy's local C2 system.

4-213. The synchronization between indirect fires and maneuvering forces is critical. As maneuver forces approach the enemy defense, the commander uses triggers to shift fires and smoke to maintain continuous suppression and obscuration of the enemy. Proper timing, adjustment of fires, and detailed triggers dictated by risk estimate distances enable a secure closure by the maneuver force on the enemy's positions. The commander must monitor the success of the preparatory fires to determine whether adequate conditions exist for commitment of the force. Reconnaissance and surveillance elements provide BDA to the commander to assist him in making this decision. The commander may need to adjust the tempo of the battalion's approach to the objective based on the BDA.

Fixation of Enemy

4-214. The battalion can fix the bulk of the enemy forces into given positions or pursue a COA that limits the options available to the enemy.

4-215. In limiting or changing the options available to the enemy, the objective is to increase the uncertainty during the battle for the enemy. The primary goal at the point of attack is to isolate the unit targeted for destruction by preventing the enemy from repositioning and preventing another element from reinforcing it.

4-216. A company normally fixes the enemy force by attacking an objective that isolates a portion of the enemy's defense. In open terrain, the most common task for the shaping force is to fix the enemy with direct and indirect fire. In more complex terrain, the shaping force might have to seize terrain or destroy key enemy forces in limited objective attacks to pass the main effort to their objective. This ensures that the main effort does not have to fight their way and lose combat power en route to their objective. Demonstrations and feints may be used to fix the enemy; although, these shaping operations should exercise economy of force as they can usurp combat power from the decisive operation. The use of indirect fires and fixed wing and rotary wing CAS is vital in attacking enemy forces and reserves in depth to reduce their effectiveness or prevent their commitment against the battalion.

4-217. Before commitment, forces remain dispersed and outside the enemy's direct fire range, and they avoid exposing themselves to enemy observation. Forces not yet committed use this time to conduct final preparations and make adjustments to their plans. A key action during this time is the update of intelligence on the enemy locations and activities. The S-2 should have an updated intelligence summary available just before the battalion crossing the LD. The commander can use assault positions, phase lines, a terrain index reference system (TIRS), or checkpoints to control the positioning of the forces not yet committed. Commanders throughout the battalion continuously assess the situation. The commander commits subordinate forces when he is satisfied the desired levels of enemy suppression, destruction, and obscuration are achieved. Timely reporting, cross-talk, accurate assessments, and sharing of information by subordinate commanders are paramount to the success of the operation.

4-218. Precision long range sniper fires can assist in locating and destroying key equipment and personnel that hinder or prevent effective reaction by enemy forces to the battalion attack.

4-219. The weapons company can provide mobile, heavy weapons platforms that can easily fix enemy positions through fire superiority. The company may also be used in the isolation role of preventing the withdrawal of the enemy off the objective or preventing reinforcements from counterattacking.

Decisive Maneuver

4-220. The attacker must be agile enough to concentrate his forces and mass his combat power by decisive maneuver before the enemy can reorient his defense.

4-221. Normally, the destruction of a defending enemy force dictates an assault of the objective. The shaping force shifts direct and indirect fires and repositions as required to support the maneuver of assaulting forces. As the assaulting force is committed, the battalion commander and staff ensure that information is available and current on the following:

- Locations and type of enemy contact on the objective.
- Locations of reconnaissance forces.
- Locations of lanes and obstacles, to include lane markings.
- Recognition signals and guides.
- Specific routes for the approach.
- Locations and orientation of fires from friendly forces.
- Additions or modifications of graphic control measures.

4-222. The previously dispersed assaulting force assembles into combat formations and maneuvers to destroy the enemy forces and clear assigned objectives. The assaulting force moves along covered and concealed routes to an exposed enemy flank, created penetration, or other position of advantage. Smoke assists with concealing the movement of assaulting forces. The assault includes destruction of defending forces and clearance of trenches and fortifications at the point of attack. The commander's main focus is maintaining the momentum and security of the assaulting force. The reconnaissance and surveillance effort continues to report enemy repositioning, BDA, and enemy counteractions to the assault. The battalion limits enemy repositioning and massing against assaulting forces through intense supporting fires and CAS, a rapid assault, and employment of smoke. Once the assault force is through the point of attack, follow-on forces quickly move through the penetration and disperse to prevent enemy forces from concentrating fires on the battalion.

FORCE-ORIENTED ATTACK AGAINST A MOVING ENEMY FORCE

4-223. The battalion is likely to attack a moving enemy force, especially during a counterattack, spoiling attack, exploitation, or after a movement to contact.

Planning Considerations

4-224. The battalion in a force-oriented attack against a moving enemy force normally organizes in the same manner as a movement to contact and can be envisioned much like an ambush. Key planning considerations are outlined below (Figure 4-17).

Determination of Where to Fight Enemy

4-225. The decision on where to fight the enemy requires that the commander have information dominance over the enemy. The commander bases his decision on a clear understanding of the effects of the terrain, the enemy situation, and what the enemy is expected to do. The commander and his staff select the most advantageous location to fight the engagement and then determine other possible locations where the engagement may occur based on a slower- or faster-than-expected enemy advance or the enemy's use of an unlikely avenue of approach. They identify these areas as objectives, intermediate objectives, or engagement areas (EAs). The commander and staff develop control measures to help coordinate actions throughout the battalion's AO. The commander, primarily assisted by the S-3 and S-2, develops DPs for the commitment of the battalion to each location based on relative locations and rates of movement of the battalion and the enemy. The S-2 carefully selects NAIs to identify the enemy's rate and direction of movement to support the commander's decision of where to fight the engagement.

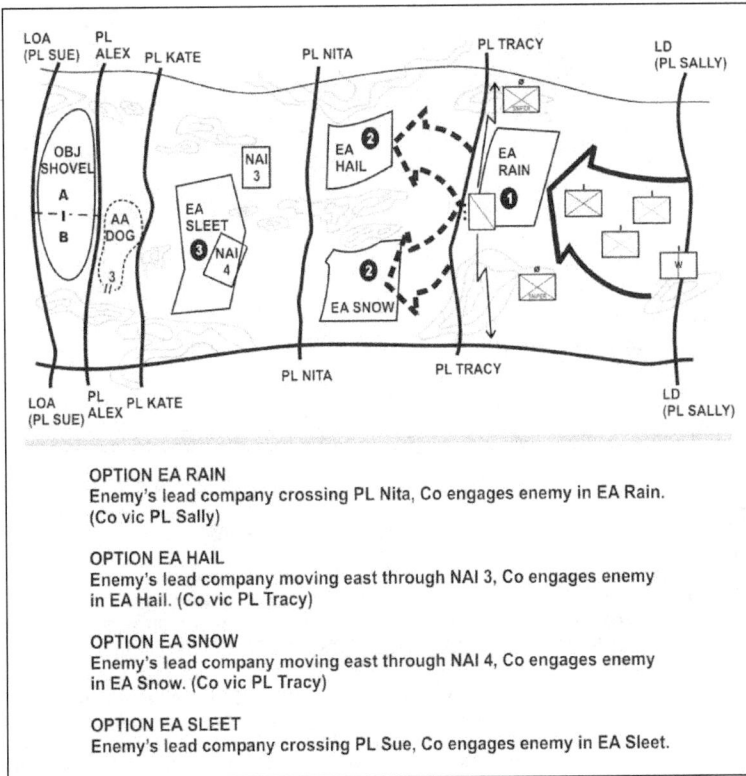

OPTION EA RAIN
Enemy's lead company crossing PL Nita, Co engages enemy in EA Rain.
(Co vic PL Sally)

OPTION EA HAIL
Enemy's lead company moving east through NAI 3, Co engages enemy
in EA Hail. (Co vic PL Tracy)

OPTION EA SNOW
Enemy's lead company moving east through NAI 4, Co engages enemy
in EA Snow. (Co vic PL Tracy)

OPTION EA SLEET
Enemy's lead company crossing PL Sue, Co engages enemy in EA Sleet.

Figure 4-17. Planning the attack.

Terrain Advantages

4-226. The commander uses the terrain to maximize the battalion's freedom of maneuver and lethality while limiting the freedom of maneuver available to the enemy. He looks for avenues of approach that allow the battalion to strike the enemy from a flank or the rear. One or two companies block the enemy's advance while the other companies attack into the enemy's flank. In this example, the terrain prevents the enemy from moving away from the main attack while also protecting the battalion's flank from an enemy attack (Figure 4-18).

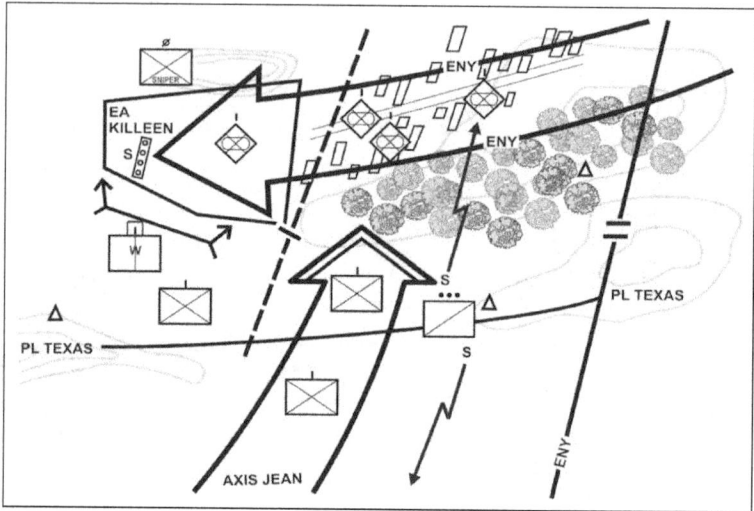

Figure 4-18. Example of a battalion flank attack.

4-227. Although he develops plans to fight the enemy at the most advantageous location for the battalion, the commander retains enough flexibility to attack the enemy effectively regardless of where the engagement develops. The scheme of maneuver includes provisions to fight the enemy at other possible locations. For simplicity, the commander seeks to keep the scheme of maneuver in each location as similar as possible.

4-228. In some situations, such as a movement to contact, the battalion may have constraints in the time or ability to select when and where to fight a moving enemy force. If so, the commander issues a FRAGO for an attack based on his his physical view and knowledge of the battlefield. As the ISR assets gather information, the commander quickly deploys and maneuvers the battalion to develop the situation and defeat the enemy.

Fire Support

4-229. The following are key considerations for the FS plan:

- Use fires to affect the enemy's maneuver well forward of the battalion to disrupt the enemy's formations and timetable.
- Destroy high-payoff targets (HPTs) and security forces.
- Carefully plan triggers, observer locations, and targets to maintain flexibility and ensure achievement of required effects before contact with the enemy.
- Coordinate and synchronize with brigade the movement and positioning of artillery to support EFSTs within each engagement location and to engage HPTs before the enemy enters the selected area. Coordinate terrain requirements.
- Retain flexibility to mass fires at the decisive point in any location where the engagement may occur.
- Plan triggers to put targets into effect and cancel them based on the battalion's movement and the commander's decision of where to fight the enemy.

- Synchronize the mortar platoon's movement, positioning, and fires with the scheme of maneuver.

Movement and Maneuver

4-230. The weapons company gives the commander considerable options:

- He can use the weapons company as the fixing force because of their fire capability.
- He can use the weapons company as the assaulting force because of their speed and mobility.
- He may choose to task organize elements of the weapons company to the Infantry companies to create balanced forces that can execute a variety of missions during the attack of a moving enemy.

4-231. The following are key considerations for the scheme of engineer operations.

- Task-organize engineer forces well forward to support breaching
- Assign normal priority of support is to the lead company.
- Prepare to bypass or breach enemy situational obstacles.
- Integrate situational obstacles with fires and triggers to affect the movement of the enemy and support flank security in support of the commander's intent.
- To support flank security, plan obstacle belts and measures, and plan situational obstacles.
- Develop and adjust obstacles and triggers for execution based on the battalion's movement and the enemy situation.

Protection

4-232. The ADA element supporting the BCT operates DS to the battalions with the normal priority of protection to the decisive operation. The ADA assets shift locations on the battlefield as required by the phase of the operation to maintain adequate air defense coverage of critical forces and events. AD coverage increases in areas and activities most vulnerable to air attack such as breaching operations or movements through restricted terrain.

4-233. The CBRN assets are employed in a similar manner to their employment in an attack against a stationary force. Obscurants and CBRN reconnaissance assets typically support the decisive operation.

Sustainment

4-234. The following are key considerations for the sustainment plan:

- Continuously update it. Ensure the sustainment plan is responsive and flexible enough to support all maneuver options. Plan support from initiation of the operation to the final objective or LOA.
- Integrate resupply operations with the scheme of maneuver.
- Weight the risk the extended distances create for security of MSRs and sustainment assets based on the potential of undetected or bypassed enemy forces.
- Use all available assets to develop and maintain an accurate enemy picture behind the lead maneuver elements.
- Plan and rehearse for enemy contact.
- Plan and coordinate the locations, displacements, and routes of sustainment assets to maintain responsive support.
- Develop triggers based on the battalion scheme of maneuver to activate/deactivate collection points and LRPs.
- Plan CASEVAC, resupply, and equipment recovery for engagements in each potential location.

Preparation

4-235.   Preparation for an attack against a moving enemy force is limited because the opportunity to attack the enemy at the appropriate time and place depends on the enemy's movement. This forces the battalion to focus the preparation on executing fires and maneuver actions within each location. The commander prioritizes each area to ensure the battalion prepares for the most likely engagements first. The commander ensures all subordinate companies and supporting forces understand their role in each area and the decision point for execution at each area. The leaders of the battalion rehearse actions in each area against various enemy conditions to promote flexibility and initiative consistent with the commander's intent. Repetitive rehearsals against likely enemy actions are essential for success at all levels.

Reconnaissance

4-236.   The reconnaissance and surveillance effort focuses on answering the CCIR to support the commander's decisions on when and where to initiate fires, where to fight the enemy, and how best to maneuver the battalion against the enemy. The S-2 develops NAIs to identify enemy actions and decisions that indicate the enemy's selected COA. The following are key intelligence considerations for attacking a moving enemy force.

Anticipate Enemy COA

4-237.   The IPB details how the enemy is likely to move and fight. It emphasizes the enemy's likely formations and routes and how he will try to fight the ensuing meeting engagement. The analysis shows the enemy's expected rate of movement and how the enemy force is likely to be arrayed. This information is based on a detailed terrain and time-distance analysis. The enemy normally has three general COAs—

- Assume a defense either before or after initial contact to retain control of defensible terrain or limit the advantages the battalion may have.
- Attack to defeat or penetrate the battalion.
- Try to delay or bypass the battalion.

4-238.   The S-2 develops enemy COAs based on the enemy's likely objective, capabilities, strengths, and known tactics. The S-2 determines those enemy actions that may indicate the enemy's selection of a COA and ensures observers are positioned to detect and report these indicators. The S-2 must always portray the enemy's flexibility, likely actions, and available maneuver options. The goal is to identify the enemy's most likely COA and have the battalion anticipate and prepare for it.

Gain and Maintain Contact

4-239.   Preferably, the battalion establishes contact with the enemy using digital sensor platforms well before it makes physical contact.

4-240.   The battalion, with support from the brigade, receives information from battlefield surveillance assets such as radar, UAS, access to joint surveillance target attack radar system (JSTARS), battlefield surveillance brigade assets, and other JIIM and SOF sensors used to track the moving enemy force. Intelligence produced from the information gathered by these sensors helps the battalion direct ground reconnaissance assets to advantageous positions to physically observe and report information on the enemy. Once made, the battalion maintains contact.

4-241.   The information gained from the sensors as well as ground reconnaissance elements must be shared with all elements of the battalion as quickly as possible. Information requirements normally include—

- The enemy's rate and direction of movement.
- The enemy's formation, strength, and composition to include locations of security forces, main body, reserves, and artillery formations.

- Enemy actions and decisions that indicate a future enemy action or intention.
- Location of enemy HPTs.
- Enemy vulnerabilities such as exposed flanks or force concentrations at obstacles.

Support Battalion Movement

4-242. Reconnaissance and surveillance forces move well forward of the battalion. They reconnoiter obstacles and areas that may slow the battalion's movement and disrupt the timing and planned location of the attack. They seek to detect obstacles, contaminated areas, enemy security forces, and suitable routes for the battalion's use. Once contact is established, the reconnaissance and security force may then be used to secure a flank of the attacking force.

Execution

4-243. The following considerations apply to the conduct of the attack:

Approach to Objective

4-244. The battalion moves with deliberate speed. By gaining contact with the enemy force through the reconnaissance and surveillance force, the brigade can use long-range fires and CAS to destroy and disrupt the enemy throughout his formation.

4-245. The battalion deploys, attacks from unexpected and or multiple directions, masses effects, and destroys the remaining enemy before he can adequately react. The commander adjusts the speed of the battalion to ensure that fires have set appropriate conditions and that the battalion arrives at the designated location at the proper time in relation to the enemy. Effective reporting and analysis of the enemy's rate and direction of movement by reconnaissance and surveillance elements are critical to the timing of the attack.

4-246. The commander seeks to conceal the movement of the battalion from the enemy to maintain surprise. The battalion moves dispersed. It masks its movement and uses covered and concealed routes. A robust reconnaissance detects and destroys enemy security forces that could otherwise warn the enemy force of friendly actions.

Action on Objective

4-247. The battalion creates favorable conditions for decisive action by weakening and disrupting the enemy's formation, destroying his security forces, and fixing the enemy's main body. The battalion main body attacks and destroys, disintegrates, or dislocates the enemy.

Disrupt Enemy Formation

4-248. The battalion employs indirect fires reinforced with situational obstacles to set the conditions for the EA or objective fight, disrupting and weakening the enemy before he gets to the area. Indirect fires should provide time for the battalion to deploy before contact. Reconnaissance elements normally control these initial fires.

Defeat Enemy Security Forces

4-249. Normally, the enemy employs security forces to protect his main body. The enemy's ability to seize the initiative often depends on his security forces. The battalion must avoid, destroy, or fight through the enemy's security forces to gain contact with the bulk of the enemy force. The commander employs fires in conjunction with his advance guard to defeat the enemy's security forces so the battalion's main body can decisively attack the bulk of the enemy force. Ideally, the battalion's advance guard attacks the enemy's forward or flank security forces to develop the situation. The commander weights the advance guard with maneuver forces and indirect fires in order to destroy the enemy's security force and gain contact with the enemy's main body before the enemy can effectively react.

Fix Enemy

4-250.   The battalion normally fixes the enemy's assault force to create the conditions for the battalion's main body attack. Normally, the battalion's advance guard executes this task once it destroys the opposing enemy security force. Indirect fires against the lead enemy forces allow the advance guard to deploy and gain contact with the enemy main body. The advance guard commander keeps the battalion commander informed of the enemy's strength and actions. It is paramount that the battalion commander receives accurate, timely reports and analysis of the enemy situation. Reconnaissance elements assist the advance guard commander in providing accurate information to the battalion commander. The battalion commander must know the enemy main body's strength, disposition, and reactions. He uses this information to make final adjustments to the main body's attack.

Maneuver Main Body

4-251.   As the advance guard develops the situation, the commander begins to maneuver the main body to a favorable position for commitment.

4-252.   The commander positions the battalion to attack the enemy formation from an assailable flank where the battalion's total combat power can be massed against an enemy weakness to reach a quick decision. Rapid movement and massed fires characterize this attack. Indirect fires shift to suppress the enemy force that directly opposes the main body's attack. The main body strikes the enemy force with overwhelming strength and speed. As the main body maneuvers against the enemy, the battalion FSO adjusts FSCMs to provide continuous support and ensure force protection.

4-253.   If the commander determines the enemy force is trying to bypass or avoid contact, he directs indirect fires to delay and disrupt the enemy's movement away from the battalion. The commander maneuvers his forces to destroy or penetrate any enemy forces trying to fix or delay the battalion and strikes the bulk of the evading enemy force from the flank or rear.

TERRAIN-ORIENTED ATTACKS

4-254.   Terrain-oriented attacks require the battalion to seize and retain control of a designated area to support future operations. The battalion attacks to seize terrain-oriented objectives for many reasons, for example—

- To seize key terrain or structures such as bridges, airfields, or public services to support follow-on operations.
- To seize terrain such as a chokepoint or route. It does this to block enemy withdrawals, reinforcements, or movements against the brigade's decisive operation; or to facilitate friendly force passage.
- To secure an area, such as a lodgment area, for future operations.

4-255.   The battalion plans and executes terrain-oriented attacks in the same manner as attacks against enemy forces (Figure 4-19). The major distinction in a terrain-oriented attack is that the battalion focuses its efforts on the seizure and control of terrain instead of effects on the enemy. The commander plans and directs the attack to gain control of the terrain as quickly as possible and conducts only necessary actions against the enemy. Success of the mission does not normally entail decisive action against all enemy forces within the AO.

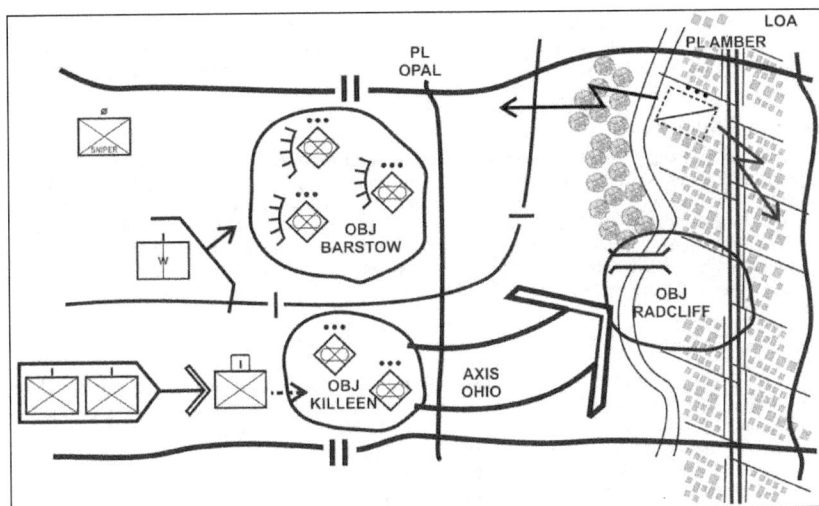

Figure 4-19. Terrain oriented attack.

4-256.   The battalion attacks only the enemy who directly affects the seizure of the objective or who might affect the future operation. Commanders must understand that seizure of terrain-oriented objectives, likely key terrain, will probably dislocate the enemy force. Therefore, the enemy might try to counterattack to dislodge and defeat the friendly forces. Other key planning considerations that differ from force-oriented attacks include--

Reconnaissance and Surveillance

4-257.   The reconnaissance and surveillance effort, as in other attacks, capitalizes on all the battlefield surveillance assets available to the brigade, as well as those that belong to the battalion, to identify the enemy situation on the objective and any sizable enemy forces within the battalion's battlespace. Battalion ground reconnaissance elements occupy advantageous positions to gain observation and report information on the enemy.

4-258.   The commander, assisted by the S-2, must consider enemy forces within his battlespace, specifically in areas outside his AO but inside his AI, that may react to the battalion's seizure of the objective. Once the battalion locates enemy forces, reconnaissance forces try to determine the enemy's strength and disposition as well as possible bypasses the battalion could exploit. This helps the S-2 develop enemy COAs and identify indicators of the enemy's commitment to a future action. The S-2 normally considers enemy actions to defend in place; reinforce threatened enemy units; counterattack; delay; or possibly withdraw.

Degree of Risk

4-259.   The commander must determine the degree of risk he is willing to accept by leaving or bypassing enemy forces in the battalion's AO. He bases this decision on the higher commander's intent and established bypass criteria, the enemy's capabilities, and the commander's assessment of the situation. The commander must recognize the potential effects that bypassed enemy forces may have on the battalion's sustainment operations and future operations. The commander normally employs economy of force missions to contain, destroy, or fix bypassed enemy forces. The risk imposed by these bypassed forces is reduced by accurate and timely reporting of their locations and status throughout the battalion, especially to the elements moving behind the maneuver forces in the battalion's AO. Once the battalion secures the objective, other forces or fires can destroy bypassed enemy forces or force their surrender.

Seizure of Objective

4-260. Once it seizes the objective, the battalion conducts a defense of the area to prevent the enemy from recapturing it. The commander seeks to position his forces in a manner that best defends the objective while allowing a rapid transition to follow-on operations. Reconnaissance and security forces establish a screen force forward of the secured objective to provide security and early warning to the battalion to prevent a surprise counterattack by the enemy. Engineers provide countermobility and survivability support as time and resources allow. Indirect fire assets reposition to support extended coverage of the defense and shift to targets beyond the objective.

EXPLOITATION

4-261. Exploitation is not normally conducted below the BCT level. Exploitation often follows a successful attack to take advantage of a weakened or collapsed enemy. The purpose of exploitation can vary, but it generally focuses on capitalizing on a temporary advantage or preventing the enemy from establishing an organized defense or conducting an orderly withdrawal. To accomplish this, the BCT (or higher level unit) attacks rapidly over a broad front to prevent the enemy from establishing a defense, organizing an effective rear guard, withdrawing, or regaining balance. The BCT secures objectives, severs escape routes, and destroys all enemy forces. Failure to exploit success aggressively gives the enemy time to reconstitute an effective defense or regain the initiative by a counterattack.

4-262. The conditions for exploitation develop very quickly. Often the lead battalion in contact identifies the collapse of the enemy's resistance. The BCT commander must receive accurate assessments and reports of the enemy situation to capitalize on the opportunity for exploitation. Typical indications of good conditions for exploitation include—

- A significant increase in EPWs.
- An increase in abandoned enemy equipment and material.
- The overrunning of enemy artillery, C2 facilities, and logistics sites.
- A big decrease in enemy resistance or in organized fires and maneuver.
- A mixture of support and combat vehicles in formations and columns.
- An increase in enemy movement rearward, especially of reserves and FS units.

4-263. Should the battalion conduct exploitation as part of a larger operation, it might receive the mission to seize a terrain-oriented objective. In this case, the battalion avoids decisive engagement and moves to the objective as quickly as possible. If assigned a force-oriented objective, the battalion seeks and destroys enemy forces anywhere within its AO. The exploitation ends when the enemy reestablishes its defense, all organized enemy resistance breaks down, or the friendly force culminates logistically or physically.

PURSUIT

4-264. The battalion does not conduct a pursuit as an independent action. Even at the BCT level, the risk associated with a pursuit operation generally outweighs the benefits. However, if provided aviation assets or additional ground maneuver units, the BCT can conduct a pursuit. If so, the battalion can serve as the direct-pressure force or the encircling force.

4-265. A pursuit is ordered when the enemy can no longer maintain a coherent position and tries to escape. Unlike in an exploitation, the BCT's mission in a pursuit is the destruction of the enemy rather than avoiding enemy contact.

4-266. The direct-pressure force organizes a movement to contact and prepares to conduct a series of attacks. Encirclement results when a force is able to destroy enemy communications and prevent his reinforcement or escape. The encircling force, usually made up of uncommitted forces, must be more mobile than the enemy. It must also be strong enough to protect itself from the enemy's reserves and what is left of the enemy's main body. The direct-pressure force must track and coordinate with the encircling force. Timing is critical. Information systems are vital to this synchronization. The encircling force should be prepared to conduct a defense until the direct-pressure force succeeds in destroying or forcing the enemy to surrender. The goal of a pursuit is to fix the enemy between the direct-pressure force and the encircling force, and then to destroy him.

SPECIAL PURPOSE ATTACKS

4-267.   The battalion can launch attacks with various purposes to achieve different results. These special purpose attacks include raids, feints, demonstrations, counterattacks, and spoiling attacks.

Raid

4-268.   A raid is a deliberate attack that involves the swift, temporary penetration of enemy territory for a specific mission. A raid usually ends with a planned withdrawal. Raids are usually small-scale attacks requiring detailed intelligence, preparation, and planning. Typical raid missions are—

- Capture prisoners, installations, or enemy materiel.
- Destroy enemy materiel or installations.
- Obtain specific information on an enemy unit such as its location, disposition, strength, or operating scheme.
- Deceive or harass enemy forces.
- Liberate captured friendly personnel.

4-269.   The raiding force may vary in size from an Infantry platoon to a reinforced company. It may operate within or outside the battalion's supporting range. The raiding force moves to its objective by land, air, or water for a quick, violent attack. Once it completes the raid mission, the raiding force quickly withdraws along a different route. Specific planning considerations include the following:

4-270.   Conduct detailed reconnaissance and maintain constant surveillance of the raid objective to ensure the enemy situation remains unchanged and within the capability of the raiding force. Support from outside the battalion helps to provide the intelligence needed to plan and conduct a raid successfully.

4-271.   Position fire support systems to provide immediate responsive fires during the approach, actions on the objective, and withdrawal. Interdiction fires, deception fires, counterfires, and situational obstacles reduce the enemy's ability to react to the raid.

4-272.   Security is vital because the raiding force is vulnerable to attack from all directions.

- Establish clear abort criteria for the raid based on CCIR. These criteria may include loss of personnel, equipment, or support assets, and changes in the enemy situation.
- Develop contingency plans for contact before and after actions on the objective.
- Plan casualty evacuation and raiding force extraction throughout the entire depth of the operation.
- Plan rally points for units to assemble to prepare for the attack or to assemble after the mission is complete and the force is ready to withdraw.

4-273.   Logistical considerations include the type and number of weapons that the raiding party will have, movement distance, length of time the raiding party will operate in enemy territory, and expected enemy resistance. Aircraft or linkup provides CASEVAC or resupply of the raiding force, if required, during the withdrawal.

4-274.   Withdrawal should be over a different route than that used to approach the objective.

Feint

4-275. A feint is a form of an attack intended to deceive the enemy and draw attention and combat power (if possible) away from the decisive operation.

4-276. Feints must be of sufficient strength and composition to cause the desired enemy reaction. Feints must appear real; therefore, some contact with the enemy is necessary. The feint is most effective under the following conditions:

- When it reinforces the enemy's expectations.
- When the enemy perceives it as a definite threat.
- When the enemy has consistently committed a large reserve early.
- When the attacker has several feasible COAs.

4-277. The purposes of a feint may include the following:

- To force the enemy to employ his reserves away from the decisive operation.
- To force the enemy to remain in position.
- To attract enemy supporting fires away from the decisive operation.
- To force the enemy to reveal defensive fires or weaknesses.
- To accustom the enemy to shallow attacks in order to gain surprise with another attack.

4-278. Planning for a feint mission follows the same sequence as any other attack. Special planning considerations include the following:

- Resource the feint so it looks like the decisive operation or at least like a significant threat.
- Establish clear guidance regarding force preservation.
- Ensure adequate means of detecting the desired enemy reaction.
- Designate clear disengagement criteria for the feinting force.
- Assign attainable objectives.
- Issue clear follow-on missions to the feinting force.

Demonstration

4-279. A demonstration is a form of an attack used for deception. It is made with the intention of deceiving the enemy; however, contact with enemy forces is not sought. Demonstrations support a BCTs or higher level units' plan; battalions do not conduct demonstrations alone. Demonstrations must be clearly visible to the enemy without being transparently deceptive in nature. Demonstration forces use fires, movement of maneuver forces, smoke, EW assets, and communication equipment to support the deception plan. Planning considerations include the following:

- Establish an LOA for demonstration forces that allows the enemy to see the demonstration but not to engage it effectively with direct fires.
- Establish other security measures necessary to prevent engagement by the enemy.
- Employ demonstrations to reinforce the enemy's expectations and contribute to the decisive operation.
- Develop contingency plans for enemy contact and to avoid becoming decisively engaged.
- Issue clear follow-on missions to the demonstration force.
- Establish the means to determine the effectiveness of the demonstration and assess its effect on the enemy.

Counterattack

4-280. A counterattack is an attack launched from the defense aimed to defeat an attacking enemy force or regain key terrain and ultimately regain the initiative. The counterattack is often the deciding action in the defense and becomes the decisive operation upon commitment. The battalion is best suited for this role in restricted terrain. In unrestricted terrain, the battalion is vulnerable to indirect fires and only possess, with the weapons company, the mobility and potential firepower of a combined arms or Stryker battalion. The commander may plan counterattacks as part of the battalion's defensive plan, or the battalion may be the counterattack force for the brigade or division.

Spoiling Attack

4-281. A spoiling attack is an attack launched from the defense to disrupt the enemy's attack preparations. Spoiling attacks focus on the enemy's critical systems and forces that have the greatest impact on the enemy's ability to mount an attack. Lucrative targets include C2 systems, intelligence assets, FS, and logistics. Spoiling attacks may be conducted as often as needed to deny adequate attack preparation to the enemy. Normally, the battalion conducts a spoiling attack as part of the higher headquarters operation. Spoiling attacks are planned and executed in the same manner as an attack.

Section VI. PLANNING CONSIDERATIONS

The battalion's ability to access information available at higher echelons may alter the manner in which the battalion actually plans, prepares for, and executes an attack. The amount of information and intelligence the battalion receives affects adjustments to the reconnaissance effort, the size of the reserve element, movement formations and techniques, security operations, and the tempo of operations. This can create unique planning considerations. For example, the battalion generally avoids linear actions, stable fronts, and extended pauses between operations. The battalion overloads the enemy by presenting an overwhelming number of actions from multiple directions throughout the depth, width, and height of the battlespace. The battalion has the flexibility to attack through varying types of terrain and thus to prevent the enemy from predicting the direction of attack and orienting on the avenue of approach. By massing the effects of long- and short-range area and precision fires with rapid combined arms movement, the battalion can decisively defeat the enemy. Improved navigation, target acquisition, and the information-sharing capabilities of the battalion enhance understanding and synchronization throughout offensive operations in near real time. This ability allows commanders in the battalion to share common perceptions of the battlefield.

FORCE ORGANIZATION

4-282. The commander task-organizes forces within the battalion after he chooses a scheme of maneuver. The task organization allocates sufficient combat power to allow subordinate companies to accomplish their assigned purposes.

SCOUT PLATOON

4-283. The scout platoon primarily executes reconnaissance and surveillance for the battalion. In instances where the enemy situation remains vague, additional forces are allocated to assist in the reconnaissance effort. Where the enemy mounts an effective security zone that denies the scout platoon the ability to provide the information that the commander needs to make decisions during execution, he may direct an Infantry rifle company to conduct a movement to contact or limited attacks through the enemy security zone. From the battalion commander's perspective, these operations constitute a reconnaissance-in-force and feed sufficient information to build the level of awareness, which when analyzed, leads to the situational understanding needed to facilitate his decision-making and decisive combat action.

SECURITY FORCE

4-284. Across the full spectrum of conflict, the battalion commander carefully considers security force requirements. Forces must be allocated to protect critical assets within the battalion AO against conventional and unconventional attacks. Also, the scout platoon, OPs, UAS, and other ISR assets will provide passive security through the conduct of their operations.

FLEXIBILITY

4-285. The battalion can conduct both linear and nonlinear operations within contiguous or noncontiguous areas of operation. This flexibility allows the battalion to conduct company-level operations against multiple objectives within the battalion's AO.

RESERVE

4-286. Reserves should be designated at appropriate levels to address unforeseen events. The amount of combat power allocated to the reserve depends primarily on the level of uncertainty about the enemy. The increased ability of the battalion to gain a better degree of understanding about the enemy should allow the commander to tailor the reserve to meet the specific threats and opportunities. At times, the situation may dictate that the battalion retain a small, but tailored, force as the reserve because there is little likelihood of catastrophic failure or because all of the Infantry rifle companies are conducting significant operations simultaneously. At other times, the commander may determine that his degree of understanding allows him to tailor subordinate forces to a level that will ensure their success and therefore he does not designate a reserve.

INTELLIGENCE, RECONNAISSANCE AND SURVEILLANCE

4-287. Intelligence, surveillance, and reconnaissance are a broad category of assets designed to support planning, decision-making, and targeting. The ISR effort is a combined arms maneuver operation, not just a scout platoon mission. All personnel in the battalion are required to observe, by visual or other detection methods, NAIs and TAIs in order to collect data, information, or combat information. Surveillance involves the systematic observation of a particular NAI by visual, electronic, photographic, or other means. Target acquisition by specialized/nonspecialized ISR assets detects, identifies, and locates targets in enough detail to effectively employ fire and effects. Intelligence includes processes for collecting, processing, and analyzing data and other relevant information.

INTEGRATION

4-288. The S-2 integrates IPB, the ISR matrix, event templates, and other MDMP products into the analysis of information coming into the main CP from the scout platoon, other ISR assets, and higher unit assets. The S-2 tries to answer the PIR, recommends refined PIR for the commander to consider, confirms probable enemy COAs and intentions, and explains enemy actions in relation to the current friendly operation. Ultimately, reconnaissance and surveillance operations set the conditions for the success of the unit in the close fight.

EXECUTION

4-289. The battalion conducts reconnaissance and surveillance using organic and supporting reconnaissance and surveillance and technical assets. The data, information, and combat information collected from these assets, when combined with intelligence provided by the higher headquarters, help the commander visualize a nearly complete picture of the enemy and environment within the battalion's battlespace. Specifically, the battalion employs an appropriate amount of its reconnaissance and surveillance assets throughout its AO in order to identify favorable terrain and determine the enemy's composition, disposition, activities, strengths, and possible vulnerabilities.

RECONNAISSANCE AND SURVEILLANCE ORDER

4-290. The reconnaissance and surveillance order (and collection plan) is published early in the MDMP process (not later than WARNO 2) with sufficient enemy detail and operational coordination to focus the battalion's reconnaissance and surveillance effort. This information allows the Infantry battalion to—

- Seize and maintain the initiative.
- Develop and disseminate effective maneuver and fires and effects plans before contact.
- Detect, identify, and destroy high payoff targets early.
- Allow follow-on forces to maneuver rapidly and without obstruction to the objective.
- Keep uncommitted forces available as long as possible in preparation for action at decision points.
- Recognize and exploit fleeting opportunities presented by discovered enemy weaknesses.
- Reduce the risk of surprise by enemy operations.

SCHEME OF MANEUVER

4-291. The battalion directs its decisive operation (or main effort) against an objective, ideally an enemy weakness, to cause the collapse of the enemy. By doing so, the battalion sustains the initiative and reduces its own vulnerabilities. The battalion commander seeks to identify an assailable flank, poorly defended avenue of approach, or a smaller unit lacking mutual support that he can exploit to gain a tactical advantage. When attacking a well-prepared enemy defense, the commander normally plans to isolate and then destroy vulnerable portions of the enemy defense throughout the depth of the zone of attack.

REVERSE PLANNING PROCESS

4-292. The commander and staff develop the plan using a reverse planning process that starts with the decisive point and the endstate of the operation and works back to the assembly area. They incorporate plans for exploiting success and unforeseen opportunities that may develop during execution. Emphasis is placed on synchronizing maneuver, fires and effects, and support throughout the reconnaissance and surveillance effort and the attack. Reconnaissance and surveillance facilitates maneuver, allowing combat forces to move on specific routes to objectives without significant enemy contact. The composition, disposition, strength, and capabilities of the enemy force drives the type of attack the battalion conducts (paragraph 4-35).

ENEMY CAPABILITIES

4-293. The staff considers the enemy's ability to mass combat power, reposition his forces, or commit his reserve. The battalion develops a scheme of maneuver to mass sufficient combat power to defeat the enemy. The reverse planning process is an essential tool in building an effective plan to attack an enemy. By starting with the decisive point and endstate of the operation and working back to the assembly area, the staff can allocate combat power, mobility assets, and fires and effects (suppression and smoke).

FIRE SUPPORT

4-294. Fire support planning is the process of analyzing, allocating, and scheduling both lethal and nonlethal fires support. The goal of fire support planning is to integrate both lethal and nonlethal fires into battle plans to support the battalions' scheme of maneuver. Fire support planning is performed concurrently with the MDMP. Effective fire support planning places the right elements of the fire support system in the right place at the right time IAW the commander's intent. The following basic principles of fire support planning apply—

- Plan early and continuously.
- Follow the commander's targeting guidance.
- Exploit all available targeting assets.
- Consider the use of all available fire support means.
- Use the lowest echelon capable of furnishing effective support.
- Use the most effective fire support means.
- Furnish the type of fire support requested.
- Avoid unnecessary duplication.
- Consider airspace coordination.
- Provide rapid and effective coordination.
- Remain flexible.
- Provide for the safeguarding and survivability of friendly forces and installations.

EFFECTIVENESS

4-295. The effectiveness of fire support planning and the fire support system depends on the successful performance of the four basic tasks: support forces in contact, support the concept of operations, synchronize fire support, and sustain fire support.

Support Forces in Contact

4-296. Supporting forces in contact includes the allocation of weapons systems and sorties to subordinate elements that actually engage the enemy. Supporting forces in contact usually means providing responsive fire support that protects and ensures freedom of maneuver to forces in contact with the enemy.

Support Concept of Operations

4-297. Supporting the concept of operations means providing fire support for any possible contingency. Fire support assets must be identified and marshaled for execution at the right time and place. The BCT commander must allocate enough firepower to the battalion commander so that he can influence the battle as necessary.

Synchronize Fire Support

4-298. Fire support is synchronized through fire support coordination, beginning with the BCT commander's estimate and concept of the operation. The battalion FSO helps the commander integrate all fire support, including the battalion mortars, with the appropriate battlefield systems and WFFs.

Sustain Fire Support

4-299. Combat sustainment includes all the sustainment activities necessary to support battles, engagements, and related actions. A battalion can realize the full combat potential of its forces and achieve synchronization in its operations only when combat sustainment is planned, coordinated, and executed efficiently. Planners must formulate tactical plans to reflect logistics limitations and exploit logistics capabilities.

URBAN TERRAIN

4-300. The nature of restricted and urban terrain presents some special considerations. The ability to direct and observe fires and effects within isolated compartments of restricted and urban terrain is required down to the platoon. Minimum engagement ranges are as important as maximum ranges. Considerations for the fire support plan include the following. see also Appendix L for more discussion of nonlethal capabilities):

- Moving fire support assets to enable destruction or engagement of HPTs.
- Moving fire support assets to support the reconnaissance and surveillance effort.
- Locating and employing COLTs and TACP to facilitate precision fires.
- Using deception fires to confuse the enemy as to the location of the decisive operation.
- Planning fires of suppression and obscuration at the point of penetration.
- Planning fires of suppression and obscuration in support of breaching operations.
- Planning fires in support of the approach to the objective. These fires engage enemy security forces, destroy bypassed enemy forces, and screen friendly movement.
- Synchronizing fires on the objective to suppress, neutralize, or destroy enemy forces that most affect the battalion's movement to the objective.
- Planning targets to attack repositioning enemy forces and the movement of enemy reserves.
- Planning fires beyond the objective to support an attack or defense.
- Using fires or CAS to delay or neutralize enemy reserves.
- Planning locations of critical friendly fire zones to protect critical assets such as support forces, breaching efforts, and artillery assets.
- Planning nonlethal effects on civilian populations.

Section VII. TRANSITIONAL OPERATIONS

The battalion spends minimum time after concluding an engagement or actions on the objective to consolidate and reorganize before continuing the attack. If consolidation and reorganization are required, the commander selects the best time and location to facilitate future operations and provide force protection. The battalion must maintain a high degree of security when performing consolidation and reorganization activities.

CONSOLIDATION

4-301. Consolidation is the process of organizing and strengthening a newly captured position. The battalion may need to consolidate to reorganize, avoid culmination, prepare for an enemy counterattack, or allow time for movement of adjacent units. The battalion makes consolidation plans for every mission, updates them during the attack, and passes them to units as the attack is completed. Actions during consolidation include—

- Reestablishing communications (if required).
- Eliminating pockets of enemy resistance.
- Establishing security consistent with the threat.
- Establishing contact (electronic, physical, or both) with adjacent friendly units.
- Preparing defensive positions.
- Clearing obstacles or improving lanes to support friendly movement and reorganization activities.
- Planning and preparing for future operations.
- Destroying captured enemy equipment and processing EPWs.
- Maintaining contact with the enemy and conducting reconnaissance.
- Cross-leveling and conducting emergency resupply.

4-302. The battalion maintains contact with the enemy by redirecting the scout platoon and sniper squad, establishing OPs, directing small-unit patrols, receiving the latest intelligence from the S-2, and possibly conducting limited objective attacks.

REORGANIZATION

4-303. Reorganization planning begins before and continues during the attack as losses occur. Companies must feed reports to the battalion as losses occur so that the information entered into the sustainment system allows movement of needed resupply forward so that it arrives as the battalion begins reorganization. The battalion immediately takes all measures required to maintain its combat effectiveness or return it to a specified level of combat capability. If extensive reorganization is required, the battalion conducts it during consolidation. Reorganization tasks include—

- Establishing and maintaining security.
- Reestablishing the battalion chain of command, key staff positions, and C2 facilities lost before or during the battle.
- Treating and evacuating casualties.
- Recovering and repairing damaged equipment as necessary.
- Redistributing ammunition, supplies, and equipment as necessary.
- Conducting resupply and refueling operations.
- Repositioning C2 facilities, communications assets, and logistics for future operations.
- Reorganizing companies and platoons if losses have occurred.

CONTINUATION OF OPERATIONS

4-304. For all missions assigned, the battalion should plan for exploiting success. However, at the conclusion of an engagement, the commander may be forced to defend. The commander considers the higher commander's concept of operations, friendly capabilities, and the enemy situation when making the decision to defend or continue offensive operations.

DEFENSE

4-305. The battalion conducts a defense when directed by higher headquarters, or to repel an enemy counterattack, avoid culmination, or complete reorganization activities. The battalion occupies the most defensible terrain, which may require the battalion to attack to seize defensible terrain. Normally, the battalion pushes its scout platoon out to establish a security area to provide reaction time and early warning of enemy actions. Subordinate companies occupy designated AOs, array forces, and develop fire plans.

Normally, the commander seeks to array companies to achieve an adequate level of defense and facilitate future operations. Engineers provide survivability support and emplace obstacles as required to support the defense.

This page intentionally left blank.

Chapter 5
Defensive Operations

Defensive operations defeat an enemy attack, buy time, economize forces, or develop conditions favorable for offensive operations. Defensive actions alone are not decisive; they must be combined with or followed by offensive action. Even within the conduct of the BCT defense, the battalion exploits opportunities to conduct offensive operations within its AO to deprive the enemy of the initiative, and create the conditions to assume the offensive.

Section I. FUNDAMENTALS

The battalion defends temporarily to create the conditions necessary to resume offensive operations. As part of the BCT, the battalion may defend, delay, withdraw, counterattack, or perform security operations or economy of force tasks. A defensive engagement often requires the battalion to execute several of these tasks over its course. A defense should never be a static operation. The battalion must always be prepared to maneuver to exploit enemy weaknesses. As with offensive operations; the enemy can be defeated by physical destruction, disintegration (reduction of control) and dislocation (reduction of enemy COAs, creation of new conditions), or a combination of these methods. This section discusses the fundamentals of the defense.

PURPOSE

5-1.   The main purpose of the defense is to force or deceive the enemy into attacking under unfavorable circumstances, defeat or destroy his attack, and regain the initiative for the offense. The defending commander seeks to dictate where the fight will occur, preparing the terrain and other conditions to his advantage while simultaneously denying the enemy adequate intelligence. Defense is a temporary measure used to identify or exploit enemy weaknesses. Use of the defense provides the opportunity to change to the offense. In general, the battalion defends to—

- Defeat or destroy an attacking enemy.
- Gain time to allow other units in the BCT to accomplish their missions.
- Fix or disrupt the enemy as part of a BCT operation.
- Deny enemy entry into an area or retain terrain.
- Economize forces in one area to apply decisive force elsewhere.
- Increase the enemy's vulnerability by forcing him to concentrate forces.
- Prepare to resume the offensive.
- Develop favorable conditions for offensive actions.
- Reduce the enemy's capability for offensive operations.

ORGANIZATION

5-2.   Defensive operations are organized around a framework of a security area, a main battle area (MBA).

SECURITY AREA

5-3.   The BCT normally establishes a security force with the reconnaissance squadron to provide early warning, reaction time, and initial resistance to the enemy. Security missions are usually time- or event-driven. The battalion commander clearly identifies the mission of the security force either by time, space, and amount of destruction to the enemy force, or by the type of enemy forces to destroy. Depending on the BCT commander's guidance and plan, the battalion has several possible security force missions and options. The battalion may—

- Establish a security area layered behind the BCT security area to add depth to the operation.
- Secure its own flanks and or rear while the BCT assets conduct the primary security area operation forward of the forward edge of the battle area (FEBA) in a linear defense.
- Conduct its own security operation in the absence of a higher echelon security force.
- Provide units for the BCT security force. This could include the scout platoon, sniper section, mortar platoon, or all three; maneuver platoons or companies, or the entire battalion.

Security Area Definition

5-4.   The security area begins at the FEBA and extends as far to the front and flanks as the unit deploys forces. The primary function of forces in the security area is to furnish information on the enemy; however, they also delay, deceive, and disrupt the enemy and conduct counterreconnaissance. The BCT commander normally identifies the BCT's security area, the battle handover line from the BCT to the battalion, the exact trace of the FEBA, and where he envisions the main battalion fight will occur. From this, the battalion commander can determine how to structure his security area and the array of forces to employ. If the battalion commander must organize his own security force, he chooses from many available options. These are four basic options:

- Use the scout platoon only as a screening force.
- Use the scout platoon in conjunction with maneuver elements, snipers, mortars, or all, in a screen mission. The security force can operate directly under battalion control; however, the HHC company commander or any company commander (weapons or rifle company) can command this force.
- Use a rifle company or create a company team with a combination of the scout platoon, snipers, mortars, and assault weapons platoons in a guard mission.
- Use the weapons company to establish a moving or stationary screen. The weapons company may be augmented with any combinations of mortars, snipers, or scouts.

Specific Guidance and Tasks

5-5.   No matter what task organization he implements, the commander provides the force with specific guidance and tasks. To terminate the security mission, the security force commander normally requires the permission of the main body commander to withdraw behind the rear boundary. This may include—

- Duration of the mission.
- Results to be achieved against the enemy to include specific guidance against the enemy reconnaissance forces.
- Specific CCIR with associated NAIs and TAIs and their windows of observation with indicators.
- Avenues of approach to be monitored with PIR and last time information is of value.
- Fire support, protection sustainment, and C2.
- Engagement, disengagement, and withdrawal criteria and rearward passage coordinating instructions.
- Follow-on tasks or missions.

Simultaneous Missions

5-6.   Using battalion resources to establish a security area, while simultaneously requiring the battalion to defend the MBA is risky and divides the attention of the commander. Whenever possible, this should be avoided. Figure 5-1 shows a typical organization of a defensive battlefield.

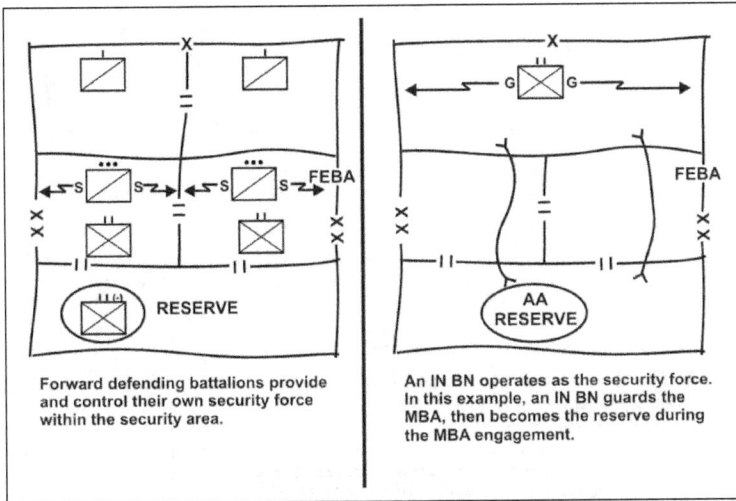

Forward defending battalions provide and control their own security force within the security area.

An IN BN operates as the security force. In this example, an IN BN guards the MBA, then becomes the reserve during the MBA engagement.

Figure 5-1. BCT organization of security zone forces.

MAIN BATTLE AREA IN A LINEAR DEFENSE

5-7.   The BCT and its battalions deploy the bulk of their combat power in the MBA. The BCT's MBA extends from the FEBA to the forward battalions' rear boundaries. Battalion MBAs are subdivisions of the BCT's MBA. The FEBA marks the foremost limit of the areas in which the preponderance of ground combat units deploy, excluding the areas in which security forces are operating. The BCT commander assigns the battalion MBAs by establishing unit boundaries. BCT and battalion commanders establish AO, BPs, or strongpoints to implement their concept of operation. As in all operations, commanders promote freedom of action by using the least restrictive control measures necessary to implement their tactical concepts (Figure 5-2).

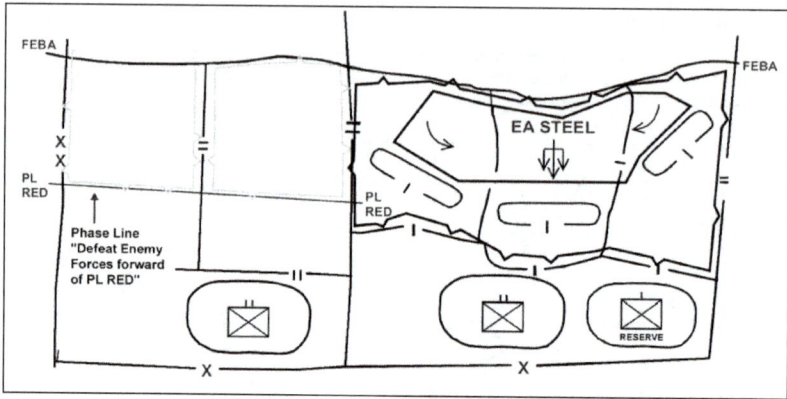

Figure 5-2. Example area defense using static and dynamic elements.

MAIN BATTLE AREA IN A NONLINEAR DEFENSE

5-8.   In a nonlinear defense, there is no cohesive battalion MBA. Company MBAs extend from the units' location to the battalion's area of influence. This battalion MBA is independent of any other unit's MBA. Noncontiguous operations place a premium on initiative, effective information operations (IO), decentralized security operations, and innovative logistics measures. Noncontiguous operations complicate or hinder mutual support of combat, sustaining operations elements because of extended distances, and security risks associated with movement between subordinate units and elements.

REAR AREA

5-9.   The Infantry battalion conducts only limited rear area operations. Although battalion does conduct sustaining operations, the locations of these operations are mainly in the security area, the MBA, or outside of the battalion AO. The BCT dircts, coordinates, and monitors most rear area operations during a linear defense. The majority of the BCT's sustaining operations occur here. Many BCT C2, protection, and sustainment units are located in the rear area as well as support elements from the Infantry battalion. Their importance and survivability is critical to sustained maneuver operations. Defense of the rear area must be planned and units must be prepared to respond to threats in the rear area. A battalion may be given a rear area protection mission from the BCT.

CHARACTERISTICS

5-10.   The characteristics of the defense are preparation, security, disruption, massing effects, and flexibility.

PREPARATION

5-11.   The battalion commander determines likely enemy avenues of approach, likely enemy schemes of maneuver, where to kill the enemy, integration of obstacles, unit positioning, and integration of indirect fires, and he assigns missions accordingly. Defensive preparations include the following:

- The S-2, S-3, and WFF representatives execute the MDMP under the XO's supervision for the commander's approval.

FM 3-21.20   13 December 2006

- Enact force protection measures that involve action against conventional threats, for example, preparation of fighting positions and digging-in C2 nodes, as well as asymmetric threats (terrorist attacks and weapons of mass destruction [WMD] employment).
- Designate a reserve.
- Conduct rehearsals to ensure synchronization. This includes employment of the reserve and counterattack forces.
- Position forces in depth.
- Reinforce terrain with obstacles that support the scheme of maneuver.
- Coordinate with BCT reconnaissance battalion or other JIIM assets to confirm limits of AOs and to deconflict direct and indirect fires.

SECURITY

5-12.   Security operations are measures taken by the Infantry battalion to protect itself against all acts designed to impair its effectiveness, and prevent the enemy from gaining an unexpected advantage. Because a force defends to conserve combat power for use elsewhere or later, commanders must secure the force. The battalion ensures security by employing reconnaissance elements throughout the depth and breadth of its assigned AO. The battalion may employ a counterreconnaissance force, combat outposts, or a screen force to provide this security. Information operations capabilities such as PSYOP, military deception, and electronic warfare can aid in securing the force and confuse the enemy as to the battalion's manner of defense. The battalion secures the force through integrated security operations tied with the BCT reconnaissance squadron and other ISR assets.

DISRUPTION

5-13.   Defenders subvert an attacker's tempo, formations and synchronization by countering his initiative and preventing him from massing overwhelming combat power. Disruption attacks the enemy's will to fight and his means of effective C2. Deep precision fires, long-range precision sniper fires, scatterable minefields (SCATMINEs), unexpected defensive positions, local counterattacks at all levels, and attacks delivered by a reserve force, combine to disrupt the enemy's attack and break his will to continue offensive operations. Repositioning forces, aggressive local force protection measures, random employment of roadblocks, ambushes, checkpoints, and information operations combine to disrupt the threat of asymmetrical attack. These attacks disrupt enemy efforts to fight as a combined-arms team. Maneuver units deceive the enemy as to the nature of their defense and employ local combined-arms counterattacks to break the tempo of the enemy's attack.

MASSING EFFECTS

5-14.   The battalion shapes and decides the battle by massing the effects of overwhelming combat power. Effects are synchronized in time and space and should be rapid and unexpected so that they break the enemy's offensive tempo and disrupt his attack. The commander employs integrated ISR to shift the effects of fires and maneuver forces so that they are repeatedly focused and refocused to achieve decisive, destructive, and disruptive effects upon the enemy's attack. The commander must be audacious in achieving overwhelming combat effects at the decisive point.

FLEXIBILITY

5-15.   The defender gains flexibility by sound preparation and task organization, disposition in depth, retention of reserves, repositioning, and effective C2. The defense is characterized by rapid, simultaneous, and collaborative planning with flexible execution. Contingency planning permits flexibility. Flexibility also requires that the commander "see the battlefield" to detect the enemy's scheme of maneuver early. Ipb determines likely enemy actions; while security elements confirm or deny those actions.

PLANNING CONSIDERATIONS

5-16.   The commander considers all the factors of METT-TC to determine how best to concentrate his efforts and economize forces. A detailed terrain analysis might be the most important process that the commander and his staff complete. A successful defense relies on a complete understanding of terrain in order to determine likely enemy COA and the best positioning of the battalion assets to counter them.

SECURITY

5-17.   One of the first planning considerations for the battalion is security operations. The scout platoon, often with augmentation, will operate forward of the maneuver battalion in order to clarify the tactical situation. The commander gives the scout platoon specific PIR to allow for an efficient occupation of the AO and to position itself for the preparation and execution of the area defense. Battalion security forces may be able to clarify enemy intentions by collecting information on the massing of forces and troop movement. On a noncontiguous battlefield, the security force is positioned between the protected force and the known or suspected enemy locations. Significant consideration must be given when planning the communications package; sustainment (with emphasis on the casualty evacuation process); mobility assets; engagement, disengagement, and withdrawal criteria; and the indirect fire support coverage for all elements participating at any time within the security area. The staff must consider redundant security and observation means in the event one of the elements is compromised or incapacitated.

MOVEMENT AND MANEUVER

5-18.   In noncontiguous operations, the battalion often must defend either on a broad front or in an AO large enough that employing units in mutually supporting positions is unrealistic. This requires a judicious effort by the commander and his staff in determining the positioning of maneuver forces. During the terrain analysis, the commander and staff must look closely for choke points, intervisibility lines, and reverse slope opportunities in order to take full advantage of the battalion's capabilities to mass fires and effects while providing protection for the units.

5-19.   Once the commander has assigned areas of operation to his companies, he determines any potential area between higher headquarters, adjacent, and subordinate units that is not assigned to any unit. Any area within the battalion AO that is not assigned to a subordinate unit remains the responsibility of the battalion. The battalion may plan to cover this area with reconnaissance assets, sensors, and UAS; however, they may also identify, analyze, mitigate, and accept risk by placing no assets to monitor or react to this unassigned area. The battalion plans local counterattacks to isolate and destroy any enemy that manages to penetrate through a gap in the AO. The commander also plans to commit the reserve element or reposition units not in contact to mass the effects of combat power against an attacking enemy.

5-20.   The need for flexibility for the companies requires graphic control measures to assist in C2 during local counterattacks and repositioning of forces. Specified routes, phase lines, attack-by-fire positions, EAs, target reference points, and other fire control measures are required for the effective synchronization of maneuver. The following are the steps for EA development (asterisks denote steps that may occur simultaneously).

- Identify enemy avenues of approach.
- Determine enemy scheme of maneuver.
- Determine where the battalion wants to kill the enemy.
- Emplace and integrate weapons systems and or direct fire. *
- Plan and integrate obstacles.*
- Plan and integrate fires.*
- Rehearse the direct fire plan and engagement criteria actions in the EA.

Reserve Force

5-21.   The commander designates and positions the reserve in a location where it can effectively execute several contingency plans. He considers terrain, potential EAs, probable points of enemy penetrations, and commitment criteria, and routes. The commander may have a single reserve under battalion control or, if the terrain dictates, the companies may designate their own reserves. The reserve should be positioned outside the enemy's direct fire range in a covered and concealed position. Information concerning the reserve must be considered essential elements of friendly information (EEFI) and protected from enemy reconnaissance. The commander may choose to position his reserve forward initially to deceive the enemy or to move the reserve occasionally in order to prevent it from being targeted by enemy indirect fires.

5-22.   The size of the reserve depends upon the size of the area covered in the defense, potential missions, and the clarity of expected enemy action. The battalion may need to defend an AO so large that only local reserves are feasible due to reaction time and the number of potential enemy COAs. BCT and battalion security forces may be able to clarify enemy intentions by collecting information on the massing of forces, electronic signals, and troop movement. The collection of information via JIIM, BCT, and battalion ISR plans allows the commander to gain an understanding of the situation and to better focus his efforts toward the size and task organization of the reserve.

5-23.   The battalion provides specific planning guidance to the reserve to include priority for planning. The reserve commander should also expect to receive specific decision points and triggers for employment on each contingency. This guidance allows the reserve commander to conduct quality rehearsals and to anticipate his commitment as he monitors the fight. Finally, the commander develops a plan to reconstitute another reserve force once the original reserve force is committed. This is most often accomplished with a unit out of contact.

Engineer Support

5-24.   Plan the transition to countermobility and survivability work in detail, ensuring adequate time for subordinate engineer troop-leading procedures.

- Site situational obstacles early. Plan multiple locations to support depth and flexibility in the defense.
- Ensure adequate time, resources, and security for obstacle emplacement systems. Integrate triggers for execution of situational and reserve obstacles in the decision support template.
- Focus the countermobility effort to shape the enemy's maneuver into positions of vulnerability.
- Ensure adequate mobility for withdrawing security forces, the reserve, and repositioning of MBA forces.
- Plan appropriately for Class IV and Class V (mines) download sites as near to the emplacement location as is practical.
- Establish early on the priority of effort and the priority of support.

Aviation Support

5-25.   In defensive operations, the speed and mobility of aviation can help maximize concentration and flexibility. During preparation for defensive operations, aviation units may support the battalion commander with aerial reconnaissance, and observed indirect fires (Appendix E).

5-26.   During the defense, aviation fires can attack deep against high-payoff targets, enemy concentrations, and moving columns and can disrupt enemy centers of gravity. Attack helicopter units can be employed in depth to attack exploitation forces or follow-on echelons before they can move forward to the close battle. Aviation forces may also conduct screening operations and may conduct guard operations of an open flank in conjunction with ground forces.

5-27.   Attack helicopters routinely support security zone operations and can mass fires during the MBA fight. Synchronization of aviation assets into the defensive plan is important to ensure aviation assets are capable of massing fires and to prevent fratricide. Detailed air-ground integration and coordination is necessary to ensure efficient use of aviation assets (Appendix E).

5-28.   If the battalion is assigned aviation assets, careful consideration must be given to EA development and direct fire planning. The supporting aviation unit, through its aviation LNO, must be involved in the battalion planning process. The aviation LNO, the S-3, and the FSO must conduct A2C2 coordination and deconfliction of the indirect fire, the UAS flight, fixed wing CAS, and the rotary wing CAS plans.

FIRE SUPPORT

5-29.   The battalion may receive priority of fires for a specific mission or phase of the defense. However, the battalion and company mortars are its primary indirect fire assets, and the commander must not rely solely on the limited indirect fire assets available to the BCT. The following are considerations for the fire support plan:

- Allocate initial priority of fires to the forward security force. Plan targets along enemy reconnaissance mounted and dismounted avenues of approach.
- Engage approaching enemy formations at vulnerable points along their route of march with indirect fires and CAS, if available.
- Plan the transition of fires to the MBA fight.
- Plan echelonment of fires.
- Incorporate existing FSCMs and detailed triggers to adjust them.
- Develop clear triggers to initiate fires and adjust priority of fires.
- Ensure integration of fires in support of obstacle effects.
- Ensure integration of fires with the battalion counterattack plans and repositioning contingency plans.
- Identify and target HPTs.
- Work in conjunction with the S-3 for A2C2 deconfliction.
- Determine multiple mortar firing points for the mortar platoon.

PROTECTION

5-30.   Key factors the battalion must consider, when AD assets are attached, include the following:

- Position AD assets and radars along air avenues of approach to provide early detection and engagement of enemy aircraft. Defeat enemy air before it enters the battalion's AO or AI.
- Provide all-round air defense protection to the battalion with mutual supporting and overlapping fires. Weight fires toward likely air avenues of approach.
- Plan primary, alternate, and supplementary firing positions to support defensive delays, positions in depth, and counterattacks.
- Reposition ADA assets to replace lost assets or to mass against significant air threats.
- Ensure adequate security, survivability support, and sustainment (especially missile caches) for ADA assets.
- Establish priorities of AD protection based on the criticality and vulnerability of units and the threat.
- Plan to defend against enemy air attacks targeting critical friendly positions such as battle positions (BPs) and start points (SPs).
- Protect the reserve, which has a critical role in the defense. The enemy will try to identify and target it to prevent its decisive employment.
- Protect C2 assets. They are normally stationary and produce a high electronic signature; thus, they are more susceptible to identification and targeting by enemy air attacks. ADA assets protecting forward maneuver forces normally provide C2 assets with incidental area coverage.

- Protect C2 assets and logistical units.
- Plan for CBRN reconnaissance at likely locations for enemy employment of chemical or biological agents.
- Use obscurants to prevent enemy observation of defensive preparation or to support disengagement or movement of forces.
- Ensure engineers integrate survivability priorities for critical systems and units.

SUSTAINMENT

5-31.   Sustainment considerations are characterized by constrained organic assets. Therefore, battalions must anticipate and plan accordingly to maintain the unit's capability to fight.

5-32.   Plan primary and alternate MSRs to support the full depth of the defense. Coordinate MSRs to avoid interfering with obstacle plans. Specify routes for contaminated equipment movement. Plan to position the combat trains where they can best support the battalion with medical, Class IV, and Class V resources. The combat trains must be able to maintain radio communications, monitor and battle track operations at all times so that it can assume the duties of the battalion TOC if required. Consider the use of preconfigured combat loads in the combat trains to expedite the process of emergency resupply. Also, consider the use of pre-stocked classes of supply (Classes IV and V) within the defense.

5-33.   Plan for medical coverage as far forward as possible to reduce the time from point of injury to Level I MTF/BAS. Considerations include—

- The use of a forward aid station (FAS) having both the FAS and main aid station (MAS) positioned forward with company trains elements.
- The use of advanced trauma life saving teams.
- The use of external support.

5-34.   The battalion should plan pick-up zones for aerial medical evacuation, and must specify routes and collection points for contaminated personnel. Other FHP considerations for defensive operations include the following:

- The heaviest patient workloads, including those produced by enemy artillery and CBRN weapons, can be expected during the preparation or initial phase of the enemy attack and in the counterattack phase.
- The enemy attack can disrupt ground and air routes and delay evacuation of patients to and from treatment elements. Plan for alternate evacuation means and routes to include preplanned pick-up zones for aerial evacuation.
- The depth and dispersion of the defense creates significant time and distance problems for evacuation assets. The FHP must be redundant and robust in evacuation assets.

5-35.   Because the enemy exercises the initiative early in the operation, it can preclude accurate prediction of initial areas of casualty density. This fact is essential to the effective integration of air assets into the medical evacuation (MEDEVAC) plan.

CIVIL CONSIDERATIONS

5-36.   Consideration of the higher headquarters ROE and limitations is necessary, particularly civilian effects and restrictions on fires and types of weapons. Civilians may be removed from the area or protected in their homes. Their movement and protection is a concern to the battalion in all cases. In some cases, the battalion may have to arrange for supply, transportation, and medical care for civilians. This can be coordinated by the CA or the civil military operations (CMO) representative if available.

5-37.   Restrictions may exist regarding use of cluster munitions, mines, nonlethal agents, obscurants, and even mortar fires. Firing into towns or near refugees may be prohibited. Historical and cultural features may be protected, and can be identified by the CA or CMO representative. All of this can influence the design of the defense.

5-38.   Consider availability of civilian assets and any limitations on use, including—

- Law enforcement support.
- Movement control.
- Transportation assets.
- Telecommunications security.
- Emergency supplies.
- Medical support.
- Decontamination support.
- Civilian labor.
- Buildings.
- Media sources.

PREPARATION

5-39.   During preparation, the commander and staff monitor preparatory actions and track the higher and adjacent unit situations and the enemy situation. They update and refine plans based on additional reconnaissance and updated intelligence information. The staff continues to disseminate these modifications through FRAGOs. They conduct much of the preparation phase simultaneously with security operations, continuing even as forward-deployed forces gain contact with the enemy. Throughout the preparation phase, the battalion commander, company commanders, and key staff members physically inspect preparatory activities. Weapons positioning, sitting of obstacles, direct and indirect fire plans and associated triggers, sustainment operations, and Soldier knowledge of their missions are all critical checks. The battalion should consider conducting spoiling attacks throughout the preparation phase to disrupt the enemy's offensive preparations.

REHEARSALS

5-40.   The battalion and subordinate units conduct rehearsals to practice their defense against multiple enemy COAs. The type of rehearsal executed must consider time, preparation activities, and OPSEC. Rarely will the battalion be able to conduct a full-force rehearsal given the tempo of operations and the potentially large size of the AO. Commanders should consider conducting key leader map and or terrain board rehearsals at night in order to focus their attention during periods of increased visibility on inspecting preparations and working with subordinate leaders. The rehearsal should cover—

- Reconnaissance and security operations.
- Battle handover and passage of lines.
- MBA engagement.
- Engagement, disengagement, reposition, and withdrawal criteria.
- Reserve employment options and their commitment criteria.
- Actions to deal with enemy penetrations, major enemy efforts along areas of risk or flank avenues of approach, and enemy actions in the rear area.
- Sustainment, particularly casualty evacuation, emergency resupply operations, and reorganization.
- Execution of routes (reposition, reserves, withdrawal, to CCPs).
- Execution of follow-on missions to exploit defensive success.
- Integration of aviation assets, if available.

MONITORING OF PREPARATION

5-41.   As subordinate units position their elements and execute defensive preparations, the battalion staff monitors and coordinates their activities and the overall situation.

5-42.   The S-2 closely monitors the enemy situation through information collected by the battalion ISR operations. The ISR matrix focuses battalion efforts on indicators that reveal the enemy's likely time and direction of attack. The staff continually analyzes this assessment to determine the effects on preparation time available and any changes to the COA. The commander updates his PIR as the situation changes and is prepared to adjust the reconnaissance and surveillance operation to answer those questions. The S-3 closely monitors the status of rehearsals and updates the plan as needed based on continuously updated intelligence and the status of preparations. The S-4 analyzes the status of logistics and maintenance of equipment within the battalion to determine any required adjustments to the plan or task organization. The engineer officer monitors the progress of all engineer efforts within the AO. He continually projects the end state of this effort based on the current and projected work rates. He identifies potential shortfalls early and determines how to shift assets to make up for the shortfalls or recommend where to accept risk.

5-43.   As the enemy closes on the battalion's AO, the battalion begins final preparations that typically include—

- Final coordinating of battle handover and passage of lines.
- Positioning of situational obstacle employment systems.
- Verifying communications status.
- Evacuating unused Class IV and V to prevent capture or loss to enemy action.
- Withdrawing engineer forces from forward areas.
- Linking up fire support, protection, and sustainment assets with reserve or other supported combat forces (if not previously accomplished).
- Reviewing reconnaissance and surveillance plan to ensure it still meets the commander's PIR.
- Final positioning or repositioning of reconnaissance and surveillance assets, security forces, and observers.
- Positioning of teams to close lanes in obstacles or execute reserve obstacles.
- Executing directed, reserve, or situational obstacles.
- Periodic situation updates and issuing of final guidance to subordinates.
- Registering indirect fire targets with mortars, if not already done. The commander may also conduct a final radio or even map rehearsal with key leaders.
- Conducting targeting meetings to continually update targets, resources, and priorities.

Section II. TYPES

There are three types of defensive actions: area defense, mobile defense, and retrograde operations. Each of these defensive actions contains elements of the others and usually contains both static and dynamic aspects. Battalions serve as the primary maneuver elements or terrain-controlling units for the BCT in all types of defensive operations. They may defend AOs, positions, or may serve as security forces or reserves, or a counterattack force as part of the BCT coordinated defense.

AREA DEFENSE

5-44.   The area defense concentrates on denying an enemy force access to designated terrain for a specific time. Outright destruction of the enemy may not be a criterion for success. The focus is on retaining terrain where the bulk of the defending force positions itself in mutually supporting positions, controlling the terrain between positions. The defeat mechanism is normally massing effects into EAs, usually supplemented by intervention of a reserve. The commander uses his reserve force to reinforce fires, add depth, block penetrations, restore positions, or counterattack to destroy enemy forces and seize the initiative. Area defenses are conducted when—

- The mission requires holding certain terrain for a specific period.
- Sufficient time remains to organize the position.
- The battalion or BCT has less mobility than the enemy.
- The terrain limits counterattacks to a few probable employment options.
- The terrain affords natural lines of resistance and limits the enemy to a few well-defined avenues of approach, thereby restricting the enemy's maneuver.

5-45.   The battalion commander normally selects one of two forms of defensive maneuver for an area defense--forward or defense in depth. However, the higher commander may define the general defensive scheme for the battalion. The specific mission may impose constraints such as time, security, and retention of certain areas that are significant factors in determining how the BCT will defend.

FORWARD DEFENSE

5-46.   The intent of a forward defense is to limit the terrain over which the enemy can gain influence or control. The battalion deploys the majority of its combat forces near the FEBA with the scout platoon establishing a relatively narrow security area (Figure 5-3). The battalion fights to retain these forward positions and may conduct counterattacks against enemy penetrations or to destroy enemy penetrations in forward EAs. Due to its inherent lack of depth, the forward defense is the least preferred option. While the battalion may lack depth, companies and platoons are expected to build depth into the defense at their levels. The battalion can expect to conduct a forward defense for protection of critical assets or other forces, or for political purposes such as defending an ally's threatened border. A battalion may defend forward under the following conditions:

- Terrain forward in the AO favors the defense.
- Strong linear obstacles such as a river are located forward in the AO.
- The assigned AO lacks depth due to the location of the area or facility to be protected.
- Cover and concealment in the rear portion of the AO is limited.
- Higher headquarters directs the battalion to retain or initially control forward terrain.

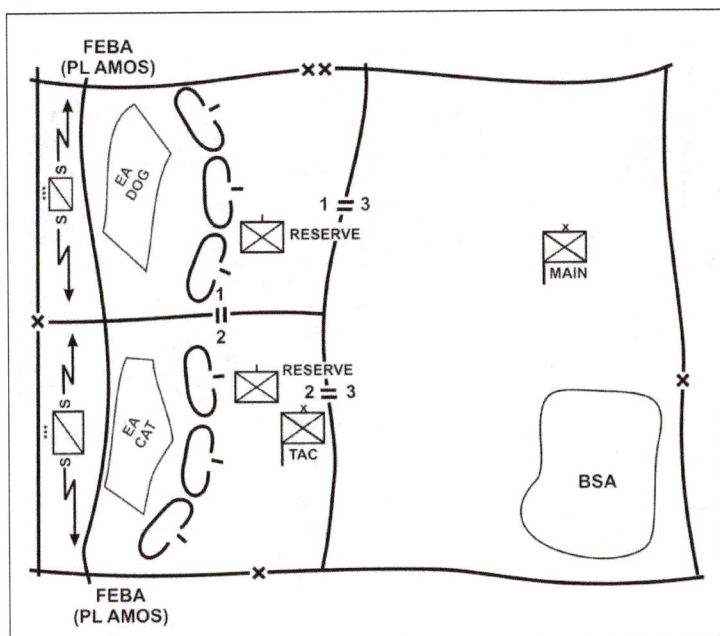

Figure 5-3. Example of a forward defense with battalions and companies defending forward.

DEFENSE IN DEPTH

5-47.   A defense in depth is the preferred option when tactical conditions allow. It reduces the risk of the attacking enemy penetrating the defense and affords some initial protection from enemy indirect fires. It also limits the enemy's ability to exploit a penetration through additional defensive positions employed in depth. The defense in depth provides more space and time to exploit ISR and fire support assets to reduce the enemy's options, weaken his forces, and set the conditions for destruction, disintegration, or dislocation. It provides the commander more time to gain information about the enemy's intentions and likely future actions before decisively committing to a plan of his own. It also allows the battalion to execute decisive maneuver by effectively repositioning companies to conduct counterattacks or to prevent penetrations (Figure 5-4).

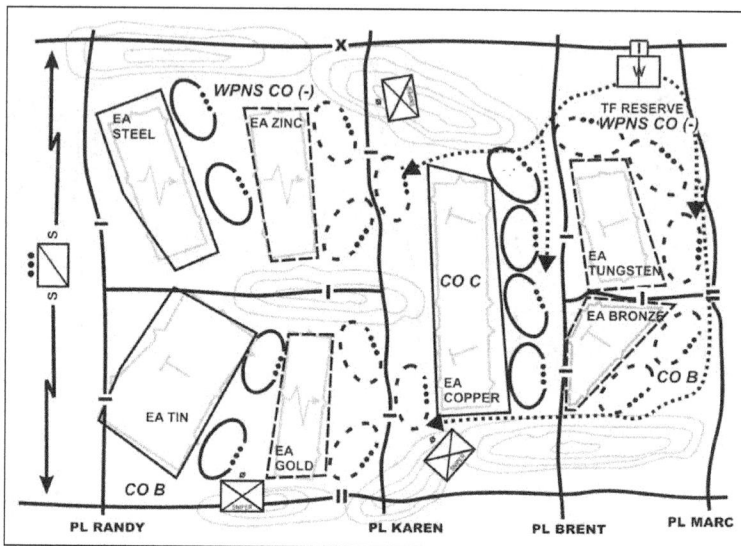

Figure 5-4. Defense in depth.

EXECUTION

5-48.   Execution and preparation activities can occur simultaneously. For example, it common that the main defense continues preparing, while the security force executes the counterreconnaissance.

SECURITY AREA ACTIONS

5-49.   Once security area forces have moved into the security area, actions in the security area predominantly focus on reconnaissance, counterreconnaissance, target acquisition, reporting, delay of the enemy main body, and battle handover. The battalion's security zone forces integrate their actions with friendly forces forward of them, maintaining information flow and security. The battalion's elements may have to execute battle handover with those forward elements and assist them in executing a rearward passage. The security zone forces must coordinate and cross-talk with the companies to their rear. Eventually, they must execute a rearward passage or move to the flanks of the MBA. On approaches that the enemy does not use, it is usually advantageous to leave elements of the security force forward to preserve observation and access to enemy flanks.

RECONNAISSANCE AND SURVEILLANCE

5-50.   The purposes of the reconnaissance and surveillance operation in the security zone are to provide the commander with information to support his decision-making, to provide early warning and reaction time, and to support target acquisition. Guided by the commander's CCIR, the ISR plan, and the fire support plan, reconnaissance and surveillance assets provide information that includes—

  • Location, movement, and destruction of enemy reconnaissance assets.
  • Speed, direction, composition, and strength of enemy formations.

- Locations of high-payoff targets such as artillery and rocket units, bridging assets, and C2 nodes.
- Enemy actions at decision points.
- Enemy flanking actions, breaching operations, force concentrations, and employment of combat multipliers.
- Battle damage assessment.
- Movement of follow-on forces.

5-51.   The staff must integrate the information provided by the security forces with information received from higher and adjacent units, other subordinate units, the BFSB, and JIIM/SOF.

5-52.   The total reconnaissance and surveillance operation must support the commander's decision-making. In an area defense, the commander's critical decisions normally include—

- Initiation and employment of direct and indirect fires against enemy formations.
- Modifications or adjustments to the defensive plan.
- Execution of situational obstacles.
- Withdrawal of forward security forces.
- Commitment of the reserve, counterattack, or both.

SECURITY AREA ENGAGEMENT

5-53.   Engagements in the battalion security area are normally limited. Counterreconnaissance forces focus on locating and destroying enemy reconnaissance elements. As the enemy closes into the area, observers initiate indirect fires and execution of reserve obstacles. The focal points are normally early warning and identification of the enemy's decisive and shaping operations, strength, and composition of threat forces, and direction of attack in order for the commander to make decisions and position forces. In the event enemy reconnaissance assets penetrate the security area, battalion forces operating in the security area must be prepared to conduct target handover with the battalion's main battle area forces.

BATTLE HANDOVER

5-54.   The battle handover is the transfer of responsibility for the battle from the BCT's or the higher unit's security zone elements to the battalions. The higher commander who established the security force prescribes criteria for the handover and designates the location where the security forces will pass through, routes, contact points, and the battle handover line. The battle handover line is normally forward of the FEBA where the direct fires of the forward combat elements of the battalions can effectively overwatch the elements of the passing unit. The BCT commander coordinates the battle handover with the battalion commanders. This coordination overlaps with the coordination for the passage of lines, and the two should be conducted simultaneously. Coordination normally includes—

- Establishing communications. This includes ensuring linkage on the tactical internet and effective information overlap.
- Providing updates on both friendly and enemy situations and the addition of appropriate command posts and leaders to the message groups on situation reports and updates.
- Coordinating passage, which includes identifying passage points and lanes, and recognition signals and exchanging or disseminating graphics of these and obstacle overlays.
- Collocating C2 elements.
- Dispatching representatives to contact points and establishing liaisons.
- Coordinating recognition signals.
- Reporting status of obstacles and routes, including overlays.
- Coordinating fire support, protection, and sustainment requirements, with particular attention given to casualty and equipment evacuation requirements.

- Coordinating actions to assist the security force with breaking enemy contact.
- Coordinating and exchanging maneuver, obstacle, and fire plans.
- Coordinating location of and communications to any stay-behind elements. These must be integrated into FSCMs to establish no fire areas (NFAs).

5-55.   Within the battalion, the battle handover between the battalion security elements and the companies is less complicated, but equally as critical and must be planned in detail. Elements must identify rearward passage points and lanes, and the passing elements need to coordinate their movement with the element(s) covering them and through which they are moving. Frequently, the first elements to displace are the maneuver forces that were executing counterreconnaissance, moving to initial defensive positions in the MBA, or acting as the battalion or BCT reserve. The scout platoon normally displaces to vantage points on the flanks, moves to establish surveillance on other avenues of approach, or infiltrates back to the battalion rear area.

5-56.   When battle handover occurs within the battalion, the MBA companies—

- Assist passage of lines and disengagement.
- Gain and maintain contact with enemy forces as battle handover occurs.
- Maintain security.
- "On order" execute reserve obstacles (battalion commander restricts authority) and "be prepared" to emplace situational obstacles (situational obstacles may or may not be executed) in the security area as the passing force withdraws. (See Chapter 2, FM 90-7.)

Main Battle Area Engagement

5-57.   The defensive battle is decided in the MBA by the actions of the battalion and its companies, and their supporting fires, protection and sustainment units. During this execution phase, it is incumbent upon the battalion staff to continue to assess the battalion's situation and update courses of action such as targeting, sustainment requirements, PIR, and adjustments of priorities for any assets.

Maneuver

5-58.   During the MBA engagement, the BCT and battalions shift combat power and priority of fires to defeat the enemy's attack. This may require—

- Adjustment of subordinates' AOs and missions.
- Repositioning of forces.
- Shifting of the main effort, if one is designated.
- Commitment of the reserve.
- Modification of the original plan.

5-59.   Forward forces, obstacles, and fires within the MBA normally break the enemy's momentum, force the enemy to deploy earlier than desired, reduce his numerical advantage, disrupt his formations and tempo, and force his troops into positions of vulnerability. The battalion masses fires (direct and indirect) and obstacles to disrupt, fix, and then destroy attacking enemy forces as they enter the EAs.

5-60.   Depending on the defensive scheme, the battalion may conduct delay operations capitalizing on movement and repeated attacks to defeat the enemy in depth or it may fight primarily from a single series of positions.

Cohesion

5-61.   The battalion must maintain a cohesive defense if it is to remain viable. This does not mean, however, that the forces must be massed close together or that companies must have mutually supporting fires. Companies can maintain cohesion with forces dispersed by cross-talk among subordinates, and continual tracking and reporting of the enemy. The staff and commanders continually assess the enemy's options and movement while identifying means to defeat them. With forces widely dispersed, continual assessment of time, distance, and trafficability factors is essential. To maintain defensive cohesion, company commanders keep their movement, positioning, and fires consistent with the commander's defensive scheme.

THREATS TO SUSTAINMENT OPERATIONS

5-62.   During the MBA fight, protection of sustainment operations and locations is necessary to ensure continuity of logistics operations. Because committing combat forces to sustaining operations and locations such as the combat or field trains diverts combat power from the MBA, the commander carefully weighs the need for such diversions against the possible consequences to the overall operation.

5-63.   Generally, sustainment nodes in the battalion area of operations or BCT rear area rely on positioning, movement, and self-protection for survival. They—

- Establish sustainment operations in covered and concealed areas away from likely enemy avenues of approach.
- Establish and maintain perimeter security and early warning OPs, integrating weapons and crews that are in the rear for repair operations.
- Keep sustainment nodes postured to move on very short notice as the security battle begins.
- Maintain internal security for any movement while executing sustaining operations.

5-64.   Early warning to sustainment units in the rear is critical to their survival in the event of a penetration of the MBA or an enemy attack from an unexpected area. Sustainment plans and rehearsals address actions to be taken in the event of attacks on sustaining operations, including defensive measures, displacement criteria, casualty evacuation, routes, rally points, and subsequent positions to which to move.

PENETRATIONS

5-65.   Unless the BCT plan makes other provisions, each battalion commander is responsible for controlling enemy advances within his AO. If the enemy penetrates the defense or a penetration appears likely, the battalion commander repositions forces or commits his reserve to block the penetration or to reinforce the area where a penetration appears imminent. Simultaneously, the battalion commander may allocate additional indirect fires to support the threatened area. He must alert the BCT commander to the threat and that he has committed his reserve force (if applicable). The battalion commander must alert the BCT commander of the situation as this may dictate when the BCT commander can commit his reserve force.

5-66.   If a penetration threatens the battalion, the commander may take several actions to counter the situation. In order of priority, he may do any or all of the following:

- Allocate priority of all available indirect fires, to include attack helicopters, and CAS, to the threatened unit. This is the most rapid and responsive means of increasing the combat power of the threatened unit.
- Direct or reposition adjacent units to engage enemy forces that are attacking the threatened unit. This may not be possible if adjacent units are already decisively engaged.
- Commit the reserve to reinforce the threatened unit.
- Commit the reserve to block, contain, or destroy the penetrating enemy force.
- Accept penetration of insignificant enemy forces and maintain contact with them as they move deeper into the MBA.
- Decide to move forces to alternate, supplementary, or subsequent positions or to withdraw forces.
- Commit attached engineers to assist in containing the penetration or constitute a new reserve from the engineers.

5-67.   When a penetration occurs, units within the MBA continue to fight, refuse their flanks, and engaging the enemy's flanks and rear. The penetrated force must try to minimize the penetration to prevent the area of penetration from widening and to protect adjacent unit flanks. Adjacent units take immediate action to secure their exposed flanks, which may include security missions or the establishment of blocking positions. Adjacent units may also need to reposition forces or direction of fire, readjust subordinate AOs and tasks, or commit their reserve. MBA forces try to reestablish contact across the area of penetration when possible.

COUNTERATTACK

5-68.   The battalion may conduct local counterattacks to restore or preserve defensive integrity. Unless defensive operations have left the battalion largely unscathed, the battalion usually lacks the ability to conduct a significant counterattack by itself. If the battalion has the ability to organize a counterattack force, this force must have mobility or be pre-positioned in a position of advantage to attack the enemy from an unexpected flank. Within the context of the BCT's operations, a defending battalion may execute a counterattack in support of the BCT's defensive posture, as part of a larger force seeking to complete the destruction of the enemy's attack, or as part of a transition to offensive operations.

MOBILE DEFENSE

5-69.   The mobile defense concentrates on the destruction or defeat of the enemy through a decisive counterattack. A mobile defense requires considerable depth in the AO in order for the commander to shape the battlefield, causing the enemy to extend his lines of communication and support, expose his flanks, and dissipate his combat power. This defense is executed at echelons above the BCT. The focus is on defeating or destroying the enemy by allowing him to advance to a point where he is exposed to a decisive counterattack by the striking force. The striking force is a dedicated force composed of the bulk of the combat power and weighted with the majority of the available combat multipliers. The fixing force shapes the battlefield and the enemy, setting the conditions for the striking force. Battalions may participate in the mobile defense as an element in the fixing force conducting a delay or area defense. Battalions may also constitute an element of the striking force conducting offensive operations. (Chapter 4 discusses offensive operations.)

RETROGRADE OPERATIONS

5-70.   The retrograde is a type of defensive operation that involves organized movement away from the enemy. The enemy may force these operations or a commander may execute them in order to overextend threat force's combat power and extend the enemy's lines of communications. In either case, the higher commander of the force executing the operation must approve the retrograde. Retrograde operations are conducted to improve a tactical situation or to prevent a worse situation from developing. Battalions normally conduct retrogrades as part of a larger force but may conduct independent retrogrades as required such as when conducting a raid. In either case, the battalion's higher headquarters must approve the operation. Retrograde operations accomplish the following:

- Resist, exhaust, and defeat enemy forces.
- Draw the enemy into an unfavorable situation.
- Avoid contact in undesirable conditions or locations.
- Gain time.
- Disengage from battle for use elsewhere in other missions.
- Reposition forces, shorten lines of communication, or conform to movements of other friendly units.

Note. Maintenance of morale is essential among subordinate leaders and troops in a retrograde operation. Movement to the rear may seem like a defeat or a threat of isolation unless Soldiers have confidence in their leaders and know the purpose of the operation and their roles in it.

PLANNING CONSIDERATIONS

5-71.   The commander determines the end state of the delay based on the higher commander's intent and specific parameters of the higher headquarters' delay order. The commander considers the factors of METT-TC, especially the effects of the terrain, to identify advantageous locations from which to engage the enemy throughout the depth of the AO. Specific delay planning considerations the commander and staff must determine include the following. (Figure 5-5 shows the three forms of retrograde operations):

- Force array and allocation of combat multipliers, particularly fires and obstacles.
- Where and when to accept decisive engagement.
- Acceptable level of risk for each subordinate force.
- Form of delay and control measures (companies delay in sector, control by BPs, or some other method).
- Integration of obstacle intent and essential fire support tasks (EFSTs).
- Numbers, locations, and preparation of alternate, supplementary, and/or subsequent positions.
- Locations of mortar firing points to provide continuous coverage to the force throughout the entire operation. This may incorporate the use of split section operations and multiple mortar firing points (MFP).
- Mobility assets to expedite movement to and from positions.
- Positioning of fire support, protection, and sustainment assets to provide continuous support throughout the operation
- Likely subsequent mission, transition point(s), and conditions.

DELAY	• Trades space for time. • Preserves friendly combat power. • Inflicts maximum damage on the enemy.
WITHDRAWAL	• Planned, voluntary disengagement from the enemy. • Conducted with or without enemy pressure.
RETIREMENT	• Organized movement to the rear by a force that is not in contact with the enemy.

Figure 5-5. Types of retrograde operation.

DELAY

5-72.   In a delay, the battalion trades space for time and inflict maximum damage on the enemy. The purpose of the delay is to control the enemy's tempo by forcing the enemy to deploy multiple times and repeatedly concentrate his combat power to defeat the delaying forces. Although the battalion must establish and maintain contact, it should avoid becoming decisively engaged. It is critical that the commander's intent defines what is more important to the mission: time, damage to the enemy, or force protection. Inflicting damage is normally more important than gaining time. The commander establishes risk levels for each delay but ordinarily maintaining freedom of action and avoiding decisive engagement is of ultimate importance. The battalion may execute a delay when it has insufficient combat power to attack or defend or when the higher unit's plan calls for drawing the enemy into an area for a counterattack, as in a mobile defense. Delays gain time to—

- Allow other friendly forces to establish a defense.
- Cover a withdrawing force.
- Protect a friendly force's flank.
- Allow other forces to counterattack.

Forms

5-73.   Based upon the commander's intent and METT-TC, a delay mission can have essentially two forms; delay within an AO or delay forward of a specific control measure.

Delay within an Area of Operations

5-74.   The battalion may be assigned a mission to delay within an AO. This operation is meant to slow and control the enemy tempo and defeat as much of the threat as possible without sacrificing the integrity of the unit. The higher commander provides guidance regarding intent and desired effect on the enemy, and he minimizes restrictions regarding terrain, time, and coordination with adjacent forces. This form of a delay is normally assigned when force preservation is the highest priority and there is considerable depth to the BCT or higher unit's AO.

Delay Forward of a Specified Line for a Specified Time

5-75.   The battalion might be given a mission to delay forward of a specific control measure for a specific period. This mission would be assigned when the BCT or battalion must control the enemy's attack and retain specified terrain to achieve some purpose relative to another element, such as setting the conditions for a counterattack, for completion of defensive preparations, or for the movement of other forces or civilians. Normally in a delay, inflicting casualties on the enemy is secondary to gaining time. It carries a much higher risk for the battalion, with the likelihood that part of, or the entire unit becoming decisively engaged. The timing of the operation is most often controlled graphically by a series of phase lines with associated dates and times to define the desired delay-until period.

Culmination

5-76.   Delay missions usually conclude in one of three ways; a defense, withdrawal, or counterattack. Planning options should address all three possibilities.

Organization

5-77.   The battalion's organization of its forces depends on how the BCT has structured its forces unless the battalion operates independently. The BCT normally organizes into a security force, main body, and reserve, but an extended AO may preclude the use of BCT-controlled security forces and reserves. In this case, the BCT may direct the battalion to organize its own security, main body, and reserve forces; the same as if the battalion was operating independently. The BCT commander can designate a battalion as the security or reserve force for the BCT. If the battalion has to establish a security force, it normally uses the Scout platoon as a screen force positioned to observe the most likely enemy avenues of approach and to initiate indirect fires to slow and weaken the enemy. Initially, the battalion main body usually locates well forward in the AO, and then fights from a series of subsequent positions. The reserve force, normally a company, is used to defeat enemy penetrations or to assist units with breaking contact.

Planning Considerations

5-78.   The delay requires close coordination of forces and a clear understanding by subordinates of the scheme of maneuver and commander's intent, and detailed mission graphics. The potential for loss of control is very high in delay operations, making cross-talk and coordination between subordinate leaders extremely important. Subordinate initiative is critical, but it must be in the context of close coordination with others. Plans must be flexible, with control measures throughout the AO allowing forces to be maneuvered to address all possible enemy options.

Battalion Order

5-79.   The battalion order must clearly articulate the parameters of the delay mission. It specifically addresses subordinate missions in terms of space, time, and friendly strength. It also provides directions for actions if the subordinate commander is unable to meet the terms of his delay mission. The following is an example of the parameters of a delay mission issued to a subordinate battalion.

EXAMPLE

Mission: Battalion 3-6 IN delays to disrupt enemy forces forward of PL Blue (Who and What) until 010400Sep2006 (When) to allow the remainder of the BCT to complete defensive preparations (Why).

Tasks to maneuver unit (3-6 IN): Retain at least 70% combat power (friendly strength). Prevent an organized platoon from penetrating PL Blue for 3 hours (When?). Force preservation is more important than time (priority). If unable to meet mission parameters, provide at least 30 minutes' warning before initiating rearward passage.

Upon completion of rearward passage, assume BCT reserve mission positioned vicinity BP 17.

Effects of Terrain

5-80.   The staff analyzes the effects of terrain and the anticipated enemy situation to identify positions that offer the best opportunity to engage, delay, and inflict damage on the enemy force. As the staff develops delay positions and control measures, it calculates enemy closure rates and compares them to friendly displacement rates between positions. Time and space factors dictate the amount of time subordinate units have to engage the enemy and move, before becoming decisively engaged. These factors are calculated for each avenue of approach. The staff develops triggers for displacement to positions in depth.

Maneuver Considerations

5-81.   The staff considers maneuver actions, fires, obstacles, and the employment of other supporting assets necessary to degrade the enemy's mobility and support friendly forces' disengagement to subsequent positions. This is especially critical at locations and times when companies or the entire battalion may become decisively engaged with the enemy. As the staff develops and refines the plan, it develops decision points for key actions. This includes triggers for the employment of fires and situational or reserve obstacles; displacement of subordinate units to subsequent positions; and movement of indirect fire assets, C2 facilities, and sustainment units. The staff also selects routes for reinforcements, artillery, CPs, and sustainment elements to use and synchronize their movements with the delaying actions of forward units.

Scheme of Maneuver

5-82.   The scheme of maneuver must allow the battalion to dictate the pace of the delay and maintain the initiative. The commander selects positions that allow his forces to inflict maximum damage on the enemy, support their disengagement, and enable their withdrawal. He may choose to delay from successive or alternating delay positions, depending on the strength of the companies and the size of the AO.

Areas of Operations

5-83.   The battalion normally assigns deep and parallel AOs to delaying companies. This provides enough terrain for companies to operate in depth, and maximizes the ability for battalion assets to simultaneously support multiple units throughout the operation. Generally, each enemy avenue of approach

---

is assigned to only one subordinate unit. The commander and his staff make provisions for coordinated action along avenues of approach that diverge and pass from one subordinate AO to another.

Control Measures

5-84.   The battalion commander may add control measures, to include BPs, EAs, or attack-by-fire positions. This allows company commanders to direct the fight more closely and give subordinates a clearer picture of how the battalion commander envisions fighting the delay. The commander may use events to control the delay. The commander must dictate specific events, for example, *enemy company penetrates PL Green, A Co in position at BP 12*, that trigger the repositioning of subordinate forces. The commander may also use phase lines to control the timing and movement of delaying units. Assigning time minimums to delays by phase line can limit company commanders to delaying on or forward of those lines, at least until the specified times. Contact points, coordination points, restrictive fire lines, coordinated fire lines, and other control measures are established to support flank unit coordination.

Delay Positions

5-85.   When determining the scheme of maneuver, positions should incorporate as many of the following characteristics as possible:

- Good observation and long-range fields of fire.
- Covered or concealed routes of movement to the rear.
- A road network or areas providing good cross-country trafficability.
- Existing or reinforcing obstacles to the front and flanks.
- Maximize use of highly defensible terrain.

Forced Enemy Deployment and Maneuver

5-86.   Engagement at maximum ranges of all weapons systems causes the enemy to take time-consuming measures to deploy, develop the situation, and maneuver to drive the delaying force from its position. An aggressive enemy commander will not deploy if he correctly determines that friendly forces are delaying; he will use his mass and momentum to develop sufficient pressure to cause friendly forces to fall back or become decisively engaged. Therefore, the delay must include the integration of direct and indirect fires and situational obstacles to make the enemy doubt the nature of the friendly mission and leave him no choice but to deploy and maneuver.

Avoidance of Decisive Engagement

5-87.   The key to a successful delay is to maintain a mobility advantage over the attacking enemy and avoid decisive engagement. The battalion seeks to increase its mobility while degrading the enemy's ability to move. The battalion improves its mobility by—

- Maintaining contact with the enemy, maintaining reconnaissance and security on flanks, and coordinating with adjacent units to prevent forces from being isolated.
- Prioritize and task-organize mobility assets in a manner which maximizes ability of the battalion to perform the delay.
- Reconnoitering routes and BPs.
- Improving routes, bridges, and fording sites between delay positions, as time and resources permit.
- Using indirect fires and obstacles to support disengagement and to cover movement between positions.
- Task-organizing and positioning breaching assets within subordinate formations to breach enemy SCATMINEs rapidly.

- Using multiple routes.
- Controlling traffic flow and restricting refugee movements to unused routes.
- Keeping logistical assets uploaded and mobile.
- Caching ammunition on rearward routes. Ensure that units know the locations of these supply points. If possible, the supply point should be guarded and prepared for destruction if not used by delaying forces.
- Task-organizing additional medical and equipment evacuation assets to the companies to increase their ability to disengage and displace rapidly.
- Positioning air defense assets to protect bridges and choke points on rearward routes.

5-88.   The battalion degrades the mobility of the enemy by—

- Maintaining continuous pressure on the enemy throughout the AO.
- Attacking logistics as well as maneuver and fire support assets.
- Securing and controlling chokepoints and key terrain that dominates high-speed avenues of approach.
- Destroying enemy reconnaissance and security forces; blinding the enemy and causing him to move more deliberately.
- Employing a combination of directed, situational, and reserve obstacles.
- Employing indirect fires, smoke, and CAS, if available.
- Using deception techniques such as dummy positions.

Order Parameters

5-89.   An order for a delay order must specify certain parameters. The parameters are normally expressed in paragraph 3, Tasks to Maneuver Units of an OPORD.

5-90.   First, it must direct one of two alternatives; delay throughout the depth of the AO or delay forward of a specific line or area for a specific period. A mission of delay within an AO implies that force integrity is a prime consideration. In this case, the battalion delays the enemy as long as possible while avoiding decisive engagement. If the delaying force is ordered to hold the enemy forward of a given phase line (PL) for a specified time, mission accomplishment outweighs preservation of the force's integrity. Such a mission may require the force to defend a given position until ordered to displace.

5-91.   The second parameter the order must specify is what is considered acceptable risk. Acceptable risk ranges from accepting decisive engagement in an try to hold terrain for a given period to avoiding decisive engagement in order to maintain the delaying force's integrity. The depth available for the delay, the time needed by the higher headquarters and subsequent missions for the delaying force determine the amount of acceptable risk.

5-92.   Third, the order must specify whether the delaying force may use the entire AO or whether it must delay from specific BPs. A delay using the entire AO is preferable, but a delay from specific positions may be required to coordinate two or more units in the delay.

5-93.   The battalion order and commander's intent define for the companies what the scheme of maneuver is, what the priorities are, and how much freedom the subordinate leaders have in maneuvering their forces. The battalion commander specifies constraints on maneuver and requirements for coordination. He defines the criteria for disengagement and movement to subsequent positions or areas and a series of BPs, checkpoints, or phase lines from which, or forward of which, the company must fight.

Alternate and Subsequent Positions

5-94.   In planning, if the commander chooses to delay using BPs, he can use either alternate positions or subsequent positions. In both techniques, the delaying forces maintain contact with the enemy between delay positions. Table 5-1 shows the advantages and disadvantages of the two techniques.

Table 5-1. Comparison of methods of delay.

Method of Delay	Use When--	Advantages	Disadvantages
Delay from subsequent positions.	• AO is wide. • Forces available are not adequate to be positioned in depth.	• Reduced fratricide risk. • Ease of C2. • Repeated rearward passages not required.	• Limited depth to the delay positions. • Easier to penetrate or isolate units. • Less time is available to prepare each position. • Less flexibility.
Delay from alternate positions.	• AO is narrow. • Forces are adequate to be positioned in depth.	• Allows positioning in depth. • Harder for enemy to isolate units. • More flexibility.	• More difficult C2; requires continuous coordination. • Requires passage of lines, increasing vulnerability and fratricide potential.

Delay from Alternate Positions

5-95.   In a delay from alternate positions (Figure 5-6), two or more units in a single AO occupy delaying positions in depth. As the first unit engages the enemy, the second occupies the next position in depth and prepares to assume responsibility for the operation. The first force disengages and passes around or through the second force. It then moves to the next position and prepares to reengage the enemy while the second force takes up the fight. Both the BCT and battalion can use this scheme of maneuver. If the AO is narrow, the battalion employs companies in depth occupying alternate positions. This enables the battalion to develop a strong delay, with forces available to counterattack or assist in the disengagement of the company in contact. At the battalion level, using alternate positions helps maintain pressure on the enemy and helps prevent platoons or companies from being decisively engaged. A delay from alternate positions is particularly useful on the most dangerous avenues of approach because it offers greater security and depth than a delay from subsequent positions. However, it also poses the highest potential for fratricide and vulnerability as units pass through or near each other.

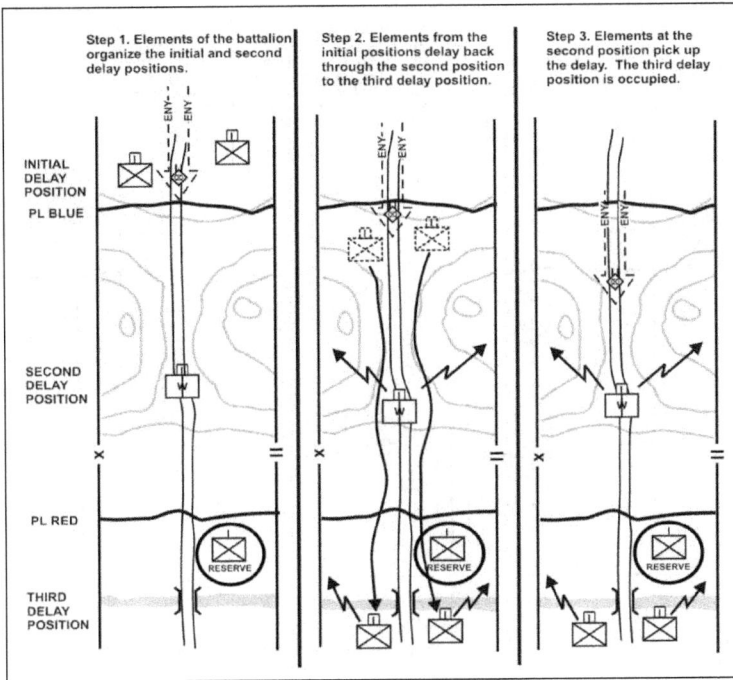

Figure 5-6. Delay from alternate positions.

Delay from Subsequent Positions

5-96.   The battalion uses a delay from subsequent positions when the assigned AO is so wide that available forces cannot occupy more than a single tier of positions (Figure 5-7). In a delay from subsequent positions, the majority of forces are arrayed along the same phase line or series of BPs. The forward forces delay the enemy from one PL to the next within their assigned AOs. At battalion level, this is the least preferred method of delaying since there is a much higher probability of forces becoming isolated or decisively engaged, particularly if the delay must be maintained over more than one or two subsequent positions. Also, the battalion has limited ability to maintain pressure on the enemy as it disengages and moves to subsequent positions unless it has been allocated additional (and adequate) indirect fire support.

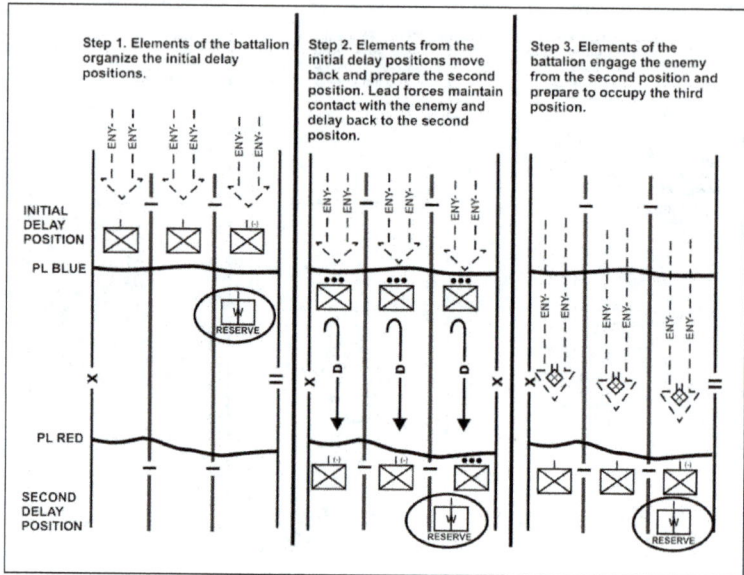

Figure 5-7. Delay from subsequent positions.

Mobility and Countermobility

5-97.   The following are key considerations for mobility and countermobility operations:

- When operating within a large AO, task-organize countermobility assets to companies; decentralizing control and execution.
- Task-organize mobility and sustainment assets to companies to support rearward breaching and reducing requirements.
- Develop the obstacle plan to support disengagement of delaying forces and to shape the enemy's maneuver to meet the commander's intent. Consider countermobility requirements for all delaying positions throughout the depth of the AO. Integrate SCATMINE at delay positions to support disengagement and movement to subsequent positions.
- Consider the impact of the obstacle effort on the movement of friendly forces and future operations. Develop obstacle restrictions, establish lanes and guides, and employ situational or reserve obstacles to support mobility requirements. Plan for closing lanes behind friendly forces with scatterable or hand-emplaced mines.
- Develop clear criteria for execution of situational and reserve obstacles. Integrate decisions for their execution in the decision support template.

Fire Support in a Delay

5-98.   The following are key considerations for the fire support plan:

- Attack the enemy throughout the AO.
- Engage the enemy with fires to inflict casualties and disrupt his approach before he gets to friendly delaying positions. Plan final protective fires (FPFs) for each series of delaying positions to support disengagement.
- Mass fires on high-payoff targets and canalizing terrain to limit the momentum of the enemy's attack.
- Plan and designate priority targets along routes from one delaying position to the next.
- Mass all available fire support to support disengagements.
- Use smoke to screen friendly movements.
- Plan appropriate MFP to provide support throughout the entire mission.
- Consider split based operations and associated security measures and risks.
- Establish clear priorities and detailed triggers to adjust them.
- Develop detailed triggers to initiate and lift fires for each target.

Protection

5-99.   Ensure adequate air defense coverage of friendly forces during movements from one delaying position to another. Consider protection along movement routes, chokepoints, and bridges that friendly forces intend to use.

5-100.   BCT planning defines CBRN operations in the delay. Battalions may coordinate for reconnaissance assets if available in the BCT. Decontamination operations in the delay focus on individual and crew operational decontamination procedures until the conclusion of the operation, when thorough decontamination can be accomplished. If smoke generators are available, the battalion may employ them for deception, obscuring movement and positions, or obscuring portions of the battlefield to reduce enemy visibility and ease of movement.

5-101.   Construct survivability positions in depth, as required, to support repositioning forces.

Sustainment

5-102.   Sustainment for a delay is particularly complex. Communication within the sustainment system, accurately tracking the battle, and anticipating support requirements are especially important. The following are key sustainment planning considerations:

- Keep the sustainment assets mobile and supplies uploaded.
- Task-organize ambulances and recovery vehicles to the companies.
- Emphasize maintenance support forward for the weapons company with short evacuation times.
- Synchronize refueling and resupply operations with the scheme of maneuver and the anticipated enemy situation to ensure continuity of support. Increase emergency Class III and V supplies positioned forward.
- Do not coordinate for throughput too far forward, which might cause assets to be caught in the fight or add to route congestion. This may not apply during the initial preparations for the delay.
- Plan routes for sustainment assets that do not conflict with maneuver elements or refugee movement.

Preparations

5-103.   Defensive preparations discussed in Section II also apply during the conduct of a delay.

Inspections

5-104.   The commander inspects planning and preparations of his subordinate units to ensure—

- Maneuver, fire, and obstacle plans are consistent with his intent.
- Flank coordination between delaying companies is conducted to maintain cohesion and mutual support during the delay.
- All leaders have a clear understanding of the scheme of maneuver including disengagement criteria, routes, triggers, and the commander's intent.

Rehearsals

5-105.   When conducting a rehearsal for a delay, key leaders practice the operation against all feasible enemy COAs to promote flexibility of decision-making, plans, and execution. The commander examines each subordinate unit commander's plan as he fights the delay during the rehearsal and pays close attention to the following:

- Direct and indirect fire instructions.
- Timing of movements (to include in limited visibility) and delaying actions from one position to the next with special attention paid to the disengagement criteria.
- Means and methods of disengaging from the enemy and maintaining contact with the enemy as the force moves to subsequent positions.
- Execution of situational and reserve obstacles to include closure of lanes.
- Movement times, routes, and positioning of fire support, protection, and sustainment assets.

5-106.   The commander also rehearses plans to deal with potential reverses such as enemy penetrations and unanticipated decisive engagement, and unanticipated opportunities to resume the offense. The rehearsal serves to further synchronize the movement of combat forces, fire support, protection, and sustainment units. It is especially important to portray movement times and required routes realistically during the rehearsal to identify potential conflicts.

Execution

5-107.   The battalion moves key forces and support assets to prepare for the delay. This initial movement includes movement into the security area and MBA.

Security Area Actions

5-108.   Delaying forces must be prepared to occupy the FLOT without a security force to their front; however, this is never the preferred option. The BCT normally uses the reconnaissance squadron to occupy the security area for a delay. The battalion may position the scout platoon or a task organized company in a screen behind the reconnaissance squadron to maintain observation, to provide early warning, and to adjust indirect fires to continue the disruption and attrition of the attacking enemy. As the enemy closes into and through the security area, the screening forces move back through or around the initial main body positions to subsequent positions that allow them to observe the MBA and assist in the disengagement and movement of forces to their next positions.

Main Battle Area

5-109.   The battalion uses fires and obstacles to force the enemy to deploy and assault. Its masses effects quickly for a short period, to inflict the maximum damage on the enemy at the maximum range. To avoid decisive engagement, the battalion must disengage before the enemy can breach obstacles or mass effective fire on the delay position. Observers positioned to the flanks in depth continue to observe and shift indirect fires as forces delay to subsequent positions. Companies may move by bounds within the battalion or company to maintain direct fires on the enemy and cover movement. Short, intense engagements at near maximum range with sustained indirect fires and covering obscurants, are the key to coercing the enemy into deploying early and often for a decisive engagement.

Control

5-110.   The battalion commander must closely control the disposition, displacement, and maneuver of his forces in order to maintain the cohesion of the delay operation and keep the entire battalion synchronized with the remainder of the BCT. Given the potential for loss of positive control, it is critical that the commander clearly establish parameters for displacement.

5-111.   As it executes the delay, the battalion and company commanders must continually assess their situations and requirements to displace with the following considerations:

- What are the size, activity, and location of attacking and adjacent enemy forces? Are elements of the battalion threatened with decisive engagement, encirclement, or bypass?
- What is the location and status of adjacent units?
- Are supporting assets, particularly artillery and mortars, postured to support movement? If not, how long will it take them to be ready?
- Are the obstacles supporting the present position still intact and effective?
- What is the ammunition status?
- Are displacement routes clear?

5-112.   The battalion must always make decisions about displacement and timing in the context of the commander's intent and priority for the delay, for example, is time more important than force preservation, or vice versa? In many instances, the battalion or elements of it must accept decisive engagement to execute the mission in conjunction with another force's counterattack.

Counterattacks

5-113.   The battalion can rarely execute a substantial counterattack during a delay by itself unless it is part of the larger BCT scheme of maneuver. Generally, counterattacks executed by the battalion, in its own scheme of maneuver, are platoon to possibly company-size counterattacks to support disengagement of forces or to destroy penetrations. Because of mobility, firepower, and range of weapons systems, the biggest asset the battalion has to execute a counterattack is the weapons company. Whenever possible, the BCT executes counterattacks to counter penetrations, to gain a temporary degree of initiative or freedom of action, and to avoid a predictable pattern of operation.

Decisive Engagement

5-114.   The battalion and companies avoid becoming decisively engaged except when necessary to prevent the enemy from reaching a specified area too early or when a part of the force must be risked to protect the entire force. If elements of the battalion are threatened with decisive engagement, or have become decisively engaged, the commander may take actions to support their disengagement and may perform any of the following:

- Allocate priority of all supporting fires to the threatened unit. This is the most rapid and responsive means of increasing the unit's combat power.
- Employ CAS or attack helicopters to suppress the enemy and restore freedom of maneuver to the battalion.

- Reinforce the unit. In a delay mission, particularly in a large AO, the battalion may not be able to do this quickly enough with ground maneuver forces.
- Conduct a counterattack to disengage the unit.

Termination

5-115.   A delay mission ends with another planned mission such as a defense, withdrawal, or attack. Ideally, a battalion that has been delaying conducts a rearward passage of lines through the established defense of another friendly force. The criteria for the termination of the delay must be detailed by the commander by time, distance, or whether the battalion defeats the enemy. If the enemy attack is defeated during the delay, the battalion may conduct one of the following:

- Maintain contact while another force counterattacks.
- Withdraw to perform another mission.
- Transition to the offense.

5-116.   In all cases, the commander must plan for the expected outcome and actions taken after termination of the delay based on the situation and the higher commander's plan.

WITHDRAWAL

5-117.   Withdrawal is a planned operation in which a force in contact disengages from an enemy force. Withdrawals may or may not be conducted under enemy pressure.

Types

5-118.   Withdrawals are either assisted or unassisted.

Assisted

5-119.   The assisting force occupies positions to the rear of the withdrawing unit and prepares to accept control of the situation. It can also assist the withdrawing unit with route reconnaissance, route maintenance, fire support, protection, and sustainment. Both forces closely coordinate the withdrawal. After coordination, the withdrawing unit delays to a battle handover line, conducts a passage of lines, and moves to its final destination.

Unassisted

5-120.   The withdrawing unit establishes routes and develops plans for the withdrawal, then establishes a security force as the rear guard while the main body withdraws. Sustainment and protection elements normally withdraw first, followed by combat forces; however, the protection and sustainment forces must continue to maintain the ability to support all elements in the battalion. To deceive the enemy as to the friendly movement, the battalion may establish a detachment left in contact (DLIC) if withdrawing under enemy pressure. As the unit withdraws, the DLIC disengages from the enemy and follows the main body to its final destination.

Organization

5-121.   The battalion normally organizes into a security force, main body, and reserve. It may elect to use a single company or elements of a company as the security or reserve force. It may also organize a DLIC or stay-behind forces if required by the enemy situation.

Security Force

5-122.   The security force maintains contact with the enemy until ordered to disengage or until another force takes over the task. It simulates the continued presence of the main body, which requires additional allocation of combat multipliers beyond that normally allocated to a force of its size. When withdrawing under enemy pressure, the security force establishes or operates as a DLIC to provide a way to break contact from the enemy sequentially. When conducting the withdrawal without enemy pressure, the security force acts as a rear guard because the most probable threat is a pursuing enemy.

Detachment Left in Contact

5-123.   The DLIC is an element that is left in contact as part of the previously designated (usually rear) security force while the main body conducts its withdrawal. Its purpose is to remain behind to deceive the enemy into believing the battalion is still in position while the majority of the unit withdraws. The DLIC should be one of the strongest of the subordinate units with the most capable leadership. It will be the unit under the greatest pressure, and the success of the withdrawal often depends on its effectiveness. The commander establishes specific instructions about what to do if the enemy attacks and when and under what circumstances to delay or withdraw. The battalion organizes a DLIC in one of three ways (Figure 5-8).

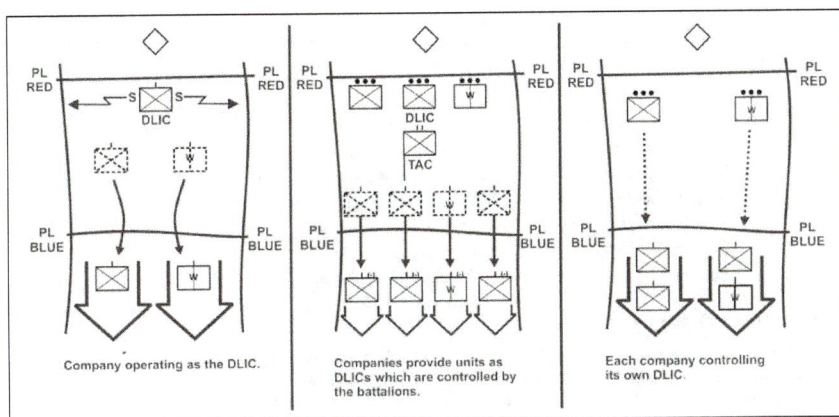

Figure 5-8. Methods for organizing the detachment left in contact.

Single Company

5-124.   A single company operates as the DLIC. This is the most effective option since it provides for effective task organization and C2.

DLIC Element Formed from each Company

5-125.   Each company provides forces for the DLIC mission. The resulting DLIC element then operates under the battalion's control. This is the least desirable option since it complicates C2 and task organization and requires significant changes to the communications architecture. The battalion most commonly uses this option when the subordinate companies have lost significant portions of their C2 capabilities.

Company Control of Separate DLICs

5-126.   Each company establishes and controls its individual DLIC. The battalion uses this option when it is operating over a wider area or one with multiple corridors in the withdrawal AO. It allows for effective dispersion of forces while maintaining standard C2 relationships.

Additional considerations

5-127.   The battalion should establish an advance guard on its route of movement. It may designate a company or the scout platoon reinforced with Infantry and mortars as the advance guard. The battalion should task-organize both the DLIC and the advance guard with engineers, with mobility assets going to the advance guard and obstacle and mobility assets going to the DLIC. The battalion main body consists of the remaining companies, command posts, sustainment assets, remaining engineers, and the mortars (if they are not task-organized to support either the DLIC or the advance guard). The battalion must ensure it provides essential communications, sustainment, and indirect fire support for the DLIC. The battalion may designate a reserve, normally a platoon or company in the main body. To create flank security, it uses the scout platoon, engineers, or elements of the main body team.

Planning Considerations

5-128.   Because the force is most vulnerable if the enemy attacks, the commander and staff normally plan for a withdrawal under enemy pressure. It also develops contingency plans for a withdrawal without enemy pressure. During planning, the commander and staff specifically consider the following:

- Disengagement criteria (time, friendly situation, enemy situation).
- Plan for a deliberate break in contact from the enemy.
- Plan for deception to conceal the withdrawal for as long as possible.
- Rapid displacement of the main body, safeguarded from enemy interference.
- Selection and protection of withdrawal routes and alternates.
- Sitting of obstacles behind the DLIC to complicate pursuit.
- Fire support remains within supporting distance.
- Sustainment assets remain within distance to support the DLIC.

Commander's Guidance

5-129.   The commander develops his vision of the battle based on withdrawing under enemy pressure. He determines the composition and strength of the security force, main body, the DLIC, and reserve. The commander clearly defines how he intends to deceive the enemy as to the execution of the withdrawal; how he intends to disengage from the enemy (use of maneuver, fires, and obstacles); and the final end state of the operation in terms of time, location, and disposition of friendly and enemy forces.

Scheme of Maneuver

5-130.   A withdrawal may be assisted or unassisted and may take place with or without enemy pressure. The plan considers which of the variations the battalion executes based on the higher headquarters' order and the enemy situation.

Assisted Withdrawal

5-131.   In an assisted withdrawal, the staff coordinates the following with the assisting force:

- Rearward passage of lines.
- Reconnaissance of withdrawal routes.
- Forces to secure choke points or key terrain along the withdrawal routes.

- Elements to assist in movement control such as traffic control points.
- Required combat, fire support, protection, and sustainment to assist the withdrawing battalion in disengaging from the enemy.

Unassisted Withdrawal

5-132. In an unassisted withdrawal, the battalion establishes its own security and disengages from the enemy. It reconnoiters and secures routes that it uses in its rearward movement while sustaining itself during the withdrawal.

Withdrawal under Enemy Pressure

5-133. In a withdrawal under enemy pressure, all units other than the rear guard or DLIC withdraw simultaneously when available routes allow. The following factors influence the decision to withdraw simultaneously:

- Subsequent missions.
- Availability of transportation assets and routes.
- Disposition of friendly and enemy forces.
- Level and nature of enemy pressure.
- Degree of urgency associated with the withdrawal.

Transition

5-134. The element that will be the DLIC or rear guard must transition to cover the battalion's AO. Simultaneously, the battalion must prepare its sustainment assets and the remainder of the force to begin a withdrawal to the rear. The battalion should seek to move on two routes to gain speed and shorten formations. Using more than two routes exceeds the ability of the battalion to maintain security. Often, only a single route will be available.

Breaking Contact

5-135. The battalion commander has essentially two options for breaking contact: break contact using deception and stealth or break contact quickly and violently under the cover of supporting fires reinforced by obstacles to delay pursuit. He bases this choice on the factors of METT-TC.

Withdrawal without Enemy Pressure

5-136. When conducting a withdrawal without enemy pressure, the commander can focus the plan on the best method to displace forces rapidly and securely. He has the option of taking calculated risks that increase his force's displacement capabilities. He may order the main body to conduct a tactical road march instead of moving in tactical formations, or he may move on as many routes as possible with reduced security in order to gain speed.

Preparation

5-137. The commander prepares the battalion for the withdrawal through inspections and rehearsals in the same fashion as discussed with other defensive operations. Inspections for this mission focus on subordinate unit preparations to ensure a clear understanding of the scheme of maneuver and his intent. During an assisted withdrawal, the commander ensures adequate coordination for battle handover and passage of lines. The focus of the rehearsal for the withdrawal is on actions to maintain security, disengagement from the enemy, and the movement of forces. When possible, key leaders or liaisons from the assisting force should attend the rehearsal. The commander ensures control measures, which include FSCMs to fully support the withdrawal. Leaders rehearse the plan against the full range of possible enemy actions. They rehearse contingencies for reverting to a delay, commitment of the reserve, and enemy interdiction of movement routes.

Execution

5-138.   Execution of the battalion withdrawal essentially follows this pattern:

- Task-organizing and positioning of security and deception forces.
- Reconnaissance and surveillance of withdrawal routes and subsequent positions.
- Preparation of obstacles to support the DLIC and withdrawal.
- Preparing wounded Soldiers and damaged equipment and nonessential supplies for movement.
- Moving nonessential protection and sustainment assets to the rear.
- Initiating movement, leading with forward security forces.
- DLIC breaks off contact and moves as a rear guard.

Disengagement

5-139.   The security force remains in position and maintains a deception while the main body moves as rapidly as possible rearward to intermediate or final positions. After the main body withdraws a safe distance, the commander orders the security force to begin its rearward movement. Once the security force begins moving, it assumes the duties of a rear guard. The security element must balance security and deception with speed as it disengages. It maintains tactical movement and security techniques until it is clear that the enemy is not pursuing and contact has been broken; it then withdraws as rapidly as possible. The main body moves rapidly on multiple routes to designated positions. It may occupy a series of intermediate positions before completing the withdrawal. Usually protection and sustainment assets move first and precede combat and fire support units in the movement formation. The staff enforces the disciplined use of routes during the withdrawal. Despite confusion and enemy pressure, subordinate units follow specified routes and movement times.

Actions on Contact

5-140.   Security forces counter the enemy's try to disrupt the withdrawal or pursue the battalion. If the security force and the reserve cannot prevent the enemy from closing on the main body, the commander commits some or all of the main body to prevent the enemy from interfering further with the withdrawal. The main body delays, attacks, or defends as required by the situation. In this event, the withdrawal resumes at the earliest possible time. If the enemy blocks movement to the rear, the battalion must adjust its order of withdrawal march to ensure protection and sustainment elements are not the primary fighting force to eliminate the threat. Friendly forces shift to alternate routes and bypass the interdicted area. Alternatively, they may attack through the enemy.

Termination

5-141.   Once the battalion successfully disengages from the enemy, it normally has the following options:

- Rejoin the overall defense.
- Transition into a retirement.
- Continue moving away from the enemy and towards its next mission area.

5-142.   The higher headquarters defines the next mission. Follow-on missions are normally planned as the withdrawal is being planned or executed.

RETIREMENT

5-143.   A retirement is a retrograde operation in which a force that is not in contact with the enemy moves to the rear in an organized manner. The battalion conducts a retirement as part of the BCT to reposition for future operations.

Organization

5-144.   The battalion may serve either as a security element for the BCT, or as a part of the main body. The battalion normally organizes itself with security, main body, and reserve elements, depending on the situation and where the battalion is in the movement scheme. The formation and number of columns employed, depend on the number of available routes and the potential for enemy interference. The commander typically wants to move his major elements to the rear, while simultaneously using multiple routes.

Planning Considerations

5-145.   The commander and staff develop a movement plan based on the friendly situation, commander's guidance, and enemy situation. The staff develops detailed movement control measures, associated graphics, and triggers to ensure the steady progress of movements and to prevent elements from congesting the routes. They develop the movement formation and order of movement to balance the need for security and speed. Security forces protect the main body from surprise, harassment, or attack by any pursuing enemy forces. Each march column normally maintains an advance guard, rear guard, and flank security, depending on the situation with adjacent friendly forces and the likelihood of enemy interference. The main body may organize into an approach march or tactical road march if speed is most important and the need for security is low.

Preparation

5-146.   During preparations, the battalion units conduct rehearsals and prepare for the movement. Units maintain OPSEC and security operations and dispatch advance parties, route security elements, and quartering parties as required.

Execution

5-147.   During a retirement, the battalions and its companies normally move to assembly areas to prepare for future operations. Companies move IAW established movement times and routes. Strict adherence to the movement plan is essential to avoid congestion or delay. The staff closely supervises the execution of the movement plan. Sustainment and protection units usually move to the rear first. The battalion may choose to provide the protection and sustainment units with security elements depending on the likelihood of enemy contact.

Section III. PLANNING CONSIDERATIONS

Planning a defensive operation is a complex effort requiring detailed planning and extensive coordination. This section contains planning considerations applicable for defensive operation. In the defense, synchronizing the effects of the battalion combat and supporting systems allows a commander to apply overwhelming combat power against selected advancing enemy forces to unhinge the enemy commander's plan and destroy his combined-arms team. All defensive operations are a mix of static and dynamic actions. As an operation evolves, the commander knows he will probably have to shift his decisive and shaping operations to disrupt and maintain pressure on the enemy, deny him freedom of maneuver, and prevent him from wresting away our initiative.

KEYS TO SUCCESSFUL DEFENSE

5-148.   The commander's keys to a successful defense are—

*   Capability to concentrate and synchronize effects.
*   Depth of the defensive area.
*   Security.
*   Ability to take full advantage of the terrain.
*   Flexibility of defensive operations.
*   Echelonment of direct and indirect fires.
*   Fire distribution and fire control measures.
*   Early identification of threat forces (UAS, counterreconnaissance, combat outposts, sensors, JIIM/SOF assets).
*   Timely resumption of offensive action.

COMMANDER'S VISION

5-149.   Initially, integrated with the staff's IPB, the commander expresses his vision of the enemy's anticipated actions. The battalion commander and staff refine the BCT IPB to focus on the details of the operation in the battalion AO. The BCT commander normally defines where and how the BCT will defeat or destroy the enemy and how he envisions the battalion executing its portion of the BCT fight.

HOW AND WHERE TO DEFEAT ENEMY

5-150.   The commander and staff base their determination of how and where to defeat the enemy, on where they believe the enemy will go, the terrain, the forces available, and the BCT commander's intent. The battalion commander may define a defeat mechanism that includes the use of single or multiple counterattacks to achieve success. The battalion commander and staff analyze their unit's role in the BCT fight, and determine how to successfully accomplish their purpose. In an area defense, the battalion usually achieves success by massing the cumulative effects of obstacles and fires to defeat the enemy forward of a designated area, often in conjunction with a BCT counterattack. In a delay operation, the battalion achieves success by combining maneuver, fires, and obstacles, and by avoiding decisive engagement until conditions are right to achieve the desired effect of gaining time or shaping the battlefield for a higher echelon counterattack.

FORCES AND ASSETS AVAILABLE

5-151.   The commander and staff analyze the forces and assets available, paying particular attention to the obstacle assets and fire support allocated by the BCT. The staff defines the engineer and fire support allocation in terms of capability, resources, and priority. For example, it should define engineer capability in terms of the number of obstacles of a specific effect engineers can emplace in the time available. Fire support analysis should include the number of targets that can be engaged with an expected result at what point in the battle.

EFFECTS

5-152.   With a definitive understanding of the assets available, the commander and staff determine what effects combat forces, fires, and obstacles must achieve on enemy formations by avenue of approach and how these effects will support both the BCT's and the battalion's defeat mechanism. They define the task(s) and purpose for subordinate units and establish priorities for protection and sustainment. They develop obstacle and fire support plans concurrently with the defensive force array, again defining a task and purpose for each obstacle and target in keeping with the commander's stated EFSTs and intended obstacle effects. The desired end state is a plan which defines how the commander intends to mass the effects of direct and indirect fires with obstacles and use of terrain to shape the battlefield and defeat or destroy the enemy.

Section IV. SEQUENCE

The battalion may assume a defensive mission following an attack of its own, or in anticipation of an enemy attack. The following general sequence of operations applies to planning and executing all defensive operations.

OCCUPATION AND ESTABLISHMENT OF SECURITY

5-153. Normally, the BCT has established some form of security with the reconnaissance squadron before the battalion moves into the area. However, the battalion must still provide its own internal security, especially on expanded or complex terrain and noncontiguous areas of operation. In order to prevent the enemy from observing and interrupting defensive preparations and identifying unit positions, the battalion establishes the security area well beyond where the MBA is desired, but within indirect fire and communications range. If they cannot push the security area forward to achieve this objective, the battalion may have to hold its positions initially, as it transitions and then withdraws units to the defensive MBA, establishing a security force in the process.

LEADERS' RECONNAISSANCE

5-154. Before occupying any position, leaders at all echelons conduct some type of reconnaissance. This reconnaissance effort is as detailed as the factors of METT-TC permit. It may consist of a simple map reconnaissance, or a more detailed leader's reconnaissance and initial layout of the new position. When feasible, the commander and subordinate leaders conduct a reconnaissance of the AO to develop the plan based on their view of the actual terrain. The commander and staff develop a plan for the leaders' reconnaissance that includes the following. When available, the commander may use aviation assets to conduct the leaders' reconnaissance:

- Provisions for security.
- Leaders and key staff members required to participate.
- Designation of a recorder.
- Areas to be reconnoitered.
- Time allocated for the reconnaissance.
- Indirect fires, communications, and CASEVAC support plans.
- Rapid reaction force to respond in the event that the reconnaissance element is compromised.

MOVEMENT INTO UNSECURED AREA OF OPERATIONS

5-155. If the battalion is moving into an unsecured AO, it may lead with the scout platoon, possibly reinforced with dismounted or weapons company elements and mortars. Depending on the situation, the battalion may send a company to secure the area. The mission of the security force is to clear the area, check for contaminated areas and obstacles, and establish security for the battalion main body. After clearing the battalion's rear area and the area where the companies will be positioned, the security force should position itself to—

- Prevent enemy observation of defensive preparations.
- Defeat infiltrating reconnaissance forces.
- Prevent the enemy from delivering direct fires or observed indirect fires into the battalion defenses.
- Provide early warning of the enemy's approach.

POSITIONING OF FORCES

5-156. The positioning of the battalion security elements must be integrated into the security operations of the BCT and adjacent battalions. In contiguous or linear defenses, the battalion commander normally organizes and defines the security area forward of the FEBA, assigning the companies AOs of the battlefield to prevent gaps in the battalion security. In non contiguous or non linear defenses, the battalion commander normally organizes and defines the security area forward of the MBA, or along likely avenues of approach. In this type of defense, companies will have more responsibility for independent security areas. The key is to integrate operations at the BCT and battalion levels and again at the company level, using all available resources to execute security operations.

SECURITY OPERATIONS

5-157. Preparation of the defense includes planning and plan refinement, positioning of forces, preparing positions, constructing obstacles, planning and synchronizing fires, positioning logistics, and conducting inspections and rehearsals. Throughout the preparation phase, security operations continue without interruption. Security forces may be assigned screen, or area security missions. The scout platoon may be positioned to screen and provide early warning along most likely enemy avenues of approach, reinforced in depth with sections or platoons from Infantry or weapons companies.

SECURITY

5-158. Security is a consideration throughout the AO. The battalion arrays security forces in depth to provide protection and to reduce the potential for enemy infiltration. It also secures the MBA to prevent enemy reconnaissance, reduction of obstacles, targeting of friendly positions, and other disruptive actions. Companies secure obstacles, BPs, and hide positions. The threat force and battlefield organization will dictate the commander's decision; whether elements in the battalion conducting sustaining operations are allocated security forces, or if they provide their own security. With extended lines of communication, the battalion may also secure logistical elements moving forward from the field trains to support the battalion.

DISPERSION

5-159. Forces should be widely dispersed and hidden, to reduce vulnerability and to aid in OPSEC. The staff must balance the benefits of dispersion against the requirements and resources for security areas. Usually, the greater the dispersion between companies, the larger the security area.

INTEGRATION

5-160. When applicable, integrate reconnaissance and ground maneuver units in the security forces. This provides the forces required for the hunter-killer technique. Use reconnaissance forces primarily to locate enemy elements and attack them with indirect fires but not to engage in direct fire attack except in self-defense. The reconnaissance force can then guide the maneuver force to destroy, neutralize, or repel threat forces with direct fires. Clearly establish the C2 headquarters and communication architecture for the security force.

SECURITY AREA ENGAGEMENT

5-161. The battalion normally does not have a significant security area engagement, as this is largely the domain of the BCT's reconnaissance squadron for shaping the battlefield and setting favorable conditions for the close fight. The battalion may execute some engagement tasks in the security area to support its own, or higher's defensive scheme.

EXECUTION OF PLANNED INDIRECT FIRES

5-162.   The battalion's planned indirect fires usually include security force elements or a fire support team (FIST), which executing indirect fire targets on a primary enemy avenue of approach. This may be in support of the higher headquarters' scheme of fires using BCT artillery, or in support of the battalion scheme with the use of organic mortars and allocated artillery fires.

EXECUTION OF SITUATIONAL OBSTACLES

5-163.   The battalion may be tasked by higher or may have integrated into a defensive scheme of its own; the use of situational obstacles to execute in the security area. These obstacles serve to disrupt the enemy and to force him to commit his engineer assets. They are usually planned and triggered relative to specific enemy attack options, and are related to accomplishing a specific essential mobility survivability tasks (EMST) and or EFST. This allows the battalion more effective engagements with indirect fires. Maneuver forces may be employed forward to cover them with direct fires, and then withdraw to positions in the MBA.

EXECUTION OF DELAY OPERATIONS THROUGH SECURITY AREA AND INTO MBA

5-164.   The battalion may support its own or higher's scheme of maneuver by fighting a delay through the depth of the security area and into the MBA. The purpose may be to take advantage of restrictive avenues of approach, to set the conditions for a counterattack, or to avoid a decisive engagement until favorable conditions have been set.

BATTLE HANDOVER

5-165.   The battalion assumes control of the FEBA fight from the security force as it completes its RPOL. Transferring responsibility from the security force to the battalion on the FEBA requires firm, clear arrangements--

- For assuming command of the action.
- For coordinating direct and indirect fires.
- For the security force's rearward passage of lines.
- For closing lanes in obstacles.
- For detailed movement planning that clears the security force from the battalion AO with minimal interference with the defense.

TRANSITION

5-166.   As security area engagements transition into the MBA, security area forces withdraw to the initial MBA, counterattack, or reserve positions. Some elements may maneuver to the flanks to maintain surveillance on enemy avenues of approach, providing early warning and execution of fires against follow-on enemy forces.

MAIN BATTLE AREA FIGHT

5-167.   The battalion seeks to defeat, disrupt, or neutralize the enemy's attack forward of or within the MBA. If the battalion can bring sufficient firepower to shape the enemy in the security zone fight, an MBA engagement may not occur. In this event, the battalion can rapidly transition and move its companies into a strong counterattack. However, the battalion and the companies normally defend over a large area, and enemy strength often forces an MBA engagement. In a non linear, non contiguous defense, dispersed companies will have a larger security area with little or no support from battalion. Therefore, companies will have a higher likelihood of having an MBA engagement. An MBA engagement is a combined-arms fight, integrating both direct fire and indirect fires, reinforced with obstacles and organic mortars.

5-168. The battalion continues to focus mortars, artillery, CAS, and attack aviation in an effort to attack the enemy continuously throughout the depth of the battlefield; therefore, fire support to the battalion and mortar support to companies, may be limited to critical points and times in the MBA fight. Combining all available fires with maneuver, obstacles, and reserve elements, the battalion commander seeks to destroy the enemy in designated EAs, or force his transition to a retrograde or hasty defense. The battalion normally specifies control measures to coordinate and focus the defensive operation. Control measures allow the commander to rapidly concentrate combat power at the decisive point, provide flexibility to respond to changes, and allocate responsibility of terrain and obstacles, and reduce tactical and accidental risk. These control measures include the security area, battle handover line (BHL), and the MBA. The commander also uses BPs and direct fire control measures, and FSCMs to further synchronize the employment of his combat power.

FOLLOW-ON MISSIONS

5-169. Following a successful defense, the attacker might have a period of confusion that the defender can exploit. Counterattacks can be executed based on branches and sequels to the plan, before the enemy can secure his gains or organize a defense. METT-TC and the higher commander's concept of operations dictate the battalion's follow-on mission. If the situation prevents offensive action, the battalion continues to defend. As in the initial establishment of the defense, gaining security zone space is critical. A local counterattack can provide space for a security zone and time to reorganize. Any attack option must pay particular attention not only to the terrain and enemy, but also to friendly obstacles (and their destruction times, if applicable) and areas where dual-purpose improved conventional munitions (DPICMs) or bomblets have been used. If the battalion cannot counterattack to gain adequate security space, then the battalion may have to direct one company to maintain contact with the enemy and guard the AO while others move to reestablish the defense farther to the rear. The battalion must reorganize whether it continues to defend or transition to offensive operations.

Section V. TECHNIQUES

The battalion normally defends using five basic techniques of defense: (1) *Defend an AO*, (2) *Defend a BP*, (3) *Conduct a Reverse slope defense*, (4) *Defend a strongpoint*, and (5) *Conduct a perimeter defense*. The BCT normally assigns the battalion an AO to defend; however, the battalion may use assign different techniques to respective companies within the same operation, for example, A Co defends an AO, B Co defends a BP, and the weapons company conducts a reverse slope defense.

DEFEND AN AREA OF OPERATIONS

5-170. A defense in an AO provides the greatest degree of freedom of maneuver and fire planning within a specific area. The battalion most often uses this method of control when it has an adequate amount of depth and width to the battlefield and does not desire decisive engagement early in the MBA fight. For a defense to be cohesive, the companies cannot maneuver with complete freedom. Phase lines, EAs, BPs, and obstacle belts help coordinate forces and achieve synchronized action. Use of AOs allows flexibility and prevents the enemy from concentrating overwhelming firepower on the bulk of the defending force. Forces defending against an enemy with superior mobility and firepower must use the depth of their positions to defeat the enemy. The depth of the defense must come from the initial positioning of units throughout the AO, not from maneuvering. A properly positioned and viable reserve enhances depth (Figure 5-9).

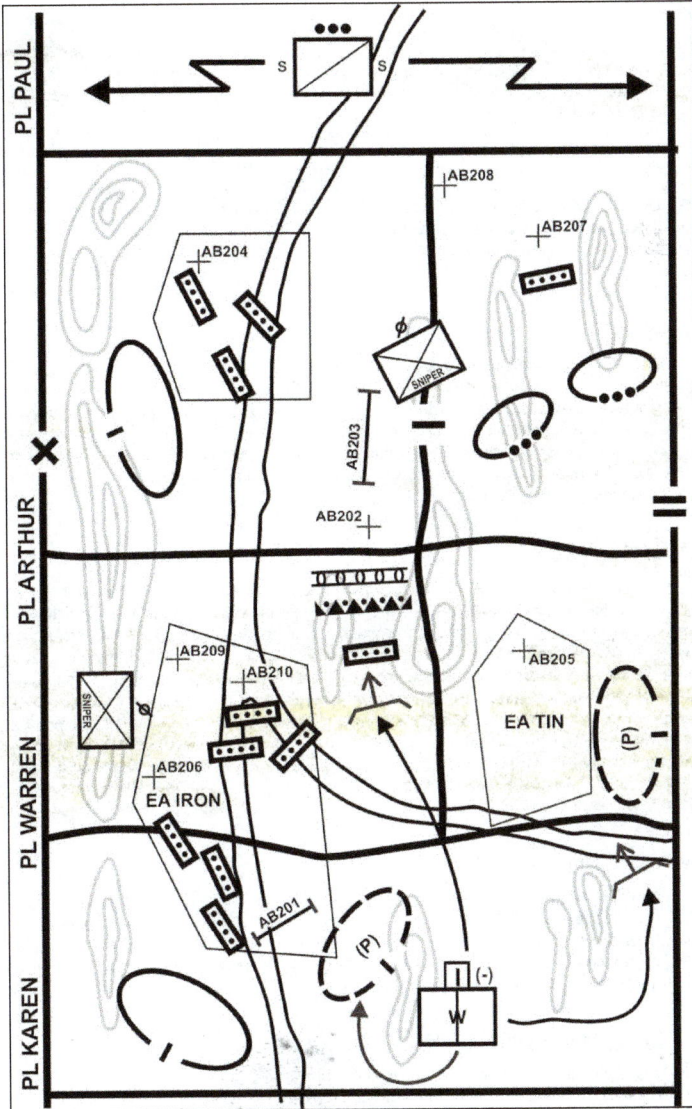

Figure 5-9. Defense of an AO.

POSITIONS

5-171. A battalion defending against a mounted enemy uses a series of mutually supporting battle positions, incorporating CCM antiarmor weapons. These positions should be located on vehicular-restricted terrain, maximize the stand-off capabilities of the CCM weapons, and strengthened by existing and reinforcing obstacles.

SECURITY

5-172. The AO defense is more effective against armor but more vulnerable to Infantry attack or combined-arms action that can be directed against one position at a time. Position preparation must emphasize all-round security and mutual support. ISR assets should be used to monitor the avenues of approach.

DEPLOYMENT IN DEPTH

5-173. Forces deployed in depth must simultaneously engage the enemy with effective fires from multiple locations as he tries to maneuver. The AO is organized around dispersed, small units that attack the enemy throughout the depth of his formations. The focus of this technique is the enemy force. Mines and other obstacles and patrols can close gaps that fire cannot cover effectively due to terrain masking or heavily wooded areas. The commander generally positions Infantry along mounted avenues of approach within restricted terrain and the weapons company along avenues of approach in unrestricted terrain; thereby, maximizing each capability.

ENGAGEMENT OPTIONS

5-174. The commander has three basic engagement options when defending an AO. He chooses the appropriate one based mainly on the restrictions of the terrain and his expectation of achieving surprise. His first option is to begin engaging at maximum optimum range, based on the terrain and available weapons systems. With this option, the commander would normally initiate with the weapons company to maximize the standoff distance. His second option is to allow the enemy to close to within direct fire range of the Infantry squads and machine guns. The defender then engages the enemy with violent, hasty, and deliberate counterattacks designed to destroy the enemy from any direction. In restricted terrain, this option denies a more mobile enemy force any firepower or mobility advantage. In the third option, the commander can task organize Infantry companies with the weapons company, to provide close combat and antiarmor capability in several locations. The commander uses this option when the enemy's courses of action are less clear. In this case, the commander normally maintains a larger reserve to react to enemy actions.

Beginning Engagement at Long Range

5-175. The defender initiates fires at long ranges with artillery, aircraft, and attack helicopters to begin to break up the continuity of the attack. As the enemy closes to within range of organic CCM antiarmor weapons, these weapons engage and further disrupt enemy synchronization by destroying key vehicles. When the enemy enters the engagement range of the battalion's organic weapons, the battalion engages him from multiple unexpected directions, and destroys him.

Allowing of Enemy into Depth of Position

5-176. This technique is offensive oriented. It allows for planned envelopments, ambushes, and counterattacks throughout the enemy formation. It is difficult for a forward array of forces to defend armor approaches. Such an array can be overrun or penetrated rapidly while under massive artillery, smoke, and direct fire suppression. To avoid penetration, the battalion must array forces in depth. Concentrating the battalion on wide fronts with a narrow depth may be risky.

DEFEND A BATTLE POSITION

5-177.   A BP is a general location and orientation of forces on the ground from which units defend. Battalion- to squad-size units can use BPs (Figure 5-10).

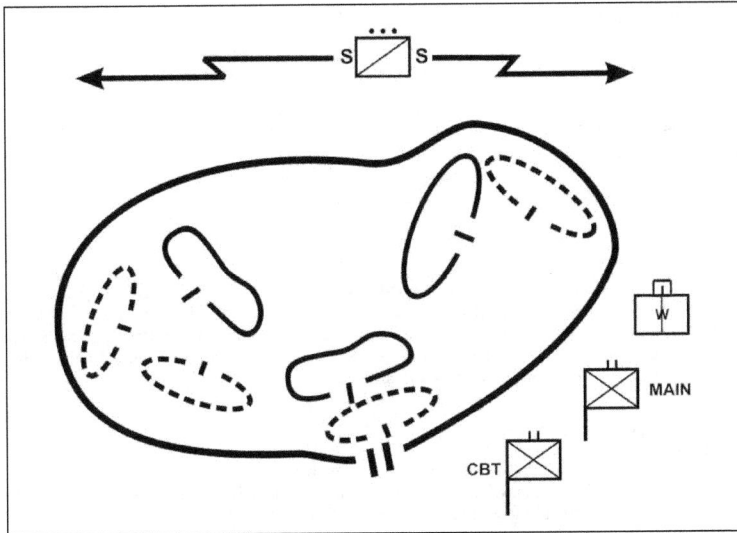

Figure 5-10. Disposition of forces in and about a BP.

USE OF BATTLE POSITIONS

5-178.   The commander's use of BPs reduces his directives to subordinate commander and gives them more freedom for placement of forces. Battle positions are graphic control measures identified by number, letter, name, or a combination of these.

THREE LEVELS OF PREPARATION FOR A BATTLE POSITION

5-179.   The three levels of preparation for a BP are: occupy, prepare, and plan. The use of on-order BPs with the associated tasks "prepare" or "planned" adds flexibility and depth to the defensive plan.

Occupy

5-180.   Occupation is complete preparation of the position where the company will initially defend. The unit fully plans, prepares, and occupies the position before the "*defend NLT*" time specified in the battalion OPORD. The company must rehearse the occupation, and the commander must establish a trigger for occupation of the position.

Prepare

5-181.   Preparation per se means that the unit fully reconnoiters the position and the corresponding EA, marking positions in the BP and fire control measures in the EA. From the BP, the unit must accomplish all actions to enable it to execute the mission immediately on occupation. Planning, coordination, and rehearsals are required for the unit to displace to the BP and accomplish the mission. Despite time constraints, the unit digs in survivability positions, constructs fighting positions, designates target reference points (TRPs), develops direct and indirect fire plans, emplaces obstacles, clears fields of fire, and prestocks ammunition. Prepare missions are normally critical to the defense. A unit assigned such a mission must maintain security on the position and on the routes to it.

Plan

5-182.   Planning means that the unit fully reconnoiters the EA and BP. They specifically plan tentative unit positions in the BP, and they establish fire control measures in the EA. They also coordinate and plan for defense from the position. Also, leaders reconnoiter, select, and mark positions, routes, and locations for security elements. Then, they coordinate movement and other actions, such as preparing obstacles and occupation plans, with other elements of the battalion.

MANEUVER

5-183.   The commander can move his elements freely within the assigned BP. To comply with the commander's intent, units can maneuver outside the BP to adjust fires or to seize opportunities for offensive action. Battalion security, fire support, protection, and sustainment assets are often positioned outside the BP with approval from the headquarters assigning the BP. Repositioning of units between BPs must be carefully coordinated to prevent fratricide.

SPACE ALLOCATION

5-184.   The commander allocates space to subordinate elements within the BP area based on the space available, terrain, and mission task. The battalion commander thinks two levels down or in terms of platoon BPs when he selects a BP for subordinate companies. When practical, he should allow enough space on each BP for dispersed primary, alternate, and supplementary positions for key weapons. The battalion commander can vary the number of maneuver elements in the battalion BP by allocating larger company BPs. Battle positions can also reflect positions in depth. They may take a shape other than the standard oblong shape, which suggests a linear defense within the BP. Large positions also increase dispersion to counter artillery and chemical munitions. The commander can combine company AO and BPs in the battalion AO to suit the tactical situation.

TYPES OF BATTLE POSITIONS

5-185.   There are five types of BPs: primary, alternate, supplementary, subsequent, and strongpoint.

Primary Positions

5-186.   Primary positions cover the enemy's most likely avenue of approach into the area. A primary position is the best position to accomplish the assigned mission. Routes between battle positions should be well known and rehearsed (optimally under the same conditions expected during execution).

Alternate Positions

5-187.   Alternate positions are those assigned for use when the primary position becomes untenable or unsuitable for carrying out the assigned task. These positions allow the defender to carry out his original task, such as covering an avenue of approach or EA, using the original direct fire plan. Alternate positions increase the defender's survivability by allowing engagement of the enemy from multiple positions and movement to other positions in case of suppressive or obscuring fires.

Supplementary Positions

5-188.   Supplementary positions are designated to cover avenues of approach that are not expected to be the enemy's primary avenue.

Subsequent Positions

5-189.   Subsequent positions are those to which the unit expects to move during the course of the engagement. The defending unit may have a series of subsequent positions (particularly in delay operations), each with associated primary, alternate, and supplementary positions.

Strongpoints

5-190.   Strongpoints are heavily fortified BPs tied into an existing or reinforcing obstacle, to create an anchor for defenses, or to deny the enemy key or decisive terrain. Strongpoints require extensive time, engineering support, and Class IV resources to construct and normally require increased Class V to defend. The battalion may be given strongpoint missions in rare instances; however, the static nature of the operation, and the resources required to conduct the strongpoint make it an unusual mission assignment.

CONDUCT A REVERSE SLOPE DEFENSE

5-191. A reverse slope defense is organized to use a topographical crest to mask the defender from the attacker's observation and from supporting direct fire (Figure 5-11).

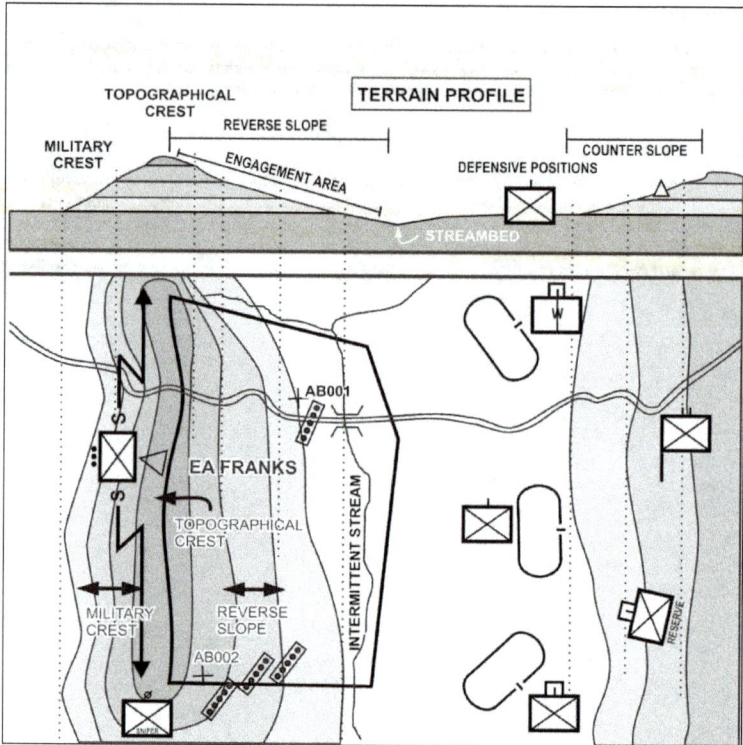

Figure 5-11. Organization of the reverse slope defense.

CONDITIONS

5-192. The battalion commander may adopt a reverse slope position for elements of the battalion when the following conditions exist. Surprising and deceiving the enemy about the true locations of the battalion defensive positions is vital:

- Enemy fire makes the forward slope untenable.
- Lack of cover and concealment on the forward slope makes it untenable.
- The forward slope has been lost or has not yet been gained.
- The forward slope is exposed to enemy direct fire weapons fired from beyond the effective range of the defender's weapons. Moving to the reverse slope removes the attacker's standoff advantage.

FM 3-21.20

- The terrain on the reverse slope affords better fields of fire than the forward slope.
- The defender must avoid creating a dangerous salient.
- The commander is forced to assume a hasty defense while in contact with or near the enemy.

ADVANTAGES

5-193. The following are some advantages of a reverse slope defense:

- Enemy ground observation of the battle area is masked, and degrades the observation capabilities of most surveillance devices and radar.
- Enemy direct fire weapons cannot effectively fire on the position without coming within range of the defender's weapons.
- The enemy must expose a majority of his force in an EA, if he wishes to mass the effects of his direct fire weapons.
- The enemy must try to breach obstacles on the reverse slope within direct fire range of all the defender's weapons. (The attacker cannot locate these obstacles until he encounters them; thus reducing his reaction time and maneuver space.)
- The enemy is deceived as to the strength and location of defensive positions.
- Enemy indirect fire is less effective since he cannot see the defender.
- The defender gains tactical surprise.
- The lack of enemy ground observation allows more freedom of movement within the battle area.
- CCM (Javelins and TOW missile systems), if positioned properly, can mass fires on the reverse military crest; Infantry small-arms weapons can contribute their close fires to the battle.
- The unit can dig in more quickly even when the enemy is approaching because the slope of the hill covers and conceals the unit from the direct fire and observation of approaching enemy ground forces. Defenders can concentrate on position preparation.

DISADVANTAGES

5-194. The following are some disadvantages of a reverse slope:

- Observation of the enemy may be limited, and the defender may be unable to cover obstacles to the front by direct fire.
- The topographical crest may limit the range of important direct-fire weapons. These weapons may have to locate separately from the Infantry elements to exploit their range.
- The enemy holds the high ground in an attack. His attack is downhill; the counterattack is uphill.
- Because the reverse military crest must be controlled, the effectiveness of the reverse slope defense is reduced during limited visibility.

ORGANIZATION OF DEFENSIVE POSITION

5-195. The battalion commander organizes the defensive position IAW procedures that apply to all defensive techniques.

Forward Edge of Position

5-196. The forward edge of the position should be within small-arms range of the crest. It should be far enough from the crest that fields of fire allow the defender time to place well-aimed fire on the enemy before he reaches friendly positions.

Flanking Fires

5-197.   A reverse slope position is most effective when units on adjacent terrain can place flanking fires on the forward slope.

Security Force

5-198.   The units should establish a security force to the front to stop or delay the enemy, to disorganize his attack, and to deceive him as to the location of the defensive position. When this security element withdraws, the unit must maintain observation, indirect fire, and security to the front. After withdrawing, the security force may either become the reserve force or move into a battle position for the main engagement. The mobility, optics, and long range direct fire capabilities of the weapons company, can provide tremendous advantages for the battalion as the security force.

Observation Posts/Combat Outposts

5-199.   The unit establishes observation posts or combat outposts on or forward of the topographical crest. This allows long-range observation over the entire front, and indirect fire coverage of forward obstacles. Observation posts or combat outposts are usually provided by the reserve, and may vary in size from a few Soldiers to a reinforced platoon. They should include forward observers. At night, their number may be increased to improve security. Depending upon their specific mission, these positions must be prepared to conduct surveillance, patrols, engage enemy reconnaissance, and engage the main body forces.

DEFEND A STRONGPOINT

5-200.   The mission to create and defend a strongpoint implies retention of terrain to stop or redirect enemy formations. Battalion strongpoints can be established in isolation when tied to restricted terrain on their flanks or on mounted avenues of approach tied to unit defensive positions on the strongpoint flanks. Strongpoints may be on the FEBA or in depth in the MBA (Figure 5-12). A bypassed strongpoint exposes enemy flanks to attacks from friendly forces inside and outside the strongpoint.

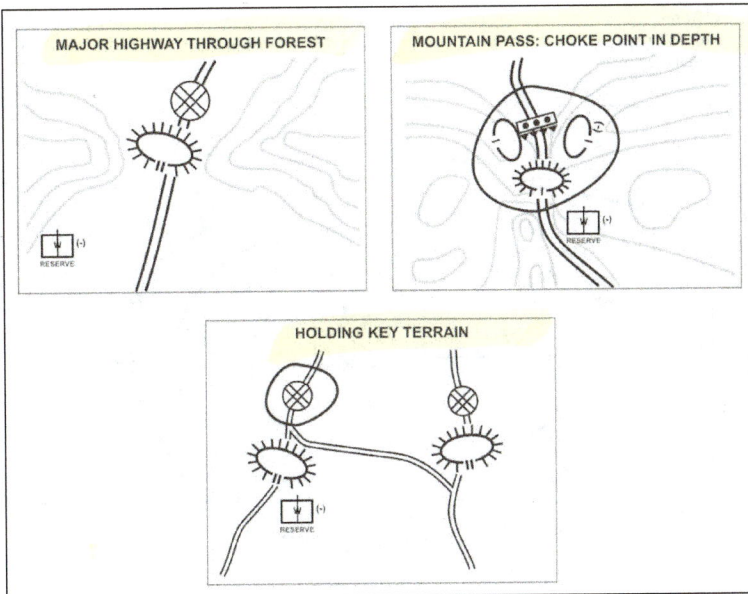

Figure 5-12. Examples of strongpoints.

PLANNING A STRONGPOINT DEFENSE

5-201. The battalion pays a high cost in manpower, equipment, material, and time to construct a strongpoint. It takes several days of dedicated work to construct a strongpoint defense.

Enemy Assault

5-202. When the enemy cannot easily bypass a strongpoint, the unit should expect and be ready to repel repeated enemy assaults. The strongpoint will probably receive intensive artillery attacks and must be prepared with overhead cover. Multiple positions in the strongpoint provide defense in depth. Combat vehicles committed to the strongpoint defense use multiple firing positions while Infantry squads use positions tied together with trenches. A battalion assigned a strongpoint mission—

- Plans movement to alternate positions in the strongpoint.
- Coordinates with forces outside the strongpoint, especially counterattack forces.
- Plans direct fires in detail and receives fire support priority.
- Establishes a small reserve to counter penetrations and, when appropriate, attacks outside the strongpoint.

Mutual Support

5-203. All positions in a strongpoint are mutually supporting (Figure 5-13). Positioning must allow massing of the fires of two or more units in the primary EA and prevent the enemy from isolating positions and defeating them in detail. Sectors of fire help coordinate and mass fires between positions. Avenues of approach into and around the strongpoint that cannot be covered by forces in primary positions must be kept under surveillance and covered by supplementary positions prepared in as much detail as time permits and occupied on order.

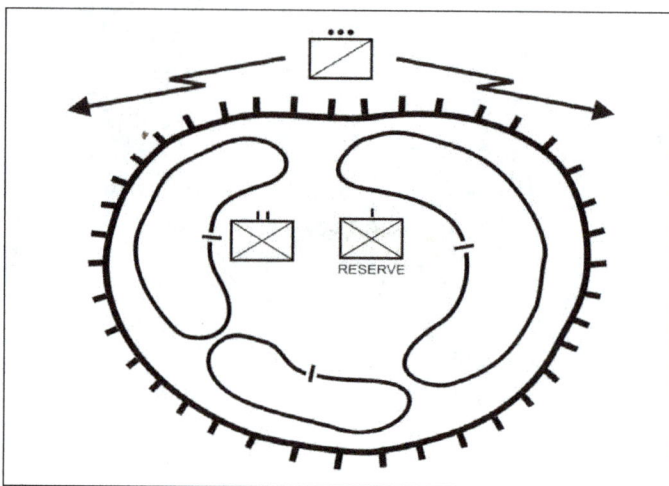

Figure 5-13. Battalion strongpoint, all forces within the strongpoint.

Forces Operating outside Strongpoint

5-204.   In some situations, the battalion defends from a strongpoint with forces operating outside the strongpoint. Security forces may operate forward or perform economy of force missions. Upon their return to the strongpoint, security forces should screen a secondary avenue of approach, occupy a position in depth, or become the reserve.

Employment Considerations

5-205.   If practical, weapons company CCM antiarmor forces occupy positions in depth to take advantage of their long-range fires. Alternate and supplementary positions are planned throughout the strongpoint and AO. Consideration should be given to operating the mortars in split section to provide greater coverage for the battalion, and avoid massing these key weapons in anticipation of great volumes of enemy artillery fires. Combat trains, with emergency resupply of Classes II and V, are placed in prepared defilade positions or buildings in the strongpoint. Supplies may be pre-positioned near primary, alternate, and successive positions. The BCT provides units to keep the main supply route open.

Security Force

5-206.   As with other types of defenses, the commander may use a company as part of the security force to provide information through contact and spot reports. The company assigned the security mission screens the battalion AO or along the most dangerous avenue of approach. This company provides early warning to the battalion, destroys enemy reconnaissance elements, and helps shape the battlefield so the enemy is directed against the strongpoint.

INTELLIGENCE SUPPORT FOR A STRONGPOINT

5-207. The strongpoint represents the culmination of the S-2's IPB and the commander's estimate of the situation. Based on a METT-TC analysis, the battalion commander identifies the piece of ground as decisive terrain. This piece of ground is the strongpoint.

Terrain Analysis

5-208. The S-2 conducts a detailed analysis of the terrain. Unlike other types of defense, the strongpoint must be defensible in 360 degrees. As a result, the terrain analysis is conducted with the understanding that enemy offensive operations, from an infiltration to a major attack, could appear from any direction (multiple avenues of approach).

Reconnaissance and Surveillance Plan

5-209. The reconnaissance and surveillance plan is essential to the strongpoint's effectiveness. Some reconnaissance assets may be able to operate outside of the position to provide initial early warning. If the strongpoint becomes encircled, the unit must be able to anticipate the actions of the enemy and respond internally. OPs positioned outside the position must be sustainable should the strongpoint become surrounded. The unit should have a plan for bringing patrols or other reconnaissance and surveillance assets into the position despite enemy presence.

Maneuver Concept

5-210. The strongpoint defense is the most labor-intensive operation a battalion commander may execute. Despite its static nature, the construction must allow for maximum flexibility. The key to an effective and sustainable strongpoint defense is to have a solid obstacle and direct and indirect fire plan coupled with properly constructed fortifications. The commander must take a personal interest in the interface between maneuver, fire support, protection, and sustainment elements.

Positions

5-211. The actual construction of the battalion EA and the direct fire control measures for a battalion strongpoint are identical to that discussed in earlier sections. After the S-2's IPB initiates the EA development process, the selection of company combat, protection, and sustainment positions is the first priority of the battalion commander. He must plan so that his weapons systems can engage the enemy effectively, along the major expected enemy avenue of approach. The S-2's line-of-sight analysis, the IPB, and the obstacle plan determine these positions. The actual construction of the battalion EA and the direct fire control measures are identical to that discussed in earlier sections. The considerations for weapons systems employment; however, may be different, particularly with respect to the lack of depth in the strongpoint. In a strongpoint, it is much more difficult to achieve depth of fires than in AO defensive operations.

Defensive Position Selection

5-212. Once the commander has determined the locations suitable for each type weapon system, he selects the company defensive positions. He addresses several considerations before finalizing the defensive positions. First, how much firepower is needed to cover the enemy avenue of approach? Second, how the defensive positions can be selected so they can be responsive to enemy attacks from other directions? Third, what task organization is best suited to the terrain and meets the security needs of the battalion?

STRONGPOINT ENGINEER SUPPORT

5-213. The supporting engineer element commander or platoon leader accompanies the maneuver commander on the reconnaissance of the strongpoint area. He helps plan indirect fires and SCATMINEs to slow, disrupt, and canalize the advancing enemy. He also prepares the position to make it physically impassable to armored or mechanized forces, severely restricted for dismounted forces, and to enhance the killing power of CCM antiarmor weapons with obstacles. The commander determines emplacement priority for fighting positions and obstacles and allocates the assets needed to accomplish the mission. Strongpoints are constructed from inside to outside. Regardless of the configuration of the strongpoint, the following are essential tasks to be performed:

- Prepare obstacles to prevent them from being overrun.
- Emplace obstacles at optimum weapon range.
- Construct protected routes between positions.
- Plan and coordinate for SCATMINEs.

RESERVE

5-214. In a strongpoint defense, it is important to maintain a reserve that can quickly react to enemy activity against the position. The reserve may—

- Block an enemy penetration of the perimeter.
- Reinforce a position or section of the defense.
- Counterattack to restore a portion of the strongpoint.

STRONGPOINT FIRE SUPPORT

5-215. If the enemy is able to reach the strongpoint in significant strength, the close-in fire support plan is essential to the integrity and survivability of the position. Fires are planned on obstacles close to the position, even if they are within minimum safe distances. Evacuation of the position may become necessary during the engagement. If fires are planned on the position, the unit can destroy the enemy and reoccupy the positions for continued defense. The indirect fires plan will normally allocate fires before, on, and beyond the strongpoint. Figure 5-14 shows the overall battalion fire support plan.

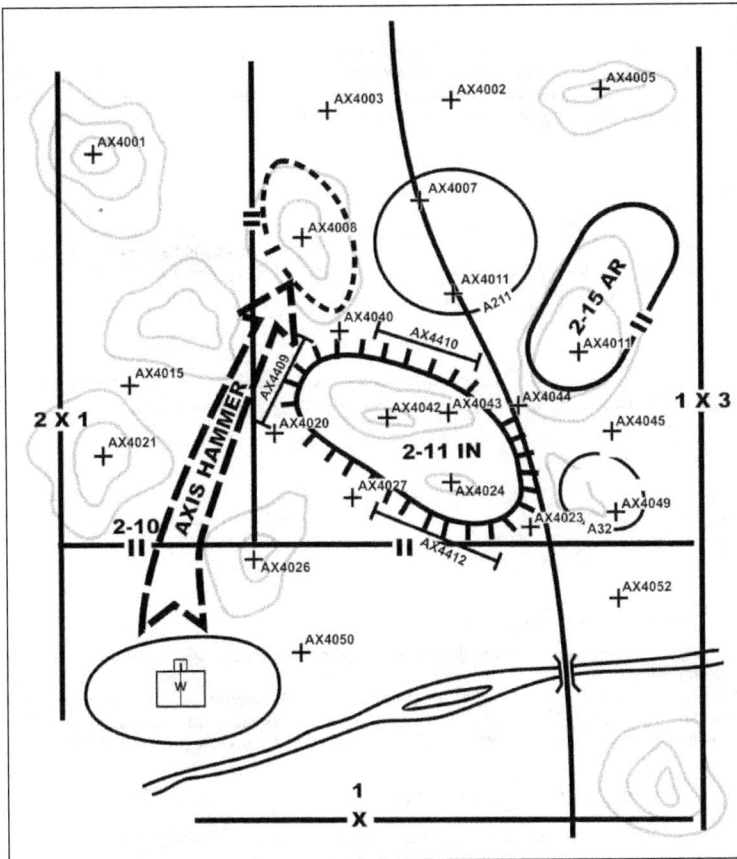

Figure 5-14. Strongpoint fire support plan.

PROTECTION

5-216. The AD commander and S-2 identify positions to facilitate engagements of enemy fixed- and rotary-wing aircraft. The AD commander ensures the engineers site actual positions properly. Engineers know how to construct positions, but the "occupant" must ensure the position is properly oriented.

STRONGPOINT SUSTAINMENT

5-217. The battalion S-4 helps plan for the following aspects of sustainment in a strongpoint.

Cache

5-218.   The S-4 examines the strongpoint construction plan and determines the best places to cache ammunition and supplies. The units refine the cache plan by positioning smaller caches adjacent to individual crew-served weapons. Once the unit caches have been identified or sited, the battalion S-4 develops a resupply plan. Battalion caches must be dispersed throughout the strongpoint to prevent a single detonation.

Medical Support

5-219.   Medical personnel must be ready to evacuate wounded from the perimeter to the aid station. The aid station is dug in, with easy access to each unit. The aid station should have access to a water supply, generators, and a bunker, if possible. In an elongated strongpoint, the aid station may split to provide support from two locations.

Refuel Points

5-220.   Even though combat vehicles in the position may be static, they still burn fuel during idling and scanning. The battalion should develop a refueling plan for the weapons company vehicles.

Combat Trains CP

5-221.   The CTCP is usually dug in separately from the battalion CP. It serves as the alternate CP should the main CP be destroyed. It is normally positioned away from the main CP but in proximity to the aid station and supply activities. The CTCP must establish redundant communications with the main CP so that direct communication is possible between the two headquarters.

STRONGPOINT COMMAND AND CONTROL

5-222.   The commander develops his strongpoint defense plan by using the terrain to its utmost advantage. His observation posts must afford the opportunity to observe the battle, and he must be able to traverse the strongpoint and respond to an attack from any direction. Communications systems must be redundant. The battalion should use all digital, FM, and wire means available. Communication wire should be buried deep in the strongpoint and field phones made available throughout the position.

CONDUCT A PERIMETER DEFENSE

5-223.   A perimeter defense is a defense oriented in all directions (Figure 5-15). The battalion uses it for self-protection. The battalion establishes a perimeter defense when it must hold critical terrain in areas where the defense is not tied in with adjacent units or existing obstacles. The battalion may also form a perimeter when it has been bypassed and isolated by the enemy and must defend in place. Unless executing a strongpoint, the perimeter defense usually does not take considerable time and resources to execute.

5-224.   These differences are in contrast to the strongpoint defense, in which the position is tied in with the rest of the defense and considerable time and resources are spent to retain key or decisive terrain.

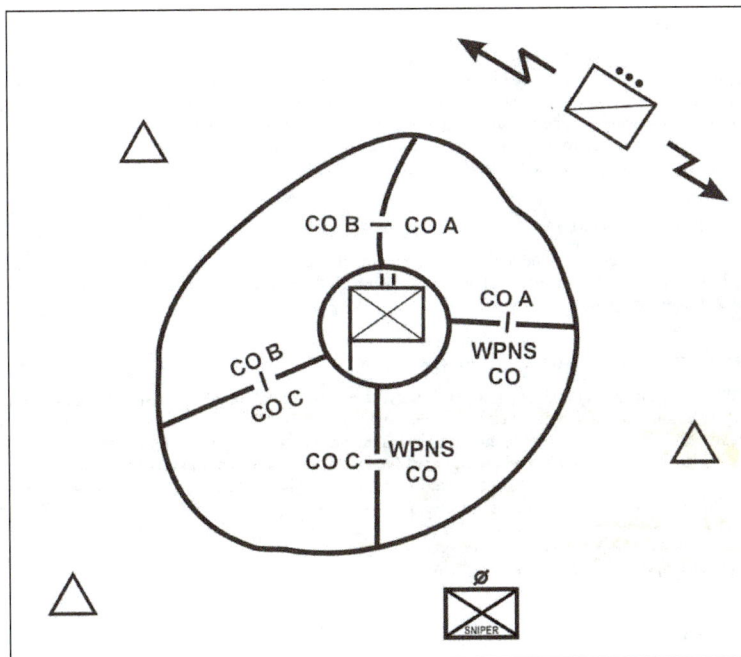

Figure 5-15. Perimeter defense.

PLANNING CONSIDERATIONS

5-225.   While in a perimeter defense, the battalion should consider the following:

- Positioning CCM antiarmor weapons systems on restricted terrain to overwatch mounted avenues of approach.
- Maximum depth allowed by the diameter of the perimeter through the location of security elements, the reserve, and secondary sectors of fire of CCM antiarmor weapons.
- Construction of obstacles to fix or block the enemy for effective engagement.
- Positioning and scheduling of ISR assets that provide 360 degree and 24 hour coverage.
- Allocation of a reserve and quick reaction forces.
- Task organization of battalion with special attention to weapons company and security force.

SECURITY FORCE

5-226.   The battalion commander employs a security force outside the perimeter for early warning. He augments the security force with patrols and OPs controlled by subordinate companies on the perimeter. Periodic patrols cover areas that stationary elements cannot observe.

BATTALION RESERVE

5-227.   The battalion reserve defends a portion of the second line of defense behind the perimeter elements. The reserve must have the mobility to react to enemy action in any portion of the perimeter. It is positioned to block the most dangerous avenue of approach and is assigned supplementary positions on other critical avenues. If the enemy penetrates the perimeter, the reserve blocks the enemy penetration or counterattacks to restore the perimeter. After committing the reserve, the commander immediately designates a new reserve force to meet other threats.

COMMAND AND CONTROL

5-228.   The battalion in a perimeter defense normally sets up two C2 operations; one for operations conducted outside the perimeter, and one to conduct base defense. See Appendix M   for more information on C2 of base operations.

FIRE SUPPORT, PROTECTION, AND SUSTAINMENT

5-229.   Fire support, protection, and sustainment elements may support from inside the perimeter or from another location depending on the mission and status of the battalion, the type of transport available, the weather, and the terrain. All sustainment assets inside the perimeter fall under the control of the battalion or base commander, and should be in a protected location where they can provide continuous support. They should also be integrated into the base security and defense plans. Since resupply may have to be done by air, the position should include or be near a landing or drop zone. The availability of LZs and DZs protected from the enemy's observation and fire is a main consideration in selecting and organizing the position. Since aerial resupply is vulnerable to weather and enemy fires, commanders must emphasize supply economy and protection of available stocks.

RESERVE

5-230.   The reserve is a force withheld from action to be committed at a decisive moment within the decisive operation. It provides the commander with the flexibility to exploit success or deal with a tactical setback and the flexibility to respond in situations where there is a great deal of uncertainty about the enemy. Normally, the battalion commander can only allocate a company as a reserve. This decreases the ability of the battalion to respond to tactical emergencies or to exploit success. It increases the significance of the BCT's reserve element, which may be only a company or a two-company battalion operating over an extended area. Situational obstacles, fires, UAS, CAS, and attack aviation can be used to augment reserve forces.

5-231.   The reserve's likely tasks are issued as planning priorities and may include one or more of the following:

- Counterattack locally.
- Defeat enemy air assaults
- Block enemy penetrations.
- Reinforce a committed company.
- Protect rear area operations.
- Secure high-value assets.

5-232.   During defensive preparations, the battalion commander may employ his reserve in other tasks such as security operations, rear area security, or obstacle emplacement. The commander must balance these uses with the needs to protect his reserve, and with the reserve commander's requirement to conduct troop-leading procedures, coordination, and reconnaissance.

5-233.   The commander and staff determine where and under what conditions the reserve force is likely to be employed in order to position it effectively and give it appropriate planning priorities. The reserve force commander analyzes his assigned planning priorities, conducts the coordination with units that will be affected by his maneuver and commitment, and provides information to the commander and staff on routes and employment times to designated critical points on the battlefield.

QUICK REACTION FORCE

5-234.   The commander may allocate a quick reaction force (QRF) if he deems it necessary. The QRF is a force withheld from action to be committed by the commander at a decisive moment within shaping, decisive, or sustaining operations. This force is usually tailored to a specific threat, and potential missions. It provides the commander with the flexibility of committing forces for emergencies throughout the battlefield, without losing the combat power of his reserve force for decisive operations.

COUNTERATTACK

5-235.   The battalion may conduct local counterattacks to restore or preserve defensive integrity or to seize initiative upon unanticipated opportunities. The counterattack force is usually pre-positioned in a location of advantage, and has mobility to respond quickly to the threat. Unless defensive operations have left the battalion largely unscathed, the battalion usually lacks the ability to conduct a significant counterattack by itself. Within the context of the BCT's operations, a defending battalion may execute a counterattack to support the BCT's defensive posture, as part of a larger force seeking to complete the destruction of the enemy's attack, or as part of a transition to offensive operations.

Section VI. MANEUVER AND PROTECTION INTEGRATION

Much of the strength of a defense rests on the integration and construction of reinforcing obstacles, exploitation of existing obstacles, and actions to enhance the survivability of the force through construction of fighting positions and fortifications. The commander's intent focuses countermobility and survivability planning through his articulation of obstacle intent (target, relative location, and obstacle effect) and priorities and establishment of priorities for survivability and countermobility. Guided by that intent, the battalion engineer (usually the DS engineer platoon leader) develops a scheme of engineer operations that includes engineer task organization, priorities of effort and support, subordinate engineer unit missions, and countermobility and survivability instructions for all units. Chapter 10 contains information on engineer systems and capabilities.

COUNTERMOBILITY

5-236.   The commander and staff develop the obstacle plan concurrently with the fire support plan and defensive scheme, guided by the commander's intent. (Figure 5-16 shows an example of a battalion obstacle plan.) They integrate into the intelligence collection plan the use of intelligent minefields such as Raptor, if allocated. The commander's intent for countermobility should contain three elements:

TARGET

5-237.   The target is the enemy force that the commander wants to affect with fires and tactical obstacles. The commander identifies the target in terms of the size and type of enemy force, the echelon, the avenue of approach, or a combination of these methods.

EFFECT

5-238.   This is the intended effect that the commander wants the obstacles and fires to have on the targeted enemy force. Tactical obstacles produce one of the following effects: block, turn, fix, or disrupt (Table 5-2). The obstacle effect drives integration, focuses subordinates' fires, and focuses the obstacle effort.

RELATIVE LOCATION

5-239. The relative location is where the commander wants the obstacle effect to occur against the targeted enemy force. Whenever possible, the commander identifies the location relative to the terrain and maneuver or fire control measures to integrate the effects of obstacles with fires.

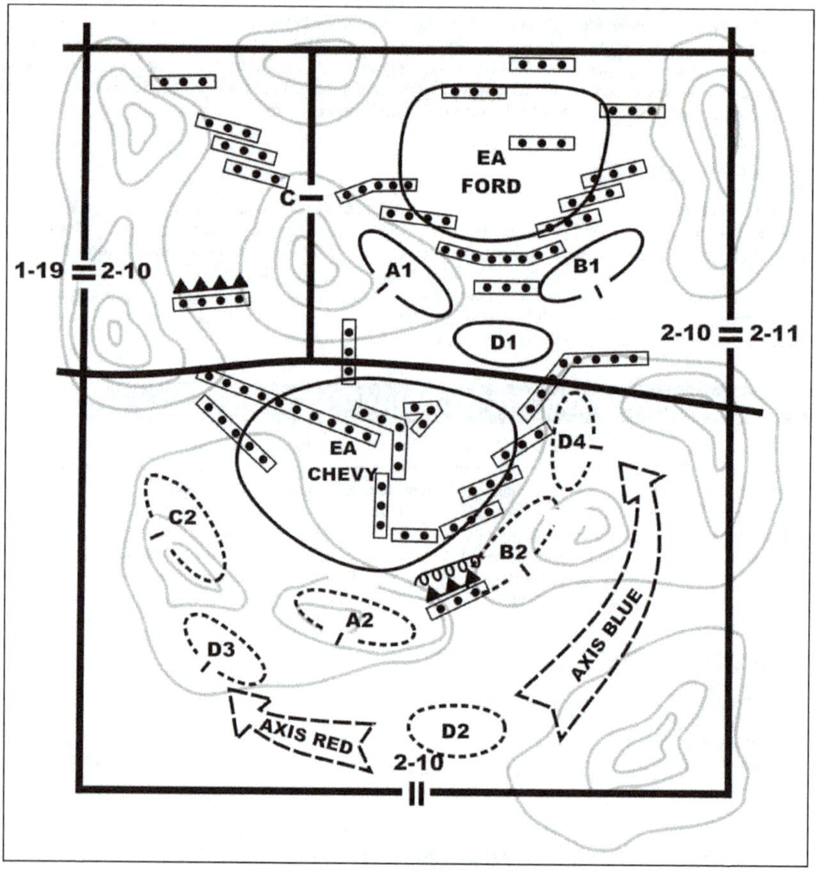

Figure 5-16. Example of a battalion obstacle plan.

Table 5-2. Obstacle effects.

Obstacle Effect	Purpose	Fires And Obstacles Must--	Obstacle Characteristics
DISRUPT	• Breakup enemy formations. • Interrupt the enemy's timetable and C2. • Cause premature commitment of breach assets. • Cause the enemy to piecemeal his attack.	• Cause the enemy to deploy early. • Slow part of his formation while allowing part to advance unimpeded.	• Do not require extensive resources. • Difficult to detect at long range.
FIX	• Slow an attacker within an area so he can be destroyed. • Generate the time necessary for the friendly force to disengage.	• Cause the enemy to deploy into attack formation before encountering the obstacles. • Allow the enemy to advance slowly in an EA or AO. • Make the enemy fight in multiple directions once he is in the EA or AO.	• Arrayed in depth. • Span the entire width of the avenue of approach. • Must not make the terrain appear impenetrable.
TURN	• Force the enemy to move in the direction desired by the friendly commander.	• Prevent the enemy from bypassing or breaching the obstacle belt. • Maintain pressure on the enemy force throughout the turn. • Mass direct and indirect fires at the anchor point of the turn.	• Tie into impassable terrain at the anchor point. • Consist of obstacles in depth. • Provide a subtle orientation relative to the enemy's approach.
BLOCK	• Stop an attacker along a specific avenue of approach. • Prevent an attacker from passing through an AO or EA. • Stop the enemy from using an avenue of approach and force him to use another avenue of approach.	• Prevent the enemy from bypassing or penetrating through the belt. • Stop the enemy's advance. • Destroy all enemy breach efforts.	• Must tie into impassable terrain. • Consist of complex obstacles. • Defeat the enemy's mounted and dismounted breaching effort.
DISRUPT	• Breakup enemy formations. • Interrupt the enemy's timetable and C2. • Cause premature commitment of breach assets. • Cause the enemy to piecemeal his attack.	• Cause the enemy to deploy early. • Slow part of his formation while allowing part to advance unimpeded.	• Do not require extensive resources. • Difficult to detect at long range.

TACTICAL OBSTACLES

5-240. Obstacles are force-oriented combat multipliers. The battalion employs tactical obstacles to attack the enemy's ability to move, mass, and reinforce directly. Tactical obstacles are integrated into the scheme of maneuver and fires to produce specific obstacle effects. Obstacles alone do not produce significant effects against the enemy; obstacles must be integrated with fires to be effective. The engineer section in Chapter 10 provides tables and specific information on engineer capabilities and obstacle effects. The following are the three types of tactical obstacles:

Directed

5-241.   The BCT directs obstacles as specified tasks to the battalion using obstacle belts. The battalion may use the same technique, but more likely will be specific about the location and type of obstacle. The commander may use directed obstacles or obstacle groups to achieve specific obstacle effects at key locations on the battlefield. In this case, the staff plans the obstacle control measures and resources as well as determines measures and tasks to subordinates to integrate the directed obstacles with fires.

Situational

5-242.   Situational obstacles are obstacles that the BCT or battalion plans and possibly prepares before an operation; however, they do not execute the obstacles unless specific criteria are met. Situational obstacles are "be-prepared" obstacles and provide the commander with flexibility for employing tactical obstacles based on battlefield developments. The commander may use engineer forces to emplace tactical obstacles rapidly, but more often, he relies on SCATMINE systems. The BCT staff normally plans situational obstacles to allow the commander to shift his countermobility effort rapidly to where he needs it the most based on the situation. Execution triggers for situational obstacles are integrated into the decision support template (Chapter 10, Section III of this manual, and FM 90-7 for situational obstacles). Situational obstacles must be well integrated with tactical plans to avoid fratricide. Given the changes in engineer force structure, tactical concepts, and capabilities, situational obstacles are increasingly used instead of conventionally emplaced obstacles.

Reserve

5-243.   Reserve obstacles are demolition obstacles that are deemed critical to the plan for which the authority to detonate is reserved by the designating commander. These are "on-order" obstacles. The commander specifies the unit responsible for constructing, guarding, and executing the obstacle. Examples of reserve obstacles include preparing a bridge for destruction or an obstacle to close a lane. Units normally prepare reserve obstacles during the preparation phase. They execute the obstacle only on command of the authorizing commander or when specific criteria are met. (See Chapter 6, FM 90-7 for specific considerations for planning reserve obstacles.) It is critical for the unit to understand and rehearse actions to execute reserve obstacles.

> *Note.* In addition to tactical obstacles, units also employ protective obstacles. Protective obstacles are a key component of survivability operations, providing friendly forces with close-in protection.

OBSTACLE GROUPS

5-244.   Obstacle groups are one or more individual obstacles grouped to provide a specific obstacle effect. Battalions integrate obstacle groups to ensure that companies plan individual obstacles that support the scheme of maneuver. Companies integrate individual obstacles with direct- and indirect-fire plans to achieve the specified obstacle group effect.

5-245.   Obstacle groups normally attack the maneuver of enemy battalions. Normally, commanders plan obstacle groups along enemy battalion avenues of approach as defined by company mobility corridors. They may plan a group along a company-size avenue of approach. Unlike obstacle zones or belts, obstacle groups are not "areas" but are relative locations for obstacle construction. Obstacle groups are represented by obstacle effect symbols (block, fix, turn, disrupt) on battalion graphics. However, if the plan requires specific obstacle types, commanders may refine obstacle group symbology with individual obstacle graphics.

5-246.   Battalion commanders plan obstacle groups within assigned obstacle zones or belts. When given a belt with an assigned effect, the battalion commander may use any combination of group effects if the sum effect of all groups achieves the overall effect of the belt.

5-247.   Obstacle groups impose strict limitations on company commanders to preserve the link between obstacle effects and the fire plan. The limitations are similar to the limitations imposed by a BP. A group does not give the exact location of obstacles in the group just as a BP does not show the exact location of each weapon in the company. The company commander and the emplacing engineer coordinate these details directly. Company commanders may make changes to obstacles and fire-control measures based on the reality of the terrain. These changes are coordinated with and tracked by the battalion commander and staff to maintain the fidelity of the desired obstacle group effect and integration into the battalion scheme of maneuver.

5-248.   Battalions do not normally assign a company more than one obstacle group; however, a company may effectively fight two groups at a time if the terrain supports it. To mass fires on an obstacle group, more than one company often covers a single obstacle group within an EA. In these cases, the commander responsible for establishing the EA is also responsible for integrating the obstacle group. Normally, the battalion commander or S-3 plays a significant role in building and synchronizing an EA covered by two or more companies.

5-249.   Obstacle groups, resource factors, and standard individual obstacles are the basis of battalion obstacle logistics planning. They enable the commander and staff to allocate the necessary resources to each obstacle group, EA, or company BP. They also enable the staff to identify critical shortfalls, plan the flow of materials within the battalion area, and schedule resupply.

TACTICAL OBSTACLE PLANNING

5-250.   Detailed obstacle planning begins during COA development. The engineer focuses on five specifics in his scheme of engineer operations for the obstacle plan.

Direct and Indirect Fire Analysis

5-251.   The direct and indirect fire analysis examines how engineers can best use obstacles to enhance the direct and indirect fire plan. The engineer must have a fundamental understanding of the direct and indirect fire and maneuver plans and the battalion's organization of the EA to integrate obstacles effectively with the direct and indirect fire plan. The engineer must consider battalion EAs, TRPs, indirect fire targets, unit locations, enemy formations, avenues of approach, and the commander's obstacle intent in order to effectively integrate obstacles. Synchronization of direct and indirect fires with obstacles multiplies the relative effect on the enemy.

Obstacle Intent Integration

5-252.   The engineer plans directed obstacle groups during the COA development process. Obstacle groups integrated into the COA sketch graphically show the commander's obstacle intent to support the maneuver plan. Obstacle groups target specific enemy elements based on the situational template. The engineer generally allocates an obstacle group against a battalion-sized avenue of approach with respect to the EAs, TRPs, indirect fire targets, unit locations, enemy formations, and avenues of approach assessed during the direct fire analysis. This process parallels the staff's placement of a company against the same size enemy force. The intent of the obstacle groups supports subordinate unit task and purpose. The engineer recommends specific obstacle group effects to the commander based on terrain, resources, time available, and the battalion commander's obstacle intent.

Obstacle Priority

5-253. The staff determines the priority of each obstacle group. The commander's intent and the most likely enemy COA clearly influence the priority. The obstacle priority should reflect the battalion's most critical obstacle requirement. The battalion engineer considers flank protection, weapons types and ranges, and the commander's overall intent for the entire force before placing obstacle priority on the main EA. Priorities assist the engineer in allocating resources and ensuring that the most critical obstacle groups are constructed first.

Mobility Requirements

5-254. The engineer identifies battalion mobility requirements by analyzing the scheme of maneuver, counterattack (CATK) options, reserve planning priorities, fire support, protection, and sustainment movement requirements, and adjacent and higher unit missions, maneuver, and movement. The engineer integrates this analysis into obstacle group planning and avoids impeding friendly maneuver whenever possible. Because the bulk of the engineer force is committed to countermobility and survivability during defensive preparation, the battalion commander uses clear obstacle restrictions on specific areas within the battalion AO to maintain mobility. Sometimes, obstacles must be constructed along a mobility corridor that primarily supports friendly movement. When this happens, a lane or gap and associated closure procedures are planned and rehearsed. These lanes or gaps may be closed with situational or reserve obstacles.

5-255. Beyond preparing and marking lanes and gaps through obstacles, engineers normally perform mobility tasks once defensive preparations are complete. Mobility assets may then be positioned to counter templated enemy situational obstacles, or be task organized to the reserve, counterattack force, or any other unit that must maneuver or move subsequent to the execution of the defense. To do this effectively, the engineers and the supported maneuver unit must integrate, prepare, and rehearse. Since this manner of mobility support is critical to the success of the maneuver plan, timely linkup and coordination is factored into the overall defensive preparation timeline.

5-256. The battalion might need significant mobility support during defensive preparation. For example, it might need route reduction or clearance, road repair or maintenance, and LZ and PZ clearance. Engineers have resources to perform these tasks, but they cannot perform them and simultaneously prepare the defense. Thus, the battalion needs augmentation from the BSTB or higher level unit multifunction engineer battalion. These engineers perform general engineering tasks, leaving the BCT engineers available to construct the battalion defense.

SURVIVABILITY

5-257. Survivability operations in support of ground maneuver elements are increasingly limited given force structure and tactical concepts. Survivability efforts within the battalion should focus on protection of assets that must remain relatively static, such as communication nodes; support of logistical and decontamination operations; and survivability for defending Infantry Soldiers.

Chapter 6
Stability Operations

This chapter discusses stability operations at the battalion level and provides planning considerations. US forces are employed in stability operations outside the US and its territories to promote and protect US national interests by influencing political, civil, and military environments and by disrupting specific illegal activities. Army forces must remain versatile and retain the flexibility to transition from the primary mission of close, personal, and brutal fighting of traditional combat to stability operations. The Infantry battalion normally performs stability operations as part of a larger, multinational, or unified team but could be required to work independently.

Army forces are highly suited for stability operations because they are trained, equipped, and organized to control land, populations, and situations for extended periods. Army forces engage in stability operations daily around the world. The depth and breadth of Army force abilities provide the combatant commander of a unified command with vital options to meet theater operational requirements. These operations enhance theater engagement and promote regional stability.

Section I. FUNDAMENTALS

Stability operations promote and protect US national interest by influencing the threat, political, and information dimensions of the operational environment. This is done through a combination of peacetime developmental, cooperative activities, and coercive actions in response to crises (FM 3-0). Army force presence promotes a secure environment in which diplomatic and economic programs designed to eliminate root causes of instability may flourish. Presence can take the form of forward basing, forward deploying, or pre-positioning assets in an AO. Army forces have the ability to establish and maintain a credible presence as long as necessary to achieve the desired results.

PURPOSE

6-1.   The overarching goal of stability operations is to promote and sustain regional and global stability. These operations may complement and reinforce offensive and defensive operations, or stability may be the decisive operation. Army forces conduct stability operations in crises and before, during, and after offensive and defensive operations. In a crisis, a stability operation can deter conflict or prevent escalation. During hostilities, it can help keep armed conflict from spreading and assist and encourage committed partners. Following hostilities, a stability operation can provide a secure environment in which civil authorities can work to regain control. Demonstrating the credible ability to conduct offensive and defensive operations underlies successful stability operations.

6-2.   Stability operations are inherently complex and place greater demands at the small-unit level. Junior leaders are required to develop engagement skills, such as cultural awareness, negotiating techniques, tactical questioning and critical language phrases, while maintaining warfighting skills. Capable, trained, disciplined, and high-quality leaders, Soldiers, and teams are especially critical to success. Soldiers and units at every level must be flexible and adaptive. Stability operations often require the mental and physical agility to shift from noncombat to combat operations and back again.

6-3.   Military forces conduct stability operations to accomplish one or more of the activities listed below. These operations demonstrate the United States' resolve through the commitment of time, resources, and forces to establish and reinforce diplomatic and military ties. stability operations can—

- Protect national interests.
- Promote peace and deter aggression.
- Satisfy treaty obligations or enforce agreements and policies.
- Reassure allies, friendly governments, and agencies.
- Maintain or restore order.
- Protect life and property.
- Demonstrate resolve.
- Prevent, deter, or respond to terrorism.
- Reduce the threat of conventional arms and WMD to regional security.
- Protect freedom from oppression, subversion, lawlessness, and insurgency.
- Promote sustainable and responsive institutions.

6-4.   Stability operations may include both developmental and coercive actions. Developmental actions enhance a host government's willingness and ability to care for its people. Coercive actions apply carefully prescribed force or the threat of force to change the security environment. For example, rapidly responding to a small-scale contingency operation can diffuse a crisis and restore regional stability.

6-5.   Stability operations complement and are complemented by offensive and defensive operations. Stability operations help restore law and order in unstable areas outside the US and its territories. Similarly, offensive and defensive operations may be necessary to defeat adversaries intending to prevent the success of a stability operation. The ability of Army forces to stabilize a crisis is related to its ability to attack and defend. For example, shows of force often precede offensive and defensive operations in tries to deter aggression and provide opportunities for diplomatic and economic solutions.

6-6.   Stability operations vary by type and are further differentiated by the specific factors of METT-TC. The battalion performs many familiar core tactical missions and tasks during stability operations. The purposes of operations, the special constraints on commanders, and the unique missions and tasks, however, differentiate stability operations from other operations.

6-7.   Ideally, the battalion receives advance notice of stability operation missions and has time to modify its mission essential task list (METL) and complete a preparatory training program before deploying. In other cases, the battalion may deploy and assume stability operations responsibilities on short notice. In those cases, the battalion relies on its training in the fundamental tasks, such as C2, patrolling, reporting, establishing OPs, and maintaining unit security, and trains to specific mission tasks during the operation.

6-8.   In stability operations, commanders must emphasize cooperating and communicating with joint headquarters, multinational units, civilian authorities, and nongovernmental organizations (NGOs). Also, commanders must empower subordinate leaders to develop close association with the population of the AOs within the ROI and typifies many stability operations. Considerations for stability operations include—

6-9.   Leverage SOF, interagency, joint, and multinational cooperation (Appendix G). As with all operations, unity of effort is fundamental to success.

6-10.   Enhance the capabilities and legitimacy of the host nation. Army forces consciously enhance host-nation credibility and legitimacy by demonstrating the proper respect for the host-nation's government, police, and military forces. Within the restrictions of international law and US policy, commanders use host-nation forces and personnel for all possible activities. Within its capabilities, a host nation should take the lead in both developmental and security activities. When host-nation capabilities prove inadequate for the task, Army forces enhance those capabilities through training, advice, and assistance.

6-11.   Understand the potential for unintended consequences of individual and small unit actions. The actions of individuals and units can have consequences disproportionate to the level of command. An individual's actions can even have strategic implications. Soldiers and leaders who are disciplined, proficient, and knowledgeable in stability operations can create the opportunity for disproportional positive consequences, while limiting the risk for negative consequences.

6-12.   Display the capability to use force in a nonthreatening manner. Army forces must be prepared for combat in stability. However, that preparedness is shown so it does not provoke potential adversaries. The force demonstrates strength and resolve, without being perceived as threatening. Consistent with mission constraints, units display preparedness by routinely conducting demanding combined arms training in the AO. The force should convey to all parties the breadth and depth of the resources available. To do so, it must be present in the communities and ensure (consistent with the demands of OPSEC) that the public knows the ROE and associated graduated response levels. The training should include challenging Soldiers to react to situations at all levels in the areas of weapons use, levels of force, and ROE.

6-13.   Act decisively to prevent escalation. The nature of stability operations ordinarily constrains forces in the ways and means available to accomplish military objectives. However, they are characterized by initiative, speed, and determination when action is necessary. Units and individuals pursue military objectives energetically and apply military power forcefully, if required. Army forces may act decisively to dominate a situation by force or negotiate to settle disputes. Without hesitation, they ensure mission accomplishment as well as protection of themselves, the people, and facilities under their charge. Decisiveness reassures allies and deters adversaries. Failure to act decisively can cause a loss of respect for the stability force. A loss of respect for the capabilities or will of the force to accomplish its mission can embolden adversaries, and therefore weaken the trust of the supported population; making the mission much more difficult.

6-14.   Apply force selectively and discriminately. Commanders ensure that their units apply force consistent with assigned objectives and not excessive. Combat power is applied selectively in accordance with assigned missions and prescribed limitations. Excessive force can lead to the loss of sympathy and support of local and international populations. Inadequate force may jeopardize mission accomplishment, and adversely affect the local populace and domestic support. Ordinarily, the local commander is best qualified to estimate the degree of force that must be used, consistent with established rules of engagement (ROE).

CHARACTERISTICS

6-15.   Stability operations are conducted in a dynamic environment. These operations are normally nonlinear and often conducted in noncontiguous AOs. They are often time and manpower intensive. Stability operations differ from the offense and defense in significant ways. Understanding their characteristics helps units successfully adapt to the special requirements presented. Some common characteristics of stability operations include: political objectives, modified concept of the enemy, joint, interagency, and multinational cooperation, risk of mission creep, noncombatants, NGOs, information intensity, constraints, and cross-cultural interaction. Although not applicable in every operation, these characteristics apply to many operations. Understanding them aids in the adjustment that units may be required to make when conducting these types of actions.

POLITICAL OBJECTIVES

6-16.   Political objectives influence stability operations at every level from strategic to tactical. These operations are distinguished by the degree that political objectives directly influence operations and tactics. Two factors about political primacy stand out. First, all military personnel should understand the political objectives and the potential impact of inappropriate actions. Having an understanding of the political objective helps avoid actions that may have adverse political effects. In such operations, junior leaders commonly make decisions that have significant political implications. Second, political objectives can be fluid. Changing objectives may warrant a change in military operations. Commanders should strive, through continuing mission analysis, to detect subtle changes that may lead to disconnects between political objectives and military operations. Failure to recognize changes in political objectives may lead to ineffective or counter productive military operations.

MODIFIED CONCEPT OF ENEMY

6-17.   Infantry units and Soldiers are naturally attuned to find, fix, and finish the enemy. Stability operations require a modified understanding of who or what is the adversary. Commanders must take care to not create an enemy where one does not exist. In situations where there is no enemy, military capability may focus on overcoming obstacles and providing support to other agencies. In some missions, such as peacekeeping, Soldiers must remain impartial.

JOINT, INTERAGENCY, AND MULTINATIONAL COORPERATION

6-18.   Stability operations typically involve unified action: joint, interagency, and multinational efforts. (See Appendix G for more information on the latter types of operations.) The increased number of participants (military and nonmilitary) and their divergent missions and methods create a coordination challenge. In this environment, the potential exists for duplicating effort and working at cross-purposes. Achieving unity of effort requires the greatest possible common purpose and direction among all agencies.

RISK OF MISSION CREEP

6-19.   Commanders and soldiers have a natural tendency to do more especially when faced with human suffering. However, well-intentioned actions can be especially dangerous in stability operations, where they can threaten impartiality as well as undermine long-term programs. There are two types of mission creep. First is the type that occurs when the unit receives shifting guidance or change in mission for which the unit is not properly configured or resourced; or if it is beyond the legal remit of the Army. The second type of mission creep occurs when a unit tries to do more than is allowed in the current mandate and mission. The best guard against mission creep is for the commander and staff to conduct a complete mission analysis, considering interim and potential political end states.

NONCOMBATANTS

6-20.   Noncombatants are a defining characteristic of most modern military operations. Their presence is unavoidable because in most cases their welfare is the reason for the operation. Noncombatants in stability operations can create various challenges. Local populations may be friendly, hostile, or indifferent to the presence of Army forces. In some cases, Army forces may have difficulty differentiating between hostile and non hostile persons.

NGOs

6-21.   The very conditions that may necessitate a stability operation—widespread human suffering, population movements, famine, human rights violations, and civil war—are also the conditions that attract the services of NGOs. Commanders must be prepared to coordinate their efforts with a myriad array of international organizations and NGOs. Each organization or agency has a different mandate, set of capacities, organizational design, and cultural orientation. An operation's success may depend on how well the commander can forge productive working relationships will all these disparate bodies.

INFORMATION INTENSITY

6-22.   All military operations are information intensive. In stability operations, this is further complicated by the numerous governmental and nongovernmental agencies involved. The scope and scale of required coordination and communication also complicate the operation. The cascading effects of events and their global magnification through the media further exacerbates this characteristic of the environment

CONSTRAINTS

6-23.   Constraints are present in all military operations; stability operations are not an exception. Constraints may arise for many reasons and may be imposed on military forces by the chain of command or by the complex nature of the environment. Army forces in these actions must typically contend with constraints such as force caps, restricted activities, restricted areas, and specific ROE.

CROSS-CULTURAL INTERACTION

6-24.   Interacting with other cultures can create a significant challenge during stability operations. Often, adjustments in attitudes or methods must be made to accommodate different cultures. Ethnocentrism and cultural arrogance can damage relationships with other forces, NGOs, or indigenous populations. The welfare and perceptions of indigenous populations are often central to the mission during stability operations. Army forces must establish good working relations with indigenous populations. Mutual trust and rapport increase the chances for mission success.

POTENTIAL USE OF NONLETHAL WEAPONS

6-25.   Stability operations require lethal force constraints due to the importance of interaction and relationship building with the local population, as well as probable media exposure. Nonlethal capabilities extend the range of firepower options (Appendix L). They augment means of deadly force. They are particularly valuable in both stability operations as they enhance the ability to apply force in proportion to the threat and allow discrimination in its use. They expand the number of options available to confront situations that do not warrant using deadly force but require soldiers to use overwhelming, decisive power to accomplish their missions.

6-26.   The use of nonlethal weapons forms the basis of a response if force is required. The use of nonlethal weapons, backed by lethal force, can defuse or deter a potentially dangerous situation involving noncombatants.

SMALL UNIT LEADER SKILLS

6-27.   Stability operations are inherently complex and place great demands on small units and small unit leaders. Small unit leaders may be required to develop or improve interpersonal skills, such as cultural awareness, negotiating techniques, and critical language phrases, while maintaining warfighting skills. They must also remain calm and exercise good judgment under considerable pressure. Soldiers and units at every level must be flexible and adaptive. Often, stability operations require leaders with the mental and physical agility to shift from noncombat to combat operations, and back again.

INTERPRETERS

6-28.   Stability operations normally require the use of language interpreters to effectively communicate with the local government officials, police, armed forces, and civilian population. In many areas of the world, the availability of qualified Army interpreters is very limited. In areas where limited military interpreters exist, local interpreters may be hired to support Infantry battalions. Some of the considerations of using local interpreters are—

- Screening potential interpreters to ensure they are trustworthy.
- If possible, use multiple interpreters working independently of each other to ensure quality of translations.

- Do not use English slang or phrases that can easily be misinterpreted.
- If possible, select older interpreters (because in most cultures, age demands respect).
- The interpreters should come from the higher social class (because they demand more respect in the community).
- If gender is a social issue, choose the interpreter whose gender carries the most respect.
- When translating a message to a local, it may be more important to convey intent, rather than a word-for-word literal translation.

Section II. TYPES OF STABILITY OPERATIONS

Stability operations typically fall into ten broad types that are neither discrete nor mutually exclusive. For example, a force engaged in a peace operation may also find itself conducting arms control or a show of force to set the conditions for achieving an end state. This section provides an introductory discussion of stability operations. For more information, see FM 3-0 and FM 3-07. (Figure 6-1 shows and the following paragraphs discuss the eleven types of stability operations.)

- Peace operations (PO)
- Foreign internal defense (FID)
- Humanitarian and civic assistance
- Foreign humanitarian assistance
- Security assistance
- Support to insurgencies
- Support to counterdrug operations
- Combating terrorism
- Noncombatant evacuation operations (NEO)
- Arms control
- Show of force

Figure 6-1. Types of stability operations.

PEACE OPERATIONS

6-29.   Peace operations (POs) support strategic and policy objectives and the diplomatic activities that implement them. POs include peacekeeping operations (PKOs), peace enforcement operations (PEOs), and support to diplomatic efforts to establish and maintain peace. Although the US normally participates in POs under the sponsorship of the United Nations (UN), a multinational organization, or a multinational force, it reserves the right to conduct POs unilaterally. Optimally, forces should not transition from one PO role to another unless there is a change of mandate or a political decision with appropriate adjustments to force structure, ROE, and other aspects of the mission. Nevertheless, just as in other operations, it is crucial that commanders and staffs continually assess the mission. In POs, this translates into planning for possible or likely transitions. Examples include: transitioning from a US unilateral operation or multinational coalition to an UN-led coalition, from combat to noncombat operations, or from military to civilian control.

6-30.   Commanders use the military decision making process to determine the appropriate force and weapons to have at the unit's disposal during peace operations. In general, peace keeping operations only allow for self-defense and peace enforcement operations require units maintain the capability to conduct combat operations.

PEACEKEEPING OPERATIONS

6-31.   PKOs are military operations conducted with the consent of all major parties in a dispute. They monitor and facilitate the implementation of agreements, such as a cease fire or truce, and they support

---

diplomatic efforts to reach a long-term political settlement (JP 3-07.3). Before PKOs begin, a credible truce or ceasefire should be in effect, and the belligerent parties must consent to the operation.

6-32.   In peacekeeping operations, the battalion must use all its capabilities, short of coercive force, to gain and maintain the initiative. The battalion may be assigned a variety of missions designed to monitor peace and stability and to improve the humanitarian environment. The following are examples of PKO missions:

- Observing, monitoring, verifying, and reporting any alleged violation of the governing agreements.
- Investigating alleged cease-fire violations, boundary incidents, and complaints.
- Conducting regular liaison visits within the operational area.
- Verifying the storage or destruction of certain categories of military equipment specified in the relevant agreements.
- Supervising cease-fires, disengagements, and withdrawals.
- Supervising prisoner of war exchanges.
- Assisting civil authorities.
- Providing military support to elections.
- Assisting in foreign humanitarian assistance.
- Assisting in the maintenance of public order.

6-33.   JP 3-07.3 and FM 3-07 provide additional details on PKO-related tasks. Army forces conducting PKOs rely on the legitimacy acknowledged by all major belligerents and international or regional organizations to obtain objectives. They do not use force unless required to defend the Soldiers or accomplish the mission. Intelligence and information operations are vital in PKOs to provide the commander with the information he needs to make appropriate decisions, protect the force, and ensure the success of subordinate PKO-related efforts.

PEACE ENFORCEMENT

6-34.   PEOs involve the application of military force or the threat of military force (normally pursuant to international authorization) to compel compliance with resolutions or sanctions designed to maintain or restore peace and order. By definition, PEOs are coercive in nature and rely on the threat or use of force. However, the impartiality with which the peace force treats all parties and the nature of its objectives, separate PEOs from war. PEOs support diplomatic efforts to restore peace and represent an escalation from peacekeeping operations.

6-35.   In PEOs, the battalion may use force to coerce hostile factions into ceasing and desisting violent actions. Usually, these factions have not consented to intervention, and they may be engaged in combat activities. A battalion conducting a PEO must be ready to apply elements of combat power to achieve the following:

- Forcible separation of belligerents.
- Establishment and supervision of protected areas.
- Sanction and exclusion zone enforcement.
- Movement denial and guarantee.
- Restoration and maintenance of order.
- Protection of humanitarian assistance.

6-36.   The nature of PEOs dictates that Army forces assigned a PEO mission be able to conduct combat operations. Maintaining and demonstrating a credible combat capability is essential for successful PEOs. The PE force normally retains the right of first use of force. Units must be able to apply sufficient combat power to protect themselves and forcefully accomplish assigned tasks. Units must also be ready to transition quickly either to PKOs or to offensive and defensive operations if required.

OPERATIONS IN SUPPORT OF DIPLOMATIC EFFORTS

6-37.   Forces may conduct operations in support of diplomatic efforts to establish peace and order before, during, and after a conflict. Military support of diplomatic activities improves the chances for success by lending credibility to diplomatic actions and demonstrating resolve to achieve viable political settlements. While these activities are primarily the responsibility of civilian agencies, the military can support these efforts within its capabilities. Army forces may support diplomatic initiatives such as preventative diplomacy, peacemaking, and peace building.

Support to Preventive Diplomacy

6-38.   Preventive diplomacy is diplomatic action taken in advance of a predictable crisis to prevent or limit violence. Army forces are not normally directly involved in preventive diplomacy but may support a State Department effort by providing transportation and communications assets. In some cases, military forces may conduct a preventive deployment or show of force as part of the overall effort to deter conflict.

Support to Peacemaking

6-39.   Peacemaking is the process of diplomacy, mediation, negotiation, or other forms of peaceful settlement that arranges an end to a dispute and resolves the issue that led to it (JP 3-07.3). Peacemaking includes military actions that support the diplomatic process. Army forces participate in these operations primarily by performing military-to-military contacts, exercises, peacetime deployments, and security assistance. Peacemaking operations also serve to influence important regional and host nation political and military groups.

Support to Peace Building

6-40.   Peace building consists of post-conflict actions (predominately diplomatic and economic) that strengthen and rebuild governmental infrastructure and institutions to avoid a relapse into conflict (JP 3-07.3). Military actions that support peace building are designed to identify, restore, and support structures that strengthen and solidify peace. Typical peace-building activities include restoring civil authority, rebuilding physical infrastructure, providing structures and training for schools and hospitals, and helping reestablish commerce. When executing peace-building operations, Army forces complement the efforts of nonmilitary agencies and local governments. Many of the actions that support peace building are also performed in longer-term FID operations.

FOREIGN INTERNAL DEFENSE

6-41.   FID is participation by civilian and military agencies of a government in any action programs taken by another government to free and protect its society from subversion, lawlessness, and insurgency (FM 1-02). The main objective is to promote stability by helping a host nation establish and maintain institutions and facilities responsive to its people's needs. Army forces in FID normally advise and assist host-nation forces conducting operations to increase their capabilities.

6-42.   When conducting FID, Army forces provide military supplies as well as military advice, tactical and technical training, and intelligence and logistics support (not involving combat operations). Army forces conduct FID operations in accordance with JP 3-07.1 and FM 3-07. Army forces provide indirect support, direct support (not involving combat operations), or conduct combat operations to support a host nation's efforts. Generally, US forces do not engage in combat operations as part of an FID. However, on rare occasions when the threat to US interests is great and indirect means are insufficient, US combat operations may be directed to support a host nation's efforts. The battalion's primary roles in nation assistance operations are usually similar to its roles in peace-building operations. If involved in these operations, battalions are most likely to provide forces rather than lead the effort themselves.

Indirect Support

6-43.   Indirect support emphasizes the principles of host nation self-sufficiency and builds strong national infrastructures through economic and military capabilities (JP 3-07.1). Security assistance programs, multinational exercises, and exchange programs are examples of indirect support. Indirect support reinforces the legitimacy and primacy of the host nation government in addressing internal problems. An example of indirect support is Infantry battalions participating in Joint Chiefs of Staff (JCS) directed or JCS exercises such as Bright Star in Egypt.

Direct Support

6-44.   DS provides direct assistance to the host nation civilian populace or military (JP 3-07.1). Examples include civil-military operations, intelligence and communications sharing, and logistics. DS does not usually involve the transfer of arms and equipment or the training of local military forces.

Combat Operations

6-45.   Combat operations include offensive and defensive operations conducted by US forces to support a host nation's fight against insurgents or terrorists. The use of US forces in combat operations should only be a temporary measure. Direct involvement by the US military can damage the legitimacy and credibility of the host nation government and security forces. Eventually, host nation forces must be strengthened to stabilize the situation and provide security for the populace independently. The use of Infantry battalions in Afghanistan, as part of Operation Enduring Freedom, is an example of combat operations in a host nation while the US Army trains the Afghan Army to take over their own national security.

6-46.   US forces must conduct FID operations while subjected to close scrutiny. Hostile propaganda will try to exploit the presence of foreign troops to discredit the host nation government and the US. Domestic and world opinion may hold the US responsible for the actions of host nation forces as well as American forces. The effective employment of PSYOP will aid in reducing this threat.

6-47.   Military support to counterinsurgencies is based on the recognition that military power alone is incapable of achieving true and lasting success. More specifically, American military power cannot ensure the survival of regimes that fail to meet the basic needs of their people. Support to counterinsurgency include, but is not limited to, FID, security assistance, and humanitarian and civic assistance (JP 3-07).

6-48.   The battalion most often support counterinsurgency operations by providing security for a host nation. The security operations include security of facilities and installations, defensive operations, and protection of the local population. Its actions directly or indirectly support the host government's efforts to establish itself with the citizens as the legitimate and competent authority in the nation.

HUMANITARIAN AND CIVIC ASSISTANCE

6-49.   Humanitarian and civic assistance (HCA) programs assist the host nation populace in conjunction with military operations and exercises. The very nature of HCA programs frequently dictates that additional engineer units and support capabilities will augment units participating in HCA operations. In contrast to humanitarian and disaster relief operations, HCA are planned activities authorized by the Secretary of State with specific budget limitations and are appropriated in the Army budget. Assistance must fulfill unit training requirements that correspondingly create humanitarian benefit to the local populace. HCA programs must comply with Title 10, United States Code, Sections 401, 401(E), (5), and Section 2551. For more information on selected sections of Title 10, US Code for medical support, see FM 8-42. See AR 40-400 for information on emergency medical treatment for local national civilians during stability operations. Humanitarian and civic actions are limited to the following categories:

- Medical, dental, and veterinary care provided in rural areas of a country.
- Construction of rudimentary surface transportation systems.
- Well drilling and construction of basic sanitation facilities.

- Rudimentary construction and repair of public facilities.
- Specified activities related to mine detection and clearance, including education, training, and technical assistance.

FOREIGN HUMANITARIAN ASSISTANCE

6-50.   US forces conduct FHA operations outside the borders of the US or its territories. This is done to relieve or reduce the results of natural or manmade disasters, or other endemic conditions such as; human suffering, disease, or deprivation that might present a serious threat to life or that can result in great damage to or loss of property.

6-51.   The US military typically supplements the host nation authorities in concert with other government agencies, NGOs, private voluntary organizations, and unaffiliated individuals. The majority of FHA operations closely resemble civil support operations. The distinction between the two is the legal restrictions applied to US forces inside the US and its territories. The Posse Comitatus Act which does not apply to US forces overseas, restricts the use of the military in federal status, and prevents it from executing laws and performing civilian law enforcement functions within the US.

6-52.   FHA operations are limited in scope and duration. They focus exclusively on prompt aid to resolve an immediate crisis. In environments where the situation is vague or hostile, FHA activities are considered a subset of a larger stability operation, offensive, or defensive operation.

SUPPORT TO INSURGENCIES

6-53.   The US supports insurgencies that oppose regimes that threaten US interests or regional stability. While any Army force can support an insurgency, Army special operations forces (ARSOF) almost exclusively receive these missions. The US supports only those forces that consistently demonstrate respect for human rights. Given their training, organization, and regional focus, ARSOF are well suited for these operations. When conventional Army forces are tasked to support an insurgency, they cooperate with insurgents under the command of a ground component or joint force commander. Conventional US forces supporting insurgencies may provide logistic and training support; however, they typically do not conduct combat operations.

SECURITY ASSISTANCE

6-54.   Security assistance includes the participation of Army forces in any of a group of programs by which the US provides defense articles, military training, and other defense-related services to foreign nations by grant, loan, credit, or cash sales in furtherance of national policies and objectives (JP 3-07). Army forces support security assistance efforts by training, advising, and assisting allied and friendly armed forces.

SUPPORT TO COUNTERDRUG OPERATIONS

6-55.   In 1986, the President issued National Security Directive 221, which defines drug trafficking as a threat to national security. It is also a threat to the stability of many friendly nations. Two principles guide Army support to counterdrug operations. The first principle is to use military capabilities both to benefit the supported agency and to train our Soldiers and units. The second is to ensure that military members do not become directly involved in law enforcement activities. Army forces may be employed in a variety of operations to support other agencies that are responsible for detecting, disrupting, interdicting, and destroying illicit drugs and the infrastructure (personnel, materiel, and distribution systems) of illicit drug-trafficking entities.

6-56.   Counterdrug operations are always conducted in support of one or more governmental agencies. These include the Coast Guard, Customs Service, Department of State, Drug Enforcement Agency, and

Border Patrol of the Immigration and Naturalization Service. When conducted inside the US and its territories, counterdrug operations are considered offensive or defensive operations under Homeland Security and Homeland Defense and are subject to restrictions under the Posse Comitatus Act. Task Force 6 is an example of US Army forces supporting the counterdrug operations along the US/Mexican border.

6-57.   Whether operating in the US or in a host nation, Army forces do not engage in direct action during counterdrug operations. Units that support counterdrug operations must be fully aware of legal limitations regarding acquiring information on civilians, both US and foreign. Typical support to counterdrug operations includes the following activities:

- Detection and monitoring.
- Host nation support.
- Command, control, communications, and computers.
- Intelligence planning, sustainment, training, and manpower support.
- Research, development, and acquisition.
- Reconnaissance.

COMBATING OF TERRORISM

6-58.   Terrorism is the calculated use of unlawful violence or threat of unlawful violence to instill fear, intended to coerce or intimidate governments or societies in pursuit of goals that are generally political, religious, or ideological (JP 3-07.2). Enemies who cannot compete with Army forces conventionally often turn to terrorism. Terrorist attacks often create a disproportionate effect on even the most capable of conventional forces. Army forces conduct operations to defeat these attacks. A battalion uses offensive operations to counter terrorism and defensive measures to conduct antiterrorism operations. The tactics employed by terrorists include, but are not limited to, the following:

- Arson.
- Hijacking or skyjacking.
- Maiming.
- Seizure.
- Assassination.
- Hostage taking.
- Sabotage.
- Hoaxes.
- Bombing.
- Kidnapping.
- Raids and ambushes.
- Use of WMD.

COUNTERTERRORISM

6-59.   Counterterrorism refers to offensive measures taken to prevent, deter, and respond to terrorism (FM 1-02). Army forces participate in the full array of counterterrorism actions, including strikes and raids against terrorist organizations and facilities. Counterterrorism is a specified mission for selected special operations forces that operate under direct control of the President or Secretary of Defense, or under a unified command arrangement. Infantry battalions generally do not conduct counterterrorism operations; however, they may conduct conventional offensive operations in support of special operations forces conducting counterterrorism operations.

ANTITERRORISM

6-60.   Antiterrorism includes defensive measures used to reduce the vulnerability of individuals and property to terrorist attacks to include limited response and containment by local military forces (FM 1-02). Antiterrorism is always a mission consideration and a component of force protection. Antiterrorism must be a priority for all forces during all operations—offensive, defensive, stability, and civil support. US units may be high priority targets for terrorists because of the notoriety and media attention that follows an attack on an American target. Experience shows that sensational acts of terrorism against US forces can have a strategic effect. The 2001 terrorist attacks against the World Trade Center and the Pentagon resulted in a change in US policy regarding proactive antiterrorism military operations. Commanders must take the security measures necessary to accomplish the mission by protecting the force against terrorism. Typical defensive antiterrorism actions include—

- Coordination with local law enforcement.
- Siting and hardening of facilities.
- Physical security actions designed to prevent unauthorized access or approach to facilities.
- Crime prevention and physical security actions that prevent theft of weapons, munitions, identification cards, and other materials.
- Policies regarding travel, size of convoys, breaking of routines, host nation interaction, and off-duty restrictions.
- Protection from WMD.

6-61.   The Infantry battalion should also conduct active defensive measures to prevent and/or deter terrorism activities in their AO. These measures include:

- Patrols.
- Cordon and searches.
- Roadblocks.

NONCOMBATANT EVACUATION OPERATIONS

6-62.   Army forces conduct noncombatant evacuation operations (NEO) to support the Department of State in evacuating noncombatants and nonessential military personnel from locations in a foreign nation to the US or an appropriate safe haven. Normally, these operations involve US citizens whose lives are in danger either from the threat of hostilities or from a natural disaster. They may also include selected citizens of the host nation or third-country nationals. The NEO may take place in a permissive, uncertain, or hostile environment and can be either unopposed or resisted by hostile crowds, guerrillas, or conventional forces. Most often, the evacuation force commander has little influence over the local situation. The commander may not have the authority to use military measures to preempt hostile actions, yet he must be prepared to defend the evacuees and his force. A key factor in NEO planning is correctly appraising the political-military environment in which the force will operate. The NEO can be a prelude to combat actions, a part of deterrent actions, or a part of peace operations.

ARMS CONTROL

6-63.   Army forces can play a vital role in arms control. Army elements may be involved in locating, seizing, and destroying WMD after hostilities, as they were following Operation Desert Storm. Other actions include escorting authorized deliveries of weapons and materiel to preclude loss or unauthorized use, inspecting and monitoring production and storage facilities, and training foreign forces in the security of weapons and facilities. Arms control operations are normally conducted to support arms control treaties and enforcement agencies. Forces may conduct arms control during combat or stability operations to prevent escalation of the conflict and reduce instability. This could include the mandated disarming of belligerents as part of a peace operation. The collection, storing, and destruction of conventional munitions and weapons systems can deter belligerents from reinstigating hostilities. Specific Army force capabilities including engineers and explosive ordnance disposal (EOD) personnel are particularly suited to these operations. Companies at checkpoints and conducting patrols have some part to play in controlling, seizing, and destroying weapons. Arms control assists in force protection and increases security for the local populace.

SHOW OF FORCE

6-64.   A show of force is an operation designed to demonstrate US resolve that involves increased visibility of US deployed forces in an try to defuse a specific situation, that, if allowed to continue, may be detrimental to US interests or national objectives (FM 1-02). The show of force can influence other government or political-military organizations to respect US interests and international law. The battalion may participate in a show of force as part of a temporary buildup in a specific region by conducting a combined training exercise or by demonstrating an increased level of readiness. The US conducts shows of force for three principal reasons: to bolster and reassure allies, to deter potential aggressors, and to gain or increase influence.

6-65.   A combatant commander may have established force deployment options as part of an existing contingency plan. These shows of force are designated as flexible deterrence options. For Army forces, show-of-force operations usually involve the deployment or buildup of military forces in an AO, an increase in the readiness status and level of activity of designated forces, or a demonstration of operational capabilities by forces already in the region. An example of a show of force operation using Infantry battalions was the deployment of 1st and 2nd Battalions of the 504th Parachute Infantry Regiment, 82nd Airborne Division, along with Soldiers from the 7th Infantry Division at Fort Ord, California in a deployment to Honduras as part of Operation Golden Pheasant in March 1988. This deployment was ordered by President Reagan, in response to actions by the Cuban and Soviet-supported Nicaraguan Sandinistas that threatened the stability of Honduras' democratic government.

6-66.   A show of force is designed to demonstrate a credible and specific threat to an aggressor or potential aggressor. The mere presence of forces does not demonstrate resolve or deter aggression. To achieve the desired effect, forces must be perceived as powerful, capable, and backed by the political will to use them. An effective show of force must be demonstrably mission-capable and sustainable.

6-67.   Although actual combat is not desired when conducting a show of force, the battalion commander must be prepared for an escalation to combat. Commanders must organize their units as if they intend to accomplish the mission by the use of force. Units assigned a show of force mission assume that combat is not only possible, but also probable. All actions ordinarily associated with the projection of a force to conduct combat operations pertain to show-of-force deployments.

Section III. PLANNING CONSIDERATIONS

Stability operations, with the exception of specific actions undertaken in combating terrorism, support to counterdrug operations, and noncombatant evacuation operations, tend to be decentralized operations over extended distances. As such, the battalion's activities consist largely of separated small-unit operations conducted across an assigned sector or AO. The battalion must conduct these operations with consistency, impartiality, and discipline to encourage cooperation from indigenous forces and garner popular support.

DECENTRALIZED OPERATIONS

6-68.   Subordinate commanders need maximum flexibility in executing their missions. Their commander should give them specific responsibilities and ensure they understand his intent. Understanding the intent is critical to successful decentralized execution of stability operations. The commander should employ centralized planning techniques, such as frequent mission briefbacks and rehearsals, to ensure his intent is understood.

6-69.   Although subordinate elements may be conducting independent operations as part of stability operations, commanders must maintain the ability to achieve mass, concentration, their objective and must not become so decentralized as to piecemeal their efforts.

6-70.   Decentralized execution at the company, platoon, and even squad level is necessary for successful execution of stability operations. As such, these small Infantry unit level leaders need, in addition to understanding the commander's intent, timely information about the friendly and enemy situations that leads to situational understanding. Well rehearsed and executed drills, SOPs, and reports also contribute to the small Infantry unit leader being able to execute timely decisions.

METT-TC CONSIDERATIONS

6-71.   The commander and staff must analyze each aspect of the mission and adapt the factors of METT-TC to fit the situation. BCT and subordinate unit missions should be viewed as decisive, shaping, or sustaining operations. Determining and executing the military actions necessary to achieve the desired end state can be more challenging than in situations requiring offensive and defensive operations.

MISSION AND ENEMY

6-72.   During all operations, the commander and his staff must constantly assess the situation in terms of the application and interrelation of the factors of METT-TC. However, stability operations often require the application of METT-TC differently than they would when conducting offensive and defensive operations. For example, the "enemy" may be a set of ambiguous but sophisticated threats and potential adversaries. The unit mission may change as the situation becomes less or more stable. A mission can be as simple as conducting a briefing to host nation forces in a military-to military exchange, or as difficult as conducting combat operations to accomplish a peace enforcement mission, or restoring the power grid and sanitation services to a country with millions of people. Stability may be threatened for a number of reasons, and the enemy may be difficult to define or isolate. Depending upon the progress of the operation, the complexity of the mission may change quickly.

TERRAIN, TROOPS, AND SUPPORT AVAILABLE

6-73.   Different factors may be important when analyzing the terrain and the troops and support available in stability operations. What constitutes key terrain may be based more on political and social considerations than on the physical features of the AOs. The troops available may include both organic units and nontraditional assets such as host nation police and conventional units, contracted interpreters and laborers, or multinational forces. The level of integration and cohesion of a force composed of diverse assets is a key consideration for mission success.

TIME AVAILABLE

6-74.   Time considerations are substantially different in stability operations. The goals of a stability operation may not be achievable in the short term. Success often requires perseverance, patience, and a long-term commitment to solving the real problem. Battalion operations may be part of the continuum of this long-term commitment. The achievement of these goals may take years. Conversely, daily operations may require rapid responses to changing conditions based on unanticipated localized conflict among competing groups.

CIVIL CONSIDERATIONS

6-75.   Civil considerations are especially critical in stability operations. Civil considerations relate to civilian populations, culture, organizations, and leaders within the AO. Commanders consider the natural environment to include, cultural sites in all operations directly or indirectly affecting civilian populations. Commanders include civilian, political, economic, and information matters as well as more immediate civilian activities and attitudes. A simple technique for analyzing civil considerations, used by untrained analysts, or when time is too short for in-depth research, is for the commander or planner to ask the following questions:

- Who are the civilians we might encounter in our AO?
- Where, why, and when might we encounter them?
- What activities are those civilians engaged in that might affect our operations?
- How might our operations affect civilian activities?

6-76. If CA support is available, they will use the preferred method of analyzing civil considerations by using the mnemonic civil, areas, structures, capabilities, organizations, people, and events (CASCOPE). More details on this method can be found in FM 3-05.401.

RULES OF ENGAGEMENT

6-77. Rules of engagement (ROE) are directives issued by competent military authority that delineate the circumstances and limitations under which United States forces will initiate and continue combat engagement with other forces encountered (FM 1-02). ROE specify when, where, against whom, and how units can use force. They may be used to control the use of force across the range of Army operations. The aggressiveness that is important in wartime must be tempered with restraint in the ambiguous environment of many stability operations.

6-78. In general, ROE in major combat operations differ from ROE in smaller scale contingencies or peacetime military engagements (PME). MCO ROE reflect the greater necessity to use force. They provide guidelines to prevent civilian casualties and limit collateral damage; however, they permit armed forces to engage all identified enemy targets, regardless of whether those targets represent actual, immediate threats. By contrast, ROE used in many stability operations merely permit engagement in individual, unit, or national self-defense. FM 3-07, Appendix C discusses ROE in greater detail.

RULES OF INTERACTION

6-79. Rules of interaction (ROI) apply to the human dimension of stability operations. They spell out with whom, under what circumstances, and to what extent Soldiers may interact with other forces and the civilian populace. ROI, when applied with good interpersonal communication (IPC) skills, improve the Soldier's ability to accomplish the mission, while reducing possible hostile confrontations. ROI and IPC, by enhancing the Soldier's persuasion, negotiation, and communication skills, also improve his survivability. ROI, founded on firm ROE, provide the Soldier with the tools to address unconventional threats such as political friction, ideologies, cultural idiosyncrasies, and religious beliefs and rituals. ROI must be regionally and culturally specific.

PROTECTION AND FIELD DISCIPLINE

6-80. Protection has four components: force protection, field discipline, safety, and fratricide avoidance. Force protection, the primary component, minimizes the effects of enemy firepower (including WMD), terrorism, maneuver, and information. Combat readiness reduces the inherent risk of nonbattle deaths and injuries. Fratricide avoidance minimizes the inadvertent killing or maiming of Soldiers by friendly fires. Force protection requires special consideration in stability operations since threats may be different and, in some cases, opposing forces may seek to kill or wound US Soldiers or destroy or damage property for political purposes. Commanders try to accomplish a mission with minimal loss of personnel, equipment, and supplies by integrating force protection considerations into all aspects of operational planning and execution. Commanders and leaders throughout the battalion deliberately analyze their missions and environments to identify threats to their units. They then make their Soldiers aware of the dangers and create safeguards to protect them. Commanders must always consider the aspects of force protection and how they relate to the ROE. Some considerations are—

- Secure the inside perimeter if the host nation secures the outside perimeter.
- Avoid becoming a lucrative target and do not become predictable.
- Include security in each plan, SOP, OPORD, and movement order.
- Develop specific security programs such as threat awareness and OPSEC.
- Restrict access of unassigned personnel to the unit's location.
- Constantly maintain an image of professionalism and readiness.
- Consider force protection throughout the range of military operations; base the degree of security established on a continuous threat assessment.
- Force protection consists of OPSEC, deception, health and morale, safety, and avoidance of fratricide.

OPERATIONS SECURITY

6-81.   OPSEC considerations include the following.

6-82.   Communications security is as important in stability operations as it is in conventional military operations. Belligerent parties can monitor telephones and radios. The need to maintain transparency of the force's intentions in stability operations is a factor when considering OPSEC.

6-83.   Maintaining neutrality contributes to protecting the force. In stability operations, the entire force safeguards information about deployment, positions, strengths, and equipment of one side from the other. If one side suspects that the force is giving information to the other side, deliberately or not, then one or both sides can become uncooperative, putting both the success of the operation and the force itself at risk.

6-84.   The single most proactive measure for survivability is individual awareness by Soldiers in all circumstances. Soldiers must look for things out of place and patterns preceding aggression. Commanders should ensure Soldiers remain alert, do not establish a routine, maintain appearance and bearing, and keep a low profile.

HEALTH AND MORALE

6-85.   Stability operations often require special consideration of Soldier health, welfare, and morale factors. These operations frequently involve deployment to an austere, immature theater with limited life support infrastructure. Commanders must consider these factors when assigning missions and planning rotations of units into and within the theater.

SAFETY

6-86.   Commanders in stability operations may reduce the chance of mishap by conducting risk assessments, assigning a safety officer and staff, conducting a safety program, and seeking advice from local personnel. The safety program should be continuous, beginning with training conducted before deployment. Training includes awareness of the safety risks in the natural environment, terrain and weather, road conditions and local driving habits, access to or possession of live ammunition, unallocated or uncleared mine fields, and special equipment such as armored vehicles and other factors that present special hazards. These other factors may include details on water or waste treatment facilities and other natural or cultural aspects of the area that may constitute a hazard to troops.

AVOIDANCE OF FRATRICIDE

6-87.   Most measures taken to avoid fratricide in stability operations are the same as those taken during combat operations. However, commanders must consider other factors, such as local hires or NGOs, or international organizations and civilian personnel, who might be as much at risk as US forces. Accurate information about the location and activity of both friendly and hostile forces and an aggressive airspace management plan assist commanders in avoiding fratricide. For more information on fratricide avoidance, see Appendix A.

SEQUENCE OF STABILITY OPERATIONS ACTIONS

6-88.   Stability operations generally follow this sequence:

- Deployment and movement into the AO.
- Establishment of a base of operation.
- Conduct of stability operations.
- Termination of operations.

6-89.   It must be remembered that offensive and defensive operations can and will often be conducted while simultaneously conducing stability operations.

DEPLOYMENT AND MOVEMENT INTO AREA OF OPERATIONS

6-90.   The commander and staff must plan, synchronize, and control the movement of forces into the AO to maintain the proper balance of security and flexibility. The commander must decide the sequence in which his forces will enter the AO. The battalion commander must consider the number of suitable routes or lift assets available to meet the movement requirements of his subordinate elements. Other considerations include—

- Entering a hostile, neutral, or permissive AO.
- Constructing, improving and maintaining roads and routes.
- Clearing obstacles.
- Repairing bridges and culverts.
- Establishing security along routes.
- Controlling traffic to permit freedom of or restriction of civilian movements along routes.
- Communications architecture.

6-91.   There may be a need to deploy an advance party heavy with logistical and engineering support into the AO initially if the AO does not have the infrastructure to support the operation. In other circumstances, it may be necessary for the commander and a small group of specialized key personnel, such as attached CA, public affairs, and or staff judge advocate, to lead an advance party. These personnel will set the groundwork for the rest of the force by conducting face-to-face coordination with local civilian or military leaders. Show-of-force operations will most likely necessitate that the commander send a large contingent of forces to act as a deterrent and to ensure initial security. In all cases, a well-developed movement order is essential.

ESTABLISHMENT OF A BASE OF OPERATION

6-92.   Often stability operations require the construction of a base of operations. A complete discussion of establishing a base of operations is in Appendix M.

CONDUCT OF STABILITY OPERATION

6-93.   After the battalion has moved into its AO and established a base for future operations, a continuation of the stability effort commences. To successfully execute the mission, commanders and leaders at all levels must clearly understand the root causes of the conflict. This knowledge enables the battalion leadership to prioritize tasks and begin stability operations. Tactical tasks executed during the stability operation will be dependant upon the factors of METT-TC. Some tasks that have been conducted during recent stability operations are as follows:

- Establishment and enforcement of buffer zones and zones of separation.

- Offensive and defensive operations including raids, checkpoints, patrols, and reconnaissance and surveillance.
- Securing lines of communication.
- Security operations.
- Treaty compliance inspections.
- Negotiation or mediation.
- Security for movement and distribution of disaster relief supplies and equipment.

TERMINATION OF STABILITY OPERATIONS

6-94.   The stability operation may be terminated in several ways. The battalion may be relieved of its mission and conduct a battle handover of the operation to a follow-on force. This force could be another US battalion, a coalition force, a UN force, or a nonmilitary organization. This requires a relief in place be conducted (chapter 8 for a complete discussion of relief operations). The situation could become stabilized and not necessitate the continuance of operations. In this case, the host nation or domestic community will assume responsibility of stability. The battalion could be redeployed with no follow-on forces and without the area being stabilized. A condition such as this would place the battalion in a vulnerable situation. Security must be intense and the protection of the force during its exit must be well planned and executed. Finally, the battalion could transition to combat operations. The commander must always ensure that the battalion maintains the ability to transition quickly and forcefully.

TRANSITION TO COMBAT OPERATIONS

6-95.   If the stability operations are unsuccessful, the battalion may be ordered to transition to tactical combat operations. The commander and staff must always keep in mind that the situation may escalate to combat operations at any time. An escalation to combat operations is a clear indicator that the peace enforcement effort has failed. The battalion must always retain the ability to conduct full-spectrum operations. Preserving the ability to transition allows the battalion to maintain the initiative while providing force protection. The commander must task organize the battalion to expeditiously transition to combat operations while maintaining a balance between conducting the stability mission and maintaining a combat posture.

TASK ORGANIZATION

6-96.   In conducting stability operations, the battalion commander organizes his assets for the type of mission he must perform, integrating attached assets and the assets from higher headquarters to accomplish the mission. The battalion organization must enable the unit to meet changing situations; thus, the commander must consider which resources to allocate to companies and which to maintain control of at the battalion headquarters. Task organization and support arrangements change frequently during long-term stability operations. Commanders must frequently shift the support of engineers, medical units, and aviation units from one area or task to another.

AUGMENTATION

6-97.   The unique aspects of stability operations may require individual augmentees and augmentation cells to support unique force-tailoring requirements and personnel shortfalls. Augmentation supports coordination with the media, government agencies, NGOs, international organizations, other multinational forces, and civil-military elements. METT-TC considerations drive augmentation.

LIAISON

6-98.   Commanders may consider task organizing small liaison teams to deal with situations that develop with the local population. Teams can free up maneuver elements and facilitate negotiation. Teams must have linguists and personnel who have the authority to negotiate on behalf of the chain of command. Unit ministry, engineers, PSYOP, CA, counterintelligence, linguistics, and logistics personnel may be candidates for such teams. Commanders must provide augmenting team members with resources and quality of life normally provided to their own Soldiers.

MEDIA CONSIDERATIONS

6-99.   See Appendix J for a complete discussion of this topic.

OPERATIONS WITH OUTSIDE AGENCIES

6-100.   US Army units conduct certain stability operations in coordination with a variety of outside organizations. These include other US armed services or government agencies as well as international organizations (including NGOs, collation, and UN military forces or agencies). Coordination and integration of civilian and military activities must take place at every level. Normally, operational and tactical headquarters plan their operations to complement those of government and private agencies. Likewise, military commanders need to make clear to other agencies their own objectives and operational schemes. Coordinating centers such as the civil-military operations center are designed to accomplish this task. These operations centers should include representatives from as many agencies as required.

Section IV. WARFIGHTING FUNCTIONS

Commanders plan for stability operations in a manner as plan for the offense and defense. The mission analysis and command estimate processes outlined in FM 5-0 are equally as important in all types of operations. Analysis using the tactical task areas outlined in FM 7-15 is helpful in focusing the planning effort. Many considerations discussed in this section also apply to offensive and defensive operations. However, they appear because the degree or manner in which they apply in these operations differs. The battalion commander must clearly understand the mission and the situation, and he must ensure his staff and subordinate units understand these as well. He must plan for continuous operations, and, as with offensive and defensive operations, planning and preparation time is often very limited. The plan must facilitate adjustment based on changes in the situation. The commander and his staff must consider—

- The mission: what the force is expected to do.
- The AO (size, location, terrain, and weather).
- The political, economic, military, and geographical situation in their AO.
- Local customs, cultures, religions, ethnic groups, and tribal factions.
- The importance of force protection, OPSEC, physical security, and permissible protection measures.
- The ROE and appropriate actions to take concerning infringements and violations of agreements.
- Physical considerations such as minefields, bridges, road conditions, and existing infrastructure.
- Security operations.
- Use of additional assets such as intelligence, public affairs, civil affairs, psychological operations, engineers, and MPs.

FIRE SUPPORT

6-101.   Although FS planning for stability operations is the same as for traditional combat operations, the use of FS may be very restricted and limited. The commander integrates FS into his tactical plan IAW the ROE and restrictions imposed by the AO such as no-fire zones, restricted fire areas, and presence of noncombatants. Special considerations include the following:

- Procedures for the rapid clearance of fires.
- Close communication and coordination with host country officials.
- Increased security for indirect firing positions.
- Restricted use of certain munitions such as dual purpose improved conventional munition (DPICM), area denial artillery munition (ADAM), or remote antiarmor mine (RAAM).

6-102.   The battalion FSE is organized to collect information from forward observers (FOs) and they can be used as observers for collecting and reporting information.

MOVEMENT AND MANEUVER

6-103.   Battalion maneuver in stability operations is similar to maneuver in traditional combat operations with extensive emphasis on security and engagement skills (negotiation, rapport building, cultural awareness, and critical language phrases). The intent is to create a stable environment that allows peace to take hold while ensuring the force is protected.

BATTALION MANEUVER

6-104.   Maneuver of the battalion in stability operations is often decentralized to the company or platoon level. As required, these units receive relief from support forces such as engineers, logistics, and medical personnel. The battalion commander must be prepared to rely on fire support, protection, and sustainment elements to assist the maneuver forces when the need arises. When new requirements develop, the fire support, protection, and sustainment elements must be ready to shift priorities.

COMBAT MANEUVER

6-105.   Maneuver may involve combat. The battalion uses only the level of force necessary to stabilize the crisis. Depending on the ROE, the battalion may precede the use of force with a warning, the use of nonlethal means (Appendix L), or a combination of the two. However, employing lethal means normally only occurs if a belligerent presents a threat to US personnel. The methods employed to reduce the crisis could take the form of separating belligerent forces or maneuvering battalion elements to provide security. A show of force or demonstration may be all that is necessary, or the battalion may employ patrolling, searches, negotiation and mediation, information gathering, strikes and raids, or combat operations to accomplish the mission.

6-106.   Often, the commander finds that he has more tasks than units, and stability operations are no exception. The function of a reserve force in a stability operation is the same as for other operations. The reserve is a portion of a body of troops which is kept to the rear or withheld from action at the beginning of an engagement, in order to be available for a decisive movement (FM 1-02). The reserve is sufficiently armed, trained, equipped, mobile, and positioned to accomplish its mission. A reserve expands the commander's ability to respond to unexpected successes and reversals. Maintaining a reserve in these operations is often difficult. Nonetheless, contingencies may arise that require using the reserve. The maintenance of a reserve allows commanders to plan for worst-case scenarios, provides flexibility, and conserves the force during long-term operations.

6-107.   The QRF differs from a reserve in that it is not in support of a particular engagement. The QRF answers to the establishing headquarters. Considerations when establishing QRF are—

- Transportation of the QRF.
- Communication equipment and procedures.
- Alert procedures.
- Training priorities.

Aviation Support

6-108.   Aviation units—which can be deployed into the AO with early entry ground forces—can be a significant deterrent on the indigenous combatants, particularly if these factions have armored or mechanized Infantry forces. Observation or attack helicopters may be employed to act as a reaction force against enemy threats. They may also conduct reconnaissance or surveillance over wide areas and provide the battalion a means for visual route reconnaissance. Utility helicopters provide an excellent enhanced C2 capability to stability operations and may be used to transport patrols or security elements throughout the AO. Medium lift helicopters are capable of moving large numbers of military and civilian peace enforcement personnel and delivering supplies when surface transportation is unavailable or routes become impassable.

Mobility and Countermobility

6-109.   Mobility within the battalion AO may be restricted due to poorly-developed or significantly damaged road systems, installations, and airfields. Before the battalion can maneuver effectively, it must prepare the AO to support that maneuver. This restricted mobility and need for the battalion to maneuver effectively, may cause higher headquarters to augment the battalion with engineer assets from the BSTB or the combat service brigade (ME).

PROTECTION

6-110.   Engineers can play a major role in stability operations by constructing base camps, upgrading the transportation infrastructure, conducting bridge reconnaissance, assisting in civic action by building temporary facilities for the civilian populace, and reducing the mine threat. Factors that help determine the amount of engineer support the battalion receives include—

- Terrain in the AO.
- Type and location of obstacles in the AO.
- Engineer assets available.
- Duration of the operation.
- Environmental considerations.
- Water supply and location.
- Sewage and garbage facilities.
- Local power facilities.
- Fire fighting capability.
- Basic country infrastructure (road, bridge, rail, airfield, and port capability) including contracted engineering support.

6-111.   Regardless of battalion requirements, there may not be enough engineer assets, including civilian contract engineer support, available. This situation requires battalion elements to construct their own fortifications and assist with other engineer tasks within their capabilities. In prioritizing the use of engineers or the use of organic forces to accomplish engineer tasks, the battalion commander emphasizes the strengthening of force protective measures.

6-112.   If attached to the battalion, an air defense officer (ADO) or NCO can analyze enemy air capabilities during the initial stages of planning. If an air threat exists or is possible, the ADO must take care to use any attached AD elements to combat the threat in full compliance with the ROE. Since a belligerent air capability can disrupt the battalion's entry and operations in the AO, the battalion must ensure any enemy air capability information remains a priority intelligence collection requirement.

COMMAND AND CONTROL

6-113. Battalions seldom function as a joint headquarters. However, a BCT HQ can function as a JTFHQ. If there is no JTF for the operation, a C2 element from a unit higher than the BCT performs the role of the JTF to integrate the other services. This allows the battalion to focus on the control of its companies.

COMMAND AND SUPPORT RELATIONSHIPS

6-114. The ambassador to the country is responsible for US operations, both civilian and military, except for military forces under the command of a regional combatant commander. The ambassador heads a country team that interfaces with civilian and military agencies. The term *country team* describes in-country interdepartmental coordination among the members of the US diplomatic mission.

6-115. The US area military commander is not a member of the diplomatic mission. The JTF interfaces with the senior military defense representative on the country team. If there is no JTF, BCT or battalion headquarters may be responsible for interface with the country team and host nation.

6-116. C2 headquarters may be unilateral or established with the host nation. An interagency headquarters of civilian and military forces also includes police, paramilitary, security, and even other US agencies. The headquarters must coordinate operations with civilian agencies to ensure no conflict of political and military objectives.

6-117. CA, CMO, and PSYOP activities require close coordination with members of the Country Team to ensure that any initiatives conducted by the Infantry Battalion do not conflict with the Ambassador's efforts. CA and PSYOP personnel attached to the Infantry battalion must ensure that their operations are closely coordinated so as not to conflict with the Country Team efforts. PSYOP approval authority by policy rests with the Ambassador whenever a US Mission (Embassy) is active in a country. PSYOP products pre-approved by the JTF and vetted with the Ambassador can be disseminated by PSYOP forces attached to the Infantry Battalion. TPTs do not have organic product development capability, and therefore must submit product requests to the next higher PSYOP element.

6-118. If a battalion follows an SOF unit or operation during a deployment, it should request a liaison before arrival in the operational area. The battalion coordinates with SOF through the JTF. If there is no JTF, the unit contacts the SOF through the security assistance office.

END STATE

6-119. To keep the battalion focused throughout the operation, the commander and his staff develop a concept of the operation that establishes objectives and timelines to meet the desired end state. The concept should cover the entire duration of the operation from deployment to the end state, defining how the battalion will accomplish its assigned mission. The commander uses FRAGOs and subsequent OPORDs to control execution of each phase of the operation and various missions as required.

6-120. The commander and his staff coordinate battalion plans and actions with the higher headquarters, adjacent units, and government and NGOs in the AO to ensure unified effort. Use of liaison officers is vital for this requirement.

COMMUNICATIONS

6-121. Communications abilities are augmented to effect long-range communications and proper liaisons. The commander and his staff consider equipment compatibility, crypto use, information sharing, and security measures when working with SOF, joint forces, and multinational forces.

INTELLIGENCE

6-122. ISR plays an important role in the battalion's accomplishment of a stability operations mission. The battalion commander uses every element available to collect information that helps him accomplish his mission. He uses these elements in compliance with the ROE. Every member of the battalion, both Soldier and civilian, plays a role in gathering information to support the battalion. The battalion commander uses his battalion S-2 and the battalion intelligence section to form a coordinated intelligence production team. They manage the information collection effort to ensure every member of the battalion understands the information required and plays an active role in the collection of that information. Information collection elements normally available to the battalion include the sniper squad, the scout platoon; maneuver companies; elements attached to or supporting the battalion; Soldiers on patrols, in OPs, and at checkpoints; small UAS, tactical HUMINT teams (THT), and other special operations forces such as CA, PSYOP and SF.

6-123. In addition to organic elements, the battalion may have interrogation, counterintelligence, other human intelligence (HUMINT) elements, or signals intelligence (SIGINT) elements from higher echelon MI units or other theater intelligence resources. The battalion will have access to the Joint Network Node as well as other intelligence sources such as SOF and JIIM.

HUMAN INTELLIGENCE

6-124. Tactical collection includes all sources. Technological capabilities may not provide a significant advantage in some environments. HUMINT is a major focus and often the main source of intelligence. An intelligence database may or may not apply or be available to the tactical commander. Every Soldier can collect and report important information. .

6-125. The attitudes and perceptions of the local populace in the AO are important in helping the battalion commander decide how to use his forces to accomplish his objectives. Human intelligence collected by battalion or other supporting or cooperating elements, is a primary means the battalion uses to understand the attitudes and perceptions of the local populace. Tactical PSYOP teams (TPTs) are an additional source for collecting information as they are in contact with local populations.

IPB APPLIED TO STABILITY OPERATIONS

6-126. The battalion commander uses the IPB process and the intelligence cycle as cornerstones for successful stability operations. They can help the commander determine who the enemy is, what capabilities the enemy has, and where he can find the enemy. They also serve as the basis for creating the battalion concept of operations and allocating combat power available to the battalion. (See FM 34-130 for IPB and how it applies to stability operations.) Although some of the traditional IPB products, such as a doctrinal template, may not apply, the method remains intact. The development of detailed PIR and IR enables all personnel in the AO to gather critical information to support the battalion. A part of IBP is to assess the area in which the battalion will be operating. (See Table 6-1 for an area assessment checklist.) The CMO estimate and the CA annex to the OPORD are products that may have already been completed and will provide an assessment of the AO. If available, CA assets can conduct detailed area assessments of the AO. For a detailed area assessment format, see FM 41-10.

Table 6-1. Area assessment checklist.

Population and Leadership	
• Is there a formal village leader? What is his/her name and what is the background? • Is there an informal village leader/tribe/clan? What is his/her/its name and background? • What language and dialect does the population speak? Are other languages and dialects used? • What is the size of the original population? • What are the size and population of the surrounding countryside the village services?	• Are there any refugees and if so, where are the refugees originally from? • What is the size of the refugee population? • Why did they come here? • What is the relationship of the village with the surrounding villages? Are they related? Do they support each other? Are they hostile? Is any portion of the population discriminated against?

Food and Water	
• What is the food and water status of the village? • Where do they get their food? • What other means of subsistence are available?	• Are the villagers farmers or herders? • What is the status of their crops or herds? • What is the quality of the water source?

Medical	
• What is the status of the public health system/services for the AO? • How many public health personnel and facilities are available and what are their capabilities? • What is the health and nutritional status of the general population or specified subpopulation?	• What are the primary endemic and epidemic diseases and what percent of the population is affected? • What is the leading cause of death for the population or specified subpopulation? • What are the names and titles of key personnel within the public and private health care infrastructure?

Civil-Military Organizations	
• What military organizations exist in the village or surrounding countryside?	• Who are their leaders?

Nongovernmental Organizations (NGOs) and International, or Other Agencies	
• What NGOs, IOs, NATO, UN, or other agencies operate in the town/village? • Who are their representatives? • What services do they provide? • What portion of the population do they service?	• Do they have an outreach program for the surrounding countryside? • Which organization, if any, does the local populace support?

Commerce	
• What commercial or business activities are present in the village?	• What services or products do they produce?

Miscellaneous	
• Determine the groups in the village in the most need. What are their numbers? Where did they come from? How long have they been there? What are their specific needs? • What civic employment projects would village leaders like to see started? • Determine the number of families in the village. What are their family names? How many in each family? • What food items are available in the local market? What is the cost of these items? Are relief supplies being sold in the market? If so, what items, from what source, and at what price?	• What skilled labor or services are available in the village? • What are the major roads and routes through the village? How heavily traveled are they? Are there choke points or bridges on the routes? Are there alternate routes or footpaths? • What is the size of any transient population in the village? Where did they come from and how long have they been there?

SEWER, WATER, ELECTRICAL, ACADEMIC, TRASH, MEDIA, AND SECURITY

6-127. The memory device for sewer, water, electricity, academia, trash, media, and security (SWEAT-MS) is useful for assessing the AO is to conduct an assessment of the local infrastructure, both physical and cultural. The physical infrastructure includes the sewer, water, electrical, academic (schools) and trash. These critical quality of life issues directly impact the lives of the population. If these issues are in need of repair it is a logical starting point for US forces to concentrate resources. Insurgents will use and exploit existing infrastructure deficiencies. A common method insurgents use to display the weakness of the current local or national government is to disrupt or destroy critical components of infrastructure They may also create additional infrastructure where gaps in government-provided services exist in order gain the good will of the local population. If successful, this demonstrates the government's inability to protect critical infrastructure components and their inability to provide basic services such as security for the population.

6-128. The cultural areas of media and security are also basic issues that need first order attention by US forces. The media can assist in informing the indigenous population of the intent of US forces. Security is critical to the safety and functioning of the US forces and the population. Like infrastructure deficiencies that may be used against the local or national government, insurgents manipulation of the media and lack of effective security can affect the effectiveness of US forces.

INFORMATION OPERATIONS

6-129. PSYOP focus on shaping the ideas, perceptions, and beliefs of select target audiences. The successful management of PSYOP gives the commander the ability to affect the perception of target audiences such as a belligerent faction or local leaders, and to accomplish the mission. Information management is critical in stability operations, and security of elements which can help manage information is essential to the success of these operations. The battalion commander may have PSYOP, CA, PA, and OPSEC elements attached or operating in support of his battalion. If he must plan for their use, he must do so in concert with the ROE, the order from higher headquarters, and his operational plan. If these elements are operating in his area, he may be responsible for providing security for them. Sources of information the battalion must use include—

- Neutral parties.
- Former warring factions.
- Civilian populace.
- Other agencies working in the AO.
- Media and information passed from organic and nonorganic assets.

SUSTAINMENT

6-130. The battalion's ability to sustain itself in the AO depends on the theater's maturity, the sustainment structure, and the time flow of forces. Refugees, an inadequate infrastructure, and demands by the host nation and coalition partners can make logistical support complex. One source of coordination and assistance with these issues is the CMOC, embedded in the CA unit supporting the battalion.

GENERAL PRINCIPLES

6-131. General principles to consider when planning sustainment for stability operations include—

- Ability of the battalion to provide its own support.
- Ability of higher headquarters to provide support.
- Availability of local supplies, facilities, utilities, services, and transportation support systems by contract or local purchase.

- Availability of local facilities such as lines of communication, ports, airfields, and communications systems.
- Local capabilities for self-support to facilitate the eventual transfer of responsibilities to the supported nation for development or improvement.
- Availability of resources.

AUGMENTATION

6-132. To make up for inadequate logistical and health service infrastructures in the AO, the battalion may be augmented with additional sustainment elements from the BSB. Some or all of these sustainment elements may precede maneuver, fire support or protection elements into the AO. In addition to supporting the battalion, sustainment elements may provide support for—

- Allied or indigenous governmental agencies.
- Allied or indigenous civilians.
- Allied or indigenous military forces.
- US governmental agencies.
- US civilian agencies and personnel.
- Other US military forces.
- US-backed personnel and organizations.
- International civilian and governmental agencies.

FORCE HEALTH PROTECTION

6-133. Specific tasks battalion FHP personnel may be required to perform in stability operations include: health and welfare inspections of detainee holding areas, inspection of food, water, and humanitarian relief supplies, inspections and recommendations for improvements to local hospitals and treatment facilities, and medical civic action program (MEDCAPS) to promote US or Coalition relations in the AO. Additional FHP requirements could include veterinary services, preventive medicine (PVNTMED), hospital, laboratory, combat and operational stress control, and dental support. For definitive information on FHP for stability operations, see FM 8-42 and FM 4-02. See AR 40-400 for information on emergency medical treatment for local national civilians during stability operations.

CONTRACTING

6-134. Contracting can be an effective force multiplier and can augment existing sustainment capabilities. Weak logistical infrastructures in the AO may make it necessary to use contracting for some supplies and services. If the commander knows that contracting functions may have to be performed, the battalion commander obtains guidance from higher headquarters concerning contracting during the initial planning stages. The CMOC has the internal and organic capability to conduct simple contracting pay agent and FOO duties. Hostilities can cause interruptions in the delivery of any contracted services, such as food and water, so the battalion must be prepared to support itself and provide necessary support to attached and supporting forces and the local populace for limited periods.

OTHER CONSIDERATIONS

6-135. The battalion commander influences and shapes the AO for mission success by effectively using buffer zones to separate belligerent factions, establishing checkpoints to control movement through and within the battalion area, and conducting cordon and search operations to isolate and locate belligerents. To plan effective stability operations, the commander must consider his AO and the environment. Diplomacy and negotiations assist the battalion in building support from the host nation, in reducing the threat of possible belligerents, and in creating an environment supportive of US actions. All planning should consider a QRF of appropriate size to react quickly to separate hostile parties before potential violent situations grow out of control. The QRF must have the ability to respond anywhere in the battalion area and handle any unforeseen crisis.

Section V. TECHNIQUES

The different techniques the battalion uses to accomplish its mission during stability operations are patrols, observation posts, providing security to officials, static security posts, searches, roadblocks, and checkpoints. Also, indigenous authorities or other high-ranking officials may require the protection of the battalion during movement through or within the AOs.

PRESENCE PATROLS

6-136.   The battalion may direct its subordinate companies to conduct specific patrols throughout the AO. Regardless of the type of patrol, patrols always have a task and purpose. Presence patrols are usually conducted overtly, using available transportation assets (air or ground) or on foot. Although the patrols are conducted overtly, the companies take all precautions to protect the Soldiers on patrol. A patrol must be readily identifiable as such by all parties and must conduct movement openly. The patrol wears distinctive items of uniform such as the American flag and nonsubdued unit patches.

6-137.   Patrols can accomplish the following:

*   Deter potential truce violations by enforcing international agreements.
*   Cover gaps between fixed observation posts.
*   Confirm reports from observation posts.
*   Investigate alleged breaches of the armistice.

6-138.   A patrol must do the following:

*   Avoid deviating from the planned route.
*   Record in writing and sketch all observations.
*   Halt when challenged, identify itself, and report any try to obstruct its progress.
*   Record any changes in the disposition of the opposing forces.

OBSERVATION POSTS

6-139.   Observation posts are an especially important element of the battalion's effort to establish and maintain security. OPs provide protection when long-range observation from current positions is not possible. The battalion can employ any number of OPs as the situation dictates.

6-140.   OPs are sited for maximum view of the surrounding area, for clear radio communications, and for defensibility. OP locations are recorded, and the commander must authorize any relocation. Soldiers man the OPs at all times. Access is limited to authorized personnel only. One squad usually mans an OP and keeps a record of all activities. Soldiers are continuously accountable for weapons and ammunition. During rotation to relieve Soldiers in an OP, the incoming and outgoing Soldiers conduct a joint inventory for the record. If Soldiers in the OP discharge weapons, they report this immediately to headquarters and make a written record of the circumstances. (SOPs include details on these and similar matters.) The mission of the OP is to report the following:

*   Movement of belligerent military forces, including unit identification, time, direction, and other details that the OP can ascertain.
*   Shooting, hostile acts, or threats directed against the peacekeeping force or civilians.
*   Any improvement to defensive positions of a former belligerent.

- An overflight by unauthorized aircraft, either military or civilian, including the time, direction, aircraft type, and nationality.
- Any observed violations of an armistice agreement.

6-141.   The peacekeeping force relies on the goodwill of the former belligerent parties for its safety. Conspicuous marking on installations, vehicles, and personnel are a source of protection. The peacekeeping force maintains its legitimacy and acceptability to the former belligerents through its professional, disinterested, and impartial conduct of the peacekeeping mission. However, factions in the former belligerents' armed forces, in the civilian population, or among other interested parties may want to disrupt the peacekeeping operation and subvert the diplomatic process. Therefore, the peacekeeping force must be prepared to defend itself.

6-142.   The battalion must strictly follow the ROE and limitations on the use of force. Each unit must maintain a ready reserve or response force that can reinforce an OP or aid a patrol in distress. Field fortifications, barriers, and well-sited weapons must protect installations, and the battalion must take precautions to protect personnel and facilities from terrorist attacks. The peacekeeping force must fight defensive engagements only if they cannot avoid such engagements. The commander must be prepared to recommend withdrawal of the force when a serious threat appears.

SECURITY OF OFFICIALS

6-143.   The battalion may be required to ensure that indigenous authorities or other high-ranking officials may move within the AO without interference from hostile agents.

6-144.   The strength of the security element required depends on the circumstances.

6-145.   The battalion security force should provide an armored vehicle as optional transportation for the official(s).

6-146.   Additional modes of transportation must provide support to the vehicle carrying the official(s) throughout the move. Each of the additional vehicles should have automatic weapons and Soldiers designated to perform specific security tasks for the officials.

6-147.   The vehicle carrying the official(s) should bear no distinguishing marks and more than one vehicle of that type should travel in the escort.

6-148.   The security element designated to accompany the official(s) must be capable of extracting the official's vehicle out of the danger area as quickly as possible in the event of an attack. The security element must develop and rehearse contingency plans, alternate routes, and actions on contact.

6-149.   Before starting the move, the security element commander briefs the official(s) about what will be done in the event of an attack. Regardless of the official's seniority, the security element commander is in command of the move.

STATIC SECURITY POSTS

6-150.   A static security post is any security system organized to protect critical fixed installations— military or civil—or critical points along lines of communication such as terminals, tunnels, bridges, and road or railway junctions (Figure 6-2).

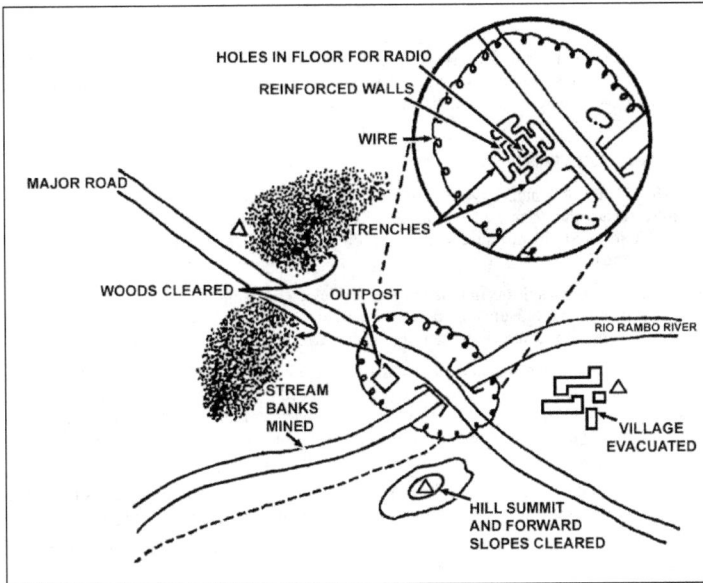

Figure 6-2. Security post.

6-151.   The size of the post depends on the mission, the size and characteristics of the hostile force, the attitude of the civilian populace, and the importance of the item being secured. The post varies from a two-Soldier bridge guard to a reinforced company securing a key communications center or civilian community. The battalion coordinates establishment of security posts with the host nation.

6-152.   The organization of a static security post varies with its size, mission, and distance from reinforcing units. For security reasons, static security posts in remote areas are larger than the same type post would be if located closer to supporting forces. It is organized for the security of both the installation and the security force. The battalion must establish reliable communications between remote static security posts and the parent unit's base.

6-153.   The battalion must control access to the security post by indigenous personnel. It screens and evacuates people living near the positions and can place informers from the local population along the routes of approach.

6-154.   The commander must give all possible consideration to Soldier comfort during the organization and preparation of the security post. Even under the best conditions, morale suffers among Soldiers who must operate for prolonged periods in small groups away from their parent organization.

6-155.   If the static security post is far removed from other battalion units and might be isolated by enemy action, the battalion prestocks sustaining supplies there in sufficient quantities. A static security post should never have to depend solely on the local populace for supplies.

SEARCHES

6-156.   Searches are an important aspect of populace and resource control. The need to conduct search operations or to employ search procedures is a continuous requirement. A search can orient on people, materiel, buildings, or terrain. A search usually involves both civil police and Soldiers.

PLANNING CONSIDERATIONS

6-157.   Misuse of search authority can adversely affect the outcome of operations. Soldiers must conduct and lawfully record the seizure of contraband, evidence, intelligence material, supplies, or other minor items for their seizure to be of future legal value. Proper use of authority during searches gains the respect and support of the people.

6-158.   Authority for search operations is carefully reviewed. Military personnel must perform searches only in areas in military jurisdiction (or where otherwise lawful). They must conduct searches only to apprehend suspects or to secure evidence proving an offense has been committed.

6-159.   Search teams have detailed instructions for handling controlled items. Lists of prohibited or controlled-distribution items should be widely disseminated and on hand during searches. The battalion contacts military or civil police who work with the populace and the resource control program before the search operations begin (or periodically if search operations are a continuing activity). Units must consider the effect of early warning on the effectiveness of their operation.

6-160.   Language difficulties can interfere when US forces conduct search operations involving the local populace. The US units given a search mission are provided with interpreters as required.

6-161.   The battalion conducts search operations slowly enough to allow for an effective search, but rapidly enough to prevent the enemy from reacting to the threat of the search.

6-162.   Soldiers use minimum-essential force to eliminate any active resistance encountered.

6-163.   The battalion should develop plans for securing the search area (establishing a cordon) and for handling detained personnel.

PROCEDURES

6-164.   Search procedures are as follows:

Search of Individuals

6-165.   In all search operations, leaders must emphasize the fact that anyone in an area to be searched could be an insurgent or a sympathizer. To avoid making an enemy out of a suspect who may support the host country government, searchers must be tactful. The greatest caution is required during the initial handling of a person about to be searched. One member of the search team covers the other member who makes the actual search. (FM 3-19.40 and STP 19-95B1-SM discuss the procedure for searching individuals.)

Search of Females

6-166.   The enemy can use females for all types of tasks when they think searches might be a threat. To counter this, use female searchers. If female searchers are not available, use doctors, aidmen, or members of the local populace. If male Soldiers must search females, take all possible measures to prevent any inference of sexual molestation or assault. A technique used by forces in Afghanistan to search women using a magnetic wand metal detector was having the husband search his wife. First, the husband was searched by the Soldiers, and then the husband used the wand on his wife. This method keeps the female individual searches within the cultural norms of the country.

Search of Vehicles

6-167. The search of vehicles may require equipment such as detection devices, mirrors, and tools. Specially-trained dogs can locate drugs or explosives. Before the vehicle is searched, occupants may need to be moved away from vehicles and individually searched. One technique is to have an occupant open all doors, the trunk, and the hood. Soldiers pull security on the occupant as he conducts these actions. Then, they move him to the individual search area and thoroughly search the vehicle. Although a thorough vehicle search takes time, leaders must consider the effect on the population. Using a separate vehicle search area can help avoid unnecessary delays.

Search of Built-Up Areas

6-168. These searches are also referred to as cordon-and-search operations. The principles, C2 and procedures for this type of search, are discussed in the following paragraph. When intelligence identifies and locates members of the insurgent infrastructure, an operation is mounted to neutralize them. All operations must be conducted legally. This may include operations conducted by police acting on warrants of a disinterested magistrate and based on probable cause. In the more violent stages of an insurgency, emergency laws and regulations may dispense temporarily with some of these legal protections. Use the least severe method to accomplish the mission adequately. Take care to preserve evidence for future legal action.

CORDON AND SEARCH

6-169. The commander should divide the area to be searched in a built-up area into zones and assign a search party to each zone. A search party normally consists of a security element (responsible for isolating the objective and specific areas within the objective), a search element (responsible for entering and searching specific focus areas and providing local security), and a reserve element (responsible for assisting either element, as required) (Figure 6-3).

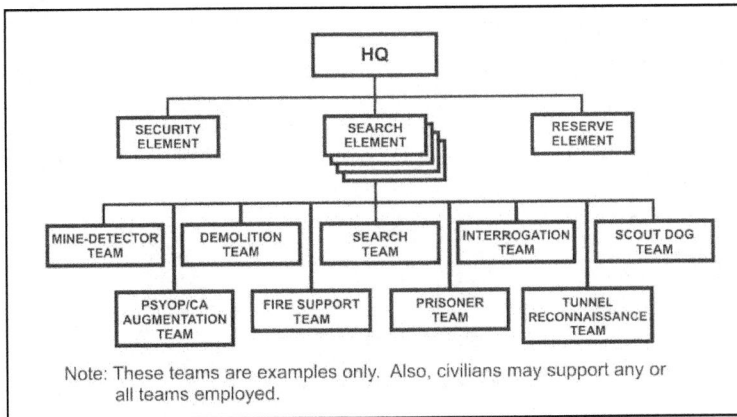

Figure 6-3. Typical organization for search operations.

Establishing Cordon

6-170. An effective cordon is critical to the success of the search effort. Cordons are designed to prevent the escape of individuals to be searched and to protect the forces conducting the operation. The cordon not only isolates the objective from individuals trying to escape, but prevents the insurgents with re-enforcements from entering the objective area. Based on factors of METT-TC, two cordons may be established: the outer cordon to focus on isolating the objective from outside, and the inner cordon to focus on keeping individuals from escaping the objective area. However, both cordon elements must focus both inward and outward for security purposes. The security element leader may have C2 of both the inner and outer cordon elements. Small UAS, scout teams, or sniper teams should be considered for use in observing the target search for enemy forces area before approach of the main body.

6-171. There are two techniques for emplacement of the cordon element(s): simultaneously or sequentially. Careful consideration must be given to both as there are advantages and disadvantages to both. Once the battalion has determined which techniques to use, ensure the order of march facilitates smooth synchronized execution (Figure 6-4).

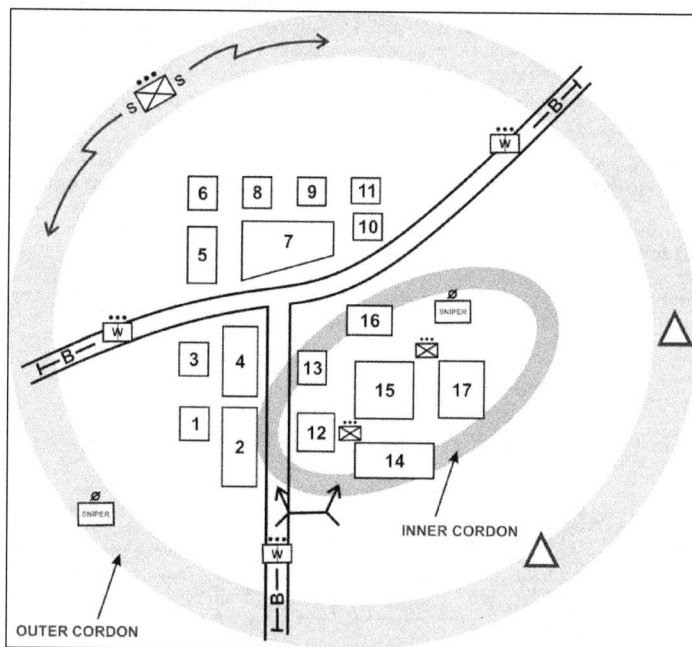

Figure 6-4. Establishment of cordon.

Outer Cordon

6-172. The outer cordon is an integral part of the security element in any cordon and search operation. Therefore, it requires detailed planning, effective coordination, and meticulous integration and synchronization to achieve the combined arms effects. Both lethal and nonlethal (Appendix L) effects should be considered by the commander.

6-173. Each subordinate outer cordon element (traffic control point or blocking position) must have a designated leader and a clear task and purpose. Units and elements to consider for establishing the outer cordon include:

- Weapons company.
- Assault platoons.
- Weapons squads (Javelin CLU equipped).
- Sniper teams.

6-174. The leader of the outer cordon maintains situational understanding in his AO to include the progress of operations for the search elements and the outer cordon. In doing so, he can anticipate threat activity, control direct and indirect fires, and facilitate the outer cordon task and purpose.

6-175. The security element of the outer cordon may include the following:

- Vehicle mounted platoons or sections.
- Interpreter(s).
- Detainee security teams.
- Crowd control teams.
- Observation posts.
- Traffic control points or blocking positions.
- Host nation security forces (military or police).
- Aviation.
- Dismounted platoons or squads.
- Female search teams.

Inner Cordon

6-176. The inner cordon may be under the control of the security element of the search element. It is normally tasked with the following actions:

- Preventing exfiltration or reposition of threat forces.
- Serving as a support by fire force for search teams.
- Maintaining communications with the search element.
- Understanding the marking system and control measures.
- Seizing supporting structures in built-up areas to overwatch target area buildings

6-177. In remote areas, the battalion may establish the cordon without being detected. The use of limited visibility aids in the establishment and security of the cordon but makes it difficult to control.

6-178. The battalion must enforce the ROE and should develop plans to handle detained personnel. Infantrymen accompany police and intelligence forces to identify, question, and detain suspects. Infantry may also conduct searches and assist in detaining suspects, under police supervision, but their principal role is to reduce any resistance that may develop and to provide security for the operation. Use of force is kept to a minimum.

Conducting Search

6-179. A search of a built-up area must be conducted with limited inconvenience to the populace; that is, enough inconvenience to discourage insurgents and sympathizers from remaining in the locale, but not enough to drive them to collaborate with the enemy because of the search. A large-scale search of a built-up area is a combined civil police and military operation. Such a search should be planned in detail and rehearsed while avoiding physical reconnaissance of the area just before the search. Aerial photographs can provide information needed about the terrain. In larger towns or cities, the local police might have detailed maps showing relative sizes and locations of buildings. As with any Army operation, mission analysis is critical. For success, the search plan must be simple and the search conducted swiftly. The search element is organized into teams. These teams can include personnel and special equipment for handling prisoners, or detainees, interrogations, documentation (using a recorder with a camera), demolitions, PSYOP and civil affairs, mine detection, military working dogs and tunnel reconnaissance, interpreters, host nation security forces, aviation assets for observation or attack, TPT, THT, and female search teams

6-180.   There are three basic methods used to search a populated area: assemble inhabitants in a central location, restrict inhabitants to their home, and control the heads of the households.

Assemble Inhabitants in a Central Location

6-181.   This method is used if inhabitants appear to be hostile. It provides the most control, simplifies a thorough search, denies insurgents an opportunity to conceal evidence, and allows for detailed interrogation. Depending on the objective of the search, a personnel search team may be necessary in this central location. This method has the disadvantage of taking the inhabitants away from their dwellings, thus encouraging looting, which, in turn, engenders ill feelings. Another disadvantage in removing inhabitants from their dwellings is that it can create an increased probability of false claims of theft and damage from the local populace. The security element is then responsible for controlling the inhabitants. The search element may escort individuals back to their dwellings to be present during the search or may leave them in the central location.

Restrict Inhabitants to Their Home

6-182.   This prohibits movement of civilians, allows them to stay in their dwellings, and discourages looting. The security element must enforce this restriction. The disadvantages of this method are that it makes control and interrogation difficult and gives inhabitants time to conceal evidence in their homes.

Control Heads of Households

6-183.   The head of each household is told to remain in front of the house while everyone else in the house is brought to a central location. The security element controls the group at the central location, controls the head of each household, and provides external security for the search team. When dealing with the head of the household, ensure that the unit leader explains the purpose of the search using an interpreter (if available). During the search, the head of the household accompanies the search team through the house. This person can be used to open doors and containers to facilitate the search. Looting is reduced, and the head of the household sees that the search team steals nothing. This is a proven method for controlling the populace during a search.

Searching a House

6-184.   The object of a house search is to look for controlled items and to screen residents to determine if any are suspected insurgents or sympathizers. A search party assigned to search an occupied building should consist of at least one local policeman, a protective escort for local security, and a female searcher. If inhabitants remain in the dwellings, the protective escort must isolate and secure the inhabitants during the search. Escort parties and transportation must be arranged before the search of a house. Forced entry may be necessary if a house is vacant or if an occupant refuses to allow searchers to enter. If the force searches a house containing property while its occupants are away, it should secure the house to prevent looting. Before US forces depart, the commander should arrange for the community to protect such houses until the occupants return.

6-185.   Make every try to leave the house in the same or better condition than when the search began. In addition to information collection, the search team may use cameras or video recorders to establish the condition of the house before and after the search. All sensitive material or equipment found in the house should be documented before it is removed or collected, to include date, time, location, the person from whom it was confiscated, and the reason for the confiscation. The use of a camera can also assist in this procedure.

OTHER CONSIDERATIONS

6-186.   The reserve element is a mobile force positioned in a nearby area. Its mission is to help the search and security elements if they meet resistance beyond their ability to handle. The reserve element can replace or reinforce either of the other two elements if the need arises. Soldiers should treat any enemy material found, including propaganda signs and leaflets, as if it is booby-trapped until inspection proves it safe. Underground and underwater areas should be searched thoroughly. Any freshly excavated ground could be a hiding place. Soldiers can use mine detectors to locate metal objects underground and underwater.

AERIAL SEARCH OPERATIONS

6-187.   Helicopter-mounted patrols escorted by armed helicopters take full advantage of the mobility and firepower of these aircrafts.

6-188.   The helicopter mounted patrols may conduct reconnaissance of an assigned area or route in search of enemy forces. When the element locates an enemy force, it may instruct the armed helicopters to engage the enemy force or they may land and engage the enemy by means of a ground assault. This technique has little value in areas of dense vegetation or when a significant man-portable air defense threat is present.

6-189.   Helicopter-mounted patrols should be used only when sufficient intelligence is available to justify their use. Even then, ground operations should be used in support of the helicopter mounted patrols.

APPREHENDED INSURGENTS

6-190.   Certain principles govern actions taken when insurgents desert or surrender voluntarily and indicate, at least in part, their attitudes and beliefs have changed. In this situation, the following guidelines apply.

- Confine them only for screening and processing, and keep them separate from prisoners who exhibit no change in attitude.
- Supervise them after their release. The supervision need not be stringent and is best accomplished by host nation authorities, if possible.
- Relocate them if they are in danger of reprisal from the enemy.
- Remember they expect any promises made to induce their defection or surrender to be met.
- Provide special handling to nonindigenous members of the insurgency who were captured.

ROADBLOCKS AND OTHER CHECKPOINTS

6-191.   A related aspect of populace and resource control mentioned previously is the control of transportation. Individuals and vehicles may be stopped during movement to assist in individual accountability or capture of enemy personnel or to control the trafficking of restricted material. The ability to establish roadblocks and checkpoints is an important aspect of movement control and area denial. The fundamentals of searches, discussed previously, also apply to roadblocks and checkpoints. (FM 3-21.8 and FM 3-21.10 provide additional information about roadblocks and checkpoints.)

6-192.   Roadblocks and checkpoints help prevent traffic in contraband and stop the movement of known or suspected insurgents. They should be manned by police or paramilitary forces, which stop vehicles and pedestrians and conduct searches as required by conditions. They must take care to maintain legitimacy by not targeting specific groups. Either host country or US Army combat forces defend these roadblocks and checkpoints from enemy attack. If police strength is insufficient for the number of positions required, the

Army can operate them. Whenever US Army forces operate roadblocks and checkpoints, host country police or other forces should be present to conduct the actual stop and search. US forces should establish communications with other elements of the site but should also remain in contact with their own chain of command. The same principles apply to waterways as to landlines of communication.

6-193.   Establish roadblocks in locations where approaching traffic cannot observe them until it is too late to withdraw and escape. Narrow defiles, tunnels, bridges, sharp curves, and other locations that channel traffic, are the preferred sites. Constructed nonexplosive obstacles slow traffic, restrict it to a single lane, and bring it to a halt. An area off the main road should be used to conduct a detailed search of suspect vehicles and people and to avoid unduly delaying innocent traffic. A small reserve using hasty field fortifications in nearby defended areas should provide immediate support to operating personnel in case of attack. A larger reserve, which serves a number of posts, should be capable of rapid reinforcement (Figure 6-4).

6-194.   US forces should fill the reserve role in combined operations with host nation personnel. The reserve is vulnerable to being set up or ambushed, especially if an enemy has observed rehearsals. The enemy may hit multiple locations simultaneously to test responsiveness or to aid his future planning. Forces should vary locations of roadblocks and routes used (Figure 6-5).

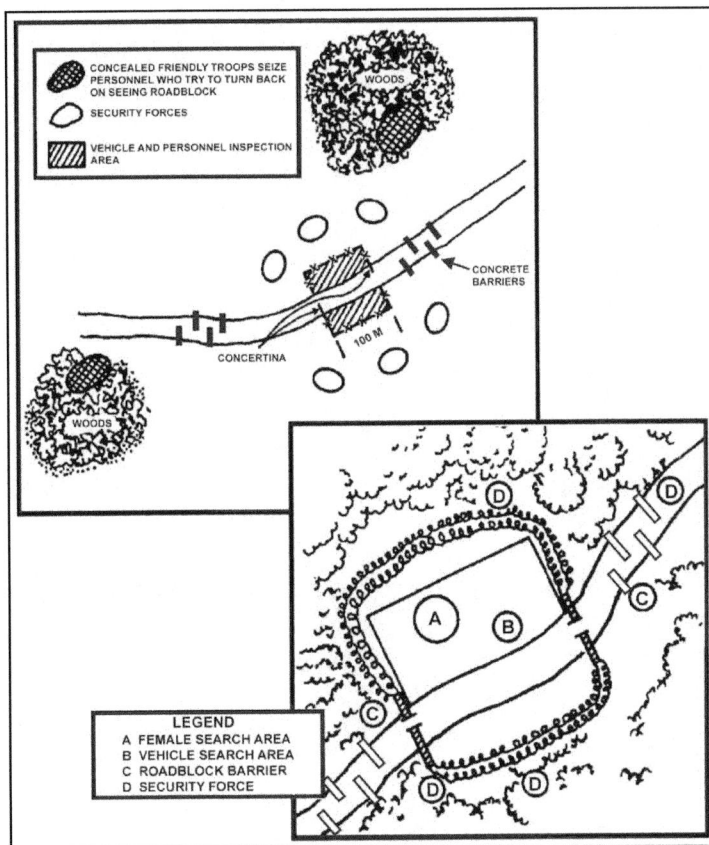

Figure 6-5. Physical layout of roadblock.

This page intentionally left blank.

Chapter 7
Civil Support Operations

The overall purpose of civil support operations is to meet the immediate needs of designated groups, for a limited time, until civil authorities can accomplish these tasks without Army assistance. Civil support operations are a subset of Homeland Security which includes Homeland Defense (offensive and defensive operations) and civil support operations. Civil support operations are only conducted inside the US and its territories.

In civil support operations, Army forces provide essential services, assets, or specialized resources to help civil authorities deal with situations beyond their capabilities. Army forces may provide relief or assistance directly, when necessary, but they normally support the overall effort controlled by another agency. In civil support operations, the adversary is often disease, hunger, or the consequences of disaster. Civil support operations for the battalion may include assisting civilians extinguish forest fires, rescue and recovery from floods or other natural disasters, or supporting security operations before, during, or after terrorist attacks.

Civil support operations vary by type and are further differentiated by the specific factors of METT-TC. Civil support operations usually require the battalion to perform common tactical missions and tasks but also call upon it to execute unique missions and tasks. The purposes of civil support operations, the special constraints they place on commanders, the location, and the types of judgments expected of battalion commanders and their subordinates, distinguish these operations from others.

Civil support operations involve Army forces providing essential supplies, capabilities, and services to help civil authorities in the US and its territories deal with situations beyond their control. In most cases, Army forces focus on overcoming conditions created by natural or manmade disasters. Army forces may provide relief or assistance directly; however, Army activities in civil support operations most often involve setting the conditions that facilitate the ability of civil authorities or NGOs, to provide the required direct support to the affected population.

Section I. FUNDAMENTALS

The US Army conducts civil support operations in the US and its territories, using active and reserve components. Domestic emergencies can require Army forces to respond with multiple capabilities and services. For this reason, they may conduct the four forms of civil support operations simultaneously, during a given operation.

PURPOSE

7-1.   Civil support operations supplement the efforts and resources of federal, state, and local governments, and NGOs within the United States and its territories. During civil support operations, the US military always responds in support of another civilian agency. Civil support operations also include those activities and measures taken by the Department of Defense (DoD) to foster mutual assistance and support between DoD and any civil government agency in planning or preparedness for, or in the application of resources for response to, the consequences of civil emergencies or attacks, including national security emergencies or major disasters. A presidential declaration of an emergency or disaster area usually precedes a civil support operation. The US military provides civil support primarily in accordance with a DoD directive for military assistance to civil authorities. The military assistance to civil authorities' directive addresses responses to both natural and manmade disasters and includes military assistance with civil disturbances, counterdrug activities, combating terrorism activities, and law enforcement. In accordance with the Constitution, civilian government is responsible for preserving public order. However, the Constitution does allow the use of military forces to protect federal and civilian property and functions. For further information, see the Posse Comitatus Act. Typically, civil support operations are conducted in response to such events as forest and grassland fires, hazardous material releases, floods, earthquakes, hurricanes, and situations resulting from an enemy attack such as terrorist activities.

ARMY ROLE

7-2.   The Army is not specifically organized, trained, or equipped for civil support operations. Instead, Army elements and forces, tailored for warfighting, rapidly adapt to dominate a crisis or disaster situation. In civil support operations, Army forces apply decisive military capabilities to set the conditions for the supported civil authorities to achieve success. Army forces have a functional chain of command, reliable communications, and well-trained, well-equipped forces that can operate and sustain themselves in an austere environment with organic assets.

MULTIPLE AND OVERLAPPING ACTIVITIES

7-3.   In most situations, Army forces involved in civil support operations execute a combination of multiple overlapping activities. Forces must conduct civil support operations with consistency and impartiality to encourage cooperation from local agencies and the population and to preserve the legitimacy of the overall effort. The actions of platoons, squads, or even individual Soldiers take place under the scrutiny of many interested groups and can have disproportionate effects on mission success. Therefore, high levels of discipline, training, and a thorough understanding of mission outcome are necessary for effective civil support operations.

MISSION TRAINING

7-4.   A sound foundation in combat mission training and in basic military skills and discipline underpins the battalion's ability to perform civil support operations missions, but many of the key individual and collective skills differ and must be trained for deliberately. Battalions use most of their regularly trained movement and security tasks in civil support operations missions, but they modify those tasks for the special conditions of their mission. They also train leaders and Soldiers for unique tasks necessary to the certain types of operation that they are assigned.

OPERATIONAL ENVIRONMENT

7-5.   The mission, the terms governing the Army's presence in the AO, the character and attitude of the population, the civilian organizations cooperating with the battalion, the physical and cultural environments, and a host of other factors combine to make each civil support mission unique. With the exception of specific actions undertaken in counterterrorism operations, support to counterdrug operations, and noncombatant evacuation operations, civil support missions tend to be decentralized and highly structured. A battalion's activities consist largely of directing the operations of its companies and supporting units within a sector or AO IAW a detailed operations order.

Most civil support operations are independent actions. Because civil support operations only occur in the United States or its territories, civil support operations rarely complement offensive, defensive, and stability operations. Civil support operations generally fall into the following four categories:

- Relief operations.
- Support to domestic chemical, biological, radiological, nuclear, and high-yield explosive consequence management (CBRNE-CM).
- Support to civil law enforcement.
- Community assistance.

RELIEF OPERATIONS

7-6.   In general, the actions performed during relief operations are identical in both civil support operations and FHA operations; however, civil support operations are performed *inside* the US and its territories and FHA *outside* the US and its territories. The actions can be characterized as either humanitarian relief, which focuses on the well-being of supported populations, or disaster relief, which focuses on recovery of critical infrastructure after a natural or manmade disaster. Relief operations accomplish one or more of the following:

- Save lives.
- Reduce suffering.
- Recover essential infrastructure.
- Improve quality of life.

DISASTER RELIEF

7-7.   Disaster relief encompasses those actions taken to restore or recreate the minimum infrastructure to allow effective humanitarian relief and set the conditions for longer-term recovery. This includes establishing and maintaining minimum safe working conditions, plus security measures necessary to protect relief workers and the affected population from additional harm. Disaster relief may involve repairing or demolishing damaged structures; restoring or building bridges, roads, and airfields; and removing debris from critical routes and relief sites.

HUMANITARIAN RELIEF

7-8.   Humanitarian relief focuses on life-saving measures to alleviate the immediate needs of a population in crisis. It often includes the provision of medical support, food, water, medicines, clothing, blankets, shelter, and heating or cooking fuel. In some cases, it involves transportation support to move affected people from a disaster area.

SUPPORT TO CBRNE-CM

7-9.   The second type of civil support operation is support to domestic chemical, biological, radiological, nuclear, and high-yield explosive consequence management (CBRNE-CM). Military operations assist civil authorities in protecting US territory, population, and infrastructure before an attack by supporting domestic preparedness and critical asset protection programs. If an attack occurs, military support responds to the consequences of the attack.

DOMESTIC PREPAREDNESS

7-10.   The Army's role in facilitating domestic preparedness is to strengthen the existing expertise of civil authorities. This is accomplished in the two primary areas of response and training. Response is the immediate reaction to an attack; training includes what happens after the attack.

PROTECTION OF CRITICAL ASSETS

7-11.   The purpose of this program is to identify critical assets and to assure their integrity, availability, survivability, and capability to support vital DoD missions across the full spectrum of military operations. Critical assets include telecommunications, electric power, gas and oil, banking and finance, transportation, water, and emergency services. An attack on any of these assets may disrupt civilian commerce, government operations, and the military.

RESPONSE TO CBRNE INCIDENTS

7-12.   The initial response to the use of WMD is primarily from local assets but sustained Army participation may be required soon afterward. The Army's capabilities in this environment are—

- Detection.
- Decontamination and medical care.
- Triage and treatment.
- MEDEVAC.
- Hospitalization (patient decontamination for self-evacuation).
- Technical consultation to commanders and local health care providers on health effects of WMD incidents.

SUPPORT TO CIVIL LAW ENFORCEMENT

7-13.   Support to domestic civil law enforcement generally involves activities related to counterterrorism, counterdrug operations, civil disturbance operations, or general support. Army support may involve providing resources, training, or direct support. Federal forces remain under the control of their military chain of command at all times while providing the support.

CIVIL SUPPORT TO COUNTERTERRORISM

7-14.   Army forces do not conduct domestic counterterrorism, but they may provide support to lead federal agencies during crisis and consequence management of a terrorist incident. They may provide assistance in the areas of transportation, equipment, training, and human resources. When terrorists pose an imminent threat to US territory, its people, or its critical assets, the US military may conduct civil support operations to counter these threats, using ground, air, space, special operations, or maritime forces. The Federal Bureau of Investigation (FBI) is responsible for crisis management in the US.

CIVIL SUPPORT TO COUNTERDRUG OPERATIONS

7-15.   Army support to domestic counterdrug operations is very limited and usually only in a support role.

CIVIL DISTURBANCE OPERATIONS

7-16.   Non federalized Army forces (National Guard) assist civil authorities in restoring law and order when local and state law enforcement agencies are unable to resolve a civil disturbance. Federal Army forces assist in restoring law and order when the magnitude of a disturbance exceeds the capabilities of local and state law enforcement agencies, including the National Guard. Army participation is to apply the minimum force necessary to restore order to the point where civilian authorities no longer require military assistance.

GENERAL SUPPORT

7-17.   The Army may also provide training, share information, and provide equipment and facilities to federal, state, and local civilian law enforcement agencies.

COMMUNITY ASSISTANCE

7-18.   Community assistance is a broad range of activities designed to strengthen the relationship between the Army and the American people. These projects should exercise individual Soldier skills, encourage teamwork, challenge leader planning and coordination skills, and result in accomplishments that are measurable. Example activities include youth physical fitness programs, medical readiness programs, and anti-drug programs.

Section III. PLANNING AND EXECUTING OF CIVIL SUPPORT OPERATIONS

The planning and execution of civil support operations are fundamentally similar to planning, preparing, executing, and assessing offensive, defensive, and stability operations. However, while each civil support operation is unique, the following four broad considerations can help forces develop mission-specific concepts and schemes for executing civil support operations.

PLANNING CONSIDERATIONS

7-19.   Whether they confront the complications of floods, storms, earthquakes, riots, disease, or other humanitarian crises, the Infantry battalion brings its strengths to civil support operations. Although it has limited numbers of medical personnel, the battalion brings to the operation its outstanding abilities to organize and supervise operations, collect and distribute information, and communicate. Finally, it brings large numbers of highly disciplined and motivated Soldiers. The following four broad imperatives help forces plan and execute civil support operations. Other special considerations, attached elements, may also apply. In addition, attached elements must be considered:

PROVIDE ESSENTIAL SUPPORT FOR LARGEST NUMBER OF PEOPLE

7-20.   Commanders must allocate finite resources to achieve the greatest good. Also, commanders require an accurate assessment of what needs to be done in order to employ military power effectively. In some cases, the battalion can accomplish this task using warfighting reconnaissance capabilities and techniques. Commanders determine how and where to apply limited assets to benefit the most people in the most efficient way. They usually focus initial efforts on restoring vital services, which include food and water distribution, medical aid, power generation, search and rescue, and firefighting.

COORDINATE ACTIONS WITH OTHER AGENCIES

7-21.   Civil support operations are typically joint and interagency (Appendix G). Unity of effort between the military and local authorities requires constant communication to ensure that tasks are conducted in the most efficient and effective way and resources are used wisely.

ESTABLISH MEASURES OF EFFECTIVENESS

7-22.   A critical aspect of mission handover is to have objective standards for measuring progress. These measures of effectiveness determine the degree to which an operation is accomplishing its established objectives. For example, a measure of effectiveness might be a decrease in the number of deaths caused by starvation. This is an indicator that food convoys are reaching the designated areas. These measures are situationally dependent, and must be adjusted as the situation changes and guidance from higher is developed.

TRANSFER RESPONSIBILITY TO CIVILIAN AGENCIES

7-23.   Civil support operations planning must always include the follow-on actions of the civilian agencies to restore conditions to normal. The following considerations determine handover feasibility:

- Condition of supported population and governments.
- Competing mission requirements.
- Specified and implied commitment levels of time, resources, and forces.
- Maturity of the support effort.

PLANNING PROCESS

7-24.   The battalion staff uses the standard Army planning process.

SPECIAL CONSIDERATIONS

7-25.   The battalion planning staff must understand the following special considerations:

- Specialized civil support operations terminology in the mission and tasks assigned to the battalion for purposes of mission analysis and COA development.
- Command relationships in support to US civil authorities.
- Presence of, activities of, and the battalion's relationship to nongovernmental organizations and private voluntary organizations in the AO.
- The political, economic, military, and environmental situation in the AO.
- Local customs, cultures, religions, and ethnic groups.
- Force protection measures.
- ROE and other restrictions on operations.
- Terrain, weather, infrastructure, and conditions unique to the AO and the nature of the operation.
- Security operations.
- Availability or need for specialized units such as public affairs, CA, chemical defense, engineers, MPs, and others.
- Support relationships when the battalion provides material aid.
- The need for liaisons with interagency, GOs, NGOs, or local/state agencies.
- Interoperability of C2 with those agencies, for example, communications, reports, and ROE.

ATTACHED ELEMENTS

7-26.   Battalions involved in civil support operations are normally reinforced with engineers and may also have troops attached. MPs, additional HSS personnel, CA, and public affairs often support battalions in civil support operations. Since these units are not organic, the staff and company commanders should learn the organizations, capabilities, limitations, and specific missions of attached organizations before employing them. In some cases, protecting those elements imposes additional loads on the maneuver companies.

WARFIGHTING FUNCTIONS

7-27.   The warfighting functions are considered during planning for civil support just as they are for other types of operations.

FIRE SUPPORT

7-28.   Basic fire planning considerations for direct and indirect fire weapons are generally no longer valid during civil support operations. FS plans in civil support operations are integrated into tactical or force protection operations as the situation warrants. The battalion FSE can be used to assist other areas requiring planning support or can be used to support unique civil support operations functions such as the establishment and operation of a civil military operations or public affairs center.

MOVEMENT AND MANEUVER

7-29.   In civil support operations, where area responsibilities, movements, and control of terrain are sensitive and hazards are sometimes widely scattered, the battalion needs detailed information on its AO and commonly uses detailed control measures. Battalion leaders must clearly delineate and ensure Soldiers throughout the battalion understand routes, installations, hazards, boundaries, and other control measures. Leaders must also clearly communicate special control measures, such as curfews, restrictions on movements, and prohibition of weapons, to all concerned.

7-30.   Also, civil support operations missions may call for dispersed operations. Digital systems organic to the battalion provide timely and accurate force tracking and facilitate reporting. Faster movement of information concerning maneuver also facilitates faster reaction to threats and allows forces in motion to be routed around new hazards.

MOBILITY AND SURVIVABILITY

7-31.   Mobility and survivability generally constitute major activities in civil support operations missions, especially at their outset. Mobility for the force and the population is also an early issue in many civil support operations as roads and bridges require repair, rubble clearing, hazardous area marking or clearing, and assessment and repair to damaged aqueducts or hydrologic control facilities. Even in mature civil support operations, engineer operations typically remain very active. They have access to topographic tools and engineer data electronically from anywhere in the world.

Engineer Digital Tools

7-32.   The engineers of digitized forces employ software that facilitates managing and recording engineer work and posting results to Maneuver Control System-Light and force XXI battle command, brigade and below (FBCB2). They also have access to topographic tools and engineer data electronically from anywhere in the world. These capabilities are of great value during civil support operations in managing engineer work, adjusting priorities, projecting needs, and informing their units and the population of the status of engineer projects.

Battalion Engineer

7-33.   Civil support operations are commonly supported with a great number of attached combat engineer units as well as construction engineers and contracted civilian engineers. Several engineer companies may support a battalion conducting civil support operations; if so, the senior engineer company commander normally serves as the battalion engineer.

COMMAND AND CONTROL

7-34.   Standard command and staff doctrine applies to civil support operations C2. Orders, estimates, planning guidance, rehearsals, and backbriefs are all useful in directing civil support operations. The need for mutual understanding between all members of the command group is as great in civil support operations as in combat operations.

Cooperation

7-35.   As in other cases, cooperation with other services or agencies imposes special requirements for training, coordination, and liaison. Multiservice operations in which the battalion controls troops of other services or are controlled by another service's, call for special attention to command relationships and limitations on the commander's prerogatives.

Communications

7-36.   The battalion's C2 systems yield significant advantages in planning and conducting civil support operations. Operation of these systems depends on communications architecture provided by the BCT or by another higher level of command. Use of nontactical or other nonstandard communications is likely in support to civil authorities in the US. If this is the case, then battalion commanders and staff leaders need training in operating these systems. In the early and concluding stages of an operation, the signal structure may permit only limited use of C2 INFOSYS if available. The battalion's plan for C2 must consider that and provide for alternate means of communication or full reliance on tactical systems.

Liaison Teams

7-37.   Liaison teams can be extremely useful in providing a common view of the situation for headquarters attached to the battalion. Battalions must staff their normal liaison teams and identify their needs for more teams as early as possible.

INTELLIGENCE

7-38.   The battalion never conducts intelligence operations during operations in the US. In some cases, intelligence operations may be replaced with neutral, self-defensive information collection operations. A coordinated intelligence, surveillance, and reconnaissance effort is as critical to the battalion's success in civil support operations as during combat operations.

Information Collection

7-39.   Information collection is a constant process that is guided by the commander's critical information requirements and is normally embodied in the ISR plan. The commander may employ his scout platoon, electronic sensors, Raven UAS (also HUNTER UAS if tasked from the BCT), patrols, engineers, liaison teams, civil affairs, and so forth to achieve his ISR aims. The battalion's scout platoon plays a special role in ISR, but every Soldier and unit in the battalion has some responsibility for observing and reporting. Therefore, the battalion commander's PIR, focus for collection, and the associated ISR tasks must be known throughout the battalion and revised as often as necessary to assure that Soldiers know what information is of greatest importance.

Collection Assets

7-40.   The battalion may request UAS and other electronic sensors to support the battalion commander's PIR. However, in order to receive useful information from those assets, the battalion must specifically request ISR support.

Human Intelligence

7-41.   Human intelligence is especially important during civil support operations. The Soldier is the most important collection asset for the battalion in these operations. The collection is focused on the effects of the disaster on the population and infrastructure. Each Soldier observes and collects information about the operational environment. In many cases, THT augmentation may be provided to the battalion. The battalion S-2 must be knowledgeable in their employment of these teams.

SUSTAINMENT

7-42.   Sustainment for civil support operations usually requires substantial tailoring to adapt to unique mission requirements; logistical requirements vary considerably between types of civil support operations. Civil support operations commonly take place in areas where local resources and infrastructure are scarce, damaged, or fully devoted to the civilian population, but resourced to a low degree.

Challenges

7-43.   The chief sustainment challenges of civil support operations are to anticipate needs and to integrate units and sources into the civil support operations. Information needs include—

- Resources available within the local area and region.
- Status of critical supply items and repair jobs.
- Nature and condition of the infrastructure.
- Capabilities of general support sustainment units.
- Mission tasks.
- Overall material readiness of the battalion.

Contracting Options

7-44.   In some cases, contracting can augment organic sustainment. Battalions may encounter or employ contractor-provided services and supply operations in civil support operations environments. The S-4 and commander must understand the terms and limitations of contractor support.

Force Health Protection

7-45.   The battalion deploys with its organic medical assets for civil support operations. The battalion may be augmented with additional HSS assets to support the battalion's mission. Civil support operations may include disaster relief and displaced personnel operations. Medical treatment provided in support of these operations must comply with Title 10 of the US Code. See FM 8-42 for FHP support of disaster relief or displaced personnel operations. The brigade support battalion's medical company may require humanitarian augmentation medical equipment sets to perform its civil support operations mission. Key personnel (health care providers) should review the requirements before deployment to provide for contingencies and modifications (add or delete items) so that the level and types of medical supplies conform to the mission requirements.

Liaison with Civil Authorities

7-46.   Nonstandard supporting relationships and close coordination with civil authorities may dictate the use of liaisons and even the creation of additional liaison teams to assure their greatest usefulness and coordination.

INFORMATION OPERATIONS

7-47.   Information operations in civil support operations is the employment of the core capabilities of computer network operations, public affairs, and operations security, in concert with specified supporting and related capabilities, to affect information and information systems and to influence decision making. The commander employs CA, public affairs, and OPSEC as part of his information operation. The battalion commander supports the higher commander's IO, carrying out tasks assigned to him and acting independently within the higher commander's intent and the constraints of his own resources.

7-48.   Because civil support operations are complex, usually decentralized, and often critical to the force's perceived legitimacy, continuity and consistency in IO are extremely important. The battalion must present its position clearly to assure that the interested public understands it. The commander must be aware of local interests, fears, and concerns of the effects of events and on the perceptions of his troops and the population in general. He must understand the positions of and information environment created by—

- The population and its major segments.
- Other agencies working in the AO.
- Organizations located outside of the AO, but have economic and political interests.
- The media.
- Information gathered by elements of the battalion.

Note. Unless PSYOP is used strictly in a public information role, civil support operations do not include PSYOP. PSYOP is prohibited from targeting US target audiences; however, they consist of public affairs and any necessary OPSEC.

Section IV. PATTERN OF OPERATIONS

While civil support operations vary greatly in every mission, the Infantry battalion can expect events to follow as broad pattern of response, recovery, and restoration.

RESPONSE

7-49.   As part of a response, the battalion enters the affected area, normally under BCT control, and makes contact with federal, state agencies and relief organizations. Planning for the operation, staging command posts into the area, establishing security, deploying the battalion, and initiating contacts with supported activities and other parts of the relief force occur during this phase of operations. The battalion may make its chief contributions in this phase. Its Soldiers are usually among the first relief forces to arrive. Its C2 structure gives it the ability to communicate and coordinate. Furthermore, the battalion's ability to reconnoiter and gather information makes it useful in the initial efforts of authorities to establish understanding and control of the area and to oversee critical actions. Typical requirements of the response period are—

- Search and rescue.
- High volume EMT.
- Hazard identification.
- Dissemination of emergency information.
- Food and water distribution.
- Collection of displaced people in temporary shelter.
- Support to law enforcement agencies.
- Repair of power generation and distribution systems.

- Clearance and repair of roads, railways, and canals.
- Firefighting, CBRNE and hazardous industrial waste decontamination, and flood control.

RECOVERY

7-50.   Once the battalion operation is underway, recovery begins. With initial emergencies resolved and a working relationship between all parties in place, there should be steady progress in relieving the situation throughout this phase of operations. The battalion is fully deployed in an AO or in an assigned task. Its work includes coordination with its parent headquarters, supported groups, and other relief forces and daily allocation of its own assets to recovery tasks. The battalion's task organization is likely to change periodically as the need for particular services and support changes. Security, maintenance, effective employment of resources, and Soldier support all need continuing attention. Medical officers should review and assist the commander in counteracting the psychological effects of disaster relief work and exposure to human suffering on the battalion's Soldiers throughout the operation. Typical tasks include—

- Continuing and modifying information operations.
- Resettling people from emergency shelters to their homes.
- Repairing infrastructure.
- Contracting to provide appropriate support (when feasible).
- Restoring power, water, communication, and sanitation services.
- Removing debris.
- Supporting law enforcement agencies.
- Transferring authority and responsibility to civil authorities.
- Planning for redeployment.
- Assisting with restoration of health care delivery system.

RESTORATION

7-51.   Restoration is the return of normalcy to the area. As civil authorities assume full control of remaining emergency operations and normal services, the battalion transfers those responsibilities to replacement agencies and begins redeployment from the area. During restoration the commander should consider issues such as—

- Transfer of authority to civil agencies.
- Transition of C2 for agencies and units that remain in the area.
- Movement plans that support redeployment and continued recovery in the area.
- Staging of C2 out of the area.
- Accountability of property or transfer of property to the community, if authorized.

Section V. SEQUENCE OF OPERATIONS

In every part of the sequence of civil support operations, special considerations apply to digitized units initiating an operation or replacing another unit that has performed the mission before them. Generally, civil support operations follow the sequence of—

- Movement into the AO.
- Establishment of a base of operations.
- Maintenance of support.
- Termination of operations.

MOVEMENT INTO AREA OF OPERATIONS

7-52.   C2 considerations normally include using advance parties or liaison teams, establishing command posts, and sequencing the arrival of key leaders. Battalion commanders must prepare a complete plan for establishing control of the AO that includes a concept for phased installation of signal and C2. Transfer of authority from the unit in place to the arriving unit and methodical, accountable handover of the AO is also of primary interest. Detailed rehearsals and mock drills held in preparation for this task are a regular part of preparatory training. Mission CCIR should guide staff specialists as they build information databases and map displays to support the operation. The commander's PIR should determine the order in which critical information, for example, a list of the locations of hazards, and of the communities in greatest need of support, is compiled and distributed.

ESTABLISHMENT OF BASE OF OPERATIONS

7-53.   Security, support, and continuous operations are the primary considerations during the establishment of a battalion base of operations. The battalion must maintain security continuously.

OCCUPATION

7-54.   During the response phase, the battalion moves in accordance with the controlling headquarters' order, employing advance parties and quartering parties as necessary. The battalion may move to an assembly area in the affected area initially or may occupy its AO directly from the march. Early priorities for the battalion include: establishing communications across the AO, refueling vehicles and recovering any inoperable equipment, establishing or coordinating with existing logistical facilities and medical aid stations, and reconnoitering the area. The battalion must complete these preliminary tasks as quickly as possible in order to assume the mission promptly. In some cases, the battalion must defer operations until it completes such tasks. For instance, a medical platoon cannot receive patients until its basic setup is complete.

BATTALION FOCUS

7-55.   The battalion commander, the principal staff officers, and the company commanders vigorously engage in making personal contact with supported groups, partners in the operation, and community representatives early in the response phase. Executive officers and staff assistants are, therefore, responsible for much of the internal activity of the battalion during response.

COMMAND POST OPERATIONS

7-56.   Organizing the command post for 24-hour operations in civil support operations also requires early attention. A detailed SOP, complete operations maps, and special provisions for communications, inspections, reporting, and adjusting security levels are necessities. Establishing a high standard for operations from the outset is key both because of the general sensitivity of civil support operations and because of the battalion's special vulnerabilities in its first days of the mission.

EQUIPMENT AUGMENTATION

7-57.   In some cases, the BCT augments the battalion with transportation assets. This is done to facilitate movement of unit troops, materiel, or displaced personnel. When this happens, driver and maintenance support is needed well before the battalion assumes the mission. The battalion might have to modify sustainment and augment the FSC to support the attached fleet.

MAINTENANCE OF SUPPORT

7-58.   Steady-state mission performance differs in each instance. The durations of civil support operations vary. They typically focus on relieving crises in an area or population.

READINESS

7-59.   During some civil support operations, the battalion must retain its readiness to transition to Homeland Defense operations. To ensure readiness, it maintains and rehearses QRF and provisions for increased levels of security in base camps, at OPs, and in patrols. Commanders continually review their operations to detect any patterns, vulnerabilities, or complacency that an opponent might exploit.

TERMINATION OF OPERATIONS

7-60.   Civil support operations end in different ways. Crises may be resolved, or continuing civil support operations may be handed over to a replacement unit, federal or state agency, a police force, or local authorities. Missions of short duration or narrow scope, such as support to civil authorities, may end with the completion of the assigned task.

WITH TRANSFER OF CONTROL

7-61.   Transferring control of an AO or an operation to a follow-on force requires detailed coordination to assure that all relevant information passes to the commander or the other authority assuming responsibility. This procedure may entail transfer of maps, inventories, records, and equipment. In cases where the battalion uses unique files and systems, staff leaders and commanders may have to go through extensive coordination to assure that their successors possess and understand all critical information.

WITHOUT TRANSFER OF CONTROL

7-62.   If the battalion leaves the AO without replacement, it must plan for an orderly, secure departure that protects the force throughout the operation and sustains sufficient C2 in the AO until withdrawal is complete. In redeployment, force protection and accountability for Soldiers, systems, and materiel are always of concern.

Section VI. TRAINING CONSIDERATIONS

The Infantry battalion must conduct civil support operations with consistency and impartiality to encourage cooperation from the population and to preserve the legitimacy of the overall effort. The actions of platoons, squads, or even individual Soldiers take place under the scrutiny of many interested groups and can have disproportionate effects on mission success. Therefore, high levels of discipline and training and a thorough understanding of mission outcome are necessary for effective civil support operations.

TRAINING PLAN

7-63.   A sound foundation in combat mission training and in basic military skills and discipline underpins the battalion's ability to perform civil support operations missions. However, many of the key individual and collective skills differ and must be deliberately trained. Battalions use most of their regularly trained movement and security tasks in civil support operations missions, but they modify these tasks for the special conditions of their specific mission. They also train leaders and Soldiers for unique tasks necessary for a certain type of operation and for civil-military interaction.

MISSION-ESSENTIAL TASK LIST

7-64.   Civil support operations tasks are not usually included in a battalion's mission-essential task list unless the battalion has been specifically assigned a civil support operations mission or its commander has determined that the likelihood of such assignment warrants dedicated training. Training for civil support operations, therefore, begins with the perception or assignment of a mission. Notification for civil support operations employment normally requires rapid reaction to an emergency but sometimes may allow for deliberate preparation.

DELIBERATE PREPARATION

7-65.   Notification for civil support operations employment normally requires rapid reaction to an emergency but sometimes may allow for deliberate preparation. In the case of deliberate preparation, a commander can anticipate a minimum of one to two weeks of mission training. This training may include a structured mission rehearsal exercise, AO orientation, and leader reconnaissance of the AO. Classes on the AO and the mission, training in the ROE and in use of special equipment, and familiarization with the other organizations present in the area may be part of this training. Reviews of Army lessons learned and preparation of families and the rear detachment also accompany this training.

IMMEDIATE RESPONSE

7-66.   When there is not enough available time (usually in an emergency), the commander may have to respond immediately to mission requirements. In cases such as Hurricane Andrew, Los Angeles riots or forest fire fighting, commanders relied on the general military skills and discipline of their troops and trained to the task as time allowed. Conditions vary from case to case in this kind of reaction, but commanders can generally draw on Army lessons learned, general purpose tactics, techniques, and procedures (TTPs), subject matter expertise from local agencies, and maps prepared for training and intelligence from the projected AO to identify the most critical training requirements. The battalion must address these in order of priority as time allows.

CIVIL SUPPORT OPERATIONS TASK ORGANIZATIONS

7-67.   Many civil support operations modify headquarters and unit organizations. New staff positions may be added to the battalion (CA, civil-military operations officer, and public affairs are common). Unfamiliar organizations may be added to the task organization and the companies, and platoons of the battalion may be re-equipped and partially reorganized to meet mission requirements or to conform to mission requirements. In such cases, conducting staff drills, training augmentees, learning to operate new equipment, and practicing operations in new unit configurations must all factor into battalion and company training plans.

BASIC SOLDIER SKILLS

7-68.   Basic Soldier skills are common to all operations and are as important in civil support operations as elsewhere. Soldiers employed in civil support operations should be trained in—

- Individual and crew-served weapons.
- Special tools, equipment, and weapons.
- Mounted (when augmented with vehicles) and dismounted land navigation.
- Observation and reporting procedures.
- First aid.
- Rules of engagement.
- Safety.
- Counterterrorist actions.

- Hazard identification.
- Appropriate handling procedures for displaced personnel.
- Communication operations.

SPECIFIC TRAINING

7-69. Training for civil support operations centers on assisting distressed populations and responding to emergencies, and it routinely requires cooperation with civil authorities. These operations typically involve operating under special legal restrictions. Civil support operations training may address the following:

- Orienting troops and leaders on legal restrictions and requirements.
- Preparing troops and leaders for hazards in the AO.
- Protecting humanitarian relief efforts.
- Organizing and conducting convoys with civilians and civilian vehicles.
- Supporting civil affairs and public affairs operations.
- Organizing and securing relief centers.
- Assisting in logistical support and construction engineer operations.
- Supporting the coordination of nonmilitary organizations.
- Familiarizing troops with mission-specific tasks such as--
  - -- Firefighting.
  - -- Flood control.
  - -- Hazardous material clean-up.
  - -- Riot control.
  - -- Protection of endangered groups or individuals.
  - -- Assistance to civilian law enforcement officials.
  - -- Resettlement actions.
- Controlling civil disturbances
- Establishing, securing, and executing distribution points

ADDITIONAL REQUIREMENTS

7-70. Almost all civil support operations have additional requirements. Some of these include—

- Orienting leaders and Soldiers to the mission.
- Familiarizing troops with the area.
- Adapting standard tactical practices to the conditions of the mission.
- Adapting fire support, protection, and sustainment operations to the limits of the mission.
- Understanding and applying ROE.
- Providing for force protection.
- Conducting effective media relations.
- Collecting information.

This page intentionally left blank.

Chapter 8
Tactical Enabling Operations

"Skepticism is the mother of security. Even though fools trust their enemies, prudent persons do not. The general is the principal sentinel of his army. He should always be careful of its preservation and see that it is never exposed to misfortune." --Frederick the Great

Tactical enabling operations are specialized missions planned and conducted to achieve or sustain a tactical advantage. When executed, these operations are also part of an offensive, defensive, stability, or civil support mission. The fluid nature of the modern battlefield increases the frequency with which the Infantry battalion plans and executes enabling operations such as passage of lines, relief operations, obstacle reduction, linkup operations, and high-value asset security. This chapter discusses techniques and procedures unique to the battalion that can be applied to these specialized missions.

Section I. SECURITY OPERATIONS

Security operations are those operations undertaken by a commander to—

- Provide early and accurate warning of enemy operations.
- Provide the force being protected with time and maneuver space within which to react to the enemy.
- Develop the situation to allow the commander to effectively use the protected force (FM 3-0).

PURPOSE

8-1.   Security operations provide reaction time, maneuver space, and protection of the force. They are characterized by reconnaissance and surveillance aimed at reducing terrain and enemy unknowns, gaining and maintaining contact with the enemy to ensure continuous information, and providing early and accurate reporting of information to the protected force. Units may conduct these operations to the front, flanks, or rear of a larger force and should be three dimensional. Security operations forces orient in any direction from a stationary or moving force. Security operations pertain to any try to defeat enemy reconnaissance and surveillance in order to deny the enemy intelligence information concerning the battalion. Security operations contain both passive and active elements and normally include combat action to seek, destroy, or repel enemy reconnaissance and surveillance units.

TYPES

8-2.   The five types of security operation are screen, guard, cover, area security, and local security (Figure 8-1). The battalion normally participates in covering force operations only as part of a larger element. The screen, guard, and cover, respectively, require increasing levels of combat power and provide increasing levels of security for the main body. However, more combat power in the security force means less for the main body. Area security preserves the commander's freedom to move his reserves, position fire support assets, provide for C2, and conduct sustaining operations, and it provides immediate protection to his force.

Level of Combat Power Required	Type	Description
LEAST	Screen	A screening operation mainly provides early warning to the protected force.
	Guard	A guarding operation protects the main body. They do this by fighting to gain time. At the same time, they observe and report information, and prevent enemy ground observation of and direct fire against the main body. Units conducting a guard mission cannot operate independently. They rely on the fires and combat support assets of the main body.
	Cover	A covering operation protects the main body. It does this by fighting to gain time. At the same time, it observes and reports information, and it prevents enemy ground observation of and direct fire against the main body.
	Area Security	An area security operation protects friendly forces, installations, routes, and actions in a specific area.
MOST	Local Security	A local security operation is are conducted and established near a unit. Its purpose is to prevent tactical surprise by the enemy.

Figure 8-1. Comparison of types of security operations.

SCREEN

8-3.   The primary task of a screening force is to observe, identify, and report information. The screening force protects the main body, impedes and harasses the enemy with supporting indirect fires, and destroys enemy reconnaissance elements within its capability. The screen can be moving or stationary depending on the posture of the main body.

BATTALION SCREEN

8-4.   At battalion level, the scout platoon normally performs screen missions. When the terrain provides multiple enemy avenues of approach, the battalion commander may provide the scout platoon additional assets, such as sniper teams and (if available) a COLT, or attach the scout platoon to a company to conduct a screen. If the anticipated enemy threat is vehicle mounted, the commander could assign the screen mission to the weapons company. The weapons company could also be task organized with truck mounted Infantry platoons. The commander might also create a company team using the HHC commander and attaching various units, for example: scouts, snipers, and an Infantry and assault platoon. The screening force generally establishes a series of OPs and conducts patrols to ensure adequate surveillance of the assigned sector.

PLANNING A SCREEN

8-5.   When assigning a screen mission to a subordinate unit, the battalion commander designates the general trace of the screen and the time it must be established. The initial screen line should be forward of the general trace but remain within range of supporting artillery. Screen lines are shown as phase lines. Passage graphics are included in the overlay.

- Designate the left and right limits of the screen as well as a phase line for the near boundary. This phase line can also become the on-order battle handover line.
- Confirm which unit has responsibility for the area between the screening force's rear boundary and the MBA. This should be the company(s) that occupies the sectors behind the screen.
- Designate general locations for OPs enabling surveillance of the avenues of approach into the sector.
- Select routes or sectors to facilitate rearward displacement.

- Augment the security force as needed to provide intelligence, engineer, air defense, signal, and sustainment. If the security force is not augmented with these assets, plans are still made and executed that provide these functions to the screening force.

INTELLIGENCE

8-6.   The S-2 designates which named areas of interest the unit must observe and when. The S-2 does not dictate the location of unit elements, nor how the unit maintains surveillance of the NAIs. If GSRs or UAS operate under battalion control to support the security effort, the S-2 positions these assets and integrates their locations and missions with the security action of the screening unit. Once the screen force commander positions his unit, he informs the S-2 of their primary, alternate, and subsequent locations.

MOVEMENT AND MANEUVER

8-7.   Generally, the best unit configuration for the screen mission is a task-organized unit. The ability to place units on the ground and conduct surveillance operations and active mounted and dismounted patrolling is an essential aspect of the screen mission.

8-8.   Generally, the mobility and countermobility efforts are dedicated to the battalion's main defensive area or main body. If available, some engineer effort may be dedicated to the screen. The screening units' obstacle plan should complement the obstacle plan in the MBA. The screening forces emplace obstacles to disrupt the enemy reconnaissance forces and fixing forces. Point-type obstacles (point AT minefields, modular pack mine systems [MOPMS], and wide area munitions) along restrictive portions of the enemy's avenues of approach are examples of obstacles that may be emplaced by screening forces and must be covered by direct and indirect fires. If emplaced obstacles are breached by enemy reconnaissance forces, the screening unit is prepared to re-emplace the obstacle and continue to cover it with direct and indirect fires.

FIRE SUPPORT

8-9.   The FSO prepares for the screen mission as he would for a defense. He uses the enemy situation template as a guide to plan fires to interdict enemy maneuver elements. He plans protective fires for all screen force positions, which helps, if the screen forces must withdraw, prevent screening force elements from becoming decisively engaged with the enemy. Accurate indirect fire is essential to the destruction of the enemy reconnaissance effort. The FSO conducts a time-distance analysis covering the enemy's probable rate of advance and the time of flight of artillery or mortars. If available, COLTs may be added to the screen force for use against enemy vehicles.

PROTECTION

8-10.   Fratricide risk is a special concern for the screen force. As enemy reconnaissance forces try to infiltrate the screen, fratricide risk is possible as elements of the screen force may engage the enemy or as the main body engages the enemy. To mitigate this risk, the screen force must conduct detailed coordination to include direct and indirect fire control measures with the main body or main defensive area units.

8-11.   The screen force task is normally to observe and report only. It engages the enemy in self-defense. As enemy elements pass through the screen line, the screening units report to the main body or main defense. The main body or main defense then destroys the enemy. This technique requires the screen force to be close to the main body or defense; however, it causes reaction time and engagement ranges to be relatively limited.

SUSTAINMENT

8-12.   The S-4 and FSC commander plans for responsive and flexible support that may require the immediate resupply of ammunition and evacuation of casualties and equipment upon contact. Lateral supply routes to a coordinated position are identified during the planning process. On-order control measures, LRPs, UMCPs, and AXPs are essential to the operation. Emergency resupply vehicles carrying ammunition and other quickly expendable supplies are prepared to respond to sudden requisitions due to enemy contact. Once the battalion begins the fight, evacuation of wounded personnel and damaged equipment occurs along lateral supply routes.

GUARD

8-13.   A guard mission is assigned to protect the force by observing the enemy, reporting pertinent information, and fighting to gain time. The guard force differs from a screen force in that it contains sufficient combat power to defeat, repel, or fix the lead elements of an enemy ground force to prevent it from engaging the main body with direct fires. The guard force normally deploys over a narrower front than a comparably sized screening force, allowing greater concentration of combat power. The guard force routinely engages enemy forces with both direct and indirect fires and operates in range of the main body's indirect fire weapons. The guard force commander must understand fully the degree of security his unit provides the larger unit. This is critical because as the battle progresses, the higher unit commander may require the degree of security to change such as from early warning to detailed and aggressive security for the main body. Three types of guard operations are conducted in support of a stationary or moving friendly force: advance, flank, and rear guard. (Figure 8-2).

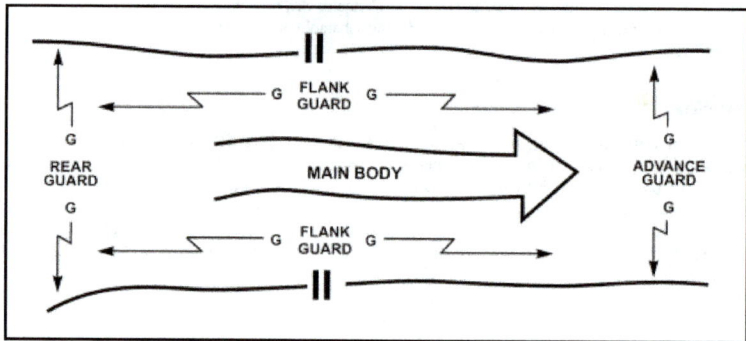

Figure 8-2. Rear, flank, and advance guard operations.

ADVANCE GUARD

8-14.   The advance guard moves ahead of the main force to ensure its uninterrupted advance, to protect the main body against surprise, to facilitate the advance by removing obstacles and repairing roads and bridges, and to cover the deployment of the main body as it is committed to action. The advance guard is a task-organized combined-arms unit or detachment that precedes a column or formation and is offensive in nature.

8-15.   The advance guard is normally conducted as a MTC. Generally, a battalion receives an advance guard mission when the BCT moves as part of a higher level unit in a MTC. In deploying a battalion as an advance guard, the BCT ensures the battalion has priority of fires. The advance guard clears the axis of enemy elements to allow the unimpeded movement of the main body battalions. The security force of the battalion, which can also be an advance guard, develops the situation to hand over the enemy to the battalion. The advance guard can conduct hasty attacks if it has sufficient combat power to destroy or fix the enemy force blocking its advance. The battalion must maintain communication and have situational awareness of the trailing battalion to prevent potential fratricide.

8-16.   Depending on the commander's assessment of the situation, a battalion conducting an advance guard normally conducts a MTC with companies advancing on axes, in zone, or (rarely) along directions of attack.

8-17.   Based on METT-TC, trail elements of the advance guard ensure they maintain adequate distance forward of the main body's lead elements to ensure freedom of maneuver for the main body. The battalion commander establishes phase lines to control the movement of the main body and the advance guard. Advance guard units remain within the supporting artillery's range.

8-18.   The advance guard force tries to destroy enemy forces through hasty attacks. It may be necessary for the battalion to mass at certain locations, destroy the enemy, report, and continue with its mission. If enemy resistance is well prepared and cannot be destroyed, the battalion reconnaissance forces try to identify a bypass route for the main body, to report enemy size and location, and (when given permission) to fix and/or bypass the enemy. The following attacking forces are responsible for destroying the fixed or bypassed enemy. The main body commander may elect not to bypass the enemy but to conduct an attack. In this case, the advance guard keeps the enemy contained and prepares to pass main body elements through to eliminate the enemy.

8-19.   An advance guard for a stationary force is defensive in nature. It defends or delays in accordance with the main body commander's intent. It is normally a task organized unit consisting of the scouts, Infantry platoons, and weapons platoons. The guard force normally constitutes its own screen force to identify enemy elements which are then destroyed by the remainder of the guard force. This necessitates the guard force to have a larger operational area compared with a screen force. However, it is equipped with sufficient combat power to destroy enemy reconnaissance and fix or delay the enemy main body.

REAR GUARD

8-20.   When a BCT, as part of a larger unit, is conducting a MTC and requires rear security, a battalion may receive a rear guard mission. The rear guard protects the rear of the main body and all fire support, protection, and sustainment elements in the main body. It may accomplish this by conducting an attack, a defense, or a delay. A battalion commander conducting a rear guard operation follows the same axis of advance as the protected force at a distance prescribed by the main body commander and normally within artillery range. The battalion commander establishes company battle positions or sectors. When using sectors, he designates phase lines and checkpoints to control movement. The rear guard's responsibility begins at the main body rear boundary and extends as far from this boundary as the factors of METT-TC allow. When conducting a rear guard action for a moving force, the main body of the protected force may move beyond supporting indirect fire range. As a result, the Infantry battalion must be prepared to fight with organic and attached indirect fire assets.

FLANK GUARD

8-21.   A battalion may receive a flank guard mission during an MTC if the BCT is part of a larger unit. The flank guard is responsible for clearing the area from the BCT and larger unit main body to the flank guard's designated positions. The battalion must be prepared to operate on a frontage greater than for other tactical operations. Usually, the area extends from the lead forward screen, along the flank of the formation, to either the FEBA or the rear of the moving formation, tying in with the rear guard. Due to the complexities of this operation, this manual provides the following detailed discussion of flank guard operations:

Engineer Support

8-22.   The battalion engineer officer has two missions to consider in planning the guard mission; mobility and countermobility operations. He concentrates his planning activities on mobility corridors or avenues of approach that allow access to the main body. When attached from the BSTB, engineers are organized as they would be for an MTC. Usually, they follow the lead element and assist in negotiating any obstacles that prevent continued advance. The obstacle plan includes rapidly emplaced obstacles through SCATMINE, Volcano (multiple delivery mine system), or other assets. Engineers also identify key bridges or other potential obstacles during the planning process so they can render them usable for friendly movement and unusable for enemy maneuver.

Protection

8-23.   The battalion plans for either active or passive air defense measures. When AD assets are DS to the battalion, the unit commander or platoon leader will assist the staff in developing a flexible plan to allow for the protection of the force as it changes posture between moving and stationary. Most AD assets are attached to maneuver elements and the main CP. Route protection or other areas go without support or rely on protection from main body AD assets. The battalion executes the air defense plan as in a MTC where a moving force may need to adopt a defensive posture quickly. Whether moving or stationary, air defense assets must be linked to the main body's air defense early warning net and the positioning of assets must protect not only the flank guard but also air approaches into the main body.

Sustainment

8-24.   The logistics planner has the same challenges as in planning a MTC. He plans for responsive and flexible support that may require the immediate resupply of ammunition and evacuation of casualties and equipment upon contact. The planner identifies lateral supply routes to the vicinity of each potential enemy engagement area during the planning process. On-order control measures, LRPs, UMCPs, and AXPs are essential to the operation. As the battalion begins its movement, the battalion trains should travel abreast of the flank guard unit (close to the main body) to avoid exposing sustainment elements to the enemy. Emergency resupply vehicles carrying ammunition and other quickly expendable supplies are ready to respond to sudden requisitions due to enemy contact. Once the battalion begins the fight, evacuation of wounded personnel and damaged equipment occurs along lateral supply routes all the way to the main body if that is where the support battalion is located. Otherwise, the evacuation is back along the axis of advance.

Orientation of Forces

8-25.   A unique aspect of the flank guard mission is the orientation of the forces and the direction they may be ordered to guard. While the force maneuvers forward along its assigned axis of advance or zone, phase lines assist in the control of movement of the company elements. Once an element detects the enemy and companies adopt hasty defensive positions, phase lines become boundaries for controlling the defensive battle. This gives the battalion commander the option of designating company sectors in addition to potential battle positions identified in zone or along the axis of advance. Similarly, control of the reserve may be accomplished through phase lines and checkpoints regardless of the actual direction of the maneuver. As a minimum, the following control measures are included:

- Phase lines (revert to boundaries on contact).
- Battle positions.
- TRPs.
- Axis of advance.
- Axis of advance of main body.
- Objectives (if used).

COVER

8-26. A covering force, unlike a screening or guard force is a self-contained force, capable of operating independent of the main body. The requirements placed upon the covering force, the C2 structure necessary for the forces involved, and the large AO involved require an adequate level of command for successful accomplishment. The battalion performs screen and guard missions. Covering force operations is normally a BCT mission. The battalion may participate in a covering force as part of a BCT operation. A covering force, or portions of it, often becomes decisively engaged with enemy forces; therefore, it must have substantial combat power to engage the enemy and still accomplish its mission.

AREA SECURITY

8-27. Area security operations may be offensive or defensive in nature and focus on the protected force, installation, route, or area. The protected force ranges from echeloned headquarters, artillery units, and reserves to the sustaining base. Protected installations can also be part of the sustaining base or they can constitute part of the area's infrastructure: areas to secure range from specific points (bridges and defiles) and terrain features (ridge lines and hills) to large population centers and their adjacent areas.

OPERATIONS IN NONCONTIGUOUS AREAS OF OPERATION

8-28. Operations in noncontiguous AOs require that commanders emphasize area security. During offensive and retrograde operations, the speed at which the main body moves provides some measure of security. Rapidly moving units in open terrain can rely on technical assets to provide advance warning of enemy forces. In restricted terrain, security forces focus on key terrain such as potential choke points.

REAR AND BASE SECURITY

8-29. A commander executes rear area and base security as part of a BCT's sustaining operations responsibilities or as part of stability and civil support operations (Chapter 6).

CIVIL CONSIDERATIONS

8-30. Since civilians are normally present within the AO, a unit may have to restrain its use of force when conducting area security operations. However, the commander always remains responsible for protecting his force and considers this responsibility when establishing his ROE. Restrictions on conducting operations and using force must be clearly explained and understood by everyone. They must realize that friendly or hostile media and enemy psychological operations organizations can quickly exploit their actions, especially the manner in which they treat the civilian population.

SAFETY

8-31. Sometimes area security forces must retain readiness over long periods without coming in contact with the enemy. This occurs most often during area security operations when the enemy knows that he is seriously overmatched in terms of available combat power. In this case, the enemy normally tries to avoid engaging friendly forces unless it is on his terms. The enemy will often use unattended mines, improvised explosive devices, and other means that minimize exposure to friendly forces combat power. Forces conducting area security should not develop a false sense of security, even if the enemy appears to have ceased operations within the secured area. The commander must assume that the enemy is observing his operations and is seeking routines, weak points, and lax security for the opportunity to strike with minimum risk.

LOCAL SECURITY

8-32.   Local security is a form of area security and includes any local measure taken by units against enemy actions. It involves avoiding detection by the enemy or deceiving the enemy about friendly positions and intentions. It also includes finding any enemy forces in the immediate vicinity and knowing as much about their positions and intentions as possible. Local security prevents a unit from being surprised and is an important part of maintaining the initiative. The requirement for maintaining local security is an inherent part of all operations. Units perform local security when conducting full spectrum operations, including tactical enabling operations. Units use both active and passive measures to provide local security.

ACTIVE LOCAL SECURITY MEASURES

8-33.   Active measures include—

- Using OPs, patrols, and UAS.
- Establishing specific levels of alert within the unit. The commander adjusts those levels based on the factors of METT-TC.
- Establishing stand-to times. The unit SOP details the unit's activities during the conduct of stand-to.

PASSIVE LOCAL SECURITY MEASURES

8-34.   Passive local security measures include using camouflage, movement control, noise and light discipline, and proper communications procedures. It also includes employing available ground sensors, NVDs, and daylight sights to maintain surveillance over the area immediately around the unit.

HIGH-VALUE ASSETS SECURITY

8-35.   Inherent within the four forms of security is the consideration of high value asset security. The increased number and importance of artillery, aviation, communications, and intelligence acquisition systems has led to increased emphasis on their security.

TYPES OF HIGH-VALUE ASSETS

8-36.   HVA security missions are not simply additional requirements. They represent an evolution in the way BCTs, and higher units fight. Systems that acquire and defeat the enemy with precision fires, at vastly extended ranges, are important warfighting tools. Types of HVAs which a battalion could secure include—

- Q36, Q37, and lightweight countermortar radars.
- MLRS battery or battalion.
- BCT or higher unit UAS site.
- Patriot battery.
- Sentinel radars.
- FARPs.
- Land-based Phalanx Weapons System (LPWS)

PLANNING CONSIDERATIONS

8-37.   The magnitude of the security requirement for HVAs varies depending on how many missions are assigned to the battalion for security of BCT and higher unit assets. Generally, these missions are kept to the minimum number possible. When securing HVAs, the commander must address information requirements. He must consider—

- What are the frequencies, locations, and linkup points of the HVA?
- What routes should be used to reach the HVA. How many unit AOs must the security force move through? Under what conditions?
- What are the mission, organizational assets, and movement and positioning plans of the HVA?
- What is the nature of the enemy threat?
- Can the HVA be detected and targeted with indirect fire? If so, the battalion needs to consider its own survivability and maintain standoff from the HVA.
- How long will the mission last (duration)? Who will determine change of mission?
- What other forces are in the area? What base clusters are nearby?
- What are the triggers to leave the security mission and enter the close fight? Is there an implied reserve mission?
- What is the mission and movement plans of the security force parent unit?
- Who is the security force's higher headquarters?
- What is the logistical support plan for the force? Who provides logistical security? Into whose communication architecture do they plug?
- How will the battalion track its forces assigned to HVA security missions and transition them back into the close fight?

Section II. RELIEF OPERATIONS

A relief is an operation in which one unit replaces another in combat. The incoming unit assumes responsibility for the mission and the assigned sector or zone of action. A relief-in-place may be conducted at any point during offensive or defensive operations. Relief operations are normally executed during limited visibility to reduce the possibility of detection. To facilitate and ensure successful operations, the linkup and relieved force commanders and staffs exchange as much information as possible to prevent the inadvertent engagement of friendly forces by either direct or indirect fire systems during relief operations. Therefore, temporary collocation of CPs is recommended.

PLANNING CONSIDERATIONS

8-38.   Upon receipt of the order to conduct the relief, the incoming battalion commander and staff establish an exchange of liaison personnel in order to exchange information pertinent to the relief operations. Commanders and staffs emphasize communications, intelligence handover, and transfer of command. If possible, the incoming unit's CP should collocate with the main CP to facilitate continuous information exchanges relative to the occupation plan, fire support plan, and intelligence updates that include past, present, and probable enemy activities. Face-to-face coordination reduces any potential misunderstandings related to relief preparation or the forthcoming operations. Responsibility for the area is transferred as directed by the senior common commander, normally when the incoming unit has a majority of his fighting force in place and all C2 systems are operating. Friendly units are vulnerable to enemy attack during this kind of operation. Care must be taken, and plans must address, screening operations that provide sufficient security to warn friendly units in case the enemy tries to take advantage of the relief.

8-39.   When planning the relief, the staff determines the most appropriate method for executing the relief by using one of the following methods:

RELIEVING UNITS ONE AT A TIME

8-40.   This method is the most deliberate and time-consuming; however, it minimizes confusion and maintains the best command, control, and readiness posture. It involves sequentially relieving maneuver companies one at a time. Separate routes to the rear of the relieved companies' locations are planned for each maneuver company and placed on the operations overlay. Routes are labeled sequentially and correspond to the order in which the company executes them during the relief. When the lead company reaches its release point (RP), its platoons move to the positions they are occupying. Crews exchange range card and fire support information, and the relieved unit then moves to the rear to its next location. When the lead company is in position, the next company moves along its designated route to relieve its counterpart: thereby repeating the relief process. This process repeats until each company has been relieved. If transfer of supplies from the relieved unit is directed, the S-4 coordinates a transfer point to execute the exchange.

RELIEVING UNITS AT SAME TIME

8-41.   This method is the quickest but risks revealing friendly unit intentions and is more difficult to control. To expedite the relief, the in-place battalion prepares overlays to show current friendly graphics, fire support measures, and the latest enemy situation update. They then pass these overlays to the relieving force before the two forces make contact. Once the command groups collocate and exchange plans, relief occurs at the same time at each location. The units of the relieving and relieved battalions execute at the same time a move along different routes. Relieved units withdraw as soon as they are relieved and do not wait for other units of the battalion to be relieved. The control measures at battalion level are identical to those used for a sequential relief (one unit at a time).

RELIEVING UNITS BY OCCUPYING IN-DEPTH AND ADJACENT POSITIONS

8-42.   This technique requires sufficient terrain to accommodate positioning of two like-sized units at the same time. In this case, the relieving unit locates where it can observe and provide protective direct and indirect fires for the relieved unit using the relieved units' fire plans. This procedure requires that relieving company and battalion commanders conduct a detailed physical reconnaissance of the position with their counterparts from the in-place unit. They enter information gathered from the physical reconnaissance, such as BPs, TRPs, and routes to and from the area, on an operations overlay and share them throughout the relieving unit during the planning and preparation process.

COMMAND AND CONTROL

8-43.   If either force gains direct fire contact with an enemy force, it immediately notifies the other unit and the higher headquarters by way of frequency modulation (FM) voice communications. If responsibility for the sector has not passed, the relieving unit becomes OPCON to the relieved unit. The assets and staff of the relieved unit become OPCON to the relieving unit when the responsibility for the sector has passed to the relieving battalion.

Section III. BATTLE HANDOVER AND PASSAGE OF LINES

Battle handover is a coordinated operation executed to sustain continuity of the combined-arms fight and to protect the combat potential of both forces involved. Battle handover is usually associated with the conduct of a passage of lines.

BATTLE HANDOVER

8-44.   Battle handover may occur during either offensive or defensive operations. During defensive operations, it is normally planned and coordinated in advance to facilitate execution and usually involves a rearward passage of lines. In the offense, it is situation-dependent and often initiated by a FRAGO. Battle handover normally occurs in the offense when one unit passes through or around another unit.

8-45.   Battle handover occurs along a line forward of the stationary force. The BCT commander establishes this line in consultation with both stationary and passing battalion commanders. The stationary battalion commander normally determines the battle handover line (BHL) location. This line could be forward of the FEBA in the linear defense (or the FLOT in the linear offense), or it could be a line determined by the common controlling headquarters in a nonlinear environment. The BHL is located where elements of the passing battalion can be effectively overwatched by direct fires or supported by indirect fires of the forward combat element of the stationary battalion until the battle handover is complete.

8-46.   Physical handover normally occurs in the battle handover zone. Events may dictate that a force break contact forward of or behind the BHL such as when a gap exists between echelons of the attacking enemy force. Close coordination--physical or by FM voice--between the battalions involved in the handover allows them to coordinate and execute this process at the small-unit level.

8-47.   The battle handover operation begins on order of the higher headquarters commander from either unit, or when a given set of conditions occurs. Defensive handover is normally complete when the passing battalion is completely clear and the stationary battalion is ready to engage the enemy. These actions may occur at the same time. Offensive handover is normally complete when the passing battalion combat elements completely cross the BHL. The BHL is normally considered the LD for the attacking battalion. Until the handover is complete and acknowledged by the commanders, the battalion commander in contact is responsible for the fight.

8-48.   Coordination for battle handover flows from the battalion commander out of contact to the battalion commander in contact. The coordination for a battle handover overlaps with the coordination for a passage of lines; the coordination for both is accomplished at the same time. The TSOP should outline these coordination requirements to facilitate rapid accomplishment.

8-49.   Each unit transmits or delivers a complete copy of their OPORD and overlays. Any changes made after initial distribution are updated immediately. The coordination effected between the two commanders includes—

- Establishing FM voice communications.
- Providing updates of both friendly and enemy situations (voice and graphical).
- Coordinating passage points and routes and ensuring these are displayed on operational overlays.
- Collocating C2 and exchanging liaison personnel (if required).
- Coordinating fires and fire control measures (direct and indirect) and ensuring these are displayed on operational overlays.
- Determining the need for and dispatching contact point representatives.
- Establishing and coordinating recognition signals.
- Exchanging locations of obstacles and related covering fires.
- Exchanging route information to include waypoints.
- Determining fire support, protection, and sustainment requirements.

PASSAGE OF LINES

8-50.   A passage of lines is the coordinated movement of one or more units through another unit. It is normally conducted when at least one METT-TC factor does not permit the bypass of a friendly unit. A passage of lines is a complex operation requiring close supervision and detailed planning, coordination, and synchronization between the battalion commanders of the unit conducting the passage and the unit being passed. The primary purpose of a passage of lines is to transfer responsibility for an area from one unit to another. The battalion or its subordinate units execute a forward or rearward passage of lines (Figures 8-3 and Figure 8-4). A passage of lines may be conducted to—

- Continue an attack or counterattack.
- Envelop an enemy force.
- Pursue a fleeing enemy.
- Withdraw covering forces or MBA forces.

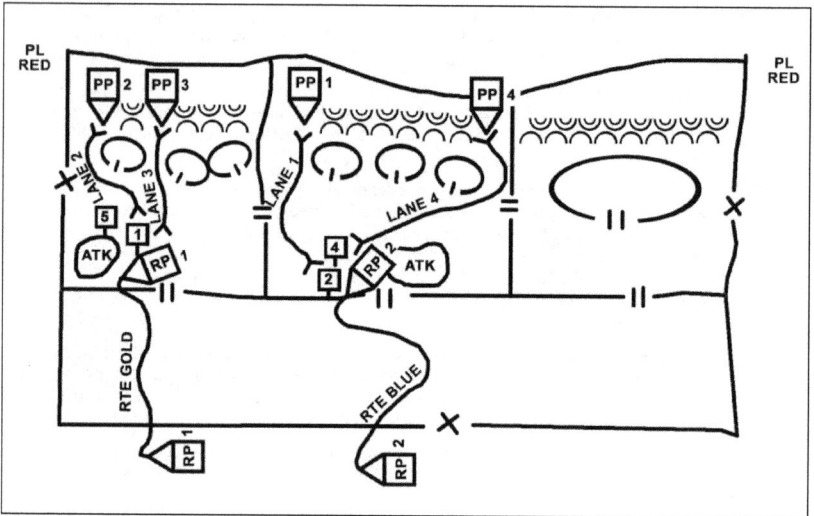

Figure 8-3. Forward passage of lines.

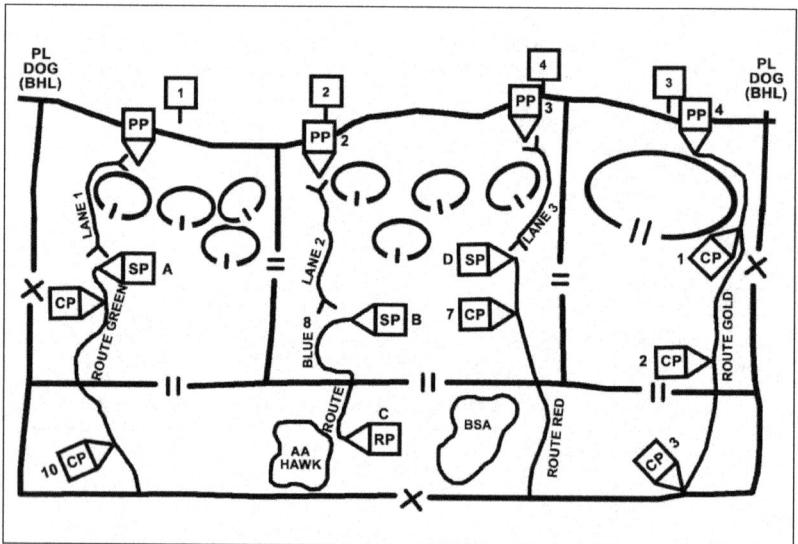

Figure 8-4. Rearward passage of lines.

Terrain Management and Control Measures

8-51.   Terrain management is critical to successful completion of a passage of lines. Terrain is controlled through the sharing of overlays that contain—

- Routes (primary and alternate).
- Checkpoint data.
- Friendly and enemy unit locations and status.
- Passage points and lanes.
- Fire support control measures.
- Obstacle types and locations.
- Sustainment locations and descriptions.
- Contact points.

MOVEMENT AND MANEUVER

8-52.   A passage of lines may require either the reduction of some obstacles or the opening and closing of lanes through friendly obstacles. The passing battalion engineer must coordinate with the stationary unit engineer. As a minimum, this coordination must address the following:

- Location and status of friendly and enemy tactical obstacles.
- Routes and locations of lanes and bypasses through friendly and enemy obstacles.
- Transfer of obstacle and passage lane responsibilities.

FIRE SUPPORT

8-53.   The battalion FSO reviews the fire support plan of the stationary unit and conducts direct coordination to ensure that a clear understanding exists between the passed and passing units on the established FSCMs. He does so through the transfer of digital fire support overlays between the two FSEs via the Advanced Field Artillery Tactical Data System (AFATDS). Procedures to establish fire support battle handover or transfer of control are also identified and approved by the maneuver commander. Terrain and route management for artillery batteries and their support assets are especially important due to potential terrain limitations. Sufficient artillery assets must be positioned to support the passage if enemy contact is possible during the operation.

PROTECTION

8-54.   During the conduct of a passage of lines, units participating in the operation present a lucrative target for air attack. The passing commander coordinates AD protection with the stationary force commander for AD coverage during the passage of lines. This method allows the passing force's supporting air defense assets to conduct a move at the same time. If the passing force requires static air defense, then it must coordinate the terrain with the stationary battalion's S-3.

SUSTAINMENT

8-55.   The sustainment plan is integral to a successful passage of lines. Sustainment assets are positioned to support the passage. Figure 8-5 shows the sustainment plan for a rearward passage of lines.

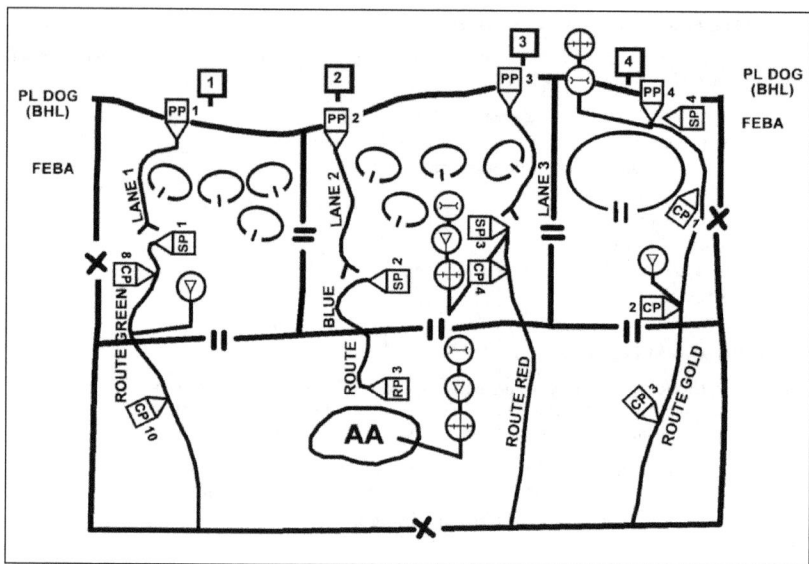

Figure 8-5. Sustainment plan for rearward passage of lines.

FORWARD PASSAGE OF LINES

8-56.   In a FPOL (conducted as part of an attack), both the stationary and passing battalion commanders must be aware of the passing battalion's objective. This awareness is especially important if the stationary battalion must provide supporting fires. The stationary battalion and forward passing unit share data needed to affect a passage of lines in a timely and safe manner.

8-57.   On receipt of an order, the passing battalion commander begins preparing his passage of lines plan by conducting a reconnaissance while concurrently updating the information received from the stationary battalion. For example, the passing battalion receives an operations overlay from the stationary battalion that delineates routes to the contact points as well as the location of the actual linkup site. The battalion commander and staff of the passing unit meet representatives from the stationary battalion at designated contact points to conduct coordination.

8-58.   During the physical reconnaissance, the S-3 from the passing battalion updates the initial operations overlay, incorporating information received from the stationary battalion by adding pertinent control measures. Upon completion, the S-3 forwards this overlay to the main CP. Based on this information; the staff completes development of the plan. Once approved by the commander, additional control measures are added to the operations overlay as necessary to complete the plan.

8-59.   The main CP forwards the validated operations overlay update from the stationary and passing battalion, BCT, and subordinate units to the liaison teams. This technique allows the S-3 and battalion commander to develop their scheme of maneuver for the passage of lines overlay concurrent with reconnaissance. At the conclusion of the reconnaissance and subsequent coordination with the stationary battalion, the revised battalion plan is distributed to subordinate units and higher headquarters.

REARWARD PASSAGE OF LINES

8-60.   Typically, a rearward passage of lines occurs within a defensive framework in which elements of the security force operate forward of the MBA. The main battle area forces are the stationary unit in a rearward passage of lines. The covering force withdraws through them, handing off control of the fight at the battle handover line.

8-61.   To facilitate a rearward passage of lines, the stationary force commander designates—

- The battle handover line.
- Contact points forward of the BHL.
- Passage points along the FEBA.
- Lanes to the rear of the MBA.

8-62.   Once he prepares the overlay, the stationary commander provides it and any amplifying information to the passing force commander.

8-63.   The stationary and passing commanders determine the best method of exercising C2 to avoid slowing the tempo of the operation and to reduce fratricide potential.

REHEARSAL

8-64.   During the rehearsal for a passage of lines, the battalion commander ensures that each organization knows when and where to move as well as how to execute the required coordination. Rehearsal items include—

- Fire support observation plan, target execution, communication linkages, and mutual support operations. Confirm fire support control measures. Review unit routes and positioning.
- Locations and descriptions of obstacles, lanes, bypasses, and markings. Confirm locations of any engineer stockpiles.
- Responsibility by unit for closing passage lanes after the passage of lines is complete.
- Air defense weapons locations, early warning communications, air threat, and weapons control status.
- Passage points, routes, and recognition procedures. Rehearse route management, contact points, and use of guides.
- Locations for and movement of sustainment units: rehearse these, along with mutual support arrangements and any transfer of supplies.
- Locations of aid stations, ambulance exchange points, and casualty evacuation procedures (rehearse these).

Section IV. LINKUP OPERATIONS

Linkup operations, which join two or more friendly forces, are conducted to—

- Complete the encirclement of an enemy force.
- Assist breakout of an encircled friendly force.
- Join an attacking force with a force operating in the enemy's rear area.
- Make contact with other forces on a noncontiguous battlefield.
- Join reconnaissance elements with the main body.

PREPARATION

8-65.   Before commencing a linkup operation, the headquarters elements of the stationary force and linkup force must share information including COMSEC procedures and graphic overlays consisting of—

- Primary and alternate linkup points.
- Checkpoint and waypoint information.
- Unit disposition and activity (friendly and enemy).
- Locations and types of obstacles.
- Fire control measures including RFLs and no-fire areas (NFAs).

CONTROL

8-66.   The stationary and linkup force must maintain positive control during linkup operations to prevent inadvertent fratricidal engagements. They use FM voice systems as required to share combat information and to identify friend from foe positively. It is imperative that both the linkup and stationary units conduct precombat communications checks before the operation begins.

FORMS OF LINKUP

8-67.   Linkup operations take one of two forms; linkup of a moving force and a stationary force or linkup of two moving forces.

LINKUP OF A MOVING FORCE WITH A STATIONARY FORCE

8-68.   To ensure the forces join without engaging one another, linkup points are selected at locations where the axis of advance of the linkup force intersects the security elements of the stationary force (Figure 8-6). These points must be readily recognizable to both forces and should be posted on overlays. When possible, the moving force should halt short of the linkup point and send a smaller force forward to pinpoint the linkup point. Alternate points are chosen so the units are prepared in case enemy activities cause linkup at places other than those planned. The number of linkup points selected depends on the terrain and number of routes used by the linkup force.

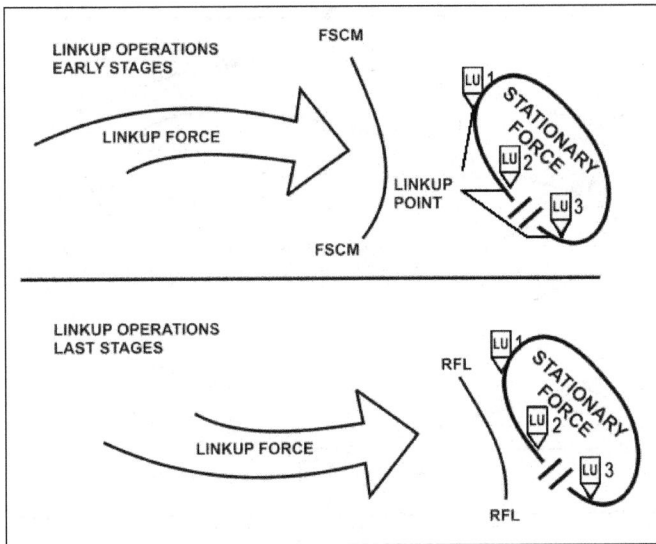

Figure 8-6. Linkup of a moving force with a stationary force.

8-69.   Communications are critical to linkup operations.

8-70.   To facilitate a rapid passage of lines and to avoid inadvertent engagement of friendly forces, personnel in the linkup force must be thoroughly familiar with recognition signals and plans. As required, stationary forces assist in the linkup by opening lanes in minefields, breaching or removing selected obstacles, furnishing guides, providing routes with checkpoints, and designating assembly areas.

8-71.   When linking up with an encircled force, the battalion carries as much materiel as possible during the linkup operation. This materiel includes Classes I, V, and VIII. If an enemy force has encircled the stationary force, the battalion carries additional supplies and materiel requested through to the brigade S-4 and BSB before the linkup takes place. The battalion S-4 ensures that each company has received the sustainment overlay showing MSRs, traffic control points, AXPs, and UMCPs.

LINKUP OF TWO MOVING UNITS

8-72.   Linkup between two moving units is one of the most difficult operations (Figure 8-7). It is normally conducted to complete the encirclement of an enemy force. Primary and alternate linkup points for two moving forces are established on boundaries where the two forces are expected to converge. As linking units move closer, positive control is coordinated to ensure they avoid firing on one another and to ensure the enemy does not escape between the two forces.

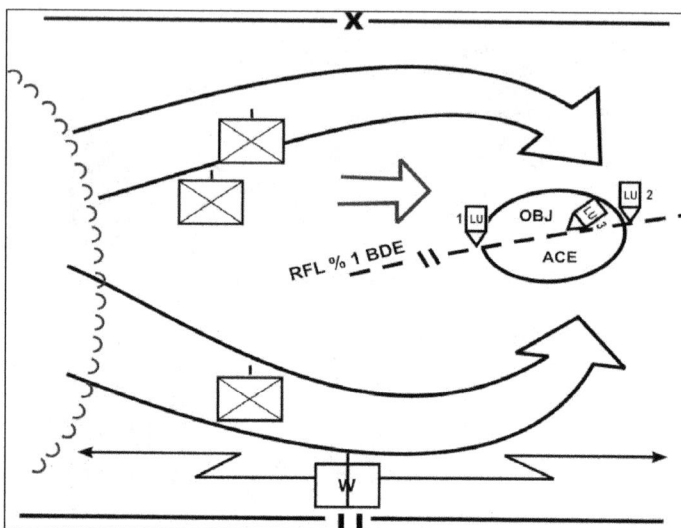

Figure 8-7. Linkup of two moving units.

ACTIONS FOLLOWING LINKUP

8-73.   When the linkup is complete, the linkup force may join the stationary force, pass through the stationary force, go around the stationary force, or continue the attack.

8-74.   If the linkup force is to continue operations with the stationary force, a single commander for the overall force is designated. Objectives for the linkup provide for dispersion in relation to the stationary force. The linkup force may immediately pass through the perimeter of the stationary force, be assigned objectives within the perimeter, or be assigned objectives outside the perimeter, depending on the mission.

8-75.   When the BCT directs a linkup operation, it normally establishes a restricted fire line for both battalions to ensure positive control and reduce the risk of fratricide. It transmits these RFLs to both units, and they are subsequently adjusted and overlays updated as one force moves toward the other. This process continues until a single RFL is established between the forces. Usually, this is the point on the ground where the two forces plan to establish contact.

PLANNING

8-76.   If possible, the two units establish liaison during planning and continue it throughout the operation. Liaison parties must have the capability to communicate with their parent unit. As the distance closes between the forces, the necessity to track movement and maintain close liaison increases. Use of Army aircraft and UAS can improve and expedite this process.

8-77.   Linkup operations frequently require a passage of lines. Once through friendly lines, and to affect the linkup, the battalion moves out as in an exploitation; speed, aggression, and boldness characterize this action. If possible, the linkup force avoids enemy interference with its mission and concentrates its efforts on completing the linkup. If enemy forces threaten the successful accomplishment of the mission, they are either destroyed or bypassed and reported.

8-78.   The headquarters directing the linkup operation must establish command relationships and responsibilities for the forces involved. Both the linkup force and the force with which linkup is to be made can remain under control of the directing headquarters. Operational plans must prescribe the primary and alternate day and night identification and recognition procedures, vehicle systems, and manmade materials used to identify friend from enemy.

8-79.   The communication plan includes all essential frequencies and secure variables to maintain communication between the two forces.

8-80.   Logistical support requirements may be greater during linkup operations than during other offensive actions. Additional considerations for planning logistical support in linkup operations include—

- Resupply of stationary unit.
- Duration the objective is to be held (METT-TC).
- Operations after the linkup is completed such as attack, withdraw, or defend.
- Transportation requirements for special purpose forces such as air assault and SOF.
- Lines of communication security requirements.

8-81.   Supply requirements for a linkup operation may exceed the transportation capability of the battalion. The battalion may have to request additional vehicles from higher headquarters, Army aviation support, or both.

8-82.   In linkup operations involving airborne and air assault units, the units assaulting the objective area have priority for supply by air. Supplies for the ground linkup forces normally move by land transportation. However, when the linkup and an airborne or air assault force plan to defend the objective area jointly, supplies for the linkup force may be flown or dropped into the objective area and stockpiled.

8-83.   Evacuation of equipment, WIAs, and EPWs may create major problems for the linkup force. If supply routes are open, normal evacuation procedures apply. When ground routes are not secure, helicopters or intra-theater fixed wing aircraft are used for the evacuation of casualties and prisoners. Damaged equipment may be moved forward with the linkup forces until it can be evacuated at the first suitable opportunity.

PREPARATION

8-84.   If time is available, he conducts a rehearsal at higher headquarters. If time is not available, the commander walks the linkup commander through the operation. He stresses the linkup and coordination required to reduce the potential for fratricidal engagements between the linkup forces. In addition, he ensures that each company commander is prepared to respond to an enemy meeting engagement or attack before the linkup.

EXECUTION

8-85.   Depending on the enemy situation and METT-TC, the initial conduct of the linkup operation may be identical to an exploitation or attack. During the operation, the commander monitors the progress and execution to ensure that the established positive control measures are followed or adjusted as required. Adjustments made to the OPLAN are coordinated and synchronized.

8-86.   As the linkup forces begin their maneuver, they establish FM voice communications and maintain them throughout the operation. As each force maneuvers, progress is tracked and adjustments to the linkup plan are made as METT-TC dictates. For example, if two forces are involved in the operations and one is unable to travel at a speed commensurate with the plan, the linkup location may require adjustment.

8-87.   As the linkup forces near each other, the tempo of the operation may be slowed to maintain positive control and to prevent fratricide. In this case, commanders must be vigilant and ensure enemy forces do not slip between the two closing forces. If possible, one of the units should establish a hasty defense and act as a stationary unit.

8-88.   The battalion FSE changes or activates the FSCMs established for the operation based on the progress of the forces and the enemy situation. All changes are provided to the FSEs of the maneuver units involved in the linkup. As the maneuver units draw closer to each another, coordinated fire lines (CFLs) are canceled, and an RFL is placed into effect to prevent fratricide between the converging forces. Once the linkup has occurred, fire support for the battalion is organized as per the higher headquarters plan for future operations.

8-89.   The battalion commander positions himself to observe the progress of the operation and maintains FM voice communications with the S-3. The battalion S-3 is positioned based on the operational concerns expressed by the battalion commander. For example, if a certain flank is of concern to the commander during the operation, or a shaping attack is required to penetrate the enemy's lines, then the battalion S-3 locates where he can best observe the battalion's secondary action.

Section V. RIVER-CROSSING OPERATIONS

A hasty river crossing is a continuation of an attack across the river with no intentional pause at the water to prepare so that there is no loss of momentum. This technique is possible when enemy resistance is weak and the river is not a severe obstacle. The three types of river crossing operations are hasty, deliberate, and retrograde. Battalions do not make deliberate or retrograde crossings independently; these are centralized operations where the controlling echelon is a BCT or higher unit. (For a detailed discussion of these operations, see FM 90-13.)

PLANNING CONSIDERATIONS

8-90.   Battalions routinely make hasty crossings and reorganize in order to maintain the momentum of operations. River crossing operations are planned and executed as for any other obstacle. The breach fundamentals; suppress, obscure, secure, reduce, and assault (SOSRA) always apply; however, they are adapted to the varying factors of METT-TC.

8-91.   Battalions cross in their respective zones at multiple points and as quickly as possible. The battalion may require the use of existing or expedient crossing means. Additional support from the BCT or higher level unit may be necessary if bridging requirements exceed the capability of engineers augmenting the battalion. Bridge companies are normally controlled at levels above the BCT. Their support is available only when headquarters have taken purposeful action to position the assets at the right time and place to assist a battalion's hasty crossing. The battalion must coordinate for support through the BCT early in the planning process.

8-92.   Small gaps, rivers, and streams that prohibit the advance are encountered more frequently than large gaps and rivers that require extensive bridging. When terrain or enemy conditions dictate, each battalion should request mobile crossing assets that enable it to install bridges quickly, cross small gaps, and recover the bridges for future crossings. Follow-on bridges, such as the medium-girder bridge (MGB), may need to be positioned at these gaps before assault bridges are removed so that following forces and support units can maintain the pace of the battalion. The two types of hasty crossings are dry-gap and wet-gap crossings.

HASTY DRY-GAP CROSSING

8-93.   Antitank ditches and craters are normally what battalions encounter as a dry-gap obstacle. The battalion may use expedient crossing means if they are readily available and can be transported to the crossing site. Reconnaissance elements should note material or existing features that can be used as expedient crossing devices.

HASTY WET-GAP CROSSING

8-94.   Bank conditions, the depth and width of the wet gap, and the current velocity determine whether the battalion can cross fording and whether bridging assets are required. Identifying wet gaps early and deploying the required resources allow hasty crossings of known or anticipated gaps to occur.

8-95.   When selecting a fording site in a wet-gap crossing, the depth of the water is the most significant factor. The depth of the water in one crossing area may change due to bottom surface mud or irregularities (boulders and potholes).

8-96.   If possible, the battalion crosses the water obstacle at multiple points across a broad front. It makes the crossing as soon as its elements reach the obstacle. As the bulk of the battalion crosses the water, minimum forces remain to secure the crossing sites.

8-97.   As with a hasty dry-gap crossing, the battalion may use expedient crossing means if they are readily available and can be transported to the crossing site. Reconnaissance elements should note material or existing features that could be used as expedient crossing devices.

8-98.   A well-practiced SOP reduces the necessary planning and preparation time. A concise order clearly articulating the commander's intent allows exploitation wherever subordinate units successfully force a crossing. When possible, advance elements seize existing crossing means intact and ahead of the main body.

8-99.   When facing negligible or light enemy resistance on both banks, the force does not have to clear all enemy forces from the river to conduct a hasty crossing. It capitalizes on the speed of the crossing and the limited ability of the enemy to oppose the crossing effectively.

ASSAULT OF CROSSING SITE

8-100.   A battalion assault across a river normally begins with an attack to secure terrain on the exit bank. This may involve an air assault, an assault crossing using pneumatic boats, or an infiltration by swimming or rope bridges.

AIR ASSAULT CROSSING

8-101.   An air assault is the fastest and most preferred crossing method. The following considerations apply when planning an air assault as part of the battalion river crossing (See Appendix C and FM 90-4 for more information on air assault operations.) Helicopters—

- Require indirect approaches to avoid detection.
- Provide the element of surprise.
- Give greater flexibility for emplacement of personnel and equipment.
- Provide the rapid insertion of forces into the area where the enemy is located, if a LZ is available.
- Are greatly affected by weather conditions.
- Must have a high suppression of enemy air defense (AD) priority at the river, requiring suppression of enemy AD effort.
- Are vulnerable to armored counterattacks and require a quick ground linkup.

RUBBER BOAT CROSSING

8-102.   The following considerations apply when using rubber boats in an assault crossing. Rubber boats—

- Offer great opportunity for surprise in a silent-paddle crossing.
- Provide a relatively fast means of crossing, especially when using outboard motors.

- Maneuver well in the water.
- Require limited, if any, entry-bank preparation and no preparation on the exit bank.
- Have limited carrying capacity, particularly for AT weapons.
- Provide limited protection, mobility, firepower, and communications on the exit bank.

ORGANIZATION FOR BOAT CROSSING

8-103.   The specific organization used for a boat crossing depends on METT-TC factors, particularly the size of the bridgehead, the distance to exit-bank objectives, and the nature of the enemy's defense. Regardless of these factors, the battalion organizes into support and assault forces and is assisted in the assault by other units in support-by-fire positions.

Support Force

8-104.   This force establishes a support-by-fire position along the friendly bank before the assault. It uses night vision and thermal sights to locate enemy positions. It also develops a fire plan to engage these positions and to provide suppressive fires on all suspected positions. When directed to engage, the support force destroys all known and suspected positions. The assault force commander (usually the battalion commander) directs the support force commander (usually the XO) to cease or shift suppressive fires as necessary. Supporting artillery and the mortar platoon provide indirect fire support and effects. Consideration of indirect fire REDs should be considered depending on the proximity of the friendly forces to the crossing site.

Assault Force

8-105.   The initial assault force moves across covertly if possible. This force tries to provide sufficient security on the far shore so that subsequent crossings can proceed if surprise is lost. Reconnaissance and security forces are pushed out as soon a possible to provide early warning and expansion of the lodgment for more crossing forces. The engineers help the assault force establish hasty defenses after it has seized its objectives. The initial assault force is normally composed of—

- Rifle platoons.
- Attached assault engineers.
- FOs.
- The command group.
- Assault platoons (if fordable).

Subsequent Crossings

8-106.   The subsequent crossings are composed of additional combat support and sustainment assets and may include the battalion command group. Subsequent crossings also transport additional material and ammunition that is not required for the initial assault but is necessary to establish a defense or continued offensive operations. This may include anti-armor weapons, mortars, ammunition, laser designators, mines, or pioneer tools. The immediate movement of some AT weapons across to support the assault element is essential if an armor threat exists. As vehicles carry all heavy AT weapons, engineers concentrate on moving antiarmor systems or vehicles carrying heavy weapons across immediately after the second wave. For a detailed description of assault crossing techniques and procedures, see FM 90-13.

Section VI. COMBINED-ARMS BREACHING OPERATIONS

Obstacle breaching is the employment of a combination of tactics and techniques to project combat power to the far side of an obstacle. Breaching is a synchronized combined-arms operation under the control of a maneuver commander. Breaching operations begin when friendly forces detect an obstacle and initiate breaching fundamentals; they end when the enemy is destroyed on the far side of the obstacle or battle handover has occurred between a unit conducting the breaching operation and follow-on forces. Breaching is an inherent part of maneuver. Effective breaching operations allow friendly maneuver in the face of obstacles.

TENETS

8-107.   Successful breaching operations are characterized by the application of breach tenets. These tenets are applied whenever an obstacle is encountered, whether friendly forces are conducting an attack or route clearance operations. The breach tenets are—

- Intelligence.
- Breaching fundamentals.
- Breaching organization.
- Mass.
- Synchronization.

INTELLIGENCE

8-108.   The ability to identify how the enemy applies obstacles to the terrain is critical to a commander's success. The commander and staff conduct intelligence preparation of the battlefield to develop initial situational templates and priority intelligence requirements. Intelligence gathered by reconnaissance forces is essential to developing a finalized situational template and final point of breach locations. Unverified enemy situational templates may cause friendly forces to deploy to reduce obstacles early, waste mission time trying to locate nonexistent obstacles, develop COAs using ineffective obstacle reduction methods, and fail to locate bypasses or become surprised by an obstacle. Augmentation of reconnaissance forces by engineer squads or sections may be used as part of the overall ISR plan. Examples of obstacle intelligence (OBSTINTEL) requirements include—

- Location of existing or reinforcing obstacles.
- Orientation and depth of obstacles.
- Soil conditions (determines ability to use mine plows, if available).
- Lanes or bypass locations.
- Composition of minefields (buried or surface laid antitank and antipersonnel (AP) mines.
- Types of mines and fuses (determines effectiveness of mechanical or explosive reduction techniques).
- Composition of complex obstacles.
- Location of direct and indirect fire systems overwatching obstacle.

BREACHING FUNDAMENTALS

8-109.   The breach fundamentals; suppress, obscure, secure, reduce, and assault (SOSRA) always apply; however, they are adapted to the varying factors of METT-TC.

8-110.   Suppression protects friendly forces reducing and maneuvering through an obstacle. Successful suppression typically initiates the rest of the actions at the obstacle. In some situations, the weapons company may be ideal to provide suppression.

8-111. Obscuration degrades observation and target acquisition of the enemy forces while concealing friendly force reduction and assault activities. Obscuration planning factors include wind direction, type of obscuration systems available (mechanical smoke, artillery delivered, mortar delivered, smoke pots), and the capabilities and limitations of these systems. Normally, obscuration starts with smoke delivered by indirect fire that builds quickly, followed by mechanical or smoke pots that have a longer duration but take more time to place and build. Typically, the most effective placement of obscuration is between the obstacle and the overwatching enemy forces.

8-112. Friendly forces secure the point of breach to prevent enemy forces from interfering with the reduction of lanes and passage of assault forces. The breach force must be resourced with sufficient combat power to secure the point of breach.

8-113. Reduction is the creation of lanes through an obstacle. Reduction cannot be accomplished until effective suppression and obscuration is achieved and the point of breach secured. The breach force will reduce, proof, and mark the required number of lanes to pass the assault force through the obstacle. Follow-on forces will continue to improve and reduce the obstacle when required. When possible, the breach force should also try to secure a foothold to assist in the passage of the assault force.

8-114. The assault force's primary mission is to seize terrain on the far side of the obstacle in order to prevent the enemy from placing or observing direct and indirect fires on the reduction area.

BREACHING ORGANIZATION

8-115. Commanders develop COAs that organize friendly forces into a support force, a breach force, and an assault force to quickly and effectively execute the breach fundamentals (Table 8-1).

Table 8-1. Breaching organization.

Breaching Organization	Breaching Fundamentals	Responsibilities
Support Force	• Suppress • Obscure	• Suppress enemy direct fire systems covering the reduction area. • Isolate by preventing enemy forces from repositioning or counterattacking to place direct fires on the breach force.
Breach Force	• Suppress (provides additional suppression) • Obscure (provides additional obscuration in the reduction area) • Secure (provides local security) • Reduce	• Create and mark the necessary lanes in an obstacle. • Secure the near side and far side of an obstacle. • Defeat forces that can place immediate direct fires on the reduction area. • Report the land status and location.
Assault Force	• Assault • Suppress	• Destroy any enemy forces capable of placing direct fires on the reduction area from the far side of an obstacle. • Assist the support force with suppression if the enemy is not effectively suppressed. Be prepared to breach follow-on and protective obstacles after passing through the reduction area.

8-116.   Support force responsibilities are to isolate the reduction area with direct and indirect fires, suppress enemy's direct and indirect fire at the point of breach, and control obscuration.

8-117.   The breach force must have sufficient combat power to secure the point of breach as well as sufficient reduction assets to reduce required number of lanes through the obstacle. CFZs should be activated at the point of breach before commitment of the breach force to protect it from enemy indirect fires.

8-118.   The assault force's primary mission is the destruction of enemy forces on the far side of the obstacle to prevent the enemy from placing direct fires on the breach lanes.

MASS

8-119.   The support force achieves mass by fixing and isolating enemy forces on the far side of the obstacle. The breach force achieves mass by planning redundancy of breach assets, creating one lane per each assaulting company-sized element, and creating two lanes separated by 800 to 1,000 meters (terrain dependent) to pass the battalion. The assault force achieves mass by projecting a 3:1 combat power ratio at the point of penetration (typically one isolated enemy platoon in an enemy company-sized defense for a battalion breach).

8-120.   In addition to direct fires and massing the breach force, the battalion masses indirect fires, attack helicopters and close air support to suppress and isolate the breach site.

SYNCHRONIZATION

8-121.   Synchronization of combined-arms elements to successfully achieve the breach fundamentals is essential. Commanders achieve synchronization through detailed reverse planning of offensive operations (from the objective back to the assembly area), by issuing clear subordinate unit instructions, planning effective C2, and ensuring their forces are well rehearsed.

8-122.   Detailed reverse planning is initiated during IPB and development of enemy situational template. The scheme of maneuver, engineer operations, fires, air defense, and actions at the obstacle are all based upon this common situational template. Actions on the objective determine the size and composition of the assault force based upon desired 3:1 combat power ratio. The size and composition (Infantry, wheeled, armor) of the assault force determines the number and location of breach lanes required. Lane requirements and disposition and composition of the obstacles determine the mobility asset requirement of the breach force. The enemy's ability to interfere with the breach force at the point of breach determines size and composition of the security element within the breach force. The enemy's ability to mass fires on the point of breach determines the amount of suppression required as well as the size and composition of the breach force. Battalion reverse planning begins with actions on the objective and continues to its deployment from tactical assembly areas in order to identify all requirements. Reverse planning should include enemy special munitions capabilities and effects (Figure 8-8).

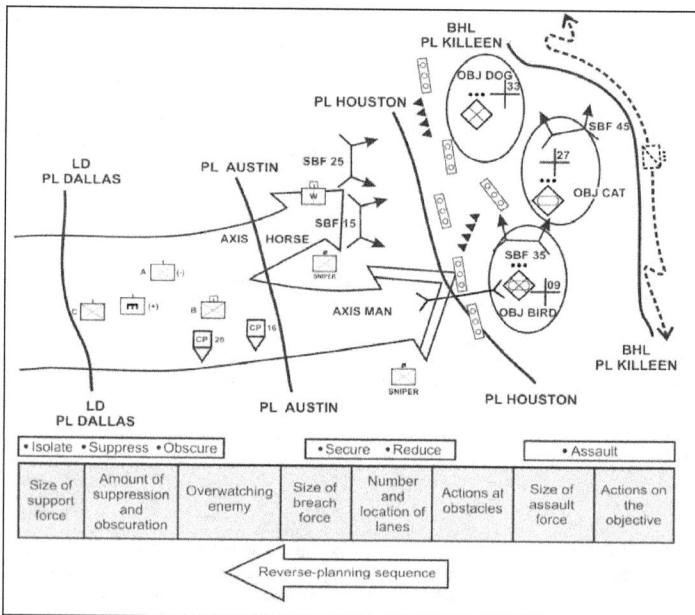

Figure 8-8. Reverse planning sequence.

DELIBERATE OPERATIONS

8-123.   The following paragraphs discuss the detailed planning, preparation, and execution necessary in conducting a combined-arms breach during deliberate operations.

PLANNING CONSIDERATIONS

8-124.   Planning a breaching operation begins with the command and engineer estimates. The battalion S-2 templates the enemy's order of battle (OB), and the engineer officer assesses its engineer capabilities. The enemy's tactical and protective obstacles are doctrinally templated by the S-2 and engineer. The staff develops COAs using the templates, and the engineer develops his scheme of engineer operations for each COA. After selecting a COA, the commander allocates available assets to the breach, assault, and support forces to ensure that they can accomplish their assigned tasks.

8-125.   Identifying the enemy's vulnerability is important so that the force can mass direct and indirect fires and maneuver against that weakness. The battalion isolates a portion of the enemy to achieve the desired combat ratio at the point of assault. It achieves mass by directing fire on the enemy from multiple directions and by narrowing attack zones to concentrate its force against a smaller defending element.

8-126.   When the attack requires breaching two or more complex obstacle systems, the commander must retain enough engineers and sufficient breaching assets to reduce subsequent obstacles. The commander must not commit all the engineers to breach the first obstacle system unless he is willing to risk his capability to breach follow-on obstacles. Depleted engineer forces need significantly more time to conduct follow-on breaches.

8-127.   The breach and assault forces may require fires and smoke under their control in addition to that controlled by the support force. The support, breach, and assault forces place direct fires on enemy positions. This makes synchronization of direct and indirect fires extremely complex. Fire control is planned in detail using SDZs, REDs, MSDs, well-understood control measures, and triggers that are carefully rehearsed.

8-128.   When a battalion conducts a combined-arms breach during a deliberate operation or plans to conduct a passage of lines of a large force after a breach, breach plans must include detailed planning for the staging and movement of follow-on forces and equipment. The plan should consider improvements to:

- The breach lanes.
- Markings of the lanes.
- Contact points and guides.
- Preparation for an enemy counterattack.
- Repositioning of indirect fire assets to provide extended coverage.
- Control measures for follow-on forces to continue the attack.

PREPARATION

8-129.   The battalion continues an intelligence collection plan using the scout platoon, snipers, UAS, attached engineers, patrols, and aerial reconnaissance. The S-2 and the battalion engineer continually refine the template based on intelligence. The battalion may adjust task organization as it uncovers more details of the defense and obstacle system. It also uses this information during the combined-arms rehearsals.

8-130.   The battalion meticulously plans, manages, and controls the rehearsals. The battalion S-3 allocates time for each unit to perform a combined-arms battalion rehearsal. When possible, the force rehearses the operation under the same conditions expected during the actual engagement, including battlefield obscuration, darkness, CBRN posture, and inclement weather. The rehearsal site reflects the actual obstacle system in as much detail as possible. The force chooses terrain as similar as possible to that of the operational area and constructs a practice obstacle system based on OBSTINTEL. Rehearsals include a leader and key personnel walk-through as well as individual rehearsals by support, breach, and assault forces.

8-131.   When the force commander rehearses the breaching operation, he also rehearses several contingency plans. The contingencies should include possible enemy counterattacks and attack by enemy indirect fire systems (artillery, rockets, attack helicopters, and other air assets). Rehearsals also include enemy use of CBRN munitions.

COLLECTION OF OBSTACLE INTELLIGENCE

8-132.   The success of combined-arms breaching during a deliberate operation depends heavily on the success of the ISR plan. The S-2 develops the collection plan, with the scout platoon and snipers concentrating on confirming enemy locations. The engineers focus on gathering intelligence on obstacle orientation and composition as well as on the types of fortifications the battalion may encounter. UAS can gather information on approaches to and composition of the obstacles, mine fields, and enemy reserve forces locations and composition. Intelligence is used to refine the task organization of support, breach, and assault forces and the scheme of maneuver.

EXECUTION

8-133.   The force crosses the line of departure organized to conduct the combined-arms breach. If the battalion encounters obstacles en route, it executes the breach with this organization. On arrival, the battalion's scout platoon and snipers adjusts artillery fires on the enemy positions to cover deployment of the support force. Snipers engage key targets to reduce enemy C2, and destroy antitank and crew served weapons. The support force moves into position and establishes its support by fire (SBF) position. Breach and assault forces move into position and prepare to execute their tasks. The battalion commander continues to incorporate last-minute information into his plan and makes final adjustments of positions and locations.

8-134.   The support force occupies its SBF position and immediately begins suppressing the enemy. The support force FSE and battalion FSO execute group targets planned on enemy positions. Mortar and artillery smoke are adjusted to provide initial obscuration of the breaching site from enemy target acquisition. Depending on the wind conditions, the support force or the breach force will provide mechanical smoke or emplace smoke pots to continue obscuration. The breach force begins movement once suppression and smoke are effective, based on clearly defined commitment criteria. Timing is critical since the high volume of suppressing fires and smoke can be sustained only for a short duration. SBF positions have interlocking sectors of fires and are positioned to ensure suppression of the enemy's positions.

8-135.   Once suppression and obscuration have built to effective levels, the breach force moves forward to the breaching site. The engineers create the lanes while the combined-arms breach force provides for local security. As they finish the lanes, engineers mark the lanes to assist the assault and following forces in maneuvering to the lanes. The assault force penetrates the objective after receiving the order from the battalion commander. The assault force must seize and clear the objective, prepare for counter attacks and be prepared to pass additional forces for attacks beyond the objective. Due to the complexity of the breach, the C2 systems spread out to ensure synchronization. The battalion S-3 controls the multicompany team support force while the battalion commander positions himself where he can best control the entire breaching operation.

CONTINUATION OF ATTACK

8-136.   The obstacle system acts as a choke point and is dangerous even after the battalion has overcome the defenses.

8-137.   The battalion constructs additional lanes to speed the passage of follow-on forces. Next, it widens the lanes to allow two-lane traffic through the obstacles and constructs switch lanes to prevent blocking by disabled vehicles or artillery fires. Deliberate marking and fencing systems are installed, and military police establish the necessary traffic control. Eventually, rear-area engineer forces clear the obstacles and eliminate the choke point. After passage through the lanes, the maneuver force continues its mission.

8-138. Both the breaching and follow-on force must be aware of the potential for the enemy to reseed breached obstacles with remotely delivered SCATMINEs or other rapidly emplaced obstacles. The breaching commander may develop a response plan and position remaining mobility assets near the breach lane(s) to rebreach, repair, or improve lanes as necessary. In addition, the commander may develop a reaction plan for maneuver or other forces that encounter a reseeded portion of the obstacle while passing through the lane. The commander of the follow-on force, regardless of the reported status of the breach lanes he is about to pass through, should organize mobility assets forward in his formation that are prepared to rebreach, repair, or improve these lanes as necessary.

HASTY OPERATIONS

8-139. Hasty operations are conducted when the enemy situation is vague and the commander may be required to execute the combined-arms breach with his current task organization. Therefore, the battalion commander must either task-organize his subordinate company teams with sufficient combat power to conduct company team-level breaching operations or have a plan that allows for the flexible application of combat power necessary to execute breaching operations. When conducting offensive operations such as a MTC, while participating in an exploitation or pursuit, and when conducting passage of lines (forward or rearward) and movements through defiles, the battalion commander must address breaching operations. The battalion breach planning considerations and process discussed previously apply to combined-arms breach planning during hasty operations as well. The only difference is the organizational echelon at which the breach is planned, prepared for, and executed.

BATTALION TASK ORGANIZATION

8-140. Subsequent to COA development, the commander and staff anticipate where units are most likely to encounter obstacles based on the scheme of maneuver and situational template. From this analysis, the commander refines his task organization, if necessary, in order to apply the combat power required for executing the templated breach. Also, the engineer recommends a task organization of engineer platoons and critical breaching equipment to create enough lanes for the breaching unit. He maintains a mobility reserve under his control that can create additional lanes for follow-on forces. This mobility reserve can also mass mobility assets if the battalion must transition to a deliberate operation. The battalion FSO designs his fire plan to provide priority of fires and smoke to company teams likely to conduct a breach. Above all, the commander task-organizes company teams for the mission first. He then modifies the task organization where necessary to provide company teams with the additional forces needed to conduct independent breaching operations as part of the battalion effort.

This page intentionally left blank.

Chapter 9
Command Posts

Echeloned C2 facilities control with varying levels of staff participation at each echelon. The battalion command group operates forward and consists of the commander and those selected to go forward to assist in controlling maneuver and fires during the battle. The command group normally includes the S-3, FSO, and ALO but there is no requirement for these people to collocate. For example, the commander may be in one part of the AO while the S-3 is in a different area. The commander determines the composition, nature, and tasks of the command group based on METT-TC analysis. The commander and S-3 also monitor the battle, develop the situation, analyze COA, and control subordinate units. As a minimum, the command group—

- Synchronizes combat assets in support of close operations.
- Controls close operations.
- Maintains the current operational situation.
- Provides close situation information to the main CP.

Section I. FACILITIES

Command and control facilities consist of the vehicles and locations where the commander, (assisted by his staff) directs the battle and sustains the force. These facilities include the following command posts: main, tactical, and combat trains. All three CPs have the ability to track the battle and assume control of the current fight.

SURVIVABILITY

9-1.   CP survivability depends mostly on concealment and mobility. The best way to protect a CP is to prevent the enemy from detecting it. Good camouflage and proper noise, light, and signal discipline enhance the security provided by a good location.

LOCATION

9-2.   The best location for CPs is determined by a METT-TC analysis. Built-up areas can be good locations for CPs because they provide cover and concealment, access to electricity and other services, and good access and regress routes. However, they also can put indigenous populations at risk and can provide enemy units covered and concealed positions to monitor and attack the CP. Locating a CP in built-up areas for longer periods tend to degrade its ability to displace quickly. A CP not in a built-up area should be located on a reverse slope with cover and concealment. Avoid key terrain features such as hilltops and crossroads. Locate CPs on ground that is trafficable, even in poor weather. Other actions when positioning CPs include—

- Ensure line-of-sight FM communications with higher, lower, and adjacent units.
- Use terrain to mask communications signals from the enemy.
- Use terrain for passive security, that is, for cover and concealment.

- Collocate with tactical units for mutual support and local security.
- Avoid possible enemy TRPs templated for enemy artillery and CAS.
- Locate the CP near an existing road network, out of sight from possible enemy observation.

ACCESS

9-3.   CPs should be near, but not next to, a high-speed avenue of approach with no more than one or two routes leading into the CP. These routes should provide cover, concealment, and access to other routes of communication. When possible, a helicopter landing zone should be nearby.

SIZE

9-4.   The area selected must be large enough to accommodate all CP elements including liaison teams and attachments from other units, communications support, and eating, sleeping, latrine, and maintenance areas. Sufficient space must be available for positioning security and vehicle dismount points and parking.

SHELTER

9-5.   Dryness and light are vital when working with maps and producing orders and overlays. CPs should be sheltered from weather conditions and should have lights for night work (exercising proper light discipline.) Buildings are the best choice but if none are available, CPs can operate from their organic vehicles or tents.

OPERATIONAL SECURITY

9-6.   OPSEC considerations for positioning CPs include--

- Avoid posting signs advertising CP locations. Disperse CP vehicles and thoroughly camouflage all vehicles and equipment. Maintain noise and light discipline.
- Employ a security force and provide communications between it and the CPs. Establish security force positions as in any defensive position, with a 360-degree perimeter and far enough out to prevent enemy fires on the CPs.
- Ensure the security force has available CCM systems and other weapons, based on the potential enemy threat. Establish a reaction force and rehearse the execution of the perimeter defense.
- Positioning C2 assets off major enemy avenues of approach reduces the probability of detection.
- Use an OP to secure any remote antennas located outside the perimeter.
- Sound proof and dig in generators, if possible.
- Provide all subordinate units and elements of the CP with near and far recognition signals. Ensure the CP uses these signals, challenges, and passwords to control access into its perimeter.
- In case of artillery or air attack, designate a rally point and an alternate CP, and ensure all members of the unit know their locations.

DISPLACEMENT

9-7.   CPs may displace as a whole or, more often, by echelon. Displacement as a whole is normally reserved for short movements with communications maintained by alternate means and minimal risk of degrading CP operations.

9-8.   A portion of the CP, called a jump CP, moves to the new location, sets up operations, and takes over operational control of the battle from the main CP. The remaining portion of the CP then moves to rejoin the jump CP. The jump CP consists of the necessary vehicles, personnel, and equipment to assume CP operations while the remainder moves.

9-9.   The XO or S-3 selects a general location for the jump CP site. The jump CP can be accompanied by a quartering party, which may consist of a security element and personnel and equipment for quartering the remainder of the CP. The signal officer, who is usually part of the quartering party, ensures communications on all nets are possible from the new site. When the jump CP becomes operational, it also becomes the net control station for the unit. The remainder of the CP then moves to rejoin the jump CP.

9-10.   Another technique is to hand off control to the command group or the CTCP and move the main CP as a whole. The command group can also split, with the commander moving with the decisive operations (or main effort) and the S-3 moving with a shaping effort.

Section II. OPERATIONS

Each CP must be organized to permit continuous operations and the rapid execution of the C2 process. SOPs for each CP should be established, known to all, and rehearsed. These SOPs should include at a minimum--

- Organization and setup of each CP.
- Plans for teardown and displacement of the CP.
- Eating and sleeping plans during CP operations.
- Command post shift manning, shift changes and operation guidelines.
- Physical security plans for the CP.
- Priorities of work during CP operations.
- Loading plans and checklists.
- Orders production.
- Techniques for monitoring enemy and friendly situations.
- Posting of CP map boards.
- Maintenance of CP journals and logs.
- Usation of a planning SOP (if separate from the TSOP).

COMMUNICATIONS

9-11.   Command posts monitor communications nets, receive reports, and process information to satisfy commander needs or CCIR. This information is maintained on maps, charts, and logs. Each staff section maintains daily journals to log messages and radio traffic. For more information, see Section III.

MAPS

9-12.   CPs maintain information as easily understood map graphics and charts. Status charts can be combined with situation maps to give commanders friendly and enemy situation snapshots for the planning process. This information is updated continuously.

9-13.   For simplicity, all map boards should be the same size and scale, and overlay mounting holes should be standard on all map boards. This allows easy transfer of overlays from one board to another.

9-14.   The following procedures for posting friendly and enemy information on the map will aid commanders and staff officers in following the flow of battle.

- All graphics should be posted on an overlay. Friendly and enemy unit symbols should be displayed on clear acetate placed on the operations overlay. These symbols can be marked with regular stick cellophane tape or with marking pen.
- Units normally keep track of subordinate units two levels down. This may be difficult during the conduct of combat operations. It may be necessary to track locations of immediate subordinate units instead.

BATTLE CAPTAIN

9-15.   The CP staff focuses on collecting the critical information the commander needs to fight the battle. Information flow is a constant challenge, especially since everyone in the CP must maintain a COP. The battle captain's essential function is like that of a conductor in an orchestra with regards to the COP. The battle captain's role is to plan, coordinate, supervise, and maintain communication flow throughout the CP to ensure the successful accomplishment of all assigned missions. The CP battle captain assists the commander, XO, and S-3 by being the focal point in the CP for communications, coordination, and information management. The battle captain is also the CP officer in charge (OIC) in the absence of the commander, XO, and S-3.

9-16.   The battle captain has the overall responsibility for the smooth functioning of the CP facility and its staff elements. This range of responsibility includes—

* Maintaining continuous operations of the CP while static and mobile.
* Battle-tracking the current situation.
* Ensuring communications are maintained with and between all stations, and that all messages and reports are routed and logged per SOP.
* Assisting the XO information management and coordination of CP staff functions to ensure a smooth and continuous information flow between the staff sections of the CP.
* Processing essential data from the incoming flow of information to ensure all tactical and logistical information is gathered and provided to the CP staff, S-3, and XO on a regular basis.
* Tracking CCIR and providing recommendations to the commander and XO.
* Approving fabrication and propagation of manual unit icons.
* Sending reports to higher and ensuring relevant information is passed subordinate units.
* Providing security for the CP, including its physical security and maintenance of noise and light discipline.
* Ensuring mobility of the CP, including configuration, equipment, and training, to facilitate rapid movement.
* Conducting CP battle drills and enforcing CP SOP.

9-17.   The battle captain ensures all staff elements in the CP understand their actions in accordance with the TSOP and OPORD, and provides coordination for message flow, staff briefings, updates to CP charts, and other coordinated staff actions. As a focal point in the CP, the battle captain processes essential information from incoming data, assesses it, ensures dissemination, and makes recommendations to the commander, XO, and S-3. Dissemination to the staff of important events is critical. In doing so, the battle captain assists in synchronization of staff actions.

9-18.   Information management in the CP can include processing journals, message forms, reports, FRAGOs, and requests for information. The battle captain ensures the consistency, accuracy, and timeliness of information leaving the CP, including preparing and dispatching FRAGOs and warning orders. In addition, he monitors and enforces the updating of charts and status boards necessary for battle management and ensures this posted information is timely, accurate, and accessible.

9-19.   To function effectively, the battle captain must have a working knowledge of all elements in the CP, understand unit SOP, and ensure the CP staff uses them. He must know the current plan and task organization of the unit and understand the commander's intent. In addition, the battle captain must understand the limits of his decision-making and action authority.

9-20.   The battle captain is integrated into the decision-making process and knows why certain key decisions were made. He must know the technical aspects of the battle plan and understand the time-space relationship to execute any specific support task. He must understand and enforce the battle rhythm; the standard events or actions that happen during a normal 24-hour period; and ensure that the CP staff is effective throughout the period. Battle captains use their judgment to adjust CP activities and events to accomplish the CP mission across different shifts, varying tactical circumstances, and changes in CP location.

Section III. COMMUNICATIONS

Command and control is exercised through communication. Communications is the means by which the commander projects his C2 across the width and depth of the battlefield. Lines of communications must go up, down, and laterally. The commander—

- Provides for redundancy in communications means by having backup at key locations.
- Makes sure subordinates know what to do during interruptions in communications. Ensure SOPs specify immediate actions in case of jamming, including prearranged frequencies to switch to and code words.
- Avoids overloading the communications systems. Use them only when necessary. Practice disciplined communications procedures by eliminating nonessential conversations.

RESPONSIBILITIES

9-21.   The sequential order of responsibilities for communications is—

- Senior to subordinate.
- Supporting to supported.
- Reinforcing to reinforced.
- Passing to passed (for forward passage of lines).
- Passed to passing (for rearward passage of lines).
- Left to right.
- Rearward to forward.

9-22.   All units take immediate action to restore lost communications. These responsibilities apply to establishing liaison between headquarters.

MEANS OF COMMUNICATION

9-23.   All standard communications means are available to the Infantry battalion. These include, wire, couriers, sound and visual signals, telephones, and radios. Although not part of the Infantry battalion TOE, single-channel tactical satellite (TACSAT) radios may also be available.

RADIO TRANSMISSIONS

9-24.   Radio transmissions should be brief to reduce the EW signature. Using secure operational and numerical codes reduces the chance of enemy detection. Use low-power transmissions and terrain to mask signals from enemy direction-finding equipment. Use couriers or wire for lengthy messages. Units must practice using SOP, operational terms and other common abbreviation techniques such as the terrain index referencing system.

INFORMATION STORAGE MEDIA

9-25.   Modern electronic information storage systems are prolific on the battlefield. Compact disks, flash memory drives, thumb drives, and hard drives can store vast amounts of information. They are routinely used to store and transfer data, including classified information. Because of their small size, they are easy to misplace, duplicate, and even steal. Management of these devises poses a new but not unique problem for physical security personnel. Care, storage and inventory management must be addressed in unit SOPs and these devises should be considered sensitive items.

SYSTEMS

9-26.   Communications currently available to the battalion fall under one of the subsets of the ABCS:

- Combat net radio.
- Army Common User System (ACUS).
- Army Data Distribution System (ADDS).

COMBAT NET RADIO

9-27.   The primary means of communication for the maneuver battalion is combat net radio (CNR). This family of push-to-talk radios includes SINCGARS, improved high frequency radio (IHFR), and TACSAT radios (when authorized).

ARMY COMMON USER SYSTEM

9-28.   The joint network node and the command post node (JNN/CPN) provide the Army Common User System (ACUS) at echelon, corps, and below (ECB). The JNN/CPN provides the higher bandwidth and Army battle command systems services required by maneuver commanders. Services range from secure internet protocol router (SIPR) and nonsecure internet protocol router (NIPR), to video teleconferencing (VTC). The equipment also enables both circuit switching and internet protocol-based networking. It works with MSE (mobile subscriber equipment) through the "Vantage" switching technology. The Vantage provides seamless interface between Voice over IP and tactical networks through the use of two dedicated MSE trunks.

ARMY DATA DISTRIBUTION SYSTEM

9-29.   The ADDS provides rapid battlefield information dissemination of products up and down the chain of command and to adjacent units. Three critical components of the ADDS at the Infantry battalion level are the tactical internet, FBCB2 and EPLRS.

TACTICAL INTERNET

9-30.   The tactical Internet (TI) is a collection of interconnected tactical radios and computer hardware and software providing seamless C2 INFOSYS data exchange between movement and maneuver, sustainment, and C2 INFOSYS platforms. The TI's primary function is to provide a more responsive information exchange capability to support battle command at BCT level and below.

9-31.   The TI consists of FBCB2 computers, the enhanced position location and reporting system (EPLRS) very high speed integrated circuits (VHSIC), the SINCGARS SIP, and other supporting communications equipment. It is an automated, router-based communications network using commercial Internet standard protocols to move data vertically and horizontally through the BCT area and to higher-level echelons using the JNN/CPN. Automated network management tools provide TI planning, monitoring, and reconfiguring capabilities.

9-32.   The TI is divided into two subareas: autonomous systems and routing areas. An autonomous system is a collection of networks, under a common administration, that shares a common routing strategy. An autonomous system can consist of one or many networks, and each network may or may not have an internal structure. A routing area is a network in an autonomous system. Routing areas and the autonomous system share the same routing strategy.

FORCE XXI BATTLE COMMAND BRIGADE AND BELOW

9-33.   The FBCB2 hardware is a mix of commercial, ruggedized, and militarized computers installed in vehicles at BCT level and below or issued to individuals as dismounted Soldier system units (DSSUs).

When available, the FBCB2 can be connected to the GPS and other embedded platform interfaces. FBCB2 is common to all aspects of the digitized battlefield; selected individuals in all platoons and companies have one. They are in most C2 INFOSYS platforms and CPs.

9-34.   FBCB2 uses the variable message format (VMF) to send and receive messages horizontally and vertically on the battlefield, irrespective of task organization. VMF improves current configurations in which the WFF automation systems do not communicate to each other. Digitization provides communication and processing capabilities to the warfighter, which yields significant advantages in two key areas.

Situational Understanding

9-35.   Situational understanding is a state of understanding gained from knowledge based on accurate and real-time information of friendly, enemy, neutral, and noncombatant locations and terrain. It consists of a COP of the battlefield scaled to specific levels of interest and needs.

Command and Control

9-36.   C2 is direction by a commander over assigned forces in accomplishing a mission. A commander employs C2 functions as he plans, directs, and controls forces and operations to accomplish a mission.

9-37.   FBCB2 provides each echelon with the COP two echelons up and down and one adjacent unit left and right. FBCB2 significantly improves the effectiveness of the force.

9-38.   FBCB2 provides up-to-date combat situation information based on echelon and location of—

- Friendly and enemy positions.
- Air and ground unit positions.
- Maps, terrain, and elevation.

9-39.   FBCB2 provides rapid generation and dissemination of messages and acknowledgments of—

- Orders and requests.
- Fires and alerts.
- Reports.
- Overlays on the situation picture.
- Semiautomatic exchange of selected mission-critical data between the FBCB2 and the ABCS component systems.

9-40.   FBCB2 hosts must receive new initialization data for each task reorganization affected. Transfer of the modified initialization data to the ultimate users occurs through signal channels.

ENHANCED POSITION LOCATION REPORTING SYSTEM WITH VERY HIGH SPEED INTEGRATED CIRCUITS

9-41.   Battalion C2 INFOSYS platforms employ EPLRS VHSIC as their primary data communications link to company and platoon platforms. It serves as a position location, navigation, identification, and communications system. Its primary components are the NCS and the radio sets. The NCS is the centralized control element used for system initialization, monitoring, and control. The radio sets are the radio receiver-transmitters provided to EPLRS VHSIC users. The battalion uses EPLRS VHSIC to provide wide area network connectivity down to platoon and up to the BCT. The antenna used with the system is an omni-directional dipole. The planning range is three to ten kilometers between radios, depending on power output settings and terrain.

DIGITAL COMMAND AND CONTROL SYSTEMS AND ARCHITECTURE

This paragraph provides basic information on the digital C2 systems and architecture.

Army Battle Command System Components

9-42.   The ABCS consists of the five ABCS subcomponents, the FBCB2 system, and the tactical Internet. The ABCS components have traditionally been "stovepipe" systems in their development, with very limited interface capability to other digital systems. The ABCS components are the primary digital communication systems between command posts. FBCB2 is the primary digital system for communication and transmission of data at battalion level and below.

Maneuver Control System

9-43.   The MCS is the hub of the ABCS component in each command post. It is the primary system for the creation and dissemination of orders, graphics, and operations-related reports. Embedded battle command (EBC) is a software subcomponent of MCS-light. It is a derivative of FBCB2 software and allows MCS-light to exchange reports and graphics with FBCB2 systems.

9-44.   At battalion level, MCS-Light performs the following primary functions:

- Receives orders and graphics from higher and adjacent units.
- Creates and disseminates orders and graphics to subordinate, higher, and adjacent units. (While platform EBC is limited, the MCS has near-term ability to interface graphics and orders to FBCB2.)
- Extracts information from other systems to display a picture of the battlefield that may include friendly and enemy positional information, terrain, friendly graphics, artillery range fans, AD umbrellas, obstacles and contaminated areas, C2 INFOSYS nodes, and supply nodes.
- Sends and receives reports.

9-45.   Future system capabilities should allow for MCS to support COA analysis, wargaming, and digital rehearsals.

9-46.   Two MCS-Light systems are located in the CP. One is used primarily for generation and transmission of orders and messages; the other is normally set to display the enemy and friendly COP and friendly graphics to allow the staff to track the battle.

9-47.   There are limitations in the automatic generation of friendly locations. Obviously, forces that are not equipped with FBCB2 or are not transmitting to the TI will not automatically appear in the COP picture and must be manually input into MCS by the operations section. Operators may also manually input friendly icons through FBCB2.

All-Source Analysis System

9-48.   All-source analysis system (ASAS) supports intelligence operations, providing linkage to strategic and tactical intelligence sensors and sources. ASAS primary functions include—

- Data access, databasing, and correlation capabilities.
- Creation and dissemination of intelligence reports, templates, and annexes.
- Receipt of intelligence reports from a variety of sources (including FBCB2 and other digital systems and display and management of the enemy COP).
- Collection management.
- Support of targeting functions.

9-49.   The S-2 uses ASAS to receive intelligence reports from all sources and to create and manage the correlated COP, which the other ABCS components in the CP can access. Also, the S-2 routinely sends the ASAS picture he generates down to subordinate units through FBCB2. He also sends it to the higher headquarters.

Advanced Field Artillery Tactical Data System

9-50.   The AFATDS provides automated capabilities to control fire support operations. Located in the FSE platform at the CP and in the supporting artillery battalion CP, the system provides the ability to—

*   Create and disseminate fire support orders, graphics, and control measures.
*   Receive and process calls for fire from other digital systems and target acquisition radars.
*   Manage mission allocation.
*   Monitor firing unit status and locations.
*   Transmit and receive reports and free-text messages.
*   Display the enemy and friendly COP from MCS-Light and ASAS-Light.
*   In conjunction with ASAS, provide integrated fires and IEW management.

Air and Missile Defense Workstation

9-51.   The air and missile defense workstation (AMDWS) is a collaborative battlespace awareness information management system that contributes to combat effectiveness by retrieving, fusing, and distributing time-sensitive information necessary to achieve decision-cycle dominance. AMDWS retrieves battlespace awareness information from many sources: joint headquarters, the ABCS network, national intelligence assets, all-source centers, and tactical and strategic sensors. AMDWS uses this information to provide an area-complete, combat-operations display that combines ground, air, and space-based sensor inputs and command and staff data with automated planning tools. Distribution is accomplished over tactical and special purpose communications in near-real time, while supporting concurrent interaction with joint C2 networks, sensor sources, and ABCS systems. The AMDWS is the force operations system of the forward area air defense command, control and intelligence network system supporting short-range air defense units. Some of the system capabilities include but are not limited to—

*   Sending and receiving messages and defense plans.
*   Maintaining human resource and logistics databases and status for the air defense unit.
*   Developing and running airbattle scenario.
*   Maintaining situation awareness of the hostile air threat.
*   Providing data required for air IPB.
*   Maintaining situational awareness during ongoing air defense operations.
*   Providing for the interface and data exchange between the tactical command system and other elements of the ABCS.
*   Planning defense design.

Battle Command and Sustainment Support System

9-52.   The battle command sustainment and support system (BCS-3) provides logistics status and information in support of sustainment planning and operations. The system receives subordinate unit logistical reports from FBCB2 and other BCS3 terminals, and transmits reports and requirements to echelons-above-brigade support elements. The S-1 and S-4 sections in the CTCP have a BCS3 terminal with FBCB2. It uses this terminal to receive digital logistical and situation reports from units within the battalion and to input data into the BCS3 network to conduct human resource transactions and to request, coordinate, and receive supplies.

9-53.   BCS3 provides a logistics picture for WFF information in support of the ABCS common operating picture of the battlefield. The system provides information on all classes of supply, maintenance, medical services (a desired future capability), human resources, and movements to commanders and staffs. This information is consolidated and collated into situation reports and planning estimates for current and future operations. This capability provides a concise picture of unit requirements and support capabilities that commanders have deemed crucial to the success of an operation and will have joint application.

9-54.   BCS3 integrates a COP of the following key logistics mission areas:

- Arming the force.
- Fueling the force.
- Manning the force.
- Fixing the force.
- Moving the force.

Internet Controller

9-55.   FBCB2 receives data across the tactical Internet through the Internet controller (INC). The INC is a tactical router built into the SINCGARS radio system. The EPLRS data radio and the SINCGARS radio transmit and receive digital information between vehicles.

Digital Command and Control Techniques

9-56.   This paragraph discusses considerations and techniques for digital C2 procedures and for integrating analog and digital units. The potential of these systems to contribute to battlefield lethality, tempo, and ability to dominate is enormous. Digital C2 systems bring a dramatic increase in the level of informational dominance units may achieve. They can significantly speed the process of creating and disseminating orders, allow for extensive databasing of information, and increase the speed and fidelity of coordination and synchronization of battlefield activities. At the same time, achieving the potential of these systems requires extensive training, a high level of technical proficiency by both operators and supervisors, and the disciplined use of detailed SOPs. Communications planning and execution to support the digital systems is significantly more demanding and arduous than is required for units primarily relying on FM and JNN/CPN communications.

FM or Digital

9-57.   Whether to use FM or digital means for communication is a function of the situation and SOPs. Some general considerations can help guide the understanding of when to use which mechanism at what time. FM is normally the initial method of communications when elements are in contact. Before and following an engagement, the staff and commanders use digital systems for disseminating orders and graphics and conducting routine reporting. During operations, however, the staff uses a combination of systems to report and coordinate with higher and adjacent units.

9-58.   FM is the primary method of communications between battalion and the BCT when elements are in contact throughout the battalion. Before and following an engagement, the staff and commanders use digital systems for disseminating orders and graphics and conducting routine reporting. During operations, however, the battalion staff uses a combination of systems to report and coordinate with higher and adjacent units.

9-59.   The Infantry battalion staff must remain sensitive to the difficulty and danger of using digital systems when moving or in contact. They should not expect digital reports from subordinate units under such conditions. Other general guidelines include the following:

- Initial contact at any echelon within the battalion should be reported on FM voice; digital enemy spot reports should follow as soon as possible to generate the enemy COP.
- Elements moving about the battlefield (not in command posts) use FM voice unless they can stop and generate a digital message or report.

- Emergency logistical requests, especially casualty evacuation requests, should be initiated on FM voice with a follow-up digital report, if possible.
- Combat elements moving or in contact should transmit enemy spot reports on FM voice; their higher headquarters should convert FM reports into digital spot reports to generate the COP. At company level, the XO, the first sergeant, or the company CP converts the reports.
- Calls for fire on targets of opportunity should be sent on FM voice; FISTs submit digitally to AFATDS.
- Plan calls for fire digitally and execute them by voice with digital back-up.
- Routine logistical reports and requests should be sent digitally.
- Routine reports from subordinates to battalion before and following combat should be sent digitally.
- Orders, plans, and graphics should be done face-to-face, if possible. If these products are digitally transmitted, they should be followed by FM voice call to alert recipients that critical information is being sent. Also, the transmitting element should request a verbal acknowledgement of both receipt and understanding of the transmitted information by an appropriate Soldier (usually not the computer operator).
- Obstacle and CBRN-1 reports should be sent initially by voice followed by digital reports to generate a geo-referenced message portraying the obstacle or contaminated area across the network.

Friendly COP

9-60.   The creation of friendly COP is extensively automated, requiring minimal manipulation by command posts or platform operators. Each platform creates and transmits its own position location and receives the friendly locations, displayed as icons, of all the friendly elements in that platform's wide area network. This does not necessarily mean that all friendly units in the general vicinity of that platform are displayed, however, because some elements may not be in that platform's network. For example, a combat vehicle in a battalion will probably not have information on an above BCT level artillery unit operating nearby because the two are in different networks. The COP generated from individual FBCB2 platforms is transmitted to command posts through the TOC server to MCS-Light. The other ABCS components can access the friendly COP through MCS.

Limitations

9-61.   Commanders must recognize limitations in the creation of the friendly COP which results from vehicles or units that are not equipped with FBCB2. The following are two aspects to consider:

- Not all units will be equipped with all ABCS components for some time, particularly in the reserve component. It is likely analog units will enter the BCT and battalion AOs.
- Most dismounted Soldiers will not be equipped with a digital device that transmits information.

Solutions

9-62.   The following are ways to overcome these limitations:

- A digitally-equipped element tracks the location of specified dismounts and manually generates and maintains an associated friendly icon.
- The main CP tracks analog units operating within the area and generates associated friendly icons. Also, the main CP must keep the analog equipped unit informed of other friendly units' locations and activities.
- A digitally-equipped platform acts as a liaison or escort for analog units moving or operating in the area. Battalion and higher elements must be informed of the association of the LNO icon with the analog unit.

- Do not use friendly positional information to clear fires because not all elements will be visible! Friendly positional information can be used to deny fires and can aid in the clearance process, but it cannot be the sole source for clearance of fires. This holds true for all ABCS systems.

Enemy COP

9-63.   The most difficult and critical aspect of creating the COP is creating the picture of the enemy. The enemy COP is the result of multiple inputs (FM spot reports, UAS and JSTAR reports, reports from FBCB2-equipped platforms in subordinate units, electronic or signal intelligence feeds) and inputs from the S-2 section. Enemy information generation is a complex process that is partially automated but requires a great deal of work and attention to detail to get right.

9-64.   Generation of the enemy COP occurs at all echelons. At battalion level and below, the primary mechanism for generating information is FBCB2. When an observer acquires an enemy element, he creates and transmits a spot report, which automatically generates an enemy icon that appears network-wide. Only those in the address group to whom the report was sent receive the text of the report, but all platforms in the network can see the icon. As the enemy moves or its strength changes, the observer must update this icon. If the observer must move, he ideally passes responsibility for the icon to another observer. If multiple observers see the same enemy element and create multiple reports, the S-2 (or some other element that has the capability) must eliminate the redundant icons.

9-65.   Unit SOPs must clearly establish who has the ability, authority, and responsibility to create and input enemy icons. Without the establishment of these procedures, it is highly probable that the enemy COP will not be accurate.

9-66.   FBCB2 spot reports must include the higher headquarters S-2 in the address group for the data to be routed through the CP server into ASAS-light to feed the larger intelligence picture. FM reports received at a command post can be manually inputted into the ASAS-light database by the S-2 section. FBCB2 and FM voice reports are the primary source of enemy information for fighting the close and rear battles.

9-67.   The BCT S-2 section and the supporting analysis control team support the Infantry battalion by receiving ASAS intelligence feeds from higher and adjacent units along with feeds from JSTARS, UAS, and the common ground station. They enter enemy information from these sources into the ASAS database and send this information through FBCB2 to the battalion S-2s. These feeds, along with FM voice and FBCB2 reports, are the primary sources of the enemy COP for executing the BCT deep fight and providing battalions a picture of what is coming into their areas.

9-68.   Fusion of all the intelligence feeds is normally done at BCT and higher levels. The BCT S-2 routinely (every 30 minutes to every hour) sends the updated enemy picture to subordinate units down to platform level. Since the fused ASAS database is focused on the deeper areas of the battlefield and its timeliness may vary, subordinate battalion elements and the reconnaissance units normally use only the FBCB2-generated COP. Companies should stay focused entirely on the FBCB2-generated COP. Battalion leaders and staffs refer occasionally to the FBCB2-generated intelligence picture to keep track of enemy forces they might encountered in the near future, but that are not yet part of the battalion close fight.

9-69.   As systems develop further in the future, the generation of the enemy COP will be increasingly automated. However, the success of the intelligence effort depends primarily on the ability of staffs to analyze enemy activities effectively, to develop and continuously refine effective IPB, and to create and execute effective collection management plans.

9-70.   Automation and displays contribute enormously to the ability to disseminate information and display it in a manner that aids comprehension; however, information generation must be rapid for it to be useful. Information must also be accompanied by analysis; pictures alone cannot convey all that is required nor will they be interpreted the same by all viewers. S-2s must be particularly careful about spending too much time operating an ASAS terminal while neglecting the analysis of activities for the battalion and subordinate commanders and staffs.

Graphics and Orders

9-71.   All ABCS components effectively support the creation and transmission of doctrinal field orders. The staff sections normally develop their portions of orders and send them to the S-3 where they are merged into a single document. The S-3 deconflicts, integrates, and synchronizes all elements of the order. Once the order is complete, it is transmitted to subordinate, higher, and adjacent units. In creating orders, remember that the tactical Internet does not possess high transmission rates like civilian e-mail. Orders and graphics must be concise to reduce transmission times. Orders transmitted directly to FBCB2-equipped systems (as all subordinate leaders in the battalion have) must meet the size constraints of the order formats in FBCB2. Graphics and overlays should be constructed with the same considerations for clarity and size.

Graphics

9-72.   Digital graphics must interface and be transmittable. The interface and commonality of graphics will continue to evolve technologically and will require further software corrections. The following guidelines apply:

- Create control measures relative to readily identifiable terrain, particularly if analog units are part of the task organization.
- Boundaries are important, especially when multiple units must operate in close proximity or when it becomes necessary to coordinate fires or movement of other units.
- Intent graphics that lack the specificity of detailed control measures are an excellent tool for use with warning and fragmentary orders and when doing parallel planning. Follow them with appropriately detailed graphics, as required.
- Use standardized colors to differentiate units. This should be articulated in the BCT SOP and established at BCT level. For example, BCT graphics may be in black, battalion A in purple, battalion B in magenta, and battalion C in brown. This adds considerable clarity for the viewer. Subordinate company/team colors should be specified.
- Use traditional doctrinal colors for other graphics (green for obstacles, yellow for contaminated areas, and so forth).

Overlays

9-73.   In order to accelerate transmission times when creating overlays, use multiple smaller overlays instead of a single large overlay. System operators can open the overlays they need, displaying them simultaneously. This technique also helps operators in reducing screen clutter.

9-74.   The S-3 should create the initial graphic control measures (boundaries, objectives, and phase lines) on a single overlay and distribute it to the staff. This overlay should be labeled as the operations overlay with the appropriate order number.

9-75.   Staff elements should construct their appropriate graphic overlays using the operations overlay as a background but without duplicating the operations overlay. This avoids unnecessary duplication and increase in file size and maintains standardization and accuracy. Each staff section labels its overlay appropriately with the type of overlay and order number such as fire support, OPORD X-XX.

9-76.   Before overlays are transmitted to subordinate, higher, and adjacent units, the senior battle captain or the XO checks them for accuracy and labeling. Hard copy (traditional acetate) overlays are required for the CPs and any analog units.

9-77.   Transmit graphics for on-order missions or branch options to the plan before the operation as time permits. If time is short, transmit them with warning orders.

Acetate Maps

9-78.   The advent of digitization does not mean that acetate and maps have no use and will disappear, at least not in the near future. Maps still remain the best tools when maneuvering and fighting on the battlefield, and for controlling and tracking operations over a large area. The combination of a map with digital information and terrain database is ideal; both are required and extensively used.

SOP Considerations

9-79.   This paragraph contains information regarding digital operations that is relevant for the BCT and battalion tactical SOPs. Most of the digital operating procedures must be established at the BCT level to achieve standardization and effective C2 INFOSYS. As units have different mission requirements and technical changes occur, they should experiment with these guidelines.

Filter Settings

9-80.   To create a common picture, all FBCB2 and EBC platforms must have the same information filter settings. This is particularly important for the enemy COP so that as icons go stale, they purge at the same time on all platforms. Standard filter settings based upon the nature of the enemy's operation should be established in unit SOPs and be the same throughout the BCT. For enemy offensive operations, the filter setting times should be short; for enemy defensive operations, the setting times should be longer, reflecting the more static nature of the enemy picture.

9-81.   The standardization of friendly and enemy situational filter settings is of great importance in maintaining a common COP throughout the force. FBCB2 provides three methods for updating individual vehicle locations: time, distance, and manually. When the system is operational, it automatically updates friendly icons using time, distance traveled, or both, based on the platform's friendly situational filter settings. The unit should standardize filter settings across the force based on both the mission and the function of the platform or vehicle. Use shorter refresh rates for combat vehicles and vehicles that frequently move and longer refresh rates for static vehicles such as CPs. Tailoring the frequency of these automatic updates reduces the load on the tactical Internet, freeing more capacity for other types of traffic.

9-82.   The BCT node is probably the most effective place to standardize the situational filter settings using the BCT tactical SOP. There are no set rules for what these settings should be; The commander must establish them based on the unit's experience using FBCB2 and the capacity of the tactical Internet. The battalion should use the capability to update a vehicle's position manually only when a platform's system is not fully functional and it has lost the ability to maintain its position within the system automatically.

Reporting and Tracking of Battles

9-83.   Having all platforms on the battlefield send spot reports digitally may result in mass confusion. However, in order to eliminate reporting confusion, there should be one designated person within the unit who is authorized to initiate digital spot reports. While the designated person will be somewhat removed from the fight, they can assist those who execute the direct fire fight by filtering multiple reports of the same event.

9-84.   Another technique that can be used to eliminate reporting problems is to limit the creation of enemy icons through digital spot reports to reconnaissance elements and the company leadership (commander, XO, or 1SG). Others report on FM to their higher headquarters, which creates and manages the icon. At company level, the XO, 1SG, or CP personnel become the primary digital reporters. These assignments cannot be completely restrictive. Unit SOPs and command guidance must allow for and encourage Soldiers who observe the enemy and know they are the sole observer (because there is no corresponding enemy icon displayed in the situational COP) to create a digital spot report. BCT and battalion SOPs should define the schedule for report submissions, the message group for the reports, and the medium (digital system or verbal) to be used.

9-85.   Battle tracking is the process of monitoring designated elements of the COP that are tied to the commander's criteria for success. Battle tracking requires special attention from all staff officers, and is normally done both digitally and manually with situation maps and boards. The XO and S-3 must continue to monitor the progress of the operation and recommend changes as required.

Updates

9-86.   Establish a routine schedule of system updates. For example, the S-2 section should continuously update the ASAS database and should transmit the latest COP to the network every 30 minutes during operations if the battalion commander, S-3, or reconnaissance elements need it. Also, staff sections should print critical displays on an established schedule. These printed snapshots of the COP can be used for continuity of battle tracking in the event of system failures, and can contribute to AARs and unit historical records.

Orders and Overlays

9-87.   SOPs should define the technical process for creating, collating, and transmitting orders and overlays, both analog and digital.

Filing System and Naming Convention

9-88.   For interoperability and clarity, BCT SOPs should define the naming convention and filing system for all reports, orders, and message traffic. This significantly reduces time and frustration associated with lost files or changes in system operators.

Databases

9-89.   C2 INFOSYS will inevitably migrate to a web-based capability, allowing information to be entered into a database and then accessed by users as needed or when they are able to retrieve it. For example, the S-2 may transmit an intelligence summary to all subordinates, and inevitably some will lose the file or not receive it. The S-2 can simultaneously post that same summary to his "homepage" so users can access it as required. If this technique is used, there are a few key things to consider—

- Posting a document to a homepage does not constitute communications. The right people must be alerted when the document is available.
- Keep documents concise and simple. Elaborate PowerPoint slide briefings will take longer to transmit, causing delays in the tactical Internet.
- The amount of information entered in a database and personnel who have access must be carefully controlled, both to maintain security and to keep from overloading the tactical Internet.
- Assign responsibility to the person(s) who is authorized to input and delete unit (both friendly and enemy) icon information.

Integration of Digital and Analog Units

9-90.   It will be several years before the majority of the Army is digitally equipped. Procedures for integrating digital and analog units are essential and should consider the following:

- FM and JNN/CPN are the primary communications mediums with the analog unit.
- Hard copy orders and graphics are required.
- Graphical control measures require a level of detail necessary to support operations of a unit without situational information. This generally requires that more control measures be tied to identifiable terrain.
- LNO teams are critical.
- The staff must recognize that integrating an analog unit into a digital unit requires retention of most of the analog control techniques. In essence, both digital and analog control systems must be in operation, with particular attention paid to keeping the analog unit apprised of all pertinent information that flows digitally.

This page intentionally left blank.

Chapter 10
Warfighting Functions

To accomplish the assigned mission, the Infantry battalion commander must integrate and synchronize his WFF as combat multipliers to enhance the combat power of his maneuver companies. This chapter describes the six WFFs: movement, maneuver (mobility and countermobility), fire support, protection, command and control, intelligence, and sustainment.

Section I. FIRE SUPPORT

FS is the collective and coordinated use of indirect fire weapons and armed aircraft in support of the battle plan. FS planning is the process of analyzing, allocating, and scheduling FS assets. FS assets include mortars, field artillery cannons and rockets, and CAS. The FS system acquires and tracks targets, delivers timely and accurate lethal fires, provides counterfire, and plans, coordinates, and orchestrates full-spectrum FS. Desired effects from FS assets can be achieved through a combination of both lethal and nonlethal (Appendix L) means. The integration of FS assets is critical to the success of the combat mission. The Infantry battalion FSO receives guidance from the commander (in coordination with the plans developed by the Infantry battalion S-3) and from higher HQ, then plans and coordinates FS assets to achieve the desired effects and support the Infantry battalion commander's concept of the operation.

INDIRECT FIRE SUPPORT SYSTEMS

10-1.   The majority of FS to an Infantry battalion is provided by indirect FS. Indirect FS systems include both field artillery cannon and rocket systems and mortars. Indirect FS systems may be under direct command of a maneuver unit or may be in a supporting role.

FIELD ARTILLERY

10-2.   Field artillery cannon systems include both 105-mm and 155-mm howitzers. Table 10-1 lists the capabilities of the field artillery cannon indirect fire systems that may support an Infantry battalion.

Table 10-1. Types and characteristics of field artillery cannon systems.

CANNON SYSTEM	M119	M198	M109A6
Caliber	105 mm	155 mm	155 mm
Maximum Range (for HE) (m)	14,000	24,000	24,000
Planning Range (m)	11,500	14,600	14,600
Minimum Range (m)	DIRECT FIRE	DIRECT FIRE	DIRECT FIRE
RATE OF FIRE			
Maximum (rpm)	6 RPM for 3 min	4 RPM for 3 min	4 RPM for 3 min
Sustained (rpm)	3	2	1
PROJECTILE			
Type	HE M760, ILLUM, HEP-T, APICM, CHEM, RAP	HE, WP, ILLUM, SMK, CHEM, NUC, RAP, FASCAM, CPHD, AP/DPICM	HE, WP, ILLUM, SMK, CHEM, NUC, RAP, FASCAM, CPHD, AP/DPICM
Fuzes	PD, VT, MTSQ, CP, MT, DLY	PD, VT, CP, MT, MTSQ, DLY	PD, VT, CP, MT, MTSQ, DLY
LEGEND			

AP..............armor piercing
APICM..............antipersonnel improved conventional munitions
chem..............chemical
CP..............concrete Piercing
CPHD..............Copperhead
DLY..............delay
DPICM..............dual purpose improved conventional munitions
FASCAM..............family of scatterable mines
HE..............high explosive
HEP-T..............high-explosive plastic-- tracer
illum..............illumination
min..............minute

MO..............multioption. VT, PD, DLY
MT..............mechanical time
MTSQ..............mechanical time super quick
NUC..............nuclear
PD..............point detonating
RAP..............rocket-assisted projectile
RD..............round
RP..............red phosphorus
RPM..............rounds per minute
SMK..............smoke
TIME..............adjustable time delay
VT..............variable time
WP..............white phosphorus

BATTALION MORTARS

10-3.   Mortars are organic to Infantry battalions. The battalion mortar platoon provides the most responsive indirect fire available to the battalion. These assets provide the commander with close and immediate responsive fires in support of the maneuver companies. These fires harass, suppress, neutralize, or destroy enemy attack formations and defenses; obscure the enemy's vision; or otherwise inhibit his ability to acquire friendly targets. The three primary types of mortar fires are HE, obscuration, and illumination (visible and IR). Mortars also can be used for FPFs and smoke. Table 10-2 lists the capabilities of mortar systems that may support an Infantry battalion.

Table 10-2. Types and characteristics of mortar systems.

| WEAPON | AMMUNITION | | RANGE (meters) | | RATE OF FIRE |
	MODEL	TYPE	MIN	MAX	
M224	M720/M888	HE	70	3,490[(1)]	30 rounds per minute for 4 minutes[(2)]; 20 rounds per minute sustained.
	M722	Smoke (WP)	70	3,490	
60 mm	M721	Illum	200	3,490	
	M767	Illum (IR)	725	931	
M252	M821A1/M889	HE	83	5,900	30 rounds per minute for 2 minutes then 15 rounds per minute sustained.
81 mm	M819	Smoke (RP)	300	4,875	
	M853A1	Illum	300	5,100	
	M816	Illum (IR)	300	5,100	
M120/M121	M57/M933/ M934	HE	200	7,200	16 rounds per minute for 1 minute, then 4 rounds per minute sustained.
120 mm	M929	Smoke (WP)	200	7,200	
	M91/M930/ M983	Illum (visible and IR)	200	7,100	
	M971	DPICM	200	7,200	
	M984	ERMC/HERA	400	6,900	
	M395	PGMM	400	7,200	

¹ Bipod mounted, charge 4 (maximum range handheld is 1340 meters.)
² Charge 2 and over. 30 rounds per minute can be sustained with charge 0 or 1.

FIRE SUPPORT PLANNING AND COORDINATION

10-4.   FS planning is accomplished concurrently with maneuver planning at all levels. Infantry battalions typically use top-down FS planning, with bottom-up refinement of the plans. The commander develops guidance for FS in terms of tasks, purposes, and effects. In turn, the battalion FSO, in conjunction with the S-3, determines the method to be used in accomplishing each task. Individual units then incorporate assigned tasks into their FS plans. In addition, units tasked to initiate fires must refine and rehearse their assigned tasks. The commander refines the battalion FS plan, ensuring that the designated targets will achieve the intended purpose. He also conducts rehearsals to prepare for the mission and, as specified in the plan, directs subordinate units to execute their assigned targets.

BATTALION COMMANDER'S AND STAFF'S ROLE IN FIRE SUPPORT PLANNING

10-5.   The key role of the battalion commander in FS planning is to ensure the synchronization of fires with maneuver. Fires and maneuver must be thought of concurrently; therefore, the commander must—

- Decide precisely what he wants FS to accomplish.
- Take an active role in the development of the battalion's EFSTs.
- Clearly articulate to his staff, not just his FSO, the sequenced EFSTs in terms of desired effects for each target and the purpose of each target as it relates to the scheme of maneuver.
- Ensure the FSO understands his FS guidance. The guidance does not have to be any different from the guidance he gives to his subordinate maneuver commanders.
- Give doctrinally stated effects and purposes. An effect for FS describes a targeting effect against a specific enemy formation's function or capability. The purpose describes how this

effect contributes to accomplishing the mission within the intent. The FSO, along with the S-3, develops the method to achieve the desired effects and the purpose for each target.

- Ensure that FS missions are clearly synchronized with the scheme of maneuver and that movement of FS assets is synchronized with maneuver movements.

BATTALION FIRE SUPPORT OFFICER'S ROLE IN FIRE SUPPORT PLANNING

10-6.   The battalion FSO plans, coordinates, and executes FS for the maneuver commander's concept of the operation. He is the fire support coordinator for the maneuver battalion. He must—

- Advise the commander and his staff on FS matters. This includes, among other things, making recommendations for integrating field artillery assets and maneuver battalion mortars into the scheme of maneuver. He also recommends their movement within the scheme of maneuver.
- Recommend to the maneuver battalion commander how to best employ and control FIST.
- Supervise all functions of the battalion FSC.
- Ensure all FS personnel are properly trained.
- Participate in brigade and battalion combined-arms and FS rehearsals.
- Prepare and disseminate the FS execution matrix or the FS plan.
- Coordinate with the tactical air control party on CAS missions and for terminal control personnel.
- Assist in the coordination for positioning or movement of lethal and nonlethal assets in the battalion AO.
- Establish and maintain communications with supporting artillery units.
- Process requests for more FS with the brigade FSE and CAS with the TACP.
- Disseminate the approved target list and matrix to subordinate elements.
- Recommend appropriate changes in the target list and attack guidance when required.
- Determine, recommend, and process time-sensitive high payoff targets to the brigade FSE.
- Coordinate with the battalion S-2 and S-3 for target acquisition coverage and processing of battalion high payoff targets. Plan and supervise the execution of assigned and developed EFSTs.
- Participate in the targeting meeting to update targets, HPTs, priorities, and asset allocation.

ESSENTIAL FIRE SUPPORT TASK PLANNING

10-7.   An EFST is a task that a FSE must accomplish in order to support a combined-arms operation. Failure to achieve an EFST may require the commander to alter his tactical or operational plan. A fully developed EFST has a task, purpose, method, and effects (TPME). The task describes what targeting objective fires, such as delay, disrupt, limit, or destroy, must achieve on an enemy formation's function or capability. The purpose describes why the task contributes to maneuver. The method describes how the task will be accomplished by assigning responsibility to observers or units and delivery assets and providing amplifying information or restrictions. Typically, the method is described by covering three categories: priority, allocation, and restrictions. Effects quantify successful accomplishment of the task.

LINKING FIRE SUPPORT TASKS AND MANEUVER PURPOSE

10-8.   A clearly defined maneuver purpose enables the maneuver commander to articulate how he wants FS to affect the enemy during different phases of the battle. In turn, this allows FS planners to develop a FS plan that effectively supports the intended purpose. They can determine each required task (in terms of effects on target), the best method for accomplishing each task (in terms of a FS asset and its fire capabilities), and a means of quantifying accomplishment. A carefully developed method of fire is equally valuable during execution of the FS mission; it assists not only the firing elements but also the observers who are responsible for monitoring the effects of the indirect fires. With a clear understanding of the intended target effects, FS assets and observers can work together effectively, planning and adjusting the fires as necessary to achieve the desired effects on the enemy. The following paragraphs describe several types of targeting objectives associated with FS tasks and provide examples of how the battalion commander might link a target task to a specific maneuver purpose in his order.

Delay

10-9.   The friendly force uses indirect fires to cause a particular function or action to occur later than the enemy desires. For example, the commander might direct delaying fires in this manner: "Delay the repositioning of the enemy's antitank reserve, allowing Company B to consolidate on Objective Bob."

Disrupt

10-10.   Disrupting fires are employed to break apart the enemy's formation, to interrupt or delay his tempo and operational timetable, to cause premature commitment of his forces, or otherwise to force him to stage his attack piecemeal; for example, "Disrupt the easternmost first-echelon Infantry battalion to prevent the enemy from massing two Infantry battalions against Company C and Company A."

Limit

10-11.   Indirect fires are used to prevent an action or function from being executed where the enemy wants it to occur; for example, "Limit the ability of the enemy's advance guard to establish a firing line on the ridge line to the flank of the battalion axis of advance to prevent the enemy from fixing the battalion main body."

Divert

10-12.   Diverting fires are employed to cause the enemy to modify his course or route of attack; for example, "Divert the enemy's combined-arms reserve counterattack to EA Dog to facilitate its destruction by Company B."

Screen

10-13.   Screening fires entail the use of smoke to mask friendly installations, positions, or maneuver. They are normally conducted for a specified event or a specified period; for example, "Screen the movement of the counterattack force (Company B) along Route Red to attack by fire (ABF) position 21 to prevent the remnants of the enemy Infantry battalion from engaging the team."

Obscure

10-14.   Smoke is placed between enemy forces and friendly forces or directly on enemy positions, with the purpose of confusing and disorienting the enemy's direct fire gunners and artillery FOs. Obscuration fires are normally conducted for a specified event or a specified period; for example, "Obscure the northernmost Infantry company to protect our breach force until the breach site is secured." Or, "Obscure observation from the East through the Al Hab intersection to protect the movement of the weapons company."

Note. The supported commander may also designate purposes for special munitions such as area denial artillery munitions, remote antiarmor mine, Copperhead, or illumination rounds.

FIRE SUPPORT AND MDMP

10-15.   The MDMP is an adaptation of the Army's analytical approach to problem-solving and is a tool that assists the commander and staff in developing a plan. FM 5-0 details the steps of the MDMP. As a member of the battalion staff, the FSO plays a crucial role in the MDMP both as the staff FS expert and as a member of the targeting team. The MDMP process, Table 10-3, describes the sequence of inputs, actions, and outputs of FS planning. At the battalion level, there is seldom time to conduct a formal MDMP process. In most cases, the battalion commander and his staff use an abbreviated or accelerated decision-making process.

Table 10-3. Fire support planning process.

MDMP Step	Inputs	Actions	Outputs
Receipt of Mission and Mission Analysis	• Higher HQ WARNO or OPORD. • Facts from higher, lower, and adjacent FSEs. • IPB products. • Enemy COA from S-2. • High-value targets (HVTs) by phase or critical event. • Facts from FS assets.	• Understand higher maneuver and FS plan. • Organize and analyze facts. • Identify specified and implied tasks. • Translate status of FS assets into capabilities. • Analyze effects of IPB on FS. — Identify FS related CCIR. — Identify FS constraints/ restrictions. • Obtain Commander's initial targeting guidance. • Develop draft EFSTs.	• Initial WARNO, on mission receipt. • Fire support portion of mission analysis brief. • Recommended EFSTs. • Commander approval or modification of initial EFSTs. • Other FS guidance. • WARNO after mission analysis brief.
COA Development	• Outputs from previous step.	• Determine EFSTs for each COA. • Determine where to find and attack EFST formations. • Identify HPTs in those formations. • Quantify the effects for EFSTs. • Plan methods for EFSTs. • Allocate assets to acquire. • Allocate assets to attack. • Integrate triggers with maneuver COA. • Use battle calculus. • Assist S-2 in R&S development to support FS. • Prepare FS portion of COA/ sketch.	• For each COA developed: (1) Concept of fires. (2) Draft FSEM. (3) Draft target list/overlay. (4) Draft targeting synchronization matrix (TSM) or modified TSM. (5) R&S plan.
COA Analysis and COA Comparison	• Outputs from previous step.	**Targeting decisions:** • Finalize HPTL. • War-game FS plan(s) versus enemy COAs. • Modify or refine inputs as required. • Refine and test FS plan.	**Final Drafts:** • FS paragraph. • FS Annex: (1) FSEM. (2) TGT list. (3) TGT overlay. (4) TSM or modified TSM (HPTL, AGM, TSS).
COA Approval and Orders Production Staff Supervision	• Outputs from previous step.	• Brief approval. • (FS) Brief plan as part of each COA. • (FSO) present analysis as part of staff.	• (Commander) selection, modification, or approval of COA. • (FSO) Issuance of WARNO as required. • Finalized FS products. • Issuance of OPORD as part of staff. • Conduct of FS backbrief. • Management of refinement. • Rehearsal.

MORTARS IN BATTALION CLOSE FIGHT

10-16.   On the battlefield, mortars act as both a killer of enemy forces and as an enhancer of friendly mobility. Mortar fires inhibit enemy fire and movements and allow friendly forces to maneuver to a position of tactical advantage. Effective integration of mortar fires with the overall FS plan and with maneuver units is critical to successful combat. Listed below are some of the key capabilities of mortar units.

- Mortar units are organic to Infantry battalions and Infantry companies that make them always available and responsive; regardless of whether or not the battalion has allocated supporting artillery. Organic mortar fires do not have to be externally cleared when firing missions in side the battalion AO.
- Mortars provide obscuration and suppression to protect the battalion during the attack or to support it while breaking contact with the enemy in the defense or movement to contact.
- Mortars provide the commander with responsive fires to support the scout platoon's infiltration and exfiltration and the counter reconnaissance force during security operations.
- The maneuver commander can continue to use mortars for indirect FS in one part of the battle and divert field artillery fires to assist in the critical fight elsewhere.
- Mortars contribute to the battalion's direct fire fight by forcing the enemy to button up, by obscuring his ability to employ supporting fires, and by separating his dismounted Infantry from its APCs and accompanying tanks.
- Heavy mortars can penetrate buildings and destroy enemy field fortifications, preparing the way for the dismounted assault force. Precision guided mortar munitions can destroy selected high payoff targets.
- Mortars provide battalion and company commanders with the ability to cover friendly obstacles with indirect fire, regardless of the increasing calls for artillery fire against deep targets or elsewhere on the battlefield. Mortar fires combine with the FPF of company machine guns to repulse the enemy's dismounted assault. It also frees artillery to attack and destroy follow-on echelons, which are forced to slow down and deploy as the ground assault is committed. Mortars can use the protection of defilade to continue indirect fires and effects even when subjected to intense counterfire.
- Commanders and FSOs should review shell-fuse combinations to ensure they best meet intent.

ECHELONMENT OF FIRES

10-17.   Understanding echelonment of fires is critical for the indirect fire plan to be effectively synchronized with the maneuver plan. The purpose of echeloning fires is to maintain constant and overlapping fires on an objective while using the optimum delivery system up to the point of its risk estimate distance (RED) in combat operations or minimum safe distance (MSD) in training. Echeloning fires provides protection for friendly forces as they move to and assault an objective, which allows them to get in close with minimal casualties. It prevents the enemy from observing and engaging the assault by forcing the enemy to take cover, which allows the friendly force to continue the advance unimpeded.

10-18.   The concept behind echeloning fires is to begin attacking targets on or around the objective using the weapons system with the largest RED. As the maneuver unit closes the distance en route to the objective, the fires cease (or shift). This triggers the engagement of the targets by the delivery system with the next largest RED. The length of time to engage the targets is based on the rate of the friendly force's movement between the RED trigger lines. The process continues until the system with the smallest RED ceases or shifts fires and the maneuver unit is close enough to eliminate the enemy with direct fires or make its final assault and clear the objective.

10-19.   The RED takes into account the bursting radius of particular munitions and the characteristics of the delivery system and associates this combination with a percentage for the probability of incapacitation of Soldiers at a given range. The munitions delivery systems include mortars, field artillery, helicopter, and fixed wing aircraft. The RED is defined as the minimum distance friendly troops can approach the effects of friendly fires without suffering appreciable casualties of 0.1 percent or higher probability of incapacitation. Commanders may maneuver their units within the RED area based on the mission; however, in doing so, they are making a deliberate decision to accept the additional risk to friendly forces. Before the commander accepts this risk, he should try to mitigate the probability of incapacitation. For example, maneuvering units in a defilade that provides some protection from the effects of exploding munitions.

```
┌─────────────────────────────────────────────────────────────┐
│                                                               │
│                         WARNING                               │
│                                                               │
│   Risk estimate distances are for combat use and do not represent │
│   the maximum fragmentation envelopes of the weapons listed.  │
│   Risk estimate distances are not minimum safe distances for  │
│   peacetime training use.                                     │
│                                                               │
└─────────────────────────────────────────────────────────────┘
```

10-20.   The casualty criterion is the 5-minute assault criterion for a prone Soldier in winter clothing and helmet. Physical incapacitation means that a Soldier is physically unable to function in an assault within a 5-minute period after an attack. A probability of incapacitation value of less than 0.1 percent can be interpreted as being less than or equal to one chance in one thousand (Table 10-4).

Table 10-4. Risk estimate distances for mortars and cannon artillery.

System	Description	Risk Estimate Distances (Meters)					
		10.0 Percent Probability of Incapacitation			0.1 Percent Probability of Incapacitation		
		1/3 range	2/3 range	Max range	1/3 range	2/3 range	Max range
M224	60 mm mortar	60	65	65	100	150	175
M252	81 mm mortar	75	80	80	165	185	230
M120/121	120 mm mortar	100	100	100	150	300	400
M102/M119	105 mm howitzer	85	85	90	175	200	275
M109/M198	155 mm howitzer	100	100	125	200	280	450
	155 mm DPICM	150	180	200	280	300	475

10-21.   Using echelonment of fires within the specified RED for a delivery system requires the unit to assume some risks. The maneuver commander determines, by delivery system, how close he will allow fires to fall in proximity to his forces. The maneuver commander makes the decision for this risk level, but he relies heavily on the FSO's expertise. While this planning is normally accomplished at the battalion level, the Company FSO has input and should be familiar with the process because he must execute the same process with the company mortars.

EXECUTION CONSIDERATIONS

10-22.   When the lead elements of the battalion task force approach the designated phase line en route to the objective, the FSO begins the preparation. Lead element observers and or company team FSOs track movement rates and confirm them for the battalion task force FSO. The battalion task force FSO may need to adjust the plan during execution based on unforeseen changes to anticipated movement rates (Figure 10-1 through Figure 10-5 (pages 10-10 through 10-14).

10-23.   As the unit continues its movement toward the objective, the first delivery system engages its targets. It maintains fires on the targets until the unit crosses the next phase line that corresponds to the RED of the weapon.

10-24.   To maintain constant fires on the targets, the unit starts the next asset before the previous asset ceases or shifts. This ensures no break in fires, enabling the friendly forces' approach to continue unimpeded. However, if the unit rate of march changes, the fire support system must remain flexible to the changes.

10-25.   The FSO shifts and engages with each asset at the prescribed triggers, initiating the fires from the system with the largest RED to the smallest. Once the maneuver element reaches the final phase line to cease all fires on the objective; the FSO shifts to targets beyond the objective.

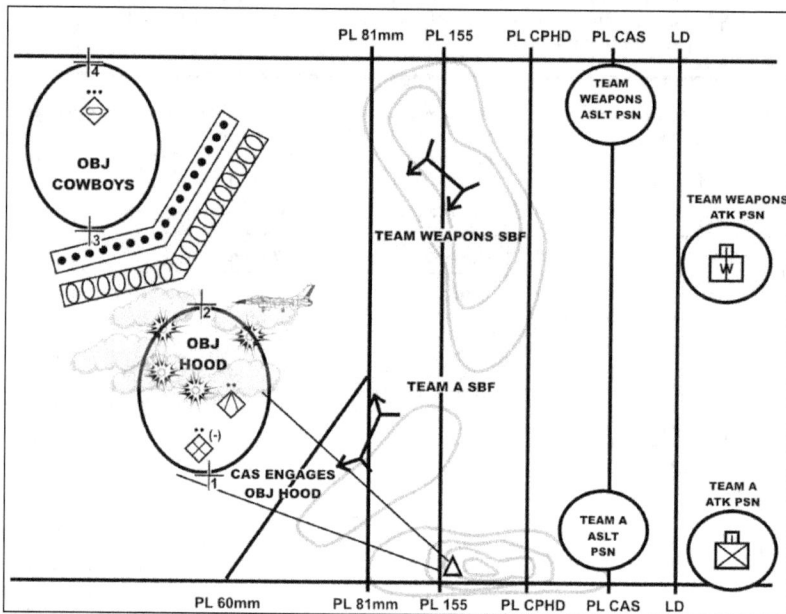

Figure 10-1. Beginning of close air support.

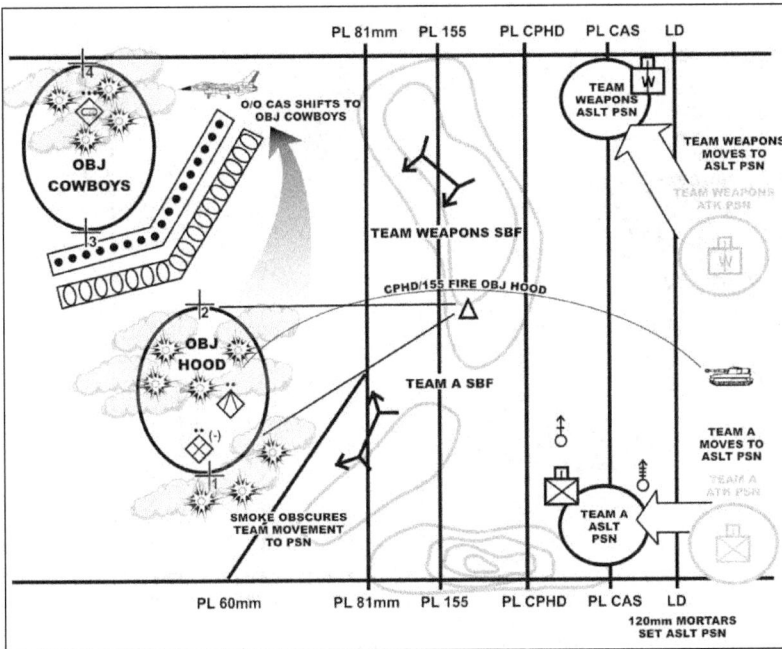

Figure 10-2. Execution of 155-mm shaping fires; shifting of close air support.

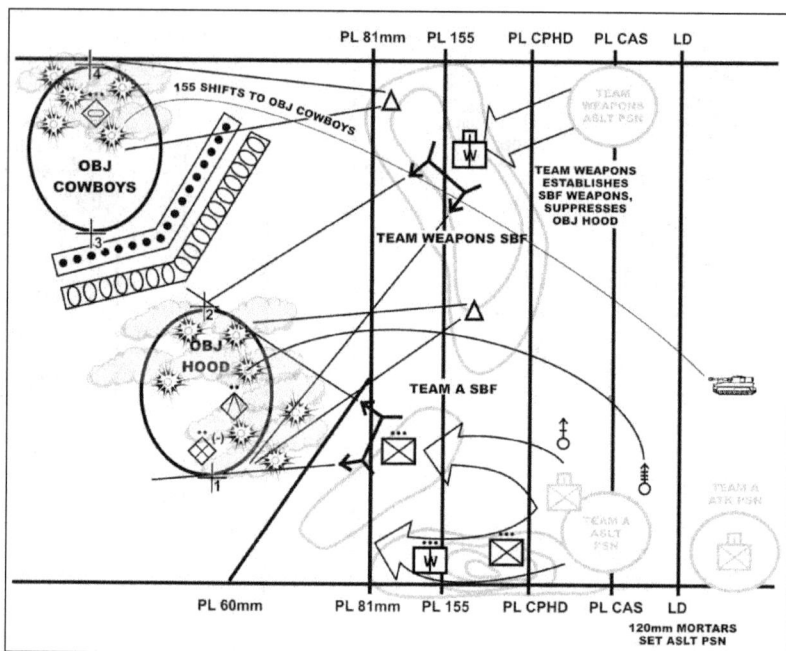

Figure 10-3. Beginning of 81-mm and supporting fires; shifting of 155-mm fires.

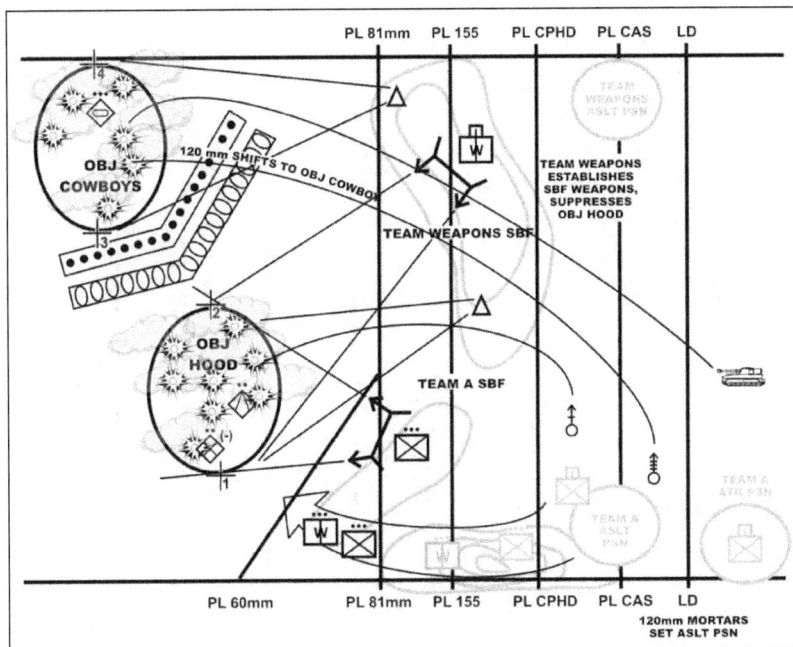

Figure 10-4. Beginning of 60-mm fires; shifting of 81-mm fires.

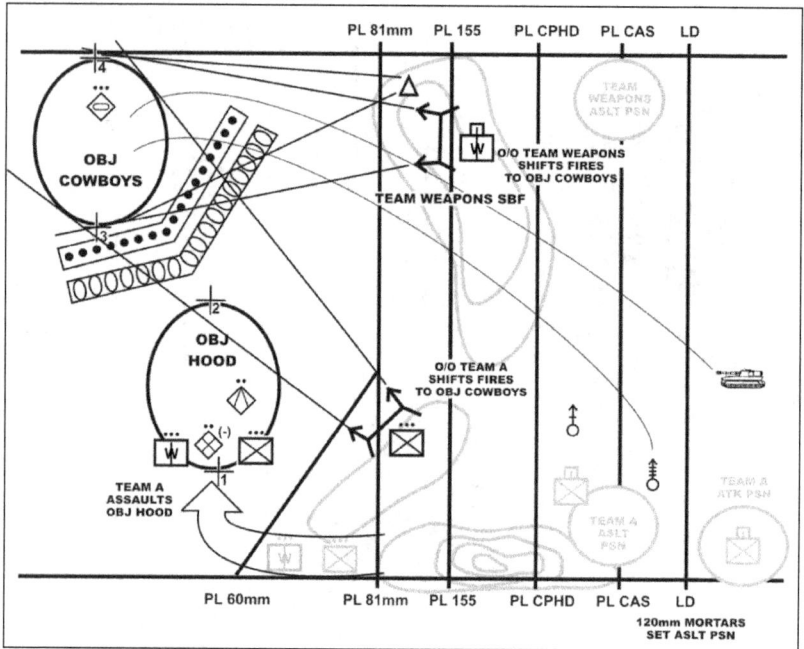

Figure 10-5. Cessation of 60-mm fires; shifting of supporting fires.

AIR SUPPORT

10-26.   Infantry battalions are generally allocated CAS sorties only. CAS is defined as air strikes on hostile surface forces that are in close proximity to friendly forces. CAS can be employed to blunt an enemy attack; to support the momentum of the ground attack; to help set conditions for battalion and BCT operations as part of the overall counterfire fight; to disrupt, delay and destroy enemy second echelon forces and reserves; and to provide cover for friendly movements. For best results while avoiding mutual interference or fratricide, aircraft are kept under "detailed integration" (part of the Air Force's combat air system). The effectiveness of CAS is directly related to the degree of local air superiority attained. Until air superiority is achieved, competing demands between CAS and counterair operations may limit sorties apportioned for the CAS role. CAS is the primary support given to committed battalions and BCTs by Air Force, Navy, and Marine aircraft. BCTs/battalions can request air reconnaissance and battlefield air interdiction missions through the next higher headquarters, but these missions are normally planned and executed at that higher unit level, with the results provided to the Infantry commanders and their staff.

MISSIONS

10-27.   The BCT normally plans and controls CAS. However, this does not preclude the battalion from requesting CAS, receiving immediate CAS during an operation, or accepting execution responsibility for a planned CAS mission. CAS is another means of indirect FS available to the battalion. In planning CAS missions, the commander must understand the capabilities and limitations of close air support and synchronize CAS missions with both the battalion fire plan and scheme of maneuver. CAS capabilities and limitations (windows for use, targets, observers, airspace coordination, and so on) present some unique challenges, but the commander and staff must plan CAS with maneuver the same way they do indirect artillery and mortar fires. When executing a CAS mission, the battalion must have a plan that synchronizes CAS with maneuver and the scheme of fires.

Preplanned Close Air Support

10-28.   Battalion planners must forward CAS requests as soon as they can be forecasted. These requests for CAS do not normally include detailed timing information because of the lead-time involved. Preplanned CAS requests involve any information about planned schemes of maneuver, even general information, which can be used in the apportionment, allocation, and distribution cycle. Estimates of weapons effects needed by percentage, such as 60 percent antiarmor and 40 percent antipersonnel; sortie time flows; peak need times; and anticipated distribution patterns. All are vital to preparing the air tasking order. ALOs and S-3s at all planning echelons must ensure that this information is forwarded through higher echelons IAW the air tasking order (ATO) cycle.

Categories

10-29.   Preplanned CAS may be categorized as either scheduled or alert missions.

- A scheduled mission is a CAS strike on a planned target at a planned time.
- An alert mission is a CAS strike on a planned target or target area executed when requested by the supported unit. Usually, this mission is launched from a ground alert (scramble), but it may be flown from an airborne alert status. Alert (on-call) CAS allows the ground commander to designate a general target area within which targets may need to be attacked. The ground commander designates a conditional period within which he later determines specific times for attacking the targets.

Request Channels

10-30.   There are specific request channels for preplanned CAS. Requests for preplanned tactical air support missions are submitted to the FSE. The commander, ALO, and S-3 at each echelon evaluate the request; coordinate requirements such as airspace, fires, and intelligence; consolidate; and, if approved, assign a priority or precedence to the request. The S-3 Air then forwards approved requests to the next higher echelon. To plan CAS, the S-3 Air must work closely with the S-3, FSO, and ALO.

Engagement Alternatives

10-31.   CAS aircraft assigned to attack preplanned targets may be diverted to higher priority targets; therefore, the FSO should plan options for the engagement of CAS targets by other FS assets.

Immediate Close Air Support

10-32.   Immediate requests are used for air support mission requirements identified too late to be included in the current air tasking order. Those requests initiated below battalion level are forwarded to the battalion command post by the most rapid means available.

10-33.   At battalion level, the commander, FSO, ALO, and S-3 consider each request. Approved immediate CAS requests are transmitted by the TACP over the Air Force air request net (Figure 10-6) directly to the air support operations center (ASOC) collocated with the corps or separate division TOC.

10-34.   The TACP at each intermediate headquarters monitors and acknowledges receipt of the request. Silence by an intermediate TACP indicates approval by the associated headquarters unless disapproval is transmitted.

10-35.   The ASOC coordinates with the G-3 Air at echelons above the BCT for all air support requests initiated by that unit. Meanwhile, intermediate TACPs pass the request to the associated headquarters G-3 or S-3 for action and coordination.

10-36.   All echelons coordinate simultaneously. If any Army echelon above the initiating level disapproves a request or substitutes another support means, such as Army aviation, or field artillery, the TACP at that headquarters notifies the ASOC at the coordinating unit and the originating TACP, which notifies the requester.

10-37.   When the coordinating unit commander or his representative approves the request, the ASOC initiates the necessary action to satisfy the request. If all distributed sorties are committed, the coordinating unit commander can request additional sorties from the next higher echelon, when appropriate. If the ASOC has no CAS missions available, it can, with Army concurrence, divert sorties from lower priority targets or request support from lateral or higher commands.

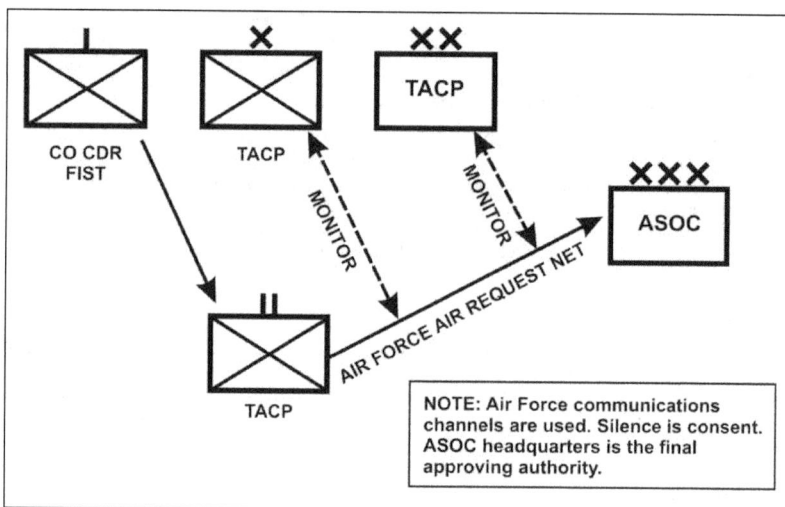

Figure 10-6. Immediate close air request channels.

PLANNING CONSIDERATIONS

10-38.   CAS mission success directly relates to thorough mission planning based on the following factors and considerations. The S-3 Air is responsible for working with the battalion ALO/ETAC before and during tactical air (TACAIR) operations. Since there are no digital links with supporting aircraft, he must consistently keep the ALO apprised of the ground tactical situation through digital and conventional means.

10-39.   When operating in the battalion's AO, CAS aircraft are under the positive control of one of the battalion's TACP forward air controllers (FACs). FACs monitor the ground tactical situation, review the COP, and monitor conventional voice radio nets of the supported ground or maneuver commander to prevent fratricidal air-to-ground or ground-to-air engagements.

10-40.   Other planning factors include time available for planning, C2 procedures, communications, and terrain.

AIR FORCE SUPPORT

10-41.   Air Force units are attached to the battalion to plan, control, and direct close air support. The TALO and the TACP are the typical air force assets attached to the battalion.

Air Liaison Officer

10-42.   TALOs are provided to Army maneuver units down to battalion. The ALO is responsible for supervising the tactical air control party and coordinating close air support with the FSE and S-3 Air. The ALO is the senior USAF representative for the TACP supporting the battalion. The ALO/ETAC is normally located with the command group during tactical operations.

Tactical Air Control Party

10-43.   TACPs are provided to Army maneuver unit headquarters down to and including the battalion level. TACPs provide direct interaction with the supported maneuver units and should be highly visible to Army commanders and readily available to assist in the integration and synchronization of air power with land-force fire and maneuver.

10-44.   The supported unit's ALO is the commander of the TACP. TACPs, at higher echelons through the BCT level, function primarily in an advisory role. These sections provide Air Force operational expertise for the support of conventional Army planning and operations. They are the point of contact to coordinate local air defense and airspace management activities. Their function is to specifically assist Army planners in the preparation of the Army's plan to integrate CAS into the overall scheme of fires and maneuver. They coordinate preplanned and immediate air requests and assist in coordinating air support missions with appropriate Army airspace command and control elements. Battalion TACPs have the added responsibility of terminal attack control.

10-45.   TACPs coordinate activities through an Air Force air request net and the advanced airlift notification net. The TACP performs the following functions:

- Serves as the Air Force commander's representative
- Advises battalion commander and staff on capabilities, limitations, and employment of air support, airlift, and reconnaissance.
- Coordinates with respective FSE and A2C2 cells.
- Helps synchronize air and surface fires.
- Helps prepare the air support plan
- Coordinates local air defense and airspace management activities.
- Integrates into the staff for air support planning for future operations.
- Advises on the joint suppression of enemy air defenses (JSEAD).
- Provides appropriate final attack control for CAS and operates the Air Force air request net.

Levels

10-46.   TACPs are generally manned at the following levels:

Two levels above the BCT

10-47.   One ALO, four fighter liaison officers (FLOs), two theater airlift liaison officers (TALOs), and six forward air controllers (FACs).

One level above the BCT

10-48.   One ALO, three FLOs, three TALOs, and six FACs.

BCT

    10-49.   One ALO, one FLO, and four FACs.

Battalion

    10-50.   One ALO and two FACs.

CLOSE AIR SUPPORT PLANNING DUTIES AND RESPONSIBILITIES

    10-51.   The ALO and members of the battalion TACP provide the necessary expertise for the control and application of tactical air power. The ALO serves as the primary tactical air power advisor for the battalion, while TACP FACs provide final control for CAS missions executed in the battalion's AO. Their collaborative working relationship established with the BCT and maneuver battalion provides a working knowledge of ground operations and enhances their ability to integrate TACAIR operations with ground schemes of maneuver effectively.

Forward Air Controller

    10-52.   The primary responsibility of TACP FACs includes the positive control of CAS aircraft flying missions in support of brigade operations. Using their knowledge of ground operations, they are also better able to provide the troop safety necessary to avoid fratricidal engagements. The following paragraphs discuss FAC procedures and responsibilities.

Troop Safety

    10-53.   The safety of ground forces is a major concern during day and night CAS operations. Fratricidal engagements are normally caused by the incorrect identification of friendly troops operating in an AO or a failure to mark the boundaries of the friendly unit adequately. The use of proper authentication and ground marking procedures assures that a safe separation exists between the friendly forces and the impact area of aerial delivered munitions. Proper radio procedures and markings assist the FACs and the strike aircraft in the positive identification of ground forces and their operational boundaries.

Identification of Friendly Forces

    10-54.   As digital technology continues to emerge and digital systems are fielded throughout combat units, the disposition and location of friendly units will become more accurate. These systems will provide enhancements to safety margins and help reduce the potential of fratricidal engagements during joint air attack team (JAAT) or TACAIR operations. Friendly unit locations and boundaries can be marked using flash mirrors, marker panels, and direction and distance from prominent land features or target marks. Strobe lights are very good markers at night and in overcast conditions. They can be used with blue or infrared filters and made directional using any opaque tube. Any light that can be filtered or covered and uncovered can be used for signaling aircraft or marking friendly locations.

Target Acquisition

    10-55.   Targets that are well camouflaged, small and stationary, or masked by hills or other natural terrain are difficult for fast-moving aircraft to detect. Marking rounds (rockets) fired from aerial platforms or artillery can enhance target acquisition and help ensure first-pass success.

Target Identification

    10-56.   Strike aircraft must have a precise description of the target and know the location of friendly forces in relation to terrain features that are easily visible from the air. Airborne FACs are generally assigned an AO and become intimately familiar with its geographical features as well as the unit operating within the AO.

Final Attack Heading

10-57.   Choice of the final attack heading depends upon considerations of troop safety, aircraft survivability, enemy air defense locations, and optimum weapons effects. Missiles or bombs are effective from any angle. Cannons, however, are more effective against the sides and rears of armored vehicles.

S-3 Air

10-58.   The S-3 Air plans for and requests the use of CAS and attack helicopters to support the commander's concept of the operation.

S-2

10-59.   The S-2 provides information on the avenues of approach, target array, terrain, and weather as it applies to the time and location of the JAAT operation.

Attack Helicopter Liaison Officer

10-60.   The Army aviation liaison officer (when attached)—

- Provides status of Army aviation assets available.
- Begins planning the air corridors and air BPs to support the operation.
- Coordinates with the FSO and the ADO to deconflict air corridors.
- Coordinates for the planned airspace coordination areas (ACAs).

Fire Support Officer

10-61.   The FSO—

- Determines the need, availability, and positioning of artillery and battalion mortars, commensurate with the enemy update, to support the JAAT.
- Coordinates with the aviation representative to provide call signs and frequencies to the supporting FDC.
- Helps the TACP deconflict the initial points from artillery positions and develop ACAs to support the mission.
- Determines the need for suppression of enemy air defense (SEAD).
- Plans and coordinates, in conjunction with the battalion staff, the use of nonlethal attack assets to complement the JAAT.
- Determines when and how priorities of fires shift.
- Recommends FSCMs to enhance the success of the mission.
- Establishes a quick fire channel if necessary.

Air Defense Officer

10-62.   The ADO—

- Coordinates to ensure that the AD assets know the location of air corridors, friendly locations, initial points, and ACAs.
- Ensures these assets are informed of friendly air operations and their integration into the battle.

Tactical Air Control Party

10-63.   The TACP—

- Develops contact points, initial points, and ACAs in coordination with the FSO and the ADO.
- Disseminates contact points, initial points, and ACAs to the ASOC for dissemination to the ground liaison officer and wing operations center for preflight briefing.
- Helps coordinate aircraft forward to the appropriate contact point or initial point (IP) and then hands them off to the aviation commander conducting the JAAT operation.

SUPPRESSION OF ENEMY AIR DEFENSES

10-64.   SEAD operations target all known or suspected enemy ADA sites that cannot be avoided and that are capable of engaging friendly air assets and systems, including suppressive fires. The FSE integrates SEAD fires into an overall fire plan that focuses fires according to the commander's guidance. Synchronization of SEAD fires with the maneuver plan is accomplished using procedural control (an H-hour sequence), positive control (initiating fires on each target as the lead aircraft passes a predetermined reference point or trigger), or a combination of the two. Regardless of the technique, the FSO planning the SEAD must conduct detailed planning and close coordination with the ALO, liaison officer (LNO), S-3 Air, S-2, ADO, FA battalion S-3/FDO, and FSE.

WEATHER

10-65.   Weather is one of the most important considerations when visually employing aerial-delivered weapons. Weather can hinder target acquisition and identification, degrade weapon accuracy and effectiveness, or negate employment of specific aerial munitions types. The S-3 Air can request IMETS data from the division G-2. This will give him highly predictive and descriptive weather information for specific times and locations in the battalion's AO. This data improves his ability to determine when close air support can be used. IMETS provides weather data based on inputs from the air weather services and meteorological sensors. This system is currently located at echelons above the BCT. It predicts weather effects on a specific mission, desired AO, or particular system. IMETS also provides weather hazards for different elevations, surface temperatures in a specific AO, and wind conditions. Meteorological satellite (METSAT) data may also be obtained to show regional cloud cover with high and low pressure systems annotated.

ARMY AVIATION

10-66.   Army aviation (rotary-wing) units perform the full spectrum of movement and maneuver, fire support, command and control, and sustainment missions. Aviation units destroy enemy forces by fire and maneuver, perform target acquisition and reconnaissance, enhance C2, and move personnel, supplies, and equipment in compliance with the overall scheme of maneuver. In support of the FS mission, aviation functions in the following roles:

- Aerial observation and calls for fire.
- Insertion of COLTs.
- Air movement of weapons systems and ammunition.
- Air reconnaissance.
- Intelligence and electronic warfare.
- Attack helicopter operations.
- Aerial mine delivery.
- Medical evacuation.
- Search and rescue.
- C2 for JAAT operations.

10-67.   Aviation has the capability to reach the battlefield quickly and move throughout the depth and breadth of the battlefield. This mobility and flexibility aid the combined-arms commander in seizing or retaining the initiative.

Section II. MOVEMENT AND MANEUVER

Engineers support the maneuver units on the battlefield through enhancements to mobility, countermobility, and protection (survivability). Mobility is the preservation of freedom of maneuver of friendly forces. Countermobility operations deny mobility to enemy forces. Survivability operations protect friendly forces from the effects of enemy weapon systems. The engineer's focus is on mobility but they also provide limited countermobility and survivability support.

MISSION

10-68.   The engineer company's primary mission is to provide focused mobility to the BCT and its battalions. The company provides combat engineering support during offensive, defensive, stability operations, and civil support operations. They also provide limited countermobility, survivability, and sustainment engineering capabilities to the battalion.

ORGANIZATION

10-69.   Engineer units are tailored to fight as part of the combined-arms team in the IBCT. Engineer units can be task-organized with equipment augmentation from engineer battalions at echelons above the BCT to provide the necessary engineer functions to fight the battle. The IBCT normally requires augmentation from other engineer units to sustain beyond 72 hours (mission, enemy, terrain, troops, and time available dependent). An engineer company is assigned to the IBCT. Depending on the level of intensity and the duration of the mission, an IBCT may require the equivalent of an engineer battalion to sustain its operations and enhance its capabilities. Engineer leaders who can accept known risks, in pursuit of mission accomplishment in line with the higher commander's intent, intensify these capabilities.

ENGINEER COMPANY

10-70.   The IBCT engineer company is assigned and executes engineer missions that are identified by the BCT commander. Their employment depends on the BCT commander's analysis of METT-TC. The engineer company commander may receive augmentation from other engineer units. He directs his unit in the execution of mission support to the BCT. The engineer company is self-sufficient for mobility. Figure 10-7 is the TOE for the IBCT engineer company.

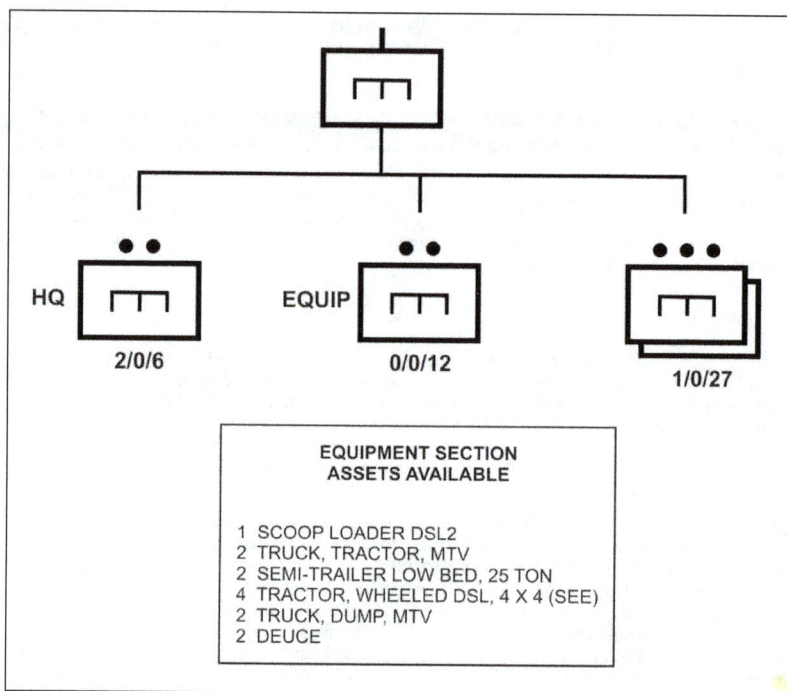

Figure 10-7. Infantry brigade combat team, engineer company.

ENGINEER PLATOON

10-71. An engineer platoon may be task organized to a battalion or company, based on the BCT commander's analyses of METT-TC. The engineer platoon can be employed to accomplish almost any engineer mission. However, the lack of organic sustainment assets and minimal depth of C2 and combat systems will likely require augmentation or external support to conduct continuous operations over a sustained period (more than 48 hrs). They may also require some augmentation to conduct combined-arms tasks such as breaching operations. The engineer platoon may receive augmentation from its engineer company or other units as required.

PLANNING CONSIDERATIONS

10-72. The maneuver battalion staff plans, integrates, and synchronizes movement and maneuver (mobility and countermobility), and protection (survivability) throughout the maneuver battalion's AO. If task-organized with engineers, the maneuver battalion engineer coordinates all military and civilian engineer efforts for the maneuver battalion. Engineering tasks include those missions that help establish and maintain infrastructure that is required to conduct and sustain military operations. Such tasks include construction and repair of lines of communication, main supply routes, airfields, utilities, and logistical facilities. FM 5-104 is the primary reference for general engineering planning. Details on staff engineer responsibilities can be found in FM 3-34.

ESSENTIAL MOBILITY AND SURVIVABILITY TASKS

10-73.   An EMST is a specified or implied WFF-specific task that is critical to mission success. Identifying the essential tasks helps to focus the development of plans, staff coordination, and allocation of resources. The staff, typically the maneuver support elements (engineer and chemical staff officers), identifies the EMSTs. Failure to achieve an EMST may require the commander to alter his tactical or operational plan.

10-74.   A fully developed EMST has a task, purpose, method, and effects. The task describes what objective (number of lanes, MSR capability, bridging capability, block, turn, fix, and disrupt, protection levels, and minimum number of survivability positions) must be achieved to support friendly formations or what it will do to an enemy formation's function or capability. The purpose describes why the task contributes to maneuver. The method describes how the task will be accomplished by assigning responsibility to maneuver units, supporting units, or delivery assets, and providing amplifying information or restrictions. The effects are a way to try to quantify the successful accomplishment of the task (lanes open, obstacles/bridging in place and MSR open).

10-75.   The approved EMSTs are described in the concept of operations in the base order. The concept of operations includes the logical sequence of EMSTs that, when integrated with the scheme of maneuver will accomplish the mission and achieve the commander's intent. The scheme of engineer operations, also in the base order, describes the detailed, logical sequence of mobility, countermobility, and survivability operations, general engineer tasks, decontamination, smoke, and force protection tasks and their impact on friendly and enemy units. It details how engineers expect to execute the mobility, countermobility, and survivability plan IAW the time and space of the battlefield to accomplish the commander's essential mobility, countermobility, and survivability tasks.

MOBILITY

10-76.   At the tactical level, superior mobility is critical to the success of the force. Mobility facilitates the momentum of forces by reducing or negating the effects of existing or reinforcing obstacles. Within this context, the emphasis of engineer integration is on mobility operations. The commander, staff, and engineers plan, organize, and prepare to perform mobility tasks using the full range of organic and augmentation mobility assets. These mobility tasks include combined-arms route clearance, combined-arms breaching, and maintaining area mobility.

Route Clearance

10-77.   Route clearance is a combined-arms operation typically executed by a maneuver company or maneuver battalion. Engineers reduce or clear obstacles as part of a route-clearance mission. Units must clear LOCs of obstacles and enemy activity that disrupt AO circulation. Units must conduct route clearance to ensure that LOCs enable safe passage of combat, fire support, protection, and sustainment organizations. Clearance operations are normally conducted in a low-threat environment. The significant difference between breaching and clearing operations is that breaching usually occurs during an attack (while under enemy fire) to project combat power to the far side of an obstacle. Route clearance focuses on opening LOCs to ensure the safe passage of combat and support organizations within an AO. Details on route clearance are covered in FM 3-34.2.

Combined Arms Breaches

10-78.   Engineers reduce lanes in obstacles as part of a combined-arms breaching operation. Because of the potentially asymmetrical, nonlinear nature of operations, engineers must be prepared to perform reduction tasks using manual, mechanical, and explosive reduction means. Through reverse breach planning, the staff identifies critical mobility tasks, allocates reduction assets, and determines the breach organization (support, assault, and breach force). Keys to allocating reduction assets include identifying all reduction tasks within the zone or axis, matching specific reduction assets to each task, and planning

50-percent redundancy in reduction assets for each task. For more specific information on combined-arms breaching, see FM 3-34.2.

Area Mobility

10-79.   Generating and sustaining combat power requires the maneuver battalion to maintain area mobility. Area mobility operations include clearing unexploded ordinance, clearing residual minefields, tracking dirty battlefield effects, and MSR repair and maintenance. Limited organic assets necessitate augmentation to preserve area mobility. The maneuver battalion staff identifies shortfalls in capability and coordinates with the BCT to request additional assets.

COUNTERMOBILITY

10-80.   Countermobility is the augmentation of natural or manmade terrain with obstacle systems integrated with direct and or indirect fire systems to disrupt, fix, turn, or block the enemy while the maneuver commander destroys the enemy's combat capabilities with increased time for target acquisition. The commander and staff integrate obstacles within the maneuver plan, enforcing adherence to obstacle emplacement authority and obstacle control measures. Task-organized engineers construct limited conventional minefields, ground emplaced SCATMINEs, special munitions, and explosive and nonexplosive obstacles in support of the scheme of maneuver. FM 3-34 is the primary reference for countermobility planning.

SURVIVABILITY

10-81.   Survivability encompasses the development and construction of protective positions such as earth berms, dug-in positions, and overhead protection as a means to mitigate the effectiveness of enemy weapon systems. Significant survivability efforts will require engineer augmentation. The staff must plan and prioritize survivability efforts. The plan should specify the level of survivability for each battle position and the sequence in which they receive support (if available). The plan should also specify the type and quantity of needed Class IV, where and when to deliver it. Additional considerations for survivability planning include command and control of digging assets, site security (including air defense coverage), sustainment (fuel, maintenance, and Class I), and movement times between battle positions. FM 5-103 is the primary reference for survivability planning.

SCATTERABLE MINES

10-82.   SCATMINEs are remotely delivered or dispensed by aircraft, artillery, missile, or ground dispensers and laid without pattern. All US SCATMINEs have a limited active life and self-destruct (SD) after that life has expired. The duration of the active life varies with the type of delivery system and mine.

10-83.   SCATMINEs provide the commander with a means to respond to a changing enemy situation with their flexibility and rapid emplacement capabilities. They enable the commander to emplace minefields rapidly in enemy-held territories, contaminated territories, and other areas where it is impossible for engineers to emplace conventional minefields. Some systems allow for rapid emplacement of minefields in friendly areas.

10-84.   During the war gaming process, the engineer, in conjunction with S-3, S-2, and FSO, identifies the requirement to respond to an enemy action with SCATMINEs. He then determines the minefield location, size, density, emplacement and SD times, delivery method, and the trigger (decision point) for execution.

CAPABILITIES

10-85.   SCATMINEs can be emplaced more rapidly than conventional mines, so they provide a commander with greater flexibility and more time to react to changes in situations. The commander can use

SCATMINEs to maintain or regain the initiative by acting faster than the enemy. Using SCATMINEs also helps preserve countermobility resources that can be used to conduct other operations on the battlefield. As with all obstacles, SCATMINES should be covered by observation and fires to be effective.

PLACEMENT

10-86.   All SCATMINEs are rapidly emplaced. This enhances battlefield agility and allows the maneuver commander to emplace mines to best exploit enemy weaknesses. SCATMINEs can be used as situational obstacles or to attack formations directly by using obstacles that disrupt, fix, turn, and block the enemy. However they are used, they must be planned and coordinated to fit into the overall obstacle plan. Modern fusing, sensing, and antihandling devices (AHDs) improve the ability of SCATMINEs to defeat enemy tries to reduce the minefield.

TACTICAL FLEXIBILITY

10-87.   Upon expiration of the SD time, the minefield is cleared by self-detonation and the commander can move through an area that was previously denied to enemy or friendly forces. In many cases, the SD period may be set at only a few hours. This feature allows for effective counterattacks to the enemy's flank and rear areas. Table 10-5 defines when certain mines begin self-destruction and when destruction is complete.

Table 10-5. Self-destruct windows.

SD Time	SD Window Begins
4 hours	3 hours 12 minutes
48 hours	38 hours 24 minutes
5 days	4 days
15 days	12 days

LETHALITY

10-88.   SCATMINEs use an explosive technique that produces a full-width kill. The effect produces a mobility kill against a vehicle's engine, track, or drive-train, or it produces a catastrophic kill by setting off the onboard ammunition, killing or incapacitating the crew, or destroying the vehicle's weapons systems. SCATMINEs are designed to destroy any tank currently available.

LIMITATIONS

10-89.   The following are limitations of SCATMINEs:

Extensive Coordination

10-90.   Because SCATMINEs are a dynamic weapon system, proper coordination with higher, adjacent, and subordinate units is extremely important. To prevent friendly casualties, all affected units must be notified of the location and the duration of SCATMINEs.

Proliferation of Targets

10-91.   SCATMINEs are regarded by some commanders as easy solutions to tactical problems. Target requests must be carefully evaluated, and a priority system must be established because indiscriminate use of weapons systems results in rapid depletion of a unit's basic load. Controlled supply rates (CSRs) are likely to be a constraint in all theaters.

Visibility

10-92.   SCATMINEs are highly effective, especially when fires and obscurants strain the enemy's C2. SCATMINEs lay on the surface of the ground, but they are relatively small and have neutral coloring.

Accuracy

10-93.   SCATMINEs cannot be laid with the same accuracy as conventionally emplaced mines. Remotely delivered SCATMINE systems are as accurate as conventional artillery-delivered or tactical aircraft-delivered munitions.

Orientation

10-94.   Between 5 and 15 percent of SCATMINEs come to rest on their edges. Mines with spring fingers are in the lower percentile, and mines landing in mud or snow more than 10 centimeters deep are in the higher percentile of mines that come to rest on their sides. When employing ADAMs or RAAMs in more than 10 centimeters of snow or mud, use high-angle fire and increase the number of mines. Melting of the snow may also cause the mines to change positions and activate AHDs.

DELIVERY SYSTEMS

10-95.   SCATMINE delivery systems include artillery, the Volcano, the GATOR, and MOPMS.

Artillery

10-96.   A 155-mm howitzer delivers ADAMs and RAAMs. Mines are contained within a projectile and are dispensed while the projectile is in the air. The wedge-shaped ADAM is a bounding-fragmentation mine that deploys up to seven tension-activated tripwires six meters away from the mine. After ground impact, tripwires are released and the mine is fully armed. The lethal casualty radius is between 6 and 10 meters. The RAAM mine uses a self-forging fragmentation (SFF) warhead, has a magnetic-influence fuze, and has a small cylindrical shape.

Multiple-Delivery Mine System

10-97.   The multiple-delivery mine system (Volcano) can be dispensed from the air or on the ground. It can be mounted on any LMTV, a heavy expanded mobility tactical truck (HEMTT), a palletized load system (PLS) flat-rack, or a UH-60 Blackhawk helicopter. The mixture of mines is fixed and cannot be altered. All canisters are capable of dispensing mines with 4-hour, 48-hour, and 15-day SD times. The SD times are field-selectable before dispensing and do not require a change or modification to the mine canister. Reload time (not including movement time to the reload site) for an experienced four-Soldier crew is about 20 minutes. The average time to emplace one ground Volcano load (160 canisters) is 10 minutes.

Gator

10-98.   The CBU-78 Gator is an aircraft delivered weapon that contains antitank and antipersonnel mines. These mines can be detonated by target sensors (magnetic field for antitank and trip line for antipersonnel) or by a disturbance/antidisturbance device. They also have a backup self-destruct time set before aircraft launch. The Gator mine system provides a means to emplace minefields on the ground rapidly using high-speed tactical aircraft. The minefields are used for area denial, diversion of moving ground forces, or to immobilize targets to supplement other direct attack weapons.

Modular Pack Mine System

10-99.   The MOPMS is a man-portable, 162-pound, suitcase-shaped mine dispenser. The dispenser contains 21 mines (17 AT and 4 antipersonnel AP) in seven tubes with three mines located in each tube. When dispensed, an explosive propelling charge at the bottom of each tube expels mines through the container roof. Mines are propelled 35 meters from the container in a 180-degree semicircle. The safety zone around one container is 55 meters to the front and sides and 20 meters to the rear.

10-100.   Mines are dispensed on command using an M71 remote-control unit (RCU) or an electronic initiating device. Once mines are dispensed, they cannot be recovered or reused. If mines are not dispensed, the container may be disarmed and recovered for later use. The RCU can recycle the 4-hour SD time of the mines three times, for a total duration of about 13 hours. Mines with a 4-hour SD time will begin to self-destruct at 3 hours and 12 minutes. All active mines must be recycled within 3 hours of the initial launch or last recycle. This feature makes it possible to keep the minefield emplaced for longer periods if necessary. The RCU can also self-destruct mines on command, allowing a unit to counterattack or withdraw through the minefield, as necessary, rather than waiting for the SD time to expire. The RCU can control up to 15 MOPMS containers or groups of MOPMS containers from a distance of up to 1,000 meters.

10-101.   The ability to command-detonate mines or extend their SD time provides an added flexibility not currently available with other SCATMINE systems. With its unique characteristics, the MOPMS is ideally suited for the following minefield missions:

- Emplacing hasty and deliberate protective minefields.
- Emplacing nuisance minefields (on trails, crossing sites, landing zones, drop zones, and road junctions).
- Emplacing tactical disrupt and fix minefields.
- Closing gaps and lanes in existing minefields.
- Temporarily closing counterattack routes.
- Supporting ambushes.
- Reseeding minefields.

COMMAND AND CONTROL

10-102.   Due to the delivery means, C2 of SCATMINEs is more complex than with conventional mines. SCATMINEs are very dynamic weapons systems because they can be rapidly emplaced and then cleared by way of their SD capability. In addition, the physical boundary of a SCATMINE is not clearly defined. These characteristics require impeccable communications and coordination to ensure that all friendly units know where mines are located, when they will be effective, and when they will self-destruct.

Emplacement Authority

10-103.   The corps commander has emplacement authority for all SCATMINEs within the corps AO. He may delegate this authority to lower echelons according to the guidelines in Table 10-6.

Table 10-6. Emplacement authority.

System Characteristics	Emplacement Authority
Ground or artillery-delivered, with SD time greater than 48 hours (long duration).	Emplacement authority may be delegated to the BCT Commander.
Ground or artillery-delivered, with SD time 48 hours or less (short duration).	Emplacement authority may be delegated to the BCT Commander and further delegated to the battalion level.
Aircraft-delivered (Gator), regardless of SD time.	Emplacement authority may be delegated to the BCT Commander and further delegated to the battalion level.
Helicopter-delivered (Volcano), regardless of SD time.	Emplacement authority is normally delegated no lower than the commander who has command authority over the emplacing aircraft.
MOPMS when used strictly for a protective minefield.	Emplacement authority is usually granted to the company or base commander. Commanders at higher levels restrict MOPMS use only as necessary to support their operations.

10-104.   Based on how the commander wants to shape the battlefield, he must specifically delegate or withhold the authority to employ SCATMINE systems.

10-105.   Due to the complete control a commander has over the MOPMS, emplacement authority guidelines do not apply to the MOPMS. It is impractical for the corps or brigade commander to authorize every MOPMS protective minefield. Therefore, authority to emplace MOPMS minefields is specifically delegated. In general, units can emplace MOPMS protective minefields as required for their own self-defense and report them as they do any protective obstacle. Any MOPMS minefield used as part of an obstacle plan must be reported as a SCATMINE.

Coordination

10-106.   Table 10-6 outlines basic responsibilities of key commands, staff elements, and units. The FSO is involved in planning artillery-delivered (ADAM and RAAM) SCATMINEs, and the air liaison officer is involved in planning air-delivered (Gator) SCATMINEs. The engineer has primary responsibility for planning and employing SCATMINE systems. It is vital that coordination be conducted with all units and subunits that will be affected by the employment of SCATMINEs. A scatterable minefield warning (SCATMINWARN) is sent to all affected units before the emplacement of the minefield.

MARKINGS

10-107.   The maneuver unit that is responsible for the area of ground in which the minefield is emplaced is also responsible for marking the minefield. This procedure normally requires direct coordination between elements of the maneuver command (usually the engineer) and the delivering or emplacing unit. However, it is unrealistic to expect units to mark artillery-delivered ADAM and RAAM, air-delivered Volcano, or Gator minefields. For this reason, units operating near these minefields must know calculated safety zones and use extreme caution.

Safety Zones

10-108.   A safety zone is an area where a stray or outlying mine has a chance of landing and laying at rest. The commander must prevent friendly forces from maneuvering into the safety zone during the minefield's life cycle. Depending on its specific location on the battlefield, the safety zone may be marked with a fence.

Fragment Hazard Zones

10-109.   If an AT mine that is oriented on its side self-destructs, the explosively formed projectile (EFP) can theoretically travel 640 meters. Tests indicate that the acceptable risk distance is 235 meters from the outer edges of the minefield's safety zone. This fragment hazard zone is also associated with Gator and MOPMS AT mines. Commanders must be aware of the fragment hazard zone when the MOPMS is used for protective minefield missions. Use Table 10-7 to determine the safety and fragment hazard zones.

Table 10-7. Safety and fragment hazard zones.

SYSTEM	SAFETY ZONE	FRAGMENT HAZARD ZONE
ADAM/RAAM	500 to 1,500 meters from aim point(s) (depends on delivery method)	235 meters from the outside dimensions of the safety zone
Gator	925 x 475 meters from aim point(s)	1,395 x 945 meters from aim point(s)
Ground Volcano	1,150 x 160 meters	235 meters from start and stop point and the center line
Air Volcano	1,315 x 200 meters	235 meters from start and stop points and the center line
MOPMS	See FM 20-32 for specific placement	235 meters from the outside dimensions of the safety zone.

ADAMs and RAAMs Safety Zones

10-110.   The FSO is responsible for obtaining safety zones. Safety zones may be computed by the BCT field artillery battalion FDC or by the FSO using a safety zone table. An alternative method is to use a mine safety template. The engineer is responsible for disseminating the safety zones to appropriate units.

Use of Mine Safety Template

10-111.   Enter the template (Figure 10-8) with the fired minefield data—

- Technique (meteorological + velocity transfer or observer adjust).
- Trajectory (high or low angle).
- Type of projectile fired (RAAM or ADAM).
- Range (to minefield center).
- Aim point coordinates (center or left and right).

10-112.   Center the selected template safety zone square over the aim point(s). Draw a square to establish the minefield safety zone.

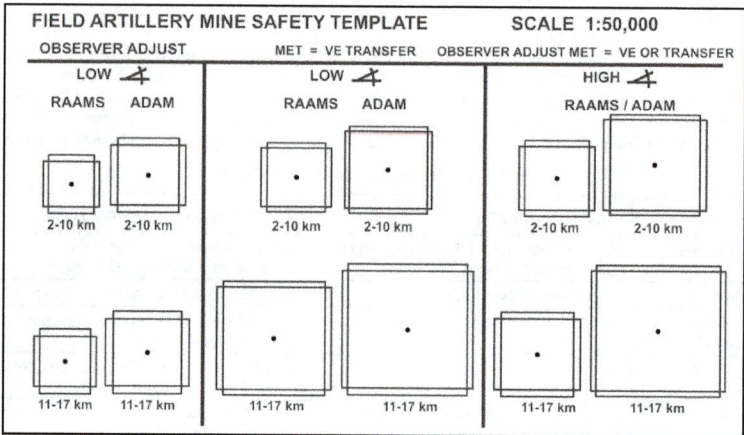

Figure 10-8. ADAMs and RAAMs minefield safety template.

Section III. PROTECTION

The objective of air defense is to limit the effectiveness of enemy offensive air efforts to a level that permits freedom of action to all friendly forces. Maneuver units who conduct close operations must be protected from the primary threat of attack helicopters, unmanned aerial systems, and high-performance aircraft. At the same time, high-priority assets in the rear must also be protected from enemy air strikes.

MISSION

10-113.   Air defense artillery protects the force and selected assets from aerial attack and surveillance. Early engagement of enemy aircraft is one of the most important SHORAD employment guidelines. The high-to-medium-altitude missile air defense (HIMAD) and joint sensors pass information to the SHORAD weapons for engagement. The primary aerial threats that must be countered by SHORAD systems are: UAS, rotary-wing aircraft, cruise missiles, fixed-wing aircraft, rocket, artillery, and mortar fires.

ORGANIZATION

10-114.   The IBCT has no organic ADA capability. ADA assets come from echelons above the BCT. ADA assets are normally deployed in the BCT AO by locating them with overlapping coverage areas. While not normally attached to the battalion, man-portable air defense (MANPAD) or Stinger teams can be deployed in Infantry battalion AOs for air defense coverage. Another ADA asset is the Avenger.

STINGER MISSILE

10-115.   The Stinger missile is usually the battalion's primary air defense weapon system. The Stinger is a short-range, heat-seeking guided missile that can be shoulder-fired. It is designed to counter the threat of advance helicopters, unmanned aerial vehicles (RPVs), high-speed maneuvering aircraft, and cruise missiles. The Stinger has a range in excess of 5 kilometers.

10-116.   The Stinger can be employed as a MANPADS. The two-Soldier Stinger team, consisting of a gunner and a crew chief, is normally transported in a HMMWV.

AVENGER

10-117.   The Avenger weapon system is a lightweight, day or night, limited adverse weather firing unit employed to counter low-altitude aerial threats. The firing unit consists of two Stinger vehicle-mounted launchers (SVMLs, located on the turret), a machine gun, a forward-looking infrared (FLIR) sight, a laser range finder (LRF), and an identification friend or foe (IFF). The gyrostabilized turret is mounted on a HMMWV. The firing unit can launch a missile or fire the machine gun on the move or from a stationary position with the gunner in the turret. It can also be remotely operated from a location up to 50 meters away. Onboard communications equipment provides for radio and intercom operations.

LAND-BASED PHALANX WEAPON SYSTEM

10-118.   The LPWS is a 20mm gun with multifrequency KU band radar for surveillance and tracking. It has a potential area defense against threat rocket, artillery, and mortars (RAM). The LPWS is an integral part of the counterrocket, artillery, and mortar (C-RAM) intercept battery. The C-RAM intercept battery, when deployed, can operate jointly with coalition forces, allies, and other services within the theater. Operationally, the C-RAM intercept battery will normally operate under a base defense operations center (BDOC) at an FOB.

PLANNING CONSIDERATIONS

10-119.   AD units may be attached to the battalion. When attached, the senior leader of the AD unit becomes the ADO for the battalion.

10-120.   AD employment guidelines are used as aids for positioning individual AD firing units. The six AD employment guidelines are—

Early Engagement

10-121.   Firing units must be positioned where they can engage enemy air platforms before the enemy can release his ordnance on or gain intelligence about friendly forces. Firing units should be located well forward and integrated into the supported battalion's scheme of maneuver. In less likely missions of defending a static asset, firing units should be positioned forward of the supported force along likely enemy air avenues of approach.

Weighted Coverage

10-122.   Once the supported force commander designates his decisive operation, stinger teams should be positioned along the most likely air avenues of approach to support the commander's scheme of maneuver. It is extremely important that detailed, in-depth air IPB is developed before deciding where to weight coverage of air defense assets.

Depth

10-123.   Depth is achieved by positioning firing units so enemy air platforms encounter a continuous volume of fire as they approach the protected force or asset. Depth is achieved by positioning assets so that they can provide continuous fires along enemy air avenues, destroying the enemy as it advances toward the protected force or asset. Depth is maximized through the integration of all air defense weapons. Additional air defense assets on the battlefield, such as other Stinger teams, Avenger firing units, HIMAD assets, and combined-arms air defense efforts from ground forces, contribute to the creation of depth on the battlefield.

Balanced Fires

10-124.   Positioning air defense weapons to distribute fire equally in all directions creates balanced fires. Except for the mission of defense of a static asset, where no clear avenues of approach are identified, this guidance is seldom employed. As an example, on a flat, open battlefield characteristic of some desert environments, no specific air corridor exists. In this situation, planning for balanced fires may be viable.

Mutual Support

10-125.   Mutual support is achieved by positioning weapons to complement fires from adjacent firing units, thus preventing the enemy from attacking one position without being subjected to fire from one or more adjacent positions. Mutual support enhances volume of fire and covers the dead space of adjacent units. The planning range for mutual support for Stinger systems is about 2,000 meters.

Overlapping Fires

10-126.   Because of the battalion's extended battlespace and a scarcity of available Stinger systems, the air defense planner should try to enhance air defense protection by positioning firing units so that engagement includes overlap. The planning range for overlapping fires for Stinger systems is about 4,000 meters.

ROLE OF AIR DEFENSE OFFICER

10-127.   When augmented with ADA assets, the unit commander or leader will serve as the battalion's air defense officer. The ADO must participate in the MDMP as an integral member of the battalion staff. The ADO should work closely with the S-2 during the IPB process. He is best suited to prepare and brief the air IPB. Airspace or the aerial dimension of the battlefield is the most dynamic and fast-paced of the three dimensions.

MISSION ANALYSIS

10-128.   The most significant threats that must be evaluated at the battalion level for aerial IPB are UAS, fixed-wing aircraft, and rotary-wing aircraft.

Air Threat Overview

10-129.   Air avenues of approach, type of air threat, probable threat objective, and potential to support the maneuver forces.

Specified, Implied, and Essential Tasks

10-130.   From the air defense perspective such as early warning.

Constraints and Restrictions

10-131.   Initial air defense warning status, weapons control status, and systems limitations.

Forces Available

10-132.   SHORAD, HIMAD, and sensor coverage.

Platoon Status

10-133.   Human resource, maintenance posture, weapons status, and missile supply.

Issues

10-134.   Coordination for related issues such as missile resupply.

ADDITIONAL RESPONSIBILITIES

- Assisting the S-3 in planning and executing the air defense portion of the operation.
- Advising the commander and S-3 on the employment of air defense assets.
- Coordinating with the S-3 air, FSO, and FAC for the appropriate air defense posture and A2C2.
- Controlling integration of air defense elements and early warning systems.
- Recommending priorities to the commander:
  - -- *Threat.* Reverse target value analysis.
  - -- *Criticality.* Force or asset that is essential to mission accomplishment.
  - -- *Vulnerability.* Susceptibility to surveillance and attack.
  - -- *Recuperability.* In terms of time and equipment.

10-135.   The ADO is also responsible for the execution of the air defense plan. He must monitor the positioning and coverage provided by his assets and other ADA assets, recommending changes to the plan based on the enemy threat and changes in the scheme of maneuver.

AIR DEFENSE TYPES

10-136.   The battalion adopts its air defense posture based on the type of supporting AD assets that are attached. The battalion always uses a combination of active and passive measures to protect itself against air attack.

PASSIVE AIR DEFENSE

10-137.   There are two types of passive air defense measures: attack avoidance and damage-limiting measures. Attack avoidance measures are used to avoid being detected by the enemy. Damage-limiting measures are those taken to avoid damage from air attack such as vehicle dispersion, camouflage, and dug-in fighting positions with overhead protection.

Attack Avoidance

10-138.   Attack avoidance involves taking the actions necessary to avoid being seen by the enemy to include concealment (the protection from observation or surveillance) and, more specifically, camouflage (the use of natural or artificial material on personnel, objects, or tactical positions with the aim of confusing, misleading, or evading the enemy). The techniques, procedures, and materials used for concealment from aerial observation are the same as those used for concealment from ground observation.

Damage-Limiting Measures

10-139.   Damage-limiting measures are an try to limit any damages if the enemy detects friendly forces. These measures are used when the troop or its platoons are located in a static position such as an assembly area or when they are maneuvering. If caught in the open, personnel should immediately execute battle drills and move to positions of cover and concealment that reduce the enemy's ability to acquire or engage them. The same measures taken to limit damage from artillery attack are used for dispersion, protective construction, and cover.

ACTIVE AIR DEFENSE

10-140.   Although passive measures are the first line of defense against air attack, troops must be prepared to engage attacking enemy aircraft. The decision to fight an air threat is based on the immediate situation and weapons system capabilities. Based on the mission, companies do not typically engage aircraft except for self-preservation or as directed by the battalion or company commander.

Crew-Served and Vehicle Weapons Systems

10-141.   Crew-served weapons and vehicle weapons systems provide a large volume and lethal means of engaging threat aircraft. When different munitions are available, use the currently loaded munitions, and then reload with the appropriate munitions to engage the aircraft.

Small Arms Used for Air Defense

10-142.   Small arms used for air defense incorporate the use of volume fire and proper aiming points according to the target. The key to success in engaging enemy air is to put out a high volume of fire. The commander must decide whether to engage and must provide the engagement command for the entire unit to fire upon the attacking aircraft rather than having Soldiers fire at the aircraft individually.

AIR DEFENSE WARNINGS AND WEAPONS CONTROL STATUS

10-143.   Battalion leaders should ensure their subordinates understand the air threat and air threat warning conditions.

10-144.   Air defense conditions are stated in the OPORD:

- *Red.* Indicates the attack is imminent.
- *Yellow.* Indicates that an attack is probable.
- *White.* Indicates that an attack is not likely.

10-145.   A local air defense warning (LADW) describes the air threat in the immediate area. LADWs are designed to alert a particular unit, several units, or an area of the battlefield of an impending air attack. AD units use LADWs to alert Army units about the state of the air threat in terms of "right here and right now." They can be used in conjunction with air defense warnings (ADWs). Examples of LADWs are described below:

- *Dynamite.* Indicates an attack is imminent or in progress.
- *Look-out.* Indicates an attack is likely.
- *Snowman.* Indicates an attack is not likely.

10-146.   Weapons control status determines the conditions for using weapons against enemy aircraft:

- *Weapons Free.* Enemy air is probable, and Soldiers may fire at aircraft not positively identified as friendly.
- *Weapons Tight.* Enemy air is possible, and Soldiers may fire only at aircraft positively identified as hostile according to announced hostile criteria.
- *Weapons Hold.* Enemy air is not likely, and Soldiers may not fire except in self-defense.

CHEMICAL, BIOLOGICAL, RADIOLOGICAL, AND NUCLEAR OPERATIONS

10-147.   Introducing CBRN weapons into conventional tactical operations results in an integrated battlefield. A battalion fights on an integrated battlefield the same as on a conventional battlefield. However, in a CBRN environment, the battalion must be ready to implement protective measures to enhance its survivability and must provide timely information to higher headquarters about possible contaminations to aid in protecting the BCT and other units.

10-148.   CBRN operations are conducted as a response to conditions on the battlefield. Chemical staff personnel adhere to the following three principles:

AVOIDANCE

10-149.   Avoiding CBRN attacks and hazards is the key to CBRN defense. Avoidance involves both active and passive measures. Passive measures include training, camouflage, concealment, hardening positions, and dispersion. Active measures include detection, reconnaissance, alarms and signals, warning and reporting, marking, and contamination control.

PROTECTION

10-150.   CBRN protection is an integral part of operations. Techniques that work for avoidance also work for protection such as shielding Soldiers and units and shaping the battlefield. Activities that comprise protection involve sealing or hardening positions, protecting Soldiers, assuming MOPP, reacting to attack, and using collective protection.

DECONTAMINATION

10-151.   CBRN decontamination prevents the erosion of combat power and reduces possible casualties resulting from inadvertent exposure or failure of protection. Decontamination allows commanders to sustain combat operations. Decontamination principles involve; conducting decontamination as quickly as possible, decontaminating only what is necessary, decontaminating as far forward as possible, and decontaminating by priority (FM 3-11.4).

CHEMICAL, BIOLOGICAL, RADIOLOGICAL, AND NUCLEAR PERSONNEL IN INFANTRY BATTALION

10-152.   The battalion chemical officer, along with the CBRN NCO, advises the commander on all CBRN matters. The chemical officer is responsible for collecting, consolidating, and distributing all CBRN reports from subordinate, adjacent, and higher units. Battalion chemical personnel inspect chemical equipment and train subordinate units on CBRN defensive tasks. As a member of the S-3 plans and operations section, the battalion chemical officer is normally found in the main CP. The chemical officer acts as the liaison with any attached chemical elements. He is required to coordinate closely with the S-2 on the current and updated CBRN threat. Together they develop CBRN NAIs. The chemical officer coordinates with the FS and aviation personnel on planned smoke operations and advises them of hazard areas. He also coordinates with the S-4 on CBRN logistics matters, such as mission-oriented protective posture, protective mask filters, and fog oil; and identifies "clean" and "dirty" routes and contaminated casualty collection points.

MILITARY POLICE SUPPORT

10-153.   MP assets may be tasked to support maneuver units to assist in maintaining maneuverability, survivability, security, law enforcement, discipline and control, and other operations. Commanders must consider where MP support would be most effective in order to maximize MP resources and must be prepared to designate other Soldiers within the battalion to assist in their execution.

MILITARY POLICE SUPPORT MISSION

10-154.   The organic BCT MP platoon provides support to the BCT and subordinate battalions through their five primary battlefield functions.

- Maneuver and mobility support.
- Area security.
- Law and order.
- Internment and resettlement.
- Police intelligence operations.

Maneuver and Mobility Operations

10-155.   MPs can support maneuver and mobility functions by expediting forward and lateral movement of combat resources. MPs used in the circulation control role can perform the following functions.

- River crossing operations, breaching operations and passage of lines.
- Route reconnaissance and security.
- MSR regulation and enforcement.
- Straggler control.
- Dislocated civilian control.

Area Security

10-156.   MPs provide area security and force protection to enhance the maneuver unit's freedom to conduct missions. Area security actions include zone and area reconnaissance; counterreconnaissance activities; and security of designated personnel, equipment, facilities, and critical points. These actions also include convoy and route security. Specific actions include the following:

- Reconnaissance operations.
- Area damage control.
- Base and air base defense.
- Response force operations.
- Critical site, asset, and high-risk personnel security.

Law and Order Operations

10-157.   MPs conduct law and order operations when it becomes necessary to extend the combat commander's discipline and control. These operations consist of those measures necessary to enforce laws, directives, and punitive regulations, conduct military police investigations, and to control populations and resources to ensure the existence of a lawful and orderly environment for the commander. Evolving criminal threats impact military operations and require the commander to minimize the threat to forces, resources, and operations. Close coordination with host-nation civilian police can enhance MP efforts at combating terrorism, maintaining law and order, and controlling civilian populations. Law and order operations include the following:

- Law enforcement.
- Criminal investigations.
- US customs operations.

Internment and Resettlement Operations

10-158.   MPs support tactical commanders by undertaking control of populations (EPW and dislocated civilians) and US military prisoners. Internment and resettlement operations include the following:

- EPW/CI handling.
- Populace and resource control.
- US military prisoner confinement.

Police Intelligence Operations

10-159.   Police intelligence operations consist of those measures to collect, analyze, and disseminate information and intelligence resulting from the other four primary MP battlefield function and other MP and Criminal Intelligence Division (CID) operations. The collection of this information is integrated into the overall ISR plan.

EMPLOYMENT AND PLANNING CONSIDERATIONS

10-160.   The factors of METT-TC must be considered when using MP support. During offensive operations, MPs best support the BCTs, and subsequently the battalion's maneuver and mobility. To do this, they control road traffic and facilitate route movement, evacuation, and control of refugees, stragglers, and enemy prisoners of war. In the defense, MPs are best employed in the area security role to enhance maneuver and mobility. MP resources must be synchronized and weighted to support the decisive operation, just as is any other asset. MP support might be unavailable or inadequate to perform all necessary MP battlefield functions at once. Commanders must prioritize those missions, and they may choose other units within the BCT, including Infantry and weapons companies and platoons, to aid in executing those missions.

Section IV. COMMAND AND CONTROL (SIGNAL)

The communications section provides the battalion with communications experts capable of supporting battalion and subordinate companies. The section provides trained communications personnel to each maneuver company who coordinate closely with the S-3 section to ensure and maintain clear lines of communication during tactical operations. The communications section is responsible for the transfer of information and the development of communications policies, procedures, and training for the battalion commander.

BATTALION SIGNAL OFFICER

10-161.   The communications section leader is the battalion signal officer (S-6) and the primary planner for battalion communication operations. He advises the battalion commander, staff, and the maneuver companies on all signal and communication matters. The duties of the battalion signal officer include—

- Plans, manages, and directs all aspects of the unit communications systems.
- Plans, supervises integration of communications with headquarters up, down, and adjacent.
- Supervises the communications activities of subordinate and attached units.
- Supervises unit maintenance of signal equipment for the unit and for subordinate units.
- Monitors status of support maintenance on unit and subordinate unit signal equipment.
- Prepares and writes the signal annex of unit orders and plans.
- Advises commander and staff on ECCM and develops MIJI reporting procedures.
- Helps the S-3 determine the location of the main, combat trains and field trains CPs.
- Ensures selected areas offer the best communications and the least interference.

BATTALION COMMUNICATIONS SECTION

10-162.   The communications section, lead by the S-6, is responsible for performing limited unit level repair and maintenance. It also conducts evacuation of the battalion's digital and wire communications equipment as well as maintenance of the digital system architecture that connects platoon, company and battalion to the BCT and higher networks; and on both secure and nonsecure local area networks. The communications section also has the capability to provide two retrans stations for the battalion, and normally provides one Soldier to each company during operations as a communications equipment expert.

Section V. INTELLIGENCE

In the Infantry battalion, the primary means to obtain information is through subordinate maneuver companies, patrols, scout platoon, snipers, OPs, and FISTs. The battalion S-2 is the primary staff officer responsible for coordination of information collection and dissemination by planning use of battalion reconnaissance and surveillance assets. The S-2 is responsible for all steps of the collection management process. The result is an ISR plan integrated into the BCT ISR plan. The BCT has robust ISR assets, and the S-2 may request additional intelligence support through the BCT. If allocated, these assets would operate normally DS or GS to the battalion.

INFANTRY BATTALION INFORMATION, SURVEILLANCE, AND RECONNAISSANCE ASSETS

10-163.   Information gathering at the Infantry battalion level is accomplished through a variety of means. The principal ISR resources available to the battalion include its organic scout platoon, snipers, and subordinate maneuver companies. Individual Soldiers, observation posts, and patrols are used and relied upon to collect and report information about the enemy, terrain, and weather. The paragraphs below discuss the assets most common to the Infantry battalion.

INDIVIDUAL SOLDIERS

10-164.   Individual Soldiers provide company and battalion commanders with a large quantity of timely combat information. They perform patrols, man observation posts, and observe enemy forces with which they are in contact. They observe and report first-hand information concerning enemy troops and equipment, patrols, reconnaissance units, and the activities of each. The size, activity, location, unit, time, and equipment (SALUTE) format for situation reports is the basis for both the training of individual Soldiers and the reporting of combat information.

OBSERVATION POSTS

10-165.   The battalion establishes OPs to observe and listen to enemy activity within particular sectors and to provide warning of the enemy's approach. Units should place OPs where they can be supported by fire and have access to covered and concealed withdrawal routes. Communications between the parent unit and each observation post are essential. Ground surveillance radars, remote sensors, UASs, and night observation devices can augment OPs.

PATROLS

10-166.   Patrols are conducted both before and during combat operations for reconnaissance, counterreconnaissance, and security purposes. They are also used to conduct small-scale combat operations. There are two categories of patrols, reconnaissance, and combat.

10-167.   Reconnaissance patrols are used to collect information and confirm or disprove the accuracy of other information gained previously. The three main types of reconnaissance patrols are—

- Route reconnaissance to obtain information about the enemy and any dominating terrain features along the route.

- Zone reconnaissance to collect the information about enemy forces and the terrain between specific boundaries.
- Area reconnaissance to gather information about the enemy or the terrain within a defined area such as a town, ridgeline, woods, or other feature critical to current or planned operations.

10-168.   Combat patrols are used to provide security and to harass, destroy, or capture enemy personnel, equipment, and installations. There are three types of combat patrols; raid, ambush, and security. The collection and reporting of combat information is usually a secondary mission for combat patrols. Captured enemy Soldiers, equipment, and documents are evacuated to the rear for exploitation at higher echelons. The results of such actions may prove to be of significant value as either tactical or strategic intelligence.

RIFLE AND WEAPONS COMPANIES

10-169.   Individual Soldiers, OPs, small UAS, and patrols are the principal means available to maneuver company commanders to gather information about the enemy, terrain, and weather in their immediate areas and to acquire targets for immediate attack.

10-170.   The Javelin command launch unit is used in all weather and visibility conditions to assist Soldiers in gathering information.

10-171.   The weapons company equipped with the TOW ITAS is also capable of information gathering in all weather and visibility conditions.

10-172.   Small/close range UAS such as the Raven UAS; provide aerial company and platoons short duration (flight time of 1 hour) and range (less than 15 kilometers) observation. Small UAS provide limited duration aerial observation, limited to fair weather, and some limited visibility operations.

SCOUT PLATOON

10-173.   As the primary intelligence-gathering asset, the mission of the scout platoon is to provide reconnaissance and security for its parent battalion and to assist in the control and movement of the battalion and its subordinate elements.

10-174.   The scout platoon is used to—

- Conduct route, zone, and area reconnaissance missions.
- Establish observation posts.
- Conduct chemical detection and radiological survey and monitoring operations.
- Screen one flank, the front, or rear of the battalion.
- Act as part of an advance, flank, or rear guard.
- Establish a roadblock.
- Provide traffic control and road guides.
- Conduct damage assessment.
- Provide contact teams, conduct liaison missions, and perform quartering functions. It also conducts limited pioneer and demolition work.

10-175.   The battalion commander may attach the scout platoon to a maneuver company for a specific operation. The battalion S-2 normally supervises reconnaissance operations. He coordinates these requirements with the battalion S-3. Security operations provide early warning of enemy maneuvers and deny information to the enemy concerning the battalion's disposition or movements. The battalion S-3 plans and supervises security operations. He coordinates with the S-2 for information on enemy activity.

SNIPERS

10-176.   The organic battalion sniper section normally operates in three man teams. They have excellend cross-country mobility and excel at surveillance as as the skilled us of cover and concealment. Inherent in

*Scout sniper qualities
high mobility, excellent cover and concealment
and razor sharp observation/surveillance*

Chapter 10

the sniper's ability to engage targets at long range, is their ability to conduct reconnaissance and surveillance in excess of their weapons range. Snipers can observe and report on NAIs and PIR. Consideration should be given to target selection engagement criteria when selecting reconnaissance and surveillance targets for snipers (Appendix F).

IBCT INFORMATION, SURVEILLANCE, AND RECONNAISSANCE ASSETS

10-177.   Ground surveillance radar teams, remote sensor teams (if available) from the BCTs military intelligence company, and UAS are also available to help satisfy the maneuver company and battalion commanders' ISR requirements.

GROUND SURVEILLANCE RADAR

10-178.   The AN/PPS-5D detects, locates, identifies, and tracks moving ground targets in an area under surveillance. The GSR detects moving ground targets only and cannot distinguish between enemy and friendly targets. GSRs provide the maneuver battalion a highly mobile, near all-weather, 24-hour capability for battlefield surveillance. They may be employed on patrols and at observation posts and are used with remote sensors and night observation devices. They may be employed near the FLOT, forward of the FLOT, on the flanks, or in the rear area. The supported battalion S-2, company commander, or scout platoon leader selects general locations where the radar may operate. The GSR team leaders select the actual site within these general locations.

10-179.   Generally, GSRs are located with or near other friendly units such as scouts and OPs. This allows mutual support, security, and complementary intelligence gathering capability.

REMOTELY-MONITORED BATTLEFIELD SURVEILLANCE SYSTEM

10-180.   The remotely-monitored battlefield surveillance system (REMBASS) can detect and classify moving targets by responding to seismic acoustic disturbances, changes to infrared energy and magnetic field changes produced by the targets. REMBASS sensors are placed along likely avenues of approach, choke points, and obstacles. (The number of sensor strings depends on the area being covered.) The first sensor is normally a seismic acoustic sensor for early warning and classification. The second sensor is normally a count indicator of the expected type of target; a magnetic sensor for vehicles and an infrared-passive sensor for personnel. The count indicator sensor provides the number of targets and direction of travel. The third sensor is also a count indicator and provides rate of speed and length of column. Once the sensors are activated, they send a burst of digital message to the monitoring station. The system requires radio LOS to transmit activations from the sensors to the monitor station. With the collected information, the operator prepares and submits a sensor activation spot report to the ISR integration section at the squadron or to the supported unit.

TACTICAL UNMANNED AIRCRAFT SYSTEMS (UAS)

10-181.   Tactical UAS see short and close range UAS that are available in the Infantry company, battalion, and BCT. Tactical UAS are organic to the IBCT and provide good observation and targeting capability under most weather conditions. They also provide IR observation capability in limited visibility. Short range UAS, also referred to as small UAS generally have a flight time of 6 to 12 hours, a range of less than 125 miles, and may have the capability to laser designate a target. Regardless of the system, tactical UAS provide Infantry units excellent observation capability to conduct reconnaissance, to observe NAIs, and collect PIR.

Section VI. SUSTAINMENT

Formerly known as *combat service support*, sustainment is the sixth warfighting function. (Chapter 10 discusses the other five.) Sustaining the force ensures units can conduct continuous combat operations. The IBCT subordinate battalions obtain their primary external support from an FSC as part of the BSB. The Infantry battalion XO, FSC commander, S-1 and S-4, along with BSB personnel, plan, coordinate, and sustain the maneuver battalion. The Infantry company commander is responsible for sustainment. The XO and the 1SG are the company's primary sustainment operators. They work closely with the battalion staff, FSC commander, and the FCS XO to ensure that the company receives the required support for its assigned operations. The concepts and organizational structures in this chapter reflect a shift from the supply-based sustainment system of the Army of Excellence (AOE). This technically enhanced, distribution-based logistics sustainment system combines information capabilities with streamlined delivery systems. The result is an efficient distribution pipeline.

ORGANIZATION AND FUNCTION

10-182.   Sustaining an Infantry battalion in a combat environment, to ensure continuous operations, is the challenge facing sustainment planners and operators. The battalion must be armed, fueled, and fixed. Its Soldiers must be sustained to ensure the battalion can plan and conduct combat operations and allow the battalion commander to take advantage of opportunities to seize the initiative. This requires that sustainment planners and operators at every level must continually anticipate needs, and ensure that the maneuver units are properly sustained in order to conduct their mission. Anticipation of future sustainment needs is critical to successful operations and to maintain the battalion's momentum.

DISTRIBUTION-BASED LOGISTICS

10-183.   Under the old AOE supply-based logistics system, units relied on stockpiles and static inventories located at each echelon. Distribution-based sustainment replaces bulk and redundancy, with velocity and control. A distribution based system relies on accuracy of reporting of requirements by the user and the logistician establishing trust within the system. Units will still maintain limited on-hand combat spares (limited prescribed load list [PLL], shop and bench stock). Once a request is submitted, it is expected that it be satisfied in a timely manner.

10-184.   Use of the BCS3 is designed to enhance establishing a logistical common operating picture (LCOP) that is accurate and timely. The distribution based logistics system combines a LCOP, in-transit visibility (ITV), total asset visibility (TAV), advanced materiel management, and advanced decision support system technology to form a seamless distribution pipeline. In essence, the supply pipeline becomes part of the warehouse which represents inventory in motion. This reduces but does not eliminate both organizational and material layering in forward areas.

10-185.   The logistics system relies on reduced order to receipt time to produce efficiency; however, it is designed with an overall intent to be effective in a combat environment. Direct throughput from the theater's sustainment brigade to the IBCT's BSB or to the FSC, or in some cases directly to the maneuver company, is a goal of distribution-based logistics. Throughput distribution bypasses one or more echelons in the supply system to minimize handling and to speed delivery to forward units. Advanced materiel management allows supplies to be tailored, packaged, and placed into configured loads (CLs) for specific supported units. This is based upon a specific time and location point of need, and is synchronized through distribution management channels based on the combat commander's mission and operation tempo. Preconfigured loads can be accomplished at every level, but only as a guide, loads should be configured at the highest level possible to minimize reconfiguring as the supplies near the end user.

10-186.   Advanced delivery platforms, such as the palletized load system (PLS) and the container roll in/roll out platform (CROP) are used to deliver materiel to supported units. Using ITV and TAV, delivery is tracked and managed from higher echelons to points as far forward as possible. Additional enablers include advanced satellite based tracking systems, movement tracking system (MTS), and radio frequency identification (RFID) devices. Radar tracking station tags, which provide detailed distribution platform interrogation of items, materials, and stocks, also provide detailed asset visibility to the distribution system managers and forward units.

GUIDELINES

10-187.   The Infantry battalion commander plans and executes sustainment operations through his XO, the battalion S-1, the battalion S-4 and the habitually associated FSC. The CTCP is the focal point of these activities. Infantry platoons and companies plan, prepare, and execute their portion of the sustainment plan and pass their requirements on to the battalion. The battalion processes these requirements and forwards them on to the BCT at the brigade support area (BSA), which encompasses the BSB. The BSB processes these requests and fills the requisitions through the FSC. In most cases, the FSC then delivers to the maneuver units through LOGPACs. Unit SOPs should address planning, implementation, and responsibilities in detail and should standardize as many routine sustainment operations as possible.

10-188.   At the BSB, the support operations officer (SPO) consolidates requisitions and transmits the order to the BSB distribution company. The BSB distribution company fills the requisition with as much as is practical, configures the supplies, and loads the contents onto its trucks. The distribution company trucks then delivers the supplies to the FSC in the battalion field trains. The FSC and the Infantry company supply sections conduct final configuration of the loads and deliver to the combat trains and/or directly to the Infantry companies by LOGPAC. When LOGPACs are delivered to the Infantry battalion combat trains, the supplies are either transloaded to FSC trucks, or used to replenish the FSC combat load. Typically, the FSC replenishes the Infantry battalion, and the BSB distribution company replenishes each FSC.

10-189.   The battalion field trains maintains the option to locate within the BSA, or to establish a field trains area somewhere between the BSA and the battalion combat trains, based on METT-TC. The commander must consider the advantages and disadvantages of efficiency, responsiveness, and security when deciding where to place his field trains. The field trains consist of the FSC(–), elements of the battalion S-1 and S-4 sections, and the company supply sections (Figure 10-9).

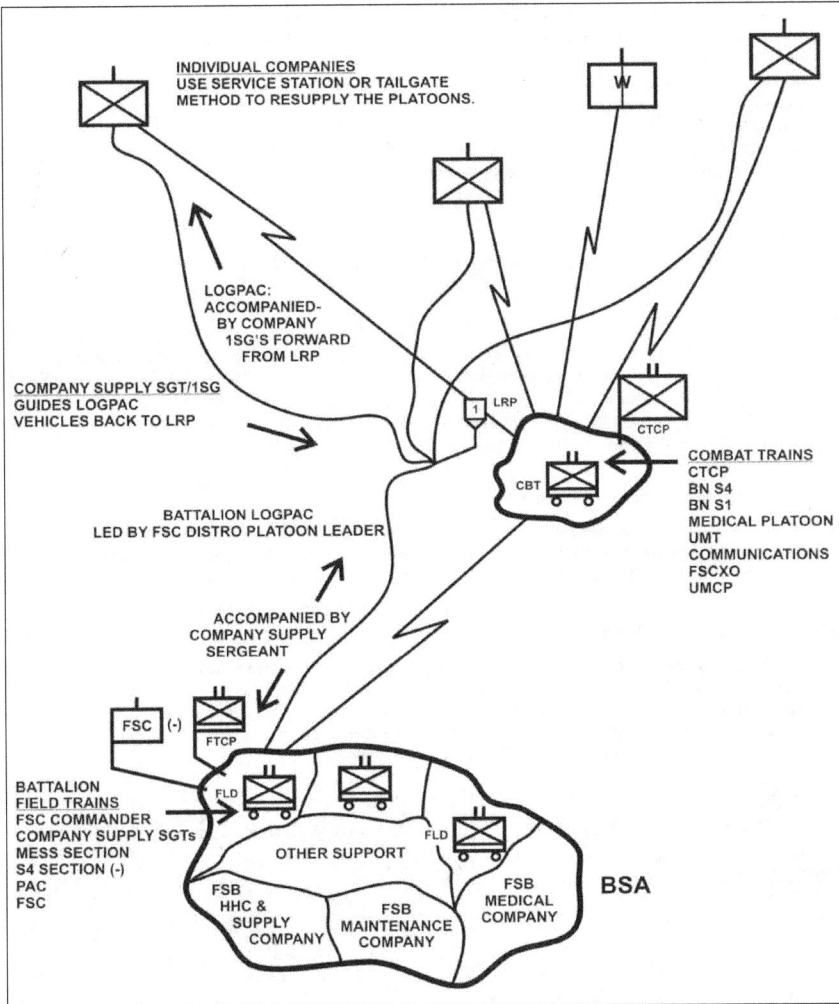

Figure 10-9. LOGPAC deliveries.

10-190.   In the IBCT, logistical loads are broken into three combat loads. The first combat load is located at the company level and is maintained by the company XO and 1SG. The second combat load is located at the Infantry battalion combat trains and loaded on the FSC distribution platoons vehicles or on the ground. The battalion S-4 manages the distribution of the load and the FSC maintains the load. The third combat load is located in the BSB, managed by the BSB SPO, and loaded on the BSB distribution company's vehicles or on the ground.

10-191.   The battalion S-4 coordinates support for the attachments and verifies who will provide this sustainment and how support for attachments is requested. When a large unit attachment joins the Infantry battalion, the attachment should bring an appropriate slice of support assets from its parent unit. These sustainment assets are controlled by the battalion XO and the FSC commander as with the rest of the Infantry battalion sustainment elements. The attached unit leader must coordinate with the battalion S-1 and furnish him a copy of his unit battle roster, as well as provide the battalion S-4 the status of all key elements of equipment. Thereafter, the attached unit submits reports and requests for resupply according to the Infantry battalion standing operating procedures (SOP).

CATEGORIES

10-192.   Sustainment operations fall into the following three general categories (Figure 10-10):

Combat Replenishment Operations

10-193.   Combat replenishment operations is defined as brief or pit-stop like events to rearm, refuel, provision essential supplies, and support the maintenance function by cross leveling and use of on-board spares with a duration of up to 3 hours. Combat replenishment operations are replenishment events executed by BCTs using organic assets to conduct internal resupply. They are executed by support sections and resupply vehicles located in the FSC.

Sustainment Replenishment Operations

10-194.   A sustainment replenishment operation is conducted within a unit's battle rhythm and that lasts from 3 to 7 hours. It can be either a deliberate or a hasty operation. Sustainment replenishment operations are executed by the BSB and may include augmentation from the sustainment brigade.

Mission Sustainment Operations

10-195.   Mission sustainment operations are intense, time-sensitive operations which include all preparations for an upcoming mission; planning, troop leading, rehearsals, training, reconnaissance, and surveillance, reconstitution, tailoring for the next mission, and information operation to ensure mission success. Mission sustainment operations are planned deliberate operations with a duration of one to three days which require support from the BSB and sustainment brigade.

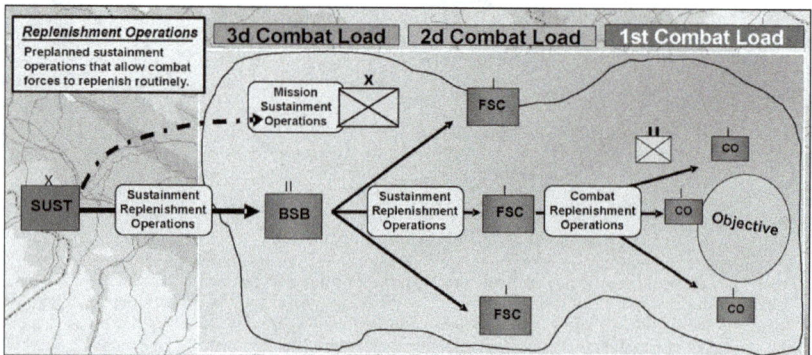

Figure 10-10. Replenishment operations.

BRIGADE SUPPORT BATTALION

10-196.   The BSB is emplaced by the supported BCT commander and controlled by the BSB commander. The BSB includes personnel and equipment to support the various classes of supply to include medical and maintenance support. Supply requirements for the maneuver battalions are collected at the BSB and as much as practical are assembled into configured loads by the distribution company. The loads are then delivered to the FSC when the two are not located at the same site. The BSB is supported by logistics units assigned to support higher level headquarters. The BSB is located in the BSA, which may also include the BCT rear CP.

FORWARD SUPPORT COMPANY

10-197.   The FSC is a multifunctional sustainment unit organized to provide habitual and direct support to the Infantry battalion (Figure 10-11). The FSC directly supports the Infantry battalion and a close SOP supported relationship exists between the units. Both the BSB and Infantry battalion commanders ensure the FSC is tightly integrated into the Infantry battalion's operations in garrison, training, and in combat. In the modular force, the FSC is responsible for conducting the majority of sustainment operations that were previously conducted by the Infantry battalion HHC. These responsibilities include—

- Field level vehicle and equipment maintenance and recovery.
- Resupply operations for all classes of supply (except medical) and water.
- Transportation for all classes of supply.
- Supplemental transportation of personnel with no organic wheel movement capability. The FSC can move one Infantry company at any one time.
- LOGPAC operations.

10-198.   The FSC commander is the senior logistics commander at battalion level. He is not the planner; however, he assists the battalion S-1 and S-4 with the battalion's logistics planning. The FSC commander is responsible for executing the logistics plan IAW the battalion commander's guidance as developed by the battalion S-1 and S-4. The FSC commander responds directly to the guidance and directives given by the Infantry battalion XO who serves as the battalion logistics integrator and assists the battalion S-1 and S-4 in logistics synchronization and troubleshooting. Many functions described in this section are a coordinated effort between the FSC commander and the battalion S-1 and S-4. The FSC commander provides information, input, or feedback to the battalion S-1 and S-4 for their use in planning and coordination. He also provides the battalion commander a LCOP. The FSC regularly interfaces with the BSB in order to provide logistics support to the battalion. He ensures requests are filled correctly by the SPO and the distribution company in the BSB.

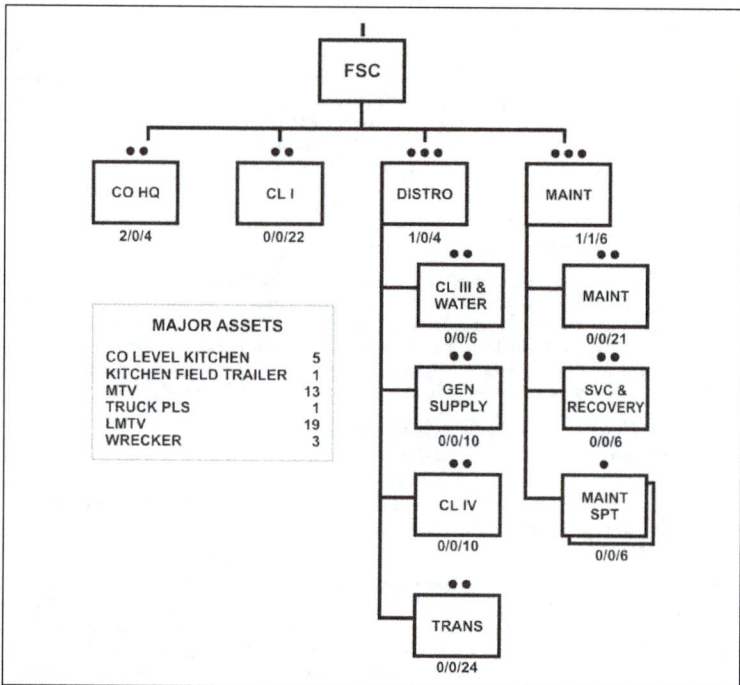

Figure 10-11. Forward support company.

10-199.   The FSC XO is the principle assistant to the FSC company commander. As second in command, he must understand both operations that provide support to the Infantry battalion, and the other functions of the FSC. He supervises the company headquarters personnel and coordinates assigned missions with subordinate elements. In accordance with commander directives, the XO formulates unit operating procedures and also supervises CP operations. He often also serves as the FSC activities coordinator at the CTCP.

10-200.   The 1SG is the company's senior NCO and typically is its most experienced Soldier. He is the commander's primary logistics and tactical advisor, and should be an expert in individual and NCO skills. He is the company's primary internal logistics operator and assists the commander in planning, coordinating, and supervising all logistical activities that support the company's mission. He operates where the commander directs or where his duties require him. Often this dictates the FSC 1SG will assist in the operation of the battalion field trains CP and FSC HQ.

10-201.   The distribution platoon provides supply and transportation support to the Infantry battalion. The distribution platoon provides Class I (to include food service support), II, III (P, B), IV, V, VI, and VII, to the battalion. The distribution section has the ability to conduct simultaneous Class III and V retail support to the maneuver companies, the Infantry battalion HHC, and the FSC itself. The distribution platoon leader of the FSC takes over the responsibilities previously held by the support platoon leader in the Infantry battalion. The key activity of the distribution platoon is the conduct of LOGPAC operations to the battalion, and acquiring replenishment sustainment stocks from sustainment brigade units through combat replenishment operations and sustainment replenishment operations.

10-202.   The FSC's maintenance platoon provides field maintenance to itself and the Infantry battalion. The platoon consists of a headquarters section and maintenance control section, recovery and service section, and two field maintenance support teams. The maintenance platoon provides C2 and reinforcing maintenance to the field maintenance support teams. The field maintenance support teams provide field maintenance and BDAR primarily to the weapons company and the Infantry battalion HHC. As the battalion commander task organizes the force, all or part of a field maintenance support team goes with the company teams in order to maintain habitual support. The maintenance platoon maintains a limited quantity of combat spares (PLL, shop, and bench stock) in the maintenance control section. The maintenance platoon's supply section can provide Class IX support (combat spares) to each maneuver company and the HHC. It maintains combat spares (PLL, shop, and bench stock) for the unit it supports and also provides exchange of reparable items.

BATTALION RESPONSIBILITIES

10-203.   The Infantry battalion headquarters is ultimately responsible for the coordination and execution of sustainment functions within the battalion. This includes conducting or supervising effective sustainment operations for all units within the battalion's AO. The primary sustainment functions required to support the Infantry battalion include treatment and evacuation of casualties, resupply operations, maintenance activities, and human resources support. The following battalion personnel have the primary responsibility for sustainment.

Commander

10-204.   The commander ensures that sustainment operations sustain his battalion's fighting potential. He integrates sustainment activities into the tactical plan and provides guidance to the sustainment operators. He tailors his sustainment operations to meet the tactical plan.

Executive Officer

10-205.   The XO synchronizes all staff actions including the battalion's logistical effort. During the planning phase, he reviews status reports from assigned and attached units; reviews the tactical plan with the S-3 to determine battalion sustainment requirements; and supervises the coordination with BCT sustainment personnel. The XO also ensures that the sustainment needs of other units in the battalion's AO are met.

Adjutant/Battalion S-1

10-206.   The battalion human resource section consists of the battalion adjutant, or S-1, and the personnel and administrative center (PAC). The section is responsible for administration of all human resource matters pertaining to the battalion and ensures assigned personnel transition smoothly into and out of the battalion.

10-207.   The S-1 section maintains unit strength reports and processes all human resource actions for assigned Soldiers to include personnel awards, orders, and finance and legal actions.

10-208.   The S-1 coordinates the special staff efforts of the chaplain, battalion surgeon, medical platoon leader, and any attached public affairs personnel. Also, the S-1 is the staff point of contact for activities such as inspector general and judge advocate general issues.

10-209.   The S-1 is responsible for supervising the casualty evacuation system and coordinates with medical platoon personnel to ensure that patient treatment and evacuation are planned, and coordinated throughout the battalion area.

10-210.   During tactical operations, the S-1 is collocated with the S-4 section in the CTCP.

10-211.   The S-1 takes part in the full range of staff officer functions which include participating in MDMP.

10-212.   The S-1 has personnel located at both the combat and the field trains. Personnel in the combat trains perform strength accounting, casualty reporting, and CP functions. Personnel in the field trains perform replacement operations, administration services, human resource actions, legal services, and finance services.

10-213.   The S-1 is also responsible for processing EPWs and tracking the status of WIAs as they are processed through the medical system.

10-214.   While the responsibility for civilians on the battlefield is a civil affairs function, in the absence of civil affairs personnel attached to the battalion, the S-1 may assume responsibility to ensure displaced civilians do not interfere with operations.

10-215.   There is no authorized public affairs officer (PAO) in the Infantry battalion. The S-1 may have the additional duty to provide information support to Soldiers and commanders in wartime. ROE and guidance from the BCT PAO and commander, dictate what Soldiers will say when approached by the media. The S-1 should manage and escort or arrange for escort of all media personnel in the battalion AO.

Logistics Officer/Battalion S-4

10-216.   The S-4 is the OIC of the combat trains and is the battalion's primary logistician. He directs actions from the CTCP and, in conjunction with the S-1, conducts sustainment functions for the battalion.

- The battalion logistics section is responsible for providing logistical planning and support to the battalion and operates in both the combat and field trains. They coordinate the sustainment functions of maintenance, supply, transportation, and services for the battalion and units operating in the battalion's AO. The S-4 normally positions his assistant at the main CP to assist the S-3's synchronization of combat and sustainment operations or at the field trains to establish coordination and provide technical support.
- The S-4 coordinates directly with the FSC commander for logistics resupply and equipment maintenance operations.
- The S-4s primary focus is on water and Classes I through V, VII, and IX.

HHC Commander

10-217.   The HHC commander's duties and areas of emphasis are assigned by the battalion commander. Depending on the emphasis in ongoing operations and guidance from the battalion commander, the HHC commander's primary duties are typically to supervise the operations of the scout and mortar platoons and the sniper section. The HHC commander will often be designated as the battalion sniper employment officer (SEO).

Medical Platoon Leader/Battalion Surgeon

10-218.   The medical platoon provides FHP to the battalion. Its personnel provide immediate trauma and combat medical treatment and MEDEVAC support to the headquarters and maneuver companies. The medical platoon's primary mission is to collect, triage, and treat patients, then make the determination to either evacuate or return them to duty.

- The medical platoon, under the direction of the medical platoon leader, who is a surgeon, operates the BAS normally located at the battalion CTCP. The medical platoon leader is assisted by a PA, a medical operations officer, and the medical platoon sergeant.
- The medical platoon leader also serves as a special staff member to the battalion commander, ensuring that battalion personnel maintain both physical and mental health.
- The medical platoon stocks and provides all Class VIII supply support for the battalion and maintains and requests repair for organic medical equipment.
- Battalion medics also provide training to combat lifesaver personnel.

Chaplain

10-219.   The unit ministry team (UMT) is composed of a chaplain and an enlisted chaplain assistant. Each UMT develops a religious support plan that details how it can best coordinate and facilitate religious support throughout the AO. The chaplain is also a special staff member who serves as a confidential advisor to the commander on the spiritual fitness and the ethical and moral health of the command.

- Battalion UMTs normally operate from the CTCP or battalion aid station.
- When not conducting combat operations, the UMT coordinates with the CTCP to be at the right place at the right time for those who need them the most. Movement with a logistics package to an LRP is an excellent way to minister and provide services to a company.
- During combat operations, the UMT's priority for religious support is care for the wounded. The team performs "religious triage" in coordination with medical treatment personnel. The UMT moves to positions where the largest numbers of casualties are to be collected, usually at BAS.
- After combat, the UMT ministers to Soldiers, paying attention to leaders and those who show signs of battle stress.
- The UMT reviews and may adjust battalion religious support plans to ensure that religious coverage is available to all, to include contractors, refugees, displaced persons, detained civilians in the AO, and enemy prisoners of war.
- Chaplains often serve as the "conscience of the command." They advise the commander on the moral and ethical nature of command policies, programs, and actions and their impact on Soldiers. The UMT is responsible for and supports the free exercise of religion. Chaplains provide support for death notifications, Red Cross notifications by command, and liaison with continental US (CONUS) and host nation clergy.

BATTALION TRAINS OPERATIONS

The logistical focal point for the Infantry battalion is the trains. Sustainment personnel and equipment organic or attached to a force that provides support, such as supply, evacuation, and maintenance services, comprise the unit trains. Whether or not battalion sustainment assets are centralized or placed in multiple locations is dependant upon the tactical needs of the battalion.

INFANTRY BATTALION TRAINS

10-220.   The battalion uses unit trains only when occupying a battalion assembly area or when the terrain restricts movement so that the battalion must depend on aerial resupply and evacuation for support. In this case, the unit trains and all sustainment assets are placed in one central location. However, the Infantry battalion normally operates in echeloned trains where the trains are split into multiple locations. Echeloned trains for the battalion normally consist of two types: the battalion combat trains and the field trains.

Combat Trains

10-221.   The battalion's combat trains are normally positioned close enough to combat elements to be responsive to forward units but beyond the range of enemy direct fires. The combat trains should not be considered a permanent or stationary support area. The battalion combat trains usually consist of the S-1, the HHC's medical platoon, the UMT, communications personnel, forward elements of the FSC, and its combat load. They are supervised by the CTCP, which is headed by the battalion S-4. The trains are positioned based upon the factors of METT-TC. The battalion's combat trains control all resupply operations for the Infantry battalion. At times, the battalion may move company supply sections forward, and an Infantry company may store its sustainment load with its company supply section in the combat trains. The company sustainment load normally consists of rucksacks, duffel bags containing extra clothing and personal items, chemical protective over garments (CPOGs), and sleeping bags. As the alternate main command post, and in the event that they must assume responsibilities as the main command post, the combat trains command post must maintain SU of current and future battalion and brigade operations

Field Trains

10-222.   The fields trains are positioned based on METT-TC considerations and often will be located in the BSA. The field trains are controlled by the FSC commander. The field trains normally consist of the FSC, Infantry battalion PAC, personnel transitioning to and from the battalion and the HHC, and Infantry company and weapons company supply sections. Usually, the Infantry and weapons companies will store its sustainment loads with its company supply section in the field trains. The units in the field trains operate as the primary direct coordination element between the Infantry companies and the BSA. The battalion S-4 coordinates all unit supply requests with the FSC commander. The FSC fills orders with on-hand stocked items. Requests for those items not on-hand in the FSC are forwarded to the brigade S-4.

Unit Maintenance Collection Point

10-223.   The UMCP is normally located near the combat trains or collocated with the combat trains for security, and should be on a main axis or supply route. The UMCP is manned by elements of the FSC. The UMCP provides vehicle and equipment evacuation, and maintenance support to the field maintenance support teams. Field maintenance support teams evacuate vehicles and equipment to the UMCP that cannot be repaired within 2 hours. Normally, vehicles or equipment evacuated to the UMCP that cannot be towed or repaired within 4-6 hours, are further evacuated to the field trains, BSB, or higher level support unit

10-224.   UMCP does not have to be located in the battalion combat trains; however, if not in the same location, the UMCP is normally in the general vicinity. The advantages to collocating the UMCP at the combat trains is for increased security, and coordination of class IX resupply. The trains must be mobile enough to support frequent changes in location, time and terrain permitting, under the following conditions when—

- Heavy use or traffic in the area may cause detection.
- Area becomes worn by heavy use such as in wet and muddy conditions.
- Security is compromised.

HHC, INFANTRY, AND WEAPONS COMPANY SUPPLY SECTIONS

10-225.   Company supply sections become the assembly point for company sustainment operations. They usually consist of the company supply sergeant and one other supply specialist, and are normally located in the battalion field trains. The section personnel are responsible for obtaining their company supply request, assembling the requested supplies into a LOGPAC, and then loading it onto an FSC distribution platoon vehicle. The company supply sergeant then accompanies the LOGPAC forward to the LRP where the company receives its supplies.

SUPPORT AREA SECURITY

10-226.   Security of sustainment elements is critical to the success of the Infantry battalion mission; therefore, trains must develop plans for continuous security operations.

Combat Trains Security

10-227.   The following should be considered when securing combat trains:

- Select good trains sites that use available cover, concealment, and camouflage. The best defense for combat trains is to avoid detection.

- Use strict movement and positioning discipline as well as noise and light discipline to prevent detection.
- Establish a perimeter defense as in an assembly area.
- Establish observation posts and patrols.
- Position weapons (small arms and machine guns) for self-defense.
- Plan mutually supporting positions to dominate likely avenues of approach.
- Prepare a fire plan and make sector sketches.
- Identify sectors of fires.
- Emplace TRPs to control fires and for use of indirect fires.
- Conduct rehearsals.
- Establish rest plans.
- Identify an alarm or warning system that allows for rapid execution of the defense plan without further guidance (normally included in an SOP).
- Designate a reaction force and ensure the force is equipped to perform its mission.

Field Trains Security

10-228. The Infantry battalion will consider the factors of METT-TC along with the considerations outlined in the previous paragraph, when determining where to position the field trains. If the field trains is located within the BSA, the FSC commander must coordinate his defense plan with the BSB commander. These defense plans must complement the plans of the other units located within the BSA.

COMMUNICATIONS

10-229. Fast and reliable communications are critical to the sustainment effort. The CTCP reports the battalion's status, including combat losses, and sends resupply and support requests to the BCT.

10-230. At the Infantry battalion level, sustainment communications may occur by any combination of FM radio, digital connectivity, courier, or wire. FBCB2 is the primary means of sustainment communication within the battalion, and the ABCS is the method to pass information to the BCT.

10-231. The CTCP is the net control station (NCS) for the battalion administrative and logistics radio network. (admin/log net) The S-4, S-1, FSC commander, maintenance platoon leader, distribution platoon leader, medical platoon leader, company 1SGs, and others (as required) operate in the Infantry battalion admin/log net. The CTCP also operates in the brigade admin/log net and in the Infantry battalion command net.

10-232. Communications are critical to expediting the sustainment effort. Unit 1SGs must report their losses and requirements as soon as it is practical to do so. When use of radio or FBCB2 is not possible, messages are sent with resupply or evacuation vehicles. The CTCP and FTCP maintain control of vehicles moving forward to the LRPs. The IBCT Infantry battalion SOP establishes procedures for resupply without request, in the event that communications fail.

SUPPLY AND TRANSPORTATION OPERATIONS

The supply system provides many types of supplies to the battalion. Generally the most important are ammunition, repair parts for weapons systems and vehicles, water, subsistence, and POL, but the mission and current situation will dictate the priority. To ensure continuous support, the leader ensures supplies are provided as far forward as the tactical situation permits and that the need for these supplies is anticipated in advance. Movement of supplies, equipment, and personnel for most companies normally come through vehicle assets from the FSC or higher. The FSC generally stocks and has for immediate issue water, fuel and packaged POL, ammunition, and repair parts.

CLASSES OF SUPPLY

11-1.   Supplies are divided into ten major categories, which are referred to as classes. There are also a few miscellaneous items that do not fit into any of the other ten supply classes (Table 10-8).

Table 10-8. Classes of supply.

SUPPLY CLASS	SYMBOL	DEFINITION
I		Subsistence items.
II		Items of equipment other than principal items.
III		Petroleum, oil, and lubricants.
IV		Construction and barrier materials.
V		Ammunition.
VI		Personal demand items normally sold through exchanges.
VII		Major end items.
VIII		Medical material.
IX		Repair parts and components.
X		Material to support nonmilitary programs.
MISC	N/A	Water, captured material, and salvage material.

ROUTINE RESUPPLY

10-233.   Routine resupply operations cover items in Classes I, III, V, IX, and water, as well as mail and any other items usually requested by the battalion. Resupply operations normally occur once a day. Whenever possible, routine resupply should be conducted daily; ideally in limited visibility.

Logistics Package Operations

10-234.   The LOGPAC technique is a simple, efficient way to accomplish routine resupply operations. Typical LOGPAC operations are shown in Figure 10-9, page 10-43.

Preparation

10-235.   Company 1SGs compile and coordinate any unique supply requests for their companies and route them through the battalion S-4 via the LOGPAC. Based on the requests and the predetermined supply needs, the requested supplies and replenishments stocks are assembled by the distribution company of the BSB. This activity is coordinated and supervised by the SPO of the BSB. The BSB distribution company configures the loads as much as practicable and prepares them for movement to the FSC. Supplies are usually configured to sustain the Infantry battalion and its companies for a 24-hour period or until the next scheduled replenishment cycle. Other items to be included in the replenishment are coordinated by the appropriate staff officer, and then delivered to the S-4 and S-1. These items may include replacement personnel and Soldiers returning from medical treatment, vehicles returning to the company area from maintenance, and mail and personnel actions.

Movement of Replenishment Load

10-236.   Replenishment loads normally follow a sequence of movement from the BSB distribution company to the FSC located in the field trains. From the field trains, the loads are then delivered by LOGPAC to the combat trains or delivered throughput directly to the companies. Throughput can be from any echelon to any lower echelon if circumstances require.

Replenishment of FSC Loads

10-237.   Once the BSB distribution company has configured the replenishment load on its organic vehicles, they are ready to move forward to the field trains under the control of FSC personnel. Once the replenishment load reaches the field trains, the supplies are downloaded or transferred to vehicles of the FSC distribution platoon.

Replenishment of Infantry Battalion Units' Loads

10-238.   The loads for the Infantry battalion's units (rifle companies, weapons company, HHC, and special platoons and sections) are configured for final delivery in the field trains by the company supply sergeants. The vehicles are lead to the LRP where they are met by the company 1SG or his representative.

Actions at LRP

10-239.   When the LOGPACs arrive at the LRP, the company 1SGs quickly assume control of the company LOGPACs and continue tactical movement to the company resupply points. The LOGPAC will stop at the LRP only when the tactical situation dictates or when ordered by the commander. Security will be maintained at all times.

Resupply Procedures

10-240.   The individual companies can use the service station or tailgate resupply method. The time required for resupply is an important planning factor. Resupply must be conducted as quickly and efficiently as possible, both to ensure operational effectiveness and to allow the company LOGPAC vehicles to return to the LRP on time. Service station resupply of the company normally takes 60 to 90 minutes but may take longer. Tailgate resupply usually requires significantly more time than service station resupply. At times, it may also be necessary to use the in-position resupply method. However, this process takes a considerable amount of time and may compromise friendly positions or activities.

Return to LRP

10-241.   Once resupply operations are complete, the LOGPAC vehicles are prepared for the return trip. Human remains and their personal effects are carried on cargo or fuel trucks. EPWs ride in the cargo trucks and are guarded by walking wounded or other company personnel. All supply requests and personnel action documents are consolidated for forwarding to the CTCP, where the appropriate staff section processes them for the next LOGPAC. The supply sergeant leads the LOGPAC back to the LRP. It is critical that the LOGPAC continue to move through the LRP as quickly as possible to avoid interdiction by enemy forces or artillery. Whenever possible, all FSC vehicles and company supply sections consolidate at a coordinated point, and the reunited LOGPAC convoy returns to the field trains together. When METT-TC dictates or when the LOGPAC arrives too late to rejoin the larger convoy, the vehicles must return to the field trains on their own in a secure manner.

EMERGENCY RESUPPLY

10-242.   Occasionally, normally during combat operations, the battalion may have such an urgent need for resupply that it cannot wait for a routine LOGPAC. Emergency resupply usually involves Classes III, V, and VIII, as well as CBRN equipment. Emergency resupply down to the company level can be conducted using either the service station or tailgate method, but more often may use the in-position method. The fastest appropriate means is normally used although procedures may have to be adjusted when the company is in contact with the enemy.

PRESTOCK OPERATIONS

10-243.   Prestock resupply, also known as pre-positioning or cache, is most often beneficial in defensive operations.

Pre-Positioned

10-244.   Normally only Class IV items are pre-positioned. Prestock operations must be carefully planned and executed at every level. All leaders must know the exact locations of prestock sites, which they verify during reconnaissance or rehearsals. The battalion and separate companies must take steps to ensure survivability of the prestock supplies. These measures include digging in prestock positions and selecting covered and concealed positions. The commanders must also have a plan to remove or destroy pre-positioned supplies to prevent the enemy from capturing them.

Caches

10-245.   A cache is a pre-positioned and concealed supply point. It can be used in any operation. Caches are an excellent tool for reducing the Soldier's load and can be set up for a specific mission or as a contingency measure. Cache sites have the same characteristics as an ORP or patrol base, with the supplies concealed above or below ground. An aboveground cache is easier to get to but is more likely to be discovered by the enemy, civilians, or animals. There is always a security risk when returning to a cache. A cache site should be observed for signs of enemy presence and secured before being used; it may have been booby-trapped and may be under enemy observation.

10-246.   In the offense, advance elements may set up a cache along the intended route of advance to the objective. Caches may also be set up in-zone to support continuous operations without allowing the enemy to locate the company through air or ground resupply. Soldier's load considerations may limit the size of caches. Do not let the cache activities jeopardize the offensive mission.

10-247.   In the defense, a defending unit may set up caches throughout the AOs during the preparation phase. A cache can be established in each alternate or subsequent position throughout the depth of the defense sector. During stay-behind operations, or in an area defense on a fluid battlefield, caches may be the only source of supply for extended periods.

Security

10-248.   While these techniques are used in both offensive and defensive operations, the transfer of supplies to the company is usually conducted from a defensive posture. As such, the security considerations for a resupply operation are like those for a perimeter defense.

NONSTANDARD SUPPLY

10-249.   The techniques described in the preceding paragraphs are the normal methods for resupply. However, a basic understanding of nonstandard techniques and different modes of delivery is also required for the successful execution of the sustainment function.

Aerial Resupply

10-250.   Air Force airlift and Army aviation assets may assist in resupply operations. The Infantry battalion must be prepared to receive both air-dropped and sling-loaded supplies. The receiving commander must consider the enemy's ability to locate his unit by observing the aircraft. Unless conducting the resupply in an area under friendly control and away from direct enemy observation (reverse slope of a defensive position with recon well forward), locate the DZ and LZ away from the main unit in an area that can be defended for a short time. The delivered supplies are immediately transported away from the DZ and LZ. Each unit must know how to select pickup and landing zones and receive aerial resupply. See FM 90-4.

Cross-Leveling

10-251.   Cross-leveling is simply a redistribution of supplies throughout the unit. Usually done automatically within companies after every engagement, the battalion may cross-level supplies between companies when resupply cannot be conducted. In some instances, supplies may not be evenly redistributed. For example, during sustainment replenishment operations, a company defending a base camp may postpone fuel resupply so that a company conducting an area presence mission is completely supplied.

TRANSPORTATION

10-252.   Movement of supplies, equipment, and personnel with the limited vehicle assets available requires careful planning and execution. Infantry companies have one organic HMMWV for C2, and one LMTV with a 400 gallon water trailer for resupply operations. The weapons company has two organic HMMWV for C2, and one LMTV with a 400 gallon water trailer for resupply operations. Additional vehicle assets from FSC or higher can be provided for company resupply operations.

10-253.   When vehicles are provided to the company, they must be employed to capitalize on their capability to execute the mission requirement, and they must be returned for follow-on company or parent-unit missions. Transportation assets are scarce, often resulting in trade-offs. For example, upload increased quantities of ammunition and less water, or carry unit rucksacks and be unavailable for resupply. Commanders must ensure that transportation assets are being employed to accomplish the most important missions. Time is critical and the company must reduce on-station time so that all company requirements can be met. Most FSC vehicles do not have radios; however, most of them do have GPS integrated into the vehicles. Vehicles leaders must ensure that drivers know where they are going and how to get there. Land navigation training, marked routes, and strip maps referenced to landmarks are all ways to keep drivers from getting lost.

10-254.   Because of the limited ground transportation, personnel must know how to conduct aerial operations. An understanding of PZs and LZs selection, sling loading, bundle drops, and allowable cargo loads may be critical to sustainment operations.

CONTRACTING AND HOST NATION SUPPORT

10-255.   The Infantry battalion is expected to use contractors, DA civilians, and host nation support in the AOs.

Contracting Support

10-256.   Though they involve a number of risks, contractors and DA civilians are playing an ever-increasing role in providing sustainment to US forces. The Army may use contractors to bridge gaps between required capabilities and actual force structure available within an AO. Contractors may be employed, subject to METT-TC, throughout the AO and in virtually all conditions. Protecting contractors on the battlefield is the commander's responsibility. When contractors are expected to perform in potentially hostile areas, the supported military forces must assure the protection of their operations and personnel. Commanders must understand that contractors are subject to the same threat as Soldiers and must plan accordingly. Contractor personnel cannot be required to perform force protection functions and cannot take an active role in hostilities but retain the inherent right to self-defense. The defense logistics agency will provide bulk fuel, water, and food to contractor personnel either through pre-positioned stocks or host-nation contracts. The logistics civil augmentation program (LOGCAP) is also available when needed.

Host Nation Support

10-257.   Host nation support is provided to Army forces and organizations located in or transiting through host nation territory and includes both civil and military assistance. This support can include assistance in almost every aspect required to sustain military operations within a theater. Planners must consider that host nation support meets local, not necessarily US, standards. Host nation support can be a significant resource provided it is available and that appropriate agreements are in place.

MAINTENANCE OPERATIONS

The maintenance of weapons and equipment is continuous. Every Soldier must know how to maintain his weapon and equipment IAW the related technical manual.

SUPPORT

10-258.   At the tactical level, the maintenance support system is designed to repair equipment as fast as possible and as near to the point of failure or damage as possible. Maintenance assets move as far forward as the tactical situation permits to repair inoperable and damaged equipment, and to return it to the battle as quickly as possible.

Vehicles

10-259.   Infantry battalions are responsible for operator and crew level maintenance on vehicles and equipment. The FSC's organic maintenance platoon and its two field maintenance support team provide field level maintenance for vehicles and equipment. Normally the field maintenance support teams are tasked to provide maintenance support to the Infantry battalion headquarters and weapons companies. If the Infantry battalion task organizes, the field maintenance support teams provide prioritized support as specified by the battalion. The BSB provides DS level maintenance and evacuation to GS and depot levels.

Other equipment

10-260.   Maintenance on other equipment such as communications equipment and weapons has limited organizational level maintenance available. Maintenance beyond the skill level of assigned personnel will need evacuation to the FSC or the BSB for repair.

REQUIREMENTS

10-261.   The maintenance of weapons and equipment is continuous. Every Soldier must know how to maintain his weapon and equipment IAW the related technical manual. The commander, XO, and 1SG must understand the maintenance concept for every piece of equipment in the battalion.

10-262.   Proper operator level maintenance is key to keeping vehicles, equipment, and other materials in serviceable condition. It is a continuous process that starts with preventive measures taken by each operator of each piece of equipment or vehicle, and continues through repair and recovery of the equipment. It includes the functions of inspecting, testing, servicing, repairing, requisitioning, recovering, and evacuating equipment.

10-263.   Maintenance functions begin with PMCS, a daily responsibility for each piece of equipment to include inspection and maintenance forms (DA Form 2404 or 5988-E [*Equipment Inspection and Maintenance Worksheet*]) when required. These forms are the primary means through which the company obtains maintenance support or repair parts. The forms follow a pathway, described in the following paragraphs, from operator/crew level to the BSA and back. The company XO or 1SG supervises the "flow" of these critical maintenance documents and parts based on the unit's SOP. These instructions must be integrated into the SOPs for patrol bases, assembly areas, defenses, and reorganization to ensure that maintenance is done without jeopardizing unit security, and to make it a habit for the Soldiers.

10-264.   In addition to operator maintenance, selected Soldiers are trained to perform limited maintenance on damaged weapons and battle damage assessment and repair (BDAR). The purpose of BDAR is to return disabled combat equipment to the tactical commander as quickly as possible. It is rapid damage assessment and repair, bypassing or temporarily fixing components, to support a combat mission or enable self-recovery. The CTCP implements the commander's guidance on whether or not to use BDAR in lieu of normal maintenance procedures. Such enabling repairs are almost always temporary, depending on the repair required. At the completion of immediate combat operations, mechanics from the FSC will make repairs that will return the equipment to fully mission-capable status. Since it may not be possible to train BDAR techniques in peacetime using actual equipment, the best substitute is to train system-oriented crews and mechanics to understand the principles associated with weapon systems. BDAR actions include—

- Using shortcuts to install or remove parts.
- Modifying and installing components designed for other vehicles or equipment.
- Using parts serving a noncritical function on a like vehicle.
- Using substitute fuels, fluids, or other POLs.
- Using readily available materials to execute a temporary repair.

10-265.   Inoperative equipment is fixed as far forward as possible. When a piece of equipment is damaged, it should be inspected to see if it could be repaired on the spot. Company armorers keep a small-arms repair kit in the company trains or on the dedicated company vehicle. If equipment cannot be repaired forward, it is evacuated immediately to the UMCP or returned with a LOGPAC. Even if the item cannot be evacuated at once, the sustainment system is alerted to prepare for repair or replacement. If a replacement is available (from an evacuated Soldier or inoperative equipment), it is sent forward. If not, the leader must work around it by prioritizing the use of remaining equipment such as using a squad radio for the company FM command net if the platoon radio is broken.

10-266.   Maintenance applies to all equipment. Items such as magazines, ammunition, and batteries are also maintained and inspected. While test firing in an assembly area, mark the magazines of weapons that have stoppages. If a magazine is marked more than twice, the magazine may be causing the stoppages.

Inspect the ammunition belts for crew-served weapons along with the weapons. Dirty or corroded ammunition may also cause weapon malfunctions.

HEALTH SERVICE SUPPORT

The medical threat to Soldiers comes from both enemy action and environmental situations that could adversely affect their combat effectiveness. Effective and timely FHP initiatives are essential factors in sustaining combat power during continuous operations. The Infantry battalion must ensure that its medical platoon coordinates with the BSB medical company for PVNTMED and combat operational stress control support. This support includes:

10-267.   PVNTMED advice and consultation in the areas of disease and nonbattle injuries (DNBI), environmental sanitation, epidemiology, entomology, and medical surveillance as well as limited sanitary engineering services and pest management.

10-268.   Training and advice in the promotion of positive combat stress behaviors. The mental health section, organic to the BSB medical company, can provide early identification, handling, and management of misconduct stress behavior and battle fatigued Soldiers. It assists and counsels personnel with personal, behavioral, or psychological problems and may refer suspected neuropsychiatric cases for evaluation.

PREVENTIVE MEDICINE AND FIELD SANITATION TEAM

10-269.   Throughout military history, the largest numbers of casualties are the result of the medical threat from DNBI. Prevention of DNBI frees medical assets to support Soldiers wounded by battle injury. The medical threat of DNBI remains the leading cause of personnel losses during military operations. Commanders are responsible for protecting their personnel against DNBI. In addition, commanders must be aware of occupational and environmental health hazards in operational areas. Commanders must also emphasize and enforce high standards of field sanitation and personal hygiene at all times to preclude DNBI from affecting Soldier readiness. Proper use of risk assessment (FM 100-14) and the subsequent risk management of those risks identified will help reduce DNBI losses to the unit. Commanders and medical personnel should receive a medical threat brief outlining the hazards.

10-270.   The use of preventive medicine measures (PMM) are used to eliminate or reduce DNBI casualties and include—

- Soldiers using individual techniques of PMM.
- Chain of command planning for and enforcing PMM.
- Leaders, at all levels, supervising and enforcing PMM at the individual and collective level.
- Unit field sanitation teams training unit members in individual PMM and advising the commander and unit leaders on implementing unit-level PMM.

10-271.   In all deployments, PVNTMED begins with the individual Soldier. No one else can better protect the individual from illness, injury, or death than the individual. PMM at the individual level defend the Soldier from a majority of the most prevalent illnesses in an AO and are easy and uncomplicated. Following them will assist the Soldier in accomplishing his mission and returning home safely from a deployment. For definitive information on PMM, see FM 21-10.

10-272.   Unit SOPs must address the following areas of concern:

- Ensure clean drinking water is supplied to and consumed by Soldiers.
- Ensure proper control of unit waste, both human waste and trash.
- Prevent weather-related problems. These include cold injuries such as frostbite, trench foot, and immersion foot, and heat injuries like heat exhaustion and heat stroke. Soldiers must understand the effects of conditions such as sunburn and wind-chill.
- Prevent battle fatigue to include strict implementation of the unit sleep plan (Appendix H).

Warfighting Functions

10-273.   Each company or troop-sized unit is required to have a field sanitation team whose members
are trained (they must attend a 40-hour course) and fully equipped according to AR 40-5. Selected
members from each company or troop unit will be designated to receive special training in DNBI
prevention so they can advise the commander in PMM for DNBI. This training enables the unit
commander to provide for arthropod control, individual and unit field sanitation, the monitoring of the
unit's water supplies, and ensuring the sanitation of the unit's food supplies. These comparatively simple
steps have resulted in commanders being able to reduce DNBI losses, and thus sustain its fighting strength.
For definitive information on unit field sanitation team operations and training, see FM 4-25.12.

SOLDIERS WOUNDED IN ACTION

10-274.   Medical treatment of wounded or injured Soldiers during combat operations is a continuous,
progressive operation that occurs in a series of separate but interconnecting stages. It involves personnel,
equipment, and facilities at virtually every level of the organization. The normal flow of medical treatment
for combat casualties is from the point of injury to the casualty collection point to the BAS to the BSB
medical company. The following paragraphs discuss responsibilities at each phase of this process:

Point of Injury

10-275.   The point of injury normally involves the action of four Soldiers; the wounded soldier
conducting self-aid, another soldier providing buddy aid, a CLS, and a combat medic. All of these Soldiers
can contribute to saving a life and reducing the extent and lasting effects of an injury. The CLS is almost
always the first person on the scene to begin treating wounded and injured personnel. The CLS is a
nonmedical Soldier trained to provide advanced first aid and or lifesaving procedures beyond the level of
self-aid or buddy aid. The CLS is not intended to take the place of medical personnel but to slow
deterioration of a wounded Soldier's condition until medical personnel arrive. Combat medics are normally
attached to each Infantry company and many Infantry platoons. They are trained in basic life saving
procedures and assist in preparing the casualty for transport to the CCP. The leader is responsible for
ensuring that all injured Soldiers receive immediate first aid and that the commander is informed of
casualties. He coordinates with the 1SG and company senior medic for ground evacuation. The leader--

- Ensures that all injured Soldiers receive immediate first aid.
- Informs the commander of casualties IAW FM 3-21.11.
- Coordinates with the 1SG and company senior medic for ground evacuation.
- Routes accurate information about each casualty to the proper channels.

Casualty Collection Point

10-276.   At the CCP, the senior medic conducts triage of all casualties, takes the necessary steps to
stabilize their condition, and initiates the process of moving them to the rear for further treatment. He
assists the 1SG in arranging evacuation via ground, air ambulance or by nonstandard means. METT-TC
dependent, the medical platoon may position a MEDEVAC vehicle ambulance with a company to provide
evacuation and en route care from the Soldier's point of injury or the company's CCP to the BAS. In mass
casualty situations, nonmedical vehicles may be used to assist in casualty evacuation as directed by the
company commander.

Note. Before casualties are evacuated beyond the CCP, leaders should remove all key
operational items and equipment IAW unit SOP. Minimum requirements of protective mask
and CPOG must stay with the individual.

Battalion Aid Station

10-277.   The BAS conducts EMT and advanced trauma treatment. Only procedures necessary to preserve life or limb or enable a patient to be moved safely are performed at the BAS. The BAS is normally positioned within 30 minutes' driving time of expected casualties. Patients normally are evacuated from the BAS by FSMC ambulances. The BSB medical company habitually positions ambulances at an ambulance exchange point collocated with or near the BAS.

> *Note.* Designated medical personnel collect DA Form 1156 at the aid station; it is forwarded through S-1 channels for processing by the PAC in the BSA.

Forward Support Medical Company

10-278.   The BSB medical company performs Echelon II FHP. This includes MEDEVAC from the BAS to the BSB medical company, patient holding, combat stress control (CSC) support, Class VIII resupply, preventive medicine support, medical equipment maintenance, x-ray, laboratory, and operational dental care. The BSB medical company also provides area medical support to BSA elements and back-up support to forward maneuver battalions. After the first 96 hours of BCT operations, the BSB medical company is normally augmented with additional forward surgical teams.

BATTALION MEDICAL PLATOON

10-279.   The medical platoon of the Infantry battalion is comprised of a headquarters, a combat medic section with 16 combat medics, an evacuation squad with four evacuation teams in medical evacuation vehicle (MEV) ambulances, and a treatment squad with two treatment teams (Figure 10-12). See Chapter 1 for a detailed discussion of the medical platoon's organization and responsibilities.

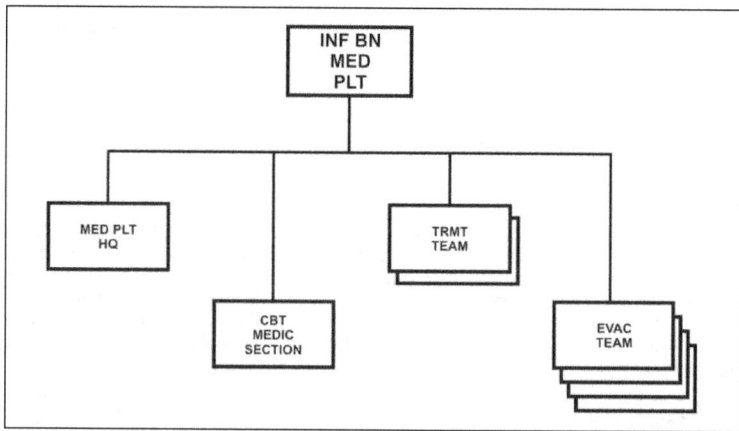

Figure 10-12. Battalion medical platoon.

COMBAT STRESS THREAT

10-280.   Many stressors in a combat situation are due to deliberate enemy actions aimed at killing, wounding, or demoralizing our Soldiers and our allies. Other stressors are due to the natural environment such as intense heat and cold, humidity, or poor air quality. Still others are due to leaders' own calculated or miscalculated choices such as decisions about unit strength, maneuver, the time of attack, and plans for medical and logistical support. Sound leadership works to keep these operational stressors within tolerable limits and prepares troops mentally and physically to endure them. In some cases, excessive stress can affect both leaders' and Soldiers' decision-making and judgment, resulting in missed opportunities, high casualties, and or failure to complete the mission.

10-281.   Some of the most potent stressors are interpersonal in nature and can be due to conflict in the unit or on the home front. In extreme cases, reactions to such stressors may involve harm to self or to others. These stressors must be identified and, when possible, corrected or controlled. For mental health or combat and operational stress control support, contact the supporting medical company through the BAS. For information on control of combat stressors and for details about specific leader and individual actions to control stress, see FM 8-51, FM 6-22.5, FM 21-10, and FM 22-51.

MORTUARY AFFAIRS

10-282.   Commanders are responsible for recovering and evacuating Soldiers killed in action to a collection point. Control of human remains and their personal effects is a systematic process. The following paragraphs discuss responsibilities at each phase of this process.

Platoon

10-283.   During reorganization, the remains of those killed in action are brought to a company collection point. DA Form 1156 is completed. All personal effects remain with the body, but equipment and issue items are turned over to the 1SG.

Company

10-284.   The supply sergeant inventories the personal effects against DD Form 1076, *Military Operations Record of Personal Effects of Deceased Personnel*. The company arranges for the remains to be transported to a MA collection point in the BSA. As a rule, remains are transported on a different vehicle than are wounded Soldiers.

Battalion

10-285.   The commander sends a letter of condolence to the Soldier's next of kin, normally within 48 hours of the death.

Brigade

10-286.   The BSB's MA NCO and the brigade S-1 section coordinate to process the human remains and supporting documentation as part of the casualty management program.

SOLDIER'S LOAD

Infantry forces are designed to be flexible and responsive in all types of terrain and environments, and for this reason, they consist mainly of foot-mobile fighters. Their success depends on the ability of Infantrymen to deliver the appropriate weapon systems and material, to the decisive place on the battlefield in a timely manner; while at the same time, maintaining the ability to defeat the enemy and survive. The Soldier's load is managed at the company and platoon level; however, standards are established at the battalion level using planning considerations to ensure Soldiers are properly equipped, and mentally and physically ready for combat.

IMPACT

10-287.   The Soldier's load is always a crucial concern to all leaders. How much is carried, how far, and in what configuration are important mission considerations, requiring command emphasis.

10-288.   The ability of an Infantry Soldier to fight is directly related to the load he must carry. An excessive load reduces energy and agility. A Soldier carrying an excessive load is at a disadvantage when they must react to enemy contact. Conversely, if the load is tailored to be light, leaders may make a decision to leave behind mission-essential or crucial equipment to balance the load. Sometimes a Soldier must carry more than the recommended combat load. However, leaders must realize how this will affect the unit's overall effectiveness. (FM 21-18 provides additional information on Soldier's load.)

PLANNING CONSIDERATIONS

10-289.   When establishing the load plan, leaders must consider what ammunition, supplies, and equipment is mission essential. Effective load planning will require the commander and his staff to take risks based on detailed estimates. The commander will also tailor his ordnance and weapons load based on the staff's estimate of the situation. The commander arranges for the remainder of the load to be secured or transported. Unit equipment and supplies are broken into one of the three echelons: combat load (fighting load or approach march), sustainment load, and contingency load.

Combat Load

10-290.   A combat load is determined by the mission commander and consists of only what is necessary to fight and survive immediate combat operations. There are two levels of combat load: fighting loads, which are carried on dynamic operations where contact with the enemy is expected, and approach march loads, which are carried when transportation cannot be provided for equipment over and above fighting loads.

Fighting Load

10-291.   A fighting load is what the Soldier carries once contact has been made with the enemy. It consists only of essential items the Soldier needs to accomplish his task during the engagement. Excessive combat loads of assaulting troops must be configured so that the excess can be redistributed, or shed (leaving only the fighting load) before or upon contact with the enemy.

Approach March Load

10-292.   An approach march load contains the operational essential equipment that Soldiers carry in addition to their fighting load. These items are dropped in an assault position, ORP, or other rally point, before or upon contact with the enemy. On extended operations, Soldiers must carry enough equipment and munitions to fight and exist until a planned resupply can take place.

Sustainment Load

10-293.   A sustainment load consists of the equipment required by the company commander for sustained operations. This equipment is usually stored by the company supply section in the field trains and brought forward when needed. A sustainment load can include rucksacks, squad duffel bags, and sleeping bags. In combat, protective items for specific threats, such as CPOGs, may be stored in preconfigured unit loads.

Contingency Load

10-294.   The contingency load includes all other items that are not necessary for ongoing operations such as extra clothing, personal items, or even Javelins in a nonarmored threat environment. The critical element for commanders is to determine what goes in these loads and who is responsible for the storage and delivery of them.

OTHER OPERATIONS

Combat operations often result in casualties to Infantry battalion Soldiers who must be replaced. These operations also result in the capture and detention of EPW and other potential enemy personnel with an undetermined status. One of the primary concerns of the Infantry battalion is to quickly and efficiently move EPWs and detainees to the rear area. All EPWs and detainees at the point of capture are treated the same.

REPLACEMENTS AND CROSS-LEVELING OF PERSONNEL

10-295.   To maintain effective, consistent combat power, the battalion must have specific plans and procedures that allow each element to quickly integrate replacement personnel and equipment. Newly arriving replacement Soldiers have a high degree of anxiety that can be reduced by well planned and executed reception operations. Unit SOPs should define how replacements and equipment are prepared for combat, including areas such as uploading, load plans, precombat inspections, and in-briefings. Replacements for wounded, killed, or missing personnel are requested through the battalion S-1. Returning or replacement personnel delivered with the LOGPAC should have already been issued all CTA-50 equipment, MOPP gear, and their personal weapons. The battalion S-1 cross-levels personnel among companies to implement the commander's guidance.

PERSONNEL REPLACEMENT

10-296.   Integrating replacements into the battalion and company is important. A new arrival on the battlefield may be scared and disoriented as well as unfamiliar with local SOPs and the theater of operations. The following procedures help integrate new arrivals.

10-297.   Units must establish SOPs for processing of new personnel. Replacements that arrive in the BSA will be fed, billeted, and equipped before being sent to their companies.

10-298.   The battalion conducts in processing through the battalion S-1 section. New Soldiers may be given a form letter to send to their next of kin. The letter should tell family members where to mail letters and packages, tell them how to use the Red Cross in emergencies, and introduce them to the chain of command. The medical platoon collects field medical records. Once assigned to a company, the battalion S-1 arranges for transportation with a LOGPAC.

10-299.   When practical, the battalion commander will introduce himself and in-brief the replacement Soldiers. This is normally done in the form of a short "welcome to the battalion" briefing. The battalion and companies must have an SOP for reception and integration of newly assigned Soldiers.

ENEMY PRISONER OF WAR AND DETAINED/RETAINED PERSONS OPERATIONS

10-300. All persons captured, detained or retained by US Armed Forces during the course of military operations are considered "detained" persons until their status is determined by higher military and civilian authorities. The BCT has an organic military police platoon organic to the BSTB to take control of and evacuate detainees (Figure 10-13). However, as a practical matter, Infantry squads, platoons, companies, and battalions capture and must provide the initial processing and holding for detainees. Detainee handling is a resource intensive and politically sensitive operation that requires detailed training, guidance, and supervision by the Infantry battalion leadership and staff.

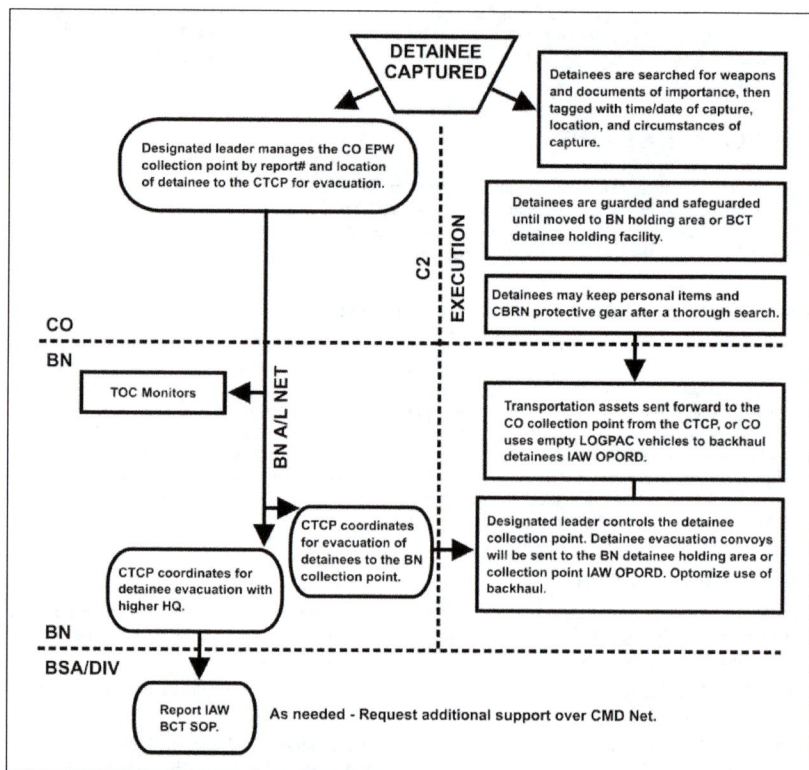

Figure 10-13. Detainee handling.

10-301. All detained persons shall be immediately given humanitarian care and treatment. US Armed Forces will never torture, maltreat, or purposely place detained persons in positions of danger. There is never a military necessity exception to violate these principles.

10-302. Field processing of detainees is always handled IAW the 5 Ss and T method:

Search

10-303. Confiscate weapons and items of intelligence value or items that might assist the detainee to escape. Let the detainee keep protective clothing, equipment, identification, and personal items. All confiscated items must be tagged.

Silence

10-304. Direct the detainees not to talk, or make facial or hand gestures. They may be gagged.

Segregate

10-305. Leaders are separated from the rest of the population. Separate hostile elements such as religious, political, or ethnic groups. Separate women and minors from adult male detainees.

Safeguard

10-306. Ensure detainees are provided adequate food, potable water, clothing, shelter, medical attention and not exposed to unnecessary danger. Do not use coercion to obtain information. Immediately report allegations of abuse through command channels.

Speed to a Safe Area/Rear

10-307. Evacuate detainees from the battlefield to a holding area or facility as soon as possible. Transfer captured documents and other property to the forces assuming responsibility for the detainees.

Tag

10-308. Use DD form 2745, *Prisoner of War (EPW) Capture Tag,* or other field-expedient means. Record the date and time of capture, location of capture, capturing unit, and circumstances of capture.

10-309. Detainees should be evacuated as soon as is practical to the BCT detainee collection point, or to a higher level facility. Circumstances sometimes preclude rapid evacuation above battalion level; however, it should never exceed 24 hours (JP 3-63). Tactical questioning of detainees is allowed relative to collection of CCIR. However, detainees must always be treated IAW the US Law of War Policy as set forth in the DoD Directive 2311.01E, *DoD Law of War Program.*

10-310. Soldiers capturing equipment, documents, and detainees should tag them using DD Form 2745 and report the capture immediately. Detainees are allowed to keep protective equipment such as protective masks. Other captured military equipment and detainee personal effects are inventoried on DA Form 4137, *Evidence/Property Custody Document.* Soldiers then coordinate with the platoon and or company headquarters to link up and turn the documents and prisoners over to designated individuals. Normally the 1SG, often assisted by the supply section, moves the detainees to the vicinity of the combat trains for processing and subsequent interrogation by battalion or MI company personnel. Crews of vehicles undergoing repair, or sustainment personnel can be used as guards.

10-311. The CTCP plans and coordinates detainee operations, collection points, and evacuation procedures. Detainees are evacuated from the battalion combat zone as rapidly as possible and moved to either the battalion detainee holding area or BCT holding facility. The battalion holding area is normally located near the CTCP or the FTCP. The BCT holding facility is normally located in the BSA, and detainees are transported on returning LOGPAC vehicles or by transportation coordinated by the battalion S-4. As necessary, the S-2 reviews and reports any documents or information of immediate value. The S-4 coordinates evacuation of large amounts of enemy equipment.

10-312. The battalion detainee holding area should be simple and easily guarded by only a few Soldiers and must include the following requirements:

- Be securable.
- Contain water.
- Have latrine facilities.
- Provide adequate shelter (trench or cover) (Figure 10-14).

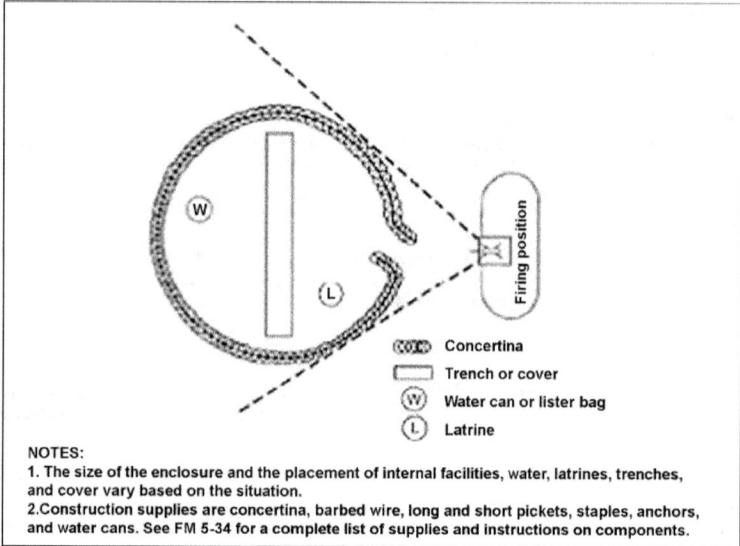

Figure 10-14. Battalion detainee holding area.

Chapter 11
Urban Operations

Urban operations (UO) are not new to the US Army. Throughout its history, the Army has fought enemies on urban terrain. However, urban areas and urban populations have grown significantly during the late twentieth century and have begun to exert a much greater influence on military operations. The worldwide shift from a rural to an urban society and the requirement to transition from combat to stability operations have affected the way US forces conduct combat operations. Companies, platoons, and squads will seldom conduct UO independently during offensive or defensive operations and will most likely conduct assigned missions as part of a battalion urban's combat operation. However, UO engagements are almost always fought by small units such as platoons and companies, due to the fragmented nature of urban terrain. During stability and civil support operations, it is likely that companies, platoons, and squads will conduct urban operations. This chapter provides the necessary background information to facilitate an understanding of how commanders plan and conduct UO.

Section I. INTRODUCTION

Urban operations are military actions that are planned and conducted on terrain, where manmade construction affects the tactical options available to the commander. An urban area is a topographical complex where manmade construction and the population are dominant features. Urban terrain confronts commanders with a combination of difficulties rarely found in other environments. Urban areas are complex, dynamic environments. However, three distinguishing characteristics can be identified as the "urban triad": The physical *terrain* of an urban area consists of three dimensional surface areas; internal and external space of buildings and structures; subsurface areas; and the airspace above the battalion AO. The noncombatant *population* is characterized by the interaction of numerous political, economical, and social activities. This population is supported by the urban area's physical and service *infrastructure*. Cities vary immensely depending on their history, the cultures of their inhabitants, their economic development, the local climate, available building materials, and many other factors. This variety exists not only among different cities but also within any particular urban area. The urban environment, like all environments, is neutral and affects all sides equally. The side that can best understand and exploit the effects of the urban area has the best chance of success.

FUNDAMENTALS

11-2.   The fundamentals described in this paragraph apply to UO regardless of the mission or geographical location. Some fundamentals may also apply to operations not conducted in an urban environment but are particularly relevant in an environment dominated by manmade structures and a dense noncombatant population. BCT and Infantry battalion commanders and staffs should use these fundamentals when planning UO.

UNDERSTAND HUMAN DIMENSION

11-3.   The human dimension of the urban environment often has the most significance and greatest potential for affecting the outcome of UO. A useful source for this information is attached PSYOP, CA or HUMINT assets. Commanders carefully consider and manage the allegiance and morale of the civilian population as these can decisively affect operations. The assessment of the urban environment must identify clearly and accurately the attitudes of the urban population toward units. Commanders and staffs make their assessments based on a thorough understanding and appreciation of the local social and cultural norms. Sound application of the understanding of the human dimension will also encourage the population to provide vital intelligence on the enemy. Well established policies, discipline, and consideration positively affect the attitudes of the population toward Army forces.

PERFORM FOCUSED INFORMATION OPERATIONS

11-4.   Information superiority efforts aimed at influencing non-Army sources of information are critical in UO. Because of the density of noncombatants and information sources, the media, the public, allies, coalition partners, neutral nations, and strategic leadership will likely scrutinize how units participate in UO.

11-5.   The proliferation of cell phones, Internet capability, and media outlets ensure close observation of unit activities. With information sources rapidly expanding, public information about Army operations will be disseminated rapidly. Therefore, units should integrate information operations into every facet and at all levels of the operation to prevent negative impacts.

11-6.   Under media scrutiny, the actions of a single Soldier may have significant strategic implications. A goal of information operations is to ensure that the information available to all interested parties, the public, the media, and other agencies is accurate and placed in the proper context of the Army's mission. (For more information, see Appendix J.)

11-7.   While many information operations will be planned at levels above the BCT, tactical units conducting UO will often be involved in the execution of information operations such as military deception, operations security, physical security, and psychological operations. BCTs and battalions must conduct aggressive ISR and security operations that will allow them to properly apply the elements of assess, shape, dominate, and transition to specific UO.

CONDUCT CLOSE COMBAT

11-8.   Close combat is required in offensive and defensive UO. The capability to conduct close combat must be present and visible in stability UO and may be required, by exception, in support UO. Close combat in UO is resource intensive, requires properly trained and equipped forces, has the potential for high casualties, and can achieve decisive results when properly conducted. Close combat in UO should be conducted by combined arms task organized units and joint fires in support. Units must always be prepared to conduct close combat as part of UO (Figure 11-1).

Figure 11-1. Soldiers conducting close combat in an urban area.

AVOID ATTRITION APPROACH

11-9.   Previous doctrine was inclined towards a systematic linear approach to urban combat. This approach placed an emphasis on standoff weapons and firepower. This approach can result in significant collateral damage, civilian casualties, destruction of vital infrastructure, a lengthy operation, and be inconsistent with the political situation and strategic objectives. Enemy forces that defend urban areas often want units to adopt this approach because of the likely costs in resources. Commanders should consider this tactical approach to urban combat only when the factors of METT-TC warrant its use.

CONTROL ESSENTIAL

11-10.   Many modern urban areas are too large to be completely occupied or even effectively controlled. Therefore, units must focus their efforts on controlling only the essentials to mission accomplishment. At a minimum, this requires control of key terrain. In the urban environment, functional, political, or social significance may determine what terrain is considered key or essential. For example, a power station or a government building may be key terrain. Units focus on control of the essential facilities or terrain so they can concentrate combat power where it is needed and conserve it. This implies risk in those areas where units choose not to exercise control in order to be able to mass overwhelming power where it is needed.

MINIMIZE COLLATERAL DAMAGE

11-11.   Units should use precision fires, information operations, and nonlethal tactical systems (Appendix L) as much as possible consistent with mission accomplishment. Commanders must consider the short- and long-term effects of firepower on the population, the infrastructure, and subsequent missions.

SEPARATE COMBATANTS FROM NONCOMBATANTS

11-12.   There is almost never a clear distinction between combatants and noncombatants. However, promptly separating noncombatants from combatants, as best as can be identified, may make the operation more efficient and diminish some of the enemy's asymmetrical advantages. Separation of noncombatants may also reduce some of the restrictions on the use of firepower and enhance force protection. This important task becomes more difficult when the adversary is an unconventional force and can mix with the civil population.

RESTORE ESSENTIAL SERVICES

11-13.   Tactical units may have to support a plan for the restoration of essential services that may fail to function upon their arrival or cease to function during an operation. Essential services include power, food, water, sewage, medical, and security. During planning for and the conduct of UO, the commander uses all available assets to minimize collateral damage to potentially vital infrastructure.

PRESERVE CRITICAL INFRASTRUCTURE

11-14.   Commanders and staffs analyze the urban area to identify critical infrastructure. Tries to preserve the critical elements for post-combat sustainment operations, stability operations, or the health and well being of the indigenous population may be required. This requirement differs from simply avoiding collateral damage because units may have to initiate actions to prevent adversaries from removing or destroying infrastructure that will be required in the future. In some cases, preserving critical infrastructure may be the assigned objective of the UO.

TRANSITION CONTROL

11-15.   UO of all types are resource intensive and thus commanders plan to conclude UO expediently yet consistent with successful mission accomplishment. The end state of all UO transfers control of the urban area to another agency or returns it to civilian control. This requires the successful completion of the mission and a thorough transition plan. The transition plan may include returning control of the urban area to another unit or agency a portion at a time as conditions permit.

PLANNING CONSIDERATIONS

11-16.   Throughout history, military planners have viewed cities as centers of gravity and sources of national strength. Cities are distinguished as population centers; transportation and communication hubs; key nodes of industrial, financial, and information systems; seats of government; and repositories of wealth. Because of the changing nature of society and warfare, deployments into urban environments have become more frequent, and this trend is likely to continue. The purpose of such deployments will be to neutralize or stabilize extremely volatile political situations, to defeat an enemy force that has sought the protection afforded by urban terrain, or to provide assistance to allies in need of support. This chapter provides guidance necessary for planning and executing missions in an urban environment. The BCT is the primary headquarters around which units are task-organized to perform UO.

11-17.   The increasing world population and accelerated growth of cities makes UO in future conflicts very likely. Operations in urban areas usually occur when—

- The assigned objective lies within an urban area and cannot be bypassed.
- The urban area is key (or decisive) in setting or shaping the conditions for current or future operations.
- The urban area is in the path of a general advance and cannot be surrounded or bypassed.
- The urban area is small enough to be bypassed or isolated by rapidly advancing units but still needs to be occupied because it lies near or on logistics lines of communications.

- Political or humanitarian concerns require the control of an urban area or necessitate operations within it.
- An urban area is between two natural obstacles and cannot be bypassed.
- Defending from urban areas supports a more effective overall defense or cannot be avoided.
- Occupation, seizure, and control of the urban area will deny the enemy control of the urban area and the ability to impose its influence on both friendly military forces and the local civilian population, thereby allowing friendly forces to retain the initiative and dictate the conditions for future operations.

ORGANIZATION

11-18. The Infantry battalion is well suited as a basic building block for UO because of its organizational structure, precision weapons systems, and the numerous Infantry-specific tasks associated with UO.

ROLE OF INFANTRY BATTALION

11-19. The Infantry battalion achieves tactical successes by means of combined-arms at the company level focused on dismounted assault. Combined-arms integration is vital to support dismounted operations by squads, platoons, and companies, including dispersed actions. Supported by direct fires from organic weapons, antiarmor weapons, and heavy forces, the battalion incorporates engineers, COLT fire support teams, mortars, artillery, and joint fires and effects to provide the appropriate systems required for this integration.

ISOLATION

11-20. An incontrovertible fact in UO is that isolation is a key to victory. If the attacker fails to isolate the urban area, the defender can reinforce and resupply his forces, thus protracting the operation and significantly decreasing the attacker's resources and will to continue. If the defender is isolated, the attacker seizes the initiative and forces the defender to take high-risk actions, such as a breakout or counterattack, to survive. Mounted forces are optimal for executing isolation operations because they possess the speed, agility, firepower, and protection necessary to successfully shape the urban area for offensive or defensive operations.

CLOSE COMBAT

11-21. Historically, the close fight in urban combat has consisted of street-to-street fighting resulting in high casualties and high expenditure of resources. Well executed combined arms operations can reduce the high casualty rate traditionally associated with UO.

TACTICAL CHALLENGES

11-22. The battalion faces a number of challenges during the planning and execution of UO. The most likely challenges are discussed in the following paragraphs.

CONTIGUOUS AND NONCONTIGUOUS AREAS OF OPERATIONS

11-23. The battalion must be prepared to conduct UO operations in both contiguous and noncontiguous areas of operations.

11-24. Contiguous operations are military operations that the battalion conducts in AOs that facilitate mutual support of combat, CS, and sustainment elements at varying levels. Contiguous operations have traditional linear features including identifiable, contiguous frontages and shared boundaries between forces. For battalions, relatively close distances among adjacent battalions, supporting assets, and subordinate units and elements characterize contiguous operations.

11-25. In noncontiguous operations, the battalion may be required to operate independently, removed from BCT CS and sustainment assets by distance and time. Also, subordinate companies may operate in isolated pockets, connected only through integrating effects of an effective concept of operations. Noncontiguous operations place a premium on initiative, effective information operations, decentralized security operations, and innovative logistics measures. Noncontiguous operations complicate or hinder mutual support of combat, CS, and sustainment elements because of extended distances between subordinate units and elements.

SYMMETRICAL AND ASYMMETRICAL THREATS

11-26. In addition to being required to face symmetrical enemy threats, the battalion must be prepared to face enemy threats of an asymmetrical nature.

11-27. Symmetrical threats are generally "linear" in nature and include those enemy forces that specifically confront the battalion's combat power and capabilities. Examples of symmetrical threats include conventional enemy forces conducting offensive or defensive operations against friendly forces.

11-28. Asymmetrical threats are those that are specifically designed to avoid confrontation with the battalion's combat power and capabilities. These threats may use the civilian population and infrastructure to shield their capabilities from battalion fires. Asymmetrical threats are most likely to be based in and target urban areas to take advantage of the density of civilian population and infrastructure. Additional examples of asymmetrical threats include terrorist attacks, WMD, electronic warfare (to include computer-based systems), criminal activity, guerilla warfare, and environmental attacks.

QUICK TRANSITION, FROM STABILITY OPERATIONS, TO COMBAT OPERATIONS AND BACK

11-29. Stability operations are missions that may escalate to combat. The battalion must always retain the ability to conduct offensive and defensive operations. Preserving the ability to transition allows the battalion to maintain initiative while providing force protection. Commanders should consider planning a defensive contingency with on-order offensive missions in case stability operations deteriorate. Subordinate commanders and leaders must be fully trained to recognize activities that would initiate this transition.

RULES OF ENGAGEMENT

11-30. UO are usually conducted against enemy forces fighting in close proximity to civilians. ROE and other restrictions on the use of combat power are more restrictive than in other conditions of combat (FM 3-06.11). If isolation of the enemy force from the civilian population can be achieved, this may allow for less restrictive ROE.

Section II. METT-TC

Planning and preparation for UO are generally the same as for operations on open terrain. However, in order for the commander and staff to develop viable COAs, the force must conduct ISR operations. UO require significant HUMINT reconnaissance because sensors and other technological devices are not as effective in urban environments. ISR operations can take the form of stealthy surveillance teams, tactical questioning of noncombatants and informants, and reconnaissance of key terrain and avenues of approach. Using ISR assets and satellite imagery, the staff can develop urban maps that include a common reference system, such as numbering buildings, to assist subordinate unit C2. The commander and staff also take into account special considerations when operating in this environment. This section provides special METT-TC considerations for UO.

MISSION

11-31. The battalion must close with and defeat the enemy in order to be decisive in UO. Close combat in UO is resource intensive, requires properly trained and equipped forces, and has the potential for high casualties. Therefore, the battalion must use close combat as its decisive operation only after shaping the urban area through reconnaissance and surveillance, isolation, precision fires, and maneuver.

OBJECTIVE

11-32. The commander and staff must clearly understand the purpose of the operation. The battalion's objective may be terrain or force oriented. The commander must consider whether committing his force to combat in urban areas is required or beneficial for achieving his intent.

INTENT

11-33. During planning for offensive operations, the commander and staff consider the overall purpose and intent of the operation and define what is required. For example, the commander determines if clearing means every building, block by block, or seizure of a key objective, which may require clearing only along the axis of advance. Often, the battalion can integrate urban areas into the defensive scheme to develop a stronger defense.

ENEMY

11-34. The battalion commander and staff consider the strength, composition, disposition, and activities of the enemy. They consider both conventional and unconventional enemy forces and the tactics the enemy may employ. Enemy tactics may range from ambushes and snipers to large-scale conventional actions conducted by heavy forces. The IPB addresses the known and potential tactics and vulnerabilities of all enemy forces and threats operating within and outside the urban area. The IPB considers the three-dimensional environment of urban areas: airspace, surface, and subsurface. It also considers the political, racial, ethnic, tribal, and religious factors that influence the enemy. (See Chapter 2, FM 3-06.11, for a detailed discussion of urban intelligence preparation of the battlefield.)

11-35. The increasing availability of sophisticated technology has created unorthodox operational approaches that can be exploited by potential opponents. These approaches seek to counter the technological and numerical advantages of US joint systems and forces, and to exploit constraints placed on US forces due to cultural bias, media presence, ROE, and distance from the crisis location.

11-36. Offsetting their inherent weaknesses, enemy forces use asymmetrical means to seek an advantage in urban terrain to remain dispersed and decentralized, adapting their tactics and weapons to provide the best success in countering a US response. Threats, in addition to conventional forces, may consist of—

- Unconventional forces.
- Paramilitary forces.
- Militia and special police organizations.
- Organized criminal organizations.

11-37. These forces range from units equipped with small arms, mortars, machine guns, antiarmor weapons, field expedient weapons such as Molotov cocktails and mines to very capable mechanized and armor forces equipped with current generation equipment. Urban environments also provide many passive dangers such as disease from unsanitary conditions and psychological illnesses. While the active threats vary widely, many techniques are common to all. The enemy may employ the following seven techniques during UO.

Use Population to Advantage

11-38.   The populace of a given urban area represents key terrain which gives the side that manages it best a distinct advantage. Future urban battles may see large segments of the populace remain in place, as they did in Budapest, Grozny, and Mogadishu. Battalions involved in UO must be prepared to conduct missions in and among the residents of the area.

11-39.   Enemy forces may use the population to provide camouflage, concealment, and deception for their operations. Guerrilla and terrorist elements may look the same as any other members of the community. Even conventional and paramilitary troops may look "civilian." Western military forces adopted the clean-shaven, close-cut hair standard at the end of the nineteenth century to combat disease and infection, but twenty-first century opponents might very well sport beards as well as civilian clothing and other "nonmilitary" characteristics.

11-40.   The civilian population may also provide cover for enemy forces, enhancing their mobility close to friendly positions. Enemy forces may take advantage of US moral responsibilities and try to make the civilian population a burden on the Army's logistical and force protection resources. They may herd refugees into friendly controlled sectors, steal from US-paid local nationals, and hide among civilians during operations.

11-41.   The civilian population may also serve as an important intelligence source for the enemy. Local hires (serving among US Soldiers, civilians with access to base camp perimeters, and refugees moving through friendly controlled sectors) may be manipulated by enemy forces to provide information on friendly dispositions, readiness, and intent. In addition, enemy special purpose forces and hostile intelligence service assets may move among well-placed civilian groups.

Win Information War

11-42.   Enemy forces may try to win the information war in direct opposition to the battalion's operations. Portable video cameras, Internet access, commercial radios, and cellular telephones are all tools that permit enemy forces to tell their story. American "atrocities" may be staged and broadcast. Electronic mail may be transmitted to sympathetic groups to help undermine resolve. Internet websites provide easy worldwide dissemination of enemy propaganda and misinformation. Hackers may gain access to US sites to manipulate information to the enemy's advantage.

11-43.   The enemy may make skillful use of the news media. Insurgent campaigns, for example, need not be tactical military successes; they need only make the opposition's campaign appear unpalatable to gain domestic and world support. The media coverage of the Tet Offensive of 1968 affected the will of both the American people and their political leadership. Although the battle for Hue was a tactical victory for the US, the North Vietnamese clearly achieved strategic success by searing the American consciousness with the high costs of urban warfare (Appendix J).

Manipulate Key Facilities

11-44.   Enemy forces may identify and seize control of critical components of the urban area to help them shape the battlespace to their own ends. Telephone exchanges provide simple and reliable communications that can be easily secured with off-the-shelf technologies. Sewage treatment plants and flood control machinery can be used to implement WMD strategies or to make sections of the urban area uninhabitable. Media stations significantly improve the information operations position of the controlling force. Power generation and transmission sites provide means to control significant aspects of civilian society over a large area.

Use Three Dimensions of Urban Terrain

11-45.   The enemy thinks and operates throughout all dimensions of the urban environment. Upper floors and roofs provide the urban enemy forces excellent OPs and BPs above the maximum elevation of many weapons. Shots from upper floors strike friendly armored vehicles in vulnerable points. Basements also provide firing points below many weapons' minimum depressions and strike at weaker armor. Sewers and subways provide covered and concealed access throughout the AOs. Conventional lateral boundaries often do not apply as enemy forces control some stories of a building while friendly forces control others floors in the same building.

Employ Urban-Oriented Weapons

11-46. Whether they are purpose-built or adapted, many weapons may have greater than normal utility in an urban environment while others may have significant disadvantages. Urban enemy weapons are much like the nature of urbanization and the urban environment: inventive and varied. Small, man-portable weapons, along with improvised munitions, can dominate the urban environment. Examples of enemy weapons favored in UO include—

- Weapons with no minimum depression or no maximum elevation.
- Weapons with little or no backblast (gas-metered, soft launch, and so forth).
- Mortars.
- Sniper rifles.
- Machine guns.
- Grenades.
- Grenade launchers.
- Flame and incendiary weapons.
- RPGs and other shoulder-fired antitank guided missiles (ATGMs).
- Riot control and tranquilizer agents.
- Mines and booby traps.

Engage Entire Enemy Force

11-47. Enemy forces may "hug" battalions operating in an urban area. They may also try to keep all or significant portions of the battalion engaged in continuous operations to increase the battalion's susceptibility to combat stress. UO, by their nature, produce an inordinate amount of combat stress casualties, and continuous operations exacerbate this problem (Appendix H). The enemy may maintain a large reserve to minimize the impact of this on their own forces.

Focus Attacks on Service Support and Unprotected Soldiers

11-48. Enemy forces may prey on Soldiers poorly trained in basic Infantry skills. Ambushes may focus on these Soldiers while they are conducting resupply operations or moving in poorly guarded convoys. UO are characterized by the isolation of small groups and navigational challenges, and the enemy may use the separation this creates to inflict maximum casualties even when there is no other direct military benefit from the action.

URBAN MAPPING PROCEDURES

11-49. Before entering an urban environment, the battalion obtains or develops urban maps to assist in C2. The brigade should try to gain access to city planner or civil engineer maps to provide detailed information of the urban area. The urban maps, whether digital or sketched, include a reference system to identify buildings and streets (Figure 11-2). Naming conventions should be simple to allow for ease of navigation and orientation in the urban environment (odd number buildings on left side of street, even numbers on right side). Street names should not be used as references because the enemy can remove or change street signs to confuse friendly forces.

11-50. Initial map and aerial photograph reconnaissance can identify key terrain and other important locations in the AO.

Safe Havens

11-51.   Safe havens include areas such as—

- Hospitals.
- Police stations.
- Embassies.
- Other (friendly) facilities.

Hazardous Areas

11-52.   Hazardous areas include construction sites, dangerous intersections, bridges, and criminal areas.

Major Terrain Features

11-53.   Major terrain features include such areas as parks, industrial complexes, and airports.

Subterranean Features

11-54.   Subterranean features include sewers and utility systems, subway systems, and underground water systems.

Figure 11-2. Initial photo reconnaissance of urban area of operations.

11-55.   The urban map also facilitates control by providing a tool for tracking units in detail and obtaining precise location updates. The battalion uses ISR assets to confirm and update their urban maps. These improved maps are critical since most existing maps do not provide the level of detail necessary to conduct tactical operations. Specifically, the BCT assesses avenues of approach in the urban AO. Included with the maps are overlays that categorize sections of the urban area by ethnicity, religious affiliation, and other prevailing characteristics that could affect operations (Figures 11-3 through 11-6, pages 11-11 through 11-14).

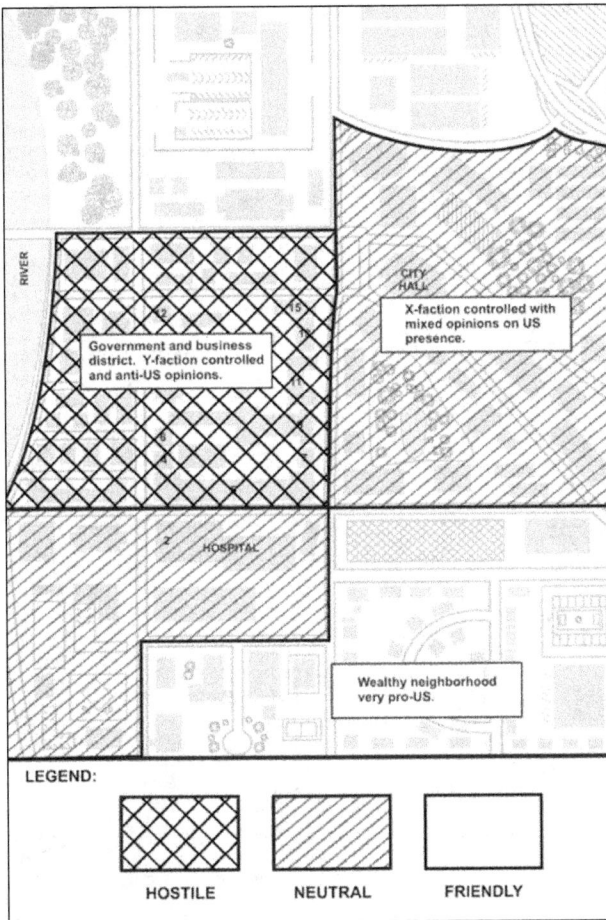

Figure 11-3. Example of population status overlay.

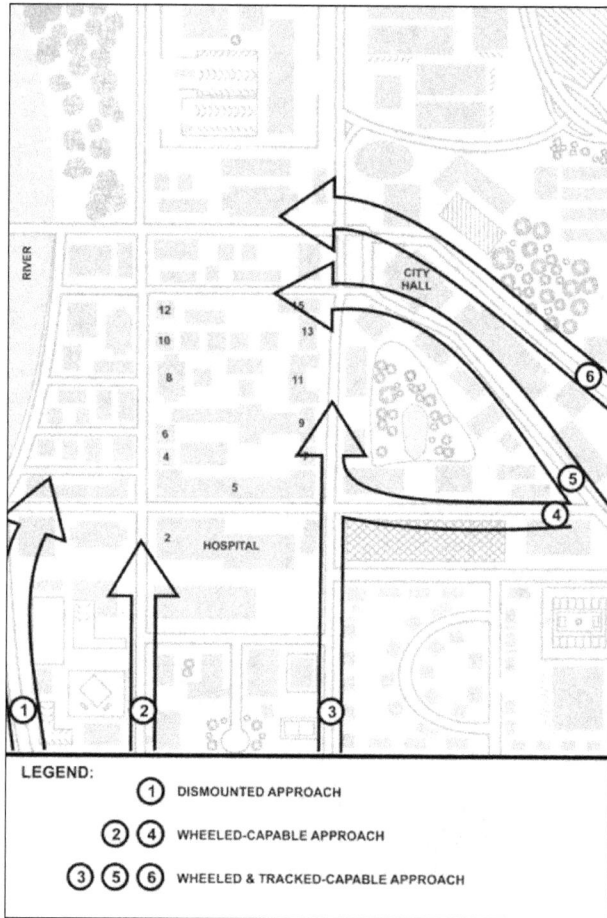

Figure 11-4. Avenues of approach in the urban area.

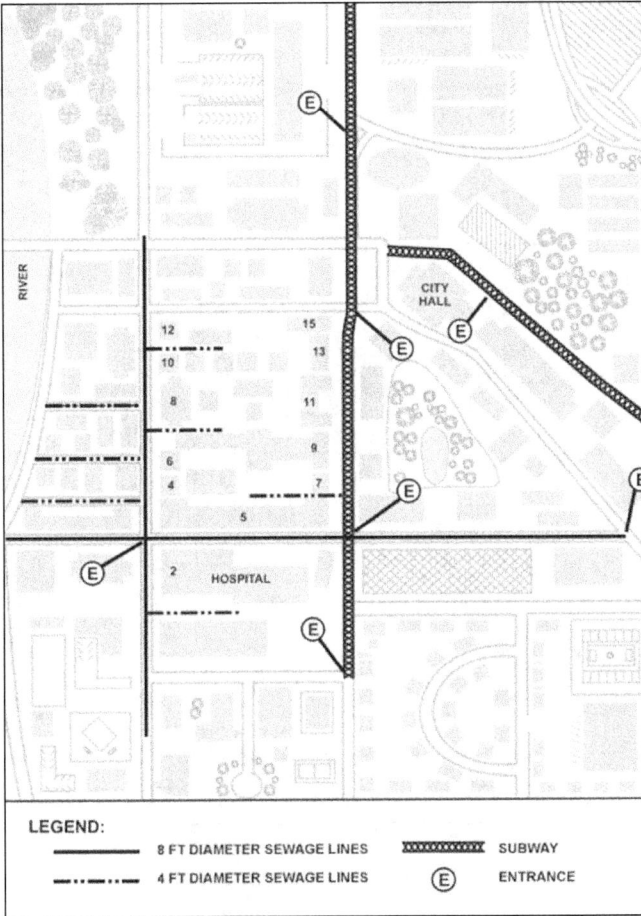

Figure 11-5. Sewer and subterranean overlay.

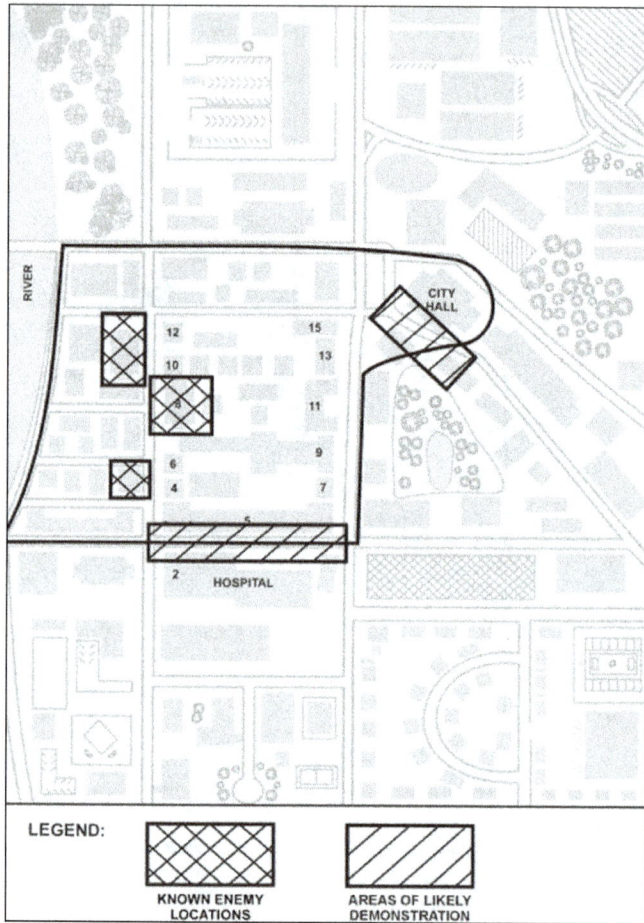

Figure 11-6. Enemy overlay.

TERRAIN AND WEATHER

11-56.   An urban area is a concentration of structures, facilities, and people that form the economic and cultural focus for the surrounding area. Battalion operations are affected by all categories of urban areas (Table 11-1). Cities, metropolises, and megalopolises with associated urban sprawl cover hundreds of square kilometers. Battalions normally operate in these urban areas as part of a larger force. Extensive combat in these urban areas involves units of division level and above.

Table 11-1. Categories of urban areas.

Category	Population	Considerations
Village	Up to 3,000	The battalion's AO can contain many villages. Battalions and companies bypass, move through, defend from, and attack objectives within villages as a normal part of operations.
Town	Between 3,000 and 100,000	Operations in such areas normally involve BCT-sized or larger units. Battalions can bypass, move through, defend in, or attack enemy forces in towns as part of larger unit operations. Operations in these areas normally require the full commitment of the BCT or higher echelon formations.
City	Between 100,000 and 1,000,000	Extensive combat in large cities involves multiple BCT formations. Battalions can fight adjacent to, on the edges of, or inside cities.
Metropolis	Between 1,000,000 and 10,000,000	Extensive combat in large cities involves multiple BCT formations. Battalions can fight adjacent to, on the edges of, or inside cities.
Megalopolis	Over 10,000,000	Extensive combat in large cities involves multiple BCT formations. Battalions can fight adjacent to, on the edges of, or inside cities.

TERRAIN

11-57.   A detailed analysis of the urban area and surrounding terrain is vital to the success of any operation in an urban area (FM 34-130 and FM 3-06.11). The battalion commander must understand the elements of the urban infrastructure that are necessary for achieving the intent and end state of the BCT's mission. Military maps normally do not provide sufficient detail for terrain analysis of an urban area. Recent aerial photographs and other current intelligence products are critical. Maps and diagrams of the city from other sources, such as local governments, tourist activities, or law enforcement services, can be useful. Products that can be developed by the National Imagery Mapping Agency (NIMA) can be specifically tailored for the AOs.

11-58.   The S-2 should obtain maps and diagrams of the following:

- Subway systems, railways, and mass transit routes.
- Underground water, sewer, and utility systems.
- Electrical distribution systems, power stations, and emergency services.
- Fuel supply and storage facilities.
- Facilities for mass communications such as cell phones, computer hubs, radio, and telephone.
- Public administration buildings, hospitals, and clinics.

11-59.   The terrain analysis should also identify the following:

- Structural characteristics of buildings, bridges, and transportation networks.
- Roads, highways, rivers, streams, and other waterways that may be used as high-speed avenues of approach.

- Analysis of the natural terrain surrounding the urban area (observation and fields of fire, avenues of approach, key terrain, obstacles and movement, and cover and concealment [OAKOC]).
- Analysis of the urban area itself, to include street patterns, structure types, and available maneuver space (FM 34-130).
- Covered and concealed approaches to the urban area.
- Key and decisive terrain inside and outside of the urban area.
- Identification of buildings, areas, or facilities protected by the law of land warfare or restricted by current ROE, such as places of worship or shrines, medical facilities, historic monuments, and other facilities dedicated to arts and sciences, provided they are not being used for military purposes (FM 27-10).
- Stadiums, parks, open fields, playgrounds, and other open areas that may be used for landing zones or holding areas.
- Location of prisons and jails.
- Potential host nation support facilities such as quarries, lumber yards, major building supply companies, and warehouses.
- Power lines, telephone lines, and raised cables that may be hazards to helicopters.
- Significant fire hazards and locations of other toxic industrial materials (TIMs).
- Weather effect products from topographic models or historical sources such as the effects of heavy rains on local areas.

11-60.   A close relationship with the local government and military forces can be very beneficial. They can provide information about population, fire-fighting capabilities, police and security capabilities, civilian evacuation plans, location of key facilities, and possibly current enemy activities. They may also be able to provide translators and informants for gathering of HUMINT.

11-61.   An infrastructure analysis of the urban area is also important. Because urban infrastructures vary greatly, a comprehensive list cannot be provided. However, common characteristics include—

- Urban street patterns and trafficability.
- Sources of potable water.
- Bulk fuel and transport systems.
- Communications systems.
- Rail networks, airfields, canals and waterways, and other transportation systems.
- Industries.
- Power (to include nuclear) and chemical production facilities and public utilities.

WEATHER

11-62.   Weather analyses that are important to battalion operations include visibility, winds, precipitation, and temperature and humidity.

Visibility

11-63.   Light data have special significance during UO. Night and periods of reduced visibility (including fog) favor surprise, infiltration, detailed reconnaissance, attacks across open areas, seizure of defended strongpoints, and reduction of defended obstacles. However, the difficulties of night navigation in restricted terrain force the battalion to rely on simple maneuver plans with easily recognizable objectives.

Winds

11-64.   Wind chill is not as pronounced in urban areas. However, the configuration of streets, especially in close orderly block and high-rise areas, can cause wind canalization.

Precipitation

11-65.   Rain or melting snow often floods basements and subterranean areas, such as subways, and makes storm and other sewer systems hazardous or impassable. Chemical agents and other TIMs are washed into underground systems by precipitation.

Temperature and Humidity

11-66.   Air inversion layers are common over cities, especially cities located in low-lying "bowls" or in river valleys. Inversion layers trap dust, chemical agents, and other pollutants, reducing visibility and often creating a greenhouse effect, which causes a rise in ground and air temperature. The heating of buildings during the winter and the reflection and absorption of summer heat make urban areas warmer than surrounding open areas during both summer and winter. This difference can be as great as 10 to 20 degrees and can reduce the effectiveness of thermal sights and imaging systems.

TROOPS AND SUPPORT AVAILABLE

11-67.   During UO, the battalion is often augmented with additional assets. Heavy forces (tanks, Infantry fighting vehicles, Strykers), Engineers, ADA Army aviation, FA, MP, public affairs, PSYOP, civilian affairs, smoke, decontamination, and long-range surveillance (LRS) assets, and special operations forces, when available, may also support the battalion. Heavy forces will, in most circumstances, be OPCON to an Infantry battalion which requires the parent unit to provide logistical and maintenance support that is normally not available in the Infantry battalion or the IBCT. (See Figure 11-7 and Figure A-3 for example task organizations. Actual task organizations depend on the factors of METT-TC.)

TROOP DENSITY, EQUIPMENT, AND AMMUNITION

11-68.   Troop density for offensive missions in urban areas can be as many as three to five times greater than for similar missions in open terrain. Troops require additional equipment such as ladders, ropes, grappling hooks, and other entry equipment. The ammunition consumption rates for small arms, grenades (all types), Claymore mines, antitank guided missiles, .50 caliber, MK 19, mortars, and explosives can be four times the normal rate. The staff must ensure the continuous supply of Classes I, III, V, and VIII and water to forward units. Supplies should be configured for immediate use and delivered as far forward as possible to supported units. Support units are particularly vulnerable in UO and the commander must consider security plans for logistics bases and resupply operations.

STRESS

11-69.   The commander and staff must consider the effects of prolonged combat on Soldiers. Continuous close combat produces high psychological stress and physical fatigue. Rotating units committed to combat for long periods can reduce stress. Leaders should take extra effort and time to train and psychologically prepare Soldiers for this type of combat (Appendix H).

DISCIPLINE

11-70.   Maintaining discipline is especially important in UO. All commanders must ensure that their Soldiers understand and follow the established ROE. The law of land warfare prohibits unnecessary injury to noncombatants and needless damage to property. This prohibition may restrict the commander's use of certain weapons, munitions, and tactics.

TIME

11-71.   Combat in urban areas has a slower tempo and an increased use of methodical, synchronized missions. In planning UO, the commander and staff must consider these factors. Planning must allow more time for thorough reconnaissance, subordinate unit rehearsals, demolitions, breaching, fire fighting, entry and movement techniques, fighting position construction, booby trap recognition and neutralization, combat lifesaver training, and crowd control.

CIVIL CONSIDERATIONS

11-72.   The commander and staff must understand the composition, activities, and attitudes of the civilian population, within the urban area, to include the political infrastructure. Various options are available to the commander to control the impact of civilians on the operation. These include screening civilians, prohibiting unauthorized movement, diverting or controlling refugee movements, and evacuating. Understanding the urban society requires comprehension of—

- Living conditions.
- Cultural distinctions.
- Ethnicity.
- Factions.
- Religious beliefs.
- Political affiliation and grievances.
- Attitudes toward US forces (friendly, hostile, or neutral).

CURFEW AND EVACUATION

11-73.   A commander with the mission of defending an urban area may need to establish a curfew to maintain security or to aid in control of military traffic. (Curfews are not imposed as punishment. They are normally established to reduce noncombatant casualties and provide a measure of force protection.) A commander can require civilians to evacuate towns or buildings if the purpose of the evacuation is to use the town or building for imperative military purposes, to enhance security, or to safeguard those civilians being evacuated. If the commander takes this action, he must specify and safeguard the evacuation routes. If civilians are evacuated, there may also be a need to provide temporary housing and sustainment for them. This is best coordinated with and conducted by other government agencies or nongovernmental organizations. However, before the evacuation begins, the commander should ensure these plans are in place so as not to cause overdue hardship and animosity among the civilian population. Battalions may also be involved in securing routes and possibly safeguarding food, clothing, medical, and sanitary facilities. Evacuated civilians must be transferred back to their homes as soon as hostilities in the area have ceased. The staff must plan for and coordinate the movement and evacuation of civilians to ensure their actions do not interfere with the military operation. The battalion staff and supporting civil affairs units working with local officials coordinate the movements of civilians.

RESISTANCE GROUPS

11-74.   The battalion may encounter civilian resistance groups whose actions may range from providing the enemy with supplies, services, and noncombat support to actively fighting against friendly forces. Members of such resistance groups should be dealt with IAW applicable provisions of the law of war. Commanders should seek guidance from the judge advocate general (JAG) concerning the detention and disposition of persons participating in acts harmful to friendly forces. The S-2 must work with PSYOP and CA units to identify these threats and recommend, within the ROE, the appropriate preemptive action or response. The activities of resistance groups may also benefit friendly forces. They may be a potential source for TAC HUMINT assets; act as guides, liaisons, or translators; and provide subject-matter expertise on local public facilities such as refineries, power plants, and water works. They may also provide active resistance against the enemy.

Section III. COMMAND AND CONTROL

UO require centralized planning and decentralized execution; therefore, the staff must develop a detailed plan that synchronizes the WFF in order to meet the commander's intent and provide subordinate units with the means to accomplish the mission.

ENEMY FOCUS

11-75.   During the mission analysis, the plan should focus on the factors of METT-TC. The commander orients the plan on the enemy rather than terrain. He uses terrain factors to defeat the enemy. Considerations include, but are not limited to, the following:

11-76.   Thorough evaluation of the urban area's related terrain and enemy force may take much longer than in other environments. This time factor also affects friendly planning efforts.

11-77.   Determine the enemy's location, strength, and capabilities. Develop a plan that defeats his direct and indirect fire systems.

11-78.   Focus the axis of advance on the enemy's weaknesses while maintaining adequate force protection measures. When possible, employ multiple and supporting axes of advance.

11-79.   Divide the objective area into manageable smaller areas that facilitate company maneuver.

11-80.   Isolate the objective area and establish a foothold at the point of entry. The location chosen for the foothold must allow for expansion.

11-81.   The BCT and battalion maneuver plans directly affect the company schemes of maneuver. Every platoon within the battalion must know what enemy targets will be engaged by BCT and battalion assets.

COMMANDER'S CRITICAL INFORMATION REQUIREMENTS

11-82.   The commander's critical information requirements directly affect his decisions and dictate the successful execution of tactical operations. The battalion staff must develop the components of the CCIR that facilitate the commander's ability to make decisions affecting the plan during UO. Essential elements of friendly information (EEFI) address the enemy commander's PIR. Friendly forces information requirements are items that cause the commander to make decisions that affect the plan. The following are examples of PIR, EEFI, and FFIR that would help the commander in an urban environment.

PRIORITY INFORMATION REQUIREMENTS

11-83.   These are intelligence requirements that a commander has anticipated and that have stated priority in task planning and decision making. Examples include—

- Is the enemy using avenue of approach 1 to infiltrate into the battalion AOs?
- Does mobility corridor three (3rd Street) restrict movement of friendly armored and wheeled vehicles?
- Is there an enemy strongpoint located between 3rd Street and 5th Street along 3rd Avenue?
- Does the enemy have ADA assets positioned along air avenue of approach 2?
- Is the enemy using the subway station at Maple and Grand Avenues as an assembly area for their reserve?

ESSENTIAL ELEMENTS OF FRIENDLY INFORMATION

11-84. These are critical aspects of a friendly operation that, if known by the enemy, would subsequently compromise, lead to failure, or limit the success of the operation. Therefore, they must be protected from detection. Examples include—

- Have any of the battalion command nets been compromised?
- Has my LOC been disrupted, and where?
- Has the enemy located my Q36?

FRIENDLY FORCES INFORMATION REQUIREMENTS

11-85. This is information the commander and staff need about the friendly forces available for the operation. Examples include—

- Reconnaissance elements captured or compromised.
- Main bridge locations along the ground route that have been destroyed.
- OPORD compromised.
- Loss of cryptographic equipment.
- Expected personnel and equipment replacements that did not arrive.

TASK ORGANIZATION

11-86. UO may require unique task organizations. For example, UO provide one of the few situations where Infantry and armor elements may be effectively task-organized below platoon levels. Battalion commanders consider providing assets where they will be needed to accomplish specific tasks. All phases of mission execution are considered when developing task organization. Changes in task organization may be required to accomplish different tasks during mission execution. Figure 11-7 (page 11-21) shows an example task organization for an Infantry battalion task force conducting offensive UO that consist of a main effort, three supporting efforts, and a reserve.

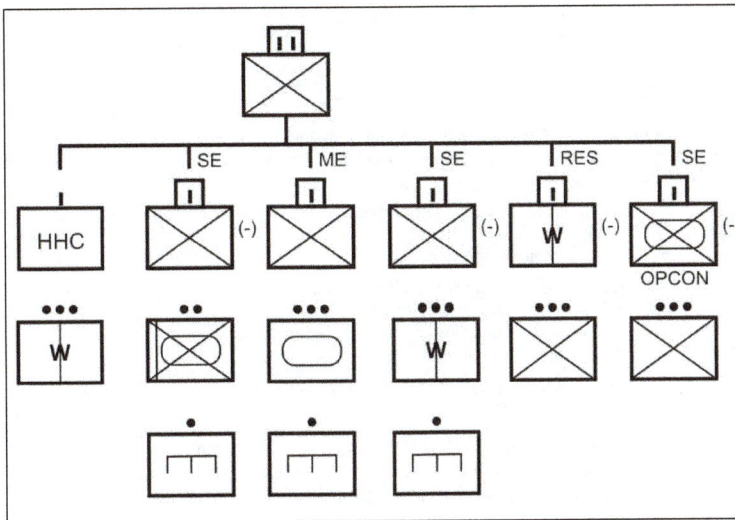

Figure 11-7. Example offensive task organization.

Note. The task organization shown in Figure 11-7 may change after the assault when the battalion reorganizes for follow-on missions.

REHEARSALS

11-87.   After developing a thorough, well-synchronized plan, battalion commanders require subordinate units to conduct combined-arms rehearsals at the levels at which the operations will occur, to include all phases of the operation. When conducted properly, combined-arms rehearsals identify potential problems in the synchronization of the plan between maneuver, CS, and sustainment elements. Rehearsals provide a means for units that seldom operate together to train collective skills. Rehearsals should start early in the troop-leading process. Some rehearsals can start shortly after receipt of warning orders. Subordinate units can rehearse drills, such as breaching, clearing buildings, and moving between buildings, before receiving a detailed plan. Infantry can also rehearse aspects of operating close to armored vehicles. The battalion commander and staff must allocate sufficient time to subordinate units to conduct rehearsals. Rehearsals for subordinate units to consider include, but are not limited to the following:

- Communications procedures.
- Direct fire control plan.
- Fires and effects.
- Breaching.
- Maneuver.

FIRE SUPPORT

11-88.   Often, the role of fires in UO is to get the maneuver force into or around the urban area with minimal casualties so that the commander has the maximum combat power to close with the enemy and finish the fight. Civil affairs and PSYOP assets should be coordinated with the appropriate command and control warfare or information operations planning headquarters.

FIELD ARTILLERY

11-89.   Appropriate FSCM are essential because fighting in urban areas results in opposing forces fighting in close combat. When planning for fire support in an urban area, the battalion S-3 and FSO should consider the following:

11-90.   Target acquisition may be more difficult because of the increased cover and concealment afforded by the terrain. Ground observation is limited in urban areas. Adjusting fires is difficult since buildings block the view of adjusting rounds; therefore, the lateral method of adjustment may be most useful.

11-91.   Initial rounds are adjusted laterally until a round impacts on the street perpendicular to the FEBA. Airburst rounds are best for this adjustment. The adjustments must be made by sound. When rounds impact on the perpendicular street, they are adjusted for range. When the range is correct, a lateral shift is made onto the target, and the gunner fires for effect.

11-92.   Special considerations apply to shell and fuze combinations when buildings limit effects of munitions:

- Careful use of variable time (VT) is required to avoid premature arming.
- Indirect fires may create unwanted rubble and collateral damage.
- The close proximity of enemy and friendly troops requires careful coordination.
- White phosphorous may create unwanted fires and smoke.
- Fuze delay is used to penetrate fortifications.
- Visible illumination rounds can be effective; however, friendly positions should remain in shadows and enemy positions should be highlighted. Tall buildings may mask the effects of visible illumination rounds. Infrared illumination rounds may be more effective if the enemy force does not possess night vision devises.
- VT, time, and improved conventional munitions (ICMs) are effective for clearing enemy positions, observers, and antennas off rooftops.
- Swirling winds may degrade smoke operations.
- Scatterable mines may be used to impede enemy movements. SCATMINE effectiveness is reduced when delivered on a hard surface.

11-93.   Target acquisition is difficult in urban terrain because the enemy has many covered and concealed positions and movement lanes. The enemy may be on rooftops, in buildings, and in sewer and subway systems. Aerial observers are extremely valuable for targeting because they can see deep to detect movements, positions on rooftops, and fortifications. Targets should be planned on rooftops to clear away enemy FOs as well as communications and radar equipment. Targets should also be planned on major roads, at road intersections, and on known or likely enemy positions. Consider employing artillery in the direct fire mode to destroy fortifications, especially when assaulting well-prepared enemy positions. Also, restrictive FSCM, such as a restrictive fire area or no-fire area, may be needed to protect civilians and critical installations.

- 155-mm howitzers are effective in neutralizing concrete targets with direct fire. Concrete-piercing 155-mm rounds can penetrate 36 inches of concrete at ranges up to 2,200 meters. Howitzers must be protected by Infantry when used in the direct-fire mode since they do not have any significant protection for their crews.
- Forward observers must be able to determine where and how large the dead spaces are. This area is a safe haven for the enemy because he is protected from indirect fires. For low-angle artillery, the dead space is about five times the height of the building. For high-angle artillery, the dead space is about one-half the height of the building. Positioning of artillery should consider their ability to shoot high angle fire to reduce the dead space effect of tall buildings.

- Aerial observers and tactical UAS are effective for seeing behind buildings immediately to the front of friendly forces. They are extremely helpful when using the ladder method of adjustment because they may actually see the adjusting rounds impact behind buildings. Aerial observers can also relay calls for fire when communications are degraded due to power lines or masking by buildings.
- Radar can locate many artillery and mortar targets in an urban environment because of the high percentage of high-angle fires. If radar is sited too close behind tall buildings, it loses some effectiveness.
- The use of airburst fires is an effective means of clearing snipers from rooftops.
- Artillery should be well practiced and prepared to conduct dangerously close fire missions.

MORTARS

11-94. Mortars are the most responsive indirect fires available to Infantry commanders and leaders. Their mission is to provide close and immediate fire support to the maneuver units. Mortars are well suited for combat in urban areas because of their high rate of fire, steep angle of fall, short minimum range and the smaller bursting radius of 60mm and 81mm mortar ammunition. Commanders must ensure that mortar support is integrated into all fire support plans. (See FM 3-06.11 for detailed information on the tactical employment of mortars in the urban fight.)

ROLE OF MORTAR UNITS

11-95. The role of mortar units is to deliver suppressive fires to support maneuver, especially against dismounted Infantry. Mortars can be used to obscure, neutralize, suppress, or illuminate during urban combat. Mortar fires inhibit enemy fires and movement, allowing friendly forces to maneuver to a position of advantage. The most common and valuable use for mortars is often harassment and interdiction fires. One of their greatest contributions is interdicting supplies, evacuation efforts, and reinforcement in the enemy rear just behind his forward defensive positions. During World War II and the recent Middle East conflicts, light mortar HE fires have been used extensively during urban combat to deny the use of streets, parks, and plazas to enemy personnel. Light mortars have also been used effectively as final protective fires because of their relatively small bursting radius. Finally, mortars can be used, with some limitations, against light armor and structures. Effectively integrating mortar fires with dismounted maneuver is critical to successful combat in an urban area.

POSITION SELECTION

11-96. The selection of mortar positions depends on the size of buildings, the size of the urban area, and the mission. Rubble can be used to construct a parapet for firing positions. Positions are also selected to reduce effectiveness of enemy counterbattery fire.

Existing Structures and Masking

11-97. The use of existing structures, such as garages, office buildings, or highway overpasses, is recommended to afford the best protection for positions, and lessen the amount of camouflage needed. Proper masking enhances survivability. If the mortar is fired in excess of 885 mils to clear a frontal mask, the enemy counterbattery threat is reduced. These principles are used in both the offense and the defense.

Placement

11-98. Mortars are not usually placed on top of buildings because lack of cover and mask makes them vulnerable. They should not be placed inside buildings with damaged roofs unless the structure's stability has been checked. Overpressure can injure personnel, and the shock on the floor can weaken or collapse the structure. Overhead clearance must be verified before emplacing mortars. For example, overhead telephone and electrical wires can interfere with the round when fired.

COMMUNICATIONS

11-99. Communication transmissions in urban areas are likely to be erratic. Structures reduce radio ranges; however, remoting the antennas to upper floors or roofs may improve communications and enhance operator survivability. The use of radio retransmissions is another technique that may apply in urban areas. A practical solution is to use existing civilian systems to supplement the unit's capability, understanding that this is a nonsecure method of communication. Hard wire communication may be the most suitable means of communication in an urban environment.

MAGNETIC INTERFERENCE

11-100. In an urban environment, all magnetic instruments are affected by surrounding structural steel, electrical cables, and automobiles. However, when laying guns, digital compasses are not affected by these urban environment restrictions and have been used effectively to overcome these problems.

HIGH-EXPLOSIVE AMMUNITION

11-101. Mortar HE fires are used more than any other type of indirect fire in urban combat. Although mortar fires often target roads and other open areas, the natural dispersion of indirect fires results in many hits on buildings. To minimize collateral damage in UO, leaders must use care when planning mortar fires.

11-102. HE ammunition, especially the 120-mm projectile, gives good results when used against lightly built structures within cities. However, it does not perform well against reinforced concrete found in larger urban areas.

11-103. When using HE ammunition in urban fighting, only point detonating fuzes should be used. The use of proximity fuzes should normally be avoided because the nature of urban areas causes proximity fuzes to function prematurely. Proximity fuzes, however, are useful in attacking some targets such as OPs on tops of buildings.

ILLUMINATION

11-104. In the offense, illuminating rounds are planned to burst above the objective. If the illumination was behind the objective, the enemy troops would be in the shadows rather than in the light. In the defense, illumination is planned to burst behind friendly troops to put them in the shadows and place the enemy troops in the light. Buildings reduce the effectiveness of the illumination by creating shadows. Continuous illumination requires close coordination between the FO and FDC to produce the proper effect by bringing the illumination over the defensive positions as the enemy troops approach the buildings (Figure 11-8).

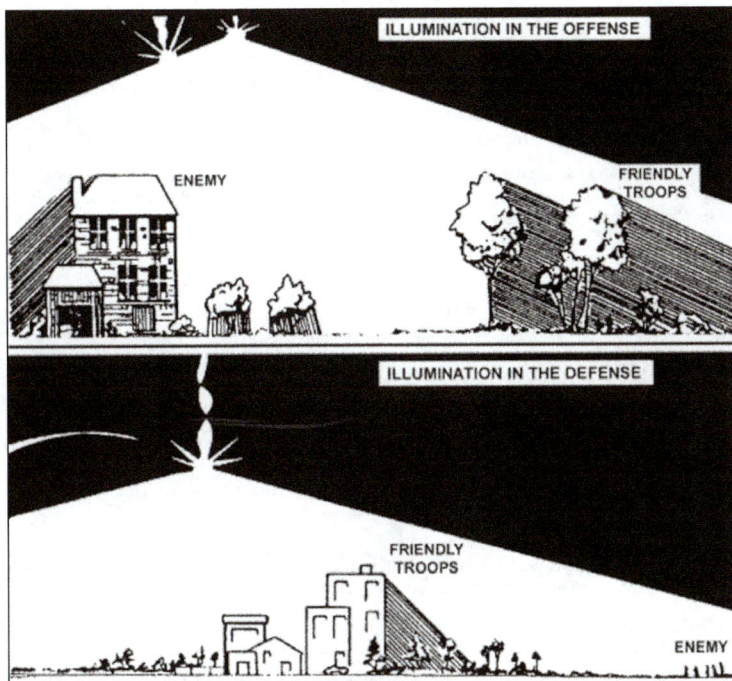

Figure 11-8. Illumination during urban operations.

SPECIAL CONSIDERATIONS

11-105. When planning the use of mortars, commanders must consider the following:

- Observer positioning.
- Ammunition effects to include white phosphorous and red phosphorous and the effects of obscurants.
- Dead space.
- Security for mortar crews.
- Displace of the mortars.

COMMUNICATIONS

11-106. One of the biggest challenges for a battalion staff is to maintain communications with subordinate elements. Buildings and electrical power lines reduce the range of FM radios. Remoting radio sets or placing antennas on rooftops can solve the range problem for CPs and trains. Companies do not have the assets to ensure continuous communications, so the battalion staff must plan for continual movement of battalion assets to support company operations.

WIRE

11-107. Wire is a secure and effective means of communications in urban areas. Wires should be laid underground, overhead on existing poles, or through buildings to prevent vehicles from cutting them.

MESSENGERS AND VISUAL SIGNALS

11-108. Messengers and visual signals can also be used in urban areas. Messengers must plan routes that avoid the enemy. Routes and time schedules should be varied to avoid establishing a pattern. Visual signals must be planned so they can be seen from the buildings.

SOUND

11-109. Sound signals are normally not effective in urban areas due to the amount of surrounding noise.

EXISTING SYSTEMS

11-110. If existing civilian or military communications facilities can be captured intact, they can also be used by the battalion. An operable civilian phone system, for instance, can provide a reliable, although nonsecure, means of communication. Use of news media channels in the immediate AOs for other-than-emergency communications, must also be coordinated through the S-1 or civil affairs officer.

WEAPONS EFFECTS

11-111. The characteristics and nature of combat in urban areas affect the results and employment of weapons. Leaders at all levels consider the following factors in various combinations.

SURFACES

11-112. Hard, smooth, flat surfaces are characteristic of urban targets. Rarely do rounds impact perpendicularly to these flat surfaces. They usually hit at an angle. This reduces the effect of the round and increases the threat of ricochets.

RANGES AND ENGAGEMENT TIME

11-113. Engagement times are short, and ranges are close in urban areas. About 90 percent of all targets are located 50 meters or less from the identifying Soldier. Minimum arming ranges and troop safety from backblast or fragmentation effects must be considered.

DEPRESSION AND ELEVATION LIMITS

11-114. Depression and elevation limits for some weapons create dead space. Tall buildings form deep canyons that are often safe from indirect fires. Some weapons can fire rounds to ricochet behind cover and inflict casualties. Target engagement from horizontal and vertical oblique angles demands superior marksmanship skills.

OBSCURATION

11-115. Smoke from burning buildings, dust from explosions, shadows from tall buildings, and the lack of light penetrating inner rooms combine to reduce visibility and increase a sense of isolation. Added to this is the masking of fires caused by rubble and manmade structures. Targets, even those at close range, tend to be indistinct.

CONFUSION

11-116. Urban fighting often becomes confused melees with several small units attacking on converging axes. The risks from friendly fires, ricochets, and fratricide must be considered during planning. Control measures must be continually adjusted to lower the risks. Soldiers and leaders clearly mark their locations IAW unit SOP to avoid fratricide (Appendix A). Armored vehicle crews will likely operate from a full protected mode decreasing the crew's ability to observe and protect the vehicle from rocket propelled grenades (RPGs), antitank guided missiles (ATGMs), and mines. Infantry and armored vehicle crews must have practiced, and redundant communications SOP established, to aid in enemy identification, engagement, and prevention of fratricide.

BUILDINGS

11-117. Both the shooter and target may be inside or outside the buildings. They may both be inside the same or separate buildings. The enclosed nature of combat in urban areas means the weapon's effect, such as muzzle blast or backblast and penetration from room to room or floor to ceiling, must be considered as well as the round's impact on the target. Usually, manmade structures must be attacked before enemy personnel inside are attacked. Weapons and demolitions may be chosen for employment based on their effects against masonry and concrete rather than against enemy personnel.

Section IV. OFFENSIVE OPERATIONS

Offensive operations in urban areas are based on offensive doctrine modified to conform to the urban terrain. Urban combat also imposes a number of demands that are different from other field conditions such as combined-arms integration, fires, maneuver, and use of special equipment. As with all offensive operations, the commander must retain his ability to fix the enemy and maneuver against him. Offensive UO normally have a slower pace and tempo than operations in other environments. Missions are more methodical. The battalion must be prepared to conduct different missions simultaneously. For example, a battalion may establish checkpoints in one section of a city and simultaneously clear enemy in another section.

"From 1942 to the present, shock units or special assault teams have been used by attackers (and often by defenders) with great success. These assault teams are characterized by integration of combined-arms. Assault teams typically contain Infantry with variable combinations of armor, artillery, or engineers."--US Army Human Engineering Laboratory

OFFENSIVE FRAMEWORK

11-118. Figure 11-9 shows the urban operational framework as it applies to offensive operations and shows the tactical tasks of subordinate units. While the elements of the operational framework are not phases, tactical tasks may become phases at the battalion level and below, based on the factors of METT-TC. Properly planned and executed offensive operations involve all tactical tasks shown. They may be conducted simultaneously or sequentially, depending on the factors of METT-TC. During offensive operations, the BCT commander's intent normally include the following (also Appendix L):

- Synchronizing fires, information operations, and nonlethal capabilities.
- Isolating decisive points to dominate the urban area.
- Using superior combat power to destroy high pay-off targets.
- Using close combat, when necessary, against decisive points.
- Transitioning to stability operations.
- Using detailed intelligence, surveillance, and reconnaissance plan to assess the situation.

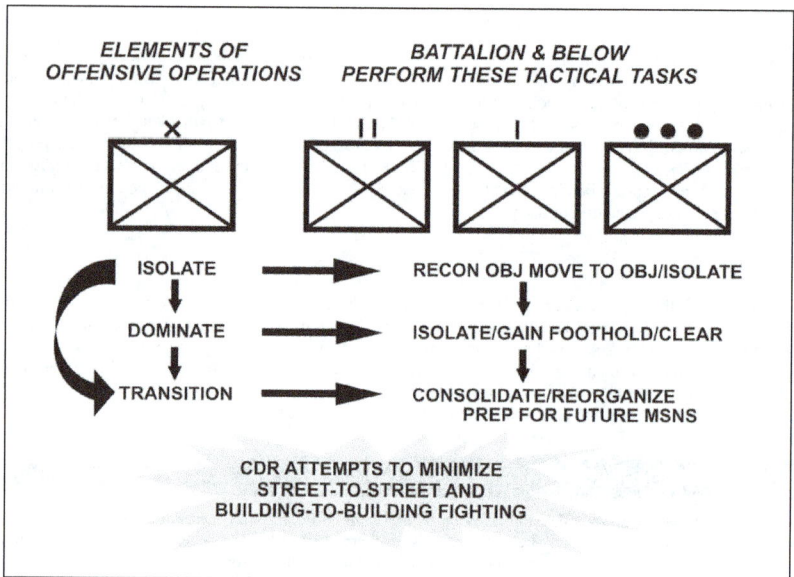

Figure 11-9. Offensive urban operational framework.

TYPES OF OFFENSIVE OPERATIONS

11-119. Offensive operations in an urban area are planned and implemented based on the factors of METT-TC. At the battalion level, the offense takes the form of either a deliberate or hasty operation such as an MTC or attack. The battalion may also be given the mission to conduct special purpose attacks such as a raid, demonstration, spoiling attack, or counterattack.

HASTY OPERATIONS

11-120. The battalions conduct hasty offensive operations after a successful defense or as part of a defense; because of a MTC, meeting engagement, or chance contact during a movement; or in a situation where the unit has the opportunity to attack vulnerable enemy forces. The attack in an urban area differs because of the close, complex nature of the terrain makes command, control, and communications, as well as massing fires to suppress the enemy, more difficult. In urban areas, incomplete information, intelligence, and concealment may require the maneuver unit to move through, rather than around, the friendly unit fixing the enemy in place. Control and coordination become important to reduce congestion at the edges of the urban area.

DELIBERATE OPERATIONS

11-121. A deliberate offensive operation is a fully synchronized operation that employs all available assets against the enemy's defense, IAW with the ROE. Deliberate operations are characterized by detailed planning based on available information, thorough reconnaissance, preparation, and rehearsals. Given the nature of urban terrain, the attack of an urban area is similar to the techniques employed in assaulting a strongpoint. At the battalion level, an attack of an urban area usually involves the sequential execution of the following tactical tasks.

Reconnoiter Objective

11-122. This involves making a physical reconnaissance of the objective with battalion assets and those of higher headquarters, as the tactical situation permits. It also involves making a map reconnaissance of the objective and all the terrain that will affect the mission and an analysis of aerial imagery, photographs, or any other detailed information about the building(s) and other appropriate urban terrain. Also, any other information collected by reconnaissance and surveillance units, such as the battalion scout platoon, snipers and tactical UAS is considered during the planning process.

Move to the Objective

11-123. This may involve moving through open terrain, urban terrain, or both. Movement should be made as rapidly as possible without sacrificing security. Movement should be made along covered and concealed routes and can involve moving through buildings, down streets, in subsurface areas, or a combination of all three.

Isolate Objective

11-124. Isolation begins with the efforts of SOF units controlled by higher headquarters to influence enemy and civilian actions. The battalion commander can use PSYOP teams, if available, to direct the civilian population to move to a designated safe area through the use of loudspeaker broadcasts, dissemination of print products or other methods.

11-125. In certain situations requiring precise fire, snipers can provide an excellent method of isolating key areas while simultaneously minimizing collateral damage and noncombatant casualties (Appendix A.)

11-126. Isolating the objective also involves seizing terrain that dominates the area so that the enemy cannot supply, reinforce, or withdraw its defenders. It also includes selecting terrain that provides the ability to place suppressive fire on the objective. Battalions may be required to isolate an objective as part of the overall BCT operation or to do so independently. Depending on the tactical situation, companies within the battalion may have to isolate an objective by infiltration.

Secure a Foothold

11-127. Securing a foothold involves seizing an intermediate objective that provides cover from enemy fire and a location for attacking troops to enter the urban area. The size of the foothold depends on the factors of METT-TC.

11-128. As a company attacks to gain a foothold, it should be supported by suppressive fires and smoke. In the example shown in Figure 11-10, the center battalion conducts a supporting attack to seize OBJ DOG. (The battalion commander has determined that two intermediate objectives are necessary in order to seize OBJ DOG.)

11-129. One company secures a foothold in OBJ Y. As a follow-on mission, the same company either seizes OBJ Z and supports the battalion main effort by fire or facilitates the passage of another company through OBJ Y to seize OBJ Z and support the battalion main effort by fire.

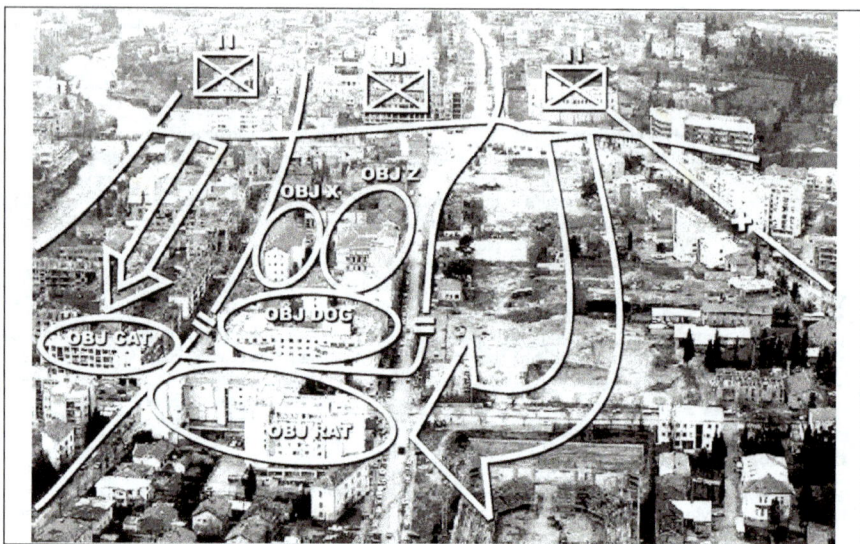

Figure 11-10. Security of a foothold in a battalion attack.

Clear an Urban Area

11-130. The commander may decide to selectively clear only those parts necessary for the success of his mission if—

- An objective must be seized quickly.
- Enemy resistance is light or fragmented.
- The buildings in the area have large open areas between them. (In this case, the commander clears only those buildings along the approach to his objective or only those buildings necessary for security.)

11-131. The mission may require the battalion to systematically clear an area of all enemies. Through detailed analysis, the battalion commander may anticipate that he will be opposed by a strong, organized resistance or will be in areas having strongly constructed buildings close together. He may assign his company zones within the battalion zone or AO in order to conduct systematic clearing (Figure 11-11).

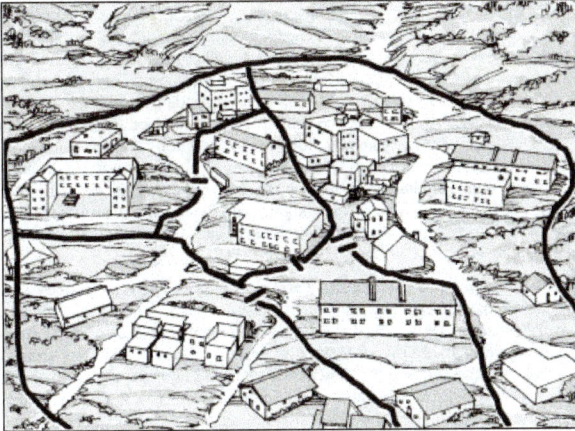

Figure 11-11. Systematic clearance within assigned areas.

Consolidate or Reorganize and Prepare for Future Missions

11-132. Consolidation occurs immediately after each action. Reorganization and preparation for future missions occurs after consolidation. Many of these actions occur simultaneously.

11-133. Consolidation provides security, facilitates reorganization, and allows the battalion to prepare for counterattack. Rapid consolidation after an engagement is extremely important in an urban environment.

11-134. Reorganization actions (many occurring simultaneously) prepare the unit to continue the mission. The battalion prepares to continue the attack or prepares for future missions, including the possible transition to stability operations.

Note. FBCB2 assets significantly improve friendly force situational understanding in digitally equipped units.

11-135. During urban combat, units rely heavily on self-aid, buddy aid, and aid from combat lifesavers to provide basic medical care until casualties can be evacuated. There are differing types of injuries and wounds that occur during urban operations, including a high percentage of orthopedic, blast, fire, and crushing injuries. The unit's force health protection plans strive to minimize the effects of wounds, injuries, disease, urban environmental hazards, and psychological stresses on unit effectiveness, readiness, and morale. Historically, the urban environment has had three to six times greater casualty rates than other combat environments.

11-136. Casualty evacuation in an urban environment presents many challenges in the location, acquisition, and evacuation of patients. Techniques may require modification to acquire and evacuate casualties from above, below, and at ground level. Furthermore, during UO, the environment (rubble and debris) may dictate that evacuation be accomplished by litter carriers rather than by vehicle or aircraft. Commanders should consider using armored vehicles for evacuation. Commanders should also be prepared for evacuation from within buildings and for the possibility that medical evacuation by Army air may not be available due to the fragility of the aircraft and their susceptibility to small arms fire. Treatment facilities may have to be moved much farther forward than usual. Units need specific medical policies, directives, and SOPs for dealing with noncombatants.

11-137. First aid training has increased significance in UO. The compartmented nature of UO, transportation restrictions, communications difficulties, and the finite number of company and platoon medics may limit the urban casualty's initial treatment administered by nonmedical personnel. Units identify and train combat lifesavers (CLSs) to perform in the absence of medics. The CLSs must have adequate supplies of Class VIII. Positioning of medical personnel, identification of CCP, positioning of medical evacuation (MEDEVAC) ambulance and locating treatment teams with supported units may mitigate some risk to injured and wounded Soldiers. In addition, the increased potential for delayed evacuation during UO mandates that medical personnel be skilled in prolonged casualty care. During the 3-4 October 1993 battle in Somalia, seven medics managed 39 casualties for more than 14 hours before they could be evacuated. Evacuation delays also significantly increase potential infection. Such delays may cause more casualties dying of their wounds; therefore, trauma specialist/company/platoon medics should also be skilled in administering antibiotics on the battlefield.

11-138. All health care providers can recognize and treat injuries due to incendiary or fuel-air explosives (also known as thermobaric weapons) a cloud of volatile gases, liquids, or powders; and then ignite, creating a fireball consuming oxygen and creating enormous overpressure. When employed in an urban structure, the blast wave or overpressure is greatly amplified. Injuries resulting from these weapons are massive burns, broken or crushed bones, concussions, missile injuries, and internal injuries. Health care providers can easily overlook internal injuries (at least initially) unless they are trained, prepared, and expecting them. The increased use of body armor during UO will help prevent penetrating chest and abdomen wounds. Medical personnel should expect more groin, pelvis, and extremity injuries. Furthermore, when fighting Soldiers that are known to use body armor, an enemy (particularly snipers) can be expected to target the head and face more often than other anatomic areas resulting in more head injuries. Lastly, hearing loss may increase particularly when firing recoilless weapons in enclosed spaces with little ventilation.

TRANSITION

11-139. During transition, the battalion continues to use all CS and sustainment assets consistent with the mission end state and ROE to move from offensive operations to stability operations. The ultimate goal is to return the urban area to civilian control. During this step, the roles and use of SOF, (especially CA and PSYOP) CS, and sustainment units (medical, and military police) become more important with the requirements to maintain order and stabilize the urban area. These assets normally support the battalion's transition efforts under BCT control. The battalion staff, in coordination with the BCT staff, prepare to transition from being a "supported" force to being the "supporting" force.

MOVEMENT TO CONTACT

11-140. Figure 11-12 shows a MTC in an urban area using the search and attack technique. The battalion uses this technique when the battalion commander does not have adequate information and a clear vision of the enemy situation and the information cannot be gathered by BCT or higher echelon elements. The battalion normally employs this technique against a known weak enemy force that is disorganized and incapable of massing strength, for example, urban insurgents or gangs. The battalion divides its portion of the AO into smaller areas and coordinates the movement of companies. It can either assign sectors to specific companies or control their movement by sequential or alternate bounds within the battalion sector. In the example shown in Figure 11-13, page 11-34, companies would find, fix, and finish the enemy, or they would find and fix the enemy and the battalion would assign another company the task of finishing the enemy (sequential or alternate bounds). During a mission of this type, the urban environment makes finding, fixing, and finishing the enemy difficult for conventional Infantry forces. For example, movement of units may become canalized due to streets and urban "canyons" created by tall buildings. The application of firepower may become highly restricted based on the ROE. The use of HUMINT in this type of action becomes increasingly more important and can be of great assistance during the "find" portion of the mission.

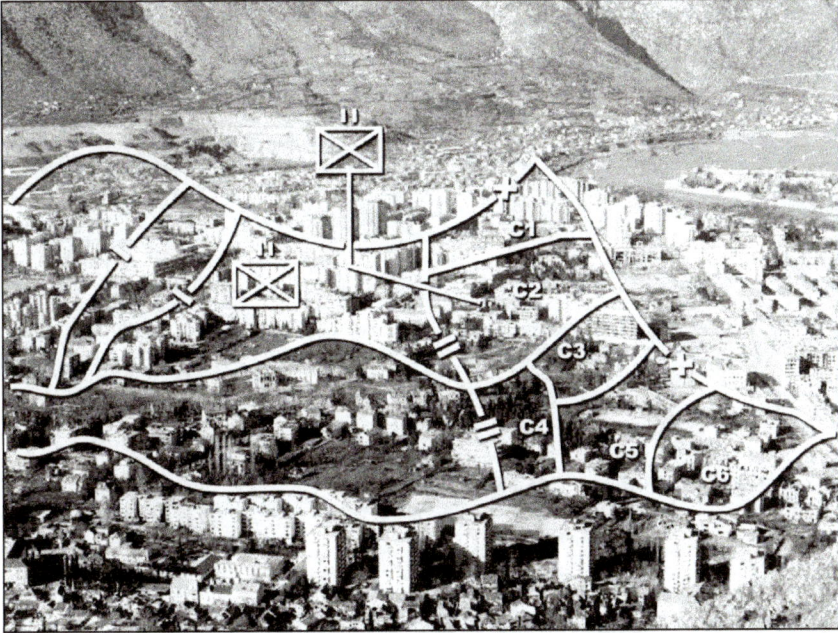

Figure 11-12. Search and attack technique.

INFILTRATION

11-141. The following is an example that describes the actions of an Infantry battalion conducting an infiltration with engineers attached.

11-142. The outskirts of a town may not be strongly defended. Its defenders may have only a series of antiarmor positions, security elements on the principal approach, or positions blocking the approaches to key features in the town. The strongpoints and reserves are normally deeper in the city.

11-143. A battalion may be able to seize a part of the town by infiltrating platoons and companies between those enemy positions on the outskirts. Moving by stealth on secondary streets using the cover and concealment of back alleys and buildings, the battalion may be able to seize key street junctions or terrain features, to isolate enemy positions, and to help following units pass into the urban area. Such an infiltration should be performed when visibility is poor and no civilians are in the area.

11-144. The Infantry battalion is organized into infiltration companies with engineers and a reserve consistent with METT-TC. Each company should have an infiltration lane that allows infiltration by company-size or smaller units. Depending on the construction of the urban area and streets, the infiltration lane may be 500 to 1,500 meters wide.

11-145. The infiltrating companies advance on foot using available cover and concealment. Mortar and artillery fire can be used to divert the enemy's attention and cover the sound of infiltrating troops.

11-146. Armored vehicles and antiarmor weapons are positioned to cover likely avenues of approach for enemy armored vehicles. The battalion commander may position attached antiarmor units to cover the likely avenues of approach. In addition, weapons company antiarmor systems can support by fire if the situation provides adequate support-by-fire positions.

11-147. As the companies move into the built-up area, they secure their own flanks. Security elements may be dropped off along the route to warn of a flank attack. Engineers assist in breaching or bypassing minefields or obstacles. Enemy positions are avoided but reported.

11-148. The infiltrating companies proceed until they reach their objective. At which time, they consolidate, reorganize, and arrange for mutual support. They patrol to their front and flanks and establish contact with each other. The company commander may establish a limit of advance to reduce chances of enemy contact or to ensure safety from friendly forces.

11-149. If the infiltration places the enemy in an untenable position and he must withdraw, the rest of the battalion is brought forward for the next phase of the operation. If the enemy does not withdraw, the battalion must clear the urban area before the next phase of the operation. If the enemy counterattacks, the battalion may establish a hasty defense (Figure 11-13).

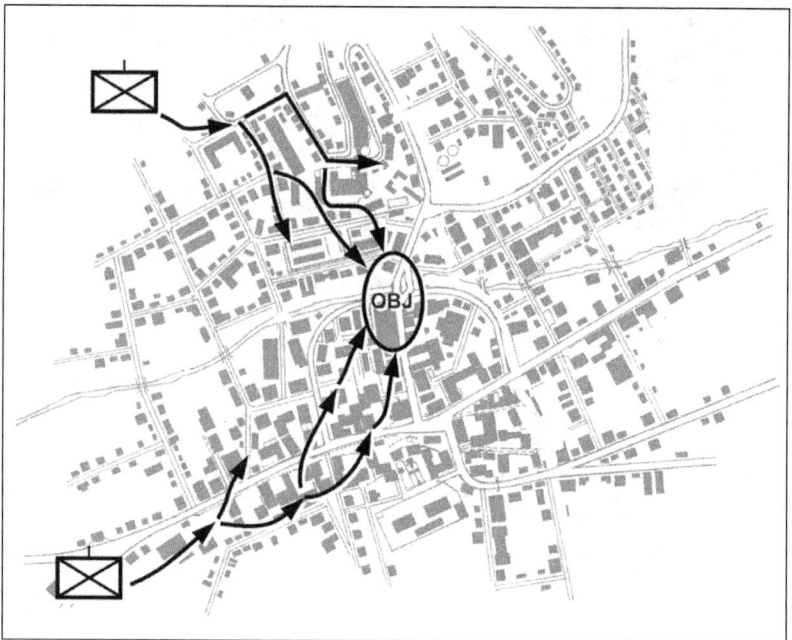

Figure 11-13. Infiltration.

ATTACK OF A VILLAGE

11-150. The battalion may have to conduct either a hasty or deliberate attack of a village that is partially or completely surrounded by open terrain (Figure 11-14). After considering the factors of METT-TC, the battalion performs the following tactical tasks:

- Reconnoiter the objective.

- Move to the objective.
- Isolate the objective.
- Secure a foothold.
- Clear the objective.
- Consolidate, reorganize, and prepare for future missions.

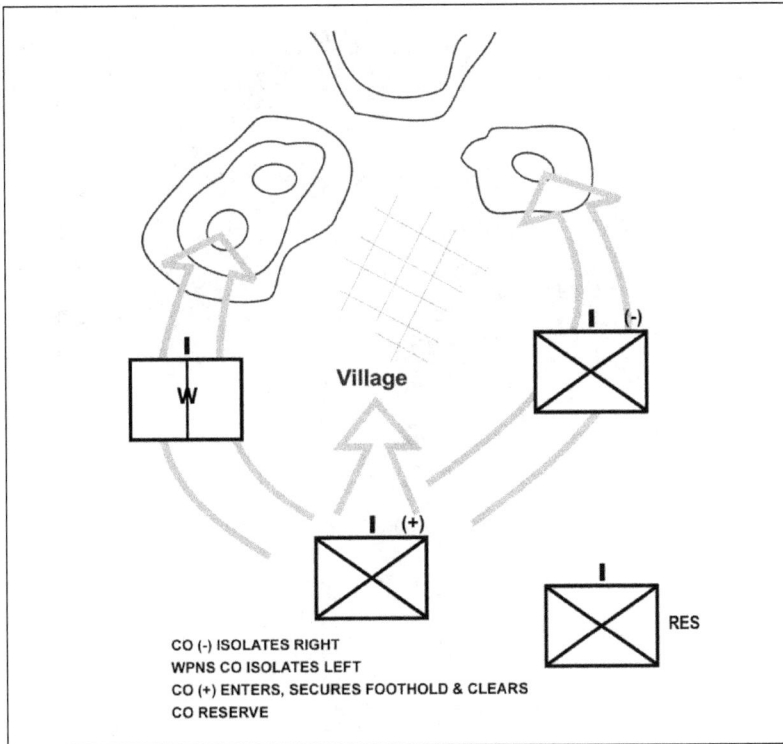

Figure 11-14. Attack of a village.

NODAL ATTACK

11-151. The battalion may receive the mission to seize a key node (or nodes) as part of the BCT operation. In certain situations, the battalion may have to seize nodes independently. Nodal attacks are characterized by rapid attacks followed by defensive operations. The enemy situation must permit the attacking force to divide its forces and seize key nodes. Multiple attacks, as shown in Figures 11-15 and 11-16, require precise maneuver and supporting fires. The battalion may receive a nodal attack mission before an anticipated sustainment replenishment operation or when isolation of an urban area is required so other units can conduct offensive operations inside the urban area. Figure 11-15 shows a BCT conducting multiple nodal attacks. Figure 11-16 (page 11-37) shows a battalion executing a nodal attack. Nodal attacks are used to deny the enemy key infrastructure. They may require a designated rapid response element (or elements) in reserve in the event that enemy forces mass and quickly overwhelm an attacking battalion. Normally, the reserve is planned at BCT level. Battalions executing a nodal attack independently must plan for a designated rapid response reserve element. The duration of this attack should not exceed the battalion's self-sustainment capability.

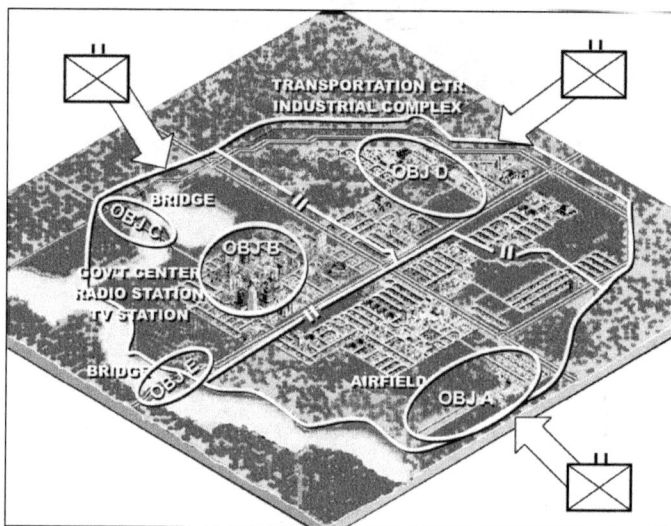

Figure 11-15. Brigade scheme of maneuver, nodal attack.

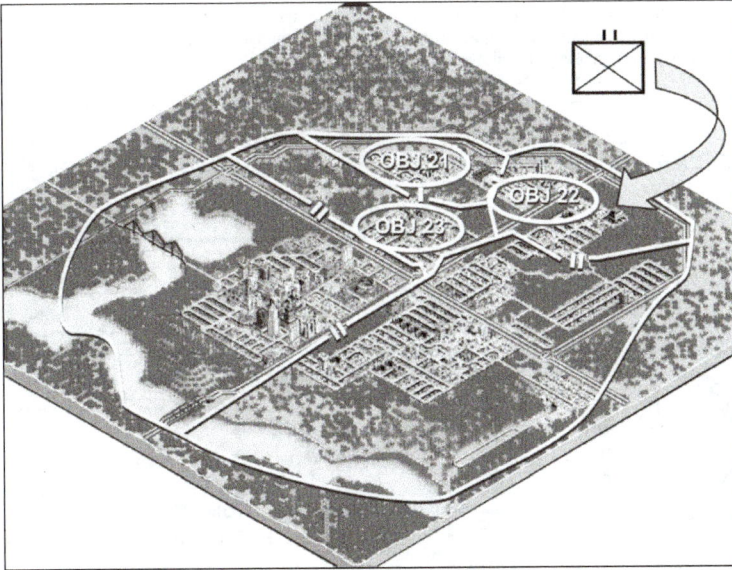

Figure 11-16. Battalion nodal attack.

Section V. DEFENSIVE OPERATIONS

An area defense concentrates on denying an enemy force access to designated terrain for a specific time and is the type of defense most often used for defending an urban area. The mobile defense concentrates on the destruction or defeat of the enemy through a decisive counterattack. Multiple BCTs units are most often required to conduct a mobile defense, with a single BCT and its battalions participating as an element in the fixing force conducting a delay or area defense or as an element of the striking force conducting offensive operations. In an urban area, the defender must take advantage of the abundant cover and concealment. He must also consider restrictions to the attacker's ability to maneuver and observe. By using the terrain and fighting from well-prepared and mutually supporting positions, a defending force can inflict heavy losses upon, delay, block, or fix a much larger attacking force.

DEFENSIVE FRAMEWORK

11-152. Normally, the battalion conducts defensive operations as part of the BCT. The BCT can conduct the full range of defensive operations within a single urban area or in an AO that contains several small towns and cities using the elements of the urban operational framework shown in Figure 11-17. The BCT avoids being isolated through its security operations. It assigns defensive missions to subordinate battalions in order to achieve the commander's intent and desired end state. Well-planned and executed defensive operations have four elements: assess, shape, dominate, and transition. During defensive operations, the BCT commander seeks to—

- Avoid being isolated by the enemy.
- Defend key and decisive terrain, institutions, or infrastructure.
- Use offensive fire and maneuver to retain the initiative.

11-153. Battalions conduct defensive operations by conducting counterreconnaissance missions and patrols (avoiding isolation); assigning BPs or sectors to companies (defending); and consolidating or reorganizing and preparing for follow-on missions (transitioning).

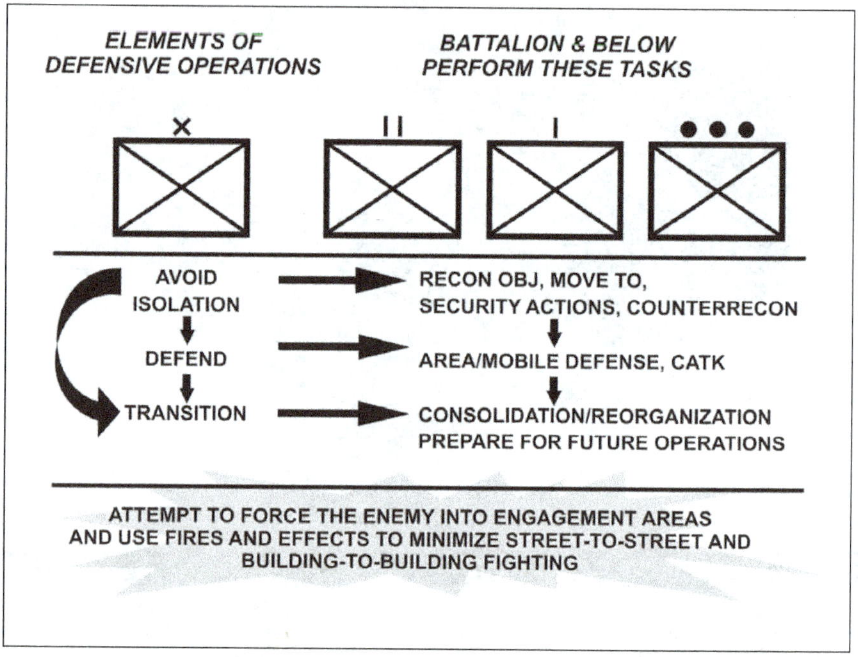

Figure 11-17. Defensive urban operational framework.

DEFENSIVE PLANNING

11-154. Battalions defending in urban areas prepare their positions for all-round defense. Subordinate units must employ security operations that include surveillance of surface and subsurface approaches. Battalions constantly patrol and use OPs and sensors to maintain effective security. Special measures are taken to control enemy combatants who have intermixed with the local population and civilian personnel who may support the enemy.

11-155. Defensive fire support in UO must take advantage of the impact of indirect fires on the enemy before he enters the protection of the urban area. FSOs at all levels coordinate and rehearse contingencies that are inherent to nonlinear FSCM and clearance of fires.

11-156. In planning a defense in an urban area, the battalion staff identifies the following:

- Positions and areas that must be controlled to prevent enemy infiltration.
- Sufficient covered and concealed routes for movement and repositioning of forces.
- Structures and areas that dominate the urban area.
- Areas such as parks and broad streets that have fields of fire for tanks and antiarmor weapons.

- Command and control locations.
- Protected areas for sustainment activities.
- Engagement areas, including employment and integration of obstacles with direct and indirect fires.
- Sniper engagement criteria.
- Suitable structures that are defensible and provide protection for defenders.
- Contingency plans in the event that the battalion must conduct breakout operations.
- Plans for rapid reinforcement.

INTEGRATION OF URBAN AREA

11-157. The battalion may integrate villages, strip areas, and small towns into the overall defense, based on higher headquarters' guidance and applicable ROE (Figure 11-18). A defense in an urban area or one that incorporates urban areas normally follows the same sequence of actions and is governed by the principles contained in Chapter 5. When defending predominately urban areas, the battalion commander must consider that the terrain is more restricted due to buildings that are normally close together. This usually requires a higher density of troops and smaller company sectors or BPs than in open terrain.

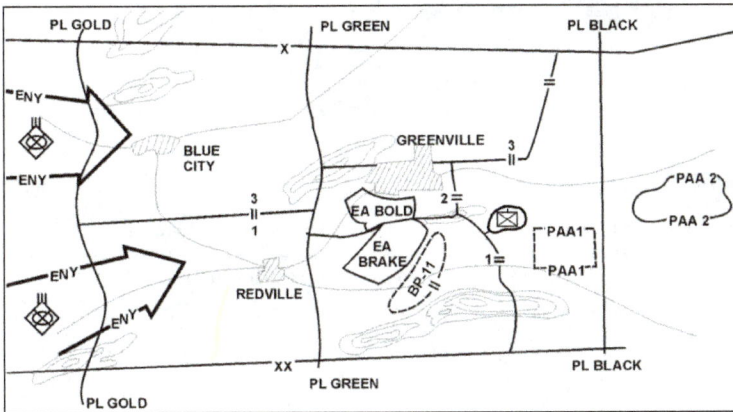

Figure 11-18. Integration of urban areas into a defense.

NODAL DEFENSE

11-158. Figure 11-19 shows a transitional situation where the battalion moves from an offensive to a defensive operation. The BCT mission may contain factors that require varying defensive techniques by the subordinate battalions under BCT control. Figure 11-20 shows a nodal defense where battalions employ different defensive techniques in order to achieve the BCT commander's desired end state. The BCT commander's intent is to safeguard the key nodes seized during the offensive operation in order eventually to return the infrastructure of this particular urban area back to civilian control. A combination of sectors, BPs, strongpoints, roadblocks, checkpoints, security patrols, and OPs could be employed within the battalion sector or AO. Figure 11-20, page 11-41, shows the changed battalion task organizations, the extended boundaries, and the directed OPs.

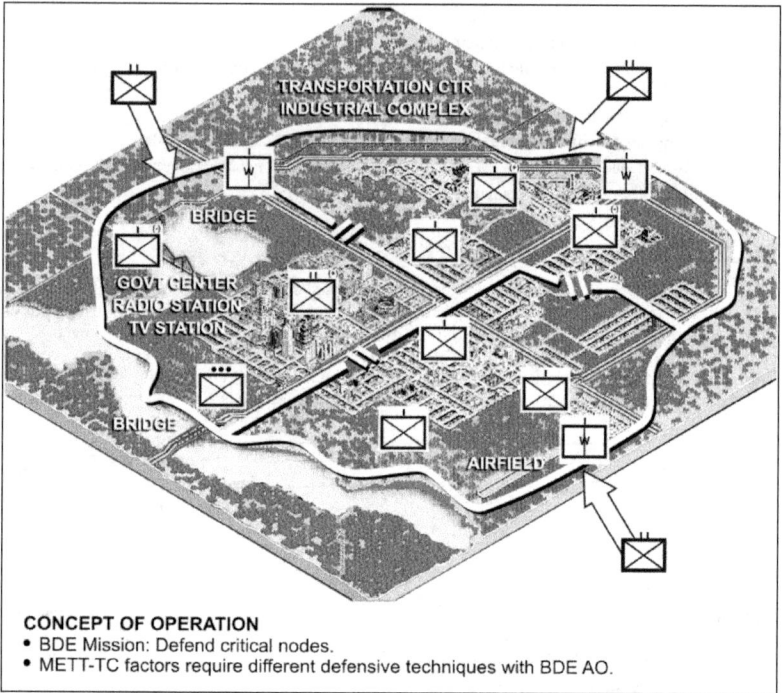

CONCEPT OF OPERATION
- BDE Mission: Defend critical nodes.
- METT-TC factors require different defensive techniques with BDE AO.

Figure 11-19. Nodal defense, transitional situation.

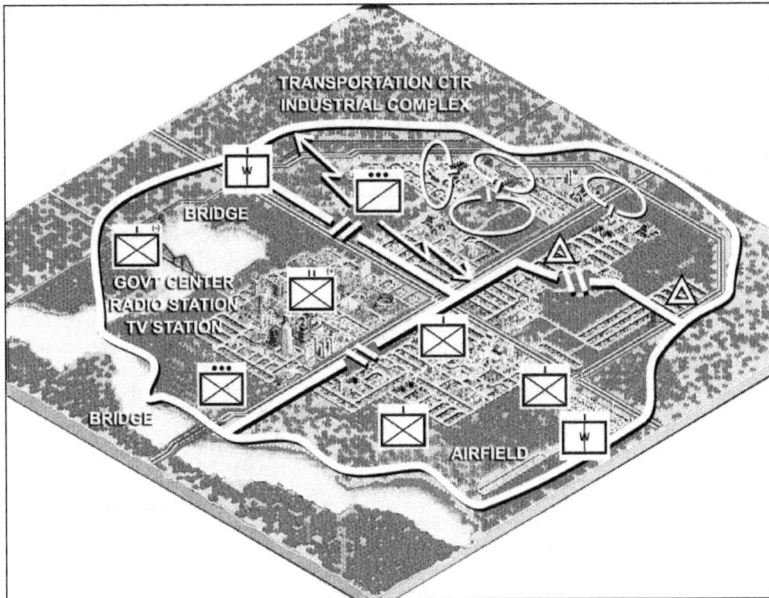

Figure 11-20. Nodal defense, different defensive techniques.

TASK ORGANIZATION

11-159. Companies may have to be task-organized to conduct the specific missions assigned by the battalion commander in a nodal defense.

SYMMETRICAL AND ASYMMETRICAL THREATS

11-160. The battalion is likely to respond to both symmetrical and asymmetrical threats within the AOs. The defensive techniques chosen by subordinate companies should allow them to respond to the specific threats in their respective AOs, BPs, or sectors.

BOUNDARY CHANGES

11-161. Based on the battalion commander's intent and the defensive scheme of maneuver, boundary changes may be required in order to give companies more or less maneuver space.

ROE MODIFICATION

11-162. The ROE may require modification based on the type of mission to be conducted. The ROE may become more or less restrictive based on METT-TC factors. Commanders and leaders must ensure that the ROE are clearly stated and disseminated at the beginning and conclusion of each day.

DELAY

11-163. The purpose of a delay is to slow the enemy, cause enemy casualties, and stop the enemy (where possible) without becoming decisively engaged or bypassed. The delay can be oriented either on the enemy or on specified terrain such as a key building or manufacturing complex.

AMBUSHES AND BATTLE POSITIONS

11-164. The battalion conducts a delay in an urban area from a succession of ambushes and BPs (Figure 11-21). The size of the battalion AO depends on the amount of force available to control the area, the nature of the buildings and obstacles along the street, and the length of time that the enemy must be delayed.

Ambushes

11-165. The battalion plans ambushes on overwatching obstacles. Ambushes are closely coordinated but executed at the lowest levels. The deployment of the battalion is realigned at important cross streets. The battalion can combine ambushes with limited objective attacks on the enemy's flanks. These are usually effective at the edge of open spaces (parks, wide streets, and so forth).

Battle Positions

11-166. The battalion should place BPs where there is good observation and fields of fire. Such locations are normally found at major street intersections, in parks, and at the edge of open residential areas. The battalion prepares BPs carefully and deliberately, reinforces them with obstacles and demolished buildings, and supports them using artillery and mortars. The battalion positions BPs to inflict maximum casualties on the enemy in order to cause him to deploy for a deliberate attack.

TWO DELAYING ECHELONS

11-167. The battalion is most effective when deployed in two delaying echelons that alternate between conducting ambushes and fighting from BPs. As the enemy threatens to overrun a BP, the company disengages and delays back toward the next BP. As the company passes through the company to the rear, it establishes another BP. The battalion uses smoke and demolitions to aid in the disengagement. Security elements on the flank can help prevent the enemy from out-flanking the delaying force. An adequate reserve can react to unexpected enemy action and conduct continued attacks on the enemy's flank.

ENGINEERS

11-168. The engineer effort should at first, be centralized to support the preparation of BPs, and then decentralized to support the force committed to ambush.

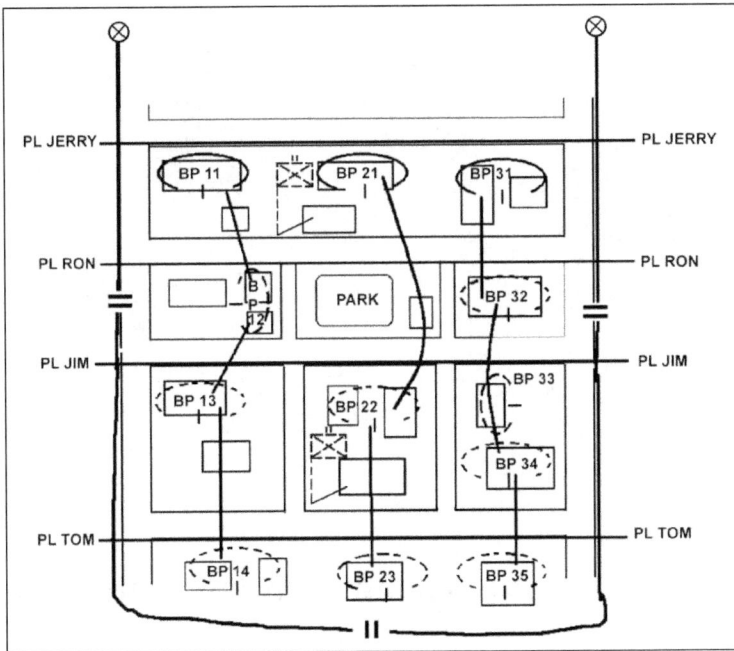

Figure 11-21. Battalion delay in an urban area.

This page intentionally left blank.

Appendix A
Risk Management and Fratricide Avoidance

The primary objective of risk management and fratricide avoidance is to help units protect their combat power through risk reduction, which enables them to win the battle quickly and decisively with minimum losses. This appendix focuses on two topics: risk management, which includes tactical and accidental risk, and the avoidance of fratricide. Risk is the chance of injury or death for individuals and of damage to or loss of vehicles and equipment. Risk, or the potential for risk, is always present across the full-spectrum of operations. Risk management takes place at all levels of the chain of command during each phase of every operation and is an integral part of planning. The BCT commander, battalion commanders, staffs, company commanders, and all Soldiers must know how to use risk management (coupled with fratricide avoidance measures) to ensure the battalion executes the mission in the safest possible environment within mission constraints. (For more information on risk management, see FM 100-14.)

Section I. RISK MANAGEMENT

Risk management is the process of identifying and controlling hazards to conserve combat power and resources. Leaders (to include the staff) must always remember that the effectiveness of the process depends on their understanding of the situation. They never approach risk management with "one size fits all" solutions. Leaders should also consider the essential tactical and operational factors that make each situation unique. This five-step risk management process is integrated into the military decision-making process (Table A-1).

TACTICAL RISK

A-1. Tactical Risk is a risk concerned with hazards that exists because of the presence of either the enemy or an adversary. Intelligence plays a critical role in identifying hazards associated with tactical risk. Intelligence preparation of the battlefield (IPB) is a dynamic leader process that continually integrates new information and intelligence that ultimately becomes input to the leaders risk assessment process. Intelligence assists in identifying hazards during operations by—

- Identifying the opportunities and constraints the battlefield environment offers to threat and friendly forces.
- Thoroughly portraying threat capabilities and vulnerabilities.
- Collecting information on populations, governments, and infrastructures.

ACCIDENT RISK

A-2. Accident risk includes all operational risk considerations other than tactical risk. It includes risks to the friendly force and also includes risks posed to civilians by an operation, as well as an operational impact of each hazard on the operation. The risk assessment provides for enhanced awareness of the current situation. The awareness builds confidence and allows Soldiers and units to take timely, efficient, and effective protective measures.

Table A-1. Risk management steps correlated with MDMP tasks.

Military Decision-Making Process	Risk Management Steps				
	Step 1 Identify Hazards	Step 2 Assess Hazards	Step 3 Develop Controls and Make Risk Decisions	Step 4 Implement Controls	Step 5 Supervise and Evaluate
Mission Receipt	X				
Mission Analysis	X	X			
COA Development	X	X	X		
COA Analysis	X	X	X		
COA Comparison			X		
COA Approval			X		
Orders Production				X	
Rehearsal[1]	X	X	X	X	X
Execution and Assessment[1]	X	X	X	X	X

[1] All boxes are marked to emphasize the continued use of the risk management process throughout the mission.

STEP 1--IDENTIFY HAZARDS

A-3. A hazard is a source of danger. It is any existing or potential condition that could result in injury, illness, or death of personnel; damage to or loss of equipment and property; or some other form of mission degradation. Hazards arise in both tactical and training operations. Leaders identify the hazards associated with all aspects and phases of the operation, paying particular attention to the factors of METT-TC. Risk management is not an afterthought; leaders begin the process during MDMP (troop-leading procedures for company and below) and continue it throughout the operation. Table A-2 lists possible sources of risk the battalion might face during a typical tactical operation. The list is organized according to the factors of METT-TC.

Table A-2. Examples of potential hazards.

MISSION	• Duration of the operation. • Complexity or clarity of the plan, that is, whether the plan is well-developed and easily understood. • Proximity and number of maneuvering units.
ENEMY	• Knowledge of the enemy situation. • Enemy capabilities. • Availability of time and resources to conduct reconnaissance.
TERRAIN AND WEATHER	• Visibility conditions including light, dust, fog, and smoke. • Precipitation and its effect on mobility. • Extreme heat or cold. • Additional natural hazards such as broken ground, steep inclines, or water obstacles.
TROOPS AND EQUIPMENT	• Equipment status. • Experience the units conducting the operation have working together. • Danger areas associated with the platoon's weapons systems. • Soldier and leader proficiency. • Soldier and leader rest situation. • Degree of acclimatization to environment. • Impact of new leaders or crewmembers. • Friendly unit situation. • NATO or multinational military actions combined with US forces.
TIME AVAILABLE	• Time available for TLP and rehearsals by subordinates. • Time available for PCCs/PCIs.
CIVIL CONSIDERATIONS•	• Applicable ROE or ROI. • Potential stability or civil support operations, such as NEOs, refugee or disaster assistance, or counterterrorism, that involve contact with civilians. • Potential for media contact and inquiries. • Interaction with host nation or other participating nation support.

STEP 2--ASSESS HAZARDS TO DETERMINE RISKS

A-4.   Hazard assessment is the process of determining the direct impact of each hazard on an operation (in the form of hazardous incidents). Use the following steps:

- Determine which hazards can be eliminated or avoided.
- Assess each hazard that cannot be eliminated or avoided to determine the probability that the hazard will occur.
- Assess the severity of hazards that cannot be eliminated or avoided. Severity, defined as the result or outcome of a hazardous incident, is expressed by the degree of injury or illness (including death), loss of or damage to equipment or property, environmental damage, or other mission-impairing factors such as unfavorable publicity or loss of combat power.
- Taking into account both the probability and severity of a hazard, determine the associated risk level (extremely high, high, moderate, or low). Table A-3 summarizes the four risk levels.
- Based on the factors of hazard assessment (probability, severity, and risk level, as well as the operational factors unique to the situation), complete risk management worksheet. Figure A-1 shows an example of a completed risk management worksheet.

Table A-3. Risk levels and impact on mission execution.

Risk Level	Mission Effects
Extremely high (E)	Mission failure if hazardous incidents occur in execution.
High (H)	Significantly degraded mission capabilities in terms of required mission standards. Not accomplishing all parts of the mission or not completing the mission to standard (if hazards occur during mission).
Moderate (M)	Expected degraded mission capabilities in terms of required mission standards. Reduced mission capability (if hazards occur during the mission).
Low (L)	Expected losses have little or no impact on mission success.

A. Mission or Task: Conduct a deliberate attack	B. Date/Time Group Begin: 010035R May XX End: 010600R May XX	C: Date Prepared: 29 April XX

D. Prepared By: (Rank, Last Name, Duty Position)   CPT Smith, Cdr

E. Task	F. Identify Hazard	G. Assess Hazard	H. Develop Controls	I. Determine Residual Risk	J. Implement Controls (How To)
Conduct obstacle breaching operations	Obstacles	High (H)	Develop and use obstacle reduction plan	Low (L)	Unit TSOP, OPORD, training handbook
	Inexperienced soldiers	High (H)	Additional training and supervision	Moderate (M)	Rehearsals, additional training
	Operating under limited visibility	Moderate (M)	Use NVDs, use IR markers on vehicles	Low (L)	Unit TSOP, OPORD
	Steep Cliffs	High (H)	Rehearse using climbing ropes	Moderate (M)	FM 3-97.6, Mountain Operations; TC 90-6-1, Mountaineering
	Insufficient planning time	High (H)	Plan and prepare concurrently	Moderate (M)	OPORD, Troop-leading procedures

K. Determine overall mission/task risk level after controls are implemented (circle one)

LOW (L)   MODERATE (M)   HIGH (H)   EXTREMELY HIGH (E)

Figure A-1. Example of completed risk management worksheet.

STEP 3--DEVELOP CONTROLS AND MAKE RISK DECISIONS

A-5.   Step 3 consists of two substeps: develop controls and make risk decisions. This step is done during the COA development, COA analysis, COA comparison, and COA approval of the military decision-making process.

DEVELOP CONTROLS

A-6.   Controls are the procedures and considerations the unit uses to eliminate hazards or reduce their risk. After assessing each hazard, develop one or more controls that will either eliminate the hazard or reduce the risk (probability, severity, or both) of potential hazardous incidents. When developing controls, it is important to consider the reason for the hazard and not just the hazard itself.

MAKE RISK DECISIONS

A-7.   A key element in the process of making a risk decision is determining whether accepting the risk is justified or unnecessary. The decision-maker must compare and balance the risk against mission expectations, then decide if the controls are sufficient and acceptable and whether to accept the resulting residual risk. If the risk is determined unnecessary, the decision-maker directs the development of additional controls or alternative controls; as another option, he can modify, change, or reject the selected COA for the operation.

STEP 4--IMPLEMENT CONTROLS

A-8.   Implementing controls is the most important part of the risk management process. It is the chain of command's contribution to the combat readiness of the unit. Implementing controls includes coordination and communication with appropriate superior, adjacent, and subordinate units and with individuals executing the mission. The commander must ensure that specific controls are integrated into OPLANs, OPORDs, SOPs, and rehearsals. The critical check for this step is to ensure that controls are converted into clear, simple execution orders understood by all levels. If the leaders have conducted a thoughtful risk assessment, the controls will be easy to implement, enforce, and follow. Examples of risk management controls include the following:

- Thoroughly brief all aspects of the mission, including related hazards and controls, and ensure that subordinates know the plan.
- Allow adequate time for rehearsals at all levels.
- Drink plenty of water, eat well, and get as much sleep as possible (at least 4 hours in any 24-hour period).
- Enforce movement safety procedures.
- Establish recognizable visual signals and markers to distinguish maneuvering units.
- Enforce the use of ground guides in assembly areas and on dangerous terrain.
- Limit single-vehicle movement.
- Establish SOPs for the integration of new personnel.

STEP 5--SUPERVISE AND EVALUATE

A-9.   During mission execution, leaders must ensure their subordinates properly understand and execute risk management controls. Leaders must continuously evaluate the unit's effectiveness in managing risks to gain insight into areas that need improvement.

SUPERVISION

A-10.   Leadership and unit discipline are the keys to ensuring implementation of effective risk management controls. All leaders are responsible for supervising mission rehearsals and execution to ensure standards and controls are enforced. In particular, NCOs enforce established combat readiness policies as well as controls developed for a specific operation or task. Techniques include spot checks, inspections, SITREPs, confirmation briefs, and supervision. During mission execution, leaders continuously monitor risk management controls to determine whether they are effective and to modify them as necessary. Leaders anticipate, identify, and assess new hazards. They ensure that imminent danger issues are addressed on the spot and that ongoing planning and execution reflect changes in hazard conditions.

EVALUATION

A-11. Whenever possible, the risk management process should also include an AAR to assess unit performance in identifying risks and preventing hazardous situations. Leaders incorporate lessons learned from the process into unit SOPs and plans for future missions.

COMMANDERS GUIDANCE

A-12. The BCT commander gives the battalion commanders and staff direction, sets priorities, and establishes the command climate (values, attitudes, and beliefs). Successful preservation of combat power requires him to imbed risk management into individual behavior. To fulfill this commitment, the commander must exercise creative leadership, innovative planning, and careful management. Most importantly, he demonstrates support for the risk management process. The commander and others in the chain of command establish a command climate favorable to risk management integration by—

- Demonstrating consistent and sustained risk management behavior through leading by example and stressing active participation throughout the risk management process.
- Providing adequate resources for risk management. Every leader is responsible for obtaining the assets necessary to mitigate risk and for providing them to subordinate leaders.
- Understanding their own and their Soldier's limitations, as well as their unit's capabilities.
- Allowing subordinates to make mistakes and learn from them.
- Preventing a "zero defects" mindset from creeping into the unit's culture.
- Demonstrating full confidence in subordinates' mastery of their trades and their ability to execute a chosen COA.
- Keeping subordinates informed.
- Listening to subordinates.

LEADER RESPONSIBILITY

A-13. For the commander, his subordinate leaders, and individual Soldiers alike, responsibilities in managing risk include—

- Making informed risk decisions; establishing and then clearly communicating risk decision criteria and guidance.
- Establishing clear, feasible risk management policies and goals.
- Training the risk management process. Ensuring that subordinates understand the who, what, when, where, and why of managing risk and how these factors apply to their situation and assigned responsibilities.
- Accurately evaluating the unit's effectiveness, as well as subordinates' execution of risk controls during the mission.
- Informing higher headquarters when risk levels exceed established limits.

Section II. FRATRICIDE AVOIDANCE

Fratricide avoidance is a complex problem defying simple solutions. Fratricide can be defined broadly as employing friendly weapons and munitions with the intent of killing the enemy or destroying his equipment or facilities but resulting in unforeseen and unintentional death or injury to friendly personnel. This section focuses on actions leaders can take to reduce the risk and occurrence of fratricide using current resources.

MAGNITUDE OF PROBLEM

A-14.   The modern battlefield is more lethal than any in history. The tempo of operations is rapid, and the nonlinear nature of the battlefield creates C2 challenges for unit leaders.

A-15.   The accuracy and lethality of modern weapons make it possible to engage and destroy targets at extended ranges. However, the ability of US forces to acquire targets using thermal imagery and other sophisticated sighting systems exceeds its capability to identify these targets accurately. Consequently, friendly elements can be engaged unintentionally and destroyed in a matter of seconds. Added to this is battlefield obscuration, which becomes a critical consideration whenever thermal sights are the primary source of target identification. Rain, dust, fog, smoke, and snow degrade identification capability by reducing the intensity and clarity of thermal images. On the battlefield, positive visual identification cannot be the sole engagement criteria at ranges beyond 1,000 meters.

A-16. It is likely that the Army will regularly conduct close combat operations in an urban environment. UO is characterized by intense short range engagements in close proximity to friendly and enemy forces. These operations are compounded in complexity because of the three dimensional nature of UO (airspace, surface, and subsurface), the compressed terrain, intermixing of civilians, and a restrictive ROE. These factors all indicate a high probability of fratricide.

A-17. An accurate COP is essential and must be maintained throughout any operation. FBCB2 and other technical enhancing systems enable the commander to have a more accurate COP. However, risk identification and mitigation still play a vital and preventive role in fratricide avoidance.

RISK IDENTIFICATION AND PREVENTIVE MEASURES

A-18. Reduction of fratricide risk begins during the planning phase of an operation and continues through preparation and execution.

A-19. Leaders consciously identify specific fratricide risk for any operation. Using this structured approach, commanders can predict the most likely causes of fratricide and take action to protect their Soldiers. Whether used for an actual combat operation or a training event, this thought process complements the troop-leading procedures and analysis of METT-TC factors in planning.

A-20. The fratricide risk assessment matrix shows an approach to assess the relative risk of fratricide for combat maneuver (Figure A-2). To assign a risk value to each direct cause of fratricide, pair the most critical METT-TC contributing factors associated with each cause. For each primary cause, favorable conditions lead to a lesser risk value, found in the cell on the left side of the corresponding submatrix. As a contributing factor becomes unfavorable, risk increases. The worst precondition for each kind of fratricide is represented by the risk value in the cell on the right side of the submatrix. Figure A-2 is an example of a fratricide risk assessment matrix that should be used in assessing every mission. For a detailed explanation of how to use this matrix, see Section II of Handbook No. 92-3.

A-21. Risk identification must be conducted at all levels during each phase. The results must be clearly communicated up and down the chain of command so risk assessment can begin. The following paragraphs cover considerations influencing risk identification and focus on measures the leader can implement to make the identification process more effective and help prevent friendly fire incidents from occurring:

SITUATION AWARENESS

FIRE & MANEUVER CONTROL			RATING
DENSITY OF FORCES	CLARITY OF THE SITUATION		
	Maintain Force Separation	Forces Converge	Forces Intermingle
Heavy	5	7	9
Normal	3	5	7
Sparse	1	3	5

FIRE DISTRIBUTION PLAN			RATING
PREP TIME REHEARSAL & DISSEMINATION	COLLECTIVE PROFICIENCY		
	Strong SOPs Hab Attchmnts	Mod Trained of Fam Tsk Org	Unseasoned & Unfam Tsk Org
Brief back Rehearsals	3	4	5
Reduced Force Rehearsals	2	3	4
Full Force Rehearsals	1	2	3

LAND NAVIGATION			RATING
EXTENT OF RECON & IPB	VISIBILITY & NAVIGATION DIFFICULTY		
	Ample Controls High Competence	Confidence With Much Effort	Very Difficult Low Confidence
Minimal	3	4	5
Limited	2	3	4
Extensive	1	2	3

FIRE CONTROL & BATTLE TRACKING			RATING
CLEARANCE OF FIRES	COMMO & CROSSTALK		
	Reliable Redundant	Adequate Means	Unreliable No Backups
Passive Only	21	23	25
Positive	1	3	5

BATTLEFIELD HAZARDS			RATING
USE OF ADDL DUD-PRODUCING MUNITIONS	KNOWLEDGE OF EXISTING HAZARDS		
	Extensive	Partial	Extremely Limited
Unknown	3	4	5
Major	2	3	4
Minor	1	2	3

POSITIVE IDENTIFICATION

COMBAT IDENTIFICATION			RATING
ENGAGEMENT RANGES & FIELDS OF FIRE	VISIBILITY & NAVIGATION DIFFICULTY		
	Practiced Very Effective	Expedient Some-what Effective	Marginally Effective
ID Unlikely	3	6	7
Marginal ID	2	4	6
Optimal ID	1	2	5

DISCIPLINE

FIRE CONTROL DISCIPLINE			RATING
COMMAND & CONTROL OR SUPERVISION	CLARITY OF THE SITUATION		
	Complete & Effective	Complete Some-what Effective	Expedient Untested
Ad Hoc Improvised	4	6	7
Attached	2	4	5
Organic	1	2	3

TROOPS

SOLDIER & LEADER PREPAREDNESS			RATING
MISSION-RELATED EXPERIENCE & COMPETENCE	SOLDIER & LEADER FATIGUE		
	Rested Low Exertion	Mod Rest & Exertion	Limited Rest High Exertion
Unseasoned	5	7	9
Moderate Experienced	3	5	7
Highly Experienced	1	3	5

LOW RISK	CAUTION	HIGH RISK	TOTAL
8 to 20	21 to 30	>30	

Figure A-2. Example format for fratricide risk assessment matrix.

PLANNING PHASE

A-22.   A thoroughly developed, clearly communicated, and completely understood plan helps minimize fratricide risk. The following factors affect the potential for fratricide in a given operation:

- Clarity of the enemy situation.
- Clarity of the friendly situation.
- Clarity of the commander's intent.
- Complexity of the operation.
- Planning time available at each level.

A-23.   Graphics are a basic tool commanders at all levels use to clarify their intent, add precision to their concept, and communicate their plan to subordinates. Graphics can be a very useful tool in reducing the risk of fratricide. Each commander must understand the definitions and purposes of operational graphics and the techniques of their employment. (See FM 1-02 for the definition of each type of graphic control measure.)

PREPARATION PHASE

A-24.   Confirmation briefings and rehearsals are primary tools for identifying and reducing fratricide risk during the preparation phase. The following are considerations for their use:

- Confirmation briefings and rehearsals ensure subordinates know where fratricide risks exist and what to do to reduce or eliminate them.
- Briefbacks ensure subordinates understand the commander's intent. They often highlight areas of confusion or complexity or planning errors.
- The type of rehearsal conducted determines the types of risks identified.
- Rehearsals should extend to all levels of command and involve all key players.

A-25. The following factors may reveal fratricide risks during rehearsals:

- Number and type of rehearsals.
- Training and proficiency levels of units and individuals.
- The habitual relationships between units conducting the operation.
- The physical readiness (endurance) of the troops conducting the operation.

EXECUTION PHASE

A-26. During execution, in-stride risk assessment and reaction can overcome unforeseen fratricide risk situations. The following are factors to consider when assessing fratricide risks:

- Intervisibility between adjacent units.
- Amount of battlefield obscuration.
- Ability or inability to identify targets positively.
- Similarities and differences in equipment, vehicles, and uniforms between friendly and enemy forces.
- Vehicle density on the battlefield.
- The tempo of the battle.
- Civilians on the battlefield.
- Rules of engagement.

A-27. Maintaining an awareness of the COP at all levels and at all times is another key to fratricide reduction as an operation progresses. Units develop and employ effective techniques and SOPs to aid leaders and Soldiers in this process, to include—

- Monitoring the next higher radio net.
- Radio cross-talk between units.
- COP updates.
- Accurate position reporting and navigation.
- Training, use, and exchange of liaison officers.

FRATRICIDE REDUCTION MEASURES

A-28. The following measures provide a guide to actions that can reduce fratricide risk. Use of these measures is not required, nor are they intended to restrict initiative. Leaders should apply them as appropriate based on the specific situation and METT-TC factors.

- Identify and assess potential fratricide risks in the estimate of the situation. Express these risks in the OPORD or FRAGO.
- Maintain awareness of the current situation, focusing on areas such as current intelligence, unit locations and dispositions, denial areas (minefields and scatterable munitions), contaminated areas such as improved conventional munitions, CBRN reports, SITREPs, and METT-TC factors.

- Ensure positive target identification. Review vehicle and weapon ID cards. Know at what ranges and under what conditions positive identification of friendly vehicles and weapons is possible.
- Establish a command climate that stresses fratricide prevention. Enforce fratricide prevention measures and emphasize the use of doctrinally sound tactics, techniques, and procedures. Ensure constant supervision in the execution of orders and the performance of all tasks and missions to standard.
- Recognize the signs of battlefield stress. Maintain unit cohesion by taking quick, effective action to alleviate it.
- Conduct individual, leader, and collective (unit) training covering fratricide awareness, target identification and recognition, and fire discipline.
- Develop a simple, decisive plan.
- Give complete and concise mission orders.
- Use SOPs that are consistent with doctrine to simplify mission orders. Periodically review and update SOPs as needed.
- Strive for maximum planning time for you and your subordinates.
- Use common language and vocabulary and doctrinally correct standard terminology and control measures such as fire support coordination line, zone of engagement, and restrictive fire lines.
- Ensure thorough coordination is conducted.
- Plan for and establish effective communications (to include visual).
- Plan for collocation of CPs when appropriate to the mission such as during a passage of lines.
- Designate and employ LNOs as appropriate.
- Ensure ROE are clear.
- Include fratricide risk as a key factor in terrain analysis (OAKOC).
- Conduct rehearsals whenever time permits.
- Be in the right place at the right time. Use position location and navigation devices (GPS and POSNAV); know your location and the locations of adjacent units (left, right, leading, and follow-on). Synchronize tactical movement.
- Plan and brief OPSEC (challenge and password, sign and countersign).
- Include discussion of fratricide incidents in after-action reports.
- Ensure fire commands are accurate, concise, and clearly stated. Make it mandatory for Soldiers to ask for clarification of any portion of the fire command that they do not completely understand.
- Stress the importance of the chain of command in the fire control process; ensure Soldiers get in the habit of obtaining target confirmation and permission to fire from their leaders before engaging targets they assume are enemy elements.
- Know who will be in and around the AO.
- Know and understand the danger and caution areas of the weapons systems being employed. For example, M1 Armor Piercing Fin Stabilized Discarding Sabot Tracer (APFSDS-T) round pedals have a danger area to Soldiers of 90 degrees from the muzzle out to 1,000 meters. There is also a firing noise and overpressure danger area out to 50 meters from the vehicle.

FRATRICIDE RISK CONSIDERATIONS

A-29.   Figure A-3 parallels the five-paragraph OPORD and contains key factors and considerations in fratricide prevention. This is not a change to the OPORD format, but a guide for use during OPORD development to ensure fratricide prevention measures are included. It is not a strict directive. The factors and considerations are listed where they would likely appear in the OPORD, but they may warrant evaluation during preparation of other paragraphs.

```
Task Organization
  • Has the Unit worked under this task organization before?
  • Are SOPs compatible with the task organization (especially with attached units)?
  • Are special markings or signals, such as cat's eyes, chemlights, or panels, needed for
positive identification of uniforms and equipment?
  • What special weapons and equipment are to be used? Do they look or sound like enemy
weapons and equipment?

1.Situation.
  a.Enemy Forces.
    (1) Weather.
      • What are the expected visibility conditions (light data and precipitation) for
the operation?
      • What effects will rain, heat, and cold have on Soldiers, weapons, and equipment?
    (2) Terrain.
      • What is the topography and vegetation (urban, mountainous, hilly, rolling, flat,
desert, swamp/marsh, prairie/steppe, jungle, or open woods) of the expected AO?
      • Has the terrain been evaluated using the factors of OAKOC?
  b.Friendly Forces.
    • Among the allied or coalition forces, are there differences (or similarities with
enemy forces) in language, uniform, and equipment that could increase fratricide risk
during combined operations?
    • Could differences in equipment and uniforms among US forces increase fratricide risk
during joint operations?
    • What differences in equipment and uniforms can leaders stress to help prevent
fratricide?
    • What is the friendly deception plan?
    • What are the locations of your unit and adjacent units (left, right, leading, and
follow-on)?
    • What are the locations of neutrals and noncombatants?
    • What are the locations of your own forces?
    • What is the status of training activities?
    • What are the levels of individual, crew, and unit proficiency?
    • Will fatigue be a factor for friendly forces during the operation? Has an effective
sleep plan been developed?
    • Are friendly forces acclimated to the AO?
    • What is the age (new, old, or mixed) and condition of equipment in friendly units?
    • What is the status of new equipment training?
    • What are the expected MOPP requirements for the operation?
  c.Attachments and Detachments.
    • Do attached elements understand pertinent information regarding enemy and friendly
forces?
    • Will gaining units provide this pertinent information to detached elements?
    • Are communications systems compatible (digital/analog)?

2.Mission. Do all elements clearly understand the mission and all associated tasks and
purposes?

3.Execution.
  a.Concept of the Operation.
    (1) Maneuver: Are decisive and shaping operations identified?
    (2) Fires (Direct and Indirect):
      • Are priorities of fires identified?
      • Have target lists been developed?
      • Have the fire execution matrix and overlay been developed?
      • Have locations of denial areas (minefield and FASCAM) and contaminated areas (ICM
and CBRN) been identified?
      • Are the locations of all supporting fire targets identified in the OPORD and
OPLAN overlays?
```

Figure A-3. Fratricide prevention checklist.

• Are aviation and CAS targets clearly identified?

• Has the direct fire plan been developed?

• Have FPFs been designated?

• Are the requirements for accurate predicted fire met or do fire adjustments have to be made?

(3) Engineer Tasks:

• Are friendly minefields, including FASCAM and ICM dud-contaminated areas, known?

• Have obstacles and the approximate time needed for reduction or breaching of each been identified?

(4) Tasks to each subordinate unit: Are friendly forces identified, as appropriate, for each subordinate maneuver element?

(5) Tasks to protection and sustainment units: Have locations of friendly forces been reported to protection and sustainment units?

b. Coordinating Instructions.

• Are rehearsals to be conducted? Are they necessary? Are direct and indirect fires included?

• Is a confirmation brief necessary?

• Are appropriate control measures clearly explained and shown in the OPORD and overlays? Have they been disseminated to everyone who has a need to know? What is the plan for using these control measures to synchronize the battle and prevent fratricide?

• Are the locations for higher echelonment slice elements in the BCT battlespace posted and disseminated?

• Have target and vehicle identification drills been practiced?

• Do subordinate units know the immediate action, drill, or signal for "CEASE FIRE" and "I AM FRIENDLY" if they come under unknown or friendly fire? Is there a backup?

• Is guidance in handling dud munitions, such as ICM and cluster bomb units (CBU), included?

4. Service Support.

• Does everyone know trains locations and identification markings?

• Do medical and maintenance personnel know the routes between trains units?

5. Service Support.

a. Command.

• What are the locations of the commander and key staff members?

• What are the chain of command and the succession of command?

b. Signal.

• Do instructions include backup code words and visual signals for all special and emergency events?

• Do instructions cover how air assets identify friendly forces and how friendly forces identify friendly aircraft?

• Do they include backup code words and visual signals for all special and emergency events?

• Are SOI distributed to all units with a need to know such as higher, lower, adjacent, leading, and follow-on elements?

Figure A-3. Fratricide prevention checklist (continued).

Appendix B
Movements and Assembly Areas

The movement of troops from one location to another is inherent in any phase of a military operation. Mission accomplishment relates directly to the ability to arrive at the proper place, at the proper time, in effective condition, and in the formation best suited for the assigned mission. Infantry battalions must conduct tactical road marches and assembly area operations to achieve their missions.

Section I. TACTICAL ROAD MARCH

The Infantry battalion conducts two kinds of movement; administrative and tactical. An *administrative movement* considers tactical implications, but its primary emphasis is on expediting movement and conserving time and energy. Administrative movements are based on the assumption that contact with the enemy during or shortly after the move is unlikely. A *tactical road march* is a rapid movement used to relocate units in a combat zone in order to prepare for combat operations. Although hostile contact is not anticipated, the unit maintains security measures and is prepared to act upon enemy contact. At battalion level and higher, the S-3 is responsible for planning tactical road marches. The S-4 has primary staff responsibility for planning administrative movements, but he coordinates his plans with all other staff members.

MARCH ELEMENTS

B-1.   The elements of a road march include the march column, serial, and march unit.

MARCH COLUMN

B-2.   A march column includes all elements using the same route for a single movement under control of a single commander. A battalion may march over multiple routes to reduce closing time. A large march column may be composed of a number of subdivisions, each under the control of a subordinate commander.

SERIAL

B-3.   A serial is a subdivision of the march column. It consists of elements of a march column moving from one area over the same route at the same time. All the elements move to the same area and are grouped under a serial commander. A serial may be divided into two or more march units.

MARCH UNIT

B-4.   A march unit is the smallest subdivision of a march column. It is normally a squad, section, platoon, or company. It moves and halts under control of a single commander using voice and visual signals. It uses radio only when it can use no other means of communication.

Before Movement

B-5.   Before starting a march, each march unit of a serial reconnoiters its route to the start point and determines the exact time to reach it. The movement order states the unit's arrival and clearance times at the start point. The serial commander then determines and announces the times for march units of his serial to arrive at and clear the start point. Arrival time at the start point is critical. Each march unit must arrive at and clear the start point on time; otherwise, movement of other elements may be delayed.

During Movement

B-6.   During movement, march units move at the constant speed designated in the order, maintaining proper interval and column gap. Elements in a column of any length may simultaneously encounter many different types of routes and obstacles, resulting in different parts of the column moving at different speeds at the same time. This can produce an undesirable accordion-like action or whip effect. March units report crossing each control point as directed by the march order. They maintain air and ground security during the move.

MARCH COLUMN ORGANIZATION

B-7.   March columns, regardless of size, are composed of four elements: reconnaissance party, quartering party, main body, and trail party. March columns are organized to maintain unit integrity and to maintain a task organization consistent with mission requirements. All march units must provide their own security.

RECONNAISSANCE PARTY

B-8.   The reconnaissance party may be augmented by engineer and other protection assets. It performs route reconnaissance to determine travel time; it identifies critical points, including choke points and obstacles. Route reconnaissance confirms and supplements data from map studies, higher headquarters, and air reconnaissance. Instructions to the reconnaissance party should state the nature and extent of information required and the time and place the report is to be submitted.

QUARTERING PARTY

B-9.   The quartering party normally consists of representatives from companies or attached units. It reconnoiters the new area, marking unit positions and guiding the march column elements into these new positions as they arrive. (See Section II for more information on quartering party responsibilities when occupying an assembly area.)

MAIN BODY

B-10.   March units of the main body consist of individual maneuver units with their trains, battalion mortars, any attachments, the battalion CP, and the battalion trains.

TRAIL PARTY

B-11.   The trail party normally consists of elements of the FSC and medical support and is a march unit in a battalion serial.

PLANNING CONSIDERATIONS

B-12.   Road marches require extensive planning. Commanders and staff use the military decision-making process to determine how best to execute a move from one point to another. (See FM 4-01.30 for a detailed discussion of movement planning considerations, terms, and movement time computation.)

FACTORS FOR CONSIDERATION

B-13.   Consider the following factors in road march planning:

 • Requirements for the movement. (Refuel requirements, time distance between march units considering vehicle capacity and time required at the refuel site and time to clear choke points).

- Organic and nonorganic movement capabilities; determine external movement requirements.
- Unit movement priorities.
- Enemy situation and capabilities, terrain conditions, and weather.
- Organization of the battalion.
  - -- Positioning recovery vehicles throughout the march unit's flow to provide flexibility and timely push/pull recovery to close all vehicles on the destination.
  - -- Ensure all march units have security and firepower.
- Security measures before and during the movement and at the destination.
- Assembly of the march units.
- Fire support coverage during movement and at the destination.
- Communications; particularly units without FBCB2.
- Actions at the destination.

SEQUENCE OF ROAD MARCH PLANNING

B-14.   When preparing for a tactical road march, the battalion uses the following sequence of march planning, as time permits:

- Prepare and issue an oral warning order as early as possible to allow subordinates time to prepare for the march.
- Analyze routes designated by higher headquarters and specify organization of the march serial.
- Prepare and issue the march order.
- Prepare a detailed movement plan and assembly area plan.
- Organize and dispatch reconnaissance and quartering parties as required.

MOVEMENT ORDER

B-15.   The movement order format is the same for administrative and tactical movements, in accordance with FM 5-0. The movement order is prepared as an annex to an operation order, as a separate operation order, or as a FRAGO.

CONTROL MEASURES

B-16.   The commander uses the control measures discussed in the following paragraphs to assist in controlling the battalion during the road march.

GRAPHICS

B-17.   Road march graphics should include, at a minimum, the start point, release point, and route. The battalion strip map should show the following (Figure B-1, page B-5).

- Start point.
- Release point (RP).
- Scheduled halts.
- Routes.
- Major cities and towns.
- Critical points and checkpoints.
- Distance between CPs.
- North orientation.

Start Point

B-18.   A start point is a well-defined point on a route at which units fall under the control of the movement commander. It is at this point that the column is formed by the successive passing, at an appointed time, of each of the elements comprising the column. The SP should be an easily recognizable point on the map and on the ground. It should be far enough from the assembly area to allow units to be organized and moving at the prescribed interval when the SP is reached.

Release Point

B-19.   A release point is a well-defined point on a route at which the elements comprising a column return to the authority of their respective commanders. At the RP, each element continues its movement toward its own destination. Multiple movement routes from the RP enable units to disperse rapidly and navigate to their assembly areas or AO.

Scheduled Halts

B-20.   Scheduled halts may be needed to provide rest, mess, and medical evaluation.

Critical Points and Checkpoints

B-21.   Critical points or checkpoints on a route are places used for information references, places where obstructions or interference with movement might occur, or places where timing may be a critical factor. They are also used as a control measure for control and maintenance of the schedule. Guides or signs may be used at designated critical points/checkpoints to ensure the smooth flow of movement.

Strip Map

B-22.   All overlay data should be entered into FBCB2 so that vehicles equipped with the system can maintain awareness of the current situation.

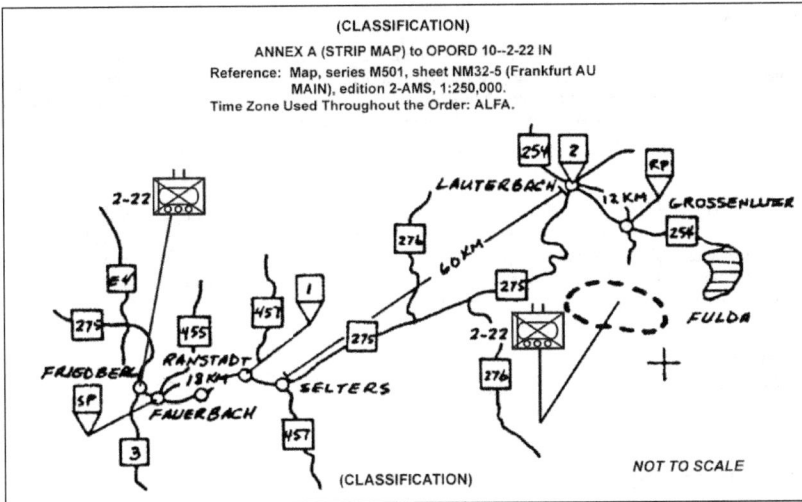

(CLASSIFICATION)

ANNEX A (STRIP MAP) to OPORD 10--2-22 IN
Reference: Map, series M501, sheet NM32-5 (Frankfurt AU
MAIN), edition 2-AMS, 1:250,000.
Time Zone Used Throughout the Order: ALFA.

(CLASSIFICATION)

NOT TO SCALE

Figure B-1. Example battalion strip map.

COMMUNICATIONS

B-23.   Messengers and visual signals are excellent means of communication during road marches. The battalion generally uses radio only in emergencies and when it can use no other means of communication. The battalion can also use road guides to pass messages from one march unit to a following march unit. Road guides are important in controlling march units and the interval between them.

TRAFFIC CONTROL

B-24.   The headquarters controlling the march may post road guides and traffic signs at designated traffic control points. At critical points, guides assist in creating a smooth flow of traffic along the march route. Military police or designated elements from the quartering party may serve as guides. They should have equipment or markers that will allow march elements to identify them in darkness or other limited visibility conditions. There is normally an RP for every echelon of command conducting the road march.

SECURITY

B-25.   During the movement, march units maintain security through observation, weapons orientation, dispersion, and camouflage. Commanders assign sectors of observation to their personnel to maintain 360-degree observation. Main weapons are oriented on specific sectors throughout the column. The lead elements cover the front, following elements cover alternate flanks, and the trail element covers the rear.

HALTS

B-26.   While taking part in a road march, the march elements must be prepared to conduct both scheduled and unscheduled halts. In either case, vehicles should move to the side of the road while maintaining vehicle dispersion. Security at halts is always the first priority.

AIR DEFENSE

B-27.   Planning for AD and implementing all forms of AD security measures are imperative to minimize the battalion's vulnerability to enemy air attack. The battalion commander must integrate his fire plans effectively with any attached or supporting AD assets. Furthermore, he must ensure the battalion plans and uses all passive and active AD measures that can be implemented at company level.

OBSTACLES

B-28.   The battalion should bypass obstacles reported by the scout platoon, if possible. If it cannot bypass obstacles, the lead march unit goes into a hasty defense to cover and overwatch and breaches the obstacle, working with engineers if available. As the lead march unit breaches the obstacles, the other march units move at decreased speed or move off the road and monitor the battalion command net. The location of the obstacle should be posted on FBCB2 as soon as the situation allows.

ENEMY INDIRECT FIRE

B-29.   Should the battalion come under attack by enemy indirect fire during the road march, the unit in contact continues to move. The remainder of the battalion tries to bypass the impact area.

ENEMY AIR ASSAULT

B-30.   Should hostile aircraft attack the battalion during the march, the march unit under attack moves off the road into a quick defensive posture and immediately engages the aircraft with all available automatic weapons. The rest of the battalion moves to covered and concealed areas until the engagement ends.

RESTRICTIONS

B-31.   Restrictions are points along the route of march where movement may be hindered or obstructed. The march planner should stagger start times or adjust speeds to compensate for restrictions, or he should plan to halt the column en route until the restriction is over.

LIMITED VISIBILITY

B-32.   Units must be able to operate routinely under limited visibility conditions caused by darkness, smoke, dust, fog, heavy rain, or heavy snow. Limited visibility decreases the speed of movement and increases the difficulty in navigating, recognizing checkpoints, and maintaining proper interval between units. To overcome C2 problems caused by limited visibility, commanders may position themselves just behind lead elements. More restrictive control measures, such as additional checkpoints, phase lines, and use of a single route, may become necessary.

Section II. ASSEMBLY AREA OPERATIONS

An assembly area is a location where a force prepares or regroups for future action. While in assembly areas, units execute the organization, maintenance, resupply, and personnel actions necessary to maintain the combat power of the force. Designation and occupation of an assembly area may be directed by a higher headquarters or by the unit commander during relief or withdrawal operations or unit movements.

TYPES OF ASSEMBLY AREAS

B-33.   The battalion may establish administrative or tactical assembly areas.

ADMINISTRATIVE ASSEMBLY AREAS

B-34.   Administrative assembly areas are established where the likelihood of enemy contact is remote and the commitment of the force from the assembly area directly to combat is not anticipated. Examples of administrative assembly areas include; seaport debarkation, pre-positioned materiel marshaling areas, and assembly areas occupied by units in reserve. Battalions may occupy administrative assembly areas alone or as part of a larger force.

B-35.   Ideally, administrative assembly areas provide—

- Concealment from air and ground observation.
- Terrain masking of electromagnetic signal signature.
- Sufficient area for unit dispersion, consistent with the degree and type of rear area or air enemy present.
- Buildings for maintenance, billeting, mess, and headquarters. Optimally, buildings will have light, heat, and wire communications.
- An area suitable for a utility helicopter LZ.
- Suitable entrances, exits, and internal routes. Ideally, unit personnel can easily secure entrances and exits.
- Good drainage and soil conditions.

B-36.   Administrative assembly areas are organized and occupied with an emphasis on unit integrity, ease of operation, C2, and efficient use of facilities. Tactical dispersion and protection from ground or air attack are lesser considerations in an administrative assembly area. Units are typically grouped tightly together and placed at lower readiness conditions.

B-37.   Units that are occupying administrative assembly areas and do not have an assigned reserve mission, are typically preparing to move forward to a tactical assembly area in preparation for employment in combat operations. Forces may occupy administrative assembly areas to await arrival of other units before moving forward.

TACTICAL ASSEMBLY AREAS

B-38.   Tactical assembly areas are areas occupied by forces where enemy contact is likely and commitment of the unit directly from the assembly area to combat is possible or anticipated. Examples of units likely to be in tactical assembly areas include units designated as tactical reserves, units completing a rearward passage of lines, units preparing to move forward to execute a forward passage of lines followed by offensive operations, units performing tactical movements, and units conducting reconstitution. Tactical assembly areas should provide—

- Concealment from air and ground observation.
- Cover from direct fire.
- Terrain masking of electromagnetic signal signature.
- Sufficient area for the dispersion of subunits consistent with the enemy and friendly tactical situation.
- Areas for unit trains, maintenance operations, and C2 facilities.
- Suitable entrances, exits, and internal routes. (Optimally, at least one all-weather paved surface road transits the assembly area and connects to the MSR in use.)
- Terrain allowing the observation of ground and air avenues of approach into the assembly area.
- Good drainage and soil conditions.

ORGANIZATION

B-39.   Battalion tactical assembly areas may be organized using one of three methods.

METHOD 1

B-40.   The battalion may occupy a portion of the perimeter of an assembly area. It does so by arraying companies, generally on a line oriented on avenues of approach into the assembly area. Leftmost and rightmost units tie in their fires and areas of observation with adjacent units of other battalions. Depending on the tactical situation and width of the area assigned to it, the battalion may maintain a reserve. Battalion trains are located to the rear of the companies. The battalion mortar platoon and the main CP are located centrally in the assembly area where they can communicate and support units by fire. The scout platoon screens along the most likely or most dangerous avenues of approach.

METHOD 2

B-41.   The battalion may assign sectors to subordinate companies and require them to tie in their fires and observation with each other. The main CP, trains, and mortar platoon are located near the center of the assembly area. Ideally, company sectors are assigned to balance the task organization against the appropriate enemy avenues of approach The scout platoon occupies observation posts at key points around the entire perimeter of the battalion or screens along the most dangerous or likely enemy avenues of approach. This method configures the battalion in a perimeter defense with companies oriented outward. This is the most common organization of battalion assembly areas.

METHOD 3

B-42.   The battalion may assign separate individual assembly areas to subordinate companies, which establish their own 360-degree security. Areas between companies are secured through surveillance and patrolling. The main CP, trains, and heavy mortar platoon establish positions central to outlying companies. If the battalion is dispersed over a large area, SHORAD assets (if available) may need to collocate with companies for adequate AD.

QUARTERING PARTY

B-43.   A quartering party is a group of unit representatives dispatched to a probable new site of operations to secure, reconnoiter, and organize an area before the main body's arrival and occupation. Unit SOPs establish the exact composition of the quartering party and its transportation, security, communications equipment, and specific duties. Quartering parties typically reconnoiter, to include CBRN reconnaissance, and confirm the route and tentative locations previously selected from map reconnaissance. Quartering parties also serve as a liaison between their parent headquarters and the quartering party of their higher headquarters to change unit locations in the assembly area based on the results of their reconnaissance.

PLANNING CONSIDERATIONS

B-44.   The S-2 routinely receives intelligence information from BCT headquarters throughout the battalion's deployment and operations. From this information, the S-2 determines the characteristics and likelihood of the air and ground threat to the quartering party during its movement to and occupation of the assembly area. This information assists the battalion staff and the quartering party OIC in determining the security required and the desirability of maintaining the quartering party in the assembly area during the movement of the rest of the battalion.

B-45.   For security, it may move with another subunit quartering party, depending on the likelihood of enemy contact. Ideally, the quartering party moves over the routes to be used by the battalion and executes a route reconnaissance and time-distance check.

B-46.   The quartering party typically includes an OIC or noncommissioned officer in charge (NCOIC) and representatives from the battalion main CP, battalion trains, and the battalion's subunits. The S-3 air, HHC CDR, XO, S-1, S-3 sergeant major (SGM), and CSM are potential quartering party leaders.

B-47.   Composition of the maneuver company quartering parties is usually determined by the company commander but may be specified by the battalion commander. HHC representatives typically include NCOs from key support sections such as communications or supply. Representatives from the mortar platoon and the scout platoon are also represented in the quartering party.

B-48.   The main CP quartering party identifies potential CP locations based on tactical requirements such as cover and concealment and the line-of-sight signal requirements of FM radios.

B-49.   If planning time is short, key members of the staff can move with the quartering party. This enables the staff to begin detailed planning immediately upon arrival in the assembly area. This technique also facilitates transitions to new missions by pre-positioning key staff members so planning can occur concurrently with the movement of the main body.

B-50.   If the battalion moves and occupies its assembly area as part of a BCT, the BCT makes all coordination for fire support. If the battalion moves and occupies the assembly area without FS planning by its higher headquarters, it conducts its own FS coordination.

B-51.   During its planning, the staff determines sustainment requirements for the quartering party. The estimate of necessary supplies and equipment covers the entire quartering party, including accompanying staff section representatives and fire support, protection, and sustainment assets.

B-52.   The quartering party may move under radio listening silence or other emission restrictive posture, especially during movement to tactical assembly areas.

PREPARATION

B-53.   The quartering party OIC or NCOIC plans his operations through coordination with battalion staff officers.

Intelligence

B-54.   The S-2 ensures the quartering party OIC/NCOIC is aware of the current enemy situation, probable enemy courses of action, the weather forecast, and the terrain and vegetation likely en route to and in the new assembly area.

Movement and Maneuver

B-55.   The OIC or NCOIC coordinates with the S-3 to determine the mission of the quartering party, whether or not the quartering party is to remain in the assembly area and await the remainder of the battalion, and the route and movement restrictions to be used by the quartering party. The OIC or NCOIC ensures subordinate unit quartering parties know where and when the battalion quartering party will be located in the assembly area.

B-56.   The battalion S-3 determines whether sending engineer personnel with the quartering party for the reconnaissance and evaluation of routes, bridges, and cross-country mobility is recommended or required.

Protection

B-57.   AD units, when available, may move with the quartering party en route to and in the new tactical assembly area. If AD assets move with the quartering party, the AD unit leader ensures he knows both the current and projected weapons control status (WCS) and AD warning.

Command and Control

B-58.   After the OIC or NCOIC finishes planning, he gathers the quartering party where and when he chooses to brief them. His briefing follows the standard five-paragraph field order format. In it, he emphasizes actions at halts and critical areas, actions of the quartering party in the assembly area, contingency plans, and procedures to request and receive fire support, protection, and sustainment. He covers in detail MEDEVAC procedures, actions on contact, and actions to take if separated from the quartering party.

EXECUTION

B-59.   The following considerations apply to quartering party execution.

Movement and Maneuver

B-60.   The quartering party navigates to the assembly area, generally along one route. If the quartering party moves along a route to be used by the main body and the main body has not yet sent a reconnaissance party forward, the quartering party conducts a route reconnaissance during its movement. The quartering party may also execute a time-distance check of the designated route. He reports these times and distances to the main CP after moving through the RP.

B-61.   Upon arrival in the assembly area, the quartering party navigates to assigned positions and executes the required reconnaissance. The quartering party also has the following responsibilities at the assembly area:

- Determines locations for squads and above.
- Identifies unit left and right limits of fire, records this information, and sends updates to the unit's commander.
- Determines the location for the main CP and records it.
- Verifies subordinate unit locations and sectors of fire to ensure there are no gaps in coverage.
- Transmits changes or updates to the main CP to alert the main body to changes in the route and assembly area.

B-62.   If reconnaissance of proposed locations reveals the area is unsuitable for occupation, the quartering party OIC or NCOIC tries to adjust unit locations in the assigned area. If such adjustments do not correct the problem, he immediately notifies the S-3 or commander.

B-63.   If an element of the main CP has accompanied the quartering party, it moves to the location reconnoitered by its representative and establishes forward C2 for the battalion. If AD assets have accompanied the quartering party, they occupy advantageous firing positions oriented on air avenues of approach. Representatives organize their respective areas by selecting and marking positions for vehicles and support facilities. If designated, guides move on order to preselected checkpoints or RPs to await main body march unit elements.

B-64.   If the battalion quartering party is not going to remain in the assembly area, it does not depart the assembly area until all subordinate unit quartering parties have reported. The unit quartering parties should provide the results of their reconnaissance and identify requested changes to their tentative locations.

B-65.   Each commander or unit leader must decide if guides are needed to assist in occupying the assembly area. Normally, the leader plans the use of guides for occupation in limited visibility.

Sustainment

B-66.   Sustainment assets may accompany the quartering party. Sustainment elements generally conduct resupply operations for the quartering party at scheduled halts or in the new assembly area.

OCCUPATION

B-67.   Units position themselves in assembly areas in accordance with their parent unit's tentative plan. Quartering parties typically guide units into position. The units accomplish occupation smoothly from the march without halting or bunching of units at the RP. Subordinate units normally establish routes and separate SPs and RPs for march elements that extend from the march column's route or RP toward the march units' assembly area positions. This technique clears the route quickly, maintains march unit C2, and prevents bunching of units at the march column RP. The battalion begins movement to the assembly area with an updated movement route, and a confirmed defensive scheme for occupation of the assembly area. This enables the battalion to transition quickly from the road march into the actual occupation while maintaining overall security for the main body.

INTELLIGENCE

B-68.   The S-2 assists in planning the assembly area occupation by identifying enemy avenues of air and ground approach into the new assembly area and the degree and type of rear area threat to the battalion in its new location. The S-2 also identifies and disseminates the security requirements for the battalion and begins preparing the reconnaissance and surveillance plan for the assembly area. In coordination with the S-3, the S-2 makes preliminary plans for reconnaissance and surveillance tasks to be assigned to subunits in the battalion, including the reconnaissance platoon.

MOVEMENT AND MANEUVER

B-69.   The commander or S-3 chooses a method for occupation (whole battalion assembly area or separate subunit assembly areas) and tentative subunit locations based on METT-TC. He then considers selecting tentative assembly area locations. To operate effectively in the assembly area, selected subunits may have specific positioning requirements such as being near mess units, near water for decontamination, or on hard stand for maintenance. Based on METT-TC, the commander or S-3 develops contingency plans that address the possibility of significant enemy contact in the assembly area. Time available and the likelihood of enemy contact determine the level of detail in contingency plans. These plans typically include fire support plans and alternate assembly areas or rally points in case the battalion is forced out of its initial assembly area.

B-70.   The type and extent of engineer support required in the assembly area depends on the anticipated length of stay, type, and degree of enemy threat, terrain in the assembly areas, and the follow-on mission of the battalion. Mobility and countermobility tasks include improving and controlling access routes into the assembly area.

FIRE SUPPORT

B-71.   Fire support requirements are coordinated with units already positioned near the new assembly area. Support shortfalls between requirements and availability are coordinated with either higher or adjacent units. Fire support planning includes support for battalion contingency plans in case of enemy ground contact.

PROTECTION

B-72.   AD planning when available for the tactical assembly area focuses on the selection of SHORAD firing positions that will allow the engagement of enemy aircraft, along identified air avenues of approach. Depending on the commander's stated priority of protection, assets available, and task organization, AD units may locate with supported battalion subunits or in separate locations under battalion control.

B-73.   Survivability tasks are also dependent upon the length of time the assembly area is to be occupied. At a minimum, individual fighting positions are dug and improved as time permits. Hardening of C2 facilities is also a priority.

SUSTAINMENT

B-74.   The S-4 recommends sustainment positioning and typically positions the combat trains near the battalion main CP. HHC and FSC support elements position themselves in relation to the battalion TOC and the mortar platoon.

COMMAND AND CONTROL

B-75.   The XO and S-2 determine tentative locations for battalion C2 facilities from map or imagery reconnaissance based on METT-TC. The overriding consideration for selecting these locations is the ability of the various CPs to communicate higher, lower, and laterally. Establishing the main CP in the new assembly area should occur early in the occupation so subunit CPs can locate based on their requirement to communicate with the main CP.

ACTIONS IN ASSEMBLY AREA

B-76.   The battalion focuses all actions in the assembly area on preparing for future operations to include resupply, personnel replacement, maintenance, reorganization, rest, and the planning of future operations.

B-77.   The battalion initiates human resource actions in the assembly area if time permits.

B-78.   Maintenance activities concentrate on deadline faults and those degrading the unit's ability to shoot, move, and communicate. The unit pays special attention to those maintenance tasks that are too time-consuming or difficult to perform during combat operations.

B-79.   The units conduct resupply actions in the assembly area to replenish items used in previous operations, to assemble stocks for future operations, and to replace damaged and contaminated supplies as required.

B-80.   The unit conducts planning and preparation for future operations concurrently with maintenance and administrative activities.

B-81.   The unit may require training if issued new or modified equipment while in the assembly area. Small unit training may be necessary if replacement personnel are introduced into the unit, especially if significant numbers of key leaders are replaced.

SECURITY

B-82.   Security comprises measures taken by a military unit to protect itself against surprise, observation, detection, interference, espionage, sabotage, or annoyance that may impair its effectiveness. Security is essential to the protection and conservation of combat power. It may be achieved by establishing and maintaining protective measures or through deception operations designed to confuse and dissipate enemy tries to interfere with the force being secured. Effective security prevents the enemy from gaining an unexpected advantage over friendly forces.

SECURITY IN ASSEMBLY AREA

B-83.   Forces in tactical assembly areas are provided a degree of security by their separation from the line of contact and by the presence of other units between them and the enemy. In keeping with their mission and the tactical situation, units in tactical assembly areas employ active security measures. These measures include reconnaissance and patrols, visual and electronic surveillance of ground and air avenues of approach, and establishment of OPs. Regardless of the security that may be provided by other units or agencies, the commander takes whatever actions or precautions he deems necessary to secure his command.

POSITIONING OF COMPANIES

B-84.   The battalion positions companies with respect to avenues of approach and access routes into the assembly area. Companies tie in their fires, observation, and patrolling with one another. This is simple for the battalion, because the companies typically occupy a portion of a battalion perimeter and are adjacent to another company. Companies exchange sector sketches, fire plans, and patrolling plans with adjacent units.

POSITIONING OF SCOUT PLATOON

B-85.   The scout platoon may be positioned in one of three ways to enhance the security of the battalion. It can form a screen astride the most likely or dangerous avenues of approach; it can establish several temporary OPs and conduct patrols between them to provide a thin screen line that surrounds the entire assembly area; or it can be positioned to observe an area that cannot be seen by other units in the assembly area. Companies may also be repositioned to observe these areas. Battalion organic snipers, UAS, GSRs, and surveillance assets allocated from the BCT may be retained under battalion control. More often, they are attached to the scout platoon to augment the screen or employed as additional OPs.

OPERATIONS SECURITY

B-86.   Operations security (OPSEC) includes active and passive measures that try to deny the enemy information about friendly forces. Units in the battalion practice noise and light discipline, employ effective camouflage, eliminate or reduce radio traffic, and use wire communications or messengers. Other electronic transmissions such as jammers and radar may be restricted. Units may construct and employ unidirectional antennas to reduce electronic signatures.

NONCOMBATANTS

B-87.   Movement of civilians and refugees near assembly areas is strictly controlled to prevent enemy sympathizers or covert agents from obtaining information about the battalion. Units may remove unit markings and uniform patches in some cases to retain unit anonymity. When possible, the unit conducts rehearsals in areas not subject to enemy observation and performs extensive movements and resupply under limited visibility. OPSEC measures vary because of higher headquarters deception efforts.

RECONNAISSANCE AND SURVEILLANCE PLAN

B-88.   The battalion reconnaissance and surveillance plan directs the employment of intelligence assets under battalion control and assigns intelligence and security tasks to subordinate units. Companies typically provide security patrols to their fronts and establish OPs IAW the reconnaissance and surveillance plan. The scout platoon also conducts reconnaissance and security tasks in accordance with the reconnaissance and surveillance plan. Patrols may be established to maintain contact between units when companies occupy separate assembly areas.

DEPARTURE FROM ASSEMBLY AREA

B-89.   The planning considerations for occupying the assembly area are based largely on the anticipated future missions of units. Units are positioned in the assembly area so they can depart the assembly area en route to their assigned tactical missions without countermarching or moving through another unit.

PLACEMENT OF SP

B-90.   Units departing the assembly area must hit the SP at the correct interval and time. To achieve this, the SP must be located a sufficient distance from the assembly area to allow units to maneuver out of their positions and configure for the road march before reaching the SP. The SP for a battalion movement should be located an adequate distance from the assembly area to permit the companies to attain proper speed and interval before crossing it.

LIAISON OFFICERS

B-91.   When unit-to-unit dispersion or terrain in the assembly area prohibits visual contact, LNOs maintain contact between departing units and return to their parent units to initiate movement at the correct time.

Appendix C
Air Assault Operations

When the Infantry battalion executes an air assault operation, Infantry companies form the primary air assault force. Usually one or two companies form the basic air assault force; however, the may be tasked organized with the weapons company if close combat missile, antitank or heavy machinegun fires are anticipated to be needed on the landing zone (LZ). Higher headquarters provide the additional assets required to execute an air assault mission. In most cases, the operation concludes with a linkup operation between Infantry and mounted forces.

Section I. CONSIDERATIONS

Situations favoring an air assault operation for the Infantry battalion include those in which the enemy has a vulnerable area suitable for air assault, surprise can be achieved, and enemy air defenses are weak and vulnerable, or can be effectively suppressed.

AIR ASSAULT MISSION ANALYSIS AND CONSIDERATIONS

C-1.   Typical air assault operations conducted by the battalion include river-crossing operations, seizure of key terrain, rear area combat operations, and raids. The mobility and speed helicopters can be exploited to—

- Secure a deep objective in the offense.
- Reinforce a threatened sector in the defense.
- Place combat power at a decisive point on the battlefield.

C-2.   For this reason, the Infantry battalion must be proficient in conducting air assault operations. Considerations for air assault operations include the following. For all other mission analysis factors, see FM 90-4:

- Ground mobility is limited once the unit is inserted unless vehicles are provided.
- Communication range may be limited to that of portable radios.
- CS and sustainment are austere.
- Air lines of communication must be planned for sustainment.
- Disposition of 81-mm and 120-mm mortars depends on the ability to displace the tubes and ammunition.

AIR ASSAULT BATTALION ORGANIZATION

C-3.   As with all air assault operations, the battalion is organized to meet METT-TC and operational considerations.

ACTIONS OF BATTALION (–)

C-4.   The OPORD should reflect detailed planning for actions of the entire force; not only the air assault element, but also the battalion (–) or battalion (–) stay behind. This planning should emphasize command and control relationships and linkup procedures. If the battalion (–) is tasked to perform linkup operations with their deployed Infantry, then both (1) operational issues, such as time, place, and method of linkup, and (2) change of command for operation and maneuver control must be carefully planned.

Section II. PLANNING CONSIDERATIONS

The battalion commander and staff review the following planning considerations during the military decision-making process leading to an air assault operation. For a detailed discussion of air assault planning, see FM 90-4.

INTELLIGENCE

C-5.   The primary enemy tactics against air assault operations can be broken down into the following four major areas:

- Air defense fires (including small arms).
- Fixed- and rotary-wing aircraft.
- Electronic warfare.
- Enemy reaction to LZ operations.

C-6.   The commander and staff must understand the capabilities and limitations of enemy aircraft in the AO and take all measures to minimize the risk of encounter. They must analyze enemy capabilities to interdict friendly LZs with ground forces, artillery, and CAS during the planning phase of the operation.

MOVEMENT AND MANEUVER

C-7.   Habitual relationships and the integration of Infantry and Army aviation, allow Infantrymen and supporting fires to strike rapidly over extended distances. To provide surprise and shock effect, the required combat power should be delivered to the objective area as early as possible, consistent with aircraft and pickup zone capabilities. Attack helicopters, if available, are integrated into the tactical plan of the ground force commander. During air assault operations, they additionally support the lift and assault force by direct and indirect fires. Air assault forces operate relatively free of the terrain influences that restrict surface operations. Air assault forces are best employed to locate and defeat enemy forces and installations, or to seize terrain objectives to prevent enemy withdrawal, reinforcement, and supply, and to prevent the shifting and reinforcement of enemy reserves.

C-8.   Engineers in an air assault operation assist mobility by constructing or expanding helicopter LZs and FARPs, and by rehabilitating existing forward operational facilities. Engineers assist in breaching obstacles and fight as Infantry when required.

FIRE SUPPORT

C-9.   FS planning provides for suppressive fires along flight routes and near LZs. Priority of fires must be the suppression of enemy air defenses. Displacement of FS assets and resupply depends on helicopters as prime movers unless prime movers are lifted into the area. Suppression of suspected ADA sites along flight routes is vital to the success of an air assault operation. Naval gunfire (NGF) support and USAF CAS may be available to augment available artillery.

PROTECTION

C-10.   AD assets provide protection against low-flying aircraft and attack helicopters. Early warning of enemy air is broadcast over the unit early warning net. Avengers, if available, are used in support of the maneuver battalions and to protect C2 and static assets.

SUSTAINMENT

C-11.   Support of organic aviation units is extensive. FARPs are necessary to maintain the fast pace of air assault operations. The battalion's organic assets push supplies, material, and ammunition forward by helicopter to support the air assault operation.

COMMAND AND CONTROL

C-12.   The key to successful air assault operations lies in precise, centralized planning and aggressive, decentralized execution. The availability of aviation assets is normally the major factor in determining task organization. Task organization is determined and announced early in the planning process. Units must maintain tactical integrity throughout an air assault operation. Squads are normally loaded intact on the same helicopter to ensure unit integrity upon landing.

Section III. AIR ASSAULT PLANNING STAGES

The successful execution of an air assault depends on a careful mission analysis by the commander and staff and a detailed, precise reverse planning sequence. The five basic plans that constitute an air assault operation are the ground tactical plan, the landing plan, the air movement plan, the loading plan, and the staging plan (Figure C-1). In operations involving units with organic combat vehicles, the ground tactical plan must also include a linkup plan. Air assaults are planned in reverse order, beginning with the ground tactical plan and working backwards to the staging plan.

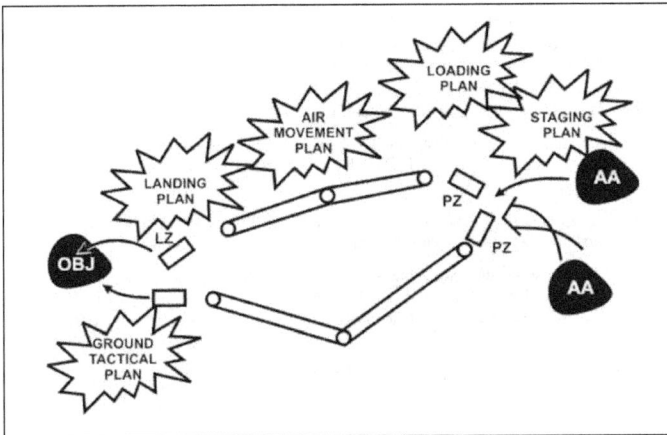

Figure C-1. Air assault planning process.

AIR ASSAULT BATTALION TASK FORCE KEY PERSONNEL

C-13.   The battalion staff is responsible for planning the air assault operation and the accompanying battalion minus operations, developing the air assault in conjunction with the assault helicopter unit, synchronizing all elements of the combined arms team, and allocating the necessary resources to the air assault force to ensure successful execution of the operation.

AIR ASSAULT TASK FORCE COMMANDER

C-14.   The air assault task force commander (AATFC) is normally the battalion commander. He has overall responsibility for the air assault task force's (AATF's) planning and execution. The BCT commander may decide to assume this role.

AIR MISSION COMMANDER

C-15.   The supporting helicopter unit provides an AMC. For air assaults conducted by an aviation company, the aviation battalion commander may designate a company commander or platoon leader to be the AMC.

AVIATION LIAISON OFFICER

C-16.   The supporting aviation unit should provide an aviation liaison officer to the AATF. He is considered a special staff officer. His role is to advise the AATFC on all matters relating to Army aviation and to jointly develop, along with the AATF staff, the detailed plans necessary to support the air assault operation. During the execution phase, he should be available to assist the AATFC or S-3 in coordinating the employment of aviation assets.

PICK-UP ZONE CONTROL OFFICER

C-17.   The pickup zone control officer (PZCO) organizes, controls, and coordinates operations in PZs selected by the AATFC. (The S-4 selects and controls logistical PZs.)

C-18.   To manage operations, the PZCO forms a control group to assist him. The control group normally includes air traffic control, subordinate units, and support personnel (manpower to clear the PZ and security). The PZCO selects a central location to position the group. The PZCO is designated by the AATFC, usually the S-3 Air. For battalion air assault operations, each company commander appoints a PZCO who operates a company PZ for the battalion.

C-19.   The PZCO should communicate on two primary radio frequencies: one to control movement and loading of units, and one to control aviation elements (combat aviation net). Alternate frequencies are provided as necessary.

C-20.   The PZCO plans fires near PZs to provide all-round protection (from available support) without endangering arrival and departure of troops or aircraft.

C-21.   The PZCO ensures that adequate security is provided. Security protects the main body as it assembles, moves to the PZ, and is lifted out. Security elements are normally provided by other forces if the PZ is within a friendly area. Security comes from AATF resources if it is to be extracted from the objective area.

C-22.   The PZSO clears the PZ of obstacles and marks the PZ.

AIR ASSAULT ROLES

C-23.   Utility helicopters and cargo helicopters are the primary aircraft used in air assault operations.

UTILITY HELICOPTERS

C-24.   The primary mission of the utility helicopter in the air assault is to move troops. With the seats installed, the allowable cabin load (ACL) for the UH-60 is 11 combat-loaded Soldiers. If the seats are removed, the ACL increases. The ACL then depends on the type of equipment being carried by the troops. For planning purposes, a UH-60 can transporting about 16 combat-loaded troops.

CARGO HELICOPTERS

C-25.   The CH-47D helicopter provides the AATFC with the capability of moving troops and equipment in support of the air assault. In a troop-carrying mode, the CH-47D can transport up to 31 combat-loaded troops.

GROUND TACTICAL PLAN

C-26.   The foundation of a successful air assault is the ground tactical plan. All other air assault planning stages are based on the ground tactical plan, which specifies actions in the objective area that will lead to accomplishment of the mission. The ground tactical plan addresses the following areas:

- Missions of all battalion elements and methods for employment.
- Zones of attack, sectors, or areas of operations with graphic control measures.
- Task organization to include command relationships.
- Location and size of reserves.
- Fire support to include graphic control measures.
- Sustainment.

Note. The AATF staff prepares this plan with input from all battalion elements and in sufficient detail to facilitate understanding by subordinate commanders. It is imperative that all aircrews know this ground tactical plan and the ground commander's intent.

COMMANDER'S INTENT

C-27.   The AATFC articulates his intent for the air assault early in the planning process. Air assault planning often begins after the AATFC issues his intent even though the ground tactical plan may not be complete. The commander's intent for the air assault allows planners to understand the method and end state and to begin to piece together the subsequent plans. The commander's intent for the air assault includes things such as whether the assault force will land on the objective or land near it and maneuver to it. The commander's intent for the air assault may include surprise as a critical element, which leads to the development of fire support and SEAD plans.

ORGANIZATION FOR COMBAT

C-28.   The mission, enemy situation, terrain, maneuver forces, and fire support assets all help air assault planners determine the battalion organization for combat. Planners emphasize—

- Maximizing combat power in the assault to heighten surprise and shock effect. This is especially important if the air assault force plans to land on or near the objective.
- Ensuring the battalion inserts the minimum essential force to accomplish initial objectives quickly. The air assault force must be massed in the LZ and build up significant combat power early to prevent being defeated by repositioning enemy forces.
- Ensuring the air assault force has sufficient assets to sustain it until linkup.

SCHEME OF MANEUVER

C-29.   The AATFC develops a scheme of maneuver to accomplish his mission and seize assigned objectives. Scheme of maneuver development by the battalion headquarters allows subsequent planning phases of the air assault to be accomplished and must be done before development of the air assault. Development of the battalion ground tactical plan need not be complete to begin air assault mission planning. As a minimum, the AATFC must provide the ground scheme of maneuver for air assault planning to begin. Battalion planners should not wait for the completed assault force OPORD to begin planning. The battalion staff and aviation units can begin air assault planning as soon as the assault force commander approves the general scheme of maneuver.

FIRE SUPPORT

C-30.   The amount of artillery available to support the air assault and the locations of supporting artillery units are critical factors in determining the ground tactical plan. Once the initial assault force has deployed to the LZ, they are often out of range of conventional artillery. Indirect fire support planning should include mortars, MLRS or ATACMS, and close air support.

ATTACK HELICOPTERS IN SUPPORT OF GROUND TACTICAL PLAN

C-31.   During the ground fight, attack helicopters may assist the assault force commander by providing reconnaissance near the LZs, destroying repositioning forces, destroying counterattacking forces, and calling for and adjusting fire on targets of opportunity. A shift in C2 from the AMC to the assault force commander is critical and must be planned and rehearsed in detail. During an air assault with multiple lifts, the attack helicopters support the air assault and ground fight. (Some elements provide reconnaissance and security for the air assault; other elements screen for the assault force.) Synchronization of the attack assets must be precise and detailed to eliminate confusion and to avoid disrupting the air assault flow.

LANDING PLAN

C-32.   The scheme of maneuver and ground tactical plan directly affects the selection of LZs, the landing formation, and the amount of combat power air assaulted into the LZ. The landing plan is planned in conjunction with the development of the ground tactical plan and supports the assault force commander's intent and scheme of maneuver. The landing plan outlines the distribution, timing, and sequencing of aircraft into the LZ.

LZ SELECTION

C-33.   In coordination with the AMC and LNO, the AATFC selects primary and alternate LZs. The number of selected LZs is based on the ground scheme of maneuver and LZ availability. The aviation planners advise the AATFC on LZ suitability. The considerations for selecting suitable landing zones are—

Location

C-34.   The LZ must be in an area supporting the ground tactical plan of the AATFC. It may be located on the objective, close by, or at a distance.

Capacity

C-35.   The selected LZ must be big enough to support the number of aircraft the AATFC requires on air assault lifts.

Enemy Disposition and Capabilities

C-36.   The AMC must consider enemy air defense locations, weapons ranges and the ability of the enemy to reposition ground forces to react to the air assault.

Unit Tactical Integrity

C-37.   Squads land in the LZ intact, and platoons land in the same serial. Vehicle crews land with their vehicles. This ensures fighting unit integrity during the air assault.

Supporting Fires

C-38.   LZs selected must be in range of supporting fires (artillery, CAS, and naval gunfire).

Obstacles

C-39.   LZ selection includes existing obstacles on the LZ as well as plans for reinforcing them. LZs should be selected beyond enemy obstacles.

Identification from Air

C-40.   The LZ should be identifiable from the air, if possible.

ATTACK HELICOPTERS IN SUPPORT OF LANDING PLAN

C-41.   During execution of the landing plan, attack helicopters can provide overwatch of the LZs, conduct a reconnaissance of the egress flight routes, call for fire (if designated to do so), and set up a screen for supporting the assault force commander during the ground tactical plan. The AMC must ensure that the missions of the attack aircraft are synchronized with the assault helicopters.

AIR MOVEMENT PLAN

C-42.   The air movement plan is based on the ground tactical and landing plans. It specifies the schedule and provides instructions for the movement of troops, equipment, and supplies from the PZ to the LZ. It provides coordinating instructions regarding air routes, air control points (ACPs), aircraft speeds, altitudes, formations, and fire support. The AATFC develops the air movement plan in conjunction with the AMC and flight lead. The air movement plan results in the production of the air movement table.

C-43.   Selection of flight routes is always based on the factors of METT-TC. The battalion staff and the AMC consider the location of friendly troops, enemy disposition, air defense systems, terrain, and the locations of the PZ and LZ to select the best flight route. Selected flight routes should always be laid over the enemy situational template produced by the S-2 to ensure that the flight route selected avoids known or suspected enemy positions.

C-44.   The battalion staff and the AMC select primary and alternate flight routes. Alternate flight routes provide the assault force a preplanned, precoordinated method of moving from the PZ to LZ if the primary route becomes compromised.

C-45.   Flight routes that pass through adjacent unit sectors must be coordinated and approved by the adjacent unit to avoid potential fratricide.

C-46.   When selecting flight routes, the AMC and battalion staff must consider—

- Airspace management.
- Support of the landing plan.
- Enemy capabilities.
- Fire support.
- Flight route distance.
- Number of aircraft.

C-47.   Attack helicopters can be used in support of the air movement plan. During the air movement phase, the air assault security forces provide reconnaissance and security for the assault helicopters.

LOADING PLAN

C-48.   The AATFC bases the loading plan on the air movement and ground tactical plans. The loading plan ensures troops, equipment, and supplies are loaded on the correct aircraft. It establishes the priority of loads, the bump plan, and the cross loading of equipment and personnel. Detailed load planning ensures the battalion arrives at the LZ configured to support the ground tactical plan. A bump plan that ensures essential troops and equipment are loaded ahead of less critical loads. Planning for the loading plan must include the organization and operation of the PZ, the loading of aircraft, and the bump plan.

PICKUP ZONE SELECTION

C-49.   The first step in the loading plan is selection of suitable primary and alternate PZs. Selection of PZs is based on—

- METT-TC.
- Commander's intent.
- Location of assault forces in relation to PZs.
- Size and capabilities of available PZs.
- Number of PZs.
- Proximity to troops.
- Accessibility.
- Vulnerability to attack.
- Surface conditions.

PICKUP ZONE CONTROL

C-50.   Once the AATFC selects the PZ, the PZ control officer (PZCO) organizes, controls, and coordinates PZ operation.

AVIATION INVOLVEMENT

C-51.   The assault helicopter unit must ensure aviation expertise is present on the PZ.

PICKUP ZONE COMMUNICATIONS

C-52.   Communications must use the most secure means available. PZ operations may be conducted under radio listening silence to avoid electronic detection. This requires detailed planning. If under radio listening silence, it is imperative that aircrews remain on schedule to allow the PZCO to keep a smooth flow of troops from the PZ. PZ communications are accomplished on the established FM PZ control net, with transmissions kept to a minimum.

PICKUP ZONE MARKING

C-53.   The PZCO directs the marking of the PZ so the PZ is identifiable from the air. Far and near recognition signals are needed, especially at night, to allow pilots to orient on the PZ quickly. Touchdown points must be clearly marked. The PZCO must ensure no other lighting is on the PZ.

DISPOSITION OF LOADS ON PICKUP ZONE

C-54.   Personnel and equipment must be positioned on the PZ to conform to the landing formation. Flight crews must understand the loading plan on the PZ and be prepared to accept troops and equipment immediately upon landing. PZ sketches showing locations of loads in the PZ assist flight crews in loading troops and equipment quickly once the aircraft arrive in the PZ. Flight crews should be provided a PZ diagram.

ATTACK HELICOPTERS IN SUPPORT OF LOADING PLAN

C-55.   During the loading phase, attack helicopters assist by providing overwatch of the PZs and conducting a route reconnaissance of the air assault flight routes.

STAGING PLAN

C-56.   The staging plan is based on the loading plan and prescribes the proper order for movement of personnel and aircraft to the PZ. Loads must be ready before the aircraft arrive at the PZ. During mission planning, the PZCO determines the time required for setting up the PZ, and selects times the PZ will be established (based upon the air assault H-hour).

MISSION PLANNING

C-57.   Mission planning includes coordination between the battalion and the AMC, development of the aviation OPORD, issuance of the OPORD, and rehearsals.

ROUTES TO PICKUP ZONE

C-58.   The AMC must select flight routes to the PZ that allow the aircraft to arrive at the PZ on time and in the proper landing direction and configuration to accept loads.

This page intentionally left blank.

Appendix D
Heavy and Stryker

Employing Infantry forces with heavy and Stryker units is a combat multiplier. These operations take advantage of the Infantry unit's ability to operate in severely restricted terrain, such as urban areas, forests, and mountains, combined with the mobility and firepower inherent in heavy and Stryker units. To ensure heavy, Stryker and Infantry assets are integrated and synchronized, forces should be mutually supporting based on the commander's concept of employment. This appendix addresses conditions Infantry commanders must consider when planning and executing tactical operations with heavy, or Stryker forces, operating as part of an HBCT or SBCT. The following terms are used throughout the appendix:

Heavy   Refers to units with BFVs or M1 Abrams tanks.

Stryker   Refers to units with Stryker Infantry carrier vehicles (ICVs) and Stryker mobile gun system (MGS) vehicles.

Mounted   Refers to units with BFVs or M1 Abrams tanks, and both Stryker vehicles.

Infantry   Refers to all Infantry, including air assault and airborne trained Infantry, and Ranger units.

Section I. MISSIONS, CAPABILITIES, AND LIMITATIONS

Across the spectrum of operations, there is an overlap in which heavy, Stryker and Infantry forces can operate. The use of a mixed force in this overlap takes advantage of the strengths of the forces and offsets their respective weaknesses. Heavy/Infantry operations occur when an Infantry force is supporting a heavy force. Infantry/heavy operations occur when an heavy force is supporting an Infantry force. Motorized unit operations occur when, due to mission requirements, some type of army unit gets a mission requiring the use of wheeled vehicles for movement. The unit can be a wheeled vehicle-equipped unit such as a Stryker unit or one augmented with wheeled vehicles. The addition of wheeled vehicles provides the unit with increased agility and provides them the flexibility to accomplish their missions. The integration of heavy, Stryker, and Infantry forces enhances the friendly force ability to take advantage of the enemy force's structure and to attack its weaknesses and seize the initiative. Table D-1, page D-2, compares the capabilities of the IBCT Infantry battalions, the HBCT Combined Arms Battalions, and the SBCT Infantry battalions; Table D-2, page D-3, compares their limitations.

Table D-1. Infantry battalion capabilities

CAPABILITIES		
IBCT INFANTRY	*HBCT COMBINED ARMS*	*SBCT INFANTRY*
Conduct offensive, defensive, stability operations and civil support operations in all types of environments. Specially suited for restricted and severely restricted terrain.	Conduct offensive, defensive, stability operations, and civil support operations in most environments. Specially suited to defeat heavy enemy forces and provide mobile protected firepower in urban terrain.	Conduct offensive, defensive, stability operations, and civil support operations in most environments. Specially suited for rapid entry and provide mobile, limited protected firepower.
Screen and guard friendly units.	Conduct security operations [screen, guard, and cover (as part of the HBCT)] for a larger force.	Screen and guard friendly units.
Exploit success and pursue limited mobility opponents.	Exploit success and pursue a defeated enemy as part of a larger formation.	Exploit success and pursue a defeated enemy as part of a larger formation.
Can move through any terrain.	Accomplish rapid movement and limited penetrations.	Tactically mobile.
Seize, secure, occupy, and retain terrain.	Seize, secure, occupy, and retain terrain.	Seize, secure, occupy, and retain terrain.
Destroy, neutralize, suppress, interdict, disrupt, block, canalize, and fix enemy forces.	Destroy, neutralize, suppress, interdict, disrupt, block, canalize, and fix enemy forces.	Destroy, neutralize, suppress, interdict, disrupt, block, canalize, and fix enemy forces.
Breach enemy obstacles.	Breach enemy obstacles.	Breach enemy obstacles.
Reconnoiter, deny, bypass, clear, contain, and isolate (terrain or enemy).	Reconnoiter, deny, bypass, clear, contain, and isolate (terrain or enemy).	Reconnoiter, deny, bypass, clear, contain, and isolate (terrain or enemy).
Weapons company allows significant task organization options.	Combined Arms Battalions have assigned tank, mechanized and engineer companies that habitually work together.	Assigned companies are built as combined arms teams.
Operate in conjunction with SBCT/HBCT, joint, interagency, multinational, or Special Operations Forces.	Operate in conjunction with IBCT/SBCT, joint, interagency, multinational, or Special Operations Forces.	Operate in conjunction with IBCT/HBCT, joint, interagency, multinational, or Special Operations Forces.
Conduct small-unit operations in all types of environments.	Conduct small-unit operations in most types of environments.	Conduct small-scale operations in all types of environments.
Conduct amphibious operations.		Conduct amphibious operations.
Conduct air assault (and airborne, for selected units) operations.	Conduct limited air assault operations.	Conduct air assault operations.
High strategic mobility.	High tactical mobility.	Good mix of strategic mobility and tactical mobility
Requires relatively small resupply.	Assigned sustainment can resupply for 24-48 hours.	Conduct sustained combat operations for 72 hours in all environments.

Table D-2. Infantry battalion limitations.

LIMITATIONS		
IBCT INFANTRY	**HBCT COMBINED ARMS**	**SBCT INFANTRY**
Especially vulnerable to enemy fires, CBRN, and enemy air.	Heavily reliant on lightly armored sustainment vehicle support (especially CL III) to conduct sustained operations.	Vulnerable to enemy direct fires, CBRN, and enemy air.
Sustainment structure may require external support for independent operations.	Large volume sustainment transport vulnerable to enemy action; sustainment activities require large footprint.	Sustainment structure may require external support for full-spectrum operations.
Lacks the firepower, mobility, and protection to conduct sustained combat against an armored force.	Mobility and firepower are reduced by restricted and severely restricted terrain.	Dense jungles and forests, very steep and rugged terrain, and significant water obstacles.
Foot mobile; organic vehicles cannot move all Soldiers at one time.	Strategic mobility is limited by substantial quantities of heavy equipment.	Vehicles are designed for transport more than direct fires engagement against conventional forces.
Excellent mobility through all terrain limited by slow rate of movement.	Fewer riflemen on the ground than IBCT or SBCT Infantry Battalions	Reduced C2 during dismounted operations.
Soldiers very dependent on resupply.	Consumption of supply items is very high, especially Classes III, V, and IX.	Consumption of supply items is high, especially Classes III, V, and IX.

MOUNTED AND INFANTRY

D-1.   The potential to use mounted and Infantry forces at the same time as part of a military operations is unlimited. Their synergistic efforts build on their strengths and offset their weaknesses.

MISSIONS

D-2.   The ability to interject Infantry forces into a theater of war dominated by friendly mounted forces gives the commander a *flexible* response to increasing tensions and a *rapid* response in the face of a sudden all-out attack. Mounted and Infantry forces are routinely cross-attached and task-organized from the BCT level down to the platoon and even section level. The decision to task-organize forces is based on echelons above the BCT or JTF-level war planning, or on a subordinate commander's request for augmentation. In all cases, METT-TC drives the decision to use mounted and Infantry forces together.

CAPABILITIES

D-3.   An advantage of mixing mounted and Infantry forces is greater tactical flexibility for the maneuver commander. In the offense, the Infantry force can infiltrate by ground or air to seize and hold restricted and severely restricted terrain, allowing the mounted force to move faster. Also, Infantry can execute tasks that mounted forces might lack the manpower or training to perform such as attacking in restricted terrain to defeat enemy Infantry in prepared positions. In the defense, the Infantry force can defend in restricted and severely restricted terrain and allow the mounted force to mass its systems along the enemy's primary mounted avenue of approach. Along with such flexibility, the integrated force also has the advantage of the mobility and firepower inherent in mounted units.

LIMITATIONS

D-4.   The challenge of combining mounted and Infantry is to understand the capabilities and limitations of each type of force structure (Table D-1 and Table D-2); then planning and executing to compensate for these challenges. Two major challenges are to understand and adjust for the differences in operational tempo and sustainment requirements.

MOUNTED ONLY

D-5.   An IBCT or smaller Infantry unit operating with mounted forces should consider the following missions, capabilities, and limitations of armored forces. For a comparison with the other types of Infantry forces, see Table D-1 (capabilites) and Table D-2 (limitations):

MISSIONS

D-6.   The missions given to mounted forces are best suited for unrestricted terrain.

CAPABILITIES

D-7.   Mounted forces have the capability to—

* Conduct sustained combat operations in all environments.
* Accomplish rapid movement and deep penetrations.
* Exploit success and pursue a defeated enemy as part of a larger formation.
* Conduct security operations (advance, flank, and rear guard) for a larger force.
* Conduct defensive operations or delay in sector over large areas.
* Conduct offensive operations.
* Conduct operations with Infantry and special operations forces.
* Conduct stability operations and civil support operations.
* Heavy forces can deploy personnel task-organized to an AO onto pre-positioned equipment.
* Currently, all Stryker forces have an enhanced common operational picture.

LIMITATIONS

D-8.   Mounted forces in general, have restricted mobility in jungles, dense forests, steep and rugged terrain, built-up areas, and water obstacles. The following are other limitations of mounted forces:

* They have a high consumption rate of supply items, especially Classes III, V, and IX.
* They are vulnerable to antiarmor weapons and mines.
* Heavy forces, and to a lesser degree Stryker units, are not organized to conduct long duration or continuous dismounted Infantry operations.
* Mounted forces require a secure ground line of communication.
* Heavy forces have limited strategic mobility.

INFANTRY ONLY

D-9.   The Infantry organizations vary in capabilities and limitations and in their impact on the heavy force. For a comparison with the other types of Infantry forces, see Table D-1 (capabilites) and Table D-2 (limitations).

MISSIONS

D-10.   The missions given to an IBCT must consider the enemy's armored superiority in mobility and firepower. The IBCT must offset its vulnerabilities with dispersion, cover and concealment, and use of close and hindering terrain to slow the enemy. Table D-3 provides examples of possible light Infantry tasks.

Table D-3. Examples of possible tasks.

Mounted Battalion Missions	Infantry Company Task
Movement to Contact	Clear and secure restricted areas; follow and support.
Attack	Air-assault to fix or destroy enemy targets; infiltrate or air-assault to seize objectives; breach obstacles; create a penetration.
Exploitation	Secure LOC; air-assault to seize terrain or attack enemy forces.
Pursuit	Clear bypassed forces; air-assault to block enemy escape.
Follow and Support	Secure key terrain and LOC; provide rear security.
Defense	Block dismounted avenues; perform security tasks; occupy strongpoint; ambush; provide rear area security; conduct urban operations.
Linkup	Serve as follow-up echelon.
Demonstration	Conduct display operations.
Retrograde Operations	Provide rear security, clear routes and occupy positions in depth; perform reconnaissance or deception; conduct stay-behind operations.

CAPABILITIES

D-11.　Infantry forces have the capabilities to perform the following actions:

- Seize, occupy, and hold terrain.
- Move on foot or by aircraft, truck, or amphibious vehicle.
- Move in all types of terrain.
- Conduct operations with heavy and Stryker forces.
- Conduct covert breaches.
- Conduct air assault and airborne (training dependent) operations.
- Take part in counterinsurgency operations within a larger unit.
- Rapidly accept and integrate augmenting forces.

LIMITATIONS

D-12.　Infantry forces have the following limitations:

- They must depend on nonorganic transportation for rapid movement over long distances.
- They require external support when they must operate for an extended period.
- Unless dug in with overhead cover, they are extremely vulnerable to indirect fires.
- Unless dug in, they are vulnerable in open terrain to long-range direct fires.

Section II. PLANNING CONSIDERATIONS

Employment of mounted and Infantry forces requires thorough integration of the operating systems of all units. Cross attaching Infantry and mounted forces only to the BCT level, leads to less than optimal mission accomplishment. Task organizing Infantry and mounted forces to the battalion/task force and even to the platoon and section levels can take full advantage of the capabilities of the different forces. However, task organizing at each lower level causes increasing strain on the WFF, especially the sustainment WFF system and it must be planned and executed with increased commander's emphasis. This section focuses on planning considerations for each of the seven operating systems.

FIRE SUPPORT

D-13.   The mounted force must recognize that Infantry operations focus on stealth, which might not allow for preparatory and other preliminary fires. Fire support available to each force must be integrated into the fire support plan. Planners must know the organizations, capabilities, and limitations of all forces involved, particularly digital and nondigital capabilities. In addition, planners should consider the possibility of limited continuous fire support for the Infantry. Fire support from the Infantry's DS artillery may be interrupted due to the battalion's towed howitzers operating in a mounted/Infantry force offensive operation. During planning and preparation, a liaison team helps synchronize fire support. Restricted fire control measures must be jointly developed and understood by everyone.

MOVEMENT AND MANEUVER

D-14.   Either the Infantry or mounted force can fix the enemy which allows the other force to maneuver. Whether it conducts the fixing operation or maneuver, the Infantry force requires the advantage of restricted terrain. The following maneuver considerations apply during employment.

OPERATIONAL TEMPO

D-15.   The differences between the operational tempo of Infantry and that of mounted forces are always a key consideration, as are rehearsal schedules. An early rehearsal may be required, both to allow units to take part jointly and to resolve the operational differences effectively.

EMPLOYMENT

D-16.   Infantry is best suited to restricted and severely restricted terrain in that it can impede the enemy's mobility, and nullify his ability to use long-range weapons and observation assets.

MOVEMENT

D-17.   To help prevent detection, leaders should plan the movement to coincide with limited visibility conditions such as darkness, severe weather, smoke, or fog.

D-18.   A common obstacle plan must be developed for all operations. Infantry forces may be used to reduce obstacles and clear choke points for the mounted forces. In breaching operations, Infantry forces must ensure the breach is large enough for the widest vehicle in the operation.

FIRES

D-19.   Direct and indirect fires should be mutually supporting during integrated operations. The mounted forces can use their long-range direct fires to provide suppression, allowing Infantry units to maneuver. Conversely, Infantry forces can provide overwatch or support by fire to the mounted forces, which allows M1s, BFVs, Stryker ICVs and MGSs to maneuver in restricted terrain.

INFILTRATION

D-20.   Mounted forces can assist infiltration of the Infantry forces by augmenting security at the LD. They can use their thermal capability to scan the area for enemy forces and can provide direct fire support as necessary.

PROTECTION

D-21.   Air defense assets may be deployed to fight and provide protection within the scope and design of any organization. Because Infantry forces frequently maneuver in restricted terrain, Avenger coverage may not be feasible. In such operations, man-portable Stingers should be allocated to support the Infantry.

D-22.   The Infantry force lacks decontamination equipment and is more limited in a CBRN environment than the mounted force. The need to carry protective clothing in addition to standard loads affects the mobility of the Infantry force Soldiers. When the IBCT and the higher echelon headquarters cannot provide transportation assets, and enemy CBRN use is possible, planners should consider using HBCT/SBCT assets to transport the Infantry force equipment. HBCTs and SBCTs have water-hauling capabilities they can use to offset Infantry shortfalls. Transporting such items with these assets reduces the load of Infantry units. Commanders must consider METT-TC and must plan linkup points to ensure the Infantry unit obtains these critical items as it needs them.

D-23.   Survivability remains the priority for Infantry forces, which must prepare to take advantage of the engineer assets available to the mounted forces and the engineer company that normally supports a combined arms battalion.

COMMAND AND CONTROL

D-24.   The directing HQ designates command relationships between the forces. The command relationship between units can be either attached or OPCON. An Infantry unit attached to a mounted unit can normally be adequately supported. Attachment of a mounted unit to an Infantry unit, however, requires considerable maneuver and sustainment support from the mounted unit's parent organization or from higher-level support assets.

COMMUNICATIONS

D-25.   Infantry units normally have considerably less digital and long-range communications capability than mounted forces. The controlling unit must therefore thoroughly analyze the communication requirements of an attached Infantry unit.

LIAISON OFFICERS

D-26.   Units normally exchange LNOs, who assist in operational planning, coordinate the development of orders and overlays, and serve as advisors to the counterpart units. In addition, leaders from the attached unit may be required to perform special functions in the different organizational configurations.

INTELLIGENCE

D-27.   Detailed intelligence is critical in integrating Infantry with mounted forces. Infantry forces orient on concentrations of enemy units, including counterattack forces and artillery and air defense assets; they also focus on the enemy's Infantry assembly areas, LZs and PZs.

SUSTAINMENT

D-28.   Infantry units are not organized, equipped, or trained to meet the support requirements of a mounted force. The Infantry force relies on considerable assistance from the mounted support elements and/or from support assets at echelons above the BCT. Mounted units, however, should be able to provide support to an Infantry element. For a more detailed discussion of sustainment considerations, see Section V of this appendix.

DISMOUNTED INFANTRY MOVEMENT RATES

D-29.   Commanders of mounted forces often overestimate the speed with which Infantry can move. Numerous factors can affect the rate of march for the Infantry forces; tactical considerations, weather, terrain, march discipline, acclimatization, availability of water and rations, morale, individual Soldiers' self-confidence, and individual loads. Table D-4 summarizes dismounted rates of march for normal terrain. The normal distance covered by a dismounted force in a 24-hour period is from 20 to 32 kilometers, marching from 5 to 8 hours at a rate of 4 kilometers per hour. A march in excess of 32 kilometers in 24 hours is considered a forced march. Forced marches increase the number of hours marched, not the rate of march, and can be expected to impair the unit's fighting efficiency. Absolute maximum distances for dismounted marches are 56 kilometers in 24 hours, 96 kilometers in 48 hours, or 128 kilometers in 72 hours.

Table D-4. Dismounted rates of march (normal terrain).

	ROADS	CROSS-COUNTRY
Day	4.0 kph	2.4 kph
Night	3.2 kph	1.6 kph

TANK MOUNTED INFANTRY

D-30.   An additional maneuver consideration for an Infantry mounted or mounted Infantry operation is the decision of whether to physically move Infantrymen on tanks. This mode of transportation can be difficult but is not impossible; it does, in fact, afford some significant advantages. The mounted Infantry can provide additional security for the tanks. When the team conducts a halt or must execute a breach or other tactical tasks, Infantry assets are readily available to provide support and security. The commander must weigh the potential dangers of carrying tank-mounted Infantrymen against the advantages of mobility and security they can provide. For specific procedures and safety considerations involved in mounting Infantry on tanks, see FM 3-20.15.

SAFETY

D-31.   Initially, most Infantrymen are not familiar with the hazards that may arise during operations with M1s, BFVs, Stryker ICVs, Stryker MGS and other armored vehicles. The most obvious of these include the dangers associated with main-gun fire and the inability of mounted vehicle crews to see people and objects near their vehicles. Leaders must ensure that Soldiers understand the following points of operational safety.

DISCARDING SABOT

D-32.   M1 and MGS sabot rounds and BFV armor piercing rounds discard stabilizing petals when fired creating a downrange hazard for Infantry. The aluminum petals of the tank rounds are discarded in an area extending 70 meters to the left and right of the gun-target line, out to a range of 1 kilometer (Figure D-1). The danger zone for BFV rounds extends 60 degrees to the left and right of the gun-target line for the plastic debris out to 100 meters and 7 degrees to the left and right of the gun target line for the aluminum base out to 400 meters (Figure D-2). Danger zone data for the MGS is not yet available, but can be assumed to be similar to the danger area for the M1. Infantrymen should not be in or near the direct line of fire for the M1 or MGS main gun or BFV cannon unless they are under adequate overhead cover.

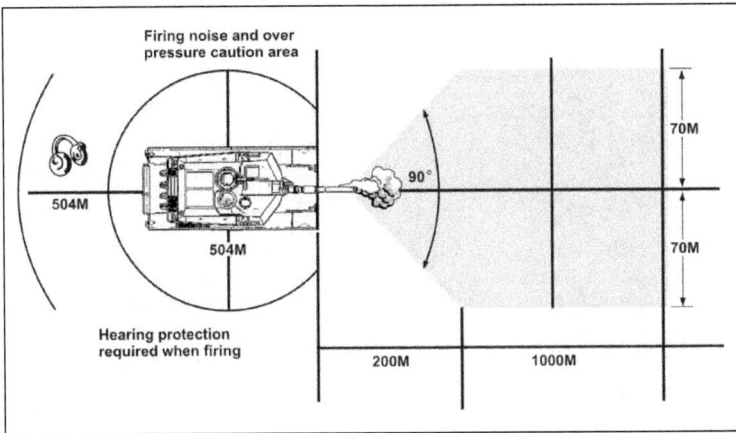

Figure D-1. M1 tank danger zone.

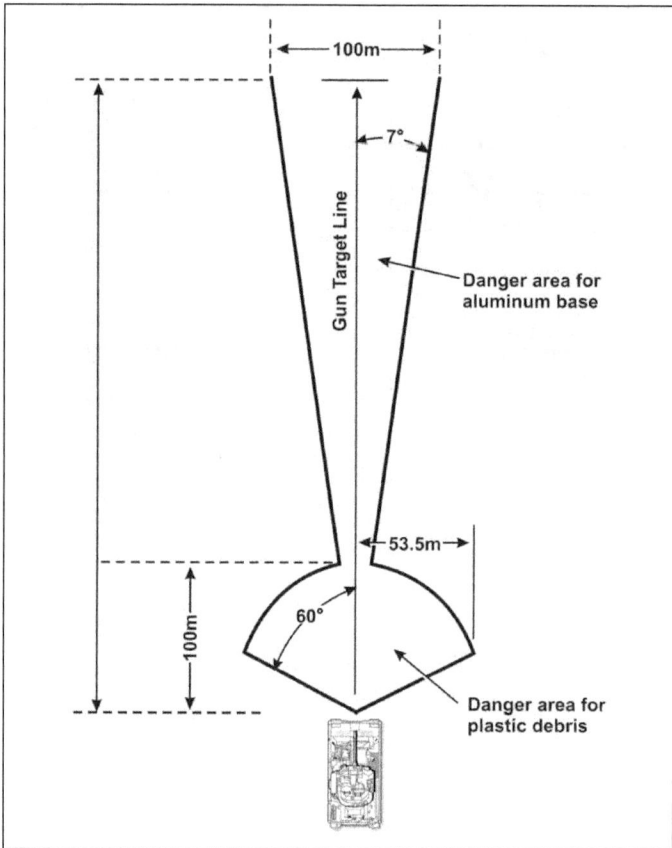

Figure D-2. BFV danger zone.

NOISE

D-33.   Tank main guns create noise in excess of 140 decibels. Repeated exposure to this level of noise can cause severe hearing loss and even deafness. In addition, dangerous noise levels may extend more than 600 meters from the tank. Single-layer hearing protection such as earplugs allows Infantrymen to work within 25 meters of the side or rear of the tank without significant hazard.

GROUND MOVEMENT HAZARDS

D-34.   Crewmen on mounted vehicles have very limited abilities to see anyone on the ground to the side or rear. As a result, vehicle crews and dismounted Infantrymen share responsibility for avoiding the hazards this may create. Infantrymen must maintain a safe distance from mounted vehicles at all times. In addition, when they work close to a mounted vehicle, dismounted Soldiers must ensure that the vehicle commander knows their location at all times.

Note. A related hazard is that M1-series tanks are deceptively quiet and may be difficult for Infantrymen to hear as they approach. As noted, vehicle crews and dismounted Infantrymen share the responsibility for eliminating potential dangers in this situation.

WARNING

M1 Exhaust Plume Hazard

M1-series tanks have an extremely hot exhaust plume that exits from the rear of the tank and angles downward. This exhaust is hot enough to burn skin and clothing.

TOW MISSILE SYSTEM

D-35.   The TOW missile system has a dangerous area extending 75 meters to the rear of the vehicle in a 90-degree "cone." The area is divided into a 50-meter danger zone and a 25-meter caution zone (Figure D-3). The danger area for the TOW systems mounted on HMMWVs and Strykers is the same as for BFVs.

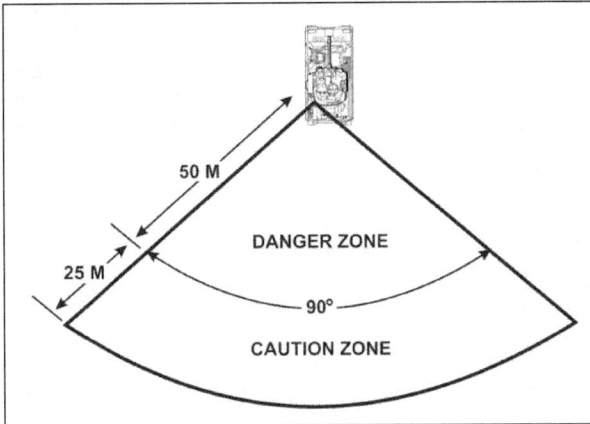

Figure D-3. BFV TOW backblast danger zone.

Section III. OPERATIONS

This section focuses on tactical employment of mounted and Infantry forces during combat operations.

OFFENSIVE OPERATIONS

D-36. The fundamentals, principles, and concepts discussed in Chapter 4 apply to Infantry and mounted force offensive operations. While combining these forces in the offense can work well in many different ways, the following are some of the most common examples.

MOUNTED FORCE SUPPORT, INFANTRY ASSAULT

D-37. M1s and BFVs or Stryker ICVs and MGSs support by fire while the Infantry assaults the objective. The vehicles fire from hull-defilade positions until the Infantry masks their fires. This is the most effective method for BFVs, Stryker ICVs and MGSs and may be used with M1s when antitank weapons or obstacles prohibit them from moving to the objective.

D-38. This method may incorporate a feint to deceive the enemy as to the location of the decisive effort. If so, the shaping efforts are timed to divert the enemy's attention from the Infantry's assault. The fires of the mounted force may also cover the sound of the Infantry's approach or breach. Close coordination is vital for effective fire control.

D-39. This method may vary when either the terrain or disposition of the enemy limits the mounted force's ability to support the Infantry's attack. In this case, the mounted force may be tasked to suppress or fix adjacent enemy positions or to accomplish other tasks to isolate the objective area.

SIMULTANEOUS ASSAULT

D-40. With this method, Infantry and mounted forces advance together, and the Infantry and vehicles move at the same speed. The vehicles may advance rapidly for short distances, stop and provide overwatch, then move forward again when the Infantry comes abreast. Tanks are best suited to assault under fire. BFVs, Stryker ICVs and MGSs may also be used in this manner but only when the threat of antitank fires is small. If an antitank threat exists, Infantry usually lead while the vehicles follow to provide fire support.

Note. Leaders must consider the safety risks when Infantry and mounted forces work in close proximity due to main gun overpressure and sabot debris.

D-41. This method may be used when the enemy situation is vague, when the objective is large and consists of both unrestricted and restricted terrain, and/or when visibility, fields of fire, and the movements of the mounted force are restricted. These conditions exist in limited visibility and in restricted terrain such as in urban areas and wooded areas. The vehicles provide immediate close protected direct fires, and the dismounted Infantry protects the vehicles from individual antitank measures.

D-42. This method sometimes requires Infantry to follow a safe distance behind the M1s, BFVs, Stryker ICVs or MGSs for protection from frontal fires. This is true when the main enemy threat is small-arms fire. From behind the vehicles, the Infantry can protect the flanks and rear of the vehicles from handheld antitank weapons.

D-43. This method may require assaulting forces to advance together in operations that require long, fast moves. Infantrymen may ride on the tanks or other vehicles until they make contact with the enemy. Although this is a quick way to move, it exposes the Infantry to enemy fire, particularly airburst munitions, and may interfere with the operation of the vehicles.

ASSAULT FROM DIFFERENT DIRECTIONS

D-44.   With this method, mounted and Infantry forces converge on the objective from different directions. Mounted and Infantry forces advance by different routes and assault the objective at the same time. For this synchronization to succeed, the Infantry elements maneuver and close on their assault position, ideally under cover of darkness or poor weather. The synchronization of the assault provides surprise, increases fire effect, and maximizes shock action. Planning, disseminating, and rehearsing the coordination of direct and indirect fire measures are critical in this type of operation.

D-45.   This method is effective for mounted forces when the following two conditions exist:

*   Terrain must be at least partly unrestricted and free from mines and other vehicle obstacles.
*   Supporting fires and smoke must effectively neutralize enemy antitank weapons; during the brief period required for the mounted forces to move from their assault positions to the near edge of the objective.

D-46.   This method requires coordination of Infantry and mounted forces to provide effective fire control on the objective. When conditions prohibit mounted force vehicles from advancing rapidly, Infantry should accompany them to provide protection.

EXPLOITATION

D-47.   Exploitation follows success in battle. The mounted force is usually the most capable exploitation force. It takes full advantage of the enemy's disorganization by driving into his rear to destroy him. A mounted force operating as a team (BFV/Stryker ICV- and M1/MGS-equipped units) may exploit the local defeat of an enemy force or the capture of an enemy position. The purpose of this type of operation is to prevent reconstitution of enemy defenses, to prevent enemy withdrawal, and secure deep objectives. A common combination is a mounted battalion or task force reinforced by an Infantry unit, engineers, and other supporting units. The Infantry may be transported in armored vehicles or trucks, or may ride on the tanks. Riding on tanks reduces road space, decreases supply problems, and keeps the members of the team together; however, it exposes the riding Infantry to enemy artillery fire. The Infantry leaders ride with the corresponding mounted unit commanders. The mounted force battalion commander must weigh the likelihood of enemy contact against the need for speed.

DEFENSIVE OPERATIONS

D-48.   The combination of Infantry and mounted forces is well suited to conduct defensive operations. The mounted force provides a concentration of antiarmor weapons and the capability to counterattack by fire or maneuver rapidly. The Infantry force can occupy strongpoints, conduct spoiling attacks, and conduct stay-behind operations. The fundamentals, principles, and concepts discussed in Chapter 5 apply to combined Infantry and mounted force defensive operations.

INFANTRY FORCE IN DEPTH, MOUNTED FORCE FORWARD

D-49.   The mounted unit covers forward of an Infantry unit's defense, masking the location of the Infantry unit. While passing through the Infantry unit's positions, mounted units provide most of their own overwatch protection. Careful planning is required for battle handover to the Infantry unit. The Infantry unit's direct fire overwatch weapons that are able to support from inside the battle handover line are limited to the long-range antitank fire from the weapons company. To alleviate this problem, the mounted force can provide some of its antiarmor assets to the Infantry. Usually, these assets are provided at company level and above.

INFANTRY FORCE FORWARD WITH MOUNTED FORCE IN DEPTH

D-50.   The mounted force assumes positions in depth behind the Infantry unit's defense. The Infantry unit's forward deployment shapes the battlefield for decisive action by the mounted forces. The Infantry unit leaves an assembly area and moves into the mounted force's objective area. At the same time, the Infantry unit prevents the enemy from using restricted and severely restricted terrain. If the enemy penetrates the Infantry unit, the mounted force counterattacks, destroying the enemy or blocking him until additional units can be repositioned to destroy him. To support the counterattack, the Infantry unit identifies the location of the enemy's main effort, slows his advance, and disrupts his C2, fire support and protection elements. The Infantry unit can guide the counterattacking force through restrictive terrain to surprise the enemy on his flank.

INFANTRY FORCE TERRAIN-ORIENTED, MOUNTED FORCE ENEMY-ORIENTED

D-51.   Terrain-oriented refers to area defense whereas enemy-oriented refers to mobile defense-like mission oriented posture. With this method, the entire force defends along the FEBA. The Infantry force (whether used as a flanking or covering force or positioned in depth) places its elements to use restrictive terrain effectively. The mounted force keeps its freedom of maneuver. To protect the Infantry unit, contact points between units should be in restrictive terrain. The Infantry unit may defend to retain key or decisive terrain while the mounted force maneuvers to destroy the enemy from the flanks or rear.

STRONGPOINT

D-52.   The Infantry unit, with additional assets and sufficient time, occupies a strongpoint. The strongpoint forces the enemy into the mounted force's EA, or the enemy attacks the strongpoint with its main effort allowing the mounted force to attack an assailable flank.

STAY-BEHIND OPERATIONS

D-53.   The Infantry unit occupies hide positions well forward of the FEBA. As the enemy passes, the Infantry force attacks the enemy's C2, fire support, protection or sustainment elements. The mounted force defends against enemy maneuver forces.

RETROGRADE OPERATIONS

D-54.   Retrograde operations include delays, withdrawals, and retirements, which gain time and avoid decisive action. During retrograde operations, mounted forces are normally employed against the enemy forces and likely avenues of advance that most threaten the operation. To assist in movement to subsequent positions, Infantry forces often need additional transportation assets. Basic movement techniques include bounding and bounding overwatch. Mounted forces with small Infantry force units mounted, along with Infantry scout platoons and weapons company elements, move to subsequent delay positions under the cover of mutually supporting forces.

SUSTAINMENT

D-55.   Sustainment planning and execution are critical elements for integration of Infantry and mounted forces. IBCTs are not organized, equipped, or trained to meet the support requirements of a mounted unit. The Infantry battalion is not structured to provide maintenance support to a mounted unit; however, they can provide limited Class V (5.56 mm, 7.62 mm, 50 cal, mortars, and antitank missiles) support. Sustainment may be further complicated if the mounted force is operating across a large geographical area to meet the demands of a decentralized mission. The following discussion covers sustainment considerations that may affect Infantry/mounted and mounted/Infantry operations:

PLANNING AND INTEGRATION

D-56.   Infantry/mounted operations may require the mounted team to integrate into the IBCT organization early in the deployment phase. This, in turn, may require sustainment assets to move into the theater of operations very early as well, usually at the same time as the command and control elements. Specific support requirements, including needed quantities of supplies, depend on the mission and must be planned and coordinated as early as possible. In addition, because the IBCT does not possess the required logistical redundancy to sustain the mounted unit, it is imperative that mission requirements calling for higher echelon unit sustainment assets be identified early in the planning process.

OPERATIONAL CONSIDERATIONS

D-57.   A mounted unit can satisfy the sustainment needs of an Infantry unit more easily than an IBCT can satisfy the needs of a mounted unit. The size and composition of the mounted force will provide insight as to the magnitude of the requirement.

Mounted Battalion with an Infantry Company

D-58.   Except for 60 mm mortar rounds, the combined arms battalion can provide all munitions the Infantry company needs. The S-4 must plan to receive and move 60-mm mortar munitions and possibly increase the anticipated usage for small arms ammunition. The Stryker battalion has 60 mm mortars and would only need to adjust consumption rates.

IBCT with a Mounted Unit

D-59.   Adding a mounted force to an IBCT significantly increases the POL, ammunition, and maintenance that must be delivered to the FSC and the BSB. The IBCT lacks the transportation required to support more than a company size mounted unit. The IBCT has no organic heavy equipment transporters (HETs) for heavy vehicle evacuation. The mounted unit battalion S-4 must constantly anticipate the unit's needs to allow the IBCT S-4 more time to react. Support packages may be required for the mounted element that is attached or under OPCON of the Infantry force. The preferred method of command relationship is OPCON, which permits the mounted unit to continue receiving support from its parent BSB. The mounted unit should always come to the Infantry unit with its FSC or a dedicated support package. The support package should include fuel trucks and operators, HETs with drivers, tracked ambulances, and maintenance support teams.

SUPPLY REQUIREMENTS

D-60.   Operations with an IBCT create many unique supply considerations for the mounted battalion. The sheer bulk and volume of supplies required by a mounted unit merits special attention during the planning and preparation phases—the following paragraphs examine some of these supply-related considerations:

Class I

D-61.   Class I food requirements are determined based on the unit's personnel strength reports. This process may be complicated by unique mission requirements imposed on the unit such as rapid changes in task organization or dispersion of subordinate companies over a wide area.

Class II

D-62.   Many Class II items required by mounted crews, such as specialized tools and fire-resistant clothing, may be difficult to obtain in an Infantry organization. Although the unit can order such items through normal supply channels, the mounted unit may face significant delays in receiving them. To overcome this problem, the mounted unit should identify any potential shortages and arrange to obtain the needed supplies before leaving its parent organization.

Class III

D-63.   The fuel and other POL products required by the mounted unit are bulky; they present the greatest sustainment challenges in planning and preparing for Infantry/mounted operations. Transportation support must be planned carefully. For example, planners must consider the placement of fuel transport vehicles during all phases of the operation. They must also focus on general-use POL products such as lubricants, which are seldom used in large quantities by the IBCT. As noted previously, the mounted unit should stock its basic load of these items, as well as make necessary resupply arrangements, before attachment to the IBCT.

Class IV

D-64.   The mounted unit does not have any unique requirements for barrier or fortification materials. The main consideration is that any Class IV materials that the commander wants may have to be loaded and carried before attachment.

Class V

D-65.   Along with POL products, ammunition for the mounted force presents the greatest transportation challenge during combat operations. Planning for Class V resupply should parallel that for Class III.; key considerations include: anticipated mission requirements, the availability of Class V transport vehicles, 120 mm main gun (M1), 105-mm main gun (MGS) and 25-mm (BFV). Ammunition may be prestocked based on expected consumption rates in the BSB along with additional transportation assets.

Class VII

D-66.   Class VII consists of major end items. The handling of these items requires thorough planning to determine transportation requirements and positioning in the scheme of the operation.

Class IX

D-67.   Repair parts for vehicles are essential to the sustainment of the mounted force. Repair parts stockage levels must be carefully considered before operations begin. Mounted forces may find it advantageous to prestock selected items to meet anticipated needs. The BSB and FSC will need to order and stock an increased number of repair parts and many repair parts will be of significant size and weight. Repair operations for mounted forces may also dictate that civilian contractors accompany the IBCT and should be considered in the planning process.

Appendix E
Army Aviation Support for Ground Operations

Army aviation's greatest contribution to the battlefield is providing the ground maneuver commander the ability to apply decisive combat power at critical times virtually anywhere on the battlefield. This combat power may be in the form of direct fire support from aviation maneuver units or the insertion of Infantry forces or artillery fires delivered via air assault. This versatility gives the maneuver commander a decisive advantage on the battlefield. However, Army aviation support has limitations that must be considered when planning and executing operations; the most significant being limitations due to weather conditions and enemy air defense capability. Ground maneuver commanders synchronize aviation maneuver with ground maneuver to enhance operations across the COE. Aviation support to operations allows the ground maneuver commander the ability to gain awareness and SU, shape the battlefield, and to influence events throughout his AO.

MISSIONS

E-1.   Aviation units operate within the framework of the commander's concept of operations. As a fully integrated member of the joint, interagency and multinational team, aviation units gather intelligence and information, move and sustain forces, provide fire support and overwatch, evacuate casualties and assist in command and control functions 24 hours a day across the entire spectrum of operations.

MOVEMENT AND MANEUVER, AND FIRE SUPPORT

E-2.   Aviation maneuver and fire support missions include—

- Reconnaissance and surveillance.
- Security.
- Escort of air assault or air movement aircraft.
- Special operations.
- Attack by fire and support by fire.
- Air assault.
- Air movement.
- Aerial mine warfare (Volcano).

PROTECTION

E-3.   Aviation protection missions include theater missile defense.

SUSTAINMENT

E-4.   Aviation sustainment missions consist of the assistance provided by aviation forces to sustain combat forces. These include—

- Aerial sustainment.
- Casualty evacuation.

COMMAND AND CONTROL, AND INTELLIGENCE

E-5.   Aviation C2 and intelligence missions include—

- Command, control, communications, and intelligence (C3I).
- Air traffic services (ATS).

OTHER ATTACK HELICOPTER MISSIONS

E-6.   In addition to the missions listed above, attack helicopters may be called on to perform some additional, nontraditional roles. This is particularly true during stability operations and civil support operations. Additional missions may include the following:

- Assisting, for limited periods, in the control and coordination of fires with the maneuver of ground forces.
- Providing limited relay of radio messages from isolated ground units.
- Marking or identifying specific buildings and areas by smoke, fires, or targeting lasers.
- Videotaping routes or objectives for later analysis by ground commanders.
- Providing navigational and directional assistance to ground units.
- Providing limited area illumination by infrared or white light using either on-board sources or illumination rockets.

OTHER LIFT/CARGO HELICOPTER MISSIONS

E-7.   In addition to the missions listed above, lift/cargo helicopters may be called on to emplace large or heavy obstacles such as abandoned vehicles and concrete dividers.

AVAILABLE ASSETS

E-8.   Any rotary-wing aircraft can conduct reconnaissance operations since they all greatly increase the range at which enemy movement can be detected. However, the aircraft primarily dedicated to reconnaissance and security operations are AH-64A, AH-64D, and OH-58D (Table E-1).

AH-64A Apache

E-9.   The AH-64A is a twin-engine, tandem-seat, four-bladed attack helicopter with a crew of two rated aviators. The pilot occupies the rear cockpit, and the copilot-gunner occupies the front cockpit. The aircraft has day, night, and limited adverse weather fighting capabilities. The aircraft is equipped with a laser range-finder/designator (LRF/D). The LRF/D is used to designate for the firing of a Hellfire missile and provides range to target information for the fire control system. (See FM 1-112 for a detailed explanation of the aircraft.)

AH-64D Longbow Apache

E-10.   The AH-64D is a variant of the AH-64A. The AH-64D is designed to provide increased effectiveness over the capabilities of the AH-64A while greatly reducing the AH-64A's limitations. The AH-64D has several key improvements, including fire control radar (FCR), radio frequency Hellfire (fire and forget) missile system, digital communications, and other significant features. The day, night, and limited adverse weather fighting capabilities of the AH-64A are significantly enhanced in the AH-64D.

OH-58D Kiowa Warrior

E-11.   The OH-58D (I) Kiowa Warrior provides the maneuver commander with a versatile platform; it can be armed with various weapons systems and is suitable for employment in numerous types of situations and operations. The aircraft features a stabilized mast-mounted sight with a low-light television sensor (TVS), thermal imaging system (TIS), and LRF/D. See FM 1-114 for a detailed explanation of the aircraft.

Table E-1. Rotary-wing aircraft.

Aircraft Type*	Hellfire	2.75" (70-mm) Rockets	M2 .50 Caliber Machine Gun (Rounds)	30-mm Chain Gun (Rounds)
AH-64A/D	16	76	---	1,200
OH-58D **	4	14	500	---
Max Range	8 km	8 km	2 km	4 km

NOTES: * Numbers in each column indicate the maximum load for each system. The total amount of ordnance carried will vary based on METT-TC and selected weapon configuration.
        ** One weapon system per side for Hellfire and 2.75-inch rocket.

E-12.   Maximum weapon ranges specified in Table E-1 above are based on "best-case" function of the system. Maximum ranges should not be the only criteria used in the establishment of EAs to BPs, or attack- or support-by-fire positions. Ranges to target engagement distances are affected by the factors of METT-TC, and the single most important factor is weather because of the limiting impact on visibility and thermal sensors. Examples of some normal engagement weapon ranges are listed in Table E-2.

Table E-2. Examples of normal weapon engagement ranges.

Weapon	Range
Hellfire	1,000 to 6,000 meters (day)
	1,000 to 4,000 meters (night)
Rocket	1,000 to 6,000 meters
30 mm	500 to 3,000 meters
.50 cal MG	500 to 1,500 meters

OFFENSIVE OPERATIONS

E-13.   Aviation assets contribute during offensive operations by assisting the ground maneuver commander in finding, fixing, and engaging the enemy.

MOVEMENT TO CONTACT

E-14.   During MTC operations, aviation assets can find, fix, and destroy the enemy. This allows the maneuver commander to further focus ISR on finding the enemy in an expedited manner, thus allowing him to develop the situation early, without premature deployment of the main body.

E-15.   AH-64 Apache and OH-58D helicopters are extremely effective during MTC operations due to their night-vision capabilities.

E-16.   During MTC operations, aviation assets may perform additional tasks, to include—

- Conducting armed reconnaissance or reconnaissance in force to gain and maintain enemy contact.
- Screening the front, flank, or rear of the ground maneuver unit.
- Acting as the rapid reaction force to conduct hasty attacks during a meeting engagement.
- Providing suppressive fires to allow for disengagement of friendly forces.
- Conducting air movements for resupply.
- Conducting CASEVAC, if necessary.

ATTACK

E-17.   During attack operations, aviation assets can assist the ground maneuver commander in destroying targets in the close or deep fight. The commander may employ aviation assets to—

- Provide direct and indirect fires.
- Overwatch assault objectives.
- Attack the enemy's flank or rear to divert his attention away from the decisive or shaping attack. Conduct forward, flank, or rear screening.
- Act as the TCF for rear operations.
- Attack deep to destroy follow-on echelons or reserves.
- Conduct air assaults to seize key terrain.
- Conduct air movement of REMBASS equipment to assist in enemy detection.
- Provide air assault security.
- Conduct CASEVAC operations.
- Conduct reconnaissance operations.
- Conduct deception operations to prevent detection of the ground maneuver force.
- Enhance C2 by providing an aerial platform for commanders.
- Provide pinpoint laser guidance for artillery fires.
- Conduct air movements for resupply.

EXPLOITATION

E-18.   During exploitation operations, aviation assets can assist the ground maneuver commander in maintaining the momentum gained by the attacking forces. The commander may employ aviation assets to—

- Attack the enemy's flanks and rear to maintain constant pressure on the defeated force.
- Attack rear area C2 and sustainment assets.
- Act as reserve to blunt any counterattacks or to provide the decisive blow by attacking to destroy lucrative targets.
- Screen vulnerable flanks.
- Conduct air assaults to seize key terrain and maintain momentum.
- Provide air assault security.
- Conduct CASEVAC operations.
- Enhance C2 by providing an aerial platform for commanders.
- Provide pinpoint laser guidance for artillery fires.
- Conduct air movements for resupply.

PURSUIT

E-19.   As the success of the exploitation develops, the speed of Army aviation is ideally suited to maintain enemy contact, develop the situation, and deliver precision fires on enemy areas of resistance. The commander may employ aviation assets to—

- Attack to destroy, disrupt, or reduce the effectiveness of counterattacking or reserve forces.
- Attack to fix withdrawing forces.
- Screen pursuing ground maneuver forces.
- Conduct air assaults to seize key terrain.
- Conduct air movement operations to resupply committed forces rapidly and maintain the momentum.

- Conduct CASEVAC operations.
- Enhance C2 by providing an aerial platform for the commander.
- Provide pinpoint laser guidance for artillery fires.
- Conduct air movements for resupply.

AIRCRAFT POWER LIMITATIONS AND TIME ON STATION

E-20.   The need to deliver hovering fires from temporary BPs may require the aircraft to carry less than a full load of munitions or fuel. This is especially true in hot climates and high altitudes. Reduced loads mean more frequent trips to forward area refuel and rearm points and less time on station. Long route distances during air movements may require the establishment of forward arming and refuel points along the route before operations. Climate will also affect the number of troops or amount of supplies the aircraft can transport.

DEFENSIVE OPERATIONS

E-21.   During defensive operations, the speed and mobility of aviation assets can help maximize concentration and flexibility. Aviation has the capability to be the most responsive direct fire asset available to the commander to react to unanticipated enemy actions.

AREA DEFENSE

E-22.   During an area defense, aviation assets can support the ground maneuver commander's preparation and defensive efforts. The ground maneuver commander may employ aviation to—

- Attack to fix enemy forces in the security zone.
- Screen during ground movement.
- Conduct reconnaissance, counterreconnaissance, and security operations, especially at night.
- Conduct air movement operations.
- Conduct CASEVAC operations.
- Emplace minefields using the Volcano mine system.
- Enhance C2 by providing an aerial platform for commanders.
- Provide pinpoint laser guidance for artillery fires.
- Conduct air movements for resupply.

MOBILE DEFENSE

E-23.   During a mobile defense, aviation assets can work in conjunction with ground maneuver forces to create a more lethal striking force to bring simultaneous fires to bear upon the enemy from unexpected directions. In a mobile defense, the ground maneuver commander may employ aviation to—

- Attack to fix enemy forces in the security zone.
- Screen during ground movement.
- Conduct reconnaissance, counterreconnaissance, and security operations, especially at night.
- Conduct air movement operations.
- Conduct CASEVAC operations.
- Emplace minefields using the Volcano mine system.
- Enhance C2 by providing an aerial platform for commanders.
- Provide pinpoint laser guidance for artillery fires.
- Conduct air movements for resupply.

RETROGRADE OPERATIONS

E-24.   During retrograde operations, aviation assets can assist the ground maneuver commander in movement away from an enemy force or to the rear.

DELAY

E-25.   In a delay operation, the ground maneuver commander trades space for time and preserves friendly combat power while inflicting maximum damage on the enemy. Aviation forces can assist the ground maneuver commander by—

- Concentrating fires to allow disengagement and repositioning.
- Conducting surprise attacks to confuse advancing enemy forces.
- Emplacing Volcano minefields to supplement obstacles or to impede or canalize enemy movements.
- Conducting air assaults to move ground forces between delaying positions.
- Providing a C2 platform.

WITHDRAWAL

E-26.   During a withdrawal, the ground maneuver commander voluntarily disengages the enemy. This withdrawal may be conducted with or without enemy pressure. Aviation forces can assist the ground maneuver commander in a withdrawal by—

- Using attack helicopters in an offensive manner to attrit enemy maneuver and fire support units.
- Providing security for withdrawing friendly units.
- Acting as the reserve.
- Conducting CASEVAC operations.
- Providing a C2 platform.

RETIREMENT

E-27.   During retirement operations, a unit that is not in contact with the enemy moves to the rear in an organized manner. Retirement operations are normally conducted during the hours of darkness. This makes aviation's ability to maneuver on the battlefield rapidly to find, fix, and destroy the enemy during the hours of darkness a decisive advantage to the ground maneuver commander. Aviation forces can assist the ground maneuver commander during a retirement by—

- Providing security of routes during the retirement.
- Conducting hasty attacks to destroy enemy elements.
- Providing a C2 platform.

COMMUNICATIONS

E-28.   Successful employment of aviation assets is possible only if they are able to communicate with the other members of the combined arms team. The primary means of communications with helicopters is FM frequency hop secure. To help reduce the load on the FM radios, all helicopters have UHF and VHF radios. Table E-3 shows the number and type of radios in Army rotary-wing aircraft.

Table E-3. Number and types of radios.

Aircraft Type	FM	VHF	UHF	HF (ALE)
AH-64A	** 1 (2)	** 1 (0)	1	
AH-64D	2	1	1	*1
CH-47D	*** 0, 1, 2	*** 2, 1, 0	1	*1
OH-58D	2	1	1	
UH-60	2	1	1	*1

Notes: * CH47D and F, UH60A/L/M, AH64D Lot 7 and above.
** Configuration is 2 FM and 0 VHF *or* 1 FM and 1 VHF.
*** Configuration is 2 FM and 9 VHF *or* 1 FM and 1 VHF *or* 0 FM and 2 VHF.
ALE (automatic link establishment): Selects the best frequency based on atmospheric conditions.

AIR-GROUND INTEGRATION

E-29. Direct fire aviation missions in the close fight differ greatly from engagements in a cross-FLOT operation. In a cross-FLOT operation, attack aircraft can benefit from deliberate planning and freely engaging at maximum ranges with minimal concern of fratricide. Engagements in the close fight, on the other hand, often result in engagements within enemy direct fire weapons system ranges that are in close proximity to friendly units. The hasty attack in the close fight typically lacks proper coordination between air and ground elements. The following paragraphs focus on the hasty attack within an air-ground integrated attack. Effective coordination between ground maneuver units and attack aviation maximizes the capabilities of the combined arms team while minimizing the risk of fratricide. To ensure adequate and effective air-ground integration, the following major problem areas should be addressed:

- Ensure aircrews understand the ground tactical plan and the ground maneuver commander's intent.
- Ensure adequate common control measures are used to allow both air and ground units maximum freedom of fire and maneuver.
- Ensure aircrews and ground forces understand the methods of differentiating between enemy and friendly forces on the ground.

AIR-GROUND COORDINATION

E-30. Effective integration of air and ground assets begins with the supported ground maneuver element. When the aviation brigade or a subordinate battalion must quickly assist a ground unit engaged in close combat, the initial information provided by the unit in contact should be sufficient to get the aviation attack team out of the aviation tactical assembly area to a holding area in order to conduct direct coordination with the engaged maneuver unit. To ensure the air and ground forces exchange essential information, planners should use the following five-step procedure:

- BCT planning requirements.
- Battalion close fight SITREP.
- Attack team check-in.
- Coordination for aviation direct fire.
- Battle damage assessment and reattack.

STEP 1--MANEUVER PLANNING REQUIREMENTS

E-31. The ground unit, through its aviation liaison officer, provides the necessary information to meet planning requirements to the aviation brigade headquarters (Figure E-1). The initial planning and information to be passed to the aviation brigade headquarters includes the location of the holding area, air axis, and route or corridor for entry and exit through the AO. The holding area should be in the sector of the ground maneuver battalion involved in close combat. The holding area may be a concealed position or an aerial holding area that allows for final coordination between the attack team leader and the ground unit leader. It must be located within FM radio range of all units involved. Alternate holding areas, along with ingress and egress routes, must be designated if occupation is expected to last longer than 15 minutes. The ground maneuver battalion also provides the call signs and frequencies or SINCGARS hopsets and COMSEC information regarding the battalion in contact. If the unit is SINCGARS-equipped, the attack team must also have the common "time," which may be taken from GPSs. In addition, the BCT provides a current situation update for its AO and specifically for the supported battalions in the AO. This update includes a recommended EA that will allow for initial planning for BPs or ABF or SBF positions and possibly prevents unintentional overflight of enemy positions.

---

1. **Current situation:** This should include friendly forces location and situation, enemy situation highlighting known ADA threat in the AO, and tentative engagement area coordinates.

2. **Battalion-level graphics update:** It updates critical items such as LOA, fire control measures, and the base maneuver graphics to facilitate better integration into the friendly scheme of maneuver.

3. **Fire support coordination information:** This includes call signs and frequencies and locations of supporting and organic artillery, organic mortars, and TUAV flight areas and times.

4. **Ingress and egress routes into the AO:** This includes PPs into the AO and air routes to the holding area.

5. **Holding area for face-to-face coordination between the attack team and the battalion in contact:** A holding area equates to an assault position. It must be out of enemy mortar range, out of range of enemy direct fire systems, and adequate in size to accommodate the number of aircraft assigned the mission.

6. **Call signs and frequencies of the battalion in contact down to the company in contact:** Air-ground coordination on command frequencies is necessary to provide a current understanding of the situation for all elements involved.

7. **SINCGARS:** Synchronize time.

Figure E-1. Minimum aviation brigade planning requirements.

STEP 2--INFANTRY BATTALION CLOSE FIGHT SITREP

E-32.   En route to the holding area, the attack team leader contacts the ground maneuver battalion on its FM command net to receive a close fight SITREP (Figure E-2). This SITREP verifies the location of the holding area and a means to conduct additional coordination. The attack team leader receives an update from the ground maneuver battalion on the enemy and friendly situations. The battalion also verifies frequencies and call signs of the unit in contact. By this time, the ground maneuver battalion has contacted the ground maneuver unit leader in contact to inform him that attack aviation is en route to conduct a hasty attack.

---

1. Enemy situation: focuses on ADA in the AO, type of enemy vehicles and or equipment position (center mass), and direction of movement; if dispersed, provides front line trace.

2. Friendly situation: provides location of company in contact, mission assigned to it, and method of marking its position.

3. Call sign and frequency verification.

4. Holding area verification: if intended to be used for face-to-face coordination, a sign/countersign must be agreed upon; for example, using a light/heat source to provide a recognizable signature answered either by aircraft IR lights or visible light flashes to signify which aircraft to approach.

Figure E-2. Battalion close fight SITREP.

Note. The examples of simulated radio traffic in this appendix show what might occur:

EXAMPLE OF SIMULATED RADIO TRAFFIC

Attack Team	Ground Maneuver Battalion
"Bulldog 06 this is Blackjack 26, over."	"Blackjack 26 this is Bulldog 06, over."
"Bulldog 06, Blackjack 26 en route to HA at grid VQ98453287, request SITREP, over."	"Blackjack 26 this is Bulldog 06, enemy Situation follows: Hardrock 06 is taking direct fire from a platoon size armor element at grid VQ96204362. Hardrock 06 elements are established on phase line Nevada center mass VQ96000050, holding area VQ94004000 expect radio coordination only. Contact Hardrock 06 on GH 478. Over."

E-33.   Upon receiving the required information from the ground maneuver battalion, the attack team leader changes frequency to the ground company's FM command net to conduct final coordination before ingressing on attack routes to BPs or ABF or SBF positions. Coordination begins with the ground maneuver company commander and ends with the leader of the lowest-level unit in contact.

E-34.   When the attack team leader conducts coordination with *any* key leader, the ground command net is the most suitable net on which both air and ground elements can conduct the operation. It allows all key leaders on the ground, including the fire support team chief and the attack team leader and his attack crews, to communicate on one common net throughout the operation. Operating on the command net also allows the attack team to request responsive mortar fire for either suppression or immediate suppression of the enemy. The AH-64A Apache is limited to only one FM radio due to aircraft configuration. However, the OH-58D is dual-FM capable, which gives the attack team leader the capability to maintain communications with the ground maneuver company as well as its higher headquarters or a fire support element.

STEP 3--ATTACK TEAM CHECK-IN

E-35.   Upon making initial radio contact with the ground maneuver unit in contact, the attack team leader executes a succinct check-in (Figure E-3). This check-in includes the attack team's present location, which is normally its ground or aerial holding area; the attack team's composition; its armament load and weapons configuration; total station time; and its night-vision device capability. If not using a ground holding area due to METT-TC considerations, the attack team selects and occupies an aerial holding area within FM communications range until all required coordination is complete. The attack team leader and ground unit's key leaders consider the effects on friendly forces of the various weapons carried by the attack aircraft before target selection and engagement. Weapons systems and munitions selection for a given engagement depend on the factors of METT-TC. Point target weapons systems, such as Hellfire, are the preferred systems for armor or hardened targets when engaging targets in the close fight. The gun systems and the 2.75-inch rockets are the preferred systems and munitions for engaging troops in the open, soft targets such as trucks, and trench works. These area fire weapons systems pose a danger to friendly Soldiers who may be in the lethality zone of the rounds or rockets. If this danger exists, the leader on the ground must be very precise in describing the target he wants the aircraft to engage.

1. Aircraft present location.
2. Team composition.
3. Munitions available.
4. Station time.
5. Night-vision device capable and type.

Figure E-3. Attack team check-in.

STEP 4--COORDINATION FOR AVIATION DIRECT FIRES

E-36.   Time is the primary constraining factor for coordinating aviation direct fire in the hasty attack. When possible, coordinate aviation direct fire face-to-face using the aviation direct fire coordination checklist (Figure E-4). If time is not available for face-to-face coordination, then use radio-only communications and the request for immediate aviation direct fire (Figure E-5, page E-20). The request for immediate aviation direct fire may also be used when targets of opportunity require engagement through a target handoff between the ground and aviation elements after face-to-face coordination has been conducted. Although face-to-face coordination is preferred, the factors of METT-TC dictate how the commander in contact and the attack team leader conduct coordination. A major benefit of face-to-face coordination is the attack team's ability to talk to the ground commander with a map available and integrate into the ground scheme of maneuver. This also provides an opportunity for the attack team to update its maps with the maneuver battalion's latest graphics.

1. *Enemy situation: specific target identification.

2. *Friendly situation: location and method of marking friendly positions.

3. *Ground maneuver mission and scheme of maneuver.

4. Attack aircraft scheme of maneuver.

5. Planned engagement area and BPs or SBF positions.

6. Method of target marking.

7. Fire coordination and fire restrictions.

8. Map graphics update.

* To employ immediate aviation direct fire, the ground commander must brief the essential elements from the coordination checklist (in bold) via radio as a SITREP.

Figure E-4. Aviation direct fire coordination checklist.

Face-to-Face Coordination

E-37.   Once they receive the flight check-in, the ground company commander and attack team leader meet at the holding area and use the aviation direct fire coordination checklist to plan their attack (Figure E-4).

E-38.   There are several key elements of coordination to complete at the holding area:

- The target is identified and its activity explained.
- The friendly forces' positions are identified on a map with a method of visually marking those positions passed on to the flight.
- If not previously done, the EA is verified or defined.
- After defining the EA, the attack team leader establishes BPs and SBF positions.
- The scheme of maneuver for the ground elements is explained with the commander's intent and description of what is considered the decisive point on the battlefield. With that information, the attack team provides an integrated scheme of maneuver.
- Existing or required fire control measures are planned for and used to minimize the potential for fratricide.
- Key maneuver graphics that are required to support or understand the scheme of maneuver are passed between the ground commander and attack team leader.
- A method of marking targets, such as laser pointers and tracers, is determined.

E-39.   After completing this coordination, forces execute the synchronized attack plan. Even with carefully thought out plans, however, situations will arise during the attack that require flexibility and possibly the need to mass effects against targets of opportunity at a new location within the supported unit's sector or zone. Ground and air forces attack these targets of opportunity on a case-by-case basis using the request for immediate aviation direct fire (FM 3-04.111).

E-40.   Ground and air commanders consider the time available for this coordination. If they remain in the holding area for greater than 15 minutes, they must accept increased risk of holding area compromise. The factors of METT-TC dictate the extent of preplanning they can accomplish and the length of time they should occupy the holding area.

Radio-Only Communications Coordination

E-41.   When using radio-only communications coordination, leaders use a request for immediate aviation direct fire (FM 3-04.111). As previously discussed, leaders employ immediate aviation direct fire under two different conditions: the first is when they have already conducted face-to-face coordination and targets of opportunity arise. In this case, the ground element uses a request for immediate aviation direct fire for target handoff. The second condition is when time is not available for face-to-face coordination. In this case, the request for immediate aviation direct fire may be used as a stand-alone method of engagement where the call is used for communicating attack requirements from ground to air via radio only.

E-42.   When employing the request for immediate aviation direct fire under the first condition, it is assumed that air and ground units have exchanged all essential elements from the coordination checklist during face-to-face coordination at the holding area. During the attack, the ground commander calls the attack team leader and requests immediate aviation direct fires for targets of opportunity. In this manner, the forces accomplish target handoff and the attack team leader redistributes fires accordingly.

E-43.   When employing the request for immediate aviation direct fire under the second condition, the ground commander in contact briefs only essential elements from the aviation direct fire coordination checklist as a SITREP via radio. He transmits this SITREP before a request for immediate aviation direct fire. Once he receives the flight check-in, the ground maneuver leader then provides a situation update, METT-TC permitting, containing essential elements from the aviation direct fire coordination checklist. After sending the SITREP, the ground commander calls the attack aircraft forward from their holding area or aerial holding area using a request for immediate aviation direct fire. Whether the attack team uses a holding area or aerial holding area to conduct radio coordination depends on its abilities to maintain FM communication with the ground element in contact.

E-44.   As the attack team maintains position at an aerial holding area or within a holding area, the ground maneuver leader succinctly outlines the concept of his ground tactical plan. He includes updates on enemy composition, disposition, and most recent activities, particularly the location of air defense weapons. He also provides an update on the friendly situation to include the composition, disposition, and location of his forces and supporting artillery or mortar positions. After providing this information, the ground maneuver leader uses the request for immediate aviation direct fire format for attack and for subsequent re-attacks.

EXAMPLE SIMULATED RADIO TRAFFIC

Attack Team	Ground Manuever Battalion
"Hardrock 06, Blackjack 26. Roger."	"Blackjack 26, Hardrock 06, stand by for update. Friendly platoon in contact.
Standing by at HA for aviation direct fire request. Over."	Located at VQ 96000050, marked by IR strobes. Enemy platoon size armor element is 800 meters due north. There has been sporadic heavy machine gun fire and main tank gun fire into our position. Fire appears to be coming from road intersection vic VQ 96204362. Negative knowledge on disposition of enemy AD. I'll be handing you down to Hardrock 16 for the aviation direct fire request. Over."

E-45.   After receipt of a request for immediate aviation direct fire, the attack team leader informs the ground unit leader of the BP, support-by-fire position, or the series of positions his team will occupy. These are the positions that provide the best observation and fields of fire into the engagement or target area. The BP or SBF position is the position where the attack aircraft will engage the enemy with direct fire. It includes a number of individual aircraft firing positions and may be planned in advance or established as the situation dictates. Its size varies depending on the number of aircraft using the position, the size of the EA, and the type of terrain. The BP or SBF position is normally offset from the flank of the friendly ground position, but close to the position of the requesting unit to facilitate efficient target handoffs. This also ensures that rotor wash, ammunition casing expenditure, and the general signature of the aircraft does not interfere with operations on the ground. The offset position also allows the aircraft to engage the enemy on its flanks rather than its front and lessens the risk of fratricide along the helicopter gun target line.

E-46.   The attack team leader then provides the ground maneuver unit leader with his concept for the team's attack on the objective. This may be as simple as relaying the attack route or direction from which the aircraft will come, the time required to move forward from their current position, and the location of the BP. Only on completion of coordination with the lowest unit in contact does the flight depart the holding area for the BP. As the attack team moves out of the holding area, it uses nap of the earth (NOE) flight along attack routes to mask itself from ground enemy observation and enemy direct fire systems. The attack team leader maintains FM communications with the ground unit leader while he maintains internal communications on either his VHF or UHF net.

<table>
<tr><td colspan="2">EXAMPLE SIMULATED RADIO TRAFFIC</td></tr>
<tr><td>Attack Team</td><td>Ground Manuever Battalion</td></tr>
<tr><td>"Hardrock 16, Blackjack elements will attack from the southeast. Turn on IR strobes at this time; we will establish a BP to the 100 meters west of your position. Over."</td><td>"Blackjack 26, Hardrock 16. Stobes on at this time. Over."</td></tr>
<tr><td>"Roger Hardrock, Blackjack has your position. En route for attack 30 seconds. Over."</td><td>"Hardrock 16. Roger."</td></tr>
<tr><td>"Hardrock 16, Blackjack 26, engagement complete. Two T-180s destroyed. Over."</td><td>"Blackjack 26, Hardrock 16, Roger two T-80's destroyed. End of mission. Out."</td></tr>
</table>

Note. This scenario was written without friction, as though conditions were perfect. Grid locations may be difficult for the ground maneuver unit to provide, depending on the intensity of the ongoing engagement. Also, actual FM communications between the ground and air may not work this well.

STEP 5--BATTLE DAMAGE ASSESSMENT AND REATTACK

E-47.   After completing the requested aviation direct fire, the attack team leader provides a battle damage assessment to the ground maneuver commander. Based on his intent, the ground maneuver commander determines if a reattack is required to achieve his desired end state. Requests for aviation direct fire may continue until all munitions or fuel is expended. Upon request for a reattack, the attack team leader considers the effects on duration and strength of coverage he can provide the ground maneuver commander. The attack team may need to devise a rearming and refueling plan; maintaining some of his aircraft on station with the unit in contact while the rest of the team return to the forward arming and refueling point. Beyond the coordination with the ground maneuver unit in contact, the attack team leader must coordinate this effort with his higher headquarters.

EMPLOYMENT

E-48.   All aircrew and ground maneuver leaders should understand the strengths and weaknesses of available aviation sensors when employed in conjunction with target-marking equipment. This paragraph addresses several factors operators consider when marking targets for varied aviation optics. The equipment covered includes target-marking devices, NVG, forward looking infrared radar (FLIR), TIS, TV/electro-optical (EO), electronic beacons, and laser designators.

TARGET IDENTIFICATION AND FRIENDLY POSITION MARKING

E-49.   The method of marking friendly positions is a critical piece of planning that must be considered thoroughly regardless of time available to the ground and air commanders. The ability of the aircrews to observe and identify ground signals easily is critical in preventing fratricide and maximizing responsive aerial fires. The signal or combination of signals is based on items commonly carried by ground maneuver units, must be acquirable by the night-vision or thermal imaging systems on the aircraft, and must be recognizable by the aircrew.

E-50.   Determine all required identification and marking procedures before starting a mission. Accurate and detailed maps, charts, or imagery facilitates aircrew orientation to the friendly scheme of maneuver. Aircrews continue to work closely with the ground forces to positively identify friendly positions.

E-51.   Visual signaling or marking positions helps determine the disposition of friendly forces. Often, the simplest methods are the best. Traditional signaling devices, such as flares, strobes, and signaling mirrors, may be quite effective. Target marking, or orientation on enemy positions, may also be accomplished by signaling. Common techniques include the use of smoke, laser pointers, or tracers. Other devices are available to aid in the recognition of friendly forces and equipment where the fluid tactical situation and intermingling of forces in the close fight may make identification difficult. The use of glint tape, combat identification panels (CIPs), and infrared beacons assists in the clear identification of friendly ground forces, but ground lighting, thermal contrast, and intermediate obstructions influence the effectiveness of these devices.

E-52.   The proximity of friendly forces to targets requires positive identification and makes marking of friendly units and targets critical. All participants must clearly understand the procedures and be issued the appropriate devices. The fire support assets must also be familiar with the friendly marking system. Aircrews require positive identification of the target and friendly positions before firing. The methods to mark and identify targets are limited only by the creativity of the ground forces and aircrews. Commanders should use Table E-4 as a reference but should not limit themselves to only these methods. Methods employed are adapted to the conditions prevalent at the time. Positive air-to-ground communications are essential to coordinate and authenticate marks.

E-53.   Time permitting, attack aircraft may input a target grid into the aircraft GPS or inertial navigation system (INS). The target grid can provide fire control cues (range, heading, and time to the target) to aid in quicker target acquisition and help distinguish friendly from enemy. Because aviation direct fire missions may be "danger close" with short firing ranges, tracking time is minimal and therefore so is the time available to optimize the sensor.

Table E-4. Target and friendly marking methods (continued).

METHOD	DAY (D)/ NIGHT (N)	ASSETS	FRIENDLY MARKS	TARGET MARKS	REMARKS
Smoke	D/N	All	Good	Good	Easily identifiable. May compromise friendly position, obscure target, or warn of fire support employment. Placement may be difficult due to structures.
Smoke (IR)	D/N	All/NVD at night	Good	Good	Easily identifiable. May compromise friendly position, obscure target, or warn of fire support employment. Placement may be difficult due to structures. Night marking is greatly enhanced by the use of IR reflective smoke.
Illum Grnd Bst	D/N	All	N/A	Good	Easily identified, may wash out NVDs.
Signal mirror	D	All	Good	N/A	Avoids compromise of friendly location. Dependent on weather and available light and may be lost in reflections from other reflective surfaces (windshields, windows, water, and so forth).
Spot light	N	All	Good	Marginal	Highly visible to all. Compromises friendly position and warns of fire support employment. Effectiveness depends on degree of urban lighting.
IR Spot Light	N	All NVD	Good	Marginal	Visible to all with NVG. Less likely to compromise than overt light. Effectiveness depends on degree of urban lighting.
IR Laser Pointer (below .4 watts)	N	All NVG	Good	Marginal	Effectiveness depends on degree of urban lighting.
IR Laser Pointer (above .4 watts)	N	All NVD	Good	Good	Less affected by ambient light and weather conditions. Highly effective under all but the most highly lit or worst weather conditions. IZLID-2 is the current example.
Visual Laser	N	All	Good	Marginal	Highly visible to all. Risk of compromise is high. Effectiveness depends on degree of urban lighting.
Laser Designator	D/N	PGM- or LST-equipped	N/a	Good	Highly effective with PGM. Very restrictive laser acquisition cone and requires line of sight to target. May require coordination of laser codes.
Tracers	D/N	All	N/a	Marginal	May compromise position. May be difficult to distinguish mark from other gunfire. During daytime use, may be more effective to kick up dust surrounding target.
Electronic Beacon	D/N	See remarks	Excellent	Good	Ideal friendly marking device for AC-130 and some USAF fixed-wing aircraft (not compatible with Navy or Marine aircraft). Least impeded by urban terrain. Can be used as a TRP for target identification. Coordination with aircrews essential to ensure equipment and training compatibility.
Strobe (Overt)	N	All	Marginal	N/A	Visible by all. Effectiveness depends on degree of urban lighting.
Strobe (IR)	N	All NVD	Good	N/A	Visible to all NVDs. Effectiveness depends on degree of urban lighting. Coded strobes aid in acquisition.
Flare (Overt)	D/N	All	Good	N/A	Visible to all. Easily identified by aircrew.
Flare (IR)	N	All NVD	Good	N/A	Visible to all NVDs. Easily identified by aircrew.
Glint/IR Panel	N	All NVD	Good	N/A	Not readily detectable by enemy. Very effective except in highly lit areas.
Combat Identification Panel	D/N	All FLIR	Good	N/A	Provides temperature contrast on vehicles or building. May be obscured by urban terrain.
VS17 Panel	D	All	Marginal	N/A	Only visible during daylight. Easily obscured by structures.
Chemical Heat Sources	D/N	All FLIR	Poor	N/A	Easily masked by urban structures and lost in thermal clutter. Difficult to acquire. Can be effective when used to contrast cold background or when aircrew knows general location.
Spinning chemlight (Overt)	N	All	Marginal	N/A	Provides unique signature. May be obscured by structures. Provides a distinct signature easily recognized. Effectiveness depends on degree of urban lighting.
Spinning chemlight (IR)	N	All NVD	Marginal	N/A	Provides unique signature. May be obscured by structures. Effectiveness depends on degree of urban lighting.

LASER DESIGNATION

E-54.   A major challenge for a gunner is achieving and keeping LOS with a target or friendly position from a moving aircraft. Helicopters may use hover capabilities but only in the most permissive environments. Laser designation requires uninterrupted LOS to identify and engage a target. This may mean the lasing platform, must be very near the target—possibly within enemy direct fire ranges, danger-close distances, or weapon arming distances—to keep the spot on the target until ordnance impact, especially in complex (urban) terrain. Smoke from burning vehicles or other fires may drift across the laser to the target line causing laser dispersion. Most laser designating platforms cannot actually see their laser spot on a target. Lasers are often boresighted to other supporting sensors like FLIR/TIS or TV/EO. If the supporting sensor cannot see a target, the laser cannot effectively mark the target. Further, even though a FLIR/TIS may "see" a target, the laser may not be capable of guiding ordnance against it since smoke, invisible to the FLIR/TIS, may attenuate the laser energy.

E-55.   The most significant contributor to laser attenuation, or nonselective scattering, is water vapor or absolute humidity. The impact of humidity on FLIR/TIS performance is greater than its impact on the laser. In other words, if you can detect the target in clear air, then the laser should provide sufficient laser energy for seeker acquisition. As a rule of thumb, if you detect a target with a visual sensor and consistently determine a range to it with a laser range finder, then you can likely designate it satisfactory for a laser-guided weapon. For low and medium threats where a great amount of time is available to use the FLIR/TIS to point the laser, the methods are simple. As the threat escalates and the time available for target acquisition shrinks, targeting with the FLIR/TIS becomes more difficult, and the delivery accuracy of the laser munitions may be degraded significantly.

TELEVISION/ELECTRO-OPTICAL

E-56.   TV/EO sensors are subject to many of the same limitations as the naked eye, particularly TVS with no low-light capability. Aircrews may not be successful in acquiring a target and achieving lock-on if smoke, buildings, or other factors repeatedly interrupt line of sight. Low-light or all-light TV/EO sensors may require frequent gain and filter changes to accommodate varying light levels. Normal means of target and friendly identification many prove ineffective. Infrared strobes or even overt strobes normally visible to TV/EO sensors may be lost in the light clutter. Laser pointers will suffer the same type of degradation. TV/EO resolution is typically not sufficient at medium and extended ranges to discriminate between a friendly position or a target and its surrounding features. Ground personnel may need to use more aggressive and overt means of identifying their position and that of the target if TV/EO sensors are to be used to identify, track, and engage targets.

MANEUVER HEADQUARTERS LNO PLANNING REQUIREMENTS

E-57.   The following list is not all-inclusive but further defines the maneuver headquarters LNO's planning requirements in support of aviation integration in the close fight. Many of these requirements require the assistance of the maneuver battalion staff. Proper planning requires the integration of the aviation brigade headquarters or battalion as early as possible in the MDMP.

- Coordinate airspace usage and control with the BCT S-3, aviation brigade S-3 Air, FSO, and AD liaison officer.
- Coordinate for land usage within the supported unit's area of operations for forward assembly areas, holding areas, and forward arming and refueling points.
- Coordinate for suppression of enemy air defenses.
- Ensure that the supported commander understands the number of aviation assets available and duration of coverage provided. If required to support the operation, begin coordination to ensure a FARP is available to support the mission.
- Provide the aviation unit with the most current update on the enemy situation, with additional emphasis on air defense assets.

- Provide the aviation unit with fire support assets (not just SEAD) available. Provide call signs, frequencies, priorities of targets, and any special instructions.
- Coordinate air routes into the BCT sector and FLOT-crossing procedures in both directions, if required (passage points, alternate passage points, crossing times, SEAD windows, altitudes, and airspeeds).
- Ensure that the ground commander is briefed on fighter management considerations.
- Coordinate for COMSEC, Have Quick sequences (through the ALO) and IFF fills. Ensure that changeover times are the same between supporting and supported units and that both elements understand the communications requirements, capabilities, and limitations of the other.
- Ensure method of target marking and friendly position marking is passed to aviation brigade.
- Prepare a mission statement for the attack unit to include the target, target location, and the expected results of the attack (destroy, attrit, disrupt, overmatch, or deny or delay avenue of approach).
- Designate an axis of advance, separate from the ground maneuver forces' axis, for each attack helicopter unit.
- Coordinate for establishment and protection of BPs or ABF positions. To take advantage of helicopter mobility, BPs should be planned for rear and flank shots into EAs, if possible. LNOs should not try to pick individual firing positions but should use the guidelines in the acronyms BRASSCRAF and NORMA (FM 1-112, Appendix A) to select BPs in conjunction with the aviation brigade or battalion staffs.

E-58. Coordinate for fire control in EAs. Establish target priorities for attack helicopters. Inform the ground commander that by doctrine, the target priorities for any attack helicopter are (in order)—

- Immediate threat to self.
- Immediate threat to platoon or company.
- Immediate threat to other friendly forces.
- Established target priorities.

E-59. Coordinate for joint air attack team operations if CAS will be available.

E-60. Coordinate laser codes, especially when working with compatible nonaviation laser systems such as Copperhead, GLAD, Pave Penny, Maverick, and laser-guided bombs.

ARMY AVIATION MANEUVER SUPPORT IN URBAN OPERATIONS

E-61. Effective combined arms employment in urban areas requires that aviation and ground maneuver forces synchronize their operations by operating from a common perspective. This paragraph highlights some possible procedures that will aid in creating a common air-ground perspective.

GENERAL

E-62. Army aviation's primary role during UO is the support of shaping operations. Aviation operating on the urban periphery effectively enhances isolation, reconnaissance, resupply, troop movement, evacuation, and support by fire for ground forces. Army aviation also enhances the combined arms team's ability to quickly and efficiently transition to new missions. Aviation forces are more vulnerable in urban terrain due to the high risk of being engaged by enemy forces in close proximity. However, when aviation forces operate in urban areas during UO, special measures and thorough risk analysis is conducted to minimize the associated dangers. The following missions are commonly performed during UO.

Assess

E-63.   Identify the portion(s) of the urban area essential to mission success. Aviation forces provide reconnaissance capability, security to ground forces, movement of troops and supplies, and augmentation of communication and surveillance capabilities

Shape

E-64.   Isolate those areas essential to mission success or avoid isolation while in the defense. In the offense, aviation forces attack to isolate the objective, move troops and supplies, enhance C2, conduct reconnaissance, and augment ground forces. In the defense, aviation forces act as a maneuver element to set the conditions for the main battle and prevent isolation.

Dominate

E-65.   In order to dominate the area, precisely mass the effects of combat power. Army aviation supports the ground maneuver commander's intent and scheme of maneuver by providing maneuver and support assets. Aviation supports the combined arms effort by providing support by fire, movement of troops and supplies, enhanced C2, air assaults, reconnaissance, and continued isolation of the objective.

Transition

E-66.   Transition the urban area to the control of another agency and prepare for follow-on operations. Aviation forces conduct WFF missions that facilitate the combined arms transition to follow-on operations.

COMMAND AND CONTROL

E-67.   Army aviation forces may be employed organic to a command level higher than the BCT to conduct maneuver or provide support (DS or GS). Aviation forces may also be attached or under operational control of another command. Operational control of attack helicopter units will remain at the level of battalion or higher; however, attack helicopters may conduct direct air-to-ground coordination with companies and platoons during combat operations.

MANEUVER GRAPHIC AIDS

E-68.   One of aviation's greatest strengths—its ability to maneuver three dimensionally—can also be a detriment. The associated challenge is that aircrews have different visual cues and perspectives than do ground forces. Common graphics and sketches can help alleviate these differences. A network route structure, an ACP, and routes (preferably surveyed) may be used to facilitate route planning, navigation, and C2. Sketches help correlate air and ground control measures with predominantly urban features. The area sketch offers the ground commander and the aircrew a means of identifying friendly and enemy locations for planning and coordination (Figure E-5). The area sketch is best used for smaller towns and villages but can be applied to a certain EA or specific area of operations in a larger city. The area sketch captures the natural terrain features, manmade features, and key terrain in that area and designates a letter or numeric code to each. Buildings are coded and each corner of the building is coded. This gives the aircrews an accurate way to target specific buildings as requested by the ground unit commander or to identify friendly locations. Inclusion of maneuver graphic, fire support control measures, and airspace control measures (ACMs) allows aircrews and maneuver elements to better visualize the urban portion of the AO. Units must ensure they use the same area sketch for accurate coordination.

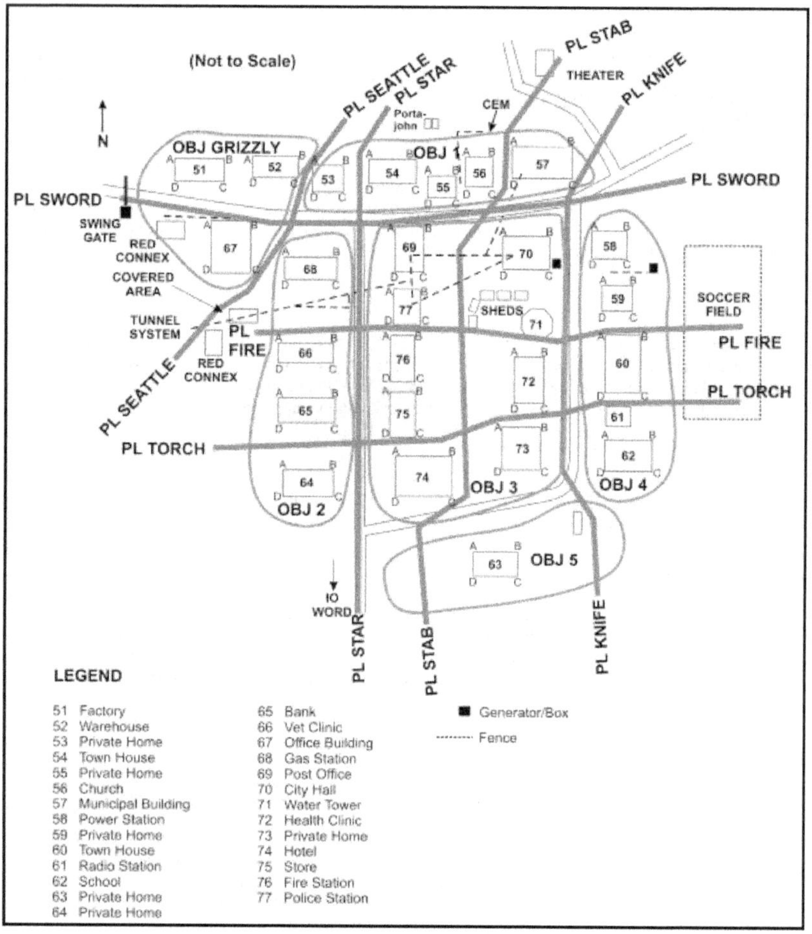

Figure E-5. Area sketch (simplified).

IDENTIFYING FRIENDLY POSITIONS, MARKING LOCATIONS, AND TARGET ACQUISITION

E-69.   In the urban environment, friendly, enemy, and noncombatants may operate in close vicinity. Furthermore, structures and debris can cause problems with identifying precise locations. Reliable communication is essential to ensure aircrews know the locations of all participants in UO. To further enhance air-ground coordination, methods are established to allow aircrews to visually identify key locations. See Table E-3 for methods of marking.

Targeting Grids and Reference Techniques

E-70. Ground maneuver elements generally use a terrain-based reference system during urban operations. Military grid reference system (MGRS) coordinates have little meaning at street level. Common control methods include urban grid (Figure E-6), bull's-eye/checkpoint targeting (Figure E-7), objective area reference grid (Figure E-8), and TRPs (Figure E-9). These techniques are based on the street and structure pattern present, without regard to the MGRS grid pattern. Aircrews must plan to transition to the system in use by the ground element upon arrival in the objective area. For example, references to the objective or target may include local landmarks such as, "The third floor of the Hotel Caviar, south-east corner." This transition should be facilitated by using a "big to small" acquisition technique.

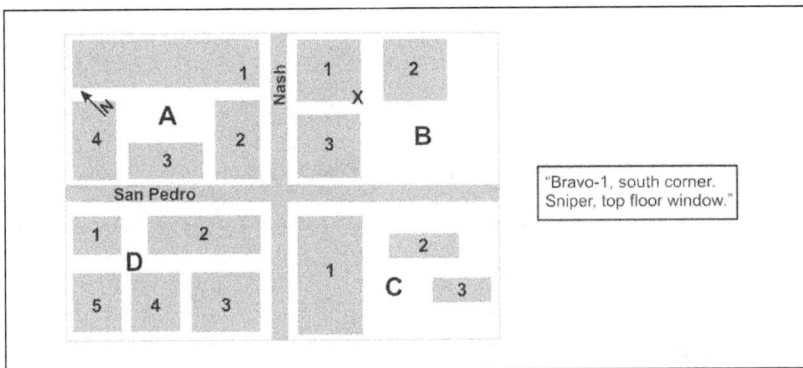

Figure E-6. Urban grid.

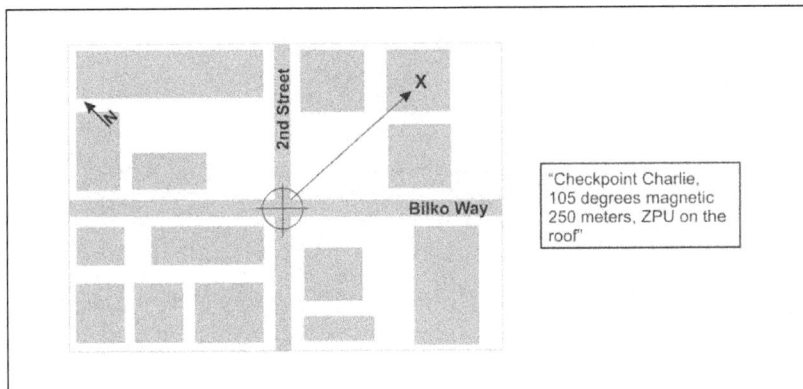

Figure E-7. Bull's-eye/checkpoint targeting.

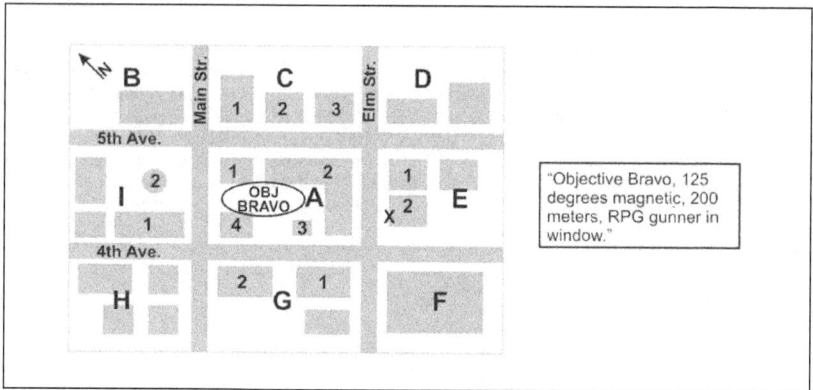

Figure E-8. Objective area reference grid.

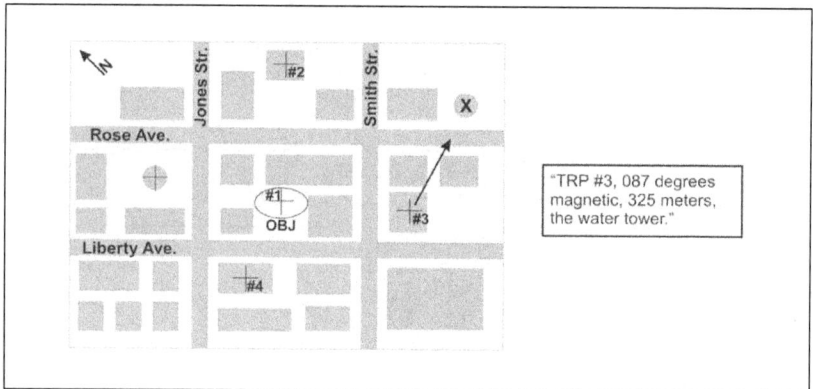

Figure E-9. Target reference points.

Additional Cues

E-71. Physical terrain features and visual markings provide additional guidance for identification purposes.

Roof Characteristics

E-72. Flat roofs, pitched roofs, domed roofs, and roofs with towers or air conditioning units on top will aid in visual and thermal acquisition. Additional structural features revealed in imagery will aid in confirmation. This method of terrain association will prove invaluable for visual engagement or reconnaissance since structures are often too close to rely on mere grid coordinates.

Visual Markings

E-73.   The visual signaling or marking of positions allows more ease in determining the location of friendly forces. During building clearing operations, the progress of friendly units--both horizontally and vertically--may be marked with spray paint or material hung out of windows. The simplest methods are often the best. Traditional signaling devices, such as flares, strobes, and signaling mirrors, may be effective as well. Target marking or an orientation on enemy positions may also be accomplished using signaling procedures. The use of GLINT tape, combat identification (ID) panels, and infrared beacons assists in the ID of friendly ground forces on urban terrain. Standardized usage of ground lighting, thermal contrast and interposition of structures, influence the effectiveness of these devices.

Shadows

E-74.   During both high and low ambient light conditions, expect to see significant urban shadowing from buildings when cultural lights are present. Shadows will hide personnel and or vehicular targets, like the shadows that hide small hills against the background of larger mountains. Shadows will hide non-thermally significant targets, but thermal targets should still be seen. A combination of sensors will need to be used to acquire and identify the target; therefore, a sensor hand-off plan must be thoroughly briefed.

Global Positioning System

E-75.   The use of aircraft with integrated GPS will reduce the amount of time spent finding the target area. If ground forces can provide accurate coordinates, inputting a target grid into the GPS or inertial navigation system will provide fire control cues (range, heading, time) to the target that will aid in quicker target acquisition and help distinguish friendly forces from enemy forces.

ATTACK HELICOPTER ENGAGEMENT

E-76.   Attack helicopters will conduct a variety of TTPs to engage targets in the urban area. Techniques range from support by fire/attack by fire at maximum standoff ranges to running/diving fire and close combat attack at minimum engagement ranges. Coordination is imperative to ensure positive ID of the target as well as friendly locations.

E-77.   Urban terrain introduces a unique challenge to aircrews and ground personnel alike with the notion of the urban canyon. Simply stated, an urban canyon exists when a target or target set is shielded by vertical structures. Unlike most natural terrain, the vertical characteristics of urban terrain can greatly affect delivery options. Urban terrain typically creates corridors of visibility running between structures. Street level targets are only visible along the street axis or from high angles. The interposition of structures around a target interrupts LOS from many directions. The presence of buildings and other structures in urban terrain creates corridors of visibility along streets, rivers, and railways. LOS must be maintained for enough time to acquire the target, achieve a weapons delivery solution, and fly to those parameters. This timeline is reduced during the employment of the AH-64D. A precise navigation system enables the aircraft to slave its sensors and weapons to a stored target, thereby significantly reducing target acquisition times. In some cases, the AH-64D may employ the gun or folding fin aerial rockets (FFARs) in an "indirect" mode and never have to expose the aircraft to the target area. (*Ground forces should make every try to pass along accurate 8-digit grid coordinates as the AH-64D can easily and accurately engage targets using this method.*)

E-78.   Visibility limitations on marking devices in the urban environment are geometric in nature. The use of any pointer or laser requires LOS. In addition, the aircraft must have LOS with the target to see the mark. Urban terrain severely limits LOS opportunities. Due to the close proximity of structures to one another, there may be very narrow fields of view and limited axes of approach. The high number of reflective surfaces in an urban setting presents an additional challenge. Laser energy can be reflected and present multiple false returns. For these reasons, fire support can be expected to be more time consuming and be much more dependent on good communications.

E-79.   Combinations of marking devices and clear talk-on procedures will be essential to safe and effective fire support. Ground forces consider using buddy lasing or remote lasing tactics for laser guided munitions when urban effects preclude the attacking aircraft from maintaining LOS with the target until ordnance impact. However, if designating with a ground-based laser along a narrow street bounded by tall buildings, LOS geometry may allow the weapon to receive reflected laser energy. Aircrews must also consider the potential miss distances for "precision" munitions when their guidance source is interrupted or removed.

E-80.   Armed helicopters can carry a mix of weapons. Commanders choose the weapons to use on a specific mission based on their effects on the target, employment techniques, and the target's proximity to ground forces. Planners must consider proportionality, collateral damage, and noncombatant casualties. Planners and aircrew must consider the following when choosing weapons.

- Hard, smooth, flat surfaces with 90 degree angles are characteristic of man-made targets. Due to aviation delivery parameters, munitions will normally strike a target at an angle less than 90 degrees. This may reduce the effect of munitions and increase the chance of ricochets. The tendency of rounds to strike glancing blows against hard surfaces means that up to 25 percent of impact-fused rounds may not detonate when fired onto areas of rubble.
- Identification and engagement times are short.
- Depression and elevation limits create dead space. Target engagement from oblique angles, both horizontal and vertical, must be considered.
- Smoke, dust, and shadows mask targets. Also, rubble and man-made structures can mask fires. Targets, even those at close range, tend to be indistinct.
- Urban fighting often involves units attacking on converging routes. The risks from friendly fires, ricochets, and fratricide must be considered during the planning of operations.
- The effect of the weapon and the position of friendly and or enemy personnel with relation to structures must be considered. Choose weapons for employment based on their effects against the building material composition rather than against enemy personnel.
- Munitions can produce secondary effects such as fires.

Appendix F
Sniper Employment

Scout snipers and sniper/observers play a critical battalion task force role. The Infantry unit TOE authorizes snipers to provide the commander accurate, discriminating long-range small-arms fire, and direct observation of key terrain and avenues of approach. Snipers can engage targets beyond the range of squad riflemen and automatic weapons. They provide precise, deadly fires that can augment other weapons systems or engage targets when and where other weapons are not effective. Snipers are able to observe and report critical, detailed enemy information about the enemy. Commanders should judge the efffectiveness of snipers by more than just the casualties they inflict. Snipers also affect enemy activities, morale, and decisions. Knowing US snipers are present hinders the enemy's movement, creates confusion and continuous personal fear, disrupts enemy operations and preparations, and compels the enemy to divert forces to deal with them (FM 3-22.10).

PERSONNEL SELECTION CRITERIA

F-1.   The standards of training and the independent nature of a sniper mission require the commander to screen sniper candidates carefully. He looks for evidence of potential aptitude as a sniper. A Soldier will need high motivation and the ability to learn a variety of skills to withstand the rigorous training program and the increased personal risk and rigors of the job. The aspiring sniper must also have an excellent personal record. The commander considers the following factors before selecting a Soldier to be a sniper or recommending him for the US Army Sniper School.

BASIC QUALIFICATIONS

F-2.   The following are basic guidelines used to screen sniper candidates.

Marksmanship

F-3.   The sniper trainee must be an expert marksman. He must have scored expert on repeated annual qualification fires. As an expert, he has learned the fundamentals for long-range engagements.

Physical Condition

F-4.   The sniper is often employed in extended operations with little sleep, food, or water. This requires him to be in outstanding physical condition. Good health indicates good reflexes, muscular control, and stamina. Also, the self-confidence and control that Soldiers gain from athletics, especially from team sports, prove definite assets to a sniper trainee.

Vision

F-5.   Excellent vision is the sniper's prime tool. Therefore, a sniper must have vision correctable to 20/20, or better. However, wearing glasses can become a liability if the glasses are lost or damaged. Color blindness is also a liability to the sniper, since this prevents him from detecting concealed targets that blend in with the natural surroundings. Therefore, a sniper must have vision correctable to 20/20, or better.

Tobacco Use

F-6.   The sniper should not be a habitual smoker or user of smokeless tobacco, even if he stops for the mission. Smoke, or an unsuppressed smoker's cough, can reveal the sniper's position. Also, the efficiency of a Soldier who has quit using tobacco only for the mission is impaired by involuntary nervousness and irritation.

Mental Condition

F-7.   A psychological examination can help the commander answer questions that indicate whether the candidate has the right qualities to be a sniper—

- Will the candidate pull the trigger at the right time and place?
- Is he reliable?
- Has he demonstrated initiative, loyalty, discipline, and emotional stability?

Intelligence

F-8.   A sniper must be able to learn the following:

- Ballistics.
- Ammunition types and capabilities.
- Adjustment procedures for optical devices.
- Radio operation and procedures.
- Observation and adjustment of mortar and artillery fire.
- Land navigation skills.
- Military intelligence collecting and reporting.
- Identification of threat uniforms and equipment.

SPECIAL QUALIFICATIONS

F-9.   The sniper must be self-reliant, with good judgment and common sense. He also needs emotional balance and fieldcraft skills.

Emotional Balance

F-10.   The sniper must be able to calmly and deliberately eliminate targets that may not pose an immediate threat to him. It is much easier to kill in self-defense or in the defense of others than to do so without apparent provocation. The sniper must not be susceptible to emotions such as anxiety or remorse. Candidates whose motivation toward sniper training rests mainly in the desire for prestige may be incapable of the cold rationality that the sniper's job requires.

Fieldcraft

F-11.   The sniper must know and feel comfortable spending long periods in the field. An extensive background in the outdoors and knowledge of natural occurrences in the outdoors will help him in many of his tasks. A Soldier with this kind of background often has great potential as a sniper.

COMMANDER RECOMMENDATION AND SNIPER SCHOOL PREREQUISITES

F-12.   Commander involvement in personnel selection is critical. See FM 3-22.10 for specific recommended sniper selection criteria.

SNIPER EMPLOYMENT OFFICER

F-13.   Each Infantry battalion should designate a sniper employment officer (SEO). The SEO's primary duty is to advise the unit commander on the employment and control of the sniper squad and teams.

SELECTION

F-14.   The individual the commander selects as the SEO depends on the type of unit, and the level of the officer's knowledge of sniper employment. The SEO can be the HHC commander, the XO, the scout platoon leader, or any other officer. In the SEO's absence, either the sniper squad leader or the individual sniper team leader can represent himself during mission planning and coordination with the battalion staff.

DUTIES AND RESPONSIBILITIES

F-15.   The responsibilities of the SEO are remembered by using the mnemonic "KACTIS."

K	Know sniper capabilities and limitations.
A	Advise battalion and company commanders.
C	Coordinate all aspects of the sniper mission.
T	Train snipers whether they are deployed or in garrison.
I	Issue orders.
S	Supervise mission planning, preparation, and rehearsals.

Knowing

F-16.   The SEO must know the capabilities and limitations of the sniper and the weapons systems in order to participate in sniper training at every opportunity. He must also ensure that snipers are trained in reconnaissance and surveillance as well as sniper skills.

Advising

F-17.   The SEO must know how to employ snipers effectively in support of various operations so that he can advise the commander. When given a mission to support a company or platoon, the SEO represents the sniper team and advises the supported unit commander on what the assigned team can do for him. Coordinating with the supported commander gives the SEO an opportunity to—

• Explain proper scout-sniper employment and tactics.
• Clarify misconceptions about the capabilities, limitations, and differences of scout and sniper assets. All officers in the battalion should attend training provided by the SEO on sniper operations.

Coordinating

F-18.   Coordinating starts during mission planning and includes—

• Assigning teams to missions to support units or to serve as a part of the overall ISR mission. If the team is assigned to a subordinate unit for an operation, the SEO and subordinate unit commander must meet face to face, so that the SEO can advise the commander on sniper employment.
• Discussing the use of terrain and sectors of operation. This ensures that both parties understand the other's mission, prevents fratricide, and protects the integrity of the mission.
• Arranging for the insertion, resupply, and extraction of sniper teams operating independently of a larger unit.

Training

F-19. The SEO ensures that training is challenging, realistic, and varied. He schedules and conducts enough sniper training to maintain the sniper team's proficiency. He also trains snipers to gather battlefield information.

Issuing Orders

F-20. Orders are formal or informal in that they are either given as a full five-paragraph OPORD, or given as a FRAGO. Missions should be assigned one at a time, with succeeding missions issued as FRAGOs. This allows sniper teams to focus on planning and executing each mission.

Supervising

F-21. The SEO provides general overall supervision to the mission planning and briefbacks, including details such as team SOPs, techniques, route plans, load tailoring, time management, and cross-loading. However, he leaves the detailed supervision of the conduct of the mission planning and execution to the team leader. The SEO should also supervise the debriefing and AARs for each team following the end of the mission.

SNIPER TEAMS

F-22. Snipers avoid sustained battles. They operate in two- or three-Soldier teams, each consisting of a senior sniper, a sniper, and an observer/security/driver; all are normally cross-trained. The senior sniper carries a M16 or M4; the sniper carries the sniper weapon system (M24 or M107, arms room concept), and each member has a side arm. Each team has an organic third team member that normally carries a M16 or M4 with a M203. Each team also has a HMMWV assigned to the team by TOE. Team members help each other with range estimation, round adjustment, and security.

EMPLOYMENT

F-23. The commander, S-3, a designated SEO, or the sniper squad leader, controls sniper teams from a central location while conducting operations. Once deployed, sniper teams generally operate independently. They must understand the commander's intent, his concept of the operation, and the purpose for their assigned tasks to accomplish the assigned unit mission. Snipers are effective only in areas that offer good fields of fire and observation. They must have the freedom of action to choose their own positions once on the ground. The number of sniper teams participating in an operation depends on their availability, the expected duration of the mission, and the enemy's strength and disposition.

SECURITY ELEMENT

F-24. Sniper teams should move with a security element (squad or platoon) whenever possible. This allows the teams to reach their areas of operation faster and safer than if they operate alone. The security element also protects the snipers during operations. When moving with a security element, snipers adhere to the following guidelines:

- The leader of the security element leads the sniper team.
- Snipers must appear to be an integral part of the security element. Whenever possible, based on METT-TC, snipers conceal sniper-unique equipment, such as optics, radios, and ghillie suits, from view.
- Sniper uniforms must be the same as that of security element members. Snipers and element members maintain proper intervals and positions in the element formation.

SNIPER ESTIMATE

F-25.   Commanders should be knowledgeable on the proper use of snipers. If commanders know the abilities and limitations of a sniper, the sniper can contribute significantly to the ISR collection plan and the fight.

Mission

F-26.   The sniper's primary mission is to support combat operations by delivering precise long range rifle fire from concealed positions. The mission assigned to a sniper team for a particular operation consists of the task(s) the commander wants the sniper team to accomplish and the reason (purpose) for it. The commander must decide how he wants his sniper team to affect the battlefield. Then he must assign missions to achieve this effect.

F-27.   The commander assigns target priorities so snipers can avoid involvement in sustained engagements. Sniper teams are free to change targets to support the commander's intent.

F-28.   The commander describes the effect or result he expects and allows the sniper team to select key targets. Because the sniper teams have both the M24 and M107 systems, the team can select the best weapon to use to achieve the desired effect. For example, the M107 can effectively disable lightly armored enemy equipment as well as personnel.

F-29.   The commander may assign specific types of targets to achieve an effect. He may task snipers to kill bulldozer operators or disable the bulldozer and other engineer equipment operators to disrupt enemy defensive preparations. He may task snipers to disable enemy command or supply vehicles, or engage Soldiers digging defensive positions.

F-30.   The commander may assign specific point targets such as vehicles, equipment, bunkers, command posts, or crew-served weapons positions. These can include enemy leaders, command and control operators, antitank guided missile gunners, the antitank guided missile system, armored-vehicle commanders, or weapons crews. Snipers can engage selected individuals. Snipers may be assigned countersniper roles.

Enemy

F-31.   The commander must ask the following questions when determining the characteristics, capabilities, strengths, weaknesses, and disposition of the enemy:

- Is the enemy force heavy or light, rested or tired, disciplined or not?
- Is the enemy traveling on motorized Infantry or towed artillery?
- Is the enemy well supplied or short of supplies?
- Is the enemy patrolling aggressively or lax in security?
- Is the enemy positioned in assembly areas or dug in?

F-32.   The answers to questions like these help the commander determine the enemy's susceptibility and reaction to effective sniper operations. A well-rested, well-led, well-supplied, and aggressive enemy with armored protection poses a greater threat to snipers than one that is tired, poorly led, poorly supplied, lax, and unprotected. The commander needs to know if enemy snipers are present and effective since they can pose a significant danger to his operations and his snipers. The commander must consider the enemy's directed energy weapons capability since snipers are particularly vulnerable to these due to their use of optical devices.

Terrain

F-33.   The commander must evaluate and consider the terrain in and en route to the sniper's area of operations, the time and effort snipers will expend getting into position and the effects of weather on the sniper and his visibility. Snipers prefer positions at least 300 meters from their target area. Operating at this distance allows them to avoid effective fire from enemy rifles while retaining much of the 800- to 2,000-meter effective range of two models of the sniper rifles. Snipers need areas of operations with adequate observation, fields of fire, and good firing positions.

Troops

F-34.   The commander must decide how many sniper teams to use depending on their availability, the duration of the operation, expected opposition, and the number and difficulty of tasks and targets assigned. Commanders must consider the snipers' level of training and physical conditioning and remember the effects of these human factors on sniper operations.

F-35.   The Infantry battalion sniper squad is designed to field three 3-Soldier sniper teams. Under this organization, the commander can generally assign continuous missions to all three teams for a maximum of 24 to 48 hours. After this time, the teams will need to rest and rotate teams conducting missions.

F-36.   During critical actions, and depending on the training of the squad members, it is possible to field up to five, 2-Soldier sniper teams with a combination of M24 and M107 sniper systems. However, only three teams will have organic vehicle movement capability and these operations should not exceed 24 hours in duration.

Time Available

F-37.   The commander must consider how much time the snipers will have to achieve the result he expects. He must allocate time for snipers to plan, coordinate, prepare, rehearse, move, and establish positions. The commander must understand how the snipers' risk increases when they lack adequate time to plan or to perform other tasks such as move to the area of operations. The amount of time a sniper team can remain in a position without loss of effectiveness due to eye fatigue, muscle strain, or cramps depends mostly on the type of position it occupies. Generally, snipers can remain in an expedient position for 6 hours before they must be relieved. They can remain in belly positions or semi-permanent hides for up to 48 hours before they must be relieved. Normal mission duration times average 24 hours. (FM 3-22.10 provides guidance on sniper position considerations, construction, and preparation and occupation times.) Movement factors for snipers moving with a security element are the same as for any Infantry force. When snipers move alone in the area of operations, they move slowly; their movement can be measured in feet and inches. The sniper team is the best resource in determining how much time is required for their movement.

Civil Considerations

F-38.   The commander must give clear guidance on ROE and ROI. Civilians on the battlefield pose a special threat to sniper teams because snipers are highly dependent on stealth in all phases of their operations. The commander must give specific mission abort criteria if the team is compromised by civilians.

OFFENSIVE EMPLOYMENT

F-39.   Offensive operations carry the fight to the enemy to destroy his capability and will to fight. Snipers play a major role in offensive operations by killing enemy targets that threaten the success of the attack. Snipers can also contribute to the ISR plan. They can be tasked to observe and report on enemy activities near NAIs to collect PIR. Follow-on sniper missions should be considered when assigning intelligence collection missions. For example, if a sniper team is tasked to collect PIR on an objective, the follow-on mission during the attack might be to kill machine gun crews once the assault on the objective begins.

OFFENSIVE MISSIONS

F-40.   During offensive operations, snipers—

- Conduct countersniper operations.
- Overwatch movement of friendly forces and suppress enemy targets that threaten the moving forces.
- Place precision fire on enemy crew-served and antitank weapons teams and into exposed apertures of bunkers.
- Place precision fire on enemy leaders, armored-vehicle drivers or commanders, FOs, and other designated personnel.
- Place precision fire on small, isolated, bypassed forces.
- Place precision fire on targets threatening a counterattack or fleeing.
- Assist in screening a flank using supplemental fires.

MOVEMENT TO CONTACT

F-41.   During a movement to contact, snipers move with the lead element, or they can be employed 24 to 48 hours before the unit's movement to—

- Select positions.
- Gather information about the enemy.
- Deny enemy access to key terrain through controlled precision fires, preventing enemy surprise attacks.

ASSAULT

F-42.   Snipers can provide effective support during an assault.

F-43.   Snipers placed with lead elements move to positions that allow them to overwatch the movement of the element and provide long-range small-arms fire. Sniper teams are most effective where supporting vehicles cannot provide overwatching fires.

F-44.   Snipers may also be placed in a position to suppress, fix, or isolate the enemy on the objective. The sniper rifle's precision fire and lack of blast effect allow the sniper to provide close supporting fires for assaulting Soldiers.

F-45.   If time permits, snipers may be deployed early in the operation. Because the snipers' weapons have better optics and longer ranges than other types of small arms, they can provide additional long-range observation, reporting and precision fire on any enemy targets that may appear. Snipers will often move with scouts during ISR operations and then once near their objective area, move to separate positions.

F-46.   Snipers may move with the assault force toward the objective, occupy a close-in support-by-fire position where they can help suppress or destroy targets threatening the assault force, or move onto the objective to provide close-in precision fire against enemy fortified positions, bunkers, and trench lines. Selection of the sniper support-by-fire position depends on METT-TC. The closer snipers are to the objective area, the greater the chance they will be discovered and lose their effectiveness.

F-47.   If elements appear on the battlefield at the same time snipers arrive, the snipers' security and potential for surprise are degraded. To increase security and surprise, snipers may move covertly into position in an objective area well before the main attack arrives. Ideally, a sniper team going in early moves with infiltrating dismounted Infantry, or mounted scouts. These infiltration methods are faster and more secure than moving alone. After the snipers are in position, Infantrymen may remain nearby as additional security, but they are more likely to have other supporting tasks to perform. The battalion fire support officer ensures indirect fire support for sniper teams, and he ensures that friendly troops know the sniper's positions. This helps prevent fratricide.

F-48.   After their fires are masked, snipers reposition as soon as possible. The commander must carefully evaluate where snipers will be most useful. If he wants to use snipers in several different places, or if he wants them to contribute throughout the attack, snipers use their organic transportation to enable them to move quickly, stealthily, and safely on the battlefield.

F-49.   Upon consolidation, snipers may displace forward to new positions that are not necessarily on the objective. From these positions, the snipers provide precision fire and observation against bypassed enemy positions, enemy counterattack forces, or other enemy positions that could degrade the unit's ability to exploit the success of the attack.

RAID

F-50.   During a raid, sniper teams can join with either the security element or the support element to—

- Cover avenues of approach and escape that lead in and out of the objective.
- Cover friendly routes of withdrawal to the rally point.
- Provide long-range fires on the objective.
- Snipers can move early with the scouts to observe and report on the objective, then join the security or support element.

ACTIONS AGAINST FORTIFIED AREAS

F-51.   Assaulting forces usually encounter some type of fortified positions prepared by the defending force. These can range from field-expedient hasty positions produced with locally available materials to elaborate steel and concrete emplacements complete with turrets, underground tunnels, and crew quarters. Field-expedient positions are those most often encountered. More elaborate positions are likely when the enemy has had significant time to prepare his defense. He may have fortified weapons emplacements or bunkers, protected shelters, reinforced natural or constructed caves, entrenchments, and other obstacles.

ENEMY DEFENSIVE POSITIONS

F-52.   The enemy tries to locate these positions so they are mutually supporting and arrayed in depth across the width of his sector. He tries to increase his advantages by covering and concealing positions and preparing fire plans and counterattack contingencies. Fortified areas should be bypassed and contained by a small force.

SNIPER SUPPORT

F-53.   The sniper's precision fire and observation capabilities are invaluable in the assault of a fortified area. Precision rifle fire can easily detect and destroy pinpoint targets that are invisible to the naked eye. The snipers' role during the assault of a fortified position is to deliver precision fire against observation posts, exposed personnel, and the embrasures, air vents, and doorways of key enemy positions. The commander plans the order in which snipers should destroy targets. Their destruction should systematically reduce the enemy's defense by destroying the ability of enemy positions to support each other. Once these positions are isolated, they can be reduced more easily. The commander must decide where he will try to penetrate the enemy's fortified positions and then employ his snipers against those locations. Snipers can provide continuous fire support for both assaulting units and other nearby units when operating from positions near the breach point on the flanks. Sniper fires add to the effectiveness of the entire unit; the commander can employ snipers in situations where other resources cannot be used for various reasons.

SNIPER PLAN

F-54.   The sniper team bases its plan on information available. The enemy information it needs include—

- Extent and exact locations of individual and underground fortifications.
- Fields of fire, directions of fire, locations and number of embrasures, and types of weapons systems in the fortifications.
- Locations of entrances, exits, and air vents in each emplacement.
- Locations and types of existing and reinforcing obstacles.
- Locations of weak spots in the enemy's defense.

DEFENSIVE EMPLOYMENT

F-55. Snipers may effectively enhance or augment any unit's defensive fire plan. After analyzing the terrain, the sniper team should recommend options to the commander.

DEFENSIVE TASKS

F-56. The sniper team can perform the following tasks during defensive operations:

- Cover obstacles, minefields, roadblocks, and demolitions.
- Perform counterreconnaissance (kill enemy reconnaissance elements).
- Engage enemy OPs, armored-vehicle commanders exposed in turrets, and ATGM teams.
- Damage enemy vehicles' optics to degrade their movement.
- Disable wheeled and light armored vehicles.
- Suppress enemy crew-served weapons.
- Disrupt follow-on units with long-range small-arms fire.
- Call for and adjust indirect fires.

PRIMARY POSITIONS

F-57. Snipers are generally positioned to observe or control one or more avenues of approach into the defensive position. Due to the types of weapons systems available, snipers may be used against secondary avenues of approach. Sniper employment can increase all-round security and allow the commander to concentrate his combat power against the most likely enemy avenue of approach. Snipers may support the battalion by providing extra optics for target acquisition and precise long-range fires to complement those of other weapon systems. This arrangement seeks to maximize the effectiveness of all the unit's weapons systems. Snipers in an economy-of-force role may cover dismounted enemy avenues of approach into TF positions.

ALTERNATE AND SUPPLEMENTARY POSITIONS

F-58. Snipers establish alternate and supplementary positions for all-round security. Positions near the FEBA are vulnerable to concentrated attacks, enemy artillery, and obscurants. Multiple sniper teams, if used, can be positioned for surveillance and mutual fire support. If possible, they should establish positions in depth for continuous support during the fight. The sniper's rate of fire neither increases nor decreases as the enemy approaches. Sniper teams systematically and deliberately shoot specific targets, never sacrificing accuracy for speed.

KEY TERRAIN

F-59. The commander can position snipers to overwatch key obstacles or terrain such as river-crossing sites, bridges, minefields, or anything that canalizes the enemy directly into engagement areas. Snipers are mainly used where less discriminate weapons systems are less effective due to security requirements, terrain or ROE restrictions. Even though weapons systems with greater range and optics capability than the snipers' weapons are available to the commander, he may be unable to use them for any of several reasons.

They might present too large a firing signature, be difficult to conceal well, create too much noise, potentially cause unacceptable collateral damage, or be needed more in other areas. Sniper team members provide the commander with better observation, greater killing ranges and more discriminate fires than do other Soldiers or weapons systems.

FORCE SECURITY

F-60.   Snipers can be used as an integral part of the security effort. They can help acquire and destroy targets, augment the security element by occupying concealed positions for long periods, observe and direct indirect fires (to maintain their security), and engage targets. Selective long-range sniper fires are difficult for the enemy to detect. A few well-placed shots can disrupt enemy reconnaissance efforts, force him to deploy into combat formations, and deceive him as to the location of the MBA. The sniper's stealth skills counter the skills of enemy reconnaissance elements. Snipers can be used where scout or rifle platoon mobility is unnecessary, freeing the scouts and riflemen to cover other sectors. Snipers can also be used to direct ground maneuver elements toward detected targets. This also helps maintain security so ground maneuver elements can be used against successive echelons of attacking enemy.

STRONGPOINT EMPLOYMENT

F-61.   Snipers should be tasked to support any unit defending a strongpoint. The characteristics of the sniper team enable it to adapt to perform independent harassing and observation tasks in support of the force in the strongpoint, either from inside or outside the strongpoint.

REVERSE SLOPE DEFENSE

F-62.   Snipers can provide effective long-range fires from positions forward of the topographical crest. This can include fires on the counterslope, when the unit is occupying a reverse slope defense. As the enemy force deploys on the reverse slope and is engaged by the main defense, snipers can engage targets on the counterslope. Knowing there is no sanctuary on the counterslope, sniper fires can have a significant effect on enemy morale causing confusion and disrupting the enemy attack plan.

RETROGRADE EMPLOYMENT

F-63.   The sniper team must know the concept, intent, scheme of maneuver, withdrawal times or conditions and priorities, routes, support positions, rally points, and locations of obstacles. Both engagement and disengagement criteria must be planned and coordinated to ensure snipers achieve the desired effect without compromising their positions.

FORCE ENEMY DEPLOYMENT

F-64.   Snipers can help the delaying force by causing the enemy to deploy prematurely during retrograde operations. They help by inflicting casualties with accurate, long-range small-arms fire. When the enemy receives effective small-arms fire from unknown positions, he is likely to assume he is near an enemy position and to begin maneuvering to a position of advantage against the perceived threat. Using a sniper team, the commander can achieve the same effect he could with another Infantry unit. The snipers' stealth also gives them a better chance of infiltrating out of positions close to the enemy.

REPOSITIONING

F-65.   Delaying forces risk being bypassed or overtaken by attacking enemy forces. Snipers use their organic transportation to move to successive positions. Vehicles must remain in defilade positions to the rear of the sniper position, or they must occupy different positions away from the sniper's area of operations to avoid compromising the sniper's position. In either case, a linkup point, egress routes, and conditions for executing the linkup must be fully coordinated. Sniper team use organic communications assets to facilitate control and movement.

INFILTRATION

F-66.   Snipers may be required to infiltrate back to friendly positions. Their infiltration plans must be fully coordinated to avoid fratricide when they try to reenter a friendly position. When planning successive positions, the commander must realize the sniper team may be unavailable for use if it is destroyed or is having difficulty disengaging from an enemy force. The commander must consider carefully how and where he wants snipers to contribute to the operation. Planning too many positions for the sniper team in a fast-paced retrograde may result in failure, temporary or even permanent loss of sniper teams.

SNIPER TASKS

F-67.   Snipers may be assigned any of the following specific tasks:

- Delay the enemy by inflicting casualties.
- Observe and report enemy movement and activities along avenues of approach.
- Cover key obstacles with precision fire.
- Direct artillery fire against large enemy formations.

URBAN OPERATIONS EMPLOYMENT

F-68.   The value of the sniper to a unit conducting urban operations depends on several factors, including the type of operation, level of conflict, and ROE. Where ROE allow destruction, the snipers may be used differently since other weapons systems have greater destructive effect. Where ROE limit or prohibit collateral damage, snipers are a key asset to the commander.

URBAN TERRAIN

F-69.   Sniper effectiveness depends partly on the terrain. The characteristics of an urban area degrade control. To provide timely and effective support, the sniper must have a clear understanding of the scheme of maneuver and commander's intent.

F-70.   Observation and fields of fire are clearly defined by roadways. However, rooftops, windows, and doorways limit surveillance. The effects of smoke from military obscurants and burning buildings can degrade what otherwise appears to be an excellent observation and firing position. Integration of snipers into the operation becomes more important because the enemy can fire from many directions--including enemy snipers--and enemy infiltration tries must be countered.

F-71.   Cover and concealment are excellent for both the attacker and defender. The defender has a decisive advantage. The attacker normally reveals his position during movement through the area.

F-72.   Avenues of approach inside buildings are advantageous because movement in a building is harder to detect than movement through the streets. The sniper must be conscious of all avenues of approach and must be prepared to engage targets that appear on any of them. Sniper teams must also be prepared for close combat which is a common characteristic of urban operations.

POSITIONING

F-73.   Snipers should be positioned in buildings of masonry construction that offer long-range fields of fire and all-round observation. The sniper has an advantage because he does not have to move with, or be positioned with, lead elements. He may occupy a higher position to the rear or flanks and some distance away from the element he is supporting. By operating far from the other elements, a sniper avoids decisive engagement but remains close enough to kill distant targets threatening the unit. Snipers should not be placed in obvious positions, such as church steeples or minarets and on rooftops, since the enemy often observes these and targets them for destruction. Indirect fires can generally penetrate rooftops and cause casualties in top floors of buildings.

MULTIPLE POSITIONS

F-74.   Snipers should operate throughout the area of operations, moving with and supporting the Infantry and Weapons company teams as necessary. Some teams may operate independent of other forces. They search for targets of opportunity, especially for enemy snipers. Since a single position may not afford adequate observation for the entire team without increasing the risk of detection by the enemy, the team may occupy multiple positions. Separate positions must maintain mutual support. Each team should also establish alternate and supplementary positions.

TASKS

F-75.   The commander may assign the following tasks to snipers:

• Conduct countersniper operations.
• Kill targets of opportunity.

Note: The sniper team assigns priorities to the targets of opportunity, based on an understanding of the commander's intent. For example, they might first engage enemy snipers, and then leaders, vehicle commanders, radio operators, sappers, and machine gun crews.

• Deny enemy access to certain areas or avenues of approach (control key terrain).
• Provide fire support for barricades and other obstacles.
• Maintain surveillance of flank and rear avenues of approach (screen).
• Support local counterattacks with precision fire.

STABILITY OPERATIONS AND CIVIL SUPPORT OPERATIONS

F-76.   Snipers can be valuable to commanders in stability operations and civil support operations. Since the ROE normally limits collateral damage--and always must limit civilian casualties--snipers can selectively kill or wound key individuals who pose a threat to friendly forces. This selective engagement avoids unacceptable civilian casualties or collateral damage. Targets often hide in the midst of the civilian populace, which makes them virtually invulnerable to US forces that cannot destroy these targets without causing innocent casualties. For example: a lone gunman or bomb wielding terrorist in a crowd. The Soldiers must first identify the gunman, which is nearly impossible from their vantage points. Then, without hurting innocent bystanders, they must stop him from firing, fleeing, or detonating the bomb. This is an easier task for an overwatching sniper than for Soldiers on the ground. The sniper can look down on the crowd, use his optics to scan continuously, and employ precision fire to eliminate the identified enemy without harming bystanders. Though other unit optical systems may supplement the surveillance effort (Javelins and TOWs from the ground or from the upper floors of buildings); they avoid engaging the target due to the risk of casualties among the surrounding civilians. After identifying the target, Javelins and TOWs still need time to guide a precision weapon or maneuver a unit to address the target. The sniper rifle provides the commander the only system that can both identify and engage the target.

RIVER CROSSINGS

F-77.   Sniper teams, by virtue of their observation and precision-fire capabilities, are uniquely adaptable to the initial stages of a river crossing. They are normally employed in general support of the battalion both before and during the crossing.

POSITIONING

F-78.   If possible, snipers assume positions across the total width of the crossing area before the crossing. Their main task is to observe. They report all sightings of enemy positions and activity immediately and provide a stealthy observation capability not otherwise available to the commander. Their stealth prevents the enemy from learning key facts like what type of unit is trying to cross. The snipers supplement normal reconnaissance assets.

CROSSING SUPPORT

F-79.   Snipers provide support during the crossing by continuing to observe and suppress enemy OPs and other key targets that heavier supporting elements might overlook. The snipers' ability to continue to provide close-in suppressive fire makes continuous fire support possible up to the moment elements reach the far side and begin their movement to establish the bridgehead line. Snipers should be positioned as early as possible, preferably as part of the reconnaissance force. Their movement across the river must also be planned in advance. How they get across and where their subsequent positions are must be coordinated. Generally, they displace once friendly elements reach the far side.

INSERTED FORCE SUPPORT

F-80.   Snipers expand the capability of the inserted force to engage threatening targets at long ranges. Once on the far side, scouts and snipers may screen the flank or rear of the crossing force, infiltrate to destroy key targets, such as a demolition guard or fortified emplacement, or man OPs well to the front of the crossing force. This placement increases both early warning time and the crossing force's ability to disrupt enemy counterattack forces.

PATROLS

F-81.   With any size or type of patrol, only the terrain and the patrol leader's ingenuity limit the effective employment of sniper teams. Snipers must know and be able to apply all aspects of patrolling.

RECONNAISSANCE PATROLS

F-82.   Snipers normally remain with the security element during reconnaissance patrols. If terrain permits, snipers can provide long-range support to enable the reconnaissance element to patrol farther from the security element. To prevent compromise of the reconnaissance element's position, snipers should fire only in self-defense or when ordered by the patrol leader. Normally, the only appropriate time to fire at a target of opportunity is when extraction or departure from the position is imminent and firing will not endanger the success of the patrol.

RAID PATROLS

F-83.   Sniper employment on a raid depends on the time of day and the size of the patrol. When the patrol needs maximum firepower and its size must be limited, snipers may be excluded. If, on the other hand, the patrol needs long-range precision fire and its size permits, sniper teams may be attached to the security and/or the support element. If appropriate, the sniper team may be attached to the support element to help provide long-range supporting fires. When attached to the security element, the sniper team may provide observation, or assist in preventing enemy escape from the objective area, prevent reinforcements from coming into the objective area, and can help cover the withdrawal of the assault force to the rally point. When the element withdraws from the rally point, the sniper team may stay behind to delay and harass enemy counteraction or pursuit.

AMBUSH PATROLS

F-84.   During ambushes, snipers are positioned in areas that afford observation and fields of fire on terrain features the enemy might use for cover after the ambush has begun. The snipers' long-range capability allows them to be positioned away from the main body. Sniper fires are coordinated into the fire plan. Once the signal to initiate fires is given, snipers add their fires to the rest of the patrols. Snipers shoot leaders, radio operators, and crew-served weapons teams. If the enemy is mounted, every effort is made to kill drivers of the lead and trail vehicles to block the road, prevent escape, and create confusion. Snipers may remain in position to cover the withdrawal of the patrol.

SQUAD DESIGNATED MARKSMAN

F-85.   A squad designated marksman (SDM) can seldom perform as well as a trained sniper, so commanders and platoon leaders should avoid trying to employ him as such. However, the marksman is still a valuable asset who can contribute in many ways. Leaders should know the value of the marksman and sniper, and use each to the best of his abilities in any situation. The SDM is discussed in detail in FM 3-21.8.

Special Operations Forces and Joint, Interagency, and Multinational Operations

"The nature of modern warfare demands that we fight as a team...Effectively-integrated joint forces expose no weak points or seams to enemy action, while they rapidly and efficiently find and attack enemy weak points..."--JP 1

Section I. SPECIAL OPERATIONS FORCES

Conventional US Army forces and SOF routinely conduct operations in the same area and coordinate the execution of missions. Conventional and special operations forces in most theater campaign plans are assigned unique but complementary tasks, and when combined and coordinated, contribute to the achievement of the operational and tactical objectives. Some SOF are routinely attached to the Infantry battalion to assist in the achievement of tactical objectives.

PLANNING CONSIDERATIONS

G-1.   As part of a BCT, the Infantry battalion is likely to conduct operations with or in support of SOF in the COE. Detailed planning and coordination may often be required down to the battalion level. On today's noncontiguous modern battlefield, the battalion is likely to find SOF forces operating around or in the BCT, battalion, or Infantry company AO. To maximize the combined combat power of these forces working together, the battalion or Infantry company must appreciate the mission and purpose of each of these forces, as well as their capabilities and limitations. This appendix covers information the commander and platoon leader are likely to need to know in order to fulfill their responsibilities during such operations.

TYPES

G-2.   The United States Army Special Operations Command (USASOC) has five main organizations that are likely to operate with conventional Infantry units. These units are Special Forces (SF), the 75th Ranger Regiment, Civil Affairs, PSYOP, and the 160th Special Operations Aviation Regiment (SOAR).

SPECIAL FORCES

G-3.   Special Forces are part of USASOC:

Organization

G-4.   Special Forces operations are inherently joint and frequently controlled by higher echelons, often with minimal involvement of intermediate HQ. The basic building block of SF is the 12-Soldier Special Forces Operational Detachment-Alpha (SFOD-A), known as an ODA or A-Team. All other SF organizations command, control, and support the SFOD-A (Figure G-1).

Figure G-1. Special Forces operational detachment-A.

Capabilities

G-5.   Special forces are capable of—

- Infiltrating and exfiltrating specified operational areas by air, land, or sea.
- Conducting operations in remote areas and nonpermissive environments for extended periods with little external direction and support.
- Developing, organizing, equipping, training, advising, and directing indigenous military and paramilitary units/personnel.
- Employing foreign language ability and cultural training.
- Training, advising, and assisting allied and indigenous forces.
- Conducting reconnaissance, surveillance, and target acquisition.
- Conducting direct-action operations that include raids, ambushes, sniping, emplacing of mines and other munitions, or providing terminal guidance for precision-guided missions.
- Conducting rescue and recovery operations.
- Conducting advanced trauma life-saving care.
- Communicating with disparate joint forces via redundant systems; including TACSAT, HF, FM, VHF, and UHF.
- Employing CAS via attached Air Force combat control teams (CCTs) or by organic capabilities or qualifications.

Limitations

G-6.   SF limitations include the following:

- Depend on the resources of the theater army to support and sustain operations.
- Cannot conduct conventional combined armed operations on a unilateral basis. Their abilities are limited to advising or directing indigenous military forces or conducting these types of operations in conjunction with conventional or other joint forces.
- Do not have organic combined arms capability. They habitually require the support or attachment of other WFF assets.
- Cannot provide security for operational bases without severely degrading operational and support capabilities.

75TH RANGER REGIMENT

G-7.   Ranger organization, capabilities, and limitations are discussed below.

Organization

G-8.   The Rangers are a special operations Infantry organization. Their organization and C2 structure are configured to support the unique demands placed on them by the specialized nature of the missions they are expected to perform. They have personnel capable of serving in the role of liaisons to the BCT in the event operations or mission requirements would dictate this. Ranger operations generally set conditions for follow-on conventional forces or are independent of conventional forces, focusing on objectives above the tactical level of warfare.

Capabilities

G-9.   Rangers have all the capabilities of conventional Infantry, air assault and airborne Infantry units, with the addition of —

- Increased tactical and operational mobility due to increase in mobility assets.
- Greatly enhanced firepower due to additional organic direct and indirect fire weapon systems.
- Familiarity with planning and conducting joint operations.

Limitations

G-10.   Same as normal Infantry limitations, namely, limited sustainment.

CIVIL AFFAIRS

G-11.   Civil affairs has the following capabilities and limitations:

Organization

G-12.   Civil affairs units include designated active and reserve component forces and units organized, trained, and equipped specifically to conduct civil affairs activities and to support civil-military operations. One CA battalion is Active Duty. The others are part of the US Army Reserve. Reserve CA forces have 4 commands (CACOMs), 8 brigades, and 28 battalions. The most common CA element is CA Team Alpha. A CA Team Alpha is structured to meet the immediate needs of the host nation populace. It does this by conducting or supporting CA activities or civil military operations in support of the overall plan. At platoon level, the typical relationship consists of providing security to CA teams operating in high threat areas.

Capabilities

G-13.　Capabilities include the following:

- Providing CMO staff augmentation and CA planning and assessment support to maneuver commanders.
- Providing linguistic, regional, and cultural expertise to supported commanders.
- Planning and supporting CMO conducted by military forces.
- Conducting the six CA activities--
  - -- Populace and resource control.
  - -- Foreign nation support.
  - -- Humanitarian assistance.
  - -- Military civic action.
  - -- Emergency services.
  - -- Support to civil administration.
- Conducting liaison with civilian authorities, NGOs, and IO, often thru a CMOC.
- Minimizing civilian interference with military operations.
- Conducting area studies and area assessments.
- Providing functional specialty skills limited to functional specialty teams.

Limitations

G-14.　The small size of the CA teams usually requires security by the supported unit. Likewise, the small force size of CA may not allow support to every commander.

PSYCHOLOGICAL OPERATIONS

G-15.　PSYOP organization, capabilities, and limitations are as follows:

Organization

G-16.　Tactical PSYOP teams (TPT) normally provide PSYOP support at battalion level and below. They are the most common elements that Infantry squads and platoons are likely to come into contact with. When attached to an Infantry battalion, the TPT chief acts as the PSYOP staff advisor to the battalion commander. He also coordinates through the tactical PSYOP detachment for support in developing and producing series to meet the battalion commander's requirements. At the discretion of the battalion commander, TPTs may be attached to platoons. In these instances, platoon leaders must have a clear understanding of the commander's intent to ensure the TPT is properly employed. It is the goal of PSYOP to influence select foreign target audiences by expressing information subjectively in order to change attitudes and behavior. The TPT will support the targeting process by recommending possible psychological action (PSYACT), PSYOP-enabling actions, and targeting restrictions to be executed by the military force. The TPT will also provide public information to foreign populations to support humanitarian activities; serve as the supported military commander's voice to foreign populations to convey intent; and counter enemy propaganda, misinformation, and opposing information.

Capabilities

G-17.　PSYOP capabilities include—

- Providing PSYOP staff support to the battalion headquarters.
- Disseminating series and conducting face-to-face communications with the targeted population.
- Coordinating PSYOP support requirements with the supported commander or staff.

Limitations

G-18.   PSYOP must rely on the supported unit to provide security for teams. The PSYOP elements are dependant on the supported unit for much of their logistical support.

SPECIAL OPERATIONS AVIATION REGIMENT

G-19.   SOAR organization, capabilities, and limitations are as follows:

Organization

G-20.   The SOAR has a regimental headquarters, three special operations aviation battalions, and a special operations aviation support battalion.

Capabilities

G-21.   Special operations aviation elements normally support the Infantry battalion only on a case-by-case basis against high-payoff targets within the battalion's area of operations. The are normally used to infiltrate, resupply, and exfiltrated US SOF and other designated personnel and equipment (FM 100-25).

Limitations

G-22.   Special operations aviation elements have limited organic sustainment capabilities especially for Class III bulk handling and storage. They do not possess a food service or water storage capability. The units do not have security personnel for an adequate force protection over extended time. SOAR requires support or agumentation for airspace deconfliction and tactical air support coordination (FM 100-25).

PLANNING CONSIDERATIONS FOR INTEGRATION OF SOF

G-23.   OPCON of SOF (less CA and PSYOP in theater) normally is exercised by the theater special operations command (TSOC), through the combined joint task force (CJTF), and further through the commander of the JSOTF. Normally, C2 of a SOF is exercised by a joint force special operations component commander (JFSOCC) or CDRJSOTF.

G-24.   Whether operating independently from one another, or under either a SOF or conventional force headquarters, Infantry and SOF may conduct concurrent combat operations in the same AO. SOF may operate directly with the Infantry or within the Infantry AO as well as with Infantry units conducting operations inside a JSOA or joint operations area (JOA). Physical contact between Infantry battalions and SOF may range from short-term direct action operations to sustained combat operations. It is essential to conduct thorough coordination and integrated planning to accomplish specific missions. SOF have several elements to aid in coordination at the battalion level and above.

G-25.   During extended operations involving both ARSOF and conventional forces, combined control and deconfliction measures take on added significance. Thus, it is critical to integrate and synchronize ARSOF with other joint and conventional forces operations.

G-26.   Integration of ARSOF with conventional forces is always of critical concern for both conventional and ARSOF commanders. Areas of interest typically include but are not limited to:

- Target deconfliction.
- Command, control, communications, computers, intelligence, surveillance, and reconnaissance (C4ISR).
- Political concerns.
- Civil populace.
- Possible linkup of ARSOF with conventional forces.

- Frequency allocation and deconfliction.
- Intelligence-collection efforts.
- Surface or airspace deconfliction.
- Fire-support coordination.
- Coordination of logistics and theater support.
- CSAR.

G-27.   SOF are most effective when fully integrated into the overall campaign plan. Given the ability of SOF to operate (1) unilaterally, (2) independently as part of the overall campaign, or (3) in support of or supported by a conventional commander, effective integration is dependent on a robust C2 structure. Successful execution of operations requires centralized, responsive, and unambiguous C2. The limited window of opportunity normally associated with the majority of SOF missions as well as the sensitive nature of many of these missions require a C2 structure that is, above all, responsive to the needs of the operational unit. SOF C2 may be tailored for a specific mission or operation. In that SOF can be assigned to various commanders within the joint force, liaison between all components of the joint force and SOF, wherever assigned, is vital to the effective employment of SOF.

Request for SOF Support

G-28.   Commanders can request direct SOF support from the theater command's TSOC. The TSOC forms joint special operations task forces as required IAW the theater commander's guidance and operational needs. Based on operational needs and complexity of operations, conventional and SOF units may exchange liaison cells or, depending on proximity of headquarters and habitual relationships, commanders may be comfortable with daily coordination meetings.

Special Operations Command and Control Element

G-29.   A special operations command and control element (SOCCE) may be used as an intermediate command element between the ODAs, conventional forces, or the TSOC. The SOCCE is normally collocated at echelons above the BCT, with smaller liaison teams operating at the BCT level and below. The SOCCE normally locates at the ARFOR or Joint Force Land Component Command. A SOCCE consists of a SF company headquarters with possible augmentation from ODAs to meet the SOCCE's support requirements.

Special Forces Liaison Element

G-30.   A SFLE conducts liaison and coordination activities among US, allied, or coalition military organizations to ensure mutual understanding and unity of effort, cooperation between commanders and staffs, and tactical unity and mutual support by operational units. A SFLE may work with a BCT headquarters to synchronize or coordinate operations between SOF and conventional forces. An SFOD-A normally forms the nucleus for the SFLE. SFLEs do not command and control special forces units.

SOF Liaison Officers

G-31.   SOF LNO personnel may be present and are typically used down to BCT level. A SOF LNO package, tailored for a particular mission, could be used to the Infantry battalion level to coordinate a particular SOF-conventional operation. Like SFLEs, LNOs do not command and control special forces units.

Civil Affairs Planning Team

G-32.   CA has six different types of planning teams that support from strategic level thru operational level down to tactical level. At the battalion level, a CA Team A (CAT-A) is the designated support planning team. For more information on CA and CMO planning support, see FM 41-10 and FM 3-05.401.

Note: Army active duty Civil Affairs and Psychological Operations units are a component of the United States Special Operations Command. In some specific situations, they might be available to support conventional units. Army Reserve Civil Affairs and Psychological Operations units are in support of conventional units.

Section II. JOINT, INTERAGENCY, AND MULTINATIONAL OPERATIONS

Conventional US Army forces require joint (Navy, Marine Corps, Air Force, and Coast Guard) support and operational combinations to conduct successful operations. Increasingly, the use and support of other US government agencies, for example, CIA, State Department, and the Agency for International Development, are vital to accomplish tactical and operational objectives. Multinational operations also contribute to the achievement of tactical and operational objectives, in that multinational forces bring cultural awareness and international legitimacy to the conduct of operations.

AIR FORCE

G-33.   Air Force air platform support is invaluable in creating the conditions for success before and during land operations. Support of the land force commander's concept for ground operations is an essential and integral part of each phase of the operation. Air Force strategic and intra-theater airlift, directed by US Transportation Command, supports the movement of Army forces, especially initial-entry forces, into an AO. Air assets move Army forces between and within theaters to support JFC objectives. Fires from Air Force systems create the conditions for decisive land operations. In addition, the Air Force provides a variety of information-related functions to include intelligence, surveillance, and reconnaissance that support land operations (FM 3-0). For detailed Air Force operational and tactical planning and coordination considerations and CAS planning and considerations, see JP 3-09.3.

ORGANIZATION

G-34.   The TACP is the principal Air Force liaison element aligned with Army maneuver units from battalion level and higher. The primary mission of BCT-level and above TACPs is to advise their respective ground commanders on the capabilities and limitations of air power and assist the ground commander in planning, requesting, and coordinating CAS. The TACP provides the primary terminal attack control of CAS in support of ground forces. The following leaders are normally part of the TACP.

Air Liaison Officer

G-35.   The ALO is the senior tactical air control party member attached to a ground unit who functions as the primary advisor to the ground commander on air power. An ALO is usually an aeronautically-rated officer.

Joint Terminal Attack Controller

G-36.   The joint terminal attack controller (JTAC) is a qualified (certified) service member who, from a forward position, directs the action of combat aircrafts engaged in CAS and other offensive air operations. The JTAC is the ground commander's CAS expert. A qualified and current joint terminal attack controller will be recognized across the Department of Defense as capable and authorized to perform terminal attack control.

G-37.   The JTAC must—

• Know the enemy situation, selected targets, and location of friendly units.
• Know the supported unit's plans, position, and needs.

- Validate targets of opportunity.
- Advise the commander on proper employment of air assets.
- Submit immediate requests for CAS.
- Control CAS with supported commander's approval.
- Perform BDA.

CLOSE AIR SUPPORT

G-38.   Close air support (CAS) is air action by fixed- and rotary-wing aircraft against hostile targets that are in close proximity to friendly forces and that require detailed integration of each air mission with the fire and movement of those forces (JP 3-09.3). CAS can be conducted at any place and time friendly forces are in close proximity to enemy forces. The word *close* does not imply a specific distance; but rather, it is situational. The requirement for detailed integration because of proximity, fires, or movement is the determining factor. At times, CAS may be the best means to exploit tactical opportunities in the offense or defense. CAS provides firepower in offensive and defensive operations to destroy, disrupt, suppress, fix, harass, neutralize, or delay enemy forces. It may be used to mass the effects of combat power to exploit opportunities in any operation. Infantry units organize, train, and equip themselves to employ CAS within their roles as part of the joint force. As a result, a variety of aircrafts are capable of performing CAS. The commander and his staff must be capable of integrating all CAS capabilities into the operation.

Planning CAS

G-39.   Whether conducting offensive or defensive operations, commanders plan for CAS at key points throughout the AO. For joint operations, planning CAS starts at the operational level. The conditions for effective CAS are—

- Thoroughly trained personnel with well developed skills.
- Effective planning and integration.
- Effective command, control, communications, and computer systems.
- Air superiority (especially suppression of enemy air defenses).
- Target marking and or acquisition.
- Streamlined and flexible procedures.
- Appropriate ordnance.

G-40.   Although not a requirement for CAS employment, favorable weather improves CAS effectiveness. CAS has several planning considerations. They include the following:

- CAS can support offensive, defensive, and other military operations.
- CAS planners must account for the enemy's disposition, composition, order of battle, capabilities, and likely COAs.
- CAS planners must consider C2, intelligence, surveillance and reconnaissance, and CAS aircraft assets available.
- Terrain can affect communications and visual line of sight for identifying the target and or aircraft. Weather ceiling and visibility may affect the decision to employ low, medium, or high altitude tactics.
- Time considerations include the time available for planning and the air tasking order (ATO) planning cycle.
- Collateral damage risk to civilians, civilian structures, and properties associated with CAS attacks.

CAS Requests

G-41.   There are two types of CAS requests: preplanned and immediate. Preplanned requests may be filled with either scheduled or on-call air missions, while most immediate requests are filled with on-call missions.

Preplanned Requests

G-42.   CAS planners prepare preplanned requests by using DD Form 1972 (*Joint Tactical Air Strike Request*, shown in Figure G-2).

Immediate Requests

G-43.   Immediate requests arise from situations that develop outside the ATO planning cycle. Because these requirements cannot be identified early on, tailored ordnance loads may not be available for specified targets (Figure G-3).

JOINT TACTICAL AIR STRIKE REQUEST	See Joint Pub 3-09.3 for preparation instructions.

SECTION I - MISSION REQUEST   DATE

1. UNIT CALLED	THIS IS	REQUEST NUMBER	TIME	SENT BY

2.	PREPLANNED: **A** PRECEDENCE _____ **B** PRIORITY _____ IMMEDIATE: **C** PRIORITY _____	RECEIVED TIME BY

3.

TARGET IS/NUMBER OF

A PERS IN OPEN _____	**B** PERS DUG IN _____	**C** WPNS/MG/RR/AT _____	**D** MORTARS, ARTY _____
E AAA ADA _____	**F** RKTS MISSILE _____	**G** ARMOR _____	**H** VEHICLES _____
I BLDGS _____	**J** BRIDGES _____	**K** PILLBOX, BUNKERS _____	**L** SUPPLIES, EQUIP _____
M CENTER (CP, COM) _____	**N** AREA _____	**O** ROUTE _____	**P** MOVING N E S W _____
Q REMARKS _____			

4.

TARGET LOCATION IS   CHECKED

A _____ (COORDINATES)	**B** _____ (COORDINATES)	**C** _____ (COORDINATES)	**D** _____ (COORDINATES)	BY
E TGT ELEV _____	**F** SHEET NO. _____	**G** SERIES _____	**H** CHART NO. _____	

5.

TARGET TIME/DATE

A ASAP	**B** NLT _____	**C** AT _____	**D** TO _____

6.

DESIRED ORD/RESULTS	**A** ORDNANCE _____
B DESTROY _____	**C** NEUTRALIZE _____ **D** HARASS/INTERDICT

7.

FINAL CONTROL

A FAC/RABFAC _____	**B** CALL SIGN _____	**C** FREQ _____
D CONT PT _____		

8. REMARKS

1. IP _____

2. HDNG _____ MAG _____ OFFSET: L/R _____

3. DISTANCE _____

4. TGT ELEVATION _____ FEET MSL _____

5. TGT DESCRIPTION _____

6. TGT LOCATION _____

7. MARK TYPE _____ CODE _____

8. FRIENDLIES _____

9. EGRESS _____

THE FOLLOWING MAY BE INCLUDED IN THE "REMARKS," IF REQUIRED:

BCN-TGT _____ MAG _____ BCN GRID _____/_____

BCN-TGT _____ METERS _____ TGT GRID _____/_____

BCN ELEVATION _____ FEET MSL _____

SECTION II - COORDINATION

9. NSFS	10. ARTY	11. AIO/G-2/G-3

12. REQUEST
   APPROVED
   DISAPPROVED
	13. BY	14. REASON FOR DISAPPROVAL

15. RESTRICTIVE FIRE/AIR PLAN **A** IS NOT IN EFFECT **B** NUMBER _____	16. IS IN EFFECT **A** (FROM TIME) _____ **B** (TO TIME) _____

17. LOCATION **A** _____ (FROM COORDINATES) **B** _____ (TO COORDINATES)	18. WIDTH (METERS) _____	19. ALTITUDE/VERTEX **A** _____ (MAXIMUM/VERTEX) **B** _____ (MINIMUM)

SECTION III - MISSION DATA

20. MISSION NUMBER	21. CALL SIGN	22. NO. AND TYPE AIRCRAFT	23. ORDNANCE
24. EST/ACT TAKEOFF	25. EST TOT	26. CONT PT (COORDS)	27. INITIAL CONTACT
28. FAC/FAC(A)/TAC(A) CALL SIGN/ FREQ	29. AIRSPACE COORDINATION AREA	30. TGT DESCRIPTION	*31. TGT COORD/ELEV

32. BATTLE DAMAGE ASSESSMENT (BDA) REPORT (USMTF INFLTREP)

LINE 1/CALL SIGN _____	LINE 4/LOCATION _____
LINE 2/MSN NUMBER _____	LINE 5/TOT _____
LINE 3/REQ NUMBER _____	LINE 6/RESULTS _____
	REMARKS _____ *TRANSMIT AS APPROPRIATE

DD FORM 1972, APR 2003	PREVIOUS EDITION MAY BE USED.	Reset

Figure G-2. Preplanned CAS request form.

IMMEDIATE CLOSE AIR SUPPORT REQUEST PROCESS

15 ASSESSMENT

14 BOMBS ON TARGET

1 UNIT DETECTS TARGET

2 COMMANDER DECIDES TO REQUEST CAS

3 UNIT NOTIFIES TACP

JTAC

13 JOINT TERMINAL ATTACK CONTROLLER CONTROLS CLOSE AIR SUPPORT (CAS) AIRCRAFT

TACP

12 AIRCRAFT DEPART THE IP

INITIAL POINT (IP)

4 TACP PASSES REQUEST TO ASOC/DASC

5 INTERMEDIATE TACP MONITORS AND COORDINATES CAS REQUEST IF NEEDED

ASOC/DASC

6 ASOC/DASC COORDINATES WITH SENIOR GROUND HQS WHICH APPROVES REQUEST

11 JTAC, FAC(A) OR TAC-A BRIEFS AIRCRAFT

7 ASOC/DASC CALLS AOC/TACC TO SCRAMBLE IF NO ON-CALL AIRCRAFT
OR
ASOC/DASC CALLS WOC TO SCRAMBLE ON-CALL CAS

10 APPROACHING THE CONTACT POINT, THE CRE, AWACS, OR DASC TELLS CAS AIRCRAFT TO CONTACT FAC(A) AND PASSES CRITICAL UPDATES TO AIRCRAFT

AFAOC/TACC

8 AFAOC/TACC CALLS WOC TO SCRAMBLE IF THERE ARE NO ON-CALL AIRCRAFT

CRC

9 CRC/DASC SENDS AIRCRAFT TO A CONTACT POINT FROM AIRBORNE ALERT/DIVERT

WOC

AWACS

AFAOC Air Force Air and Space Operations Center	**FAC(A)** Forward Air Controller (Airborne)
ASOC Air Support Operations Center	**HQ** Headquarters
AWACS Airborne Warning and Control System	**JTAC** Joint Terminal Attack Controller
CRC Control and Reporting Center	**TACC** Tactical Air Command Center
CRE Control Reporting Element	**TACP** Tactical Air Control Party
DASC Direct Air Support Center	**WOC** Wing Operations Center

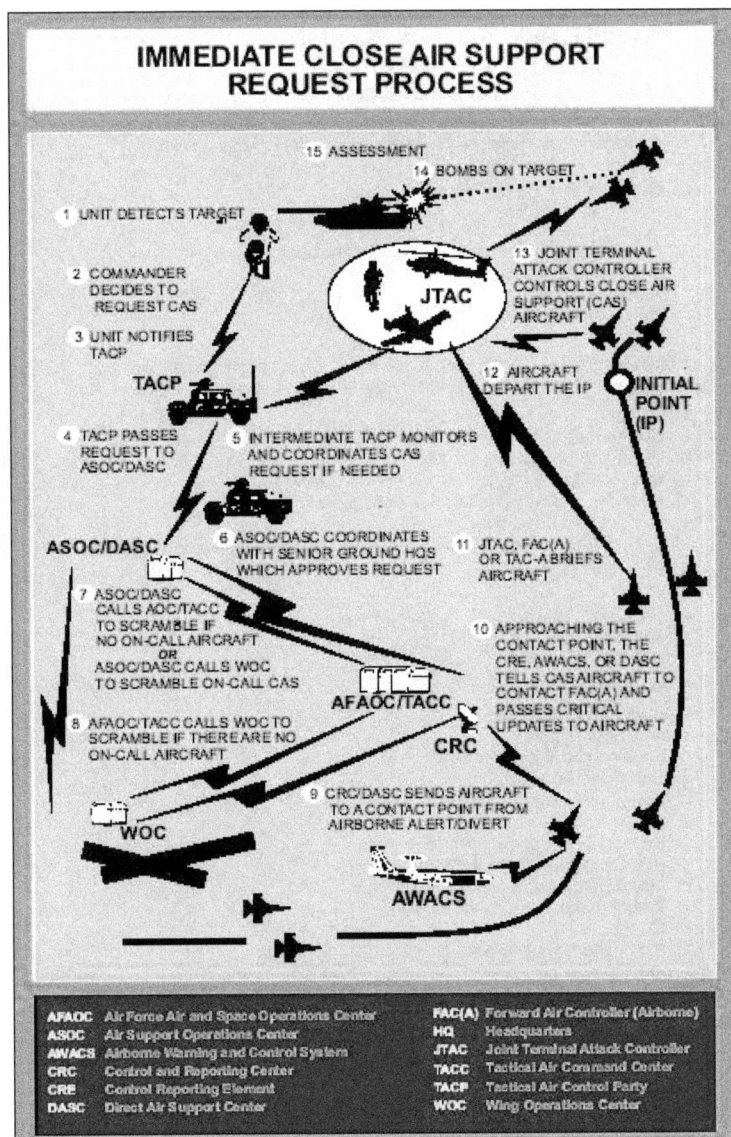

Figure G-3. Immediate CAS request process.

EXAMPLE GENERAL CAS PLANNING CONSIDERATIONS (DAY/NIGHT)

1. Ground Commander's Intent/Mission Objectives.
2. Preparation of Maps (coordinate with S-2, Intel, and S-3).
   a. Contact points, initial points, observation points, battle positions.
   b. Friendly order of battle.
      (1) Scheme of maneuver
      (2) Scheme of fires
      (3) Unit locations
      (4) Observation/terminal attack control positions
   c. Enemy order of battle.
      (1) Unit location
      (2) Target locations
      (3) Threats
3. Reviews. Review ACO, ATO, SPINS, ROE, communications plan; verify appropriate forms, worksheets, and formats in use to request and control CAS.
4. Weather.
   a. Ceiling/visibility
   b. Winds (ground and at altitude)
   c. Sunrise/begin morning nautical twilight (BMNT)
   d. Sunset/end evening nautical twilight (EENT)
   e. Solar elevation/azimuth
   f. Moon data (rise/set, elevation, azimuth, percent illumination)
5. Agency Coordination.
   a. ASOC
   b. DASC
   c. AWACS
   d. JSTARS
6. Preparation of AO Update.
7. Fire Support Coordination.
   a. ACM/FSCM plan
   b. Artillery/mortar position areas (PA)
   c. Gun-target line (GTL)
   d. Minimum/maximum ordinate
   e. Attack plan
   f. Support by fire and maneuver
   g. High-payoff target list (HPTL)
   h. Attack guidance matrix (AGM)
   i. Target marking (smoke/laser/illum)
   j. SEAD
   k. Schedule of fires worksheet
8. Fighter Holding Plan.
   a. Location
   b. Altitude
9. Rotary Aviation Coordination.
   a. JAAT opportunities
   b. Battle/firing positions
   c. Altitudes
   d. Minimum risk routes (MRR)

EXAMPLE GENERAL CAS PLANNING CONSIDERATIONS
(DAY/NIGHT, *continued*)

   e. Deconfliction plan
   f. Frequencies
   g. Downed aircrew and personnel recovery operations (CSAR assets)

10. Target Area Operations.
   a. Authentication procedures
   b. Friendly location marking procedures
   c. Prepare CAS briefing 9-Line (Figure G-4)
   d. 9-Line remarks considerations
     (1) Target description
     (2) Threats
     (3) Artillery
     (4) Clearance (final control/abort code)
     (5) Desired ordnance effects
     (6) Restrictions
     (7) Timing/deconfliction plan
     (8) Airspace coordination areas (ACAs)
     (9) Weather
     (10) SEAD and location
     (11) Laser, illumination, night vision capability
     (12) Danger close
   e. Prepare target mark devices
     (1) Artillery
     (2) Laser/IR pointers
     (3) FAC-A

11. Passing of BDA.
   a. Fighters
   b. ASOC
   c. DASC

EXAMPLE GENERAL URBAN CAS PLANNING CONSIDERATIONS

1. Effective Targeting.
   a. Large scale (1:25,000) maps with street names
   b. Gridded overhead photos
   c. UAS support
   d. Other NIMA/standardized maps with geo-ref overlay

2. Responsive C2.

3. SEAD.

4. Target Marking Capabilities.

5. Effectiveness of Weapons.
   a. Penetration capability
   b. Proportional response

6. Capability of Platforms/Sensors.

7. Proficiency and Training of Participants.

8. Rules of Engagement Considerations.

```
                FORMAT 11. CAS BRIEFING (9-LINE)
       (Omit data not required. Do not transmit line numbers. Units of
       measure are standard unless otherwise specified. *Denotes
       minimum essential in limited communications environment.
       BOLD denotes readback items when requested.)

       Terminal controller: "_____, this is _____ "
                              (Aircraft Call Sign)   (Terminal Controller)

         1.  *IP/BP: "_____ "
         2.  *Heading: "_____ " (Deg Magnetic)
                            (IP/BP to Target)
             Offset: "_____ " (Left/Right)
         3.  *Distance: "_____ "
                            (IP-to-Target in nautical miles/BP-to-Target in meters)
         4.  *Target Elevation: "_____ " (in feet/MSL)
         5.  *Target Description: "_____ "
         6.  *Target Location: "_____ "
                                 (Lat/Long, grid coords to include map datum
                                 [i.e., WGS-84], offsets or visual description)
         7.  *Type Mark: "_____ " Code: "_____ "
                            (WP, Laser, IR, Beacon)      (Actual Code)
             Laser to Target Line: "_____ Degrees"
         8.  *Location of Friendlies: "_____ "
                                 (from target, cardinal directions and distance in meters)
             Position marked by: "_____ "
         9.  Egress: "_____ "

       Remarks (as appropriate): "_____ "
       (Ordnance Delivery, Threats, FAH, Hazards, ACAs, Weather,
       Restrictions, Addtnl Tgt Info, SEAD, Laser, Illumination, Night Vision
       Capability, Danger Close [with commander's initials])

       Time on Target (TOT): "_____ "
                                        OR
       Time to Target (TTT):
       "Stand by_____ plus _____ Hack."
                  (minutes)              (seconds)

       NOTE: When identifying position coordinates for joint operations,
       include the map data. Grid coordinates must include the
       100,000-meter grid identification.
```

Figure G-4. CAS 9-line briefing.

MARINE CORPS

G-44.   The Marine Corps, with its expeditionary character and potent forcible entry capabilities, complements the other services with its ability to react rapidly and seize bases suitable for force projection. The Marine Corps often provides powerful air and ground capabilities that complement or reinforce those of Army forces. When coordinated under a joint force land component commander (JFLCC), Army and Marine forces provide a highly flexible force capable of decisive land operations in any environment (FM 3-0).

ORGANIZATION

G-45.   These are the Marine organizations that a BCT or Infantry battalion will likely encounter:

Marine Air-Ground Task Force

G-46.   The specific composition of a Marine air-ground task force (MAGTF) depends on the requirements of a particular mission, but the basic organization is standard. Each MAGTF has a command element (CE), a ground combat element (GCE), an aviation combat element (ACE), and a sustainment element.

Command Element

G-47.   The CE consists of the MAGTF commander, an executive staff, headquarters sections, communications, and other service support sections. The CE serves as the focal point for MAGTF operational execution in coordinating and directing the efforts of assigned aviation, ground, and sustainment forces.

Ground Combat Element

G-48.   The GCE is task-organized around combat, fire support and protection units and can range in capability and size from a single reinforced rifle company to one or more reinforced Marine divisions (MARDIVs).

Aviation Combat Element

G-49.   The ACE plans and executes air operations for the MAGTF. Marine aviation functions include air reconnaissance, anti-air warfare, assault support, offensive air support, electronic warfare (EW), and control of aircraft and missiles. The ACE varies in size from a reinforced helicopter squadron to one or more Marine Air Wings (MAWs). Like the GCE, the ACE is also task-organized with appropriate fire support, protection, and sustainment.

Sustainment Element

G-50.   The sustainment element is task-organized to provide the necessary sustainment to accomplish the MAGTF mission. Based on situational requirements, sustainment elements vary in size from an expansive Force Service Support Group (FSSG) that supports a Marine Expeditionary Force (MEF) to the Marine Expeditionary Unit (MEU) Service Support Group (MSSG) that supports an MEU.

Marine Expeditionary Force

G-51.   The MEF, the largest MAGTF, is the Marine Corps' primary warfighting force. The MEF may consist of one or more MARDIVs, one or more MAWs, and possibly more than one FSSG. An MEF (single-vision/wing/FSSG) features about 55,000 Marine Corps and Navy personnel, 300 fixed- and rotary-wing aircraft, 300 combat vehicles, and 72 artillery pieces.

Marine Expeditionary Brigade

G-52.   The specific composition of the Marine Expeditionary Brigade (MEB) depends on the same conditions that dictate the task organization of Army brigades. The MEB is the midsized MAGTF and is normally commanded by a brigadier general. The MEB bridges the gap between the MEU at the tip of the spear and the MEF. Like all MAGTFs, the MEB is comprised of the CE, GCE, ACE, and sustainment element. The GCE is normally a reinforced Infantry regiment while the ACE is centered on a composite Marine Aircraft Group (MAG), comprised of both rotary- and fixed-wing assets. The sustainment element is commonly referred to as a brigade service support group (BSSG) and can sustain the fighting force for about 30 days.

CAPABILITIES AND LIMITATIONS

G-53.   The Marine Corps' capabilities and limitations are listed in Table G-1.

Table G-1. Marine Corp capabilities and limitations.

Capabilities	Limitations
C2 several maneuver battalions, a Marine air group, and associated fire support, protection, and sustainment units.	Limited ground capability to counter extensive enemy armor threat.
Conduct amphibious assaults, raids, demonstrations, withdrawals, and other amphibious operations.	Limited numbers of ground mobility assets constrain tactical mobility to about one battalion by ground transport.
Seize advanced operating bases.	Limited capability to conduct mounted ground maneuver operations.
Conduct vertical assaults and envelopments.	Limited protection and decontamination capabilities in CBRN environments.
Conduct sustained combat operations ashore as part of a larger force to achieve campaign or major operations' objectives.	Limited indirect counterfire capability.
Provide close and deep air support and aerial reconnaissance.	Limited bridging capabilities. Armored vehicle launched bridges (AVLB) are in active forces while the rest of bridging is in the reserves.
Achieve local air superiority to support ground operations.	Limited organic ISR capability.
Conduct EW.	
Conduct dismounted operations in all geographic environments.	
Conduct military operations in urban terrain.	
Coordinate naval support of ground operations.	
Conduct military operations other than war.	

PLANNING CONSIDERATIONS

G-54.   The basic principle for effectively integrating and employing Army and USMC forces, as a joint warfighting team is to maximize the capabilities of one force, to counterbalance the vulnerabilities of the other. To achieve that end, requirements for more external forces and assets must be identified and resourced, command relationships must be established, and the force must be task-organized for operational planning and execution.

NAVY

G-55.   The Navy and Marine Corps conduct operations in oceans and littoral (coastal) regions. The Navy's two basic functions are: sea control operations and maritime power projection. Sea control connotes uninhibited use of designated sea areas and the associated airspace and underwater volume. It affords Army forces uninhibited transit to any trouble spot in the world (FM 3-0).

G-56.   Most joint Army-Navy operations will likely involve Marine Corps assets. In the event that Army headquarters are planning, coordinating, or directing naval assets, they are likely to fall into one of three categories: special operations (SEAL), CAS, or ship-delivered surface fires. (Ship-delivered surface fires procedures are listed in Figure G-5.) For SEAL considerations, detailed face-to-face coordination is recommended. Navy CAS is coordinated and directed in the same manner and using the same forms and calls (Figure G-6) as Air Force CAS. For detailed naval fires information, see FM 3-09.32.

NAVAL SURFACE FIRE SUPPORT

Table 6. 5"/54 and 5"/62 Gun Data	
Maximum Range:	23,100m (Full Charge) 12,200m (Reduced Charge)
Sustained Fire Rate: Maximum/Sustained	20/20 rounds per minute
Ammo:	HE, Illumination, WP
Fuzes:	quick (Q), mechanical time (MT), controlled variable time (CVT), variable time (VT), delay (del)
Illumination:	Mk 88: Height of burst (HOB) = 500m Burn Time (sec) = 45/72 Rate of Fall (m/sec) = 5m/sec Mk 91: (new round), HOB 325 Meters (65-70 second burn time) Rate of Fall = 5m/sec

NOTE: Data applies to 5"/62 firing conventional munitions.

DANGER CLOSE MISSIONS (<750m for NSFS)
Give cardinal direction and distance to friendlies. Use first salvo offset and "creeping" method for adjustments at 50 meter(m) increments.

DIRECTIONS
Directions are normally given in mils in relation to grid north. Any other combination may be used but must be specified (i.e., "direction 180 degrees magnetic").

Figure G-5. Naval surface fire support.

```
                    FORMAT 8. NSFS CALL FOR FIRE
                        (given in two transmissions)
                            (Grid Method)

"_____this is _____Fire Mission,
    (Ship Call Sign)         (Observer's Call Sign)

Target # _____, Over"
         (Assigned by Observer)

"Grid _____ Altitude _____, Direction
       (6-digit UTM)                (Meters MSL)

_____, Over"
   (mils/grid)

Target Description:      (Target Description, Size, Activity)
Method of Engagement:    (Danger Close, Ammo/Fuze Type,
                         # Salvos, # Guns, Reduced Charge,
                         TOT, Request Summit)
Method of Control:       (Fire for Effect, Ship Adjust, Spotter
                         Adjust, Cannot Observe, At My
                         Command)
```

```
                      Message to Observer

Gun-Target Line                (From Gun to Target)
Ready/Time of Flight/ Line of  (Time of Flight in Seconds)
Fire (if firing Illum)
First Salvo at Offset          (Danger Close Missions Only)
Summit                         (Max Ord in Feet for Air Spotter;
                               Meters for Ground Spotter)
"Fire"                         (Command from Spotter after
                               Message to Observer is read
                               back)
Changes to Call for Fire
```

Figure G-6. Naval call for fire, grid method.

INTERAGENCY

G-57.   The instruments of national power complement and reinforce each other. By understanding the influence of other agencies and organizations, commanders can add diplomatic, informational, and economic depth to their military efforts. US military capabilities allow other agencies to interact with foreign powers from a position of strength and security. Just as integrating different unit capabilities results in the advantages of combined arms warfare, synchronizing military power with other instruments of national power leads to dynamic strategic capabilities (FM 3-0). US forces may cooperate or synchronize with hundreds of government, nongovernment and international organizations, and agencies. The greater the command and staff understanding of these organizations, the easier it is to coordinate or deconflict operations. Usually, these agencies are receptive to Army offers of planning and coordination assistance. Such an offer normally builds a sense of trust and understanding between them. This benefits all parties. Army units can generally increase their situational understanding by communicating frequently with other agencies--especially nongovernment agencies--operating in the AO.

ORGANIZATION

G-58.   Several example interagency organizations follow:

Department of Homeland Security

G-59.   Homeland Security leverages resources within federal, state, and local governments, coordinating the transition of multiple agencies and programs into a single, integrated agency focused on protecting the American people and their homeland. More than 87,000 different governmental jurisdictions at the federal, state, and local level have homeland security responsibilities.

Coast Guard

G-60.   The coast guard is an armed force under the Department of Homeland Security. It has a statutory civil law enforcement mission and authority. The Coast Guard and Navy cooperate in naval coastal warfare missions during peace, conflict, and war. However, when directed by the President, or after a formal declaration of war, the Coast Guard becomes a specialized Navy service.

Federal Emergency Management Agency

G-61.   The Federal Emergency Management Agency (FEMA) is part of the Department of Homeland Security's Emergency Preparedness and Response Directorate. FEMA has more than 2,600 full time employees who work at FEMA headquarters in Washington D.C. They work at regional and area offices across the country, including the Mount Weather Emergency Operations Center, and the National Emergency Training Center in Emmitsburg, Maryland. FEMA also has nearly 4,000 standby disaster assistance employees who are available for deployment after disasters. FEMA often works in partnership with other organizations that are part of the nation's emergency management system. These partners include state and local emergency management agencies, 27 federal agencies, and the American Red Cross.

CIA

G-62.   The mission of the CIA is to support the President, the National Security Council, and all who make and execute US national security policy by providing accurate, evidence-based, comprehensive, and timely foreign intelligence related to national security and by conducting counterintelligence activities, special activities, and other functions related to foreign intelligence and national security as directed by the President.

FBI

G-63.   The Federal Bureau of Investigation (FBI) is the investigative arm of the US Department of Justice. The top ten priorities of the FBI are to—

- Protect the United States from terrorist attacks.
- Protect the United States against foreign intelligence operations and espionage.
- Protect the United States against cyber-based attacks and high-technology crimes.
- Combat public corruption at all levels.
- Protect civil rights.
- Combat transnational and national criminal organizations and enterprises.
- Combat major white-collar crime.
- Combat significant violent crime.
- Support federal, state, county, municipal, and international partners.
- Upgrade technology to successfully perform the FBI's mission.

United States Agency for International Development (USAID)

G-64.   USAID is an independent federal government agency that receives overall foreign policy guidance from the Secretary of State. They support long-term and equitable economic growth and advance US foreign policy objectives by supporting:

- Economic growth, agriculture, and trade,
- Global health and democracy.
- Conflict prevention and humanitarian assistance.

G-65.   They provide assistance in four regions of the world:

- Sub-Saharan Africa
- Asia and the Near East
- Latin America and the Caribbean
- Europe and Eurasia

International Red Cross

G-66.   The International Committee of the Red Cross (ICRC) is an impartial, neutral, and independent organization whose exclusively humanitarian mission is to protect the lives and dignity of victims of war and internal violence, and to provide them with assistance. The ICRC directs and coordinates the international relief activities conducted by the movement in situations of conflict. It also endeavors to prevent suffering by promoting and strengthening humanitarian law and universal humanitarian principles.

Médecins Sans Frontières

G-67.   This group is also known as MSF or Doctors without Borders. They deliver emergency aid to victims of armed conflict, epidemics, and natural and manmade disasters, and to others who lack health care due to social or geographic isolation.

CAPABILITIES AND LIMITATIONS

G-68.   There are unique capabilities and limitations for each agency. Only through detailed analysis will the commander or staff fully appreciate each. General limitations are likely to include—

- Modern and sophisticated communication assets within the agency. These assets may not be compatible with Army operational or tactical communication assets.
- Limited firepower, protection, and operational and tactical mobility compared to Infantry units.

PLANNING CONSIDERATIONS

G-69.   The intricate links among the instruments of national power demand that commanders consider how all capabilities and agencies can contribute to achieving the desired end state. Interagency coordination forges a vital link between military operations and the activities of

- Other governmental agencies (OGAs).
- Governmental agencies of the US.
- Nongovernmental organizations.
- Host nation.
- Partner nations.
- Regional, international organizations.

G-70.   Theater strategies routinely employ the capabilities of the entire US interagency network. Interagency cooperation poses challenges. Among the most difficult is lack of mutual familiarity among the various agencies. In joint operations, leaders from the different services generally share a common tradition and understanding of military matters. Interagency operations bring together leaders and staffs that often have no common experiences. The institutional values and experiences of the separate agencies and departments sometimes have few common points of reference. Some may even conflict. However, education and teamwork can create an understanding and awareness of the missions, strengths, weaknesses, and outlooks of the interagency members (Table G-2). CA assets are a vital link between the military and all other agencies, IOs, and NGOs. The CMOC is especially useful in this critical aspect of military operations. This understanding can mitigate the friction inherent in interagency operations.

Table G-2. Considerations for interagency operations.

Military	Political	Cultural
Targeting	Goals and objectives	Culture and language
Fire support coordination	National control of forces	Communication
Air and missile defense	Consensus building	Media relations
Teamwork and trust		Law enforcement
Doctrine, organization, and training.		
Equipment		

MULTINATIONAL FORCES

G-71.   Army forces will likely find themselves conducting multinational operations in future combat operations. Whether working directly with or in proximity to multinational forces, commanders must address the unique aspects associated with multinational operations.

ORGANIZATION

G-72.   Multinational forces conducting operations with Army forces may be organized in many ways. Command and support relationships may be dramatically different from what Army personnel are used to. Multinational operations are conducted within the structure of an alliance or a coalition (JP 3-16). Military alliances, such as the North Atlantic Treaty Organization (NATO), may afford participating nations time to establish formal, standard agreements for broad, long-term objectives. Alliance members strive to field compatible military systems, establish common procedures, and develop contingency plans to meet potential threats in a fully integrated manner (FM 3-0).

CAPABILITIES AND LIMITATIONS

G-73.   An Army force commander designated as a multinational force commander faces many complex demands. These may include dealing with cultural issues, interoperability challenges, and an immature theater C2 organization. Commanders may also be required to address different national procedures, the sharing of intelligence, and theater support functions. Because coalition operations are not structured around standing agreements, a preliminary understanding of the requirements for operating with a specific foreign military may occur through peacetime military engagement. These developmental activities include, but are not limited to, exercises, exchange programs, humanitarian assistance, ongoing personal contacts, and pre-positioning of equipment. Every multinational operation is different. Commanders analyze the mission's peculiar requirements so they can exploit the advantages and compensate for the limitations of a multinational force.

PLANNING CONSIDERATIONS

G-74.   Allow extra time for cultural considerations and unique C2 issues inherent in multinational forces. Be sure to—

- Plan for redundant communications and language barrier issues.
- Rehearse operations to account for differences in techniques, tactics, and procedures.
- Consider the sensitivity of multinational leaders to various nonmilitary issues such as home government and ethnic considerations.
- Develop combined planning and tactical operations centers that maintain appropriate US only OPSEC procedures.

Appendix H
Continuous Operations

The Infantry battalion often operates for extended periods in continuous operations. Continuous operations are combat operations that continue at the same high intensity level for extended periods. During continuous operations, leaders and Soldiers must think faster, make decisions more rapidly, and act more quickly than the enemy acts. Leaders must know the commander's intent. They must be able to act spontaneously and synchronously, even though the situation has changed and communications are disrupted. The continuous cycle of day and night operations and the associated stress of combat can lead to degradation in performance over time. Reducing this impact on performance is a significant challenge for the C2 system. (FM 22-51 discusses the effects of continuous operations on sleep and performance in detail.)

EFFECTS OF CONTINUOUS OPERATIONS

H-1.   Continuous operations force leaders and Soldiers to perform under adverse conditions that cause degradation in performance and may lead to combat stress. Figure H-1 shows combat stress behaviors.

CONTROL OF COMBAT STRESS

H-2.   Controlling combat stress is often the deciding factor in all forms of human conflict. It can be the difference between victory and defeat. Stressors are a fact of combat. Soldiers must face this. Controlled combat stress--properly focused by training, unit cohesion, and leadership--gives Soldiers the necessary alertness, strength, and endurance to accomplish their mission. Controlled combat stress can call forth positive stress reactions of loyalty, selflessness, and heroism. Conversely, uncontrolled combat stress causes negative, erratic, or otherwise harmful behavior, which can

- Bring disgrace, disaster, and defeat, or
- Disrupt or block accomplishment of the mission.

WILL TO FIGHT

H-3.   The art of war aims to impose so much stress on enemy Soldiers that they lose their will to fight. Both sides try to do this and at times accept severe stress themselves in order to inflict greater stress on the enemy. To win, combat stress must be controlled.

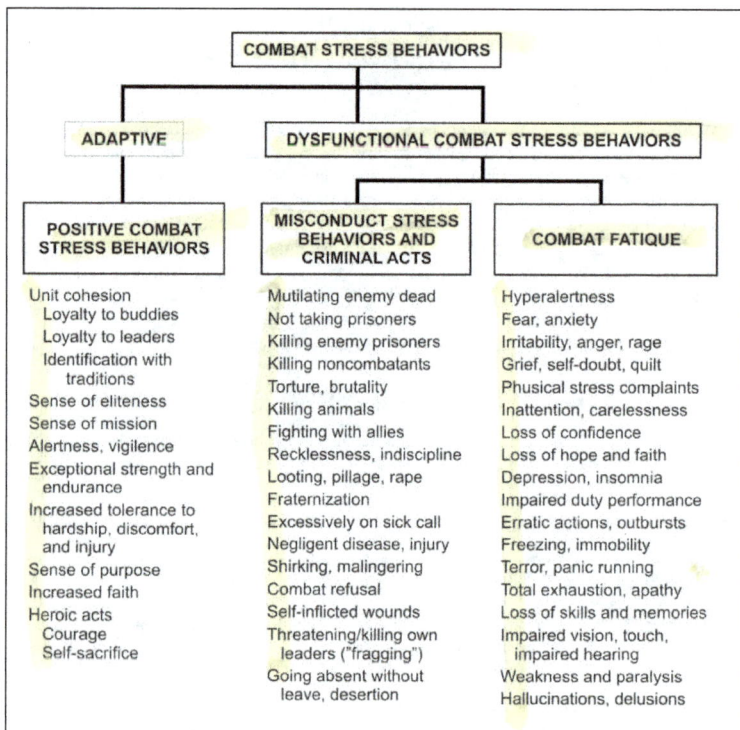

Figure H-1. Combat stress behaviors.

RESPONSIBILITY FOR CONTROL OF COMBAT STRESS

H-4.   Responsibility for combat stress control requires a continuous interaction that begins with every Soldier and his buddies. Combat stress control also includes unit combat lifesavers and trauma specialists. The interaction continues through the small unit leaders and extends up through the organizational leaders, both officers and NCOs, at all echelons.

Unit Cohesiveness

H-5.   Rigorous, realistic training for war must go on continuously to assure unit readiness. Emphasis must be placed on establishing and maintaining cohesive units. Unit training and activities must emphasize development of Soldier skills. This development should focus on building trust and establishing effective communication throughout the unit.

Senior (Organizational) Leaders

H-6.   The chain of command ensures that the standards for military leadership are met. Senior leaders provide the necessary information and resources to the junior leaders to control combat stress and to make stress work for the US Army and against the enemy. The following are some suggestions for senior leadership considerations for combat stress control.

- Demonstrate competence, commitment, courage, candor, and compassion.
- Plan to accomplish the mission with as few losses as possible.
- Set the policy and command climate for stress control, especially to build cohesive teams.
- Serve as an ethical role model.
- Make "the bureaucracy" work for the Soldiers.
- Provide resources to "take care of the Soldiers."
- Plan for and conduct tough, realistic training to include live fire.
- Provide as much information as possible to the Soldiers.
- Assure that medical and mental health/combat stress control personnel are assigned and trained with their supported units.
- Have medical and metal health/combat stress control personnel conduct regular screenings of individual Soldiers for signs of combat stress. These screenings should be immediately after operations, upon return to home station and three to six months after returning to home station.
- Plan for combat stress control in all operations.
- Provide junior leaders/NCOs with necessary guidance.
- Ensure risk assessments are conducted before all training and combat operations.
- Supervise the junior leaders/NCOs and reward their success.
- Remain visible.
- Lead all stress control by good example.
- Maintain (through positive leadership and, when necessary, with disciplinary action) the high standards of the international law of land warfare.

Junior (Direct) Leaders

H-7.   Junior leaders, and especially the NCOs, have the crucial task of applying the principles of stress control day-by-day, hour-by-hour, and minute-by-minute. These responsibilities overlap with senior leaders' responsibilities but include parts that are fundamentally "sergeants' business," supported by the officers. The following are junior leadership considerations for combat stress control.

- Be competent, committed, courageous, candid, and caring.
- Build cohesive teams; integrate new personnel quickly.
- Cross-train Soldiers wherever and whenever possible.
- Plan and conduct tough realistic training that replicates combat conditions.
- Take care of Soldiers (including leaders).
- Assure physical fitness, nutrition, hydration, adequate clothing and shelter, and preventive medicine measures.
- Make and enforce sleep plans.
- Keep accurate information flow down to the lowest level and back up again; dispel rumors.
- Encourage sharing of resources and feelings.
- Conduct after-action debriefings routinely.
- Maintain (through positive leadership and, when necessary, with disciplinary action) the high standards of the international law of land warfare.
- Recommend exemplary Soldiers for awards and decorations.
- Recognize excess stress early and give immediate support.
- Keep those stressed Soldiers who can still perform their duties in the unit and provide extra support and encourage them back to full effectiveness.
- Send those stressed Soldiers who cannot get needed rest in their small unit back to a supporting element for brief sleep, food, hygiene, and limited duty,   to return in one to two days.

- Refer temporarily unmanageable stress cases through channels for medical evacuation and treatment.
- Welcome recovered battle fatigue casualties back and give them meaningful work and responsibilities.

SLEEP

H-8.   Sleep issues include sleep deprivation (too little sleep) and degradation (poor sleep).

LOSS OF SLEEP OR SLEEP DEGRADATION

H-9.   One of the most significant factors leading to the degradation of a Soldier's performance is the loss of sleep. Table H-1 shows the effects of sleep loss. Other contributing factors include low light levels, limited visibility, disrupted sleep routines, physical fatigue, and stress.

Table H-1. Effects of sleep loss.

AFTER 24 HOURS	Deterioration in performance of tasks that are inadequately or newly learned, that are monotonous, or that require vigilance.
AFTER 36 HOURS	A marked deterioration in ability to register and understand information.
AFTER 72 HOURS	Performance on most tasks will be about 50 percent of normal.
3 TO 4 DAYS	The limit for intensive work including mental and physical elements. Visual illusions are likely at this stage, or earlier.
BETWEEN 0300 & 0600 HOURS	Performance is at its lowest ebb.

SIGNS OF SLEEP DEPRIVATION AND FATIGUE

H-10.   To minimize the effects of sleep loss, all commanders must be able to recognize the signs of sleep loss and fatigue. Table H-2 shows the indicators of sleep deprivation and fatigue.

SLEEP DENIAL

H-11.   Commanders and leaders often regard themselves as being the least vulnerable to fatigue and the effects of sleep loss. Tasks requiring quick reaction, complex reasoning, and detailed planning, however, make leaders the most vulnerable to the effects of sleep deprivation. Leaders must sleep. The display of sleep denial as an example of self-control by leaders is extremely counterproductive.

Table H-2. Signs of sleep deprivation and fatigue.

PHYSICAL CHANGES	Body swaying when standing. Vacant stares. Pale skin. Slurred speech. Bloodshot eyes.
MOOD CHANGES	Less energetic, alert, and cheerful. Loss of interest in surroundings. Possible depressed mood or apathetic and more irritable.
EARLY MORNING DOLDRUMS	Requires more effort to do a task in the morning than in the afternoon, especially between 0300 and 0600.
COMMUNICATION PROBLEMS	Unable to carry on a conversation. Forgetfulness. Difficulty in speaking clearly.
DIFFICULTY IN PROCESSING INFORMATION	Slow comprehension and perception. Difficulty in accessing simple situations. Requiring more time to understand information.
IMPAIRED ATTENTION SPAN	Decreased vigilance. Failure to complete routines. Reduced attention span. Short-term memory loss. Inability to concentrate.

REDUCTION OF IMPACT

H-12.   Table H-3 shows the measures that may reduce the negative impacts of continuous operations.

Table H-3. Reduction of the effects of continuous operations.

Sleep Scheduling		Countermeasures
Adequate	4 hours of continuous sleep in every 24 hours (likely to maintain adequate performance over several weeks).	Give simple, precise orders. Increase use of written orders. Crosscheck. Plan more time for completion of all tasks.
Sleep Wakefulness	A small amount of sleep relative to that lost is beneficial.	
Recovery	10 hours uninterrupted sleep required for full recovery after 48-72 hours without sleep.	Enforce adequate food and water intake.
Catnaps (10 To 30 Minutes)	Catnaps are beneficial, but the only truly effective remedy is sleep.	Develop and enforce sleep plans. Good physical fitness slows the effects of sleep loss and fatigue.
Timing	Consistent timing of sleep and wakeup times will contribute to successful adjustment to an arduous regimen.	Increase use of confirmation briefs.

Note: After 48 to 72 hours without sleep, Soldiers become militarily ineffective. After five to seven days of even partial sleep deprivation, alertness and performance decline to the same low level as seen after two to three days without sleep.

Appendix I
CBRN Environment Operations

The purpose of using chemical and biological weapons varies based on when employed by emerging nations and terrorist groups. Chemical weapons would most likely be used early in an operation or from its onset to hinder an enemy's momentum; disrupt its command, control, and communications; produce casualties; destroy or disable equipment; and disrupt operations. Biological weapons will target rear area objectives such as food supplies, water sources, troop concentrations, convoys, and urban and rural population centers, rather than frontline forces. Chemical and biological agents may be employed separately or together and may supplement conventional weapons.

The possibility of the use of chemical, biological, and or radiological dispersal weapons by terrorist groups can not be overlooked. Planning must routinely address the use of each of these as well as protective measures against enemy CBRN weapons. Terrorist groups who have sufficient chemical and or biological agents may use them in an operational or tactical situation. They will use persistent chemical agents to restrict air base and port operations, and nonpersistent chemical agents on bypassed troops, strongpoints, and flanks.

Section I. BATTLEFIELD

The CBRN-contaminated battlefield is the integration of CBRN weapons and contamination caused by industrial incidents into tactical operations.

COMMAND

I-1.   The battalion commander prepares his units and personnel to operate in a CBRN environment. To do this, he ensures the battalion takes the proper protective measures including—

- CBRN vulnerability analysis.
- Dispersion and use of terrain as shielding.
- Continuous CBRN monitoring with detection equipment.
- Assumption of the appropriate MOPP level.

STAFF

I-2.   For CBRN operations, the battalion chemical officer, assisted by the battalion chemical NCO provides technical advice to the battalion commander and the remainder of the battalion staff. The CBRN staff officer and NCO—

- With the S-2, templates strikes and predictecs effects of enemy CBRN on battalion.
- Disseminates information received via the CBRN warning and reporting system (CBRNWRS).
- Recommends reconnaissance, monitoring, and surveying requirements.
- Recommends MOPP and OEG based on S-2's threat analysis and higher headquarters guidance.
- Maintains records of unit contamination to include radiological dose records.
- Conducts vulnerability analysis of unit positions.
- Plans battalion decontamination operations in conjunction with the S-3.

- Coordinates for nonorganic CBRN assets (decon, smoke, and reconnaissance) support.
- Acts as the liaison between attached chemical units and the S-3.

CHEMICAL AGENTS

I-3.   Chemical agents bring about casualties, degrade performance, slow maneuver, restrict terrain, and disrupt operations (Table I-1). They can cover large areas and may be delivered as liquid, vapor, or aerosol and disseminated by artillery, mortars, rockets, missiles, aircraft spray, bombs, land mines, and covert means.

Table I-1. Characteristics of chemical agents.

AGENT	Nerve	Blister	Blood	Choking
PROTECTION	Mask and BDO	Mask and BDO	Mask	Mask
DETECTION	M8A1, M256A1, CAM, and M8 and M9 paper	M256A1, CAM, and M8 and M9 paper	M256A1	Odor (freshly mowed hay)
SYMPTOMS	Difficult breathing, drooling, nausea, vomiting, convulsions, and blurred vision	Burning eyes, stinging skin, irritated nose	Convulsions and coma	Coughing, nausea, choking, headache, and tight chest
EFFECTS	Incapacitates	Blisters skin, damages respiratory tract	Incapacitates	Floods and damages lungs
FIRST AID	Mark 1 NAAK	As for 2d and 3d degree burns	None	Keep warm and avoid movement
DECON	M291 and flush eyes with water	M291 and flush eyes with water	None	None

BIOLOGICAL AGENTS

I-4.   US forces may be faced with enemies capable of producing and employing biological agents such as disease-causing microorganisms (pathogens) and toxins. Biological agents can produce and reproduce lethal or incapacitating effects over an extensive area. The delayed onset of symptoms and detection, identification, and verification difficulties for biological agents can provide significant advantages to adversaries who decide to use them.

TOXINS

I-5.   Toxins are poisonous substances produced from living organisms. The following characteristics also apply to toxins:

- Can be synthesized (artificially produced).
- Mirror the symptoms of nerve agents.
- Present 8 to 12 hours of tactical concern (destroyed by sunlight).
- Can be fast acting (neurotoxins) or slower acting (cytotoxins).

PATHOGENS

I-6.   Pathogens are infectious agents that cause disease in man and animals. Examples of pathogens are bacteria, viruses, and rickets. Characteristics of pathogens include—

- Delayed reaction (incubation 1 to 21 days).

- Multiply and overcome natural defenses.
- Vectors (disease-infected insects) circumvent protective clothing and prolong hazards.

PROTECTION FROM BIOLOGICAL AGENTS

I-7.   Steps that can be taken to protect against biological agents include--

- Maintain up-to-date immunizations.
- Practice good hygiene.
- Maintain area sanitation.
- Maintain physical conditioning.
- Ensure water purification.

EFFECTS OF NUCLEAR WEAPONS

I-8.   Nuclear weapons are much more destructive than conventional weapons. Blast, nuclear and thermal radiation, and electromagnetic pulse are of primary concern.

BLAST

I-9.   High-pressure shock wave crushes structures and causes missiling damage.

THERMAL RADIATION

I-10.   Intense heat and extremely bright light cause burns, temporary blindness, and dazzle.

NUCLEAR RADIATION

I-11.   Energy released from nuclear detonation produces fallout in the form of initial and residual radiation, both of which cause casualties.

ELECTROMAGNETIC PULSE

I-12.   Surge of electrical power occurs within seconds of a nuclear detonation and damages electrical components in equipment, such as radios, radar, computers, and vehicles; and in weapon systems such as the TOW, Javelin, and Dragon.

PROTECTION FROM NUCLEAR ATTACK

I-13.   Cover and shielding offer the best protection from the immediate effects of a nuclear attack; this includes cover in fighting positions (18 inches overhead cover), culverts, and ditches. Soldiers should cover exposed skin and stay down until the blast wave passes and debris stops falling. Immediately after a nuclear attack, begin continuous radiation monitoring.

MONITORING TECHNIQUES

I-14.   FM 3-11.3 describes monitoring techniques, correlation factor data, and recording forms. Monitoring may be periodic or continuous.

Periodic

I-15.   Units conduct periodic monitoring during nuclear warfare. All units routinely--at least once an hour--monitor a designated point in their respective areas. The CBRN defense annex of the unit SOP gives detailed guidance on monitoring procedures.

Continuous

I-16.   All units initiate continuous monitoring when they receive a fallout warning, when a unit is on an administrative or tactical move, when a nuclear burst occurs, when radiation levels above one centigray (cGy) per hour are detected by periodic monitoring, and on order of the commander. Except for units on the move, continuous monitoring stops on instructions from the commander or higher headquarters or when the dose rate falls below one cGy per hour.

OPERATIONAL EXPOSURE GUIDANCE

I-17.   Operations in a nuclear environment are complicated by the necessity to control exposure of personnel to nuclear radiation. An OEG determines the maximum radiation dose to which units may be exposed and still accomplish a mission. Determination of this dose is based on the accumulated dose or radiation history of the unit.

Section II. DEFENSE

Protect the force by adhering to three tenets of CBRN defense: contamination avoidance, protection, and decontamination.

AVOIDANCE

I-18.   Avoiding CBRN attacks and hazards is the key to CBRN defense. Avoidance allows commanders to shield Soldiers and units, thus shaping the battlefield.

ACTIVE AND PASSIVE MEASURES

I-19.   Contamination avoidance involves both active and passive measures. Passive measures include training, camouflage, concealment, hardening positions, and dispersion. Active measures include detection, reconnaissance, alarms and signals, warning and reporting, marking, and contamination control.

CBRN RECONNAISSANCE

I-20.   CBRN reconnaissance is the detection, identification, reporting, and marking of CBRN hazards. CBRN reconnaissance consists of search, survey, surveillance, and sampling operations. Due to limited availability of the M93 FOX reconnaissance vehicle, consider alternate means of conducting CBRN reconnaissance such as reconnaissance elements, engineers, and maneuver units. As a minimum, consider the following actions when planning and preparing for CBRN reconnaissance:

- Use the IPB process to orient on CBRN enemy NAIs.
- Pre-position reconnaissance assets to support requirements.
- Establish command and support relationships.
- Assess the time and distance factors for the conduct of CBRN reconnaissance.
- Report all information rapidly and accurately.
- Plan for resupply activities to sustain CBRN reconnaissance operations.
- Determine possible locations for post-mission decontamination.

- Plan for fire support requirements.
- Plan fratricide prevention measures.
- Establish MEDEVAC procedures.
- Identify CBRNWRS procedures and frequencies.

PROTECTION

I-21.   CBRN protection is an integral part of operations. Techniques that work for avoidance also work for protection (shielding Soldiers and units and shaping the battlefield). Other forms of protection involve sealing or hardening positions, protecting Soldiers, assuming appropriate MOPP levels (Table I-2), reacting to attack, and using collective protection. Individual protective items include the protective mask, joint services, lightweight integrated suit technology (JSLIST), overboots (multipurpose rain/snow/chemical and biological overboots (MULO)), and gloves. The higher-level commander above the BCT establishes the minimum level of protection. Subordinate units may increase this level as necessary but may not decrease it. The JSLIST may be worn for 45 days with up to six launderings or up to 120 days with no launderings. The JSLIST can be worn for 24 hours once contaminated. The MULO provides 60 days of durability and 24 hours of protection against liquid chemical agents.

Table I-2. MOPP levels.

Level/Equipment	MOPP Ready	MOPP0	MOPP1	MOPP2	MOPP3	MOPP4	Mask Only
Mask	Carried	Carried	Carried	Carried	Worn	Worn	Worn***
JSLIST	Ready*	Avail**	Worn	Worn	Worn	Worn	
Overboots	Ready*	Avail**	Avail**	Worn	Worn	Worn	
Gloves	Ready*	Avail**	Avail**	Avail**	Avail**	Worn	
Helmet Cover	Ready*	Avail**	Avail**	Worn	Worn	Worn	

* Items available to Soldier within two hours with replacement available within six hours.
** Items must be positioned within arms reach of the Soldier.
*** Never "mask only" if nerve or blister agent is used in AO.

DECONTAMINATION

I-22.   Use of CBRN weapons creates unique residual hazards that may require decontamination. In addition to the deliberate use of these weapons, collateral damage, natural disasters, and industrial emitters may require decontamination. Contamination forces units into protective equipment that degrades performance of individual and collective tasks. Decontamination restores combat power and reduces casualties that may result from exposure, thus allowing commanders to sustain combat operations. Use the four principles of decontamination when planning decontamination operations:

- Decontaminate as soon as possible.
- Decontaminate only what is necessary.
- Decontaminate as far forward as possible (METT-TC dependent).
- Decontaminate by priority.

DECONTAMINATION LEVELS

I-23.   The three levels of decontamination are immediate, operational, and thorough.

Immediate Decontamination

I-24.   Immediate decontamination requires minimal planning and is a basic Soldier survival skill. Personal wipedown removes contamination from individual equipment using the M291. Operator spray-down uses the on-board decontamination apparatus with DS2 to decontaminate surfaces that an operator must touch or contact to operate the equipment.

Operational Decontamination

I-25.   Operational decontamination involves MOPP gear exchange and vehicle spray-down. MOPP gear exchange is most effective when performed within the first six hours of being contaminated. It must be completed within 24 hours of contamination. Vehicle wash-down removes gross contamination and limits the spread of contamination.

Thorough Decontamination

I-26.   Thorough decontamination involves detailed troop decontamination (DTD) and detailed equipment decontamination (DED). Thorough decontamination is normally conducted (required after six hours in a contaminated area without any decontamination performed) as part of reconstitution or during breaks in combat operations. Support from a chemical decontamination platoon is required.

PLANNING CONSIDERATIONS

I-27.   Decontamination planning considerations include the following:

- Plan decontamination sites throughout the width and depth of the AO.
- Tie decontamination sites to the scheme of maneuver and templated CBRN strikes.
- Apply the principles of decontamination.
- Plan for contaminated routes.
- Plan logistics and resupply of MOPP, mask parts, water, and decontamination supplies.
- Consider medical concerns, including treatment and evacuation of contaminated casualties.
- Plan for site security.

Appendix J
Media Considerations

In today's environment, the media are present in most military operations. In most cases, the media can immediately send, publish, or broadcast whatever they see and hear. Their words and images are powerful--and can affect national policy. Under our form of government, the media have the right to cover operations, and the public has a right to know what the media have to say. Although many members of the media lack a full understanding of the military, they are nevertheless the key transmitters of information about the Army to the public. Many good things about the Army are unknown to the public. Commanders and public affairs personnel tell the Army's story. However, the right to a free press does not outweigh the necessity for operations security and the accomplishment of the mission. This appendix covers how to deal appropriately with the media.

OBJECTIVE

J-1.   The objective of the Infantry battalion commander, and more often through the unit's personnel, in dealing with the media, is to ensure that battalion operations are presented to the American public and audiences around the world in the proper context. Commanders can best achieve this goal by educating Soldiers and subordinate leaders about the positive aspects of a well-informed public.

REALITIES

J-2.   It is impossible, in this modern era, to keep large-scale military movements quiet. The media will speculate on destinations of these moves and the likely missions, and such speculation can affect operations security (OPSEC). News coverage for deployments will be immediate and worldwide, and the messages put out by the media can change policy. The Army cannot and should not control media messages or stories. The media will go everywhere they can to uncover unique angles and stories. They will resist management and escort and will instead try to gather their information firsthand. However, many members of the media have not served in the military and do not have an in-depth understanding of military doctrine, terminology, and culture.

OBJECTIVES AND INTERESTS

J-3.   The media will want access to Soldiers and units. They will seek fresh stories every day and will expect daily authoritative briefings from operators and leaders. The media are particularly interested in excessive civilian casualties, fratricide, and the plight of noncombatants. They will want to discuss the ROE and issues related to them. Also of media interest, will be any military-civilian disagreements or conflicts such as looting, murder, rape, or mistreatment of prisoners. Civilian opinions, blaming US forces for lack of food, fuel, water, or medical care, are sure to reach the press. Looming large on the press list will be any US casualty figures, both actual and projected with little consideration for comparison or context.

J-4.   The press will also want the Soldiers' perspective and will try to accompany Soldiers on missions. The technique of embedding reporters with units should be considered if the operational conditions allow. Embedding reporters with units for extended periods has added to the media's understanding of Soldiers and the military objectives, and has produced positive coverage about the Army.

CAPABILITIES

J-5.   With available technology, the media have the capability to collect and transmit images and sound worldwide from any location. They have the ability to cover events quickly and to influence the public either positively or negatively. With interest high in worldwide deployments, the media can send large numbers of reporters to cover operations in detail.

COMMAND

J-6.   Commanders must anticipate, prepare, and respond within minutes or hours to breaking events. Otherwise, it will be difficult or impossible to explain or counter what has already appeared on the television or in print. When the released report is inaccurate, the commander should aggressively counter the false report with timely and accurate information backed up by subject matter experts. It is also important to coordinate statements among agencies. Bad news does not get better with age, and ignoring the media will not make them go away. If the commander refuses to talk to the media, he will only guarantee the military's perspective will not be seen or heard. The commander must balance his time with the news media to avoid being overexposed or ignored.

GUIDELINES

J-7.   The following are general guidelines for dealing with the media. These guidelines must be tempered with the public's right to know and the requirements of OPSEC.

SECURITY CONSIDERATIONS

J-8.   It is important that all Soldiers understand what is considered classified information and not discuss it with the press. Soldiers should also understand that they are not required to talk to the media if it is against their wishes. Precautions should be taken to protect classified information from the news media. If someone accidentally reveals classified information, the reporter should be informed and asked not to use it and explain why. All such incidents must be reported to the BCT commander. All Soldiers represent the military and they should not guess or speculate on things they do not know. Anything said could be in the hands of the enemy in minutes. In addition, grumbling or thoughtless complaining could provide the enemy with propaganda to use against the military. The media must be prevented from televising nearby recognizable landmarks, sensitive equipment, or operational or classified information contained in the CP. The reasons for interfering with the telecast should be explained to the press.

MEDIA CONTROLS

J-9.   Media in the AO should be checked to ensure that they are credentialed, and a military escort should escort them at all times for their safety. An interview should not be scheduled when it could interfere with the mission. Even when preventing the disclosure of classified information, media material or equipment should not be confiscated.

TOPICS TO AVOID DISCUSSING

J-10.   Neither the commander nor any member of his command should discuss political or foreign policy matters. These are outside the direct scope of the military and would be purely speculative. No Soldier should discuss matters in which he does not have direct knowledge. Operational capabilities, including exact numbers or troop strengths, numbers or types of casualties, types of weapons systems, and plans, should not be discussed with the press.

INTERVIEWS

J-11. The Infantry battalion commander or a senior member of the staff may be required to grant an interview. This should be considered an opportunity to ensure that the needs of the media are met by providing accurate, timely, and useful information.

MAINTAIN A PROFESSIONAL ATTITUDE

J-12. Remain in control even when the media seem aggressive or ask inappropriate questions. Be polite but firm. Be brief and concise; use simple language. Do not use jargon or acronyms; the public does not know what they mean. Tell the Army's story.

MAKE A GOOD IMPRESSION

J-13. Relax and be yourself. Ignore the cameras and talk directly to the reporter. Remove your sunglasses so the audience can see your eyes. Use appropriate posture and gestures.

THINK FIRST

J-14. Stop and think before answering; questions need not be answered instantly. Answer only one question at a time. Do not get angry. Correct answers are more important than deadlines.

KNOW QUESTION

J-15. If you do not understand the question, ask the reporter to rephrase it. Know the question you are answering. Do not answer "what if" questions or render opinions. Reporters often ask the same question in different ways so stay consistent with your answer.

EVERYTHING COUNTS

J-16. Everything is *ON THE RECORD*. You may be friendly but stick to business. The interviewer chooses the questions and you choose the answers.

QUESTIONS WILL NOT BE THERE

J-17. Videotape and print media will not include the question, just your answer. Your answer should stand alone. If the interviewer uses a catch phrase, such as "assassination squad," do *not* use the word or phrase in your answer. For example: "What are you doing about the assassination squads?" *Bad Answer:* "The assassination squads are being investigated." *Better Answer:* "We are committed to investigating this matter and will take the necessary and appropriate action."

SPEAK ABOUT WHAT YOU KNOW

J-18. If you do not know the answer, simply say, "I don't know." That answer rarely appears in print. Avoid speculation or answering a question more appropriate for the Secretary of Defense. Talk about your area of expertise.

TELL TRUTH

J-19. Tell the truth even if it hurts. Do not try to cover embarrassing events with a security classification. Never lie to the media.

KNOW, EXPRESS, AND STAY ON MESSAGE

J-20.   Generally, you will know what the media will want to ask. Decide beforehand the theme of your responses. The media will try to make you divert from your message; however, stay focused on the message.

TRAINING

J-21.   Units should train for media awareness in two parts, first in a classroom and then in the field.

CLASSROOM PHASE

J-22.   OPSEC should be covered thoroughly. Many of the things outlined in this appendix should be discussed with Soldiers and leaders. If a media card is available in the command, it should be explained in detail. Soldiers should be instructed on how to give an interview and their right to refuse to do so. Leaders should understand their responsibility to convey the Army's story truthfully so that the public will understand it.

FIELD PHASE

J-23.   Soldiers should be given an opportunity to participate in an interview using Soldiers who role-play as reporters. If possible, the role-playing Soldiers should be qualified in public affairs training. This training should be included in regular field training exercises. If a video camera is used during the interview, the tape can be replayed during an AAR. Due to possible far reaching effects of interviews, this training should receive considerable command emphasis.

MEDIA CARDS

J-24.   If higher headquarters has not developed a media card, the battalion commander should ask the PAO to develop one. If he or she does not or cannot, the commander should consider doing so for the battalion. Items to include in a media card are—

- The name of the POC and how to contact him or her if a reporter arrives in the unit's area.
- Responsibilities of a media escort.
- What information can or cannot be discussed.
- When to allow a media interview.
- How to treat reporters.
- How to conduct an interview.
- The best techniques to use in telling the Army's story.

Appendix K
Unmanned Aircraft Systems

UAS operations support battlefield commanders and their staffs as they plan, coordinate, and execute operations. UAS contribute to the SU of commanders through ISR. Army UAS can perform some or all of the following functions; enhanced targeting through acquisition, detection, designation, and BDA. Other UAS missions support the maneuver commander by contributing to the effective tactical operations of smaller units. Ground Control Stations (GCS) with common data links, remote video terminals (RVTs), portable GCSs, and Army Airspace Command and Control System (A2C2S) enhance SA and the COP, helping to set the conditions for the current and future force's success. This appendix is an introduction to rapidly developing UAS doctrine, equipment, and A2C2. It highlights capabilities of tactical UAS likely encountered at the BCT and subordinate unit levels.

DESCRIPTION

K-1.   UAS can locate and recognize major enemy forces, moving vehicles, weapons systems, and other targets that contrast with their surroundings. In addition, UAS can locate and confirm the positions of friendly forces, the presence of noncombatant civilians, and so on. However, visually locating well camouflaged enemy forces is difficult. The BCT and Infantry battalion and below units can enhance the UAS capabilities by employing it as part of an overall collection plan, integrated with and cued by other intelligence systems, in a synchronized effort to support the warfighters' needs.

FUNDAMENTALS

K-2.   All UAS organizations must be able to—

- Plan and conduct strategic deployment.
- Conduct administrative and tactical movements.
- Coordinate with supported maneuver units.
- Gather information to support the IPB.
- Use the full spectrum of communications means to satisfy internal and external requirements for combat information.
- Plan and coordinate A2C2.

K-3.   BCT and below UAS organizations must accomplish operations in any of the following conditions:

- As subordinate unit assigned, attached, OPCON, or TACON to another service.
- Near ground forces.
- Day or night.
- Limited visibility.
- CBRN (avoid intentional contamination).
- All natural environments such as desert, mountains, rolling hills, dense forests, jungles, plains, and urban areas.
- All operational environments such as contiguous, noncontiguous, linear, nonlinear, and asymmetrical.

K-4.   BCT and below UAS organizations must be proficient in the following areas:

- Call-for-fire operations.
- Reconnaissance and security operations.
- Terrain flight: low-level, contour, and NOE
- Movement techniques: traveling, traveling overwatch, and bounding overwatch.
- Airfield and FARP operations.
- Emergency procedures.
- Base defense (includes emergency evacuation under all weather conditions).
- CBRN exposure avoidance, surveys, and decontamination.

EQUIPMENT

K-5.   UAS have rapidly developed in the past few years. Systems range from those capable of extreme long distance and high altitude to resembling civilian hobby shop models. Most recently, development and deployment of UAS specifically designed to support the BCT and below now support the tactical commander.

BCT AND BELOW

K-6.   The Shadow and Raven UAS are the most common found at the BCT level and below. They are characterized by relatively short flight duration, small size, limited payload options, and are not capable of directly engaging the enemy.

SHADOW UAS

K-7.   The Shadow UAS is an effective intelligence gathering system that has been proven in combat. The Shadow's electro-optical/infrared (EO/IR) payload can produce color video in daylight operations and black and white thermal images at night. This imagery give commanders near real-time intelligence day and night. The aircraft is nearly undetectable in urban areas or other areas with ambient noise. The Shadow's operators can often identify enemy ambushes or insurgents planting improvised explosive devices (IEDs). These capabilities let the Shadow unit--

- Support conventional combat operations and raids
- Provide TA
- Follow-up BDA
- Perform countermortar operations, and
- Assist with search and rescue operations.

System Mission

K-8.   The mission of the Shadow is to provide a real-time, responsive, day and night imagery surveillance and reconnaissance capability to support SA, target acquisition, and BDA.

Fundamentals

K-9.   The Shadow is used at the BCT level, but may be allocated to support a subordinate battalion. The Shadow conducts R&S missions to protect friendly forces and can perform screen missions and participate in guard or cover missions. The Shadow provides reconnaissance and security and/or employs indirect fires and can perform near real time BDA (Figure K-1).

Figure K-1. The Shadow UAS.

Description

K-10.   The Shadow aircraft uses a twin-boom pusher design. The Shadow has a rotary engine. Its nonretractable, tricyclic landing gear allow conventional wheeled take-off and landing. However, the Shadow can also be launched from a catapult, plus it has a tail hook to catch arresting cables on a short runway. A complete Shadow system has four air vehicles and two GCSs, and the operators have full control over the air vehicle and their sensors. Both line of sight (LOS) and non-line-of-sight (NLOS) data links provide command uplink and sensor data downlink.

Navigation

- For full autonomy, the Shadow can use a GPS-based navigation system.

Tasks

- Shadow tasks include day or night reconnaissance, surveillance, TA, and BDA.

Payloads

- Block 1 (initial production) vehicles--an EO/IR sensor turret.
- Block 2 vehicles (not fielded)--are projected to use an improved EO/IR sensor.
- Other, possibly including a synthetic aperture radar/moving target indicator (SAR/MTI).

Capabilities

K-11.   Capabilities of the system include—

- Multiple payload capability.
- Modular design enables growth.
- Automatic landing and takeoff.
- Early entry capability with one C-130.
- System and maintenance section transportable on three C-130s.
- Compatible with Army battle command system (ABCS).
- EO/IR sensor.

Electro-Optical/Infrared Payload

K-12.   The EO/IR payload (Figure K-2) is a multimode, forward looking infrared (FLIR)/line scanner/TV sensor. It has a resolution sufficient to detect and recognize an armored personnel carrier sized target from operational altitudes, for example, more than 8,000 ft above ground level (AGL) day; more than 6,000 feet AGL at night; and at survivable standoff ranges (3 to 5 km) from the imaged target. Images are processed onboard the AV and passed to the GCS via the system data link. The payload can provide autonomous preplanned operation and instantaneous retasking throughout a mission. The EO/IR payload provides continuous zoom capabilities when in enemy operations mode and multiple fields of view (FOV) when in IR mode. The mission payload operator (MPO) selects the mode.

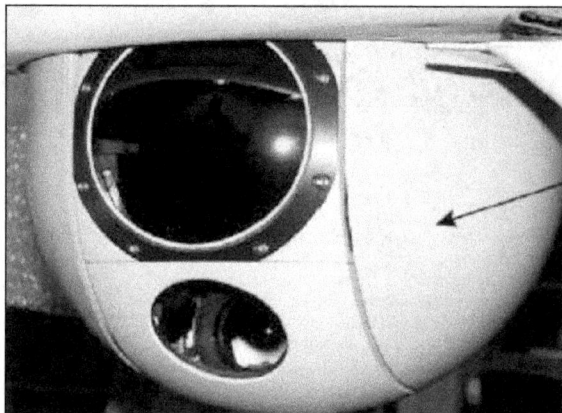

Figure K-2. Shadow mission payload.

Remote Video Terminal

K-13.   The RVT (Figure K-3) is a portable system that receives, processes, and displays near real time (NRT) video images and telemetry from the AV. The RVT receives video and telemetry signals from the AV through either the antenna or the GCS. The RVT receives direct downlink from the AV when within 50 km of the AV and displays annotated imagery to the operator (same as MPO display in the GCS). In addition, the RVT can store imagery, recall selected segments, and display NRT imagery with annotations of date/time group. It also can store selectable target locations in latitude/longitude, military grid reference system, and universal transverse Mercator coordinates when in the center FOV, north seeking arrow, AV position, and heading. The system has four RVTs to provide payload information in the AOs. Based on METT-TC, the commander allocates RVTs to support his scheme of maneuver. The RVT is "user friendly" and easy to operate. A Soldier assigned to the supported unit transports and operates the RVT. Supported units receive the RVT and operator training from the Shadow platoon.

RAVEN UAS

K-14.   Like the Shadow UAS, the Raven is a combat proven intelligence gathering system. It has seen extensive use in ongoing combat operations, enhancing the intelligence-gathering capabilities of battalions, companies, and even platoons.

System Mission

K-15.   The Raven team provides R&S and remote monitoring, day and night imagery to support SA and SU, target acquisition, and BDA down to company level.

Fundamentals

K-16.   The Raven team normally operates at the battalion level, but may be allocated to support a subordinate company or even a platoon. Ravens are deployed to conduct R&S missions and convoy security to protect friendly forces. The Raven can provide information on enemy location, disposition, activity, and/or employ indirect fires. Raven can perform real time BDA.

Figure K-3. The Raven UAS.

Description

K-17.   The Raven is a man-portable, hand-launched small UAS that is designed for reconnaissance, surveillance and remote monitoring. The Raven can be launched and recovered in minutes without special equipment on unprepared terrain. It can be either remotely controlled from the ground control unit (GCU) or fly completely autonomous missions using global positioning system waypoint navigation. The AV can be ordered to immediately return to its launch point simply by pressing a single command button.

Capabilities

K-18.   The following are some of the characteristics of the system:

- Hand launch, auto-land, or manual recovery.
- Auto navigation using military P(y)-code GPS.
- Manual navigation and flight modes.
- AV quick assembly (less than 3 minutes).
- Man-portable or backpackable.
- Quiet.

- Reusable (100 or more flights).
- Ability to climb to operational altitude in 1 to 2 minutes.

Organization

K-19. A Raven team typically consists of—

- Two operators from the unit to which the equipment is assigned.
- Three AVs.
- Three payloads.
- Three EO front and side look.
- Two IR front look.
- Two IR side look.
- One GCU.
- Remote video terminal.
- Single use and rechargeable batteries.
- Carry/protective cases.
- Battery charger and power supply.
- Field maintenance kit.
- Spare and repair parts.

Electro-Optical or Infrared Payload

K-20. The optics package includes an EO, color camera nose (side and forward look) for day operations, and two IR thermal noses (one side and one forward look) for night operations. EO IR Pixels 768H X 494V 160H X 120V Payload Nose Weight 6.2 oz 6.5 oz. The Raven aircraft carries either an EO or an IR camera in its nose. The system includes three payload noses (Figure K-4). Video clarity begins to degrade above 500 feet AGL:

- One nose holds cameras in forward and side look positions.
- One nose holds a camera in the forward look position.
- One nose holds a camera in the left side look position.

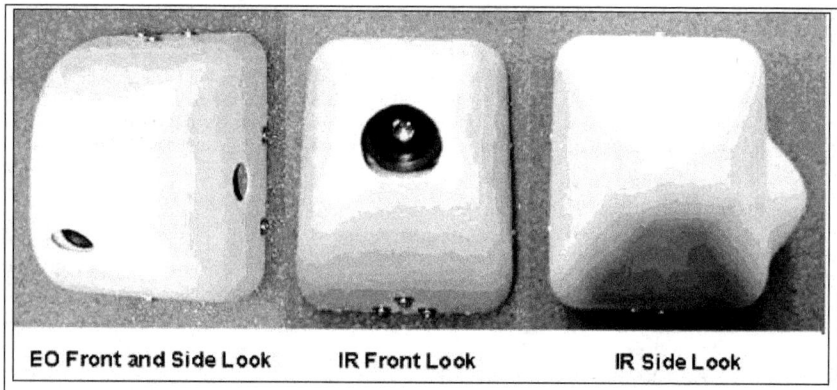

EO Front and Side Look   IR Front Look   IR Side Look

Figure K-4. Camera payloads.

Remote Video Terminal

K-21.   The UAS transmits live airborne video images and compass headings (location information) from the AV to a GCU and RVT, enabling operators to navigate, search for targets, recognize terrain, and record all information for analysis later. The RVT (Figure K-5) display is a receive-only monitor with no aircraft control functions. It can be used to view real-time video from any location within a 5 to 10 km LOS of the aircraft. A single BA- 5590 or BB-390 battery powers the RVT.

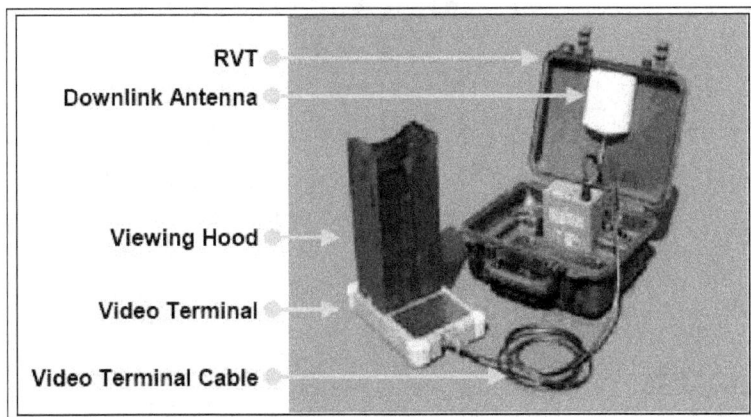

Figure K-5. Raven remote video terminal.

K-22.   Field maintenance on the Raven typically includes routine inspections, servicing, cleaning, and adjusting. Procedures that should be done at the field level do not require specialized training or tools. If the repair is not at an operator (field) maintenance level, the item should be turned in to the battalion supply S-4.

AIRSPACE CONTROL MEASURES

K-23.   UAS present significant challenges due to their small size, agility, and increasing density, as well as their limited ability to detect, see, and avoid other aircrafts. Thus, UAS pose an operational hazard to manned aircraft operating nearby. UAS flights, like manned aircraft flights, must be coordinated to avoid conflict with other airspace users. UAS missions should be coordinated with the airspace control authority, area air defense commander (AADC), and the JFACC to safely separate UAS from manned aircraft and to prevent engagement by friendly AD systems (FM 3-100.2).

PLANNED MISSIONS

K-24.   The ACA may establish specific UAS flight routes and altitudes, and publish them in the airspace control plan. The established principles of airspace management used in manned flight operations apply to UAS operations, but the JFC may waive them, if necessary. UAS missions may be both preplanned and hasty in nature. Preplanned UAS flights should be included in the ATO, special instructions (SPINS), or airspace control order (ACO). The unit should coordinate hasty UAS missions with the appropriate airspace control agencies to safely separate UAS from manned aircraft, and to prevent inadvertent engagement by friendly air defense (AD) elements. See Figure K-6.

K-25. Before launching any UAS mission, commanders must assess the training and readiness level of friendly forces. The analysis includes availability of critical systems, supporting fires, and joint support.

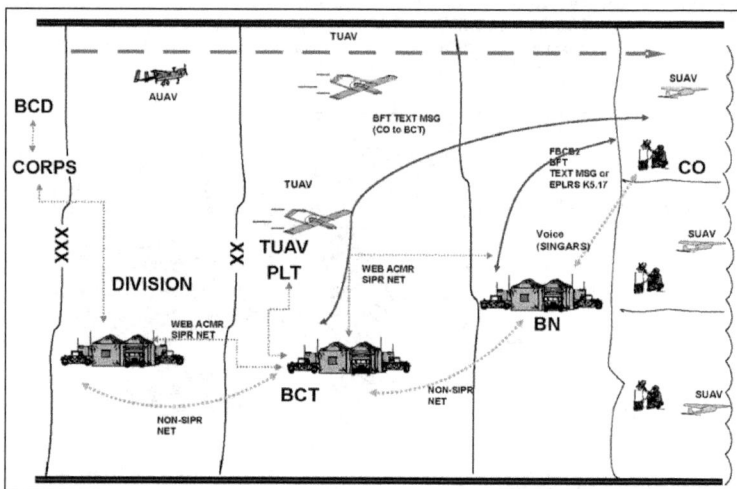

Figure K-6. UAS request flow.

Supporting Fires

K-26. The supported unit frequently has access to indirect fires from a coordinated fires network. These complementary fires could facilitate movement to the objective area through JSEADs, engage targets bypassed by UAS, or provide indirect fires on the objective. Knowing what and when FS is available are important considerations during UAS mission planning and EA development. Efforts to coordinate joint fires for actions on the objective could be critical to the success of operations in deep areas.

Airspace Control Order

K-27. The ACO is an order implementing the airspace control plan that provides details of the approved requests for ACMs. It is published either as part of the ATO or as a separate document. ACO coordination is required for any operations outside of Army controlled airspace.

Air Tasking Order

K-28. The ATO is a method for tasking and disseminating to components, subordinate units, and C2 agencies projected sorties, capabilities, and/or forces to targets and specific missions. It normally provides specific instructions to include call signs, targets, and controlling agencies, as well as general instructions.

BCT AND BELOW TASKING AND PLANNING CONSIDERATIONS

K-29. UAS units organic to or supporting BCT and below frequently team with manned systems to support ground maneuver and fire support units. UAS planners may be called upon to assist planners from other mission areas. Because of this, UAS planners must have adequate knowledge to plan operations to support a wide variety of unit missions.

Planned Mission Development

K-30.   The S-2 develops NAIs that aid in focusing collection efforts in a systematic approach to answer PIR, monitor decision points, and locate multiple high value targets (HVT). UAS can reconnoiter and expand the supported brigade's battlespace for targeting and early warning. UAS also support close combat, and assist in security and surveillance of NAIs. See Figure K-7, pages K-11 through K-15.

K-31.   UAS employment is optimized when integrated into an ISR plan that uses other collection assets to cue the UAS. Collection systems can provide single source reports that UAS can confirm; this produces reliable intelligence. Some of these collections systems are the JSTARS, GSR, improved remotely monitored battlefield sensor system (IREMBASS), and SIGINT collectors such as Prophet and Guardrail common sensor. Collection systems locate a potential enemy force; UAS then detect the enemy element and confirm its composition. The bottom line is that UAS, cued by other ISR assets enable the BCT and below to systematically gain and maintain contact with the enemy well before that enemy can range the BCT main body.

K-32.   Many BCTs have CGS access to provide JSTARS downlink and UAS imagery and data. The CGS provides the ability to view both JSTARS MTI and SAR imagery on one screen; on a second screen, it can display the UAS location, where it is looking, and its real-time video feed. Often, the UAS GCS is nearby, enabling rapid landline interface. Trojan Spirit provides another means to link the GCS and CGS. JSTARS provides the S-2 and UAS with tasking authority to monitor the big picture and fully integrate the UAS; in this way, the UAS can confirm what the JSTARS detects.

K-33.   Another BCT method for using UAS during offensive operations is to exploit the UAS ability to move quickly through the zone and observe successive NAIs in a short time. The BCT ISR plan can use the "waves" of reconnaissance method, in which ground collection assets move forward at different times. This allows information from lead elements to cue follow-on reconnaissance forces and trailing intelligence assets. If BCT UAS are in the first "wave" of reconnaissance in the synchronized ISR plan, follow-on manned reconnaissance and security assets know where to concentrate their efforts. This UAS "recon push" expedites the BCT's movement through the zone. The UAS reconnaissance that cues ground and air scouts, enables the BCT to identify the enemy's disposition, determine its weakness, and exploit that weakness.

K-34.   Before such an operation, the S-2 develops NAIs to confirm or deny the enemy defense. Just before reconnaissance assets crossing the LD, UAS launch to take an initial look at the NAIs. UAS over fly and examine ground reconnaissance infiltration routes while en route to NAIs which correspond to primary routes of advance. This allows the UAS to detect any enemy forces or obstacles that the ground reconnaissance assets will encounter en route to their observation point. Once on station, the UAS sensor is focused on each NAI. After the initial observation, the UAS may be returned to a previously observed NAI to possibly observe signs of enemy movement.

K-35.   Because the BCT and below small UAS flight duration is shorter than larger UAS, route planning is critical, and must integrate manned reconnaissance routes with reconnaissance routes. See Figure K-8, page K-15. If possible, the UAS should remain on station until the first "wave" of manned reconnaissance assets arrive at their OP locations. This assures nearly continuous surveillance of NAIs. It shortens the window between UAS reconnaissance of routes leading to an OP, and manned reconnaissance. It simplifies handover of any UAS detected targets to the manned reconnaissance and security team.

K-36.   Based on findings of this initial observation, the S-2 may refine the ISR plan. Collection assets may be focused more on certain NAIs and may focus less on others, or may be redirected to new NAIs. The commander issues a FRAGO to the ISR plan to adjust taskings. The FRAGO includes information concerning the infiltration route reconnaissance of the second "wave" of manned and unmanned reconnaissance.

K-37.   The GCS and the supported BCT tactical operations center (TOC) transmit UAS derived and other combat information and intelligence to ground units currently en route or about to cross the LD. This enables the ground units to adjust their routes and movement techniques to the threat.

K-38.   Fire support elements want dedicated UAS for target acquisition and fires. Maneuver and intelligence elements want dedicated UAS for RSTA and air-to-ground engagements. With limited brigade and below UAS capabilities, both units must compromise. The BCT commander must prioritize UAS support, while allowing the potential for both units to benefit from UAS support. Below outlines two approaches for establishing criteria for the transition of the UAS from surveillance to targeting.

K-39.   The first approach is to establish HPTs for the UAS. During war-gaming, the battle staff identifies HPTs. The staff also develops the observer plan to locate and track those HPTs for engagement and BDA. During planning, the battle staff prioritizes those sufficiently important HPTs, which, if found, will cause UAS operators to track and engage with on-call fires. In this approach, the commander consciously accepts risk to the vehicle and loss of ISR. The target's importance must justify loss of the UAS, or loss of combat information during targeting. Conversely, UAS operators know to report non-HPTs.

K-40.   An alternate approach is to have the commander specify a time or event during the battle when a transition in UAS priorities will occur. For example, once the infantry battalion security, support, and assault formations are in position to attack, the UAS may be diverted to observe the enemy reserve force.

K-41.   For the lowest echelon UAS supporting battalion and below efforts, the battalion S-2 uses ISR planning that combines BCT and above level SU with organic scouts and UAS. The battalion employs RVTs to derive information from the BCT UAS. It also employs company and below UAS to "see-over-the-next-hill" and perform more localized ISR. As with BCT level UAS planning, battalion and below may exploit other sensors and scouts to cue UAS employment.

UAVS MISSION PLANNING CHECKLIST
_____ Duty Assignments
_____ Enemy Situation
_____ Friendly Situation
_____ Mission Planning
_____ Fuel/FARP Planning
_____ Communications Plan
_____ Packet/Card Prep
Duty Assignments:
_____ Authorized MOSs on-hand
_____ Critical MOSs identified and on-hand
_____ Additional personnel necessary for 24-hour operations (if commander directed)
Enemy Situation:
_____ Unit/Order of Battle/Uniforms
_____ Battalion/Company Locations Plotted on Map
_____ Strengths/Weaknesses
_____ Most Probable Course of Action
_____ Most Dangerous Course of Action
_____ ADA Threat (For Each Weapon System)
System
Location Plotted on Map
Max/Min Range (Threat Rings Plotted on Map)
Min Engagement Altitude
Strengths

Figure K-7. Example format for UAS mission planning checklist.

UAVS MISSION PLANNING CHECKLIST

AV should avoid NBC presence
Place M9 paper on AV

Friendly Situation:
_____ Brigade Mission/Intent
_____ Battalion Mission/Intent
_____ Maps or imagery of operating area
_____ Friendly Unit Location (BN HQ Plotted on Map)
_____ Friendly Graphics Posted On Map
_____ UAVS readiness status
_____ Supported Unit Task/Purpose
_____ Adjacent Unit Task/Purpose
_____ Abort Criteria
_____ Other UAVS Units Task/Purpose
_____ Other UAVS Units Graphics Posted on Map
_____ Army Aviation/Friendly Scheme of Maneuver
_____ Rules of Engagement
_____ GCS/GCU and L/R site security
_____ Additional UAVS equipment necessary for 24-hour operations (if commander directed)
_____ Evaluate All Specified Tasks From:
     OPORD
     WARNOs
     FRAGOs
_____ Verify ACO, ATO, SPINs Requirements
     ROZ/ROA Locations/Dimensions/Freq/Call signs
     Artillery Position Area Locations Plotted
     Active Routes/ACPs Plotted
_____ Verify method of airspace control
       Positive control measures
       Procedural control measures
_____ Verify H-Hour Time
_____ Spare AV Procedures
_____ Emergency Procedures

Figure K-7. Example format for UAS mission planning checklist (continued).

K-12   FM 3-21.20   13 December 2006

UAVS MISSION PLANNING CHECKLIST

Mission Planning:
_____ Sensor selection (if not dual selectable)
      EO and IR imagery payload for day/night operations
      EO or IR (Raven only)
_____ Map Reconnaissance of Mission Area
_____ Identify terrain that will interfere with LOS data link
_____ Named Areas of Interest (NAIs)
      Grids defining NAIs
      Heading and Distance to NAI from Launch Point
      Heading and Distance between NAIs
_____ Identify/Mark Natural and Man-Made Hazards to Flight
      Local Hazards
      Sectionals
_____ Primary Route (ingress and egress)
_____ Alternate Route (ingress and egress)
_____ Threat Plotted Along Route
_____ Weather
      Clouds
      Precipitation
      Wind
      Visibility
      Temperature
      Illumination
_____ Flight Route Outside Threat Engagement Rings
_____ Route Time
_____ Loiter Time
_____ Verify grids
_____ Check all altitudes, azimuths, and distances
_____ Times Submitted to Higher HQ
_____ Waypoint Card Printed
_____ Air Control Points (ACPs) Plotted on Map
_____ Primary/Alternate Routes Plotted on Map
_____ Contingency Actions

FARP/Fuel Planning:
_____ Availability and on-hand stockage of MOGAS

Figure K-7. Example format for UAS mission planning checklist (continued).

```
UAVS MISSION PLANNING CHECKLIST
_____ Availability and on-hand stockage of batteries (Raven only)
          BB-390
          BA-5590
_____ Availability and on-hand stockage of ammunition (Hunter only)
_____ Estimated Fuel Burn Rate
_____ Estimated Battery Usage Rate (Raven only)
_____ Minimum Fuel at Departure
_____ Bingo Fuel
_____ FARP Information
_____ Location
          Frequency/Call sign
          Landing Direction
          FARP Markings
          Number of Points
          Point Numbering
          Drive Through/Nose In Landing
          Lighting Requirements
          Number of Trucks/Gallons Available
_____ Contingency Actions
          FARP Compromised
          Emergency Actions (Fire)


Commo Plan:
_____ Flight Operations
_____ TOCs, Command Nets
_____ Air Battle Net
_____ FSC Net
_____ ALOC Net
_____ ATC (airfields, approach, etc)
_____ Restricted Operating Zones
_____ LOS characteristics of terrain because AV limits of operation based on LOS data link
          Hunter        125 km (200 km with second Hunter as airborne relay)
          Shadow        50 km
          Raven         10 km
_____ Challenge and Password
_____ Contingency Actions
          Frequency Compromise
          COMSEC Compromise
          Emergency Procedures for Loss of Signal
```

Figure K-7. Example format for UAS mission planning checklist (continued).

```
                    UAVS MISSION PLANNING CHECKLIST
_____ Communication frequency bandwidth of UAVS operation
_____ Frequency management
_____ OPSEC requirements
_____ EW considerations to include friendly commo interference


_____ Packet/Card/Map Preparation:
_____ Enemy Graphics
_____ Friendly Graphics
_____ ROZ Graphics
_____ Flight Routes
_____ Crew Card
_____ Time Flow
_____ Mission Sequence
_____ Waypoint Card
_____ FARP Diagram
_____ Rehearsal Setup
```

Figure K-7. Example format for UAS mission planning checklist (continued).

Air speed/Ground speed conversion:

Note: The number 60 converts hours to minutes. The number 1.85 converts knots to knots to kilometers per hour. Round all fractions to the nearest whole minute.

Example: Given distance from OP 4 to the FARP is 50 km; average ground speed is 90 knots.

T = 50 km   x   60 = 3,000
                   -------- = 18 min flight time from OP 4 to the FARP at 90 knots
S = 90 knots x 1.85 = 166.5

Sample ground speeds in knots converted and rounded off to km/hr and km/min:

KNOTS		KM/HR		KM/MIN
65 knots	=	120.4 km/hr	=	2.0 km/min
100 knots	=	185.2 km/hr	=	3.1 km/min
80 knots	=	148.2 km/hr	=	2.5 km/min
110 knots	=	203.7 km/hr	=	3.4 km/min

Figure K-8. Example UAS flight time worksheet.

UAS Immediate or Quick Reaction Missions

K-42.   The immediate or quick reaction mission will be the one most common to the small unit commander. These missions to find out what is "over the next hill" are normally of short duration and extend over a limited range (3 to 5 kilometers). With the number of systems being introduced, it is crucial that unit commanders and UAS teams become proficient with A2C2.

K-43.   Immediate UAS mission requests do not necessarily mean the A2C2 measures have not been planned or are not already in place. For example: a restricted operations area (ROA) may have been coordinated in anticipation of the need to conduct immediate UAS missions. In this case, a UAS flight mission is cleared like that for indirect fires. The requestor calls on the battalion fire support or command net and requests clearance for the UAS flight using the format in Figure K-9.

K-44.   When the BCT or the battalion effectively owns the immediate airspace in their operations zone or area, a less restrictive technique can be used. The BCT or battalion can coordinate ahead of time the designation of a UAS "status" similar to the air defense weapons status. Normally this kind of procedure is covered in the BCT or battalion operations SOP, for example:

"UAS FREE"

K-45.   All UAS may fly with no restrictions inside the BCT/battalion operations area. UAS operators must give notice of intent to fly, when, where and time duration. Unless the higher command stops the launch, the command making the request may fly the UAS mission within the established ROA. When the UAS is launched, the operators must submit an immediate mission notification (Figure K-9). The UAS operators also announce when the UAS is over the target area and when the UAS is down.

"UAS TIGHT"

K-46.   The same general rules apply as with UAS FREE; however, the operators must receive permission to fly the UAS.

"UAS HOLD"

K-47.   No UAS flights are allowed in the specified area, and all UAS in flight must be retrieved as soon as possible.

K-48.   Figures K-9 and K-10, pages K-17 though K-18, are examples of an immediate mission checklist and A2C2 checklist list that will assist the commander and UAS team in assuring the AO is clear and safe for AV operations.

UAV IMMEDIATE MISSION CHECKLIST

_____ Restricted Operational Airspace (ROA) clearance received from Battalion/BCT
air space controlling agency.

_____ Named Area of Interest (NAI)

_____ Ingress Route Way Points (MGRS)

_____ Egress Route Waypoints (MGRS)

_____ Max/Min Altitude (AGL)

_____ L/R Site (MGRS)

_____ Route shape (Circle, Box, Track, Diamond)

_____ Call Sign

_____ Time/Date of Launch/Duration of Mission

_____ Map Reconnaissance Complete

Figure K-9. Immediate mission checklist.

Unit A2C2 Checklist

_____ Date of mission.

_____ Call sign.

_____ Time of launch.

_____ Location of L/R site, altitude, and radius around the launch site that must be avoided.

_____ Mission duration.

_____ Mission objective.

_____ Shape (circle, box, track, diamond) and location of the UAVS ROA/ROZ.

_____ Maximum Altitude (AGL).

_____ Minimum Altitude. (AGL).

_____ Time from.

_____ Time to.

_____ Operational altitudes (flight profile).

_____ Ingress Route (Azimuth, Distance, Time).

_____ Egress Route (Azimuth, Distance, Time).

_____ Air Control Points.

_____ Holding Points.

_____ Emergency Recovery Point (including route).

_____ Emergency landing site.

_____ Special requirements.

_____ Airspace Classification (See table 4).

_____ NOTAM Published (If Required).

Figure K-10. A2C2 checklist.

Appendix L
Nonlethal Capabilities

Because of the wide spectrum of threats present today and the necessity to apply the appropriate amount and type of force to accomplish the mission, force can no longer be viewed as either on or off (lethal force or no force). The ability to achieve objectives by employing nonlethal fires and weapons/munitions, allow force to be viewed as a continuum and complementary to all types of operations. First, much like a rheostat switch where power can be dialed up or down as desired, nonlethal operations provide tools to allow a commander to employ sufficient force to accomplish an objective without requiring the destruction of an enemy or the habitat. Second, nonlethal operations are used to complement lethal force to achieve the overall desired effect on the enemy. The intent of employing nonlethal capabilities is not to add another step in the progression of escalation with an adversary but to add other tools to use anywhere along that continuum.

OVERVIEW

L-1.   Military forces have long used nonlethal capabilities to influence behavior of people and nations. Combined with the use of lethal capabilities and conventional arms, nonlethal capabilities have been widely used to defeat and weaken adversaries. The following classic, nonlethal means will remain relevant in future operations and are a part of an evolutionary process of capabilities, IO, fires, and weapons/munitions development:

- Deception to prevent an enemy force from targeting actual forces,
- Jamming tactics to decrease effective command and control of enemy forces
- Shows of force to discourage and break-up protests;
- Use of physical obstacles to deny access
- Noise to create or enhance psychological impacts
- Smoke and obscurants to mask operations or defeat homing and guidance mechanisms
- Light to disorient combatants
- Leaflets to inform local populations of wanted terrorist.

DEFINITIONS

L-2.   Full spectrum operations require that adaptive leaders use the complete array of nonlethal capabilities (fires and weapons/munitions) available to the Infantry battalion to deal effectively with many situations encountered in whatever operating environment employed. There are two types of nonlethal capabilities available to the commander: nonlethal fires and nonlethal weapons/munitions.

NONLETHAL CAPABILITIES AND EFFECTS

L-3.   Nonlethal effects are any results, outcome, or consequence of the use of nonlethal capability whereby the intent is not to cause permanent harm or destruction. Nonlethal effects include elements of offensive and defensive IO. CA, CMO, public affairs, PSYOP, PSYACTs, and related supporting legal operations can have considerable impact on influencing target audiences. The term nonlethal effects is not synonymous with the term IO in that engineer operations in stability operations and civil support operations may also provide nonlethal effects, as well as other projects planned and executed by BCT units.

NONLETHAL FIRES

L-4.   Nonlethal fires are traditionally delivered by the same platforms and munitions, which deliver lethal fires. Currently, these are limited to smoke and illumination. Their employment is planned and executed in much the same manner as lethal fires. In the future, projectiles may deliver a broader range of nonlethal capabilities such as jamming, antiradiation, and incapacitating liquids.

NONLETHAL WEAPONS/MUNITIONS

L-5.   Nonlethal weapons/munitions are defined as weapons or munitions that are explicitly designed and primarily employed, at a minimum, to discourage or at most, incapacitate personnel or materiel while minimizing fatalities and undesired damage to property and the environment. Nonlethal weapons/munitions are employed with the intent to compel or deter adversaries by acting on human capabilities or materiel while minimizing fatalities and damage to equipment or facilities. The use of nonlethal weapons/munitions can assist in the application of measured force. Nonlethal weapons/munitions achieve these benefits by employing means other than catastrophic physical destruction to incapacitate their targets. The term "nonlethal" should be understood as a function of intent; zero mortality or permanent damage are goals but not guarantees of these weapons/munitions. Nonlethal weapons/munitions add flexibility to combat operations and enhance force protection by providing an environment in which friendly troops can engage threatening targets with limited risk of noncombatant casualties and collateral damage.

LETHAL VS NONLETHAL

L-6.   Nonlethal capabilities provide a wider range of options that augment but *do not replace* traditional means of lethal/deadly force. The option to resort to deadly force must always remain available when the commander believes it is appropriate to the mission. The existence of nonlethal capabilities does not represent the potential for "nonlethal war," and unrealistic expectations to that effect must be vigorously avoided. Lethal and nonlethal capabilities are most effective when used together to achieve an overall desired effect.

PLANNING CONSIDERATIONS

L-7.   Nonlethal capabilities planning is conducted by the BCT staff in the fire support cell. Infantry battalions conduct limited nonlethal planning and are normally limited to instances where CA and PSYOP teams are attached. The multifunctional IBCT fires cell structure provides the IBCT staff an organic capability to perform all tasks of a traditional fire support element, plus integrate nonlethal capabilities, primarily IO capabilities, in support of the operational plan.

BASIC COMBAT TRAINING

L-8.   The BCT commander relies on the fires cell to plan, coordinate, integrate, and synchronize in executing lethal and nonlethal capabilities to support his scheme of maneuver. This includes the massing of firepower and the massing or concentration of nonlethal capabilities to limit, disrupt, divert, destroy, or damage enemy force in depth.

L-9.   The Infantry battalion is normally responsible during operations to execute parts of the BCT nonlethal capabilities employment plan. The Infantry battalion will plan and execute nonlethal employment primarily through special staff officers attached, OPCON or DS to the battalion.

CIVIL AFFAIRS

L-10.   Civil-military operations are the activities of a commander that establish, maintain, influence, or exploit relations between military forces, government and nongovernmental civilian organizations and authorities, and the civilian populace in a friendly, neutral, or hostile area of operations in order to facilitate military operations and consolidate and achieve US objectives. Civil-military operations may include performance by military forces of activities and functions normally the responsibility of local, regional, or national government (FM 41-10).

Civil Affairs Teams

L-11.   CA teams normally consist of four Soldiers and can be attached or OPCON to an Infantry battalion for specific missions or long duration in support of ongoing stability and civil support operations. The team will have a team leader, a team sergeant, a team engineer NCO, and team medical NCO. As more CA forces arrive in theater, the team may be augmented or replaced by specific functional specialist required by the CA mission in the battalion area of operations.

Capabilities of Civil Affairs Teams

L-12.   Basic capabilities of all CA teams are to—

- Deploy rapidly, within 24 to 48 hours.
- Provide CMO staff augmentation and CA planning and assessment support to maneuver commanders.
- Maintain direct data and voice communications with conventional, SOF, and interagency elements with both classified and unclassified connectivity.
- Provide linguistic, regional, and cultural expertise to supported commanders.
- Provide general and limited technical assessments (engineering, medical, and intelligence).
- Plan and support CMO conducted by military forces.
- Identify and facilitate FNS.
- Conduct liaison with civilian authorities.
- Minimize civilian interference with military operations.
- Conduct area studies and area assessments.
- Establish and operate a CMOC.

PSYCHOLOGICAL OPERATIONS

L-13.   PSYOP are planned operations to convey selected information and indicators to foreign audiences to influence their emotions, motives, objective reasoning, and ultimately the behavior of foreign governments, organizations, groups, and individuals. The purpose of PSYOP is to induce or reinforce foreign attitudes and behavior favorable to the originator's objectives. PSYOP are a vital part of the broad range of US diplomatic, informational, military, and economic activities. PSYOP characteristically are delivered as information used during peacetime and conflict, to inform and influence. When properly employed, PSYOP can save lives of friendly and/or adversary forces by reducing adversaries' will to fight. By lowering adversary morale and reducing their efficiency, PSYOP can also discourage aggressive actions and create dissidence and disaffection within their ranks, ultimately inducing surrender (JP 3-53).

Tactical PSYOP Team

L-14.   The Infantry battalion will normally receive a TPT attached, OPCON, or DS. The TPT consists of a three man team lead by a staff sergeant. The TPT provides tactical PSYOP planning and dissemination support. The TPT's primary purpose is to integrate and execute tactical PSYOP into the supported battalion commander's maneuver plan. The TPT must also advise the battalion commander and staff on the psychological impact of their operations on the target audience in their area of operations and answer all PSYOP-related questions. The TPT can conduct loudspeaker operations, face-to-face communication, and dissemination of approved audio, audiovisual, and printed materials. They gather PSYOP relevant information, conducting town or area assessment, observing impact indicators, and gather pretesting and post testing data. TPTs also conduct interviews with the target audience. They take pictures and document cultural behavior for later use in products. TPTs often play a role in establishing rapport with foreign audiences and identify key communications that can be used to achieve nonlethal objectives.

Role of TPT

L-15.   Specifically the TPT operations can—

- Increase the supported unit commander's ability to maneuver on the battlefield by reducing or minimizing civilian interference.
- Potentially reduce the number of casualties suffered by the supported unit by reducing the number of enemy forces he must face through surrender appeals and cease resistance messages.
- Assist the supported unit commander in gaining the tactical advantage through the use of deception measures, increasing the probability of the gaining the element of surprise.

WEAPONS AND MUNITIONS

L-16.   Nonlethal weapons/munitions extend the range of firepower options. They augment means of deadly force. They are particularly valuable in both stability operations and civil support operations as they enhance the ability to apply force in proportion to the threat and allow discrimination in its use. They expand the number of options available to confront situations that do not warrant using deadly force but require Soldiers to use overwhelming, decisive power to accomplish their missions. Nonlethal capabilities must show military necessity, must be used proportionally, and must not result in unnecessary suffering.

L-17.   Nonlethal weapons/munitions have existed and been used by military forces for many years. Traditionally, nonlethal weapons/munitions have been used for crowd control or law enforcement. Ongoing technological advancements continue to refine and expand nonlethal weapons/munitions capabilities. Nonlethal weapons/munitions technology has continued to evolve with new requirements based on circumstances encountered in operations such as Operation Enduring Freedom and Operation Iraqi Freedom. The need for nonlethal weapons/munitions was clearly demonstrated by the increase in missions conducted in urban areas with large civilian populations and the need to limit collateral damage.

L-18.   The commitment of military power to resolve crises has traditionally involved the use of deadly force or the implicit or explicit *threat* of the use of deadly force. The Infantry battalion is trained, organized, and equipped for this purpose. An Infantry battalion armed only with traditional military weapons/munitions normally has two options for enforcing compliance; *threats of deadly force* and *application of deadly force*. This limitation creates a critical vulnerability that belligerents may quickly discern and use to their advantage. Nonlethal weapons/munitions, always backed by lethal force, give the battalion commander increased courses of action in planning operations.

L-19.   Noncombatant casualties, to include serious injuries and fatalities, will continue to be a regrettable but often unavoidable outcome when military power is employed, regardless of nonlethal weapons/munitions availability. Nonlethal weapons/munitions used to "augment deadly force," are now fundamental to the planning and execution of Infantry battalion operations where the employment of nonlethal capabilities is contemplated.

L-20.   The following are advantages to employing nonlethal weapons/munitions:

- Can assist in the isolation of an objective.
- Can be more humane.
- Can be more consistent with political and social considerations.
- Can be more consistent with ROE.
- Can gain advantage over enemy employing only lethal weapons/munitions because of degree of provocation.

L-21.   Nonlethal capabilities extend the range of firepower options. They augment means of deadly force. They are particularly valuable in both stability operations and civil support operations as they enhance the ability to apply force in proportion to the threat and allow discrimination in its use. They expand the number of options available to confront situations that do not warrant using deadly force but require Soldiers to use overwhelming, decisive power to accomplish their missions. Nonlethal capabilities must show military necessity, must be used proportionally, and must not result in unnecessary suffering. Nonlethal weapons/munitions capability sets can be divided into four categories: personnel protectors; personnel effectors; mission enhancers; and training devices.

PERSONNEL PROTECTORS

L-22. Personnel protectors include items, such as face shields and riot shields, which protect Soldiers from blunt trauma injuries inflicted by thrown objects like rocks, bottles, and clubs.

PERSONNEL EFFECTORS

L-23. Personnel effectors include items such as riot batons, sting grenades, pepper sprays, beanbags, foam, electric shock and high powered acoustic devices designed to either discourage or incapacitate individuals or groups.

MISSION ENHANCERS

L-24. Mission enhancers include items such as bullhorns, combat optics, spotlights, personnel, and vehicle barriers. These items are designed to facilitate target identification and crowd control. Also, these items provide a limited ability to affect vehicular movement

TRAINING DEVICES

L-25. Training devices include items such as training suits, training batons, and inert pepper sprays. They are designed to facilitate realistic hands-on scenario training in preparation for operations.

This page intentionally left blank.

Appendix M
Forward Operating Bases and Fire Bases

In some tactical situations, especially during stability or counterinsurgency operations, the Infantry battalion may establish either fire bases or forward operating bases. Bases are established and maintained as secure locations for conducting operations and logistics support activities, or delivering supporting indirect fire. Bases can be used in all types of operations; offense, defense, stability operations and civil support operations, but they are most often established during dispersed, noncontiguous, nonlinear situations. The Infantry battalion establishes and maintains bases primarily as platforms from which to conduct offensive or stability operations. In most instances, Infantry battalions are the smallest units that establish and maintain bases although it is possible for companies to establish and maintain a base for short periods. Platoons can establish temporary bases; however, if these are to be maintained for long periods they must be augmented with logistics and fire support. This appendix discusses the types of bases the Infantry battalion can establish or participate in establishing. It also discusses site selection, construction, priority of work, and continuous operations from a base.

OVERVIEW

M-1.   The use by US forces of bases has a long and varied history. Before the Civil War, Infantry and Cavalry units typically established and operated from frontier forts. These forts gave them a base to support operations over vast unmapped areas against an elusive enemy.

M-2.   The linear high-intensity combat operations of the Civil War did not often lend themselves to the use of small, dispersed bases, but immediately after the war, the US Infantry and Cavalry moved to the frontier once again. Between 1868 and 1888, the Army constructed a number of small forts from Texas to Montana, much like the forward operating bases we use today. These provided security for the population around them and supported forays to find and engage the elusive bands of hostile Indians, the premier guerrilla fighters of their day.

M-3.   After the initial pitched battles of the Spanish American War, US forces found themselves conducting a drawn-out stabilization and counterinsurgency operation in the Philippines. Once again, units established bases in remote areas from which they could patrol deeply into guerrilla territory and to which they could return to rest, recuperate, and resupply.

M-4.   In Vietnam, with long-range artillery, reliable radio communications, and unparalleled tactical mobility, the Army modified operating bases into firebases. These not only provided combat units a secure area from which to operate; they also contained powerful fire support units. With a network of firebases in place, no American unit, regardless of its location in the area of operations, faced an enemy attack without immediate and accurate indirect fire support.

M-5.   The Cold War period in Europe did not lend itself to the use of operating bases or firebases. German territorial forces secured the large rear areas, and combat forces were arrayed for linear, contiguous operations. However, in Operation Desert Shield, US Forces quickly established bases in remote desert locations. There they organized into combined arms task forces, stockpiled supplies, trained, and prepared for powerful armored thrusts deep into Kuwait and Iraq.

M-6.   Current stability and counterinsurgency operations worldwide have revived the use of operating bases and firebases in both Iraq and Afghanistan.

13 December 2006   FM 3-21.20   M-1

TYPES OF BASES

M-7.   Doctrinal names and definitions for bases (FM 1-02) are often misunderstood. Units normally establish bases for two purposes: to provide a secure site for rest and refit and as a projection platform for offensive or stability operations. Base may also be used to provide supporting fires or observation.

M-8.   Infantry battalions can establish or participate in the establishment of several kinds of bases. The most common bases are —

FORWARD OPERATING BASES

M-9.   A forward operating base (FOB) is established to provide support for tactical operations. Most often, those tactical operations are associated with stability or civil support, but that is not always the case. Facilities may be established for either temporary or long-term operations. FOBs have been used extensively by Infantry battalions in OIF and OEF as a base from which to conduct operations. A FOB provides the battalion with a secure area in which to rest, recuperate, repair and maintain equipment, plan and organize for upcoming operations. It may also be used to provide a secure environment for other agencies or units to function in specialty roles.

INTERMEDIATE STAGING BASES

M-10.   An intermediate staging base is a secure staging base established near to, but not within, the area of operations. It is normally used for a short period, just long enough for the battalion to complete its precombat preparations and to transition the bulk of its combat power into the operational area and establish effective command and control of forces.

FIRE BASES

M-11.   A fire base supports the operation's main effort with indirect fires. It is a secure location for field artillery, and sometimes mortar units, which allows the battalion to operate over large areas while still being within the weapons' range fans. Fire support bases are used in both stability and major combat operations. They provide secure, defendable hardened locations for the indirect fire units. This minimizes the amount of combat power the commander must allocate to defense and allows him to better use his forces on offense. A base may be both a fire base and an operating base at the same time.

FUNDAMENTALS OF BASE DEFENSE

M-12.   Regardless of what type of base the unit establishes, or where, it must be prepared to defeat an enemy attack. Attacks may be conventional assaults supported by indirect fire, or they may be made by unconventional means such as covert infiltration or suicide bomber. Attacks may consist solely of indirect fires or standoff attacks using small arms. The base commander organizes and controls all forces assigned to the base to capitalize on their capabilities. These forces must be trained, organized, and equipped to defend the base. Fundamentals of base defense are the same as for defensive operations with two additions—

BALANCE BASE SECURITY WITH POLITICAL AND LEGAL CONSTRAINTS

M-13.   Base security may have to be designed around numerous political constraints. For example, status of forces agreements between the United States and the host country.

KNOW RULES OF ENGAGEMENT

M-14.   Base commanders and their subordinates must comply with the ROE. They should ensure that inconsistencies among JIIM ROE are reconciled.

SITE SELECTION AND CONSTRUCTION

M-15.   The initial base site selection is critical and must meet the two fundamental purposes of a base: defense and operations projection platform. Unless both conditions are satisfied, the base cannot be used effectively.

METT-TC

M-16.   Many aspects of the establishment of a base are the same as for defensive operations; however, because a base is at least semi-permanent, different considerations apply.

Mission

M-17.   The requirement to establish a base will be the result of a mission analysis of the primary mission. The mission analysis will indicate the Infantry battalion can anticipate the conduct of operations in support of other forces, such as providing security and defense for an air assault, or will conduct operations for an extended period in the same general vicinity. A mission in support of other forces for example, might be to provide long term security and defense for a lodgment in an air assault operation requiring the building of an FOB.

Enemy

M-18.   Enemy forces will always have at least a limited capability to threaten the forces using the base. The base defense should be such that the minimum amount of combat power is required to defeat any enemy attack. This frees the rest of the force for operations.

Terrain and Weather

M-19.   Both terrain and weather are major considerations for the placement of the base.

Terrain

M-20.   The terrain selected for the base must be defensible. If possible, key terrain is a good location for the base. However, it may not always be possible to locate the base on key terrain because of other METT-TC considerations. Other primary terrain considerations are—

- Access to good road networks.
- Ease of resupply and relief
- Water, power, and sanitation sources.
- Sufficient area for anticipated expansion.
- Maximum coverage for weapons (if used as a fire base).

Weather

M-21.   The affect of adverse weather on the proposed base and the surrounding terrain is vital. For example, if the proposed base site is in a flood zone, how will flooding affect operations.

Time

M-22.   When the base is first occupied, normal priorities of work are followed for a perimeter defense. Over time, the base is continually improved so that the base can fully support the needs of the units and Soldiers.

Troops Available

M-23.   The base should be able to support and provide protected work and living areas for all the units that will potentially conduct operations at the base. Engineer unit support to establish a fully functional base is normally required.

Civil Considerations

M-24.   The base should not be too close to the civilian population to cause collateral damage and casualties, in the event the base is attacked.

PRIORITY OF WORK

M-25.   Initial priorities of work for the establishment of a base are the same as for a defense. Once the initial base defense is established, with the assistance of building assets, the priorities change to include creating infrastructure and hardening facilities.

M-26.   Occupation of a new base follows the normal priorities of work for establishing security and preparing a defensive. These include at least—

- Establishing initial base security, including observation posts and patrols outside the perimeter.
- Positioning crew-served weapons and assigning fields of fire.
- Preparing and emplacing unit CBRN detection equipment.
- Clearing fields of fire and preparing range cards.
- Preparing fighting positions.
- Installing and hardening communications.
- Emplacing obstacles and mines.
- Hardening primary fighting positions, including overhead cover.
- Preparing alternate and supplementary positions.
- Stockpiling and hardening the locations of ammunition, food, water, and medical supplies.
- Within 24 hours, providing for human waste disposal.
- Preparing routes and trenches between positions.
- Developing a counterattack plan.
- Conducting rehearsals, including rehearsals of movements to supplementary and alternate positions.

M-27.   After the initial occupation and preparation of the defense, the base priorities of work change to establishment of the infrastructure to support ongoing operations. These priorities, which are established by the base commander, include—

- Laying out base camp.
- Setting up water supply.
- Setting up waste disposal.
- Setting up electric power supply.
- Setting up dining facilities.
- Setting up fuel storage site.
- Establishing drainage patterns.
- Strengthening defenses.
- Clearing vegetation, moving earth, making earthen dikes and embankments.
- Building secured storage spaces.
- Building dispensary facilities.
- Building living facilities.

CONSTRUCTION

M-28.   From the time the area is first occupied for use as a defensive position, the base area is continually upgraded. At some point, the defensive area is transformed into a base from which to conduct continuous operations. Tasks associated with this semi-permanent construction are normally beyond the capability of the Infantry battalion, and professional engineer support is required.

Engineers

M-29.   Construction of the base normally requires the use of engineers. Engineers can be US Army construction engineers, US Navy construction engineers (SEABEEs), contracted companies, and host nation contracted support or a combination. When using contracted support, a vetting system must first be in place to ensure base construction plans are not compromised to potential enemy forces.

Planning Considerations

M-30.   A base's primary functions are for defense and as a location to prepare and execute operations. When constructing bases, these functions must remain paramount. For example, a base should have multiple entrance and exit points so units conducting operations from the base can vary routes so as not to be predicable. Also, a base should have multiple defensive lines around and inside the base as contingencies to enemy attacks. Other construction considerations include—

- Hardening all fighting positions, bunkers, and facilities. See FM 5-103.
- Providing for a BDOC.
- Providing lighting to cover the entire perimeter of the base.
- Integrating sensors into the base perimeter warning system.
- Providing a vehicle parking area well away from the perimeter for contracted workers.
- Locating indirect fire weapons where they have the capability to fire 360 degrees (if the base is also to be used as a fire base).

Entry Control Points

M-31.   The design, construction, and operation of entry control points (ECPs) are critical to base defense. Vehicle-borne and personnel carried explosive device effectiveness can be mitigated through proper ECP design, construction, and operation. The most important consideration for ECP construction is the analysis of the threats the installation is vulnerable to (Figure M-1).

Design Characteristics

M-32.   Design characteristics should consider the following:

Deterrence

M-33.   The overall ECP design, security posture, and procedures should convey to a potential aggressor a hardened access point not likely to be penetrated.

Example ECP (not to scale)

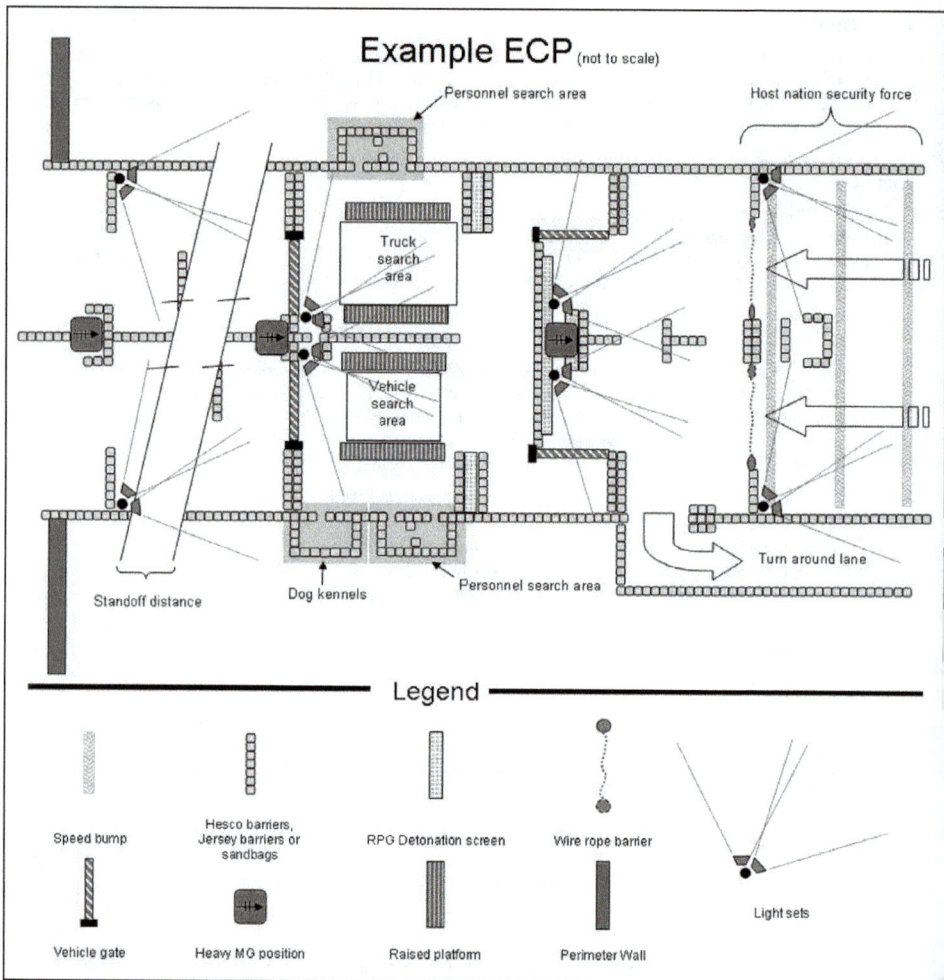

Figure M-1. Example entry control points.

Detection

M-34. Multiple measures that sense validate and communicate the presence of an aggressor to the response force. Detection measures and equipment include: cameras, vehicle passes, searches, questioning, bomb dogs, vehicle and package X-ray machines, metal detectors, and explosive compound sniffing devices.

Defense

M-35.   Active and passive measures employed to prevent an aggressor from gaining entry or to minimize the effects of an attack. Defensive measures include: drop barriers, collapsible wire-cage barriers, blast walls, stand-off, serpentines tracks, guards, RPG detonation screens, and ballistic glass.

Defeat

M-36.   The active and escalating measure of force design to defeat an aggressor. Defeat measures include: heavy machine guns, antitank weapons, and QRF.

Design Elements

M-37.   Design elements are the basic building blocks of the ECP. Each element must be effective individually and also be effective within the context of the intent of the whole ECP. The following are design elements of an ECP:

Traffic control

M-38.   The flow of vehicle, and personnel must be effectively controlled in order to efficiently segregate and process legitimate movement through the ECP. Segregate the traffic through the ECP by establishing points that check for different items. For example, ID Cards at one station and vehicle passes/registration at another station. Control the speed of movement through the ECP with speed bumps, serpentines for vehicles and turn styles for personnel. Have the ability to positively stop vehicle traffic using wire rope and drop barriers. Canalize traffic so crew served and vehicle mounted weapons systems have good fields of fire on vehicles negotiating the ECP. Provide points in the traffic control routes so unauthorized vehicles can exit from the ECP.

Threat mitigation

M-39.   Features incorporated to specifically mitigate identified threats such as, blast walls to protect from the effects of overpressure, and standoff distance for fragmentation. Hesco barriers, sandbag walls, Jersey barriers all provide some protection from explosive blasts. Shaped charged weapons effectiveness can be reduced by the emplacement of screens, such as chain link fences, which cause the predetonation of rounds like RPGs. Keeping a safe distance from explosions (brought about by vehicle-borne IEDs) saves lives and reduces blast effectiveness (Figure M-2). Consider the use of trans-load yards away from the base for equipment and supplies that are to enter the base. Ensure crew served weapons, armored vehicles, and close combat missile systems have clear fields of fire to engage targets.

Vehicle-Borne IEDs

ATF

Vehicle Description	Maximum Explosives Capacity	Lethal Air Blast Range	Minimum Evacuation Capacity	Falling Glass Hazard
 Compact Sedan	500 lbs 227 kilos (in trunk)	100 feet 30 meters	1,500 feet 457 meters	1,250 feet 381 meters
 Full Size Sedan	1,000 lbs 455 kilos (in trunk)	125 feet 38 meters	1,750 feet 534 meters	1,750 feet 534 meters
 Passenger Van or Cargo Van	4,000 lbs 1,818 kilos	200 feet 61 meters	2,750 feet 838 meters	2,750 feet 838 meters
 Small Box Van (14ft box)	10,000 lbs 4,545 kilos	300 feet 91 meters	3,750 feet 1,143 meters	3,750 feet 1,143 meters
 Box Van or Water/Fuel Truck	30,000 lbs 13,636 kilos	450 feet 137 meters	6,500 feet 1,982 meters	6,500 feet 1,982 meters
 Semi-Trailer	60,000 lbs 27,273 kilos	600 feet 183 meters	7,000 feet 2,134 meters	7,000 feet 2,134 meters

Figure M-2. Vehicle-borne IEDs.

Procedures

M-40. Operating practices should be integrated so that all processes are thorough, quick, and with some degree of overlap. Establish ECP procedures from point of entry to release from the ECP. Integrate host nation forces in to the ECP procedures where appropriate. Conduct a guard mount that ensures complacency is not established. Periodically test the procedures and conduct after action reviews to identify and correct shortcomings. Consider changing procedures periodically to keep the enemy from identifying and taking advantage of patterns in ECP procedures. Monitor reports from other ECPs and adjust procedures proactively to respond to new threats.

Defense in Depth

M-41. Allow for repeated engagement zones. If a threat breaks through one section of the ECP, the next engagement zone engages the threat. The outer perimeter of the base also establishes an engagement zone. The interior of the base should also contain engagement/defensive zones/belts established by the BDOC.

BASE DEFENSE OPERATIONS

M-42.   Defense and security of tactical units, bases and installations are integral parts of combat missions. A base defense consists of both normal and emergency local military measures to deter or reduce the effect of enemy attacks or sabotage. It ensures the continued effectiveness of its facilities and the units to fulfill their missions. A base is always assigned a base commander who may be the senior officer of the units in the base or who may be another officer specifically given that responsibility..

ORGANIZATION AND CONTINUOUS OPERATIONS

M-43.   The base commander is responsible for the perimeter defense of the base. If an Infantry battalion is located on a base by itself, the battalion commander can also serve as the base commander. The BDOC is solely responsible for base defense while the battalion CP is responsible for operations of subordinate units that conduct operations from the base.

M-44.   The BDCO has the following basic functions:

- Providing the essential C2 organization necessary to conduct coordinated base security related operations.
- Preparing comprehensive plans to implement the base commander's overall base force protection, security, and defense guidance.
- Designing, coordinating, and implementing base force protection, antiterrorism, physical security, and force protection working group.
- Monitoring the current status of assigned, attached, and tenant unit forces and resources and providing information to aid, allocate, and move forces and material to meet base security requirements.
- Identifying and communicating any base defense or area security shortfalls to the higher unit base defense commander or JSC, as well as service or applicable functional component command.
- Keeping the base commander informed of the current base security situation.
- Ensuring the participation of all units within the base perimeter in conducting active and passive defense and security measures. Monitoring and directing guard forces as necessary.
- Assessing potential conflicting interests and operational demands of base forces inherent when operating within a multiservice or multinational environment.
- Developing and executing a reconnaissance and surveillance plan to ensure proper security from standoff threats.
- Establishing and maintaining connectivity with higher level staff.
- Preparing security related operational reports as required.
- Maintaining a staff journal and displaying and filing necessary items to record operational activities of the command.
- Coordinating (when necessary) with the appropriate area commander or tenant commander to ensure that base security actions are deconflicted with ongoing or planned combat or stability operations related actions.
- Planning and coordinating the base fire support plan.
- Collecting and disseminating base emergency response capabilities to include medical support, combat engineering, EOD, and fire fighting.
- Evaluating actions to identify operational deficiencies and developing methods to improve combined operational effectiveness to include coordinating, training, and exercising base security related measures.

BASE DEFENSE

M-45.   Base commanders establish a base defense with available forces to provide all-round security. This base defense includes detailed planning and centralized control. Security measures may also include provisions to protect adjacent civilian communities. Constant and aggressive action by friendly elements against enemy forces constitutes a major element of base defense. Vigilance and sound security measures reduce enemy interference with operations at the base. It also tends to cause enemy forces to divert their operations from the area.

Security

M-46.   Early warning of pending enemy actions provides the base commander time to react to any threat. Security measures employed outside of the base are generally within direct fire range because the terrain outside of that direct fire range fan may often be assigned to a different unit. These measure may include outposts, patrols, ground surveillance and counterfire radar, military working dogs, and air R&S provide early warning. Civilian informants and actions of indigenous personnel near the base indicate pending enemy actions.

M-47.   Counterfire radars are field artillery systems that can track and locate enemy mortar, artillery, and rocket fires. Counterfire radars located in the target acquisition battery of the IBCT fires battalion. These radars are not normally located with the Infantry battalion during major combat operations, but they are routinely co-located during stability operations in order to reduce troops to tasks requirements.

M-48.   There are currently three counterfire radar systems in use: Q-36, Q-37, and Q-47. These systems do not have 360 degree coverage. The lightweight countermortar radar (LCMR) is in development and has 360 degree coverage out to 7 kilometers. The LCMR, when fielded, requires 360 degree line-of-site for full usation of the system.

M-49.   The land-based phalanx weapon system is a 20mm gun with multifrequency KU band radar for surveillance and tracking. It has the capability to defeat threat RAM. The land-based phalanx weapon system is an integral part of the C-RAM intercept battery. The C-RAM intercept battery, when deployed, can operate jointly with coalition forces, allies, and other services within the theater. Operationally, the C-RAM intercept battery will normally operate under a BDOC at an FOB.

M-50.   Security measures employed inside of the base may include guard towers, and internal roving patrols. Security measures vary with enemy threat, forces available, and other factors; all-round security is essential. The base commander establishes and maintains a guard force IAW FM 22-6.

M-51.   Other security techniques and procedures include:

- Guard shift rotations, which are determined by the BDOC, should be based on weather and light conditions, fatigue and other human factors that reduce vigilance.
- The times of shifts should change often to limit the enemy's ability to pattern the base's daily activities and battle rhythm.
- The commander of the relief and his NCOIC should constantly inspect each security position or post to ensure guards are vigilant, clearly understand the ROE, are following the ordered weapons ready posture, NVGs are present and operational and range cards are present, serviceable, and accurate.
- The commander of the relief should continuously assess the base's defensive posture to identify any possible weaknesses or vulnerabilities and report those to the BDOC.
- Inspection checklists are a valuable method to provide structure to each guard shift and should be continually assessed and updated.

M-52.   Snipers can pose a significant threat. Counter sniper measures include rehearsed responses, reconnaissance and surveillance, and well constructed and designed base defenses. ROE should provide specific instructions on how to react to sniper fire, to include restrictions on weapons to be used. The best counter to enemy snipers is another sniper. Snipers are most familiar with sniper techniques and are best able to locate and engage an enemy sniper.

Force Protection

M-53.   The BDOC establishes procedures for alerting units, individuals, and personnel accountability during periods of increased force protection levels. Individuals should have protective equipment such as body armor, and CBR protective masks readily available.

- Bunkers must be routinely inspected to ensure they are safe to occupy.
- Bunkers should have light, heat, food, and water available in the event they must be occupied for extended periods.
- Each bunker should have a means of communication to the higher unit or BDOC so that occupants can remain informed of the current situation, and for personnel accountability.
- Each living area and bunker should have a designated commander that is responsible for accountability and security.

M-54.   All units in the base area are responsible for implementing passive defense measures. Passive defense measures reduce the probability (and the effects) of damage caused by enemy attacks. Units assigned to the base, initiate passive defensive measures such as dispersion, camouflage, blackout, and use of shelters. These measures assist in preserving the operating integrity of the base and in ensuring decisive and effective action against enemy attack.

Alarms

M-55.   An SOP should be established specifying alarms for anticipated contingencies. The alarm system should be tested routinely. The alarms should be able to be heard throughout the base. Different alarms should be used to distinguish different types of attacks. For example, there should be one type of alarm for artillery, mortar, and rocket attacks and a different alarm type for ground attacks as personnel may be required to perform different actions for each type of attack. A public address system is normally used to announce the stand down from alerts.

Mutual Support

M-56.   Defending forces ensure mutual employment of defensive resources, which include fires, observation, and maneuver elements. Mutual support between defensive elements requires careful planning, positioning, and coordinating due to the circular aspects of the base area. To control gaps, forces employ surveillance, obstacles, prearranged fires, and maneuver. Defensive plans provide for the use of all available support, including attack helicopters, AC-130 and CAS.

M-57.   When defending a base, the terrain of the base is generally divided, and assigned to tenant units. Although numbering and lettering unit sectors and towers is done for simplicity and quicker situational awareness, those manning positions or towers as part of a guard shift must be controlled by one commander of the relief to ensure unity of command.

Quick Reaction Force

M-58.   The base commander forms and maintains a QRF. On a base occupied by an Infantry battalion, the QRF is normally a squad sized force, but may be larger depending on the threat. The QRF's mission is to react to small scale threats inside or in the immediate vicinity of the base.

Reserve Force

M-59.   The Infantry battalion commander normally designates a reserve force that can be used to respond to threats external or internal to the base. The reserve is normally at least an Infantry or assault weapons platoon sized unit.

Patrols

M-60.   Detailed reconnaissance and counterreconnaissance plans, based on IPB, greatly enhance the security of any base. Base defensive operations to counter small groups of enemy forces include, aggressive and frequent patrolling by squad-size and platoon-size forces. Night patrols are particularly effective as they will keep the enemy off balance and ensure that US forces can exercise freedom of maneuver under all visibility conditions. These forces detect and capture or destroy small groups of insurgents. Use of military working dogs adds security and detection ability to patrol operations.

M-61.   Attached or OPCON mounted forces or weapons company platoons can be used to patrol regions where the terrain is flat, rolling, and a mixture of open areas and small woods. The mobility and firepower of these forces allow for rapid traverse of large areas and the ability to quickly engage enemy units. The unit may patrol populated areas near the base. Also, it establishes surprise checkpoints along known or suspected routes of insurgent communications and employs IEW assets to detect insurgent use of the electromagnetic spectrum.

M-62.   If allowed by the ROE, concealed night ambush sites are randomly manned outside the base perimeter. These sites must be coordinated with adjacent units. Indigenous personnel should accompany ambushes near populated areas. Their knowledge of the local populace and terrain assists the ambush mission. Artillery and mortar targets are registered and plotted to provide rapid on-call support. NFAs must also be established on the ambush sites. The unit emplaces detectors and sensors to provide early warning.

M-63.   Reconnaissance patrols obtain target acquisition data. They may penetrate known enemy-controlled territory to install sensors that report the enemy's presence along infiltration and supply routes. Patrols observe known infiltration and supply routes, and report activity along these routes. They provide early warning of enemy assembly areas; movement of weapons, ammunition, or other supplies; and preparation of mortar, artillery and rocket firing sites. Reconnaissance patrols may also locate suspected areas where other types of surveillance or acquisition systems may be employed to obtain information. When conducting patrols outside of the base, detailed coordination must be conducted with adjacent units. Indigenous personnel are assets to reconnaissance patrols. Their knowledge of the terrain, ability to operate in the environment, knowledge of the language, and familiarity with local customs are essential.

M-64.   Units employ combat patrols in difficult terrain far from the base, but normally within range of supporting artillery. These patrols may operate out of artillery range when supported by attack helicopters, CAS aircraft, or AC-130 aircraft. They may be supplied by air and equipped to communicate with the base and supporting aircraft. Such patrols vary in size from squad to platoon and are conducted at random times so as not to set a pattern. They perform planned searches to locate areas used by enemy forces to hide supplies, regroup, rest, train, or prepare for offensive actions. Small groups of enemy forces are engaged and destroyed. Large groups are reported and kept under surveillance until they are attacked. Augmentation in the form of local paramilitary guides or trackers increases the effect of combat patrols.

Host and Third Country Forces

M-65.   The Infantry battalion commander normally considers integrating host and third country forces in the overall base defensive effort with the approval of the BCT or higher level unit commander. The commander emphasizes integration of host country forces in patrol and populace control activities. Based on his threat assessment and host nation capabilities, the base commander should rely heavily on US forces to secure US personnel and equipment. Both host and third country forces provide local security for their own units; however, all local plans should be coordinated with, and integrated in, the base defense plan. The extent of participation in base defense by host and third country forces depends on the orders and guidance of their governments.

Glossary

Section I. ACRONYMS AND ABBREVIATIONS

1SG	first sergeant

A

A2C2	Army airspace command and control
A2C2S	Army Airspace Command and Control System
AA	avenue(s) of approach
AADC	area air defense commander
AAR	after action review
AATF	air assault task force
AATFC	air assault task force commander
ABCS	Army Battle Command System
ABF	attack by fire
ACA	airspace coordination areas
ACE	aviation combat element
ACL	allowable cabin load
ACM	airspace control measures
ACO	airspace control order
ACP	air control point
ACPS	Army Civilian Personnel System
ACT	analysis and control team
ACU	Army combat uniform
ACUS	Army Common User System
AD	air defense
ADA	air defense artillery
ADAM	area denial artillery munition
ADC	area damage control
ADDS	Army Data Distribution System
ADO	air defense officer
ADW	air defense warning
A/EGM	attack/effects guidance matrix
AFATDS	Advanced Field Artillery Tactical Data System
AGCCS	Army Global Command and Control System
AGT	air ground team
AHD	antihandling device
AI	area of interest
ALE	automatic link establishment
ALO	air liaison officer
AMDWS	air and missile defense workstation

ANGLICO	air and naval gunfire liaison company
AO	area of operation
AOR	area of responsibility
APC	armored personnel carrier
APFSDS-T	armor-piercing, fin-stabilized, discarding sabot with tracer
APOD	aerial port of debarkation
APOE	aerial port of embarkation
ARFOR	Army forces
ARSOF	Army special operations forces
ASAS	All Source Analysis System
ASOC	air support operations center
ASP	ammunition supply point
ATGM	antitank guided missile.
ATM	advanced trauma management; asynchronous transfer mode
ATO	air tasking order
ATS	air traffic service
AXP	ambulance exchange point

B

BAS	battalion aid station
BCS3	Battle Command Sustainment and Support System
BDA	battle damage assessment
BDAR	battle damage assessment and repair
BDO	battle dress overgarment
BDOC	base defense operations center
BF	battle fatigue
BFSB	battlefield surveillance brigade
BFT	blue force tracking
BFV	Bradley fighting vehicle
BHL	battle hand-over line
BP	battle position
BSA	brigade support area
BSB	brigade support battalion
BSC	brigade support company
BSFV	Bradley stinger fighting vehicle
BSMC	brigade support medical company
BSSG	brigade service support group
BUA	built-up area

C

C2	command and control
C3I	command, control, communications, and intelligence
C4ISR	command, control, communications, computers, intelligence, surveillance, and reconnaissance
CA	civil affairs
CAAT	civic affairs assessment team
CACOM	civil affairs command
CAFAD	combined arms for air defense
CAS	close air support
CASCOPE	civil areas, structures, capabilities, organizations, people, and events
CASEVAC	casualty evacuation
CAT	civil affairs team
catk	counterattack
CBRN	chemical, biological, radiological, and nuclear
CBRNE-CM	chemical, biological, radiological, nuclear, and high-yield explosive consequence management
CBRNWRS	Chemical, Biological, Radiological, Nuclear Warning and Reporting System
CCIR	commander's critical information requirements
CCP	casualty collection point
CCT	combat control team
CD	counterdrug
CDRJSOTF	commander, joint special operations task force
CE	command element (marine-air-ground task force)
CFFZ	critical friendly fire zone
CFL	coordinated fire line
CFZ	critical friendly zone
cGy	centigray
CHEMO	chemical officer
CI	counterintelligence
CID	criminal intelligence division
CIP	combat identification panel
CJTF	combined joint task force
CL	configured loads
CLS	combat lifesaver
CLU	command launch unit
CMO	civil-military operations

CMOC	civil-military operations center
CNR	combat net radio
COA	course of action
COE	contemporary operating environment
COLT	combat observation and lasing team
COMSEC	communications security
CONOP	continuous operations
CONOPS	concept of operations
CONUS	continental United States
COP	common operational picture
COSCOM	corps support command
CP	command post; checkpoint
CPOG	chemical protective overgarment
C-RAM	counter rocket, artillery, and mortar
CROP	container roll in/roll out platform
CRT	combat repair team
CSC	combat stress control
CSM	command sergeant major
CSP	contract support plan
CSR	controlled supply rate
CTCP	combat trains command post
CTIL	commander's track items list

D

DA	Department of the Army
DED	detailed equipment decontamination
DISCOM	division support command
DLIC	detachment left in contact
DNBI	disease and nonbattle injury
DoD	department of defense
DP	delivery point
DPICM	dual-purpose improved conventional munition
DS	direct support
DSO	domestic support operation
DSSU	dismounted Soldier system unit
DST	decision support template
DSVT	digital secure voice terminal
DTD	detailed troop decontamination
DTSS	digital topographic support system
DVNT	digital voice nonsecure telephone
DZ	drop zone

E

EA	engagement area
EBA	engineer battlefield assessment
EBC	embedded battle command
ECB	echelons, corps, and below
ECCM	electronic counter-countermeasures
ECP	entry control point
EEFI	essential elements of friendly information
EFD	explosive-formed penetration
EFET	essential fire and effects tasks
EFP	explosively formed projectile
EFST	essential fire support task
EMST	essential mobility-survivability task
EMT	emergency medical technician
EO	electro-optical
EOD	explosive ordnance disposal
EPLRS	Enhanced Position Location and Reporting System
EPW	enemy prisoner of war
ETAC	enlisted terminal attack controller
EW	electronic warfare

F

FA	field artillery
FAC	forward air controller
FARP	forward arming and refueling point
FAS	forward aid station
FASCAM	family of scatterable mines
FASP	field artillery support plan
FBCB2	force XXI battle command brigade and below
FBI	Federal Bureau of Investigation
FCR	fire control radar
FD	financial detachment
FDC	fire direction center
FEBA	forward edge of battle area
FEC	forward error correction
FEMA	Federal Emergency Management Agency
FFAR	folding fin aerial rocket
FFIR	friendly force information requirements
FHA	foreign humanitarian assistance
FHP	force health protection

FID	foreign internal defense
FIST	fire support team
FLIR	forward looking infrared radar
FLIR/TIS	FLIR/thermal imaging system
FLO	fighter liaison officer
FLOT	forward line of own troops
FM	frequency modulation
FMC	field maintenance company
FO	forward observer
FOB	forward operating base
FOO	field ordering officer
FPF	final protective fires
FPOL	forward passage of lines
FRAGO	fragmentary order
FS	fire support
FSB	fire support base; forward support battalion
FSC	forward support company
FSCM	fire support coordination measure
FSCOORD	fire support coordinator
FSE	fire support element
FSG	family support group
FSMC	forward support medical company
FSMT	forward support MEDEVAC team
FSO	fire support officer
FSSG	Force Service Support Group
FST	forward surgical team
FTCP	field trains command post

G

GBS	global broadcast service
GCS	ground control station
GCE	ground combat element
GPS	global positioning system
GS	general support
GS-R	general support-reinforcing
GSR	ground surveillance radar

H

HA	holding area
HAZMAT	hazardous materials
HBCT	heavy brigade combat team
HCA	humanitarian and civic assistance
HCP	health and comfort pack
HE	high explosive
HEMTT	heavy expanded mobility tactical truck

HET	heavy equipment transporter		JFSOCC	joint force special operations component commander
HF	high frequency		JIIM	joint, interagency, intergovernmental, and multinational
HHC	headquarters and headquarters company			
HIMAD	high-to-medium altitude missile air defense		JOA	joint operations area
HPT	high payoff target		JP8	type of fuel
HQ	headquarters		JNN/CPN	joint network node and command post node (JNN/CPN
HSS	health service support			
HUMINT	human intelligence		JSEAD	joint suppression of enemy air defenses
HVA	high value asset		JSOA	joint special operations area
HVT	high value target		JSOTF	joint special operations task force
			JSTARS	Joint Surveillance Targeting Acquisition Radar System

I

IAW	in accordance with		JTAC	joint terminal attack controller
ICM	improved conventional munitions		JTF	joint task force
ICRC	international committee of the Red Cross			

L

ID	identification			
IDAD	internal defense and development		LADW	local air defense warning
IED	improvised explosive device		LAN	local area network
IEW	intelligence and electronic warfare		LC	line of contact
IFF	identification, friend or foe		LCOP	logistical common operating picture
IHFR	improved high frequency radio		LD	line of departure
IM	information management		LLDR	lightweight laser designator rangefinder
IMETS	Integrated Meteorological System			
INC	internet controller		LMTV	light medium tactical vehicle
INFOSYS	information system		LNO	liaison officer
INS	inertial navigation system		LOA	limit of advance
IO	information operations		LOC	line of communications
IP	initial point		LOGCAP	logistical civil augmentation program
IPB	intelligence preparation of the battlefield			
IPC	interpersonal communication		LOGSITREP	logistics situation report
IREMBASS	Improved Remotely Monitored Battlefield Sensor System		LOGPAC	logistics package
			LOS	line of sight
ISR	intelligence, surveillance, and reconnaissance		LP	listening post
			LRF/D	laser range finder/designator
ITAS	Improved Target Acquisition System		LRP	logistics release point
			LRS	long-range surveillance
ITV	in-transit visibility		LSDIS	light and special division interim sensor
			LTIOV	last time information of value

J

			LZ	landing zone
JAAT	joint air attack team			
JAG	judge advocate general		**M**	
JCS	Joint Chiefs of Staff			
JFLCC	joint force land component commander		M/S	mobility/survivability
			MAG	Marine Aircraft Group

MAGTF	Marine air-ground task force		**MSSG**	MEU Service Support Group
MANPAD	man-portable air defense		**MTC**	movement to contact
MARDIV	Marine division		**MTF**	medical treatment facility
MAS	main aid station		**MTP**	mission training plan
MAW	Marine Air Wing		**MTS**	Movement Tracking System
MBA	main battle area		**MTV**	medium tactical vehicle
MCOO	modified combined obstacle overlay		**MTW**	major theater war
			MWR	morale, welfare, and recreation
MCS	maneuver control system			
MDMP	military decision-making process		**N**	
ME	main effort		**NAI**	named area of interest
MEB	Marine Expeditionary Brigade		**NATO**	North Atlantic Treaty Organization
MEDEVAC	medical evacuation		**NC**	node center
MEF	Marine Expeditionary Force		**NCO**	noncommissioned officer
MES	medical equipment set		**NCOIC**	noncommissioned officer in charge
METL	mission essential task list		**NCS**	net control station
METSAT	meteorological satellite		**NEO**	noncombatant evacuation operations
METT-TC	mission, enemy, terrain and weather, troops and support available, time available, and civil considerations		**NFA**	no-fire area
			NGF	naval gunfire
			NGO	nongovernmental organization
MEU	Marine Expeditionary Unit		**NICP**	national inventory control point
MEV	medical evacuation vehicle		**NIMA**	National Imagery and Mapping Agency
MFP	mortar firing point			
MG	machine gun		**NLOS**	non-line of sight
MGB	medium girder bridge		**NLT**	not later than
MGRS	Military Grid Reference System		**NMC**	nonmission capable
MGS	mobile gun system		**NOE**	nap of the earth
MI	military intelligence		**NORMA**	nature of the target, obstacle clearance, range to target, multiple firing positions, adequate area for proper dispersion between aircraft
MICLIC	mine clearing line charge			
MICO	military intelligence company			
MIJI	meaconing, interference, jamming, and intrusion		**NOSC**	network operations and security center
MLMC	medical logistics management center			
			NSA	national security agency
MLO	medical logistics officer		**NSFS**	national surface fire support
MLRS	Multiple Launch Rocket System		**NTDR**	near term data radio
MMS	maneuver and mobility support		**NVD**	night vision device
MOPMS	Modular Pack Mine System		**NVG**	night-vision goggles
MOPP	mission-oriented protective posture			
MP	military police		**O**	
MRE	meal, ready to eat		**O&M**	operations and maintenance
MSD	minimum safe distance		**OAKOC**	observation and fields of fire, avenues of approach, key terrain, obstacles and movement, and cover and concealment
MSE	mobile subscriber equipment			
MSETAN	Mobile Subscriber Equipment Tactical Packet Network System			
			OB	order of battle
MSR	main supply route		**OBSTINEL**	obstacle intelligence

OCONUS	outside continental US	RAU	radio access unit
OEG	operational exposure guide	RC	reserve component
OGA	other governmental agency	RCU	remote-control unit
OI	operations and intelligence	RED	risk estimate distance
OIC	officer in charge	REMBASS	Remotely-Monitored Battlefield
OP	observation post		Sensor System
OPCON	operational control	RFI	request for information
OPLAN	operation plan	RFID	radio frequency identification
OPLAW	operational law	RFL	restricted fire line
OPORD	operation order	RI	relevant information
OPSEC	operations security	RPV	remotely piloted vehicles
		ROA	restricted operations area

P

		ROE	rules of engagement
PA	physician's assistant	ROI	rules of interaction
PAC	Personnel and Administration	ROS	reduced operational status
	Center	RP	release point
PAI	personnel asset inventory	RPG	rocket-propelled grenade
PAO	public affairs officer	RPOL	rearward passage of lines
PEO	peace enforcement operation	RSTA	reconnaissance, surveillance, and
PGM	precision guided munitions		target acquisition
PIR	priority intelligence requirements	RVT	remote video terminal
PKO	peacekeeping operation		
PL	phase line		

S

PLGR	precision lightweight GPS receiver	S-1	personnel staff officer (adjutant)
PLL	prescribed load list	S-2	intelligence staff officer
PLS	Palletized Load System	S-3	operations staff (and training)
PME	peacetime military engagement		officer
PMM	preventive medicine measures	S-4	supply officer
PO	peace operation	S-6	signal officer
POD	port of debarkation	SA	situational awareness
POV	privately owned vehicle	SALUTE	size, activity, location, unit, time,
PP	passage point		and equipment
PROFIS	Professional Officer Filler	SAO	security assistance office
	Information System	SAMS	satellite automatic monitoring
PSG	platoon sergeant		system
PSYOP	psychological operations	SARSS	standard Army retail supply
PSYACT	psychological action		subsystem
PVNTMED	preventive medicine	SBCT	Stryker brigade combat team
PZ	pickup zone	SBF	support by fire
PZCO	pickup zone control officer	SCATMINE	scatterable minefield
		SCATMINWARN	scatterable minefield warning

Q

		SCL	strategic configured load
QRF	quick reaction force	SD	self-destruct
		SDM	squad designated marksman

R

		SE	supporting effort
RAAM	remote antiarmor mine	SEABEE	construction battalion (US Navy)
RAM	rockets, artillery, and mortars	SEAD	suppression of enemy air defense

SEN	small extension node	STARFIARS	Standard Army Financial Inventory Accounting and Reporting System
SEO	sniper employment officer		
SF	Special Forces	SU	situational understanding
SFF	self-forging fragmentation	SVML	standard vehicle-mounted launcher
SFLE	special forces liaison element	SWT	scout weapons team
SFOD-A	special forces operational detachment-Alpha		

T

SGM	sergeant major		
SGT	sergeant	T&C	targeting and counterfire
SHORAD	short-range air defense	TAA	tactical assembly area
SHTU	simplified handheld terminal units	TAI	target area of interest
SIDPERS	Standard Installation/Division Personnel System	TACAIR	tactical air
		TACCS	tactical air command and control specialists
SIGINT	signals intelligence		
SINCGARS	Single Channel Ground and Airborne Radio Subsystem	TACON	tactical control
		TACCP	tactical command post
SIP	system improvement plan	TACP	tactical air control party
SIR	specific information requirements	TACSAT	tactical satellite
SITTEMP	situational template	TALO	theater airlift liaison officer
SITREP	situation report	TAV	total asset visibility
SJA	staff judge advocate	TCF	tactical combat force
SOAR	special operations aviation regiment	TDA	table of distribution and allowances
SOC	special operations command	TEWT	tactical exercise without troops
SOCCE	special operations command and control element	THT	tactical HUMINT team
		TI	tactical internet
SOCOM	Special Operations Command	TIM	toxic industrial material
SOEO	scheme of engineer operations	TIO	tactical intelligence officer
SOF	special operations forces	TIRS	terrain index reference system
SOI	signal operating instructions	TIS	thermal imaging system
SOP	standing operating procedures	TMD	tactical munitions dispenser
SOR	specific orders and request	TOC	tactical operations center
SOSRA	suppress, obscure, secure, reduce, assault	TOE	table of organization and equipment
SP	start point	TOW	tube-launched, optically tracked wire-guided missile
SPBS-R	supply property book system-revision	TPFDDL	time phased force and deployment data list
SPIN	special instruction		
SPIRIT	special purpose intelligence remote integrated terminal	TPME	task, purpose, methods, and effects
		TPN	tactical packet network
SPO	support operations officer	TPT	tactical PSYOP team
SPOD	sea port of debarkation	TPU	tank pump unit
SPOE	seaport of embarkation	T-REx	tactical range extension
SPOTREP	spot report	TRP	target reference point
SRP	soldier readiness preparation	TSC	theater support command
SSC	small-scale contingency	TSM	targeting synchronization matrix
STAMIS	Standard Army Management Information System	TSOC	theater special operations command

	TSOP	tactical standing operating procedure		**V**
	TSS	target selection standards	**VHSIC**	very high speed integrated circuits
	TTP	tactics, techniques, and procedures	**VIP**	very important person
	TV/EO	television/electro-optical	**VMF**	variable message format
	TVS	television sensor	**VT**	variable time

U

UAS	unmanned aircraft system
UMCP	unit maintenance collection point
UMT	unit ministry team
UN	United Nations
UO	urban operations (replacing term MOUT)
USAF	US Air Force
USAID	United States Agency for International Development
USAOC	United States Army Special Operations Command
USMC	United States Marine Corps
UXO	unexploded ordnance

W

WAN	wide area network; wireless area network
WARNO	warning order
WCS	weapon(s) control status
WIA	wounded in action
WMD	weapons of mass destruction
WP	white phosphorous
WFF	warfighting function

X

XO	executive officer

Section II. TERMS

Pave Penny	passive laser tracker whose current range is too short for the rounds it must track

References

SOURCES USED

These are the sources quoted or paraphrased in this publication.

DEPARTMENT OF DEFENSE PRODUCTS

DoD Directive 2311.01E	*DoD Law of War Program*, 9 May 2006.
DoD Directive 5240.1-R	*Procedures Governing the Activities of DoD Intelligence Components that Affect US Persons*, December 1982.

FIELD MANUALS

FM 3-05.70	*Survival*. 17 May 2002.
FM 3-07.31	*Multiservice TTP for Conducting Peace Operations*. 26 October 2003.
FM 3-7	*NBC Field Handbook*. 29 September 1994.
FM 3-11	*Multiservice TTP for NBC Defense Operations*. 10 March 2003.
FM 3-21.91	*Tactical Employment of Antiarmor Platoons and Companies*. 26 November 2002.
FM 3-22.27	*MK 19, 40-Mm Grenade Machine Gun, Mod 3*. 28 November 2003.
FM 3-90	*Tactics*. 4 July 2001.
FM 3-90.2	*The Tank and Mechanized Infantry Battalion Task Force*. 11 June 2003.
FM 5-170	*Engineer Reconnaissance*. 5 May 1998, with Change 1, 13 July 1998.
FM 5-250	*Explosives and Demolitions*. 30 July 1998, with Change 1, 30 June 1999.
FM 7-85	*Ranger Unit Operations*. 9 June 1987.
FM 7-98	*Operations in a Low-Intensity Conflict*. 19 October 1992.
FM 17-95	*Cavalry Operations*. 24 December 1996.
FM 31-23	*Special Forces Mounted Operations TTP*. 5 May 1999.
FM 100-25	*Doctrine for Army Special Operations Forces*, 1 August 1999.

JOINT PUBLICATIONS

JP 1	*Joint Warfare of the Armed Forces of the United States*. 14 November 2000.

OTHER

Technical Memo 5-87	*Modern Experience in City Combat*, US Army Human Engineering Laboratory, March 1987.

DOCUMENTS NEEDED

These documents must be available to the intended users of this publication.

ARMY REGULATIONS

AR 601-142	*Army Medical Department Professional Filler System*. 23 June 2004.

ARMY TRAINING EVALUATION PROGRAMS (MTPS AND DRILL BOOKS)

ARTEP 7-8-Drill	*Battle Drills for the Infantry Rifle Platoon and Squad*. 25 June 2002.
ARTEP 7-10-MTP	*Mission Training Plan for the Infantry Rifle Company*. 1 June 2002.

FIELD MANUALS

FM 1-02	*Operational Terms and Graphics.* 21 September 2004.
FM 1-112	*Attack Helicopter Operations.* 2 April 1997.
FM 1-114	*Air Cavalry Squadron and Troop Operations.* 1 February 2000.
FM 3-0	*Operations.* 14 June 2001.
FM 3-04.111	*Aviation Brigades.* 21 August 2003.
FM 3-05.401	*Civil Affairs TTP.* 23 September 2003.
FM 3-06.11	*Combined Arms Operations in Urban Terrain.* 28 February 2002.
FM 3-07	*Stability Operations and Support Operations.* 20 February 2003, with Change 1, 30 April 2003.
FM 3-09.32	*(J-FIRE) Multiservice Procedures for the Joint Application of Firepower.* 29 October 2004.
FM 3-11.3	*Multiservice TTP for CBRN Avoidance.* 2 February 2006.
FM 3-11.4	*Multiservice TTP for NBC Protection.* 2 June 2003.
FM 3-19.40	*Military Policy Internment/Resettlement Operations.* 1 August 2001.
FM 3-21.8	*Infantry Rifle, Platoon, and Squad.* TBP.
FM 3-20.15	*Tank Platoon.* 1 November 2001.
FM 3-21.11	*The SBCT Infantry Rifle Company.* 23 January 2003.
FM 3-21.10	*The Infantry Rifle Company.* TBP.
FM 3-22.10	*Sniper Training and Operations.* TBP.
FM 3-34	*Engineer Operations.* 2 January 2004.
FM 3-34.2	*Combined-Arms Breaching Operations.* 31 August 2000, with Changes 1 through 3, 15 November 2000 through 11 October 2002.
FM 3-100.2	*ICAC2 Multiservice Procedures for Integrated Combat Airspace C2.* 30 June 2000.
FM 5-0	*Army Planning and Orders Production.* 20 January 2005.
FM 4-01.30	*Movement Control.* 1 September 2003.
FM 4-02	*Force Health Protection in a Global Environment.* 13 February 2003.
FM 4-25.12	*Unit Field Sanitation Team.* 25 January 2002.
FM 5-103	*Survivability.* 10 June 1985.
FM 5-104	*General Engineering.* 12 November 1986.
FM 6-22.5	*Combat Stress.* 23 June 2000.
FM 7-15	*The Army Universal Task List.* 31 August 2003, with Change 1, 18 March 2005.
FM 8-42	*Combat Health Support in Stability Operations and Support Operations.* 27 October 1997.
FM 8-51	*Combat Stress Control in a Theater of Operations.* 29 September 1994, with Change 1, 30 January 19998.
FM 20-32	*Mine/Countermine Operations.* 29 May 1998, with Changes 1 through 5, 30 June 1999 through 1 April 2005.
FM 21-10	*Field Hygiene And Sanitation.* 21 June 2000.
FM 22-51	*Leaders' Manual for Combat Stress Control.* 29 September 1994.
FM 22-6	*Guard Duty.* 17 September 1991, with Change 1, 15 January 1975.
FM 27-10	*The Law of Land Warfare.* 18 July 1956, with Change 1, 15 July 1976.
FM 34-130	*Intelligence Preparation of the Battlefield.* 8 July 1994.

FM 41-10	*Civil Affairs Operations.* 14 February 2000.
FM 90-4	*Air Assault Operations.* 16 March 1987.
FM 90-7	*Combined Arms Obstacle Integration.* 29 September 1994, with Change 1, 10 April 2003.
FM 90-13	*River-Crossing Operations.* 26 January 1998.
FM 100-7	*Decisive Force: The Army in Theater Operations.* 31 May 1995.
FM 100-14	*Risk Management.* 23 April 1998, with Change 1, 8 August 2005.

FORMS

DEPARTMENT OF THE ARMY FORMS

DA Form 1156	*Casualty Feeder Card*
DA Form 2028	*Recommended Changes to Publications and Blank Forms*
DA Form 2404	*Equipment Inspection and Maintenance Worksheet*
DA Form 4137	*Evidence/Property Custody Document*
DA FORM 5988-E	*Equipment Inspection Maintenance Worksheet (EGA)*

DEPARTMENT OF DEFENSE FORMS

DD Form 1076	*Military Operations Record of Personal Effects of Deceased Personnel*
DD Form 1972	*Joint Tactical Air Strike Request*
DD Form 2745	*Enemy Prisoner of War (EPW) Capture Tag*

INTERNET WEB SITES

Some of the documents listed in these References may be downloaded from Army websites:

Air Force Pubs	http://afpubs.hq.af.mil/
Army Forms	http://www.apd.army.mil/usapa_PUB_formrange_f.asp
Army Knowledge Online	https://akocomm.us.army.mil/usapa/doctrine/index.html
NATO ISAs	http://www.nato.int/docu/standard.htm
Reimer Digital Library	http://www.train.army.mil

JOINT PUBLICATIONS

JP 3-07.1	*Joint TTP for Foreign Internal Defense.* 30 April 2004.
JP 3-07.2	*Antiterrorism.* 14 April 2006.
JP 3-07.3	*Joint TTP for Peace Operations.* 12 Feb 1999.

OTHER

Handbook No. 92-3	*Fratricide Risk Assessment for Company Leadership*, Section II, *Fratricide Risk Assessment*

TRAINING CIRCULARS

TC 7-98-1	*Stability and Support Operations Training Support Package.* 5 June 1997.

This page intentionally left blank.

Index

potential hazards, examples, A-3
(*illus*)
preparation for operations, 2-14
coordination and liaison,
2-15
force protection, 2-15
plan revision and refinement,
2-15
reconnaissance and
surveillance, 2-14
rehearsals, 2-16
security, 2-15
preparation, 4-7
preplanned close air support
(CAS) request form, G-10
(*illus*)
presence patrols, 6-27
protection, 1-14, 6-15, 6-21,
10-30, C-2, D-7
air defense, 10-33
chemical, biological,
radiological, and nuclear
(CBRN) operations, 10-34
military police support, 10-35
mission, 10-30
organization, 10-30
planning considerations,
10-31
role of air defense officer,
10-32

Q

quick reaction force, 5-57

R

RAAMs minefield safety
template, 10-30 (*illus*)
radios, number and type, E-7
(*illus*)
Ranger battalion, 1-4 (*illus*)
rates of march (normal terrain),
dismounted, D-8 (*illus*)
Raven remote video terminal,
K-7 (*illus*)
Raven UAS, K-5 (*illus*)
rear, flank, and advance guard
operations, 8-4 (*illus*)
rearward passage of lines, 8-12
(*illus*)
sustainment plan for, 8-14
(*illus*)
reconnaissance and surveillance,
2-14
recovery, 7-11

reduction of effects of continuous
operations, H-6 (*illus*)
reduction of impact, H-5
reference grid, objective area,
E-21 (*illus*)
rehearsals, 2-16, 11-21
relief operations, 7-3, 8-9
reorganization, 4-63
replenishment operations, 10-44
(*illus*)
reserve, 4-5, 5-56
response, 7-10
restoration, 7-11
retrograde
employment, snipers and,
F-10
operations, 5-18, 5-19 (*illus*),
D-14, E-6
reverse planning sequence, 8-26
(*illus*)
reverse-slope defense, 5-46
(*illus*)
risk estimate distances (REDs)
for mortars and cannon
artillery, 10-9 (*illus*)
risk levels and impact on mission
execution, A-4 (*illus*)
risk management, A-1
accident risk, A-1
Step 1 -identify hazards, A-2
Step 2 -assess hazards to
determine risks, A-3
Step 3 -develop controls and
make risk decisions, A-4
Step 4 -implement controls,
A-5
Step 5 -supervise and
evaluate, A-5
steps correlated with MDMP
tasks, A-2 (*illus*)
tactical risk, A-1
worksheet, example
completed, A-4 (*illus*)
river crossing operations, 8-20,
F-12
roadblocks, 6-35, 6-37 (*illus*)
roles, 2-10
rotary wing aircraft, E-3 (*illus*)
rules of engagement and
interaction, 6-15

S

safety, D-8. *See also* danger,
fratricide, risk

and fragment hazard zones,
10-29 (*illus*)
scatterable mines, 10-24
scheme of maneuver, 4-60
science of control, 2-3
search and attack, example, 4-27
(*illus*), 11-33 (*illus*)
search operations, typical
organization for, 6-31 (*illus*)
search, dispersal to, example,
4-25 (*illus*)
searches, 6-30
security, 2-15 (*See also* security
operations)
area engagement, 5-38
of a foothold in a battalion
attack, 11-30 (*illus*)
occupation and establishment
of, 5-37
of officials, 6-28
post, 6-29 (*illus*)
zone forces, BCT,
organization of, 5-3 (*illus*)
security operations, 5-38, 8-2
(*illus*)
area security, 8-7
cover, 8-7
guard, 8-4
high value assets security,
8-8
local security, 8-8
screen, 8-2
types, 8-1
self-destruct windows, 10-25
(*illus*)
sequence, 4-7
sewer overlay, 11-13 (*illus*)
Shadow
mission payload, K-4 (*illus*)
unmanned aircraft system,
K-3 (*illus*)
shaping operations, 4-4
show of force, 6-13
signal officer, battalion, 10-37
signs of sleep deprivation and
fatigue, H-5 (*illus*)
sleep, H-4
deprivation, H-5 (*illus*)
sniper(s)
actions against fortified
areas, F-8
defensive employment, F-9
employment officer, F-3
offensive employment, F-6
patrols, F-13

FM 3-21.20 (FM 7-20)
13 December 2006

By Order of the Secretary of the Army:

PETER J. SCHOOMAKER
General, United States Army
Chief of Staff

Official:

JOYCE E. MORROW
Administrative Assistant to the
Secretary of the Army

0632601

Distribution: *Regular Army, Army National Guard, and US Army Reserve:*
To be distributed in accordance with IDN 110079, requirements for FM 3-21.20.

CPSIA information can be obtained
at www.ICGtesting.com
Printed in the USA
BVHW031717100722
641780BV00011B/198

9 781536 919191